ETHICS AND VALUES
IN THE
INFORMATION AGE

ETHICS AND VALUES
IN THE
INFORMATION AGE

JOEL RUDINOW
Santa Rosa Junior College

ANTHONY GRAYBOSCH
California State University—Chico

WADSWORTH

THOMSON LEARNING

Australia • Canada • Singapore • Spain
United Kingdom • United States

WADSWORTH
THOMSON LEARNING ™

Acquisitions Editor: David Tatom
Development Editor: Scott Spoolman
Marketing Strategist: Steve Drummond
Project Manager: Suzie Wurzer
Project Editors: Jeannine Christensen and Rebekah Mercer

Manufacturing Manager: Elaine Curda
Art Director: Sue Hart
Copy Editor: Karen Keady
Compositor: GAC/Indianapolis
Printer: Malloy Lithographing

Printed in the United States of America
1 2 3 4 5 6 7 05 04 03 02 01

For more information about our products, contact us at:
Thomson Learning Academic Resource Center
1-800-423-0563

For permission to use material from this text, contact us by:
Phone: 1-800-730-2214
Fax: 1-800-730-2215
Web: http://www.thomsonrights.com

ISBN: 0-15-507956-5
Library of Congress Number: 20-01091588

Asia
Thomson Learning
60 Albert Street, #15-01
Albert Complex
Singapore 189969

Australia
Nelson Thomson Learning
102 Dodds Street
South Melbourne, Victoria 3205
Australia

Canada
Nelson Thomson Learning
1120 Birchmount Road
Toronto, Ontario M1K 5G4
Canada

Europe/Middle East/Africa
Thomson Learning
Berkshire House
168-173 High Holborn
London WC1 V7AA
United Kingdom

Latin America
Thomson Learning
Seneca, 53
Colonia Polanco
11560 Mexico D.F.
Mexico

Spain
Paraninfo Thomson Learning
Calle/Magallanes, 25
28015 Madrid, Spain

This is dedicated to the ones we love.

ABOUT THE EDITORS

Joel Rudinow received his B.A. in Philosophy from the University of California at Santa Barbara, and his Ph.D. in Philosophy from the University of British Columbia. He has held faculty appointments at the University of Western Ontario, Dartmouth College, and Sonoma State University. He is currently Chair of the Department of Philosophy at Santa Rosa Junior College and co-author of *Invitation to Critical Thinking*.

Anthony Graybosch is Professor of Philosophy at California State University—Chico. He has taught at Mount Senario College in Wisconsin and at the University of Central Oklahoma. He has held Fulbright Lectureships at Tel Aviv University, Eotvos Lorand University in Budapest, and the University of Gdansk. He received his B.A. from Fordham University and his Ph.D. from The City University of New York.

INTRODUCTION

Many significant historical moments or periods have come to be identified with some central theme or concept—the Age of Reason, the Summer of Love, the Industrial Revolution. "Information" has become the defining concept of our moment in history. We live in the information age. The label is fairly recent, only about twenty years old.[i] In part, the label points to the revolutionary explosion of information technology—so predominant in our age that it now often goes by the ironically awesome acronym IT. Thanks to IT, we now enjoy—individually as human beings, citizens, consumers, etc. and collectively as a species—capabilities to gather, store, transmit, receive, sort, analyze, and otherwise process information in quantities, at speeds, and across distances unimaginably greater than at any other time or place in world history.

To put this in perspective, consider that for most of human history—more than two million years before anyone thought of IT—oral speech and gesture were the only means of communication among humans. Writing, which allowed communication across distances in space and time, emerged about six thousand years ago. Printing, which permitted communication with mass audiences, emerged only 500 years ago in the fifteenth century. Only in the twentieth century did mass distribution of integrated audio-visual-textual (multimedia) material become possible through the development of film, video, audio-recording, radio and television broadcast technologies.[ii]

The concept of information is of course much older than the label. Steven Lubar, in his introduction to the "Information Age" exhibit at the Smithsonian Institution's National Museum of American History, notes a cartoon published in 1903 depicting a merger maniac business tycoon surrounded by "information machines. A newspaper and stock ticker brings him information from markets around the world. Two telegraph messengers have fallen asleep on a bench, exhausted from their efforts. His son, or perhaps his office assistant, is on the telephone, relaying orders to buy or sell, or perhaps sending instructions to his subordinates back at the office. His wife—or is it his secretary?—sits at a typewriter, ready to take down memos or letters."[iii] Recent technological innovations such as the microchip, fiber-optics, and satellite communications may have elevated information to Age-definitive status, but the new technologies have their Industrial Age antecedents and certainly the concept of information has had a long career.

From the Latin *informare*, "information" means literally "that which gives form to thought," but its "extensional" meaning—the things it is conventionally taken to be a label for—has evolved, especially as it has come front and center in the information age. Fifty years ago the label information would have referred to such mundane and humble matters of fact as a person's phone number or the correct answer to a question used on *Who Wants to be a Millionaire?* Now anything (text, graphics, sound, computer code, what-have-you) that can be encoded for transmission through any medium of IT qualifies as information.[iv]

Technology is certainly one important dimension of this picture. However, here we can begin to glimpse changes at a more profound level. The information age cannot adequately be characterized simply in terms of a revolution in technology. It is also, and just as importantly, a revolution in collective consciousness. Twenty years ago, who knew what e-mail or a twenty-gigabyte hard drive was? Now these and many other related neologisms are part of the shared vocabulary of much of the world's population. As one of our authors, James Boyle, observes, along with the revolution in technology a wholesale conceptual reconstruction process is now underway. This conceptual reconstruction process produces not just new words, but new conceptual schemes—new ideologies, new legislation, new justifications—for new regimes, new arrangements, new obligations; new distributions of burdens and benefits, new rights, new wrongs. It raises new ethical puzzles and dilemmas, and new versions of old ethical puzzles and dilemmas.[v] Thus the subject of this book: ethical issues in which the concept of information plays some important role.

As we shall see, this brings two significant and hitherto separate areas of applied ethics together: media ethics and computer ethics. Ethics is the branch of philosophy that has to do with morality—justice, fairness, right and wrong. Applied ethics is an approach to ethics in which abstract theoretical considerations are placed in the context of their relevance to real life situations. Both media ethics and computer ethics originated as varieties of professional ethics—ethics as applied to one or another professional, occupational, or career path. Media ethics began as a part of the training of professional journalists; and computer ethics has arisen in education for the burgeoning computer industry. Because the training for each of these occupational areas is rather specialized, courses of instruction in Media Ethics and Computer Ethics have so far generally been developed and taught separately from each other, in spite of the fact that they share information as their crucial conceptual foundation.

The centrality and importance of this common conceptual foundation can perhaps best be appreciated from the point of view of political philosophy, where it is generally understood that the flow of information is fundamental to determining the structure and exercise of political power. A basic premise, for example, of classical liberal theory of democracy is the essential value of "freedom of information." One example is Jefferson's famous reliance upon a "well *informed* citizenry" as a condition for a well functioning democracy. Jefferson famously said, "I know of no safe depository of the ultimate powers of the society but the people themselves, and if we think them not enlightened enough to exercise their control with a wholesome discretion, the remedy is not to take it from them but to *inform* their discretion by education."[vi] Thus it is easy to appreciate, from the point of view of political theory, how high-speed global access to information now made possible via the Internet gives rapid rise to a host of new ethical issues regarding security, privacy, secrecy, international sovereignty, and so on. By the same token, the central functional purposes of the press have traditionally had to do with the flow of information. Thus the central principles of a professional ethic for journalism seem also to flow naturally from an analysis of information—its nature and its importance in the conduct of human affairs.

We were made vividly aware of the convergence of media ethics and computer ethics by an episode at one of our home institutions that eventually rose to the level of a national story and a potential Supreme Court case. What began as a controversy about an advertisement in the student newspaper, and the right to publicly demonstrate in opposition to the paper's editorial policies, soon found its way into school-sponsored online discussion groups, some of which had been designated as confidential gender-exclusive chat rooms. When a "whistleblower" leaked certain personally offensive messages from one of the confidential discussions, the college became embroiled in a sexual harassment case that raised several intriguing issues all at once, some of which had Constitutional relevance and significance. Should a school-sponsored discussion be restricted by gender, or by a confidentiality rule? If so, how binding should such restrictions be? Can one conscientiously break an agreement to hold certain communications in confidence, and if so under what circumstances? Should the college faculty or administration be held responsible for offensive material published in a student newspaper? Should the college faculty or administration be held responsible for offensive messages posted to an on-line discussion group? Should an online discussion group be understood and treated in the same way as a classroom discussion, or as the letters to the editor section of the student newspaper, or as something else entirely? We will be exploring this case and the nest of issues it raises more deeply in Chapters 2 and 11. At the outset, however, let us just notice the convergence of ethical issues in journalism with ethical issues in the management of new and emerging forms of electronic communication.

A marvelous example, showing again how inextricably intertwined these two areas of applied ethics have become—if for no other reason than the degree to which information technology is revolutionizing mass media journalism—was furnished to us by the American presidential election of 2000. On November 7, election day, shortly before 8 p.m. EST, in the closest presidential race in American history, all of the major television networks estimated that Vice President Al Gore had beaten Texas Gov. George W. Bush in the key state of Florida. But as the night wore on and results came in from the state's Panhandle region, networks were forced to retract that estimate. Meanwhile, the race remained extraordinarily close across the nation. Gore took the battleground states of Pennsylvania, Michigan and Illinois; Bush claimed Ohio, Tennessee and Missouri. Eventually it became clear that whichever candidate won Florida would win the electoral votes necessary to claim the presidency. About 2:15 the following morning, the major networks called Florida and the election for Bush. Gore, hearing that he probably would lose Florida by about 50,000 votes, called Bush to concede the election. Forty-five minutes later, en route to a rally in Nashville to make a public concession speech, Gore learned that Bush's lead in Florida had shrunk dramatically to only a few thousand votes. By 4:15 a.m., the major networks were forced to retract their estimate that Bush had been elected. Questions had already arisen in public debate over how responsible the coverage of the election had been, and over the possibility that the coverage itself might have unduly influenced the electoral contest. Within hours, allegations of voting and vote-counting "irregularities," in addition to the narrow emerging margin of victory, had given rise to automatic machine recounts and requests for manual recounts in several Florida counties. Questions quickly arose in public debate over the relative reliability and integrity of machine (that is, computer) tabulation versus manual tabulation of votes. Over the next five weeks federal and state courts heard a tangle of issues and arguments in an escalating drama as gripping and difficult to follow as any of John Grisham's best stories. Finally, in an extraordinary late-night decision, a deeply divided United States Supreme Court over-ruled a deeply divided Florida State Supreme Court, saying in effect that the recounts ordered by the state Supreme Court violated the United States Constitution's Equal Protection principle, but also that too little time remained in the electoral process to conduct recounts in accordance with that principle—in effect awarding Florida's votes in the electoral college, and thus also the election, to George W. Bush. Throughout the entire process, people all around the world could log onto any of a host of web sites—the Cable News Network (CNN), National Public Radio (NPR), among many others—and follow the entire story on-line. (This narrative of the sequence of events, for example, was itself derived from CNN's on-line chronology.) Anyone with Internet access could read the full text of each court decision—complete with all of the concurring and dissenting opinions—within minutes of its release to the public. Members of the American public could sample the international coverage of their own electoral adventure in progress.

Suffice to say, we think that the time is clearly right to focus in applied ethics on the concept of information—on new ethical issues that the revolution in information technology is pushing to the top of the agenda, and on new twists older ethical issues are taking on in the information age. That is precisely what we will be doing in this book.

In Chapter 1, From Walden to DotComGuy, we give an overview of the revolution in collective consciousness brought on by the revolution in information technology. We consider the impact of information technology on ethics in business and the ethical implications of information technology's globalizing influence, as well as some of what may become lost to us through information technology's ascendancy.

In Chapters 2 and 3 we explore freedom of information as the conceptual ground of several of the fundamental principles of ethics in journalism: the principles of freedom of expression and freedom of the press, and ideals of press performance such as newsworthiness, objectivity, accuracy, impartiality, and balance.

In Chapters 4, 5, and 6 we focus on the economic structure of the institutions that have come to serve as primary information delivery systems, on the role and impact of commercial advertising in mass media, and on the preeminence of entertainment values in mass media programming. In this connection we explore some special applications of ethics to several controversial categories of entertainment and cultural material: comedy, pornography, representations of violence in the news, and in popular music.

In Chapters 7 and 8 we look at issues regarding access to information. We explore the concept of privacy, as the right to control access to information about oneself, and the closely associated concepts of secrecy and confidentiality, as these apply not only to individuals but to large organizations, including the political state. In Chapter 9 our exploration of information access extends into the area of intellectual property, as we consider the right to own information. In Chapter 10 this discussion is extended into the area of security of information, as we consider the impact of information technology on issues of national security and the conduct of warfare and other forms of conflict.

In Chapter 11 we explore the impact of information technology in several areas of intimate and otherwise personal life. We look at how information technology is affecting interpersonal relationships and communication. We explore some of the ways in which information technology is affecting the formation and maintenance of personal identity. Finally, we contemplate the future of human civilization in the unfolding age of information.

Each of the readings in this book is followed by exercises and/or case studies. Some of these are based on actual cases; some are hypothetical. They may be used as prompts for class or study group discussion activities or as essay assignments. Each chapter concludes with a short list of recommended additional readings.

Often throughout this book we refer you to Internet sites. Internet resources are inherently less stable than the book you're now holding in your hand. This is both exciting and troublesome. An exciting thing is that new information and materials are always turning up on the Internet. One of the troubles has to do with changes of Internet address, otherwise known as "broken links." We want to help our readers—both students and their instructors—make effective use of the Internet in connection with this book. To that end, here are your authors' academic and Internet addresses:

Anthony Graybosch
Department of Philosophy
CSU Chico
Chico, CA 95929-0730
email: agraybosch@csuchico.edu
Internet site:
   http://www.csuchico.edu/~graybosc

Joel Rudinow
Department of Philosophy
Santa Rosa Junior College
1501 Mendocino Ave.
Santa Rosa, CA 95401
email: jrudinow@santarosa.edu
Internet site:
   http://online.santarosa.edu/
   homepage/jrudinow/

We welcome you to visit our web sites. Look for the Ethics and Values in the Information Age (EVIA) link. We will be maintaining up to date links (as best we can) to the Internet resources referenced in the text, and we will be adding new links as we learn of them. We welcome you to contact us with suggestions for new additional links, and of course to bring broken links to our attention.

We are hoping that instructors and students of both media ethics and computer ethics will see the value in approaching their courses and studies within a framework defined by the concept of information. As a practical matter, journalistic ethics education must come to terms sooner or later with the radical transformation that the profession of journalism, like so many others, is undergoing in the information age. At the same time we suggest that computer ethics may well find itself usefully broadened and deepened by consideration of its affinities with media ethics. Beyond these two already charted areas of the curricular landscape, we see in the collection of readings assembled here the contours and outlines of an emerging area for applied philosophy generally. Although many of our selections were written by professionals and lay persons in disciplines and occupations other than academic philosophy, we have been struck by the abundant renewed relevance of traditional philosophical themes and preoccupations to the promises and challenges presented by the emerging information environment. Accordingly, it is our hope that the discipline of academic philosophy will find fertile ground in information age ethical issues for the application of its special skills and techniques.

Acknowledgments

In 1996 an adjunct professor of philosophy at a small campus of a rather large state university system organized a panel discussion at one of the three regional conferences of the American Philosophical Association (APA). The session was entitled "Promises and Pitfalls of Cyberia University." Educators and philosophers of education joined in discussing the pros and cons of "distance learning" and other initiatives incorporating new information and communications technologies into the schools and colleges. Panel leader Joel Rudinow, co-author of a textbook in critical thinking, had a few ideas about building interactive tutorial support software for his critical thinking classes. He also had some deep-seated reservations about the new technology and its impact on the highly personal processes of teaching and learning. Coincidentally, at the same conference, another panel had been assembled under the auspices of the APA's Committee on Computers and Philosophy. Two of the members of this panel, Ron Barnette of Valdosta State University in Georgia, and Jon Dorbolo, of Oregon State University, had done pioneering work developing Internet-based scholarly and instructional resources for philosophy as a discipline. The three of them wound up going out to dinner together and kicking around some ideas for various experiments in pedagogy and curriculum design involving new technologies. Inspired by these discussions, Joel Rudinow returned to Sonoma State University and wrote grant proposals for a project entitled Ethics and Values in the Information Age (EVIA). The goals of the EVIA project were to create a new college course on Information Age ethical issues and to teach the course in a multicampus learning community using as many of the new tools of information and communication technology as he could get his hands on. The next step was to enlist colleagues from other campuses of the California State University system. First to join the project was Anthony Graybosch, then Chair of the Philosophy Department and Director of Center for Applied and Professional Ethics at the Chico campus. The course was initially offered in the spring semester of 1997 on the campuses of Chico State University, Sonoma State University, and San Jose State University. This book grew out of the reading list for that initial course.

Like any project of this size, this book owes a great deal to a great many people. The EVIA project began with seed funding from the Sonoma State University Academic Innovation Fund and eventually was awarded major funding from the California State University Academic Opportunity Fund. We wish to thank these institutions for their support. In addition we wish to thank Phil Clayton, chair of the philosophy department at Sonoma State University for his early support of the project, as well as Michael Donovan and Sean Martin, for taking charge of the course and keeping it alive at Sonoma State University in subsequent years. We are grateful to our project evaluator, Michael Scriven, for his involvement, advice and encouragement. We are especially indebted to David Tatom at Harcourt College Publishers for recognizing the potential of a book to support the course, and to our development editor Scott Spoolman for his patience and support while we got the manuscript together (we are, to put it mildly, somewhat behind our original schedule). Thanks also to Jeannine Christensen and Rebekah Mercer for escorting us through the production process and for their attention to detail. We thank all of the contributors for their wonderful words and for their permission to include their works here as well as Marilyn Gallaty for transcribing Ben Bagdikian's lecture. We are grateful to Deni Elliott of the University of Montana, James Huchingson of Florida International University, Tom Mullin of Eastern Washington University, and

Robert J. Schihl, of Regent University for their comments and suggestions for improvement on the first draft of our manuscript.

NOTES

[i]Historians date the Stone Age as 2,400,000–4000 B.C.; The Metal Ages as 4000 B.C.–1000 C.E.; the Age of Water and Wind as 1000–1732; the Industrial Revolution as 1733–1878; the Age of Electricity as 1879–1946; the Electronic Age as 1947–1972; and the Information Age from 1973 on. See Bunch, Bryan H., and Alexander Hellemans, *The Timetables of Technology: a Chronology of the Most Important People and Events in the History of Technology,* (New York: Simon & Schuster, 1993).

[ii]See Robert C. Davis, "The Impact of Mass Communication," in Melvin Kranzberg and Carroll W. Pursell Jr., eds., *Technology in Western Civilization,* vol. 2, (New York: Oxford University Press, 1967), pp. 323–ff.

[iii]Steven Lubar, *InfoCulture: The Smithsonian Book of Information Age Inventions,* (Boston: Houghton Mifflin, 1993), p. 1.

[iv]Cf. Theodore Roszak, *The Cult of Information,* (Berkeley: University of California Press, 1994), Ch. 1 "Information, Please," pp. 3–20.

[v]James Boyle, *Shamans, Software, and Spleens: Law and the Construction of the Information Society,* (Cambridge, MA: Harvard University Press, 1996), pp. ix–ff.

[vi]Thomas Jefferson, "Letter to William C. Jarvis", September 28, 1806, emphasis added, in Edward Dumbauld, ed., *The Political Writings of Thomas Jefferson;* (New York: Liberal Arts Press, 1955), pp. 93–ff; Cf. Judith Lichtenberg, ed., *Democracy and the Mass Media,* (Cambridge: Cambridge University Press, 1990), pp. 81, 91, 110, 155, 290–291, 299, 361.

TABLE OF CONTENTS

1

ETHICS INFORMATIONALIZED: FROM WALDEN TO DOTCOMGUY

*My purpose in going to Walden Pond was not to live
cheaply nor to live dearly there, but to transact some
private business with the fewest obstacles; to be hindered
from accomplishing which for want of a little common
sense, a little enterprise and business talent; appeared not
so sad as foolish.[1]*

HENRY DAVID THOREAU

INTRODUCTION

Approximately one hundred fifty years ago on July 4, 1845, Henry David Thoreau retreated from Concord society and established residence in a one-room dwelling a mile outside of town. Here he pursued an experiment in living in order to determine how to spend his life. After a little more than two years he left because he "had other lives to live." Thoreau tells us that the total cost of his modest home was $28.125[2] and boasts of using borrowed material rather than purchasing all the tools needed for his home construction project. Today DotComGuy retreats into his two-bedroom townhouse from which he will broadcast his life live for a year on the Internet. DotComGuy's computer will cost significantly more than Thoreau's retreat even adjusting for inflation and including a rebate of $400 for signing a three-year Internet access contract with CompuServe. His $90,000 salary, however, is certainly higher than Thoreau's wages.

Many of us will choose to follow DotComGuy and invite a computer into our home rather than take a walk around Walden Pond. Although we could do both, the time many people spend with the computer eats into an already busy schedule. Even the trustees of Walden Pond realize that humans have little time for walks. The replica of Thoreau's cabin is placed conveniently in the parking lot and not at its original site, which would require a leisurely half hour's walk. Whatever we include also excludes. The computer takes up most of my desk; the morning e-mail from InfoBeat excludes playing with the dog, and morning chats with my e-mail friend in Germany exclude morning chats with neighbors. "Who is my neighbor anyway?" takes on new meaning in the information age.

Why do we have computers in our home? (The question conjures up visions of those we refuse entry: sales persons, police, and vampires.) A significant portion of the population works at home via computer, computes rather than commutes, but most home computer owners use the machines for access to information or entertainment. And a good deal of time spent on office computers is also dedicated to amusement. Game playing, e-mail, online shopping, pornography, and word processing are the major avocations of computer users. Games play a major role in supporting the industry. Improvements in game complexity and visual presentation require faster machines with more storage. The Internet also demands faster machines and increased bandwidth as more people seek entertaining or educational images online. The long obsolete 386 processor in your attic or garage is more than sufficient for word processing and e-mail. But it cannot handle the latest version of *Redneck Rampage*.

Take a look at the contents of your e-mail address book. If you have not activated the option to automatically add e-mail addresses of all mail you answer, you will find a snapshot of your communication habits. Perhaps your address book contains your sister who lives 2,800 miles away, friends in Boston and Berlin, acquaintances you have never met in person who share a common musical interest, several online bulletin boards dedicated to topics of professional and personal interest, and a favorite electronics outlet. It may not contain the address of any political representative or news organization. But it could. E-mail has made it possible to sustain family relationships and friendships over great distances. We use e-mail to complete shared projects and purchase items. It could facilitate communication with political representatives. Critics of computers often concentrate on the negative impact of information technology on human life, but it is useful to keep its positive potential for global and diverse access in mind while reading about its dangers to civilization. After all, the morning newspaper can be just as much an impediment to walking the dog as the morning e-mail. But it is beyond doubt that computers radically affect how we live and work. The readings in this part of the text provide an overview of the ethical issues raised, and altered, by computer-based information technology. That is why this introductory chapter is entitled Ethics "Informationalized." Computers help turn information into a more valuable commodity, introduce new forms of customer profiling, and assist those who want to find out anything about anybody. Sometimes information technology ethical issues are old issues, but sometimes the changing use of information can transform how we address ethical issues such as privacy or just cause for going to war.

1.1 THE "CULT" OF INFORMATION Theodore Roszak's introduction to the second edition of *The Cult of Information* is aptly titled "In Defense of the Naked

Mind." Roszak picks an interesting way to respond to a review of the first edition in *Business Week,* which stated that *The Cult of Information* would appeal to "closet technophobes and incipient Luddites." Roszak points out that the Luddites were desperate men fighting to feed their families. Luddites were concerned about how machines were used and for whose benefit. The group resorted to violence only when leaders of industry and government failed to address their concerns about the economic impact of technology.

Roszak dedicates his book to a discussion of the use and abuse of computers. The selection details some of his concerns about how computers affect employment, national defense, financial markets, culture, and perhaps human nature itself through genetic engineering. He frequently brings up control, ownership, and access to information. In some instances, information technology only exaggerates or facilitates already existing practices. For example, financial investors have been selling short for a long time. Short sellers sell a promise to deliver a stock or commodity at a given price at a future date. They are called short sellers because at the moment of making the promise to deliver the stock they don't actually own the stock. Short sellers make money on a transaction if the stock price goes down between selling short and fulfilling the delivery agreement. Market information and rumors affect prices. Sometimes short sellers sell in volume to produce the impression that a stock is weak. The impression leads to more sales and so drives price down. This creates a buying opportunity for short sellers to purchase the stock they have promised to supply. Information technology facilitates awareness of volume sales and hence the goal of short sellers. Recently, computer bulletin boards have been used to start rumors about stock weakness as a means of "artificially" driving stock prices down temporarily.

Roszak is also concerned by the transforming effects of information technology. Anything that can be represented in binary form is information to a computer whether it be Shakespeare or nonsense words. The volume of information and the lack of discrimination in its quality leads to a general cultural decline in which all information is equal. Society has accepted the mystique of information: that making basic judgments about information quality empties information of its meaning.

Yet Roszak holds out hope for positive outcomes from information technology. Although he seems at times to despair over the quality of contact and information provided by the Internet he acknowledges that people choose whether to use a chat room to discuss the banalities of existence or more significant matters. Thoreau's major distraction was unwelcome visitors. Nobody can make you visit DotComGuy's Web address, but here it is: www.dotcomguy.com.

QUESTIONS FOR STUDY AND DISCUSSION

Nothing is more nourishing to philosophical study than discussion. Questions for study and discussion appear before each of the readings in this book. Some of these questions are intended primarily as hints and guideposts to reading carefully and retaining important concepts. Keep them in mind as you read, mark significant passages, and pause every page or two to make margin comments and summaries on the text. Other questions will provoke further reflection and discussion of the readings. Your instructors may find it worthwhile to organize some of your class sessions around some of these questions. We encourage informal study groups to organize around these questions as well.

1. What does Roszak mean by the mystique of information? by the cult of information?
2. Some advocates of artificial intelligence predict the emergence of conscious computers that will eventually be granted human rights. Does Roszak share this view of the potential of information processors? Why or why not?
3. Roszak writes, ". . . the main effect of automation and cybernation is to deskill, disempower, and disemploy people from the assembly line up through middle management. Computers have come to play a central role in downsizing companies and in the creation of a part-time, temporary, low-paid, nonbenefited workforce." Do you agree with his diagnosis? What government action might you suggest to cushion the impact of computers on society?
4. When you surf health Web sites devoted to gout, for instance, you can expect to receive unsolicited e-mail from one or more sites. The sites often capture e-mail addresses during a visit. Is this capturing of information ethical? Is it an invasion of privacy?
5. Online shopping offers significant bargains. Roszak thinks that you should purchase from local merchants and not from online sites. Explain why. Do you agree?
6. Perform an inventory of your e-mail address book and your list of Internet bookmarks or favorites. Do you use the Internet primarily for entertainment purposes or educational purposes?

IN DEFENSE OF THE NAKED MIND[3]

THEODORE ROSZAK

The Computer and General Ludd

There are computer enthusiasts I have met who will hear no evil spoken of the machine they hold dear. They tend to regard every critic they encounter as the latest species of "Luddite" those notorious machine-wreckers of the early industrial revolution who are remembered in the textbooks as mindless enemies of progress. For example, one reviewer of the first edition of *The Cult of Information*

declared in *Business Week* that the author's views would appeal to "closet technophobes and incipient Luddites." It is a book, he said, that "caters to their hidden fears and biases about what the computer is doing to their lives."

The Luddites have come to play a peculiar role in technological history. They are usually invoked as convenient whipping boys whose function is to squelch critical discussion of machines and their uses. Once the label "Luddite" has been attached to you, the inevitable next question is, "How would you like to go back and live in a cave?"

Historians now tell us that the original Luddites may have taken a bad rap. The hard-pressed weavers of northern England who rallied around the mythical General Ludd appear to have had no grudge against technology in and of itself; their grievance was with those who used machines to lower wages or eliminate jobs. General Ludd's "army of redressers" as they named themselves, never attacked one of the new power looms unless its owner had violated the workers' interests. Though they were desperate men fighting to feed their families, their hostility was carefully targeted. They asked how the machines were being used, by whom, for whose benefit—and then normally tried negotiating a better deal with their employers. Only when that effort failed did they feel forced to resort to violence. But to begin with, theirs was essentially an appeal for justice and humane treatment.

I am quite willing to have this book seen as a "neo-Luddite" treatise in just that sense. It belongs to that same tradition of passionate but, I hope, measured criticism. In this respect, I count myself an ally of all those serious students and users of information technology who hold a reasonably balanced view of what computers can and cannot, should and should not, do. Many of those who read the first edition of *The Cult of Information* recognized that the book, far from being a wholesale rejection of high tech, sought to discriminate between the use and abuse of computers. For example, in an online conference convened in 1986 on one of the country's most respected electronic bulletin boards (The WELL, operating out

of the San Francisco Bay Area), there were some contributors who saw the book as nothing more than an outburst of technophobia; but others were sympathetic to the effort. One participant said in the author's defense:

> I'm really puzzled about why this book pissed you off so much. . . . He attacks the hype and the misuses of the technology, not what most of us are trying to do. . . . Those of us who are working on what we consider humane, democratic, decentralized projects should welcome critiques which make the public more skeptical. . . . In other hands, with only slight variations, it could be centralist and propagandist. And the myth that surrounds it—which is the true target of Roszak's critique—will determine how people will react.

Lest there be any misunderstanding, then, let me preface this edition with a clear statement of my admiration for this remarkable technology. Like all the works of *homo faber,* high tech, this latest chapter in humanity's ongoing industrial saga, deserves to be honored as a manifestation of the astonishingly inventive genius of our species. I use a computer to earn my way as a writer; I might even qualify as a highly proficient user. I marvel each time I boot the machine at the cunning that has found a way to translate so much of human culture—numbers, words, graphics, music, three-dimensional design, animation, fractals—into simple digital symbols that can be read as electrical signals. I am astonished at the speed and compaction that has been achieved by computational devices in little more than a generation. I can even understand how some might (though mistakenly, I think) identify an accomplishment of this magnitude as an incipient form of superior intelligence.

If there were not thousands already applauding the skill of those who have fashioned this technology, I might be the one to do it. But there are more than enough who stand ready to praise; indeed, one of the things that worries me most is the great number who are handsomely rewarded for doing so. The "data merchants" as I call them, find their careers or their investments tied to the extravagant promises that attach to computers; they have every reason to believe that there is nothing computers cannot do and should not be doing. The result has been the creation of a mystique of information that makes basic intellectual discriminations between data, knowledge, judgment, imagination, insight, and wisdom impossible.

Again, so that I will not be misunderstood: as a writer and a teacher, I admit to having a healthy appetite for information. I value having plenty of data readily available as much as the next person. *Unless,* that is, the next person happens to be a computer manufacturer, a software mogul, an advertising executive in charge of the IBM account, or an Artificial Intelligence expert under contract to AT&T. Whenever I hear vested interests like these speaking of information as if it were *all* the human mind needs to think with, I begin to feel as if I might have strayed into some strange sect where all about me I find people worshipping light bulbs. No question but that light bulbs are useful devices; I would not want to live without them. But I never would have thought of them as objects of veneration.

So too with information. The cultlike status it has attained both bewilders and troubles me. The eagerness some enthusiasts (as well as many academics, intellectuals, and journalists who should know better) display to globalize the word until it covers all the cultural ground in sight seems to me blatantly wrong—especially when it comes to teaching the young. If they had their way, they would flatten the natural hierarchy of the mind until people cannot tell the difference between the telephone directory and Homer's *Iliad.* So in these pages I raise a small protest on behalf of the naked human mind, its creative powers, its animal resiliency, its undiscovered evolutionary potentiality, its deep enigmas of aspiration and self-transcendence. I seek to remind readers of the obvious that so often goes unobserved. There have been works of genius, indeed whole golden ages of culture— many of them the creation of peasant peoples and tribal folk—based upon nothing more than human speech, imagination, and memory. The heights of intellect and vision have been scaled by people gathered around campfires to tell stories, by poets scratching away with a quill by candlelight, by scribes bending over a sheet of parchment, by inspired painters working on the wall of a cave. There is, of course, no reason why we should not, in our time, look for other, more expressive media of communication, but I find it important to recall that mind has never been dependent on machinery to reach the peaks of achievement.

Though that reminder is not meant as a rejection of machinery, which is itself a glory of our species, I am sure some will see it as a typical humanist response to the overweening claims of the technician. Well, perhaps it is. But where high tech is concerned the disposition of forces ought to be obvious to anyone who has as much as a passing acquaintance with the shape of the global economy. High tech is the biggest thing going in the world of financial and political decision; it enjoys the unstinting support of governments and great corporations. Billions of dollars stand behind every computer chip. There is not the least chance that the most extreme humanistic critic of these machines and their makers will register as more than a minor annoyance to economic power of this magnitude. The computer establishment is the Goliath in this confrontation; before it even the most militant critic stands like David without his slingshot.

Meanwhile, Back at the Carnival

. . . With the Cold War and the arms race generating less budgetary support, Information-the-Science may now be less compromisingly connected with Information-the-Weapon; but it still remains embarrassingly beholden to Information-the-Commodity. So the merchandising of hardware and software remains as much of a carnival act as ever, with endless new attractions along the midway, all of them being brazenly oversold. While the price of such basic items as memory chips and hard disks continues to fall, new fascinations like desktop publishing multimedia, and interactivity serve to keep the consumers consuming. New hardware and software constantly push toward the purchase of bigger, faster equipment and more complex programs, none of which is nearly as necessary to have, as cheap to buy, or as friendly to use as the advertising pretends. What P. T. Barnum earned by convincing everybody in the nation that they

just *had* to buy a ticket to see Jumbo the elephant amounts to peanuts compared to the billions that Bill Gates of Microsoft has taken in from sales of Windows, a big, expensive, and (in its early versions) clunky imitation of the Macintosh graphical user interface. What made so many people rush to buy Windows? Gates made it seem like the only relief in sight from the cumbersome DOS program he had foisted upon his customers in the first place.

And what, overwhelmingly, do the hardware and the software get used for outside their day-to-day business applications? The computer industry remains embarrassingly dependent upon much that is simply tawdry. Games and amusements continue to be the mainstay of the technology in the mass market. As of the early 1990s American parents were paying more for video games (over *$5 billion*) than for tickets to the movies. Manufacturers are hoping to increase that figure tenfold by the end of the decade by including 3-D, virtual reality, adult versions of "Star Trek" and "Yoshi's Cookies"—probably spiked with a heavy dose of pornware, or "erototronics," as it is called in *Future Sex,* a magazine that specializes in computer-mediated titillation. "Adult" bulletin boards have proven to be one of the growth areas of the technology. Advertising "A Hundred Lines of Hot Modem Fun At Your Fingertips! With Both Straight and Gay Sections," the language and imagery have grown potent enough to raise issues of censorship. Responding to police raids in some cities, system operators have addressed the question of X-rated material at conferences with some urgency. "More and more boards are including the X-rated material for a simple reason—their subscribers want it."[4] Most of these amusements are benign, if silly; some are not. In Austria kids can now purchase neo-Naziware videogames called *Aryan Test* and *KZ Manager* which allow players to run death camps and gas inferior races.[5]

Even the business community gets suckered into wasting precious resources on expensive computer digressions like chasing fonts through desktop publishing programs and cranking out 256-color graphics-laden fast-step CD-ROM "presentations" that are more sizzle than substance. One study I have come across estimates the amount of time spent fussing with in-house newsletters, especially trying out this and that font, may cost American industry tens of millions of dollars in lost time.

The electronic bulletin boards, in which some see adumbrations of a new democratic forum, are also frequently taken up with trivial or less-than-idealistic pursuits: dating services, jokes, ticket sales, soap opera summaries, investing, and, more and more often, shopping. In France, it is estimated that more than half of what passes through the national Minitel computer-telephone network is sexual banter. The Internet has set aside an entire branch of the system (Alt.Sex) for pornographic chat and pictures. Perhaps this is inevitable with a technology that shades off so abruptly into entertainment, but it is nonetheless disappointing—as if the mighty railroad train, once the leading-edge invention of civilization, had been dependent on selling cut-down versions of itself to be used as roller coasters in amusement parks. Admittedly, an objection like this is a matter of taste and should not be pressed too seriously. But I have often wondered how cognitive

scientists and idealistic hackers must feel, knowing that the technology some among them regard as the salvation of democracy and the next step in evolution is being squandered on so many unbecoming uses.

The End of the War Machine?

Another issue [is] . . . the power of the computer to concentrate ever-greater decision-making power in the wrong few hands. . . . What I refer to as "the War Machine," the computerized control of thermonuclear weaponry, has receded as a threat to our freedom and survival in recent years. Though the Russian government that has taken over from the former Soviet leadership still possesses more than thirty thousand nuclear weapons (ten thousand of them capable of reaching targets in the United States), the complex of international political changes we refer to as "the end of the cold war" has made the forty-year balance of terror seem far less terrifying. The worst danger to which I addressed myself in dealing with the military uses of high tech—that of all-out Soviet-American nuclear war initiated by computer error or by the hair-trigger response of forces kept on instant alert—has all but disappeared. . . . The underlying concern I voice in dealing with nuclear weapons is not really tied to the particular facts and figures of the arms race at a given point in history. Rather, it has to do with the overweening confidence of computer scientists in their systems—and with our willingness as a society to believe what those scientists tell us about the absolute reliability of their programs.

At the same time, we should bear in mind that much of that military technology still exists and is as error-prone as ever. In one respect, we may even be worse off than before. As nuclear weapons proliferate around the world, the chance of regional conflicts achieving nuclear proportions increases. We now have more nuclear powers than ever before, many of them living side by side in deep distrust, their armed forces on round-the-clock alert, their under-trained technicians nervously fingering the red button. As Daniel Ellsberg warns us, "Worldwide, although the risk of nuclear war between NATO and the former Warsaw Pact powers has virtually vanished, the chance that some nuclear weapons will kill humans somewhere may be higher than before."[6] Another study by Scott Sagan reminds us that computerized weapons systems must still remain a cause for serious concern precisely because the cold war has ended.

The collapse of the Soviet Union has subjected its nuclear command and control system to unprecedented and unanticipated tensions. . . . Intercontinental-range strategic nuclear weapons are likely to be deployed in Russia, Kazakhstan, and Ukraine for many years to come, and the safety of these weapons will likely be strained by emerging political, ethnic, and civil-military conflicts in the region.

Sagan observes that many of the new nuclear powers that have been created out of the fragments of the old Soviet Union "may not be able to afford even a modicum of mechanical safety devices and modern warning sensors and will therefore be more prone to accidents and false warnings."[7]

As things now stand, our military leaders can have no clear idea who controls the world's remaining thermonu-

clear weapons systems; all accountability is being lost in the progressively fragmenting international community. Nor can anybody say with certainty what programs those weapons now obey, or how competent their new and anonymous keepers may be in dealing with this delicate and deadly technology. The "War Machine" is far from being a historical curiosity.

The Advent of the Money Machine

Even as the threat of thermonuclear Armageddon lessens, in another area of our lives, almost by way of negative compensation, things have grown more menacing. To the other categories of computer abuse . . . I would now add "the Money Machine." As in the worlds of law enforcement, political campaigning, and the military, so now in the world of high finance the computer has fallen into the wrong hands and is being used in ways that have radically altered international economic affairs. Programmed trading, a form of Expert System that has been steadily under development since the 1970s by some of the best mathematical brains in the nation, has at last become a disruptive and all but dictatorial force in world finance—to such a degree that patterns of investment and speculation generated by computers have become an independent factor determining the shape of the market.

Electronic cash management and funds transfers using the speed of computers and global telecommunications networks date well back into the 1960s; but the first indication the public received that the technological magic that made same-day funds possible might be a mixed blessing came in May 1984 when, following little more than rumors in the press, Continental Illinois Bank of Chicago, the seventh-largest bank in the United States, was reported to be insolvent. Foreign banks, mainly Japanese, responding to rumors about Continental's dubious financial health, had suddenly withdrawn billions of dollars in one-day overnight deposits. A massive run on the bank had begun in the international banking community. Continental, it was feared, was carrying far too many bad loans and was not financially stable. The reports turned out to be true; the bank had made many big, bad investments, mainly in oil companies. Poor judgment in the banking world is nothing new; what was new about the story were the scale of the misjudgment and the way in which such immense mismanagement could be kept out of sight. As the story unfolded, it became clear that Continental had been covering up its true condition by using its state-of-the-art instant-communications capacity to execute the sort of rapid electronic transfers of short term funds that computers and global telecommunications make possible. The transfers amounted to as much as $8 billion in overnight funds and $35 billion in one-week deposits. Now Continental had fallen victim to its own sleight-of-hand methods; the same electronic network it had been using to stay afloat had turned against it to produce a bank failure so huge that the federal government had no choice but to bail Continental out at the public expense.[8]

A year after the collapse of Continental Illinois, a major brokerage house, E.F. Hutton, was indicted by the Justice Department in a multimillion-dollar computer scam. Hutton was caught fast-shuffling funds between scores of banks throughout the United States in such a way that the company could write checks against deposits that did not exist except as computer records flashing across the electronic network—a form of high-tech check kiting.

Front page sensations like these were the public's first significant experience of the destabilizing potential that computers had assumed in the financial markets. Over the next year, commentators raised questions about another new computer-driven business practice: programmed trading. Might it be introducing too much speed and speculation into the markets? Not everybody saw much to worry about; there was certainly nothing illegal about the practice. *Time* magazine quoted optimistic insiders who even believed the new high-speed technology represented the "threshold of a golden age of capitalism." Other observers were more skeptical; they saw in the growing use of neural networked systems ominous possibilities for new forms of financial manipulation that would be dominated by a handful of institutional investors and programmed traders equipped with the best expert investment systems money can buy.[9]

The skeptics turned out to be right. In October 1987, programmed decisions to buy and sell by large institutional investors triggered the worst collapse in the history of the New York Stock Exchange. In effect, too many of the programs that had been cleverly devised *by* the "rocket scientists" (as the hackers of the financial world are called) at major brokerage firms were doing the same thing at the same time. What each of the institutional investors was seeking to do was to protect itself by choosing the safest selection of risk-reducing options and futures: "portfolio insurance," as it is termed. But the net result was a cascading series of self-fulfilling prophecies operating as a feedback loop. The market went haywire.

After the crash, the Securities and Exchange Commission imposed "circuit-breakers" to head off any future disaster of this kind. But these are of limited value in a financial marketplace that has become round-the-clock and international; damping the panic in one stock exchange will only divert it elsewhere.

The simple fact is that, thanks to the computer, information about money has now become as valuable as money itself. And those who can process the most information the fastest are in the best position to profit—often in ways that escape any effective legal control. The computerized hand can move faster than the regulatory eye. As a result, the instability produced by high-speed computerized operations has become endemic. It has in fact been institutionalized in the signature financial instrument of the nineties: the "derivative," by far the most exotic and elusive entity ever to appear in the world of money.

Derivatives are new categories of financial "products" that could only achieve the prominence they enjoy where lightning-fast transfers are possible. They allow a variety of speculative maneuvers keyed to minute fluctuations in the price action of markets that deal in interest rates, foreign currency, stock indices, collateralized mortgages, and commodities. One observer calls derivatives "a concept out of *Alice in Wonderland*. . . . In this strange and eerie electronic world, Japanese pension funds

can buy American bonds backed not by gold or corporate assets, but by stacks of car loans made by Detroit."[10]

Interest rate swaps are among the most popular derivatives; these allow speculators to "surf the yield curve" between the day-to-day (or even hour-to-hour) differences in long-term and short-term obligations—for example, the spread between fixed and variable mortgage interest rates. Traders can make contracts on future interest rates, then trade the contracts separately from the money to which the rates were originally attached. Major banks are among the big players in these tricky games. Since the accounting practices associated with derivatives are terra incognita even to regulators, nobody knows for certain how much money is tied up in this new market, but the figure is certainly in the hundreds of billions. The credit exposure of the banks on sums like this is enough to worry *Barron's* magazine, which asks in a major editorial report if the explosive popularity of derivatives might not lead to a "meltdown" on the global market greater than the panic of '87.[11]

Those who are complacent about the risks rely heavily on the sort of "dynamic hedging" that only programmed investment can provide. This is among the chief services provided by the "quants," the computer experts who account for the ascendancy of derivatives in the markets. Creating an optimum portfolio made up of such complex abstractions requires the ability to assimilate huge amounts of information with maximum speed. So too, the split-second trading in currencies by speculators that has played havoc with monetary policy around the world is uniquely a computer phenomenon. In 1993 the French government, after expending billions in an effort to shore up the franc, was forced to capitulate and devalue its currency. The traders it was up against not only had the capital to get their way but the computer power to take instant advantage of currency fluctuations and to move funds at the push of a button.

The new masters of the universe [*Barron's* reports in its survey] are as likely to have degrees in engineering or computer science. In their high tech world of probability curves and elaborate securities pricing models incorporating lots of Greek letters, there's little room for the once-venerated qualities of trading intuition and social polish. . . . These days [the nerds] even have their own trade group—the International Association of Financial Engineers. Imagine that.

As the financier Felix Rohatyn sees it, "twenty-six-year-olds with computers are creating financial hydrogen bombs."[12]

But risk is not the only liability to these computer games; an opportunistic preoccupation with quick and massive profit-taking may pose a greater problem, especially as banks grow more and more involved with derivatives and other speculative financial products. For the high rollers in the marketplace, the temptation to make overnight billions by shuffling electronic values has become a major distraction. Most worrisomely, banks have been seduced into diverting their capital away from what Joel Kurtzman calls "the real-economy . . . where products are made, trade is conducted, research is carried out, and services rendered. The real-economy is where factory workers toil, doctors tend the sick, and teachers teach, and where roads,

bridges, harbors, airports, and railway systems are built."

But in the real-economy, profits can take a long while reporting in. These days smart guys don't waste their time in the real-economy; they vandalize it and move on across the buzzing networks. Inevitably, restless and globally footloose capital drifts toward the international electronic casino where the returns come at the speed of light. Writes Kurtzman:

> Over the years, especially during the 1980s, real-economy companies have been hit by wave after wave of corporate takeovers, with the stock market conspiring in those takeovers by camouflaging rather than revealing true value. These companies have also been handed a big bill from the firms that sell their stocks for the thrill of participating in financial markets that are rigged against real-economy companies.

So Kurtzman asks of the high-flying "megabyte marketplace" that now devours the true wealth of nations: "When the economic unit is the globe, where do people fit in?"[13]

Like the other examples I offer of computer power "in the wrong hands," the money machine raises issues about the social value of the computer that make for neo-Luddite pessimism. The question of balance once again is central. List the pros and the cons of the technology and give them their proper weight. Granted, it is now possible for concerned citizens with PCs and Macs to log into electronic conferences on their local bulletin board, to debate, to gripe, to complain and petition. On the other hand we have the money machine, which makes possible the electronic hijacking of the world's financial markets by a small number of privileged traders who play the game for paper billions. As a result, the capital resources that we need to generate paychecks, useful products, research and development, and helpful services are diverted from long-term investment to short-term speculation. What citizenly use of this technology can counterbalance a shift of power on this scale?

One comes back to the basic economic fact of the matter: computer technology, both the hardware and the software, is a commodity on sale to those who can afford it—and the most powerful machines continue to be in the wrong hands.

Edutainment

A particular interest in the 1986 edition of *The Cult of Information* was the role of the computer in education, a lively topic of discussion and promotion at that time. The computer industry continues to cultivate the field, but I would judge that a great deal of the shine that once surrounded the vision of the electronic classroom has rubbed off—at least among the educators. Even though there are more computers than ever in our schools (since the early 1980s, the number of personal computers in U.S. schools has risen from fifty thousand to 2.4 million), their place in the curriculum remains highly uncertain. Certainly the predictions that were being made a few decades ago that public education would be revolutionized by the advent of the electronic classroom have fallen flat. In 1969, for example, the National Education Association confidently predicted (in a report titled "The Teacher

and His Staff") that by 1994 every student in the United States would be equipped with "computer information bank consoles" and international video phones.

Computers are only the most recent wave of educational technology; since the 1950s educators have been through two generations of hype about all the good things they can expect from various kinds of "teaching machines." They have learned to be skeptical. As two close students of educational technology observe, "We thought that mere acquisition was sufficient to begin using these new technological delights, but have learned that there were no quick and easy roads to success. . . . We have learned that educational technology is a problem-solving process, not a product."[14]

More to the point, an increasing number of educators have begun to recognize that classroom technology is emphatically *not* neutral but carries with it significant (if subliminal) cultural, ethical, and epistemological presuppositions. The computer is inherently a Cartesian device embedded in the assumptions of a single intellectual style within a single culture of the modern world. The very metaphors that surround it bespeak a conception of the mind as logical machinery; the constant references to the "productivity" that the computer promises endorse the values of the marketplace and the western ethos of progress. In a critique that draws upon Jacques Ellul, Martin Heidegger, and Jurgen Habermas, the educator C. A. Bowers concludes that "the designers of educational software, in not being more aware of the phenomenological traditions of thought, have simply ignored the epistemological problem of how to represent the cultural foundations of a person's tacit knowledge, which is highly contextual, through a medium that decontextualizes knowledge.[15]

"There is a built-in conservatism to American public education that is deeply rooted in the professional self-interest of teachers and the entrenched localism of our country's sixteen thousand school districts. Teachers have not been quick to learn computer skills, and even less quick to redesign the chalk-and-talk curriculum in favor of confused and untested schemes—even when they come attached to free equipment like the many Apple II computers that were donated to American schools in the 1980s. None of the more radical proposals for computer-based educational reform . . . has found a solid, aggressive, and growing constituency. Instead we continue to have . . . a national hodgepodge" of ideas and prescriptions.

In large part the high-tech standoffishness of classroom teachers can be justifiably traced to a false start. In the early 1980s, "computer literacy" by and large meant teaching pupils to program in some simple language like BASIC. That orientation betrayed astonishing short-sightedness on the part of experts who should have known better. I noted . . . that the availability of well-developed application programs made programming courses a waste of time; that is even more the case now. As sophisticated software has flowed onto the market, there is little need for the sort of low-level amateur programming that can be taught on cheap equipment in limited time. Like everybody else, schools can now buy whole off-the-shelf packages for classroom use. The fact that many computer enthusiasts did not see this coming hardly inspires confidence.

Most of the packages, however, have turned out to be more hype and puffery than well-conceived instructional material. One estimate has it that of the ten thousand programs in the pedagogical marketplace as of the early 1990s, perhaps two hundred are of some value. Among these, basic word processing—a valuable but hardly exhilarating use of the technology—dominates the interest of educators. But even here, where we have a clear, practical application of computer skills, teachers report that they can spend more time teaching pupils how to find their way around the word processing program than they spend actually using the computer to improve expression and thought. This is hardly surprising; every computer program has its "learning curve." The simple fact is, when it comes to writing, learning how to use a computer takes more time than learning how to use a pencil. The same could be said about graphics and science programs in comparison to learning how to use a paintbrush, crayons, and most lab equipment. When it comes to the three Rs, only 'rithmetic clearly benefits from computerization. Placing a complex machine between the student and reading and 'riting puts more distance between intention and result.

Whatever the sources of curricular indecision and lethargy may be, the conservatism of American educators has been powerfully supplemented by a new factor: fiscal limitations. When computers first began to penetrate the classroom, the assumption was that an Apple II or an IBM PC, plus some basic software and a low-cost dot-matrix printer, represented a long-term capital investment. But machines like the aging Apple II, which still makes up some 50 percent of the installed base of school computers, are moving steadily toward obsolescence, despite the continued production of software designed for them. Teachers may be resourceful in making the most of the old machines, but both they and their students are constantly made aware that there is later and better merchandise on the market. Many of the kids are aware of that fact from the games they use at home or at the video arcade. And the latest, most eye-popping programs that have entered the educational market require hard disks and much memory, as well as CD-ROM drives. Though the cost of everything electronic continues to decline, the purchase of add-ons as costly as CD-ROM players and sound cards in any great quantity is no easy expenditure for financially strapped school systems. Even when there are ways of networking such facilities, the installation and maintenance of networks can be a heavy expense—especially in schools where the wear and tear on fragile equipment can take a fierce toll. All the money has to come from other parts of the curriculum. As long as "edutainment," as the industry calls its latest *melange* of multimedia tricks, requires as much computer power as it does, it will lie beyond the reach of many schools.

This may be the greatest obstacle computer enthusiasts now confront in touting their wares. If the data merchants have their way, the main thrust of edutaining technology will be toward ever-more-expensive gimmickry with ever-less quality control. But they are pushing a costly substitute for books and blackboards, one that many school districts, plagued by a backlog of social issues, simply cannot afford.

That factor has shown up dramatically in an unusually comprehensive and conscientious survey of computers in our schools that was sponsored in the early 1990s by *Macworld* magazine.[16] The findings were sobering. Charles Piller, who headed the study, concluded that we are rapidly creating a "technological underclass in America's public schools." While the survey did find schools where computers were being used imaginatively as an integrated part of a high-level curriculum, it found many more schools where the machines were limited to drill-and-practice sessions, and far too many where computers were simply going unused. This led to an important insight: *Mere statistics, like computer-to-student ratios, tell us nothing about the real on-site value of the technology.* Many computers that get tallied in superficial studies turn out to be broken relics stacked away in closets and storerooms. This is poignantly true of schools in minority neighborhoods. "Poor schools," the *Macworld* study observes, "tend to use computers so rigidly and ineptly as to repel students. Poor schools create refugees from technology." In a follow-up article for *The New York Times,* Piller concluded, "Instead of becoming instruments of reform, computers are reinforcing a two-tier system of education for the rich and poor."[17]

Moreover, even if the will and the skill were there to use the machines well, in many school districts the funds educators divert to computers will have to come out of urgently necessary programs like vaccinations or school lunches or campus security. There are schools where controlling the handguns on campus counts for more than teaching computer literacy. We are reminded that our nation's schools are woven into a dense political and sociological fabric that has everything to do with morale, teachability, opportunity, safety, and survival.

Social and financial problems of this magnitude would compromise effective educational use of computer technology even if what that technology offered included intellectually reputable choices. But it is not at all the case that academic quality can be guaranteed. . . . [A]s the CD disks fill up with spectacular effects, the reading habits encouraged by interactive materials—at least the versions I have seen—run the risk of over-loading and further fragmenting the attention span (already so badly battered) that is basic to intelligence. There is an unresolved tension between computer literacy (still a catchphrase in search of a meaning) and plain old print literacy that will not be resolved as long as the data merchants promote their wares for short-sighted profiteering motives.

Computers raise another issue in the classroom. By far the strongest argument for going high tech in the schools has been the promise of employment; computer literacy supposedly represents the royal road to a good job. But, by a cruel irony, in the greater global economy that surrounds our schools, the main effect of automation and cybernation is to deskill, disempower, and disemploy people from the assembly line up through middle management. Computers have come to play a central role in downsizing companies and in the creation of a part-time, temporary, low-paid, nonbenefited workforce. The brutal economic fact of life in today's marketplace is that we could generate more good jobs by outlawing computers than by multiplying them. Once again the basic truth about public education is clear: our schools do not exist in a vacuum. They are surrounded by and permeated by social and economic forces that pose more problems in the lives of our children than any machine will ever solve—unless videogames are intended to be the circus that will keep otherwise restless citizens preoccupied in the New World Order.

The Ideal of the Online Commonwealth

Does it *have* to be like this? Does this remarkable technology *have* to be swamped by silly commercial novelties and abusive social power? Of course not. There is no law that says information technology *must* fall victim to mindless consumption and technocratic manipulation. There are any number of principled, politically concerned hackers who are struggling to salvage the computer for better uses. Bulletin boards across the country are being employed as worldwide citizens' information and discussion facilities. Many see the expanding Internet . . . as the beginning of a democratic renaissance. Combined with full and free public access to government archives, the Internet may one day largely supplant newspapers and television news, with their many limitations and biases, as a customized news service. Some look forward to new forms of electronic publication that will replace print-on-the-page with new image and sound capabilities; purely electronic magazines already exist, and some authors have begun to "publish" their works over networks, requesting a voluntary fee from their readers.

Though there will always be debate about the best technology to select, the

Clinton-Gore administration, with its commitment to a public "data highway," would seem to be setting the course for a national information infrastructure. If information is what our embattled democracy needs, people—at least those who can afford the bill—should soon have no great difficulty filling the need in the "wired world" that some predict. In fact, navigating the surplus may be the great problem. There are difficulties and expenses involved in making use of the opportunity, but these need not be insurmountable. With enough skill, anyone owning a cheap second-hand computer and a modem can access many networking services. It is now possible to exchange mail, news, and expertise across the globe at a cost that may be as low as a local phone call or a subscription to a daily newspaper.

And there are other good possibilities. . . . [T]he nation's libraries might become the vital center that would provide maximum democratic access to the burgeoning electronic plenty within an ethic of public service. The libraries are, I suggest, our best hope of turning the sprawling potentiality of information technology into a true public utility.

For all the reservations I may express about computers and their uses, my heart goes out to the heroic spirits who recognize what power we have here to do the right thing—and who struggle to keep that power under democratic control. They are the conscience of the technology. . . .

Nor is the promise of computer technology limited to the political arena. At the Media Lab at the Massachusetts Institute of Technology—the Bauhaus of high tech—new artistic and expressive possibilities are being brilliantly explored. The more optimistic assessments of the electronic wonders there being created look forward to a "technological populism" and a new "computer-enhanced individuality" in which everything will be cheaply digitalized and wholly customizable.[18]

What I have seen and sampled among the new genres that Stewart Brand calls a "techno-feast of goodies" can be dazzling in the extreme. As one might predict, among all the goodies, an author would be most curious about the promise of the "electronic book." Will it inherit the future the way the printed book displaced the handwritten manuscript? The E-book is being promoted as a push-button cornucopia of spectacular multimedia effects: hypertext interactively linked at every point to film, animation, graphics, music, voice, all miniaturized to the size of a Sony Walkman, and possibly made available as a domestic production facility. Every home its own MGM.

As in the case of desktop publishing, I find it hard to imagine that the technology needed to produce the most impressive electronic results will ever be affordable by ordinary users like myself, or that the skills will be within our reach. The benefits of the E-book will most likely come to us by way of buying them ready-made—as we do the printed word. Will they be affordable? There are special problems here that are far from solution. Some are painfully ironic. It turns out that even those who would seem to have the capital and the cunning to exploit these astonishing possibilities may find the road into virtual reality blocked by one of the most traditional barriers imaginable. It is called "copyright," and it entails paying for the privilege to use created material.

The producers of E-books are entrepreneurs operating in a free, competitive market out to make all the profit they can. But they are learning that producing an E-book means entering a jungle of property rights held by those who are just as eager to turn a profit. In the cultural marketplace, everything—words, images, music, lyrics, logos, voices, photos, film footage—is property owned by somebody; entrepreneurs now routinely buy up and hoard every last seemingly worthless shred of created material. And a fully packed CD-ROM disk needs a lot of that material: hundreds of megabytes of it.

High tech comes surrounded by an aura of big bucks; precisely for that reason, everybody wants a piece of the multimedia pie, and nobody is willing to sell cheap. Software Toolworks of Novato, California, producer of the highly successful Grolier Multimedia Encyclopedia, is one of the largest CD-ROM software companies in the world. In the early 1990s, it set about producing *The Twentieth Century Video Almanac,* a five-disk interactive compendium of film, music, and graphics. The project required a feature-film-sized production team in which the writer was a minor player. Legal skill proved to be far more crucial. Why? Because rounding up all the permissions involved took as much time as the technical work; the bargaining was fierce, the prices demanded were high. Everybody who so much as appeared in the background of a picture or film clip expected to be paid. Permissions availability became the main editorial factor determining what got included; the "art" had to be worked in around the copyrights. The fees demanded might have been prohibitively high, but Software Toolworks was able to argue that its market for this CD-ROM would be quite limited, perhaps under one hundred thousand sales (at some $200 for the five disk set). But what happens if the E-book medium booms, as Software Toolworks and all its competitors hope that it will? The price of everything can only go up—and so too the cost to the buyer.[19]

Interestingly, in print publishing, standards of fair use and a scale of reasonable permission fees for graphics and illustrations have been worked out over generations; nobody expects to make a killing off somebody else's book (except perhaps for the song-lyric vendors, who are notorious bandits). But the E-book has no such tradition to draw upon. Its association is with the sky's-the-limit motion picture marketplace where all concerned expect to get rich quick. In the new, uncharted world of the E-book, where permissions wrangling and litigation are apt to go on endlessly, the CD-ROM may become the first cultural genre invented wholly for the financial benefit of lawyers.

Whenever I find myself having doubts whether increasingly powerful media like these will ever be brought under the creative control of mature aesthetic minds, I try to remind myself that once upon a time the printing press, the camera, the piano, the orchestra, and motion pictures were innovations with no cultural track record. But one thing I know for certain: the minds that use these powers well will still have to master the art of thinking. Though the medium may be zero-cost infinite bandwidth networks, the media users will have to exercise the same mental muscles as the artists of Lascaux and draw upon the same creative sources. If there is anything particularly pernicious in the lore of high tech it is the facile assumption that just maybe the machines will do the thinking (and the feeling, and the judging, and the creating) for us, and do it better. The irony behind this technology is the tendency it encourages in some of its most talented and enthusiastic developers to cheapen—or even try to replace—the mind that created the technology in the first place.

A Few Words for the Rest of Us

Despite the problems I mention here, I fully accept that information technology is here to stay—at least for as long as the world industrial economy survives. (No guarantees about that, to be sure.) It has the permanence of a mature technology.

What is a mature technology?

One that finally generates as many problems as it solves.

As we have learned from every earlier wave of invention, machines are jinnis that get out of control. They reshape the world in unforeseen ways. The railroad and the automobile "solved" the problem of rapid transportation—only to finish by depleting our store of nonrenewable fossil fuels, fouling the air, and destroying the integrity of cities. Modern medicine "solved" the problem posed by numerous infectious diseases, only to finish by giving us the population explosion, ever-more-resistant strains of bacteria, and the ethical dilemma of protracted senility.

The computer "solved" the problem of fast, cheap data processing in a business culture drowning in red tape and paperwork, only to finish by destroying the rights of privacy, concentrating the political and commercial control of information in ever fewer hands, mesmerizing our children with bad art and pernicious nonsense, and menacing us with "computer errors" vast enough to paralyze whole societies. A clever few find ways to work around these vices and maximize the advantages of each new technology; the computer-proficient can sound quite smug about their command of databases and online resources. Many earn well from new, more sophisticated media. But the sum total of good and bad gets visited on the rest of us—and especially on the generations to come, who are simply born into the technology's inevitable downside. . . .

There is the problem, right before our eyes. The machines may not be smarter than we are, but we may not be proficient enough or moneyed enough to hold our own with those who own and exploit the machines. The cult of information is theirs, not ours. They use it, and they use it against us. What "the rest of us" are offered as "access" to the information society is hardly enough to make us real citizens of the information age: it may be little more than a diversion. True, we can now use our modems to send e-mail to the new online White House, but there is no law that says anybody has to read what we send. And if there were, would it matter? We may soon have programs that make it possible to defeat the purpose of rapid, personal communications. A teaching colleague of mine, swamped by the e-mail he receives from the students in one college course—much of which he finds repetitive, garbled, or witless—has developed a program that scans what he receives for keywords and generates boilerplate responses.

"The rest of us" get games to play and programs that will balance our checkbooks and catalogue our recipes. Maybe eventually we will get 3-D subscription virtual sex. We can rent CompuServe or log onto the local electronic bulletin board to check the running file of light-bulb jokes or to flame away on an issue or two. But even if we can buy the technology, we don't own it—not in any substantial way that gives us power. I, for example, am grateful that high tech has provided me with a great substitute for my old Smith-Corona on which to write my neo-Luddite lament. Perhaps one day I will become proficient enough to find my way through a MUD (a Multi-User Dungeon) on the Internet. But all the while I keystroke away, I suspect that the data-surfers at the IRS and the FBI and TRW are gliding through every secret I ever thought I had, and that the hot young quants at Morgan Stanley are using their rather more powerful machines to vandalize the banking systems of six nations. While the rest of us cling to the margins, the power and the profit of the technology gravitate elsewhere. The solution is once again becoming the problem.

But then the history of technology has always been a faltering search for Promethean power and utopian perfection. Every mature technology brings a minimal immediate gain followed by enormous long-term liabilities. The computer is the latest entry in that history, still bright with promise for its enthusiasts but surely destined to join the lengthening file of modern technological treachery that Aldous Huxley began compiling in his prophetic *Brave New World.* By now we should know what the Luddites of old learned before us: every tool ever invented is a mixed blessing. How things will balance out is a matter of vigilance, moral courage, and the distribution of power.

Whenever I begin to despair over such matters, I conjure up a few consoling images: Charlie Chaplin sliding woefully down the gullet of the assembly line, Laurel and Hardy fleeing for their lives before a runaway trolley car. There is a certain healthy amusement to be enjoyed in the irony of seeing our species victimized by the machines we invent to liberate ourselves—*provided,* that is, we heed the great lesson that underlies the human comedy. Namely, that there will never be a machine that leaves us wiser or better or freer than our own naked mind can make us—nor any that helps us work out our salvation with diligence.

CASE STUDIES

Following each of the readings in this book you will find case studies and/or exercises to help you digest, understand, and apply the issues, concepts, and arguments presented in the readings.

Roszak believes that computers have legitimate and illegitimate uses. Which ethical values underlie the distinctions he wishes to promote between applications of technology? The values most important to ethicists are human autonomy, individual and community self-reliance, privacy, and accuracy of information. These are interrelated values and so the same case may involve more than one value issue. Roughly, *autonomy* is the ability to make informed decisions in accordance with a person's own values while free from coercion. Anything that fosters a person's ability to act autonomously respects the person and the person's characteristic ability to act freely. By fostering autonomy we show respect for a typical human ability and humanity in general. A concern for *self-reliance* recognizes the inherent satisfaction people find in self-directed personal accomplishments. A community concerned with self-reliance would supplement and preserve such individual satisfaction from personal effort in smaller communities of intimate interaction. A concern for *privacy* sometimes focuses on establishing places, such as our homes, where we need not fear surveillance. Privacy also can involve control over access to certain types of information. For instance, most people dislike having their e-mail address captured by a corporation regardless of whether they access their e-mail at home, on the job, or in a public Internet cafe. Finally, *accuracy of information* is connected to the autonomy of information consumers. But accuracy can also be important as a condition of showing respect to the people or cultures depicted.

Keep in mind the difference between judging an action as immoral and favoring legal regulation of an activity. Political and practical concerns can provide good reason not to regulate activities that conflict with ethical values. You may morally object to a practice and still not favor legal remedies.

CASE STUDY: AMATEUR CYBER-PORN

A certain Usenet group hosts explicit photos of former romantic partners. Most people would see this as a clear violation of numerous moral and ethical values such as privacy, even if the photos were originally taken with the "model's" consent. Nevertheless, the Internet hosts a great deal of voluntary pornography. *Rolling Stone* reported recently that twenty-five percent of the four-billion-dollar-a-year pornography industry is generated online.[20] "Mom-and-pop" suppliers form a significant portion of that online business. For a few thousand dollars porno entrepreneurs can purchase the technology necessary to start a Web-based business.

Discuss how you see this in light of the values mentioned above and other morally relevant concerns. Try to clarify and rank the moral values involved before discussing the morality of the practice.

CASE STUDY: THIS COKE'S FOR GEORGE

In April 1999 a group "dedicated to the sabotage of corporate products" maintained a Web site that misleadingly appeared to belong to the George W. Bush Presidential Campaign Exploratory Committee. College students who visited the site and inquired about political internships received an e-mail message explaining that resumes were being considered and requesting that the students do a little research in the meantime on how their peers felt about Bush's cocaine use. "Please ask as many of your peers as possible four or so questions about the governor's former drug use."[21]

CASE STUDY: DON'T ASK, DON'T TELL

The United States Navy has adopted a "don't ask, don't tell" policy toward sexual orientation. In June 1998, the navy pursued a sailor whose Internet name identified him as gay, intending to discharge the sailor. A naval investigator called the Internet provider, America Online, and obtained confirmation of the ownership of the Internet identification. (America Online's policy forbids giving out such information without a court order. The identification in this instance was obtained through a combination of subterfuge and customer service error.) The sailor and America Online considered this matter a violation of privacy. What do you think?[22]

1.2 THE NEW INFORMATION ETHICS   Richard T. De George is Distinguished Professor of Philosophy and Business Administration at the University of Kansas. In 1999 he was selected as the first Bell Atlantic Visiting Professor in Business Ethics and Information Technology at Bentley College. In this essay, Professor De George reflects on the transformation of business ethics in the information age. The essay calls ethicists to greater involvement in business ethics before problems emerge. Those of us working at the advent of electronic mail in business and educational institutions remember that most were using e-mail long before policies emerged regarding its use in private communication. This led to some misunderstandings on the part of employees about who owned e-mail and who had legitimate rights to access e-mail communications.

De George addresses the expansion of business information services in general, remarking on how retailers such as Wal-Mart may also be seen as information businesses. He expresses concern over the public's abdication of personal privacy in a context in which information is an increasingly valuable commodity. Concerned with the accuracy of information offered for public consumption, he offers an interesting proposal for establishing independent authenticators for Web-based information analogous to the role now played by magazines such as *Consumer Reports.*

QUESTIONS FOR STUDY AND DISCUSSION

1. Explain how the Internet affects business marketing through customer tracking. Does De George see this as a positive or negative aspect of the impact of technology upon business?
2. Why does De George consider Wal-Mart primarily in the information business?
3. What does De George mean by the myth of amoral computing and information technology? How does this myth undermine the ethical responsibility of business?
4. Does De George's suggestion of authenticators for the Internet amount to an attempt at censorship? Do you agree that authenticators are needed?
5. Does De George see a difference between truth and accurate information? If so, explain the difference. Does a commitment to accuracy involve holding business to a higher ethical standard than a commitment to truth?
6. Regardless of whether truth and accuracy are different concepts, De George holds that providing accurate information is in the interest of business. Why?

Business Ethics and the Information Age[23]

R I C H A R D   T.   D E   G E O R G E

. . . The fact that we are entering the information age is a truism, yet exactly what that means is understood differently by different people. As we enter this new age, we will face new ethical and business issues. I shall briefly present some thoughts about these issues in seven theses that I hope we can pursue in questions and comments from you. . . .

Thesis 1.

The IT head-in-the-sand syndrome:

Many businesses either fail to realize that we have entered the information age or fail to appreciate its importance.

The move of business to the information age raises many ethical issues, but has received little ethical attention, either from business or from business ethicists. Uncovering the ethical issues that grow out of information technology, facing them, and providing ethical guidelines is the major challenge for business and business ethics at the start of the new millennium.

The rise of the Internet as a locus of business is changing marketing, for instance. It makes possible one-on-one marketing by tracking the customer, recording his or her preferences and proclivities, and presenting the customer with products that he or she is likely to want to buy. Department stores and discount stores, just like TV ads, have to rely on generalizations and average wants and desires. The Internet makes possible an individual fit. As Internet sales climb, they will continue to encroach on, if not yet threaten, department stores and other stores and retail outlets. Many businesses seem not to care or worry, or else do not know how to respond effectively.

Wal-Mart is one of the few traditional firms that realizes it exists in the information age. In a real sense, Wal-Mart is not primarily in the retail business, but in the information business. It's very much like Amazon.com, except that Wal-Mart also owns its own outlets. Like Amazon.com, Wal-Mart has a database that is probably its most important asset. Because of its database, Wal-Mart can customize each of its stores to suit local shoppers and order product to point-of-delivery exactly when each store needs it—saving storage and other costs, and changing the way product is manufactured and delivered.

The effect of such time pressure on factories and workers in the plants that supply Wal-Mart, however, is uncharted territory for the business ethicist. The changes are real. But their ethical impact has yet to be assessed. The security of Internet transactions, the return of goods with which customers are dissatisfied, and the delivery of goods ordered all raise issues to be examined, and carry with them ethical implications. Similarly, how, where, and whether to tax online sellers and buyers is an unresolved question that has been temporarily put on hold by legislation. But the tax base of many cities and local communities relies on local sales taxes, which may well diminish considerably as new ways of buying goods develop in the information age.

Business via the Internet changes the relevance of location, geography, times during which businesses are open and employees work, how employees are used, and so on.

In area after area, businesses have not yet started to sort out the implications. And society has not decided whose laws should apply; what rules and regulations should be adopted; who is to decide; and who is responsible for enforcement. The pirating of software, music, books, and anything that can be put in digital form is symptomatic of a growing nest of problems.

The failure of business to recognize the move into the information age is demonstrated by its procrastination in facing up to the Y2K problem. That information technology and computer people could not get the attention of management long before the approach of the year 2000, to fix a problem the technicians knew existed and would have to be faced sooner or later, is a sad reflection on business managers. Undoubtedly, many did not understand the problem or its scope, and many who did were unwilling to spend the millions of dollars it would take to fix their systems before they had to, even though the delay added to the cost. Companies are now backing into the information age or being pulled by a technology they do not completely understand, even as they become more and more dependent on it. One result is the focus of my second thesis.

Thesis II.

The abdication of IT ethical responsibility:

The "Myth of Amoral Computing and Information Technology" permeates the public as well as the business mind, implicitly accepts the technological imperative, and undermines the ethical responsibility of business.

The lack of awareness of the ethical implications of the information age is what I call the "myth of amoral computing and information technology." The myth says that computers are not good or bad, information systems are not good or bad—they simply have a logic and rationale of their own. To speak of ethics with respect to them is to make a category mistake. Hence, when the computer is down, that is no one's fault. When programs malfunction or software has bugs, that is no one's fault. In general, anything that has to do with computers and information technology has a life of its own and is not susceptible to moral evaluation or blame or censure.

This myth is understandable in part because so few people in or out of business truly understand computing and information technology. They are tools that we non-techies like to have and use. But we do not take ethical responsibility for them, and because of our ignorance, we do not expect anyone else to take ethical responsibility for them. The result is a failure both to accept and to assign responsibility.

In businesses in the more developed countries, management for the most part still tends to think of information systems [IS] and information technology [IT] as something that is not central to the organization. Most managers do not understand them, and tend to ignore them. IS and IT offices are not typically center stage at corporate headquarters, and the typical manager is not a computer techie. The disconnect between corporate leaders and their technical divisions, which often are still off in a back set of rooms and considered part of the support structure and not part of the core business, is the clearest indication that firms have not moved consciously into the information age. Yet if we are truly in a developing information age, then IS and IT need to be at the center of things, and management has to both understand them and take responsibility for them. . . .

Thesis III.

Where are the business ethicists when you need them?

The task of the business ethicist in the present period of transition—and a task in which few are engaged—is to help anticipate the developments and ease the transition by not losing sight of the effects on people.

The transition is from the industrial age to the information age. The ethical issues in business of the industrial age are those with which we are familiar. The development of the information age came about without conscious direction. As technology developed, the transition came along as a handmaiden. One consequence is that businesses and society as a whole are following the technological imperative—what can be developed is developed and implemented. Because the transition to the information age is currently taking place, many of the ethical issues have not clearly jelled. The task of the business ethicist in this instance is to at least keep up with the technological and social developments and identify problems and potential problems before they cause great harm, and before they become embedded ways of doing business that are difficult to change.

Business ethicists and society in general could wait for ethical problems and injustices of the information age to arise, and do analysis after the fact. Far preferable, however, is to anticipate injustice, prevent it from appearing, and form structures that are ethically justifiable, rather than having to undo and attempt to reform structures that are unfair, socially disruptive, and harmful to some of the parties. We of course cannot anticipate all the ethical issues that will arise. Experience and the empirical approach are also necessary. But we can anticipate more than we might expect, and I suggest that now is the time to start this analysis as we enter the information age. We do not need a new ethics framework, but we have to apply and possibly revise our ethical concepts and norms to fit the new environment. We need an imaginative analysis of the potential harms to people—be they in the realm of privacy, property, the new surveillance sweatshops, or other areas.

Thesis IV.

Surmounting the information nexus:

In order to lay out the ethical issues of the information age in business, we must give careful attention to an analysis of the concept of information and the related concepts with which it forms a whole.

We can start by a simple analysis of information to see the virtues and the vices basic to it. A second step is to superimpose the analysis of information upon the analysis of industrialization to see how it changes production, exchange, advertising, conditions of employment, ownership rights, and so on. Each of these is transformed in the information age and the transformation requires new thinking about its effect on people.

If by "information" we mean not simply data but *useful* data, we see immediately that what we are interested in is useful information. Information, as generally used, stands for true knowledge in some area. Its opposites are disinformation, misinformation, and falsehood. Information is not simply data, but data that represents reality. It's true and not false.

Two virtues appear immediately. One is truth (and so truthfulness), the other is accuracy. It follows that the virtues necessary for the information age are not necessarily the same virtues as are or were necessary for the industrial age. In the latter, efficiency became paramount. As opposed to an agricultural age, punctuality became important and time took on critical importance. In the information age, truthfulness and accuracy take on special importance. For if the information is not accurate or truthful or correct, it is worse than useless. It's dysfunctional. It is ironic that truthfulness no longer seems to hold a place of honor in our society. We find people, including high government officials, lying. Truthfulness takes on more importance than ever.

False information is injurious to a system built on information. So we have truth as a necessary virtue and a presupposition, and distortion of the truth, lying, the spreading of false information, as vices to be guarded against. It is not only necessary for people not to lie or deceive or mislead; it's also necessary to represent reality as accurately as possible.

The enemy of accuracy is inaccuracy, which also leads to disinformation and error. These two virtues or values are basic to any system of information if it is to be socially useful and economically valuable for business, as well as for societies and the individuals within them.

Questions that immediately arise are: information of what or whom and for what or whom? Information about the world, or scientific information, is one kind of information. Information about societies, or social information, is another kind. Information about people and corporations is another kind. Important to all of them in an information age is ownership. Together with ownership goes power, and with it the dangers of control and manipulation. Truth leads to the concepts of enlightenment, education, and the potential freeing of individuals and of society. As individuals learn the truth, they are also in a position of empowerment. Politically, this makes enslavement difficult and it promotes self-rule or democracy. Nonetheless, there remains the possibility of the domination of citizens by government and of employees by employers, as well as of one society by another—for instance, through the domination of the communication resources.

Ethics is about people and their relations, and it is with this aspect of information that we can also get some inkling of problems and potential pitfalls of which we should be wary. The computer, so prominent in the information age, has the capacity to change our concept of ourselves and others—our concept of what it is to be human. Computers as tools can free human beings to be truly human. Or, if computers become the models against which we measure humanity, they can dominate our thinking and lead us to see ourselves as computers: as storers and manipulators of information, as thinking machines or robots, devoid of dignity and freedom.

Information about individuals clearly raises the issue of privacy, and information about corporations leads to the comparable problems associated with trade secrecy and espionage. As information becomes a central marketing tool, we are forced to face the harm that we can do to ourselves, society, and social relations through abuses that technology makes possible. As information becomes more and more central, we will also realize the vulnerability of networks. Unfortunately, sabotaging a corporate or national information network is easier than sabotaging the industrial network. The links are more fragile, and the interdependence greater. The need for safeguards against industrial and national information espionage and sabotage are profound and pressing.

To mention or raise these issues is not to solve them. But we can develop the analyses and begin better to understand the nature of the information age and its promises and pitfalls for individuals and for society. This is the beginning of an ethical analysis of the information age.

Thesis V.

Confronting the communication complex:

Information without communication is useless, and communication without information is empty. The ethics of communication shares the podium with the ethics of information in the new information age.

Information is not useful, even if truthful and accurate, unless it is used. Hence, it needs to be communicated. The communication process, which is developing at an exponential rate, is central to the information age. The virtues of truthfulness and accuracy carry over into communication. But there are elements of communication that pose their own ethical issues: communication of what, to whom, in what form?

In the information age, the communication explosion has resulted in information overload. There is more information than any individual can absorb. The instantaneous communication made possible by computers and the Internet opens the lines of communication to all, in an environment in which anyone can say or publish anything. There is no peer review or editorial overview before something gets published on the Web. And anonymity makes possible irresponsibility. In the name of the freedom of speech that we so cherish, more and more is posted on the World Wide Web under the guise of information. The result is that it is difficult to know what to believe and what to trust as reliable. The function that was previously filled by peer review, editors, and the cost of publication has been eradicated in Web publishing. We need some comparable authenticators, which I shall call authentication centers.

In the industrial world, *Consumer Reports* and similar independent groups could test and give impartial judgments about products. Similar independent authenticators are needed with respect to information on the Web. For instance, which Web sites that carry medical information are reliable and authoritative, and which are not? The need for centers of this type in all areas of information is crucial if people are to benefit from the information available, and if they are to be kept from being harmed by the available misinformation and falsehoods, whether deliberate or unintended.

The same is true with respect to business, both for consumers and for suppliers of information. The lines between information and advertising, between information and brainwashing or manipulation, between information and self-interest are crucial. Two examples illustrate the point.

One is the review of books that people see upon going to Amazon.com. The only way such reviews will carry weight with viewers is if they can be sure the reviews are not simply paid for by the book publisher, and that Amazon.com is not paid to promote the book. If either is the case, then the review should be identified as an advertisement, as advertisements are identified in newspapers. The function of authenticator and of advertiser must be kept separate.

The second example is search engines that bring up businesses or organizations as the first few entries in any search. These businesses or organizations pay to have their sites mentioned first. If search engines are to be trusted, they should give the Web sites closest to what one requests in a search, not the site that pays the most. If the latter is the standard, then that should be clearly stated, lest once again the distinction between authenticator and advertiser become blurred.

In this brief discussion, I have mentioned a number of other virtues besides truthfulness and accuracy—namely, trust or trustworthiness, and reliability. The four go together and form the basis for a smooth-functioning information processing system. The application of these four key virtues to business is part of the task for the business ethicist.

Thesis VI.

The American information privacy schizophrenia:

The U.S. is schizophrenic about information privacy, wanting it in theory and giving it away in practice.

Information must be communicated, but it must also be about something. Information about people has become much more important than it was previously because of the great opportunity for a revolution in marketing in which manufacturers can target potential customers in ways not previously possible.

A commonly heard issue that arises in the information age is the question of privacy—a question about which there is great confusion and about which Americans in particular may be said to be schizophrenic. The privacy that many complain is being eroded is not being taken from us. Most of us are giving it away. This privacy, which I shall call personal information privacy, is information about ourselves. Some individuals and some privacy and other groups, such as the Computer Professionals for Social Responsibility, argue in favor of legislation protecting personal information privacy and claim that everyone has a right to such privacy. But it is difficult to defend any strong sense of a right to such privacy when so many people blithely give the information away. Sometimes they do so for no return; sometimes for minimal return, such as the possibility of being notified about products they may be interested in purchasing; and sometimes for more substantial gain.

The importance of personal information to business, and one American response to privacy, is illustrated by the extraordinary offer made by the small company Free-PC.com. In February, the company offered 10,000 (eventually to go to a million) Compaq personal computers free to those willing to provide a variety of information about themselves (including their age, interests, income, and hobbies) to receive ads on the Internet, and to have their Internet activities tracked. That information is obviously worth more to the company than the price of a *333* MHz computer with a 4 GB hard drive. The computer is free. It's the information about the users that is valuable. Whether giving up a large area of personal privacy is worth a computer might be a matter of debate and of personal choice. But it is difficult to defend any strong right to personal information privacy when so many value it so cheaply.

Rather than a right to personal information privacy, what most people seem to want is protection from harm as a result of the misuse of personal information. They fear identity theft, or credit card theft, or some harm—psychological, financial, or physical—as a result of information about themselves being widely and easily available. It is not their privacy that is violated, but their sense of security. Yet the two issues are often confused and the arguments, similarly confused.

The information age is changing the nature of privacy. Nonetheless, as a society we have had almost no debate about what the legitimate limits on privacy are, why they are important, or what violates those limits. Since business is one of the two potential abusers of information—the other being government—this is a clear issue for business ethics. But it is one that has generated very little attention in the literature, and one that most businesses still do not include anything about in their codes.

Thesis VII.

Mickey Mouse isn't a program:

Information is very different from machines and tangible products, and so requires a new conception of property and property protection applicable to it.

Until fairly recently, a copyright granted protection to the expression of ideas in books and similar forms for 28 years (renewable for another 28 years). The protected period was then changed to the life of the author plus 50 years and to 75 years for a corporate author. In 1998, Congress extended the already-extended period, to the life of the author plus 70 years and to 95 years for a corporate author. The change came just in time to save Mickey Mouse from falling into the public domain, much to the pleasure of the Walt Disney Company.

On the other hand, when faced with the Y2K problem, many computer software companies claimed that their products did not have to be year 2000 compliant until 1996. Some even argued that the deadline should be 1998, because the life of a program was at best two or four years before it became obsolete. Nonetheless, computer programs are covered by copyright for the same 95 years that Mickey Mouse or the latest novel is covered. Does 95 years of protection make sense when the industry claims its products are obsolete after four years or less?

We can share information without depriving ourselves of its full use. It can be stolen from us without depriving us of its use. It is intellectual property. But just as we have not adequately discussed the changing nature of privacy, we as a society have not adequately discussed the changing nature of property applicable in the information age. We have sought to use traditional laws about copyright and patents, and have in the process caused a great deal of confusion. Instead of rethinking intellectual property in the information age, we have tried to make do with concepts and legal doctrines that were not constructed with thought of the kind of intellectual property that is emerging and that does not fit the old mold. What is fair and what is not are issues that form an important part of business ethics for the information age; these are issues that too few in the field presently address. . . .

QUESTION AND ANSWER SESSION WITH RICHARD DE GEORGE

The following questions were raised by students, faculty, and guests following his March 22 public lecture at Bentley College.[24]

Question: A lot of personal data is collected traditionally by telephone companies. For example, when you make a phone call, what number you make the phone call from, how long the phone call lasts, and so forth. And it is very protected by the Baby Bells. As the digital services have come along, I understand that more and more of the information is up for sale. And I was wondering how Bell Atlantic reconciles your philosophy, which kind of flies in the face of much of what I hear telephone companies are doing right now, with these new practices.

Richard De George: That's a valid question. Not only telephone services, but also a great many companies of all sorts, are collecting information. Most of it, at least, is supposed to be information, that is, correct data about personal use and so on. And I've suggested what happens with data collected on the Internet. Is that OK or not, from an ethical point of view? That's the question. My answer is that I can't give a hard yes or no because I have to qualify whatever I say. I would prefer to know how the information is being used, who's collecting it, what they're collecting, and what they're doing with it. And if I know that, then I would be able to say whether I approve or disapprove, whether it's OK with me.

What bothers me is that all this information about me is being collected without my knowledge and is being used in ways that I can only imagine, some of which may be harmful to me. Now, if I have a right to anything, it's a right to protect myself from harm. Consequently, I have to ask, how can I implement that right? And the only way I can implement that right is to know that I may be harmed. I have to know what people are doing that may be linked to the harm that I might suffer. So, I would like to see companies very much up-front telling us, "When you do this, that, or the other thing, we're collecting information about you. We're collecting information on use and we're going to sell that information, we hope, in ways that will bring you products we hope will interest you. But, if you're not interested, then let us know and we won't do it for you anymore. We'll take you off our list. We won't track you the way we track other people, and so on." Some companies do this.

Or, a company might say, "We collect information about you of this type, but it will just be for our own personal use, that is, company use, not for use by other corporations, and we won't sell it or give it to others without your permission." Legislation in Europe has gone in the latter direction. There's legislation that has been passed in countries of the European Union that says, if one company collects this sort of information, it's not allowed to sell it to another company. America has not come to the point where we're willing to even entertain that legislation. And if it were proposed in Congress, I doubt that it would pass, because the business interests against it are so strong. Now, what's the popular opinion on the issue? Well, I said, we're schizophrenic. There is no popular opinion. If I take one poll of this set of people and another of another set of people, I'm going to get different results. So, I think we have to decide what's really in our interest. And the only way we can decide that is by discussing the issue openly. Consequently, I'd like to see questions like yours appearing in periodicals, newspapers, and business ethics centers, in all sorts of places, so that we can talk about these things rationally rather than just letting them happen.

Question: I take it you're uncomfortable with allowing technology to find its own level. In other words, you appear to feel that there should be some government or societal regulation along the way. I'm particularly troubled about the freedom of speech aspect. . . . I'm troubled with the idea that information, which is so important and precious, faces the possibility of being controlled and not allowed to find its own level.

Richard De George: . . . First, with respect to the information issue, my claim was not that we should prevent quacks from putting out their medical remedies on the Web. Rather, we should have authentication pages that say, "If you're interested in cures for cancer, we have investigated and can report that these sites give information that is in accordance with the best known medical advances of the day." The quack sites can still operate—freedom of speech operates. Nobody says you can't have a quack site. Nobody outlaws them. Nobody does anything to them. And, if

you're interested in cures for cancer and you want to try those, you're free to do so. But it would be nice to have someplace to go to say, "Hey, how do I, a poor novice who's not a doctor, who doesn't know much about medicine, sort out what's reliable and what's not reliable out there?" Therefore, I proposed authentication centers. I didn't intend them to be censorship centers, and I didn't intend them to be run by the government.

My example with respect to products was *Consumer Reports,* which people can use or not use. It's independently funded, not sponsored by any corporation. It tries to be objective and serve a useful function. I'd like to have similar authentication centers developed in the various areas of information. So, I'm all with you about freedom of speech. I'm not in favor of outlawing that; I am in favor of letting a hundred flowers bloom. Some of them will be useful and some will not.

On the other point: Should we allow technology to go wherever it wants? Well, that's what I called the technological imperative, which says that technology has its own rationale and whatever is rational from its point of view will be developed by somebody and something will come out. The question is one that Joseph Weizenbaum, a computer scientist from MIT, raised back in the 1970s. Are there directions that we really shouldn't encourage? Maybe we can't outlaw developments, but are there directions in which we shouldn't encourage technology to go? Are there things that are obscene, that it would just be terrible to have technology develop? I think that's a legitimate question. Now, I haven't given you a definite answer. But I don't think the answer is, "Obviously no. We can't stop technological progress. Anything anybody wants to develop is OK."

In the field of cloning we've said, "Well, maybe we're not ready for human cloning yet," and some countries have imposed a moratorium on human cloning. Are there things in the technological realm that are similar to cloning, which affect human beings very centrally and very directly and about which we'll want to say "No, we don't think that should be done?" If so, we certainly shouldn't put government resources there, and we should discourage private resources from going in that direction. It would be nice to have a debate about the issue. I'd like to engage you in that debate and have you tell me why we shouldn't have any restrictions, and then see if I could propose some things that I think would be wrong to develop, and see where we get. We now say we don't want to develop biological warfare agents. Those are bad things to develop and although we find countries developing them, we say that it's a no-no. We discourage such development, and so on. We don't want countries to proliferate nuclear bombs, because they pose a big threat to us all. Are there comparable things in the information age, things that would subvert the information age itself? If there are, then we should give very serious thought to whether those things should be developed and whether we should take precautions against their being developed—or, if they are developed, precautions against their being used.

Question: My question has to do with corporations and other organizations who sometimes, and sometimes not, let employees know that they can break in, and may break in, on their e-mail and monitor it at any time, for any reason. I wonder if you could comment on the "privacy schizophrenic mode" we're in at the moment. How do you stand on that issue?

Richard De George: My basic approach is that I think what employees deserve ethically or morally is information about what the company is doing with respect to monitoring e-mail or Web use, and what use will be made of that information. If a company is continuously monitoring or randomly monitoring e-mail to see if people are using e-mail for personal instead of business reasons, and if the company has promulgated very clearly a policy that says, "You will not use e-mail for personal use. You can only use your computer at work for business reasons, and if we find that you're using it for personal reasons, we take a very dim view of that and you'll be penalized in some way or another," then I think the employees know the rules and can decide that the company is worth working for and they can live with the policy. Or they'll decide, "Hey, I don't like this company. I'll move elsewhere." Or they'll say, "Well, if they're going to take that view of e-mail, I'll use the telephone or some other means. I won't be tracked and monitored." Those are different reactions. The company has to decide on its rules, promulgate them, and then worry about the results. The employee has to obey the rules and then, if they don't like the rules, either leave or get around them in some way. And I think many of the various options can be said to be ethical. So I don't know any way to argue that every company that monitors employees' e-mail, even though it informs them of that practice, is unethical. The results may be counterproductive, bad for employee morale, or have other negative impacts, but I really cannot say that monitoring e-mail is an unethical policy. A policy of monitoring may be unwise or counterproductive, but that is another matter. Companies are within their legal rights to monitor employees' e-mail, and I believe that they have the ethical right to do so if they clearly inform the employees of the company's policy.

CASE STUDY: REALJUKEBOX

RealJukebox is a software program designed for downloading and playing music from the Internet. A Seattle-based company produced the program to report back on the musical choices of consumers without informing listeners that the information was being harvested. Because the company did claim that the information was not being used to profile individual consumers, we can assume that the Internet feedback helped create general marketing profiles. What would De George find objectionable in this case? How might he think RealJukebox should have behaved? Why? Do you agree?

CASE STUDY: A RELIABLE SOURCE?

The recent U.S.-led NATO military action against Yugoslavia was justified to a large extent by the reports of atrocities committed by Serbian forces against Albanian Kosovar civilians. However, in a recent article Philip Terzian writes

> The notorious mine shaft where 700 murdered Kosovars were said to have been thrown has been thoroughly examined by a French forensic team sent in by NATO. They found no bodies, and no evidence that bodies were ever in the mine shaft. When NATO spokesman Jamie Shea would recite horrific statistics to justify the bombing campaign against Belgrade . . . it turns out he was using figures and anecdotes supplied by the Internet site of the Kosovo Liberation Army, not the most reliable source of information. . . .
>
> President Clinton and his various spokesman (*sic*) still talk about the "tens of thousands" of Kosovar Albanians killed by Serbs in a genocidal orgy. But the United Nations International Tribunal for the Former Yugoslavia puts the number at 2,108. . . .[25]

Various kinds of reviews occur before the publication of many items in print media. For instance, professional journals require peer reviews. De George points out that anyone can place information of any kind on the Net. The Internet is the electronic equivalent of the vanity press. De George urges the remedy of authentication centers that would guide information consumers to reliable sources. Yet at the time when NATO spokesperson Shea was citing statistics supplied by the Kosovo Liberation Army (KLA), the press frequently carried stories about the KLA being a known terrorist organization. In other words, authentication centers had already publicly labeled the KLA as an inaccurate source when NATO was using the KLA as a supposed reliable source. Does this not suggest that authentication centers will only serve the converted and will be useless in combating intentional misinformation supplied by business or government advertisers? Is De George's suggestion best because it balances freedom of expression with fostering autonomy through accurate information supply? Can you think of a better solution for fostering accuracy on the Internet?

EXERCISE

Most e-mail programs come with filters that allow mail to be placed in different virtual mailboxes. Using filters enables a recipient to send some mail automatically to the trash as well as sort mail into boxes by topic or urgency. If workers use this technology to sort personal e-mail into a separate mailbox for viewing on breaks, should the employer providing the computer and Internet access respect the privacy of that e-mail by not archiving it or reading it?

1.3 TOWARD A GLOBAL INFORMATION ETHIC Elizabeth A. Buchanan draws our attention to the global impact of the new information technology. She, like De George, is concerned with how making a commodity of information ("commoditization" of information) will affect business. She also argues that the information revolution will favor the economic interests of those who are best off in society. Buchanan also voices concern over how the Internet will affect local culture and community life. Buchanan discusses the political hegemony that can emerge in a world where information is supplied largely by companies close to the interests of the political and economic elites of developed nations. She takes a critical stance toward substituting virtual communities for real ones.

Democratic theorists have long emphasized the importance of public, or third, places for a strong participatory democracy. Popular media reflect this concern with shows situated in public places such as restaurants, coffee houses, and bars "where everybody knows your name" and people from different economic classes meet as equals.

Buchanan seems to fear that virtual communities will significantly erode the communication of diverse perspectives between different economic classes and cultures. At the same time, she recognizes the inevitability of accepting virtual communities and seeks to moderate their effects through respect for cultural specificity and the economic and cultural interests of developing nations.

QUESTIONS FOR STUDY AND DISCUSSION

1. Mustapha Masmoudi cites various information inequities that persist between the developed and developing nations. What are these inequities?
2. Why does Buchanan think that continuing to develop information as a commodity (commoditization) will preserve the economic advantages of the developed nations?
3. What does Buchanan mean by "qualitatively grounded inequities" of information?
4. Explain what Buchanan means by "language imperialism" in conjunction with the prevalence of English on the Internet.
5. Buchanan uses the quote about the effects of the introduction of running water to Ibieca to illustrate the impact of technology upon community life. Explain the example. Do you think Buchanan opposes the introduction of indoor plumbing? If not, what is the argumentative purpose of including the example?

INFORMATION ETHICS IN A WORLD-WIDE CONTEXT[26]

ELIZABETH A. BUCHANAN

Alkalimat begins his eloquent essay, "The New Technological Imperative in Africa: Class Struggles on the Edge of Third-Wave Revolution" by stating the "twentieth century is ending as a global drama full of conflict and change, with humanity torn between hope and despair. For a few the new century offers the wonders of a high-tech future, with wealth amid the birth of a new civilization; but for the majority there is fear of war, starvation, homelessness, poverty, and plagues. . . ."[27] As information professionals, what are our ethical obligations in this worldwide context? Of course we play a major role in this divide between hope and despair. While one of our fundamental responsibilities continues to be free and open access to information, many circumstances seemingly beyond our control are diminishing such access. And, we are repeatedly told the world is shrinking, boundaries closing, peoples becoming one—a result of the information age and its technologies. This growing intimacy, however, does not equate with equitable access and dissemination of information. The information age is a time of mythology, a time for fantasies of wealth, power, ownership. The ethics of information services in this time, however, are very real, and don't necessarily correspond to these fantasies.

How do we as information professionals respond? Do we contribute to the fantasies? the non-truths? Or do we recognize the conditions Alkalimat describes and respond to them? What ethical considerations demand our continued and renewed attention? This overview reminds us of the many ethical issues involved in cross-cultural information transfer. This paper describes the many levels of inequity, the issues surrounding the commoditization of information worldwide, and the ethical dilemmas associated with international information transfer and service. The fantasies and myths are growing in severity, and along side these illusions, peoples and nations are suffering.

The information society (now understood as a global society) or information age possesses a number of characteristics or qualities, among them a growing reliance on computer technologies, a large knowledge sector work force, a growing division of labor—a division which has major international implications, a movement from an analog to a digital model of informational and commercial transfer, and the consideration of information as a major commodity, analogous to the physical goods of the industrial age.[28] And, nearly two decades ago, Smith recognized the global significance of information as a major commodity and defining feature of this age.[29] Smith then declared that information lay at the heart of the world economy and cannot be separated from the other conflicts of which international and national policies are composed. Thus, the information society is considered an international phenomenon, with potential benefits and detriments to the world as a whole.

. . . [New] ethical dilemmas range from the fair and equitable distribution of resources to the availability and provision of education and training, to a mutual respect and consideration of cultural specificity and values. For instance, while the information age has encouraged a major increase in the amount of information produced, in the number of available channels through which information is accessible, and the apparent ease with which information is readily available, a growing disparity continues to set apart the now all-too-familiar "haves" and the "have-nots." In agreement is Mosco who details the many *Myths Along the Information Highway:* ". . . computer communication is little more than business as usual. A world of information haves and have-nots will far more likely emerge than a global village or a world of virtual communities."[30] In other words, while the information society offers an abundance of goods to some peoples, it is contributing to an expansive "digital divide," keeping peoples and nations on unequal planes. This inequality is promulgated on a number of levels.

An Overview of Information Inequity

In 1979, Mustapha Masmoudi's seminal paper "The New World Information Order" drew attention to the growing inequities and imbalances across the world in terms of information access, control, dissemination, and content construction.[31] In it, he cites seven prominent forms of inequities existing in the world in terms of information.

1. A flagrant quantitative imbalance between North and South;
2. An inequality in information resources;
3–4. A de facto hegemony and a will to dominate;
5. A lack of information on developing countries;
6. Survival of the colonial era. An alienating influence in the economic, social, and cultural spheres.
7. Messages ill-suited to the areas in which they are disseminated.

. . . Smith highlighted cultural domination of the South by the North through the control of major media outlets, through the unstinted flow of its cultural products throughout the world, and the cultural, political, and economic powers wielded by the North over the South. Ultimately, Smith's *Geopolitics of Information* thoroughly documented the ways in which information dissemination and commoditization fuel international domination, inequality, and suppression of cultural uniqueness and traditional values. Following Masmoudi and Smith, Morehouse called attention to another level of inequity, in the quantitatively biased distribution of resources, including information-based resources, across the world; he states

> . . . the late twentieth century world is a highly unequal place in energy consumption, income distribution, materials deprivation, economic and political power, and science-based problem solving capacity. Ninety-seven percent of the world's expenditure on research and development is made by a handful of industrialized countries. . . . Technology is rapidly emerging as a major instrument for global domination as other economic and military forms of power decline for stronger nations in the international system.[32]

Nearly twenty years after Masmoudi, Smith, and Morehouse questioned the ethics of the information age and its supposed free flow of information and related commodities, the inequities in information transfer across the globe have changed very little. For example, flagrant inequities exist on a number of levels where the transfer of information or commodities is involved. Of particular significance, the unjust state of intellectual resource allocation severely affects contemporary scientists. If knowledge is power, the creation and dissemination of knowledge contribute to power. Thus, in relation to the science-based problem solving capacity to which Morehouse referred, Gibbs reviews the poor showing of third world researchers in the *Science Citation Index,* the leading index to cited scientific journal literature.[33] This poor showing has third world researchers caught in a "vicious circle."

The invisibility to which mainstream science publishing condemns most Third World research thwarts the efforts of poor countries to strengthen their indigenous science journals—and with them the quality of research in regions that need it most. . . . We [third world researchers] don't get many citations, because the journal is not well known because it is not in the international indexes . . . Since Western research libraries only acquire journals with a high impact, they do not subscribe to journals outside of the magic circle of citation analysis. . . . Being unrepresented in the SCI or INSPEC or many other databases is just another cruel fact of the way science in the world works at the moment.

Third world scientists denied the possibility to contribute suggests that their information is less valuable, or less esteemed to the western eye. Less developed countries are held at a distance in terms of research and development, forcing continuous cycles of dependence. On another level, Gibbs considers telephone access, and notably, Haywood suggests that "one approach to measuring the impact of the 'information economy' as it evolves is the rate at which a country gains access to telephone lines." A dramatic example comes from Africa, a continent representing more than one tenth of the world's population, yet the least technologically and informationally developed. "The entire continent of Africa . . . contains fewer telephone lines than does Manhattan. African customers who sign up for service today are put on a waiting list 3.6 million people deep; in sub-Saharan regions, the wait is currently about nine years." Equally dismal, Haywood relates that "portable radios are probably the most widespread technology to be found in rural Africa, but even these lie silent for want of batteries."

It is significant to note that within Africa, great inequities exist. "South Africa has 9.5 main telephone lines per hundred people, giving a teledensity twenty times higher than the rest of sub-Saharan Africa. But only 11.6% of Africans have telephones in their homes, compared with 87.4% of whites, and 47.6% of Africans have no access to any phone, compared to only 6.6% of whites." This suggests that while North to South information flow is dramatically inequitable, internal inequities exist as well. In many ways, these inequities parallel the disparity between suburban, urban, and rural regions within the United States. For specific discussions of the U.S. digital divide, see Novak and Hoffman and NTIA.[34]

Qualitatively-Grounded Inequities

While a quantitative evaluation of information equity is dim for many nations, a more qualitatively-based assessment of the information society and its international flow of information reveals an equally disturbing picture . . . .

First, information transfer from the North to the South may contribute to serious disruption in the social fabric of a nation. Given that the majority of information entering a country is from the United States or constructed with a western viewpoint, cultural values and perspectives are transferred as well. The potential for serious social fragmentation is at hand and Woodrow draws attention to four major areas of potential conflict or tension that result from this international telecommunications or transfer of information. These include conflict over basic values embedded within the information infrastructure; tensions at the industry levels, at which western corporate interest may take precedence over the indigenous interests; conflict among nations over views on liberal or conservative approaches to information dissemination; and finally, tension, which arises when information holds great economic and political power; the power remains in the hands of the developers or transmitters of information, not in the hands of the receivers.[35] Furthermore, social disruption may ensue, leading to potential dangerous situations; for instance, the Tiananmen Square incident in China was further aggravated by incoming fax memos and email messages from dissidents in the United States.[36]

In addition. . . , Shapiro warns against the dangers of social fragmentation brought on by inappropriate information transfer; he suggests "not falling prey to the illusions of cyberspace or the seduction of total individual control, and remaining committed to the uses of technology that enable diversity and interdependence rather than exclusivity and factionalism."[37] Likewise, Haywood calls for information services that "ensure the survival of cultural and ideological diversity." Interdependence will become an increasingly important relationship, as the information age continues. Interdependence must come to replace the existing forms of domination and dependency currently intact among the developed and underdeveloped societies. Information transfer affects psychological, cultural, and political realities and can easily contribute to social fragmentation or an altering of the texture of daily life within nations or communities. . . .[38]

Information Commoditization, or, "Free Is Out, Fee Is In"

Next, the commoditization of information brings potentially unnecessary or undesirable forms of information to a region or country. . . . The increasing commoditization of information is removing information from public sectors or public agencies to the private realm. . . . If we are of the belief that information wants to be free and should be free, an age old adage of librarianship, this intense commoditization of information comprises a most significant issue facing information professionals today. As wealth is concentrated in fewer and fewer hands through monopolization and centralization, information professionals must more actively seek alternative outlets of information. Uniformity and monotony dominate, as we see American and western privatization strangle choice and options. While we have hundreds of channels, millions of Internet sites, and a plethora of media outlets, we still suffer from a paucity of choice. On the global level, fewer countries, fewer cultures have a chance to promote their own forms of indigenous knowledge, and they are increasingly forced to accept irrelevant, futile, and ineffective information.

Furthermore, the continual neglect of developing nations as *potential* information suppliers smacks of imperialism and colonialism, while it continues to deny any economic power or autonomy to the developing nations. . . . The myth of the information age strikes again—providing computers to the average citizens of the third world is insufficient, at best. . . . [T]he information society is grounded in commoditization and profit for some, while simultaneously, for many, social necessities and resources are in danger. . . .

The Internet: Perpetuating Inequity World Wide

Increasingly, the information age is defined by the "world-wide" presence of the Internet. The NTIA offers a familiar sentiment "Now that a considerable portion of today's business, communication, and research takes place on the Internet, access to the computers and networks may be as important as access to traditional telephone service." The Internet has been heralded as a means to ensure equitable access to information and democratic ideals, as well as a destroyer of cultural sovereignty and polluter of values. It has been viewed as "offering great potential for global and national dialogue and participation" and it has been

viewed as a means to further "reduce participation and threaten fundamental human needs—freedom, creativity, and relationality."[39] Due to the inherent nature of the Internet, including its many-to-many mode of communication, its immediacy, and its anonymity, the world's population can potentially have access to any and all forms of information, regardless of where or when it was released, or irregardless of its subject. Yes, information might be free in the philosophical sense, but at what expense, in the monetary sense and in terms of cultural values?

Shapiro optimistically acknowledges the liberating characteristics of the Internet; these sentiments comprise the many myths surrounding the information age and its technologies.

Using the Net and other new media, individuals can take back power from large Institutions, including government, corporations, and the media. Trends like personalization, decentralization, and disintermediation . . . will allow us each to have more control over life's details: what news and entertainment we're exposed to, how we learn and work, whom we socialize with, even how goods are distributed and political outcomes are reached. . . . The Net will allow us to transcend the limitations of geography and circumstance to create new social bonds.

Conversely—some would say more realistically—the Net can contribute to "social fragmentation;" it can cause cultural splintering and loss of tradition, . . . "What happens to the special history of people situated in microsocial niches when information is directed to people en masse? Does this universality of information destroy particularity of social life?" Many issues demand the attention of information professionals in considering these questions. Firstly, the mass release of information fails to consider cultural sensitivity; peoples and nations may take objection to such forms of information as governmental, for instance.[40]

Secondly, the immediacy of the international information flow denies opportunities for peoples and nations to prepare for the onslaught of foreign cultural viewpoints, and the rapidity with which information is released denies the chance for contemplation and consideration. Haywood asserts "devising new forms of cultural protection from unwanted information flows will just get more frantic as the technology makes it more difficult to stop"[41]

Thirdly, cultural particularity is under siege by the prevalence of the English language on the Internet; some 90% of the material on the Internet is in the English language, thus raising concerns over language imperialism and literacy issues.

Fourthly, cultural specificity should be cherished and protected. With mass releases of information, information that continues to be homogenous and often monotonous, individual thought is diminishing and communal integrity is lessening, Cultural niches fight for survival in a world of sameness, and despite the many predictions and hopes of virtual communities and virtual neighborhoods, individuality in the truest sense and the communal sense is taking a severe beating. . . .

Receptivity to information between cultures is increasingly at an exciting or alarming rate, depending on your point of view. The upside of this is that different races can now understand more about each other as language barriers break down in favor of English; the downside is that, as language is the main conduit of cultural heritage and the key to distinctiveness, there will be less to fascinate and excite us because the richness of difference will be replaced by the poverty of sameness. . . .

Conclusion

Masmoudi demands a reevaluation and readjustment to the inequitable conditions surrounding information access, control, dissemination, and content construction. He suggests that "the new world information order founded on democratic principles seeks to establish relations of equality in the communications field between developed and developing nations and aims at greater justice and greater balance. Far from calling in question the freedom of information, it proposes to ensure that this principle is applied fairly and equitably for all nations."[42] This principle remains intact twenty years after it was first written. Yet, it is critical however, that developing countries make their own decisions concerning the flow of information; while no country should be denied access or control of information, cultural sensitivity demands that self-reliance and self-control dictate that flow of information. Cultural specificity demands respect. An imperialistic or colonialist approach to information will only set the worlds further apart, at a time when information and its conveyers promise to bring the world closer together.

In summary, it is useful to consider an episode which begins Richard Sclove's *Democracy and Technology:*

> During the 1970s, running water was installed in the houses of Ibieca, a small village in northeast

Spain. With pipes running directly to their houses, Ibiecans no longer had to fetch water from the village fountain. Families gradually purchased washing machines, and women stopped gathering to scrub laundry by hand at the village washbasin.

Arduous tasks were rendered technologically superfluous, but village social life unexpectedly changed. The public fountain and washbasin, once scenes of vigorous social interaction, became nearly deserted. Men began losing their sense of familiarity with the children and the donkeys that had once helped them to haul water. Women stopped congregating at the washbasin to intermix their scrubbing with politically empowering gossip about men and social life. In hindsight, the installation of running water helped break down the Ibiecans' strong bonds—with one another, with their animals, and with the land—that had knit them together as a community.

Sclove's premise in *Democracy and Technology* involves participatory design and a democratic adoption of information and technology. Participatory design and development holds the key to ensuring that all peoples will be able to choose among alternatives, these choices will reflect their personal aspirations and their view of the common good, and will contribute to the best social conditions possible according to the perspective of those affected by the information flow or technological development. Sclove asserts that participatory design and development will "ensure a more diverse range of social needs, concerns, and experiences." Such an approach is requisite if the information age is to be equitable and ethical. Consequently, information transfer in terms of access, dissemination, control, and content construction must be designed according to a principle or set of principles that respect cultural specificity, subjectivity, and values. The information age holds great potential to unite disparate peoples and ideas; nevertheless, it is imperative to safeguard the cultural uniqueness and social microcosms which furnish the regions of the world with independence, freedom of choice, and freedom of access.

CASE STUDY: THE DIGITAL DIVIDE

The National Telecommunications and Information Administration (NTIA) issued a report on access to computer information services in July 1998. (See the suggested readings at the end of this chapter to find the full report.) The report found as follows:

> Despite this significant growth in computer ownership and usage overall, the growth has occurred to a greater extent within some income levels, demographic groups, and geographic areas, than in others. In fact, the "digital divide" between certain groups of Americans has *increased* between 1994 and 1997 so that there is now an even greater disparity in penetration levels among some groups. There is a widening gap, for example, between those at upper and lower income levels.

Additionally, even though all racial groups now own more computers than they did in 1994, Blacks and Hispanics now lag *even further behind* [emphasis in original] Whites in their levels of PC-ownership and online access.

Do you think that lack of access to computers and computer-based information services places the children of the poor and minority groups in an unfair educational and financial situation that amounts to a competitive disadvantage in the emerging information based economy? What role, if any, should government take to encourage computer literacy and information access in public schools?

CASE STUDY: DEMOCRACY AND TECHNOLOGY

Discuss the implications of the example that Buchanan cites from Sclove at the end of the article for Internet communities. Do you believe that the Internet will enhance political participation through more direct access to political and business leaders? Has the Internet enhanced your understanding of other cultures?

SUGGESTED READINGS:

Dreyfus, Hubert. *What Computers Still Can't Do: A Critique of Artificial Intelligence.* Cambridge: MIT Press, 1992.

National Telecommunications and Information Administration. *Falling Through the Net 11. New Data on the Digital Divide.* 28 July 1998. http://www.ntia.doc.gov/ntiahome/net2lfalling.html

Negroponte, Nicholas. *Being Digital.* New York: Knopf, 1995.

Searle, John. *Mind, Brains, and Science* Cambridge: Harvard University Press, 1984.

Stoll, Clifford. *Silicon Snake Oil* New York: Doubleday, 1995.

Twitchell, James. *Carnival Culture* New York: Columbia University Press, 1992.

Winner, Langdon. *Autonomous Technology : Technics-out-of-control as a Theme in Political Thought* Cambridge: MIT Press, 1977.

NOTES

ETHICS "INFORMATIONALIZED": FROM WALDEN TO DOTCOMGUY

1. Henry David Thoreau, *Walden* (New York: Library of America, 1985), 338; originally published 1854.
2. Thoreau figured all expenses to the mill (one-tenth of a cent).

IN DEFENSE OF THE NAKED MIND

3. Theodore Roszak, *The Cult of Information,* 2nd ed., (Berkeley: University of California Press, 1986), xvii–xlvi, 16–19.
4. *Bay Area Computer Currents,* 7–20 September 1991, 18.
5. *Washington Post,* 10 May 1991.

6. Daniel Ellsberg, "Manhattan Project II: To End the Threat of Nuclear War," *Harvard Journal of World Affairs*, Summer 1992. On Ellsberg's project to achieve a "zero-nuclear-weapons world" also see "Undoing the Doomsday Machine," *Outlook: Washington Post*, 10 May 1993, and "Manhattan Project II," *The Progressive,* August 1993.

7. Scott Sagan, *The Limits of Safety: Organizations, Accidents, and Nuclear Weapons* (Princeton: Princeton University Press, 1993), 9–10, 266.

8. James McCollom, *The Continental Affair* (New York: Dodd, Mead, 1987), 78–80, 127–29, 315–17.

9. See "Manic Market," *Time,* 10 November 1986.

10. Joel Kurtzman, *The Death of Money: How the Electronic Economy Has Destabilized the World's Markets and Created Financial Chaos* (New York: Simon and Schuster, 1993), 19.

11. Jonathan Laing, "The Next Meltdown? Fears Grow that Derivatives Pose a Big Threat," *Barron's,* 7 June 1993, 10–34.

12. Quoted in Laing, "The Next Meltdown," 10.

13. *The Death of Money,* 12, 202–3, 205.

14. Donald Ely and Tjeerd Plomp, "The Promises of Educational Technology: A Reassessment," in *Computers in the Human Context: Information Technology, Productivity, and People,* ed. Tom Forrester (Cambridge, MA: MIT Press, 1989), 248–61.

15. C. A. Bowers, *The Cultural Dimensions of Educational Computing: Understanding the Non-Neutrality of Technology* (New York: Teachers College Press, Columbia University, 1988), 36.

16. Charles Piller et al., "America's Shame: The Creation of the Technological Underclass in America's Public Schools," *Macworld,* September 1992.

17. "America's Computer Ghetto," *The New York Times,* 7 August 1992.

18. Stewart Brand, *The Media Lab: Inventing the Future at MIT* (New York: Viking, 1987).

19. John Eckhouse, "Computer Age Goes Hollywood," *San Francisco Chronicle*, 30 August 1993.

20. Tom Samiljan, "Digitaletc," *Rolling Stone,* 28 October, 1999, 109.

21. "Electronic Bushwhacking," *Harper's,* July 1999, 23.

22. Mark Weinraub, "Navy Settles With Sailor Who Had Gay Internet Identification," *Reuters News Service,* 12 June 1998.

Business Ethics and the Information Age

23. First presented as the public lecture for the Bell Atlantic Visiting Professorship in Business Ethics and Information Technology at the Center for Business Ethics at Bentley College, Waltham, Massachusetts, 22 March 1999. Later published in *Business and Society Review: Journal of the Center for Business Ethics at Bentley College,* 104, no.3 (Fall 1999), 261–78. Copyright 1999 Center for Business Ethics at Bentley College.

24. Some questions included in the original publication have been omitted; other questions have been edited.

25. Philip Terzian, "Rwanda and Kosovo: A Tale of Two Foreign Policies," *Sacramento Bee,* 10 January 2000, B7.

Information Ethics in a World-Wide Context

26. Elizabeth A. Buchanan, "An Overview of Information Ethics in a World-Wide Context," *Ethics and Information Technology* 1 (1999), 193–201. Reprinted with kind permission of Kluwer Academic Publishers and the author.

27. A. Alkalimat, "The New Technological Imperative in Africa: Class Struggle on the Edge of Third-Wave Revolution," *Cutting Edge: Technology, Information, Capitalism, and Social Revolution* (London: Verso, 1997), ch. 15.

28. Kester takes issue specifically with the divisions of labor: "What is more clearly happening . . . is a growing division of labor between the low-paid, insecure, and often unsafe jobs in the service sector, assembly and manufacturing, and a minority of highly privileged managerial, technical, and professional positions. This is a division that is reiterated in both the local and the global level with the expansion of 'informal' economies in major American cities, fueled by immigrant labor . . . what [can be] described as 'the revival of nineteenth century seated trades in the richest cities on earth.' Grant Kester, "Access Denied: Information Policy and the Limits of Liberalism," in *Ethics, Information, and Technology,* ed. Richard Stichler and Robert Hauptman (Jefferson: NorthCarolina, McFarland, 1998), 225. See also Daniel Bell, *The Coming of Post-Industrial Society: A Venture in Social Forecasting* (New York: Basic Books, 1973); Fritz Machlup, *The Production and Distribution of Knowledge in the United States* (Princeton: Princeton University Press, 1962); and Adam Toffler, *The Third Wave* (New York: Morrow, 1980).

29. Adam Smith, *The Geopolitics of Information: How Western Culture Dominates the World* (London: Faber and Faber, 1980).

30. V. Mosco, "Myths Along the Information Highway," in *Alternative Library Literature, 1996–1997,* ed. Stanford Berman and James Danky (Jefferson, NC: McFarland, 1998.)

31. *Journal of Communications,* Spring 1979, 172–85.

32. Ward Morehouse, *Separate, Unequal, but More Autonomous: Technology, Equity, and World Order in the Millennial Transition* (New York: Institute for World Order, 1981).

33. "Lost Science in the Third World," *Scientific American* 273, August 1995, 92–100.

34. Trevor Haywood, *Info-Rich Info-Poor: Access and Exchange in the Global Information Society* (London: Bowker-Saur, 1995), 123. Leslie H. Steeves, "Sharing Information in Kenya: Communication and Information Policy Considerations and Consequences for Rural Women," *Gazette* 56 (1996), 157–81. Martin Hall, "The Virtual University: Education for All, or a Segregated Highway?" *South African Journal of Science* 94 (1998). Thomas Novak and Donna Hoffman, "Bridging the Digital Divide: The Impact of Race on Computer Access and Internet Use," *Science* 280 (April, 1998), 390–91; and "NTIA: Falling through the Net: Defining the Digital Divide." Available http://www.ntia.doc.gov.

35. Brian R. Woodrow, "Telecommunications and Information Networks: Growing International Tensions and Their Underlying Causes," *The Information Society* 6 (1989), 117–25.

36. I use this incident with caution; while I support efforts for democracy and individual empowerment, one must be prudent making judgments about other national values and political agendas to avoid overt colonialism.

37. Andrew Shapiro. *Is the Net Democratic? Yes—and No.* Berkman Center for Internet and Society [electronic bulletin board]. Available from http://cyber.law.harvard.edu/works/shapiro/net_democ.net

38. Richard Sclove, *Democracy and Technology.* (New York: Guilford, 1995).

39. Steeves, 157.

40. Steeves, 157.

41. Haywood, 141.

42. Masmoudi, 178.

2

MEDIA VALUES I: FREEDOM AND INFORMATION

*Congress shall make no law respecting the establishment of
a religion or prohibiting the free exercise thereof or
abridging freedom of speech or of the press or the right of
the people peaceably to assemble and to petition their
government for a redress of grievances.*

THE FIRST AMENDMENT TO THE
CONSTITUTION OF THE UNITED STATES OF AMERICA

INTRODUCTION

How do information and power relate? The connection between the two is important—information, or access to it, or control over access to it, is directly connected to individual and organizational power. A similar connection is often noted between power and speech—the power to speak, having a "voice," is an essential element or prerequisite of political power. Outside the realm of political affairs, advertising that promotes new information and communication technologies promises personal empowerment by means of instant unlimited access to information and communication.

We begin our exploration of the ethics of information with the principles of freedom of speech, freedom of expression, and freedom of the press, mentioned above in the First Amendment to the Constitution of the United States of America. The First Amendment was formulated in the early design stages of the American system of government. It is appropriate therefore to understand it fundamentally in terms of the construction and distribution of political power. It is carefully and explicitly worded so as to forbid the government to create any legislation that would interfere with the people's freedoms in four specific areas (the "Four Freedoms of the

First Amendment"). First, the government may not act to restrict the freedom of worship. This is expressed in the so-called establishment and free-exercise clauses of the First Amendment. Familiar policy and constitutional legal issues arise around this particular prohibition, including the status of school prayer, the "Pledge of Allegiance," and so on. Second, the government may not act to restrict the freedom of individual expression. This is expressed in the "freedom of speech" clause. Policy and constitutional legal issues arise around this particular prohibition when individuals engage in controversial forms of expression such as desecration of the flag, and other forms of political and artistic expression. Third, the government may not act to restrict the freedom to publish. This is expressed in the "freedom of the press" clause. Issues arise around this particular prohibition when the government claims that the "national security" would be compromised by the publication of certain information, for example, as it did when the "Pentagon Papers" were published. Finally, the government may not act to restrict the freedom of the people to organize collectively for political purposes, specifically to object to the established order and exercise of political power. The "freedom of assembly" clause applies, for example, when the government or its agents demand to know one's political affiliations, as often happened during the cold war years.

These "four freedoms" may appear oddly diverse, but they each serve an essential function: to reserve and secure political power and responsibility to the people collectively. The fourth freedom (freedom of assembly) relates directly to this function, and the other three only slightly less so. To understand this, let us suppose that we are trying to set up a society in which the people have the political power to appoint and direct the government and the government is responsible to the people for everything it does. In order to exercise their political power effectively and wisely, the people must be reasonably well informed about the issues they are delegating representatives to address. The freedoms of speech and of the press are essential to ensure that information is communicated by individuals speaking to each other and of course by means of publication. In order to exercise their political power effectively and wisely, the people further need access to a forum in which they may hear and evaluate competing arguments, where contending policy ideas and candidates for office are openly and freely engaged in debate. This is based on the reasonable assumption that a well-informed citizenry will, given adequate opportunity to consider competing arguments, be appropriately moved by reason to favor the most reasonable of the policy options and candidates for leadership. Freedoms of speech and press make such forums and choice making possible. Wise and effective exercise of both personal political power and political responsibility means that the people must monitor the workings of the government and the conduct of government officials in office. This is based on the reasonable assumption that corruption is inhibited by publicity. In general, it is more difficult to corrupt an office or institution whose business processes are conducted in full view of the public. Again, the freedoms of speech and press are essential. Finally, people can exercise their political power only if they can organize themselves as they see fit. Again, and for obvious reasons, the Freedoms of Speech, of the Press, and of Assembly are crucial.

What does freedom of worship have to do with all of this? Why does a constitutional guarantee that so far seems to center on freedom of communication (assembly, speech, and publication) also concern itself with creating a "wall between church and state"? The key idea here is that *all* of this revolves around freedom of *thought*—freedom of access to *ideas*. In a constitutional democracy we allow the government *no* authority to exclude *any* idea or issue from consideration, or to put it beyond the reach of reasoned debate among the people. The government should not have the power, as organized religions often do, to impose an official orthodoxy of any kind on its membership. The freedom of each member of the group to make up his or her own mind as to what to *think* or *believe* is presupposed by the fundamental principles of democratic self-government, and accordingly by each of the other freedoms enumerated in the First Amendment.

America's First Amendment is not unique. Other nations have recognized and established constitutional protections for these same freedoms. For example the Canadian Charter of Rights and Freedoms lists the following "Fundamental Freedoms: Freedom of Conscience and Religion; Freedom of Thought, Belief, Opinion and Expression, including Freedom of the Press and Other Media of Communication; Freedom of Peaceful Assembly; and Freedom of Association." These same fundamental freedoms are officially recognized and respected even in certain societies with long-standing traditions of much greater regimentation and orthodoxy than the United States or Canada. In Japan, for example, when a freedom is constitutionally protected against the enactment of restrictive legislation, it is called a "fundamental liberty" *(jiyuken)*. Japan's fundamental liberties include freedom of thought and conscience, freedom of religious faith, freedom of speech, freedom of the press, freedom of assembly, freedom of association, and academic freedom. The Japanese constitution recognizes that these "fruits of the age-old struggle of man to be free have survived the many exacting tests for durability," and goes on to "confer [them] upon this and future generations in trust to be held for all time inviolate." But although these values and principles are widely recognized and celebrated in many cultures and societies around the globe, some important differences arise. Unlike the American Bill of Rights, the Canadian Charter's recognition of these fundamental freedoms is hedged with a vaguely worded qualification: ". . . subject only to such reasonable limits prescribed by law as can be demonstrably justified in a free and democratic society." As we shall see in the readings to follow, this difference has deep and far-reaching implications.

2.1 FREEDOM OF SPEECH

2.1 FREEDOM OF SPEECH   Nat Hentoff has written extensively on jazz and is even more widely known for his advocacy of the principles of freedom of expression. He is one of the best-known and respected lay scholars of First Amendment law in the United States. Hentoff is what many writers call a First Amendment absolutist: Hentoff's general position on interpreting and applying the First Amendment is uncompromising. In his view the First Amendment must be applied consistently, even and especially where the speech in question is most objectionable, is at its most unorthodox, most hateful, most offensive, even where speech is positively harmful. Why would one be so uncompromising? In general the absolutist's worry is that *any* compromise of the First Amendment principles would destroy all their force as principles, leaving any and all speech vulnerable to censorship.

In this excerpt from his 1992 book *Free Speech for Me—But Not for Thee*—in which he catalogues threats to the First Amendment from across the entire political spectrum from the religious right to the radical left—Hentoff narrates what is perhaps the most famous test case for First Amendment absolutists, the American Civil Liberties Union (ACLU)'s defense of the First Amendment rights of the American Nazi Party to march publicly and demonstrate in predominantly Jewish Skokie, Illinois. He also explores the more contemporary issue of hate speech and speech codes on college and university campuses.

QUESTIONS FOR STUDY AND DISCUSSION

1. If you were an ACLU member, would you be able to support the ACLU position in the Skokie case?
2. What objections did ACLU members make to that organization's defense of the American Nazi Party's freedom of speech. Overall, do you find these objections or Hentoff's responses to them more convincing? Explain and be specific in your explanations.
3. According to Hentoff, how does conflict arise between "civil liberties" and "civil rights"? How in your view might conflicts between the agenda of civil rights and the principles of freedom of speech be best resolved?
4. Can you think of any type of speech, or demonstration, or expression that you believe ought *not* to be protected under the First Amendment? Be specific and explain why.
5. As you move from the Skokie case to hate speech on campus and what should be done about it, what additional considerations above and beyond those already raised by the Skokie case do you consider important?

FREE SPEECH FOR ME, BUT NOT FOR THEE[1]

NAT HENTOFF

In the spring of 1977, the Chicago-based National Socialist Party (a coven of standardly noisome Nazis) decided to focus their demonstrations on suburban areas with sizable Jewish populations. Skokie [Illinois] very much suited their provocative purpose.

The Nazis intended to march in Skokie on May 1 and July 4, but the village ob-tained a state circuit court injunction preventing the demonstrations. Enter the American Civil Liberties Union, on the side of the Nazis, followed by a series of court skirmishes leading to a July 1977 decision by the Illinois Appellate Court that the Nazis could demonstrate or march in Skokie but were absolutely forbidden to display or wear the swastika.

"The swastika," declared the court, "is a personal affront to every member of the Jewish faith, in remembering the nearly consummated genocide of their people committed within memory by those who used the swastika as their symbol." And that symbol, the court added, is not protected by the First Amendment because it could very well provoke violent reaction among certain Jews of Skokie, particularly those who had barely lived through the Holocaust.

The ACLU filed an appeal on First Amendment grounds, arguing that the swastika is as fully protected symbolic speech as were the black armbands, in the *Tinker* case, worn by the school children in Des Moines protesting the Vietnam War. To allow the state to decide which "symbols" are lawful, and which are not, is to weaken the First Amendment dangerously. After all, given that power, who can tell what the state will decide the next time controversial symbolic speech is tested?

Those supporting the village of Skokie countered by claiming that this particular form of expression was deliberately calculated to ignite violence, and surely would—as the Illinois Appellate Court had said. Indeed, Skokie officials had testified that they would probably not be able to control the town's fiercely anti-Nazi citizens if the homegrown fascists were to appear.

In answer, the ACLU pointed out that it is unconstitutional to ban speech on the basis of a "heckler's veto." If Skokie was so sure that certain hostile groups would be hard to control, the ACLU pointed out, why didn't the village seek an injunction against *them* to prohibit *their* unlawful actions? If extra police power were needed, it must be used to protect speech, even the speech of Nazis.

Also, keeping the First Amendment principle the same but changing the cast, what about historic "provocative" demonstrations? Recalling the Selma, Alabama, march led by Martin Luther King, the *Nation* noted that the Selma demonstration "would never have taken place if the authorities had been allowed to ban it on the ground that it would provoke the rage of white opponents of civil rights for black citizens and therefore endanger the peace."

This argument had no impact on the growing number of ACLU members who continued to send in their furious letters of resignation. Often they attached their membership cards—on the back of which, by the way, the First Amendment was printed. It was grotesque, many of them said, to equate the Nazis with Martin Luther King. As a letter to the *Nation* put it, "Martin Luther King's marches furthered human freedom and dignity, and aimed at spreading nonviolence, while the Nazis want to degrade and destroy freedom, and spread violence."

But nowhere in the First Amendment does it say that freedom of speech is limited only to ideas and symbols that further freedom, dignity, and nonviolence.

Those who opposed the right of the Nazis to march often offered a further argument against the ACLU position: the Nazis, they said, aim at gathering the numerical strength to tear down the very institutions and principles that the ACLU presents as a shield for the Nazis. True, this particular Chicago cadre is small, but so was another seemingly ludicrous Nazi band in Germany. The more the Nazis are allowed to gain strength here, the more the freedoms of the rest of the citizenry—particularly those of Jews and blacks at first—will be in peril.

This viewpoint is a variation of the theory that the Constitution is not a suicide pact. Should a rational society permit unfettered freedom of speech to those who exist to destroy it? If it does, is this indeed a rational society?

Judge Oliver Wendell Holmes answered that question forcefully and lucidly in a 1925 dissent *(Gitlow* v. *New York)*. Benjamin Gitlow and colleagues had been convicted of distributing literature proposing "revolutionary mass action" to replace the present government of the United States. The Supreme Court affirmed the conviction. Joined by Justice Brandeis, Holmes took another view:

> It is said that the manifesto [by Gitlow] was more than a theory, that it was an incitement. *Every idea is an incitement.* It offers itself for belief and if believed is acted on unless some other belief outweighs it or some failure of energy stifles the movement at its birth.
> The only difference between the expression of an opinion and an incitement in the narrower sense is the speaker's enthusiasm for the result . . . Eloquence may set fire to reason. But whatever may be said of the redundant [Gitlow] discourse before us, it had no chance of starting a present conflagration. *If in the long run the beliefs expressed in proletarian dictatorship are destined to be accepted by the dominant forces of the community, the only meaning of free speech is that they should be given their chance and have their way.* (Emphasis added.)

Holmes' logic is inescapable. If speech is to be free, there is always the risk that those who would destroy free speech may be sufficiently eloquent to use that constitutional freedom to end it. But if speech is to be limited to prevent that possibility, then the enemies of free expression have already won a significant victory—even as they are silenced. And once the concept of curbing speech is established, those enemies, each time the state suppresses speech, will have moved closer to their goal of destroying free speech.

And so it happened in Skokie. On May 3, 1977, in order to bar the Nazis, the village passed a set of ordinances imposing criminal penalties on certain forms of speech and assembly. Without mentioning the Nazis by name, the ordinances first required that no parade or assembly involving more than 50 persons could be held unless there was at least 30 days notice for a demonstration permit—and unless a $350,000.00 insurance policy was obtained by the demonstrators. The latter, covering public liability and property damage, cost anywhere from $100 to $900, depending on the risk. An underwriter willing to insure also had to be found, and that was not always a real possibility— especially if the group was decidedly unpopular.

Also prohibited, under any circumstances, was any demonstration that would "incite violence, hatred, abuse, or hostility toward a person or group of persons by reason or reference to racial, ethnic, national, or religious affiliation." So much for Oliver Wendell Holmes' most basic principle of the Constitution—free thought must include free thought for those whose ideas we hate.

The lengthy notice for a permit, moreover, would prevent ad hoc demonstrations—sometimes the most valuable kind, since free speech often has to be timely to be effective. In addition, the insurance provision turned the First Amendment into a document that discriminates against the lower economic classes. Suppose you don't have $100 or $900?

Obviously the ordinances, as a whole, would smother free expression. And so Skokie, in vehement reaction to the Nazis' assertion of *their* right to free speech, had managed to greatly delimit *anyone's* right to free speech in that village.

Skokie, to be sure, had generally been described as a "liberal" community. But those liberals had now constructed a law that—as the New York Civil Liberties Union's then-executive director, Ira Glasser, said—"is the same kind of law that was used in Birmingham, Alabama, and throughout the South to stop civil rights demonstrators. It is the same kind of law that was used against the Wobblies in the earlier part of the century, and by Mayor Hague in New Jersey to stop labor organizers. And it is the same kind of law that was used repeatedly only a few years before to stop anti-war demonstrations."

These Skokie ordinances—trampling the letter and spirit of the First Amendment—also became part of the litigation in which the ACLU remained stubbornly involved, despite its quite stunning loss of membership.

At the end of January 1978, one of the court battles over the Nazis and Skokie reached the highest tribunal in the state, the Illinois Supreme Court. Overruling the Appellate Court, the justices, by a 6-1 vote, declared that the Nazis had a constitutional right to display swastikas in Skokie. Upholding the ACLU, the court explained: "The display of these swastikas—as offensive to the principles of a free nation as the memories it recalls may be—is symbolic political speech intended to convey to the public the beliefs of those who display it." Furthermore, the court said that anticipation of a hostile audience cannot justify prior restraint of speech.

The Illinois Supreme Court dismissed another suit as well. Brought by an organization called Survivors of the Holocaust, the suit argued that psychological and emotional wounds caused by imprisonment in Nazi death camps would impel the survivors in Skokie to try to stop the Nazi demonstration, quite possibly by violent means. (One of the complainants noted in an affidavit that he had watched his mother being buried alive by the German Nazis.) Here again, the threat of violence, however understandable the motivation, cannot be a reason, in law, to shut off speech.

Or, as New York State Judge Charles Breitel said seventeen years earlier in another case that got the ACLU into trouble—the defense of Nazi George Lincoln Rockwell's right to speak in a New York City park—"The unpopularity of views, their shocking quality, their obnoxiousness, and even their alarming impact is not enough [to prohibit speech]. Otherwise, the preacher of any strange doctrine could be stopped; the anti-racist himself could be suppressed if he undertakes to speak in 'restricted' areas; and one who asks that the public schools be open indiscriminately to all ethnic groups could be lawfully suppressed, if only he chose to speak where persuasion is most needed."

The United States Supreme Court refused to review the decision of the Illinois Supreme Court. (Justices Harry Blackmun and Byron White dissented. They wanted to hear arguments on the limits to freedom of speech.) For the battered ACLU, the run of resignations eventually stopped. In time, the ACLU grew again, eventually reaching a higher membership than it had before. But if another Skokie were to test the membership, many are likely to again fail the test because not all members of the ACLU are primarily civil libertarians.

Skokie turned out to be a double lesson in liberty. The case itself vividly illustrated the First Amendment importance of symbolic speech and the indivisibility of all free speech. Simultaneously, the reaction to the ACLU's position by so many who considered themselves liberals and even libertarians emphasized—as no other case in many years—how fragile throughout the land is support for the still revolutionary notion that the state has no business squashing anybody's ideas or symbols. *Anybody's.*

The ACLU has won more renowned victories than its Skokie success. But the ACLU has seldom won a more vital internal battle than its decision to stay with the First Amendment rights of Nazis even if the great majority of the membership were to fall away.

Aryeh Neier, national executive director of the ACLU at the time, said: "As a Jew, and a refugee from Nazi Germany, I have strong personal reasons for finding the Nazis repugnant. Freedom of speech protects my right to denounce Nazis with all the vehemence I think proper. Despite my hatred of their vicious doctrine, I realize that it is in my interests to defend their right to preach it."

But the National Lawyers Guild, a group of lawyers on the left, which has done valuable civil rights work and has defended the civil liberties of people with whom it agrees, accused the ACLU of "poisonous evenhandedness" in the Skokie cases.

During a grim period of the ACLU, when members were resigning in angry hordes, David Goldberger, legal director of the ACLU and attorney for Frank Collin, the head of the National Socialist Party (the Nazis), wrote to many of Chicago's criminal defense lawyers for their support in order to offset fierce public criticism of the ACLU—and those membership losses. Goldberger thought that defense lawyers, above everyone else, would understand the bar's ethical responsibility to represent unpopular clients, and therefore would rise in spirited defense of the ACLU, not to mention the First Amendment.

"The response to the letter," said Goldberger, "was silence." Nor had he been able to find any volunteer attorneys.

During the long march through the courts, Goldberger, the lead lawyer on the case, suffered much verbal abuse and after a while, as I discovered, disguised his voice on the phone until he knew who was calling. He did receive a letter of support from a woman:

> I was one of the youth of Jehovah's Witnesses during World War II—stoned, spat upon, jailed without due process, urinated upon and reviled because my religion forbade me to salute the flag or buy war stamps in school. I resigned my ministry in 1951 but eleven years was long enough to learn the value of the First Amendment to a person espousing an unpopular viewpoint.

* * *

In June 1991, on the Public Broadcasting System, I was a member of a Fred Friendly seminar on "Safe Speech, Free Speech and the University." We were discussing the rising tide of college speech codes—punishing students for a wide, vague spectrum of "offensive" speech. The session was held at Stanford University, which had enacted a typically slippery code that can ensnare students who have no idea they are breaking it.

There were two Stanford students—and one recently graduated Stanford alumnus—on the panel. Two were black; the other was Asian-American. All were bright, articulate, and firmly in favor of punishing speech for the greater good of civility on campus.

During the preceding two years, I had visited over twenty colleges and universities around the country—from Penn State and Columbia to the University of Utah and the University of Tennessee. With some exceptions, I found that minority students—and women of all colors—do indeed believe that the First Amendment (and its spirit in private institutions) must bend when hate speech is at issue.

When I tell them that James Madison, the architect of the First Amendment, intended it to be of most value in times of bitter crisis, they point out, with various degrees of civility, that Madison, a dead white male, lived in a time of slavery. So he and the First Amendment are abstractions.

Many white students, faculty members, and administrators are also convinced that speech must be limited if racism, sexism, and homophobia are to be extirpated in and out of the classroom. And that includes the punishment—and if necessary—the banishment of profes-

sors infected with any or all of those viruses.

Indeed—again, with some exceptions—most of the white liberal students who consider themselves activists look at you with genuine puzzlement when you tell them how Oliver Wendell Holmes described the test of free speech:

> If there is any principle of the Constitution that more imperatively calls for attachment than any other, it is the principle of free thought—not free thought for those who agree with us but freedom of thought that we hate."

Another abstraction.

These new Jacobins are powered by a genuine faith that they are working for an undeniable good—creating and sustaining true equality on campus by eradicating speech that makes minorities, women, and gays feel unwanted. Convinced that they are occupying the moral high ground, they see their opponents as raising the issue of free speech as a cover for their own racism, sexism, or disgraceful indifference to these issues.

And they are joined by the undeniably influential editorial writers of *The New York Times* who—on May 12, 1991—described as "sloganeering" any attempts to criticize "political correctness" on campus. "The real danger," said the *Times,* "is the rising tide of hate."

The *Times* approves of campus speech codes—as if it is essential to curb speech in order to curb bigotry. Educators presumably have no other way to educate students out of what they have learned at home or among poisoned peers.

Underlying this conflict between the relatively few free-speech students and administrators, on the one hand, and the censors-for-the-common-good on the other is a deeper debate: advocates of civil rights versus advocates of civil liberties. It has hardly been mentioned in the abundance of reports on the civil wars on the campuses.

Among the law professors on the Fred Friendly panel were Thomas Grey of Stanford, who is white, and Randall Kennedy of Harvard, who is black. Grey essentially wrote the Stanford speech code, and Kennedy—usually a proponent of free speech and thought—is nonetheless in favor of college codes.

Both Grey and Kennedy served as clerks to J. Skelly Wright on the District of Columbia Court of Appeals. Wright was a courageous, indomitable defender and implementer of civil rights. Both Grey and Kennedy also served as clerks to Thurgood Marshall on the Supreme Court. Marshall, while a consistent advocate of free speech, has been most influential as a paladin of civil rights.

Throughout the country, both on campus and off, there is an intense conflict between civil rights and civil liberties students, administrators, and law professors. In the American Civil Liberties Union—whose national board finally declared its opposition to college speech codes—the legal director, John Powell, who is black, still maintains that a balance has to be struck in these matters between the First and Fourteenth Amendments. The latter guarantees everyone equal protection under the laws. Powell and the civil rights legions maintain that this means students have to be protected from demeaning and denigrating speech if they are to be—and feel—equal on campus.

This split between civil rights and civil liberties forces has been dramatically evident during debates about college speech codes on various boards of affiliates of the ACLU. Black board members, with exceptions, have called for support of the speech codes. The more fundamental issue—which will be debated for many years to come—is whether the First Amendment goes too far.

A conclusion from this division among people of good intentions is that when the First Amendment is put up against such desirable goals as the control of bigotry, it fades—for many people—in importance.

Furthermore, civil liberties have to do, most of the time, with protections of the *individual* from the government. Civil rights, on the other hand, are usually regarded, and litigated, as *group* rights that the government must implement for individuals. And that, too, is a basic conflict in the battle over curbing speech on and off campus. (With regard to pornography, for another example, those feminists who want to outlaw it base their attack on group rights claiming that pornography debases and degrades women and therefore puts them in a subordinate position in society.)

So, too, with race. On the *MacNeil/Lehrer News Hour* (June 18, 1991), Professor Molafi Asante, chairman of the African-American Studies Department at Temple University, said:

> You have certainly the individual's right to say whatever he or she pleases to say. I mean, that is fundamental to the Constitution itself. You have the other point to this, of course, which is the collective interest. . . What is the collective interest? What is best for the community? What is best for the

society? And certainly I think the whole question of insensitivity is basic to this issue. And if an individual is insensitive to his or her peers or colleagues, then I think that certainly the university should be concerned about this.

His approach—more carefully wrought than most—exemplifies the ritual of balancing free speech into the back of the bus. Yet though free speech is "fundamental to the Constitution itself," when the chips are down, the university must put "sensitivity" first.

By rather lonely contrast, there is the view—and practice—of Yale University President Benno Schmidt. The great majority of college presidents have either put a speech code in place as a quick cheap way of pretending they're doing something about bigotry on campus, or they hunker down and try to avoid the subject. Benno Schmidt continually, consistently, confronts the question of free speech versus the university-as-a-community, a community with its concerns of civility and sensitivity.

On Fred Friendly's Public Broadcasting System program Schmidt said:

> I take a completely different view of what a university is . . . I don't think the university is first and foremost a community. It's not a place, first and foremost, that is about the inculcation of thought [and] habits of mind that I might agree are correct and constructive.
>
> The university has a fundamental mission, which is to search for the truth. And a university is a place where people have to have the right to speak the unspeakable and think the unthinkable and challenge the unchallengeable.

> Now, it's not a place of violence. It's not a place for threats. . . . There's no place for violence, or threats of it, in a regime of freedom. But beyond that, I think that these [speech] codes make a terrible mistake. . . . Students think that they are codes about building communities that are based on correct thoughts, and that's antithetical, I think, to the idea of a university.

The group-rights codes have actually succeeded in helping to divide the university into a number of splintered "communities." And contrary to some of what's been written, they have not succeeded—on any campus I know of—in squashing or even intimidating conservative students. (A number of professors who march to their own drums, however, have been bedeviled into dropping courses because of the heat—including classroom disruptions by the ultra-orthodox.)

Conservative students are enjoying their role as champions of free speech, taking great sardonic pleasure in depicting the righteous left as neo-McCarthyites. On many campuses, conservatives—usually with the help of funds from highly conservative foundations—are publishing alternative papers. They tend to be quite lively and witty (humor being in exceedingly short supply among the Jacobins). And these papers take much muckraking pleasure in exposing the surrenders, small and large, of university administrators to the demands of the ultra-orthodox.

Those most stifled by the pall of orthodoxy on campus are students who are liberals but of an independent mind—and moderates. On campus after campus, from Brown to Stanford, I have talked to students who say there are some views they hold—or questions they want to ask—that they no longer bring up in class or in most places outside of class. It's not worth the hassle—or being placed in Coventry. Questions, for example, about affirmative action. How far should it go? Should the progeny of the black middle class get preference? And questions about abortion. Should the father have any say at all in what happens to the fetus?

One brave student at New York University Law School, Barry Endick, actually signed his name a few years ago to a complaint about this bristling orthodoxy in a letter in the law school student publication, *The Commentator.* He told of the atmosphere in the law school created by "a host of watchdog committees and a generally hostile classroom reception regarding any student right of center." This "can be arguably viewed as symptomatic of a prevailing spirit of academic and social intolerance of . . . any idea which is not 'politically correct.' . . . We ought to examine why students, so anxious to wield the Fourteenth Amendment, give short shrift to the First. Yes, Virginia, there are racist assholes. And you know what? The Constitution protects them, too."

Federal and state workplace rules concerning sexual harassment have been incorporated in many college speech codes—particularly sanctions for the creation of a "hostile atmosphere" for students. These codes began in response to crude racial and sexist scrawls and epithets. But indeed, the language being punished increasingly extends to any words that create a "hostile atmosphere" or any language that "involves an express or implied threat to an individual's academic efforts." Whatever that may mean.

There is also the damaging effect of these "protective" regulations on the very people who are insisting they be safe-guarded. Malcolm X used to talk about the need to learn how language works, how to dissect it, how to use it as both a shield and sword. Above all, he felt, blacks should not be fearful of language. They should not let language intimidate them but rather fight back—when words are used against them—with more powerful words of their own.

If you read Malcolm X's collected speeches and listen to his recordings, it's clear he was an extraordinarily resilient, resourceful, probing master of language. How did he get that way? Not by being protected, as he grew up, from wounding language.

I've debated black students about these speech codes. They are highly articulate and quick with polemical counterpoint. And I've asked them why on earth they are running away from language when they could turn a campus into a continuing forum on racism—by using the vicious racist language directed at them to illuminate and counter what's going on at that college.

Moreover, by turning to censorship instead of a challenge, these students can well cut off speech they themselves want to hear.

On ABC-TV's *Nightline* several years ago, debating Barbara Ransby (a Ph.D. student in political science at the University of Michigan and a founder of the United Coalition Against Racism there), I asked her to respond to this quite possible scenario. A group of black students invite Minister Louis Farrakhan to lecture in a political science class at a college. He comes and says, "I want to explain what I said about Judaism being a gutter religion. I meant it, but I want to give you the context in which I said it."

There are Jewish students in the class, and they claim that—according to the university's code, which includes outside speakers—Farrakhan has created a hostile atmosphere for them.

In my view, I said, Farrakhan ought to be able to speak anywhere he chooses, and certainly on a college campus. So long as the students have the right to question him and argue with him, they'll have something to gain from the experience. But under some of the speech codes at more and more colleges, Farrakhan—having created a "hostile atmosphere"—would quite likely not be permitted on campus again.

Is that what the black students pressing for speech codes want? To have black speakers they invite on campus rejected because of what they say and how they say it? Do women students want radical feminist Andrea Dworkin barred because of possible charges that she creates a "hostile environment" for nearly all men?

Also overlooked by students especially concerned with artistic expression is that a "hostile atmosphere" can be created by a painting or a piece of sculpture because obviously, "expression" can be graphic as well as verbal. When the University of Wisconsin's speech code was being debated before the state's Board of Regents, E. David Cronon, dean of the university's Madison College of Letters and Sciences, testified that the code would indeed chill students' rights to artistic expression.

Furthermore—and this is a poignant dimension of the rush to virtuous censorship—it won't do a bit of good. Let us suppose these codes were in place on every campus in the country. Would racism go away? Racism would go underground, in the dark, where it's most comfortable.

According to the Stanford speech code, "Speech or other expression constitutes harassment by personal vilification if it:

> a) is intended to insult or stigmatize an individual or small number of individuals on the basis of their sex, race, color, handicap, religion, sexual orientation, or national and ethnic origin; and
>
> b) is addressed directly to the individual or individuals whom it insults or stigmatizes; and c) makes use of insulting or "fighting" words of nonverbal symbols.

But how is it determined that someone *intended* to insult? Intended to "stigmatize"? Which "nonverbal symbols" can get you suspended or expelled?

And what is a "fighting word"? To whom?

Fighting words, according to the Stanford speech code, are words that by their "very utterance inflict injury or tend to incite to an immediate breach of the peace."

That hardly helps prevent you from getting into trouble unless you know, in advance, what particular set of words will ignite each particular student. The least Stanford can do is interview every student and then provide all students with a list of the specific words that will cause each of the other students to explode.

And, by the way, when does a word "tend" to incite? What measuring rod is used?

Stanford prides itself on being one of the elite universities, and yet the majority of its faculty and students have yet to learn so basic a historical truth as this— stated by Eleanor Holmes Norton, former chairwoman of the federal Equal Employment Opportunity Commission:

> It is technically impossible to write an anti-speech code that cannot be twisted against speech nobody

means to bar. It has been tried and tried and tried.

Steven Rohde, a constitutional lawyer, who was co-chairman of the Los Angeles Bar Association Bill of Rights Bicentennial Committee, points out

> A university campus, whether public or private, must be a place for robust, wide-open, and free discussion. Students bring to college all their prejudices, their fears, their doubts, their misconceptions. If they spend four years cooped up under repressive regulations, they might well dutifully obey the rules, offend no one, and leave with all their prejudices, fears, doubts, and misconceptions fully intact.
>
> Punishing bigoted speech only treats the symptoms, not the disease. It often creates martyrs and drives them underground, where they attract new, impressionable followers on the pretext that they themselves [the bigots] are an "oppressed minority," whose "truths" are so powerful they are banned by the Establishment.

Stanford has also gone beyond the continuous chill of speech codes to institute a policy that some people should have more free speech than others.

One of the leading supporters of the speech police is law professor Robert Rabin, who was chairman of the Student Conduct Legislative Council. During the debate in the Faculty Senate on whether the Stanford speech code should pass, Professor Michael Bratman offered Rabin a hypothetical:

In an angry exchange with a white student, a black student calls him a "honky son-of-a-bitch." I assume, said Bratman, that language would be prohibited under the speech code.

"No," said Professor Rabin. As reported in a document of the Student Conduct Legislative Council, Rabin went on to explain that the proposed Stanford speech policy takes the position that the white majority, as a whole, should not be protected from hateful speech as much as groups that have suffered discrimination.

Accordingly, "calling a white a 'honky,'" said Professor Rabin, "is not the same as calling a black a 'nigger.'"

The Stanford Sliding Scale of Free Speech.

Under this notion that some people deserve more free speech than others, punishment of bad speech is measured by which *groups* have been more discriminated against over time. Members of those groups get extra free speech.

One assumes, then, that a student charged with anti-Semitism will get a heavier punishment than someone who has insulted a WASP because Jews, Lord knows, have been discriminated against more often and certainly longer than any other religious group.

As for ethnicity, what about Native Americans? In view of the length of their brutal mistreatment here, shouldn't they be allowed more free speech than any other ethnic group? What about Italian Americans? They claim, with justification, that they have historically been the targets of deep-rooted discrimination. Will a Stanford student suffer greater punishment for insulting an Italian Catholic student by contrast with making a Presbyterian feel bad?

CASE STUDY: STUDENT NEWSPAPER RUNS OFFENSIVE EDITORIAL CARTOON

Now that you've read Hentoff's account of the Skokie case and his comments on campus speech codes as a remedial response to hate speech, imagine that you are the opinion page editor of the student newspaper in the following actual case. The next week's edition must devote most of its editorial space to a dispute, and you must write the lead editorial.

In November of 1990, in the run up to Operation Desert Storm (the war in the Persian Gulf) the *Star,* Sonoma State University's student newspaper, ran an editorial cartoon by syndicated cartoonist Milt Priggee. The cartoon depicted an "inner city" scene in which three young African American men hanging out along a littered sidewalk, one of them bouncing a basketball, are "advised" by an older African American man, "No job? No hope? No future? Quit worryin', there's a war on the way. . . ."

To protest what they considered racist stereotypes presented in the cartoon, members of African American fraternity Kappa Alpha Psi led a rally on the campus quad. At the rally students set fire to a trashcan full of newspapers featuring the cartoon, accused the *Star's* editorial staff of racism, and demanded a public apology.

The *Star's* editor in chief, speaking before the assembled protestors said, "[I'm] sorry that students have been offended. I respect your view, but I think that burning newspapers is an unacceptable form of censorship."

Informed of the controversy, cartoonist Priggee explained the intended message of the cartoon, "It's a slice of life in the ghetto. There's no job, no hope, no future. It's about being black and disenfranchised. A disproportionate number of blacks fought in Vietnam, and it's happening again. The black man ends up fighting the white man's war."

Follow-up Thought Experiment/Essay Question

Imagine that you are the faculty adviser to the editorial board of the newspaper. Assume that some students on the staff and editorial board side with the protestors and wish to publish strongly worded apologies and retractions; others are equally adamant about defending the cartoon and the paper's editorial judgment and are in any case opposed to publishing any "apology." Based on your understanding of Hentoff, how would you handle the situation?

2.2 LIMITING THE FREEDOM OF SPEECH University of Michigan Law School Professor Catharine A. MacKinnon is one of the world's leading feminist legal scholars. Her work has contributed to a host of recent developments in pornography law and toward establishing sexual harassment as a legal concept.

We've selected her essay "Equality and Speech," from her 1993 book *Only Words,* as an introduction to MacKinnon's work and as counterpoint to Hentoff. *Only Words* was originally presented as a series of three public lectures at Princeton University.[2] "Equality and Speech" was the third and final lecture. In *Only Words* MacKinnon argues first of all that just as sticks and stones can hurt your bones, words *can* also harm you; words have the power to cause actual injury to people. She argues further that speech is a form of action for which people may legitimately be held accountable. In "Equality and Speech" she argues against First Amendment absolutism's refusal to compromise free speech principles. Her legal argument, framed at first within American constitutional law, is also quite interesting in general philosophical terms. Her argument is based on the idea that freedom of speech is only one of several basic principles to which we are—or ought to be—fundamentally committed in a just and democratic society. Another such principle is equal protection under the law for each and every member of society. So, in addition to the First Amendment's commitment to freedom of speech, the American Bill of Rights commits us in the Fourteenth Amendment to equality before the law, guaranteeing to each citizen that no state shall "deny to any person within its jurisdiction the equal protection of the laws." MacKinnon wants us to consider what *should* happen when a fundamental principle such as this runs into conflict with freedom of speech. Based on a survey of relevant case law, including Hentoff's Skokie case, she argues that American constitutional law has not yet squarely faced this question. For contrast and as guidance she presents a famous case in Canadian constitutional law in which an anti-Semite who had been teaching Holocaust revisionism to schoolchildren in Alberta challenged Canada's hate propaganda law—under which he had been prosecuted and convicted—as a violation of his constitutionally guaranteed freedom of expression.

Questions for Study and Discussion

1. As MacKinnon's argument unfolds, reconsider the case of the editorial cartoon in the student newspaper. In light of MacKinnon's reasoning, would you, as faculty adviser, handle the situation differently?
2. How does MacKinnon characterize the First Amendment absolutist position? Do you consider MacKinnon's characterization of First Amendment absolutism *fair?* Does MacKinnon's critique of First Amendment absolutism succeed in exposing genuine weaknesses in that position? Explain.
3. Can you identify any areas or ways in which MacKinnon's argument mirrors Hentoff's? In those areas where MacKinnon and Hentoff seem to be making the same argument for opposite positions, how might we adjudicate the issues that divide them?
4. What similarities and differences can you identify between Canadian and American traditions regarding freedom of expression? Why might you prefer either the Canadian or the American traditional approach to issues of freedom of expression?

Equality and Speech[3]

C A T H A R I N E   M A C K I N N O N

The law of equality and the law of freedom of speech are on a collision course in this country. Until this moment, the constitutional doctrine of free speech has developed without taking equality seriously—either the problem of social equality or the mandate of substantive legal equality. Originally, of course, the Constitution contained no equality guarantee to serve as context, expansion joint, handmaiden, counterbalance, or coequal goal to the speech guarantee. Yet the modern doctrine of speech dates from considerably after the entrenchment of equality in the Fourteenth Amendment, and still the First Amendment has been interpreted, with a few exceptions, as if it were not there.

More precisely, the First Amendment has grown as if a commitment to speech were no part of a commitment to equality and as if a commitment to equality had no implications for the law of speech—as if the upheaval that produced Reconstruction Amendments did not move the ground under the expressive freedom, setting new limits and mandating new extensions, perhaps even demanding reconstruction of the speech right itself. The version of equality that *has* become part of First Amendment law has been negative—equally keeping law from regulating one forum or view as another—and formal—speech protected for one group or interest is equally protected for others. It is, in other words, largely redundant. The subprovince of the First Amendment that resonates in equal protection is simply an unbiased extension of precedent and the rule of law—a narrow equality supporting a shallow speech. Fourteenth Amendment equality, for its part, has grown as if equality could be achieved while the First Amendment protected the speech of inequality, meaning whenever inequality takes an expressive form, and without considering equal access to speech as central to any equality agenda.

Both bodies of law accordingly show virtually total insensitivity to the damage done to social equality by expressive means and a substantial lack of recognition that some people get a lot more speech than others. In the absence of these recognitions, the power of those who have speech has become more and more exclusive, coercive, and violent as it has become more and more legally protected. Understanding that there is a relationship between these two issues— the less speech you have, the more the speech of those who have it keeps you unequal; the more the speech of the dominant is protected, the more dominant they become and the less the subordinated are heard from—is virtually nonexistent. Issues at the equality-speech interface are not framed as problems of balance between two cherished constitutional goals, or as problems of meaningful access to either right in the absence of the other, but as whether the right to free speech is infringed acceptably or unacceptably. Equality-promoting provisions on hate crimes,

campus harassment, and pornography, for example, tend to be attacked and defended solely in terms of the damage they do, or do not do, to speech. At the same time, issues such as racial segregation in education, with its accompanying illiteracy and silence, are framed solely in equality terms, rather than also as official barriers to speech and therefore as violations of the First Amendment.

First Amendment speech and Fourteenth Amendment equality have never contended on constitutional terrain. The reason is largely that both have been interpreted more negatively than positively, prohibiting violations by government more than chartering legal intervention for social change, even as governmental inaction and the more extended consequences of governmental action undermine this distinction in both areas. It is also relevant that federal equality statutes have not been seen to arise under the Fourteenth Amendment, although it expressly authorizes them, and action by states against social inequalities needs no constitutional authority, so invokes the Constitution only when said to violate it.

This mutual one-sidedness in the law has made it virtually impossible to create a community of comprehension that there is a relation, for example, between the use of the epithet "nigger" and the fact that a disproportionate number of children who go to bed hungry every night in this country are African-American; or the use of the word "cunt" and the fact that most prostitutes are women. It creates no room to see that slave laws that make it a crime to teach a slave to read, or schools in which Black children cannot learn to write, deny them freedom of speech; or that judicially eliminating grievance procedures that recognize racist or homophobic vilification as barriers to education officially denies students equality in education.[4] The tensions and intersections between the deeper principles and wider orbits of equality and speech remain un-mapped, equality speaking and speech unequal.

The official history of speech in the United States is not a history of inequality—unlike in Europe, where the role of hate propaganda in the Holocaust has not been forgotten. In America, the examples that provide the life resonance of the expressive freedom, the backdrop of atrocities for the ringing declarations, derive mostly from attempts to restrict the political speech of communists during the McCarthy era. Through this trauma, the country relearned its founding lesson: not to stifle political dissent. Horrible consequences to careers, families, privacy, and security resulted from attempts that now look paranoid to shut up what mostly good and creative people could think and say, from academic theory to street advocacy, about the form of government and economic system we should have. The story of the First Amendment is an epic story of overcoming that, of progress, of making sure it never happens again.

The litany predicated on this experience goes like this. The evil to be avoided is government restricting ideas because it disagrees with the content of their political point of view. The terrain of struggle is the mind; the dynamic at work is intellectual persuasion; the risk is that marginal, powerless, and relatively voiceless dissenters, with ideas we will never hear, will be crushed by governmental power. This has become the "speech you hate" test: the more you disagree with content, the more important it becomes to protect it. You can tell you are being principled by the degree to which you abhor what you allow. The worse the speech protected, the more principled the result. There is a faith that truth will prevail if left alone, often expressed in an openly competitive laissez-faire model taken from bourgeois economics and applied to the expressive marketplace: the "marketplace of ideas" metaphor.[5] The marketplace becomes the battlefield when we are assured that truth will prevail while grappling in open encounter with falsehood, to paraphrase Milton, as he so often is.[6]

In this faith, restricting some speech can only eventuate in restricting more or all speech: the "slippery slope" hazard. Restricting speech is seen to be tempting, to have a seductive power that draws governments to its totalitarian—also regarded as principled—logic: if we restrict this bad thing now, we will not be able to stop ourselves from restricting this good thing later. One corollary is that everyone has an interest in everyone else's speech being free, because restriction will get around to you eventually; the less power you have, the sooner it will get around to you. Crucial is that speech cannot be restricted because you fear its consequences: the "bad tendency" or "witch-hunt" doctrine. If some speech is conceded to be risky, more speech to the contrary will eliminate that risk. Most of all, government can make no judgment as to content. For constitutional purposes, there is no such thing as a false idea,[7] there are only more or less "offensive" ones,[8] to remedy which, love of liberty recommends averting the eyes or growing a thicker skin.

Americans are taught this view by about the fourth grade and continue to absorb it through osmosis from everything around them for the rest of their lives, including law school, to the point that those who embrace it think it is their own personal faith, their own original view, and trot it out like something learned from their own personal lives every time a problem is denominated one of "speech," whether it really fits or not. Any issue that strikes this chord, however faintly, gets played this tune, even if the consequences are more like a replay of McCarthyism than resistance to it. This approach is adhered to with a fundamentalist zeal even when it serves to protect lies, silence dissent, destroy careers, intrude on associations, and retard change. At least as ironic is the fact that the substance of the left's forbidden theories, which were a kind of argument for class equality, made no impression on the law of speech at all.

Has this doctrinal edifice guaranteed free and equal speech? These days censorship occurs less through explicit state policy than through official and unofficial privileging of powerful groups and viewpoints. This is accomplished through silencing in many forms and enforced by the refusal of publishers and editors to publish, or publish well, uncompromised expressions of dissent that make them uncomfortable by challenging the distribution of power, including sexual power. Such publishing decisions, no matter how one-sided and cumulative and exclusionary, are regarded as the way the system of freedom of expression is supposed to work. Legal accountability for these decisions is regarded as fascism; social accountability for them is regarded as creeping fascism; the deci-

sions themselves are regarded as freedom of speech. Speech theory does not disclose or even consider how to deal with power vanquishing powerlessness; it tends to transmute this into truth vanquishing falsehood, meaning what power wins becomes considered true. Speech, hence the lines within which much of life can be lived, belongs to those who own it, mainly big corporations.

Refusal to publish works that criticize the sexual distribution of power in particular are often, in my experience, supported by reference to the law of libel. Libel law, just one subdivision of the law of speech which lacks sensitivity to the substance of social inequality, has become a tool for justifying refusals to publish attacks on those with power, even as it targets the powerless for liability. Its equality-blindness goes back at least to the formative *New York Times* v. *Sullivan,*[9] in which the law of libel was first recognized as coming under the First Amendment. The *New York Times* ran a civil rights fundraising ad for Black leaders that described racist misbehavior by white police in the South. On the basis of minor inaccuracies in the ad, the *Times* was successfully sued for libel under state law by the police commissioner of Montgomery, Alabama. The newspaper argued that more than minor inaccuracies should be required to sue for a form of speech. When the *Times* won this argument before the Supreme Court, a new First Amendment doctrine was born.

In reality, *Sullivan* was animated by issues of substantive equality as powerful as they were submerged; indeed, they were perceptible only in the facts. The case lined up an equality interest—that of civil rights activists in the content of the ad—*with* the First Amendment interest of the newspaper. This aligned sentiment in favor of racial equality with holding libel law to standards of speech protection higher than state law would likely enforce on racists. In other words, *Sullivan* used support for civil rights to make it easier for newspapers to publish defamatory falsehoods without being sued. This brigading of support for racial equality with enhanced power for the media to be less careful about what they publish was utterly tacit. The argument for the *Times* by Herbert Wechsler—originator of the broadside attack on *Brown v. Board of Education* which prohibited racial segregation in the public schools, as unprincipled constitutional adjudication—did not mention equality at all, while benefiting from the pro-equality wind at its back.[10]

Because the *Times* won without any acknowledgment that concern for substantive equality powered this extension of the First Amendment, the decision did not consider whether the standard of care for truth might have been drawn higher if, for example, southern racist police had been accused of libeling prominent leaders of the nascent civil rights movement in an ad with a few inaccuracies. The extent to which publishers had to know the truth before they could recklessly disregard it, as *Sullivan* newly required for libel of public figures, might have appeared especially problematic if the submerged equality issues had been exposed. Bigotry as often produces unconscious lies as knowing ones, indeed often precludes the dominant from seeing the truth of inequality being lived out beneath their station, hence vision. The implications for subordinated groups of a relaxed standard of truth for publishers—perhaps the stake of the subordinated in having publishers substantiate what they print might be as often on the other side? Perhaps media are owned and run by dominant groups who sincerely see a dominant way of seeing as the truth?—was not discussed. Nor was social inequality considered when, in the same case, the constitutional status of laws against group defamation was undermined in advance of a real case on the subject.[11]

The resulting law of libel has had the effect of licensing the dominant to say virtually anything about subordinated groups with impunity while supporting the media's power to refuse access to speech to the powerless, as it can always cite fear of a libel suit by an offended powerful individual. This situation is exacerbated by the facts that it is subordinated groups who are damaged by group defamation and mostly the privileged who can make credible threats to sue even for true statements that make them look bad. Because the *Sullivan* holding made it easier for media to get away with false and damaging statements about public figures, individuals from subordinated groups who take on dominant interests in public are left especially exposed—sexually libeled feminists who oppose pornography, for example. The assumption seems to be that anyone who stands up in public has the same power that government and its officials do, and possesses access to speech equal to that of socially privileged or unscrupulous operatives of the status quo, like pornographers.

The *Sullivan* dictum on group libel substantially undermined the vitality of an earlier case, *Beauharnais* v. *Illinois*, which had held that group defamation, including publications that expose the citizens of any race, color, creed, or religion to contempt, could be made criminal, without violating the First Amendment. *Sullivan* tilted First Amendment law in the direction of the conclusion that individual libel is actionable but group libel is not, making injury to the reputation of individuals legally real and consigning injury to the reputation of groups to legal limbo. Reputational harm to those who are allowed to be individuals—mostly white men—is legal harm. Those who are defined by, and most often falsely maligned through, their membership in groups—namely almost everyone else—have no legal claim. Indeed, those who harm them have something of a speech right to do that harm. This arrangement avoids the rather obvious reality that groups are made up of individuals. It also looks a lot like discrimination against harms done through discrimination, in favor of what are regarded by distinction as individual harms. In reality, libel of groups multiplies rather than avoids the very same damage through reputation which the law of individual libel recognizes when done one at a time, as well as inflicting some of its own.

The effectiveness of *Sullivan's* undermining of *Beauharnais* became vividly clear in the later case that arose out of the Nazis' proposed march in Skokie, Illinois, a site chosen because it was largely populated by Jewish survivors of the Holocaust. The march was found to be protected speech, invalidating a group defamation law that would have stopped it, by judges who had never faced a pogrom piously intoning how much they abhorred what the Nazis had to say, but how legally their hands were tied and how principled they were in allowing it. You can tell how principled they were because of how much they hated the speech.

Over a notable dissent by Justice Blackmun, the U.S. Supreme Court denied review, leaving this result standing and leaving unvindicated a perception of fascist speech by Justice Jackson in a dissent of a decade before: "These terse epithets come down to our generation weighted with hatreds accumulated through centuries of bloodshed. They are recognized words of art in the profession of defamation. . . . They are always, and in every context, insults which do not spring from reason and can be answered by none. Their historical associations with violence are well understood, both by those who hurl and those who are struck by these missiles." Justice Jackson was later to dissent in *Beauharnais,* but when he wrote this, he had just returned from the Nuremberg trials, facing what those who became the residents of Skokie had survived.

Nobody mentioned that to be liquidated because of one's group membership is the ultimate inequality. Constitutional equality has never been the interest that hate speech prohibitions are seen to promote.[12] No one to my knowledge has proposed that Congress prohibit hate propaganda to effectuate the Fourteenth Amendment. Instead, when hate speech regulations are assessed, the question has been: does a given law trench too far, or not too far, on the right of free speech? The political speech litany is invoked: nasty ideas that may or may not cause harm, depending on whether they are acted upon (we are supposed to wait); truth outing; more speech solving the problem; swallowing your gorge and adjusting your dignitary standards if you want to be part of the big bad real world. This, under a document that accepts balancing among constitutional interests as method.

The closest the Court has come to recognizing substantive equality in the hate speech area occurred in *Beauharnais.* Writing for the majority, Justice Frankfurter said: "[A] man's job and his educational opportunities and the dignity accorded him may depend as much on the reputation of the racial and religious group to which he willy-nilly belongs, as on his own merits." Employment, education, and human dignity are all on equal territory but went unmarked as such. Civil unrest—otherwise known as oppressed people agitating for their equality or expressing frustration at their inequality—was also noted as a possible consequence of allowing group defamation to go unchecked.

Justice Douglas, in his dissent in *Beauharnais,* came almost as close: "Hitler and his Nazis showed how evil a conspiracy could be which was aimed at destroying a race by exposing it to contempt, derision, and obloquy. I would be willing to concede that such conduct directed at a race or group in this country could be made an indictable offense. For such a project would be more than the exercise of free speech." He does not say what that more would be an exercise in. Kalven writes of this passage, "There is a germ of a powerful idea here," but he does not call that idea by its name either.[13] The statute in *Beauharnais* was not defended as an equality law, and no argument in the case located group defamation as part of social inequality.[14] Legal equality under the Fourteenth Amendment, in effect for almost a hundred years, was not mentioned.

So there never has been a fair fight in the United States between equality and speech as two constitutional values, equality supporting a statute or practice, speech challenging it. Courts have balanced *statutory* equality interests against the constitutional speech protection. Equality always won these fights until pornography, statutorily framed as sex inequality, lost to the First Amendment, and now equality is losing to speech-based attacks on hate provisions as well.[15] In other words, pornography ordinances and hate crime provisions fail constitutional scrutiny that they might, with constitutional equality support, survive. Moreover, speech is not extended that might be, as in the broadcasting or campaign financing areas.[16] If speech were seen through an equality lens, nude dancing regulations might be tailored to ending the sex inequality of prostitution, at the same time undermining the social credibility of the pimp's lie that public sex is how women express themselves. Cross-burning prohibitions would be seen as the civil rights protections they are. Women might be seen to have a sex equality right to the speech of abortion counseling. Poverty might even be seen as the inequality underlying street begging, at once supporting the speech interest in such solicitations and suggesting that equal access to speech might begin before all one can say is "spare change?"[17]

Since this perspective does not yet animate case law, speech cases that consider words as triggers to violent action instead submerge inequality issues further. In *Brandenburg* v. *Ohio,* a case that set the standard on speech and consequent conduct with regard to inflammatory advocacy, the words were Ku Klux

Klan racism.[18] *Claiborne Hardware,* a further ruling on instigating speech, questioned whether arm-twisting rhetoric of leaders of a civil-rights boycott was protected or whether the activists could be held responsible for the lost business in money damages.[19] *Brandenburg's* concern was whether the "ideas" of the Klan were a sufficient "incitement" to restrict the speech, meaning were they immediate enough to the assaults. *Claiborne Hardware* explored the parameters of holding public speakers responsible for the consequences of their persuasive advocacy. Suppressed entirely in the piously evenhanded treatment of the Klan and the boycotters—the studied inability to tell the difference between oppressor and oppressed that passes for principled neutrality in this area as well as others— was the fact that the Klan was promoting inequality and the civil rights leaders were resisting it, in a country that is supposedly not constitutionally neutral on the subject.

If this was expectable, the virtual absence of discussion of equality in recent litigation over discrimination policies that prohibit group-based harassment and bigotry on campuses was astounding. Denominated "campus speech codes" by their opponents, these regulations are formally predicated on federal laws that require equal access to an education on the basis of race and sex.[20] In challenges to these regulations under the First Amendment, which have been successful so far, the statutory equality interest is barely mentioned. That these procedures might vindicate a constitutional interest in equality which is as important as, or part of, the speech interest used to demolish them is not considered. What can one say about the failure to take seriously the educational equality these provisions exist to serve?

Nor is equality recognized as legally relevant to the problem of pornography, which is addressed instead under the First Amendment doctrine of obscenity. Obscenity law started with the "deprave and corrupt the morals of consumers" test (*they're* being hurt); moved through the censorship of literature from Joyce through Radclyffe Hall to Henry Miller, making them all bestsellers (*they're* being hurt); winding up with the Supreme Court devising its own obscenity test, which is so effective that, under it, the pornography industry has quadrupled in size (*they're* being hurt?). The ineffectuality of obscenity law is due in some part to exempting materials of literary, political, artistic, or scientific value. Value can be found in anything, depending, I have come to think, not only on one's adherence to postmodernism, but on how much one is being paid. And never underestimate the power of an erection, these days termed "entertainment," to give a thing value. Adding to the unworkability of the obscenity test is the requirement that the state prove "prurient interest": is the average person turned on? The more violent pornography is, the less willing juries and police are to say it is arousing, and more and more pornography is more and more violent, and arousing.

Equally difficult in practice has been the requirement in the obscenity test that community standards be proven violated. The more pornography there is, the more it sets de facto community standards, conforming views of what is acceptable to what is arousing, even as the stimulus to arousal must be more and more violating to work. In other words, inequality is allowed to set community standards for the treatment of women. What is wrong with pornography is that it hurts women and their equality. What is wrong with obscenity law is that this reality has no role in it. This irrelevant and unworkable tool is then placed in the hands of the state, most of whose actors have little interest in stopping this abuse but a substantial interest in avoiding prosecutions they cannot win. The American law of obscenity, as a result, is only words.

The pornography issue, far more than the political speech cases, has provided the setting for the definitive development of the absolutist approach to speech. First Amendment absolutism did not begin in obscenity cases, but it is in explaining why obscenity should be protected speech, and how it cannot be distinguished from art and literature, that much of the work of absolutism has been done, taking as its point of departure and arrival the position that whatever is expressive should be constitutionally protected. In pornography, absolutism found, gained, and consolidated its ground and hit its emotional nerve. It began as a dissenting position of intellectual extremists and ended by reducing the regulation of obscenity to window dressing on violence against women.

Concretely, observe that it was the prospect of losing access to pornography that impelled the social and legal development of absolutism as a bottom line for the First Amendment, as well as occasioned bursts of passionate eloquence on behalf of speech per se: if we can't have this, they seem to say, what can we have? During the same twenty-year period of struggle over obscenity standards, the Court was watching more and

more pornography as its mass-marketed forms became more and more intrusive and aggressive. Observing this process from its end point of state protection of pornography, I have come to think that the main principle at work here is that, once pornography becomes pervasive, speech *will* be defined so that men can have their pornography. American obscenity law merely illustrates one adaptation of this principle: some men ineffectually prohibit it while others vaunt it openly as the standard for speech as such.

Consider the picture. The law against pornography was not designed to see harm to women in the first place. It is further weakened as pornography spreads, expanding into new markets (such as video and computers) and more legitimate forums and making abuse of women more and more invisible as abuse, as that abuse becomes more and more visible as sex. So the Court becomes increasingly *unable to tell* what is pornography and what is not, a failing it laments not as a consequence of the saturation of society by pornography, but as a specifically judicial failure, then finally as an impossibility of line-drawing. The stage is thus set for the transformation of pornography into political speech: the excluded and stigmatized "ideas" we love to hate. Obscured is the way this protects what pornography says and ignores what it does, or, alternatively, protects what pornography says as a means of protecting what it does. Thus can a law develop which prohibits restricting a film because it advocates adultery, but does not even notice a film that is made from a rape.[21]

Nothing in the American law of obscenity is designed to perceive the rape, sexual abuse of children, battering, sexual harassment, prostitution, or sexual murder in pornography. This becomes insulting upon encountering obscenity law's search for harm and failure to find any. The law of child pornography, by contrast—based as it is on the assumption that children are harmed by having sex pictures made of them—applies a test developed in areas of speech other than the sexual: if the harm of speech outweighs its value, it can be restricted by properly targeted means. Given the history of the law of pornography of adult women, it is tempting to regard this as a miracle. Child pornography is not considered the speech of a sexually dissident minority, which it is, advocating "ideas" about children and sex, which it does. Perhaps the fact that boys were used in the film in the test case has something to do with it. The ability to see that child pornography is harmful has everything to do with a visceral sense of the inequality in power between children and adults, yet inequality is never mentioned.

Now, in this context of speech and equality concerns, consider again the judicial opinion on the law Andrea Dworkin and I wrote and Indianapolis passed. This law defines the documented harms pornography does as violations of equality rights and makes them actionable as practices of discrimination, of second-class citizenship. This ordinance allows anyone hurt through pornography to prove its role in their abuse, to recover for the deprivation of their civil rights, and to stop it from continuing. Judicially, this was rendered as censorship of ideas.

In *American Booksellers* v. *Hudnut*, the Court of Appeals for the Seventh Circuit found that this law violated the First Amendment. It began by recognizing that the harm pornography does is real, conceding that the legislative finding of a causal link was judicially adequate: ". . . we accept the premises of this legislation. Depictions of subordination tend to perpetuate subordination. The subordinate status of women in turn leads to affront and lower pay at work, insult and injury at home, battery and rape on the streets. In the language of the legislature, '[p]ornography is central in creating and maintaining sex as a basis of discrimination.'" Writing for the panel, Judge Easterbrook got, off and on, that "subordination" is something pornography does, not something it just says, and that its active role had to be proven in each case brought under the ordinance. But he kept losing his mental bearings and referring to pornography as an "idea," finally concluding that the harm it does "demonstrates the power of pornography as speech."[22] This is like saying that the more a libel destroys a reputation, the greater is its power as speech. To say that the more harm speech does, the more protected it is, is legally wrong, even in this country.

Implicitly applying the political speech model, Judge Easterbrook said that the law restricted the marketplace of ideas, the speech of outcast dissenters— referring presumably to those poor heads of organized crime families making ten billion dollars a year trafficking women. He said the law discriminated on the basis of point of view, establishing an approved view of what could be said and thought about women and sex. He failed to note at this point that the invalidated causes of action included coercion, force, and assault, rather a far cry from saying and thinking. He reminded us of

Sullivan, whose most famous dictum is that to flourish, debate must be "uninhibited, robust, and wide open." Behind his First Amendment facade, women were being transformed into ideas, sexual traffic in whom was protected as if it were a discussion, the men uninhibited and robust, the women wide-open.

Judge Easterbrook did not say this law was not a sex discrimination law, but he gave the state interest it therefore served—opposition to sex inequality— no constitutional weight. He did this by treating it as if it were a group defamation law, holding that no amount of harm of discrimination can outweigh the speech interests of bigots, so long as they say something while doing it. Besides, if we restrict this, who knows where it will end. He is sure it will end with "Leda and the Swan." He did not suggest that bestiality statutes also had to go, along with obscenity's restrictions on depictions of sex between humans and animals. Both restrict a disapproved sexuality that, no doubt, contains an element of "mental intermediation." Nothing in *Hudnut* explains why, if pornography is protected speech based on its mental elements, rage and sexual murder, which have mental elements, are not as well.

A dissent in a recent case invalidating sentence enhancements for crimes of bias could have been a dissent here: "The majority rationalizes their conclusion [that the statute violates the First Amendment] by insisting that this statute punishes bigoted thought. Not so. The statute does not impede or punish the right of persons to have bigoted thoughts or to express themselves in a bigoted fashion or otherwise, regarding the race, religion, or other status of a person. It does attempt to limit the effects of big-

otry. What the statute does punish is acting upon these thoughts. It punishes the act of [discrimination] not the thought or expression of bigotry."[23]

Perhaps it is the nature of legal inequality that was misused by the Seventh Circuit. Discrimination has always been illegal because it is based on a prohibited motive: "an evil eye and an unequal hand," that the perpetrator is thinking while doing, what the acts mean. Racial classifications are thought illegal because they "supply a reason to infer antipathy." A showing of discriminatory intent is required under the Fourteenth Amendment. Now we are told that this same motive, this same participation in a context of meaning, this same hatred and bigotry, these same purposes and thoughts, presumably this same intent, *protect* this same activity under the First Amendment. The courts cannot have it both ways, protecting discriminatory activity under the First Amendment on the same ground they make a requirement for its illegality under the Fourteenth. To put it another way, it is the "idea" of discrimination in the perpetrator's mind that courts have required be proven before the acts that effectuate it will be considered discriminatory. Surely, if acts that are otherwise legal, like hiring employees or renting rooms or admitting students, are made illegal under the Constitution by being based on race or sex because of what those who engage in them think about race or sex, acts that are otherwise *il*legal, like coercion, force, and assault, do not become constitutionally protected because they are done with the same thoughts in mind.

Seventh Circuit cases after *Hudnut* show that court attempting to straddle the fault lines beneath that decision without falling into an abyss. Some fancy footwork was required in a death penalty case in which a sex murderer claimed he could not be held responsible for his actions because he was a lifelong pornography consumer. To receive the death penalty, a defendant must be capable of appreciating the wrongfulness of his actions, but that is exactly what pornography was proven to destroy in the consumer by evidence in this case. Noting that the *Hudnut* court had accepted the view that pornography perpetuates "subordination of women and violence against women" yet is protected because its harm depends on "mental intermediation," this panel, which included Judge Easterbrook, faced the dilemma *Hudnut* placed them in: "It would be impossible to hold both that pornography does not directly cause violence but criminal actors do, and that criminals do not cause violence, pornography does. The result would be to tell Indiana that it can neither ban pornography nor hold criminally responsible persons who are encouraged to commit violent acts by pornography!"[24]

To get out of this, the court imagined that Indiana must have decided that rapists who are aware that a woman does not consent are not then excused by the rapists' belief that they have a right to proceed anyway. This is unsatisfying, as pornography makes rapists unaware that their victims are not consenting. As this record showed, it creates "a person who no longer distinguishes between violence and rape, or violence and sex." There will, ultimately, be no way of addressing this problem short of changing the rape law so that it turns on what the perpetrator did rather than on what he thought *and* holding the pornographers

jointly responsible for rapes they can be proven to have caused. Meantime, we kill a man rather than let his victims stop the pornography that produced him— leaving the pornographers completely off the hook. If anyone knows what they are doing, it is the pornographers.

The nude dancing case the Supreme Court ultimately resolved came from the Seventh Circuit, where it produced eight separate opinions, the majority invalidating the regulation on First Amendment grounds. Judge Posner's concurrence turned Judge Easterbrook's protected "ideas" into protected "emotions," explaining that "[m]ost pornography is expressive, indeed expressive of the same emotions that a striptease expresses." Since a videotape of nude dancing would be covered under the ordinance in *Hudnut,* and the ordinance in *Hudnut* restricted protected speech, he reasoned that nude dancing had to be protected speech as well: ". . . if this analysis is wrong, our decision in *Hudnut* is wrong." The Supreme Court found the analysis was wrong. The regulation of nude dancing was valid under the First Amendment, even though striptease was not obscene. But Judge Posner was right about the connection between that case and protecting pornography as speech: their decision in *Hudnut* is wrong.

That these tortured consequences result from the lack of an equality context in which to interpret expressive freedoms is clear from the fact that the same issues produced exactly the opposite results in Canada. Canada's new constitution, the Charter of Rights and Freedoms, includes an expansive equality guarantee and a serious entrenchment of freedom of expression. The Supreme Court of Canada's first move was to define equality in a meaningful way—one more substantive than formal, directed toward changing unequal social relations rather than monitoring their equal positioning before the law. The United States, by contrast, remains in the grip of what I affectionately call the stupid theory of equality. Inequality here is defined as distinction, as differentiation, indifferent to whether dominant or subordinated groups are hurt or helped. Canada, by contrast, following the argument of the Women's Legal Education and Action Fund (LEAF), repudiated this view in so many words, taking as its touchstone the treatment of historically disadvantaged groups and aiming to alter their status. The positive spin of the Canadian interpretation holds the law to promoting equality, projecting the law into a more equal future, rather than remaining rigidly neutral in ways that either reinforce existing social inequality or prohibit changing it, as the American constitutional perspective has increasingly done in recent years.

The first case to confront expressive guarantees with equality requirements under the new constitution came in the case of James Keegstra, an anti-Semite who taught Holocaust revisionism to schoolchildren in Alberta. Prosecuted and convicted under Canada's hate propaganda provision, Keegstra challenged the statute as a violation of the new freedom of expression guarantee. LEAF intervened to argue that the hate propaganda law promoted equality. We argued that group libel, most of it concededly expression, promotes the disadvantage of unequal groups; that group-based enmity, ill will, intolerance, and prejudice are the attitudinal engines of the exclusion, denigration, and subordination that make up and propel social inequality; that without bigotry, social systems of enforced separation, ghettoization, and apartheid would be unnecessary, impossible, and unthinkable; that stereotyping and stigmatization of historically disadvantaged groups through group hate propaganda shape their social image and reputation, which controls their access to opportunities more powerfully than their individual abilities ever do; and that it is impossible for an individual to receive equality of opportunity when surrounded by an atmosphere of group hate.

We argued that group defamation is a verbal form inequality takes, that just as white supremacy promotes inequality on the basis of race, color, and sometimes ethnic or national origin, anti-Semitism promotes the inequality of Jews on the basis of religion and ethnicity. We argued that group defamation in this sense is not a mere expression of opinion but a practice of discrimination in verbal form, a link in systemic discrimination that keeps target groups in subordinated positions through the promotion of terror, intolerance, degradation, segregation, exclusion, vilification, violence, and genocide. We said that the nature of the practice can be understood and its impact measured from the damage it causes, from immediate psychic wounding to consequent physical aggression. Where advocacy of genocide is included in group defamation, we said an equality approach to such speech would observe that to be liquidated because of the group you belong to is the ultimate inequality.

The Supreme Court of Canada agreed with this approach, a majority upholding the hate propaganda provision, substantially on equality grounds. The Court recognized the provision as a content restriction—content that had to be stopped because of its antiegalitarian meaning and devastating consequences.[25]

Subsequently, the Winnipeg authorities arrested a whole pornography store and prosecuted the owner, Donald Victor Butler, for obscenity. Butler was convicted but said the obscenity law was an unconstitutional restriction on his Charter-based right of freedom of expression. LEAF argued that if Canada's obscenity statute, substantially different from U.S. obscenity law in prohibiting "undue exploitation of sex, or sex and violence, cruelty, horror, or crime," was interpreted to institutionalize some people's views about women and sex over others, it would be unconstitutional. But if the community standards applied were interpreted to prohibit harm to women as harm to the community, it was constitutional because it promoted sex equality.

The Supreme Court of Canada essentially agreed, upholding the obscenity provision on sex equality grounds.[26] It said that harm to women—which the Court was careful to make "contextually sensitive" and found could include humiliation, degradation, and subordination—*was* harm to society as a whole. The evidence on the harm of pornography was sufficient for a law against it. Violent materials always present this risk of harm, the Court said; explicit sexual materials that are degrading or dehumanizing (but not violent) could also unduly exploit sex under the obscenity provision if the risk of harm was substantial. Harm in this context was defined as "predispos[ing] persons to act in an anti-social manner, as, for example, the physical or mental mistreatment of women by men, or, what is perhaps debatable, the re-

verse." The unanimous court noted that "if true equality between male and female persons is to be achieved, we cannot ignore the threat to equality resulting from exposure to audiences of certain types of violent and degrading material." The result rested in part on *Keegstra* but also observed that the harms attendant to the production of pornography situated the problem of pornography differently, such that the appearance of consent by women in such materials could exacerbate its injury. Recognizing that education could be helpful in contributing to this harm, the court held that that fact did not make the provision unconstitutional.

Although the Canadians considered the U.S. experience on these issues closely in both cases, the striking absence of a U.S.-style political speech litany suggests that taking equality seriously precludes it, or makes it look like the excuse for enforcing inequality that it has become. The decision did not mention the marketplace of ideas. Maybe in Canada, people talk to each other, rather than buy and sell each other as ideas. In an equality context, it becomes obvious that those with the most power buy the most speech, and that the marketplace rewards the powerful, whose views then become established as truth. We were not subjected to "Let [Truth] and falsehood grapple; who ever knew Truth to put to the worse, in a free and open encounter." Milton had not been around for the success of the Big Lie technique, but this Court had.

Nor did the Canadian Court even consider the "slippery slope," a largely phony scruple impossible to sustain under a contextually sensitive equality rule. With inequality, the problem is not where intervention will end, but when it will ever begin. Equality is the law; if the slippery slope worked, the ineluctable logic of principle would have slid us into equality by now. Also, perhaps, because the Canadian law of equality is moored in the world, and knows the difference between disadvantaged groups and advantaged ones, it is less worried about the misfiring of restrictions against the powerless and more concerned about having nothing to fire against abuses of power by the powerful.

Fundamentally, the Supreme Court of Canada recognized the reality of inequality in the issues before it; this was not big bad state power jumping on poor powerless individual citizen, but a law passed to stand behind a comparatively powerless group in its social fight for equality against socially powerful and exploitative groups. This positioning of forces—which makes the hate propaganda prohibition and the obscenity law of Canada (properly interpreted) into equality laws, although neither was called such by Parliament—made the invocation of a tradition designed to keep government off the backs of people totally inappropriate. The Court also did not say that Parliament had to limit its efforts to stop the harm of inequality by talking to it. What it did was make more space for the unequal to find voice.

Nor did the Canadians intone, with Brandeis and nearly every American court that has ruled on a seriously contested speech issue since, that "[f]ear of serious injury cannot alone justify suppression of free speech. . . . Men feared witches and burnt women." I have never understood this argument, other than as a way of saying that zealots misidentify the causes of their woes and hurt the wrong people. What has to be added to

fear of serious injury to justify doing something about the speech that causes it? *Proof* of serious injury? If we can't restrict it then, when can we? Isn't fear of serious injury the concern behind restricting publication of the dates on which troop ships sail? Is it mere "fear" of injury to children that supports the law against the use of children to make pornography? If that isn't enough, why isn't proof of injury required? "Men feared witches and burnt women." Where is the speech here? Promoting the fear? Nobody tried to suppress tracts against witches. If somebody had, would some women not have been burnt? Or was it the witches' writings? Did they write? So burning their writings is part of the witch-hunt aspect of the fear? The women who are being burned as witches these days are the women in the pornography, and their burning is sex and entertainment and protected as speech. Those who are hunted down, stigmatized, excluded, and unpublished are the women who oppose their burning.

Neither Canadian decision reduces the harm of hate propaganda or pornography to its "offensiveness." When you hear the woman next door screaming as she is bounced off the walls by a man she lives with, are you "offended"? Hate speech and pornography do the same thing: enact the abuse. Women's reactions to the presentation of other women being sexually abused in pornography, and the reactions of Jews living in Skokie to having Nazis march through their town, are routinely trivialized in the United States as "being offended." The position of those with less power is equated with the position of those with more power, as if sexual epithets against straight white men were equivalent to sexual epithets against women, as if breaking the window of a Jewish-owned business in the world after Kristallnacht were just so much breaking glass.

In the cases both of pornography and of the Nazi march in Skokie, it is striking how the so-called speech reenacts the original experience of the abuse, and how its defense as speech does as well. It is not only that both groups, through the so-called speech, are forcibly subjected to the spectacle of their abuse, legally legitimized. Both have their response to it trivialized as "being offended," and that response then used to support its speech value, hence its legal protection.[27] Both are also told that what they can do about it is avert their eyes, lock their doors, stay home, stay silent, and hope the assault, and the animus it makes tangible, end when the film or the march ends. This is exactly what perpetrators of rape and child sexual abuse tell their victims and what the Jews in Germany were told by the Nazis (and the rest of the world) in the 1930s. Accept the freedom of your abusers. This best protects you in the end. Let it happen. You are not really being hurt. When sexually abused women are told to let the system work and tolerate the pornography, this is what they are being told. The Jews in Germany, and the Jews in Skokie, were told to let the system work. At least this time around, the Jews of Canada were not, nor were sexually abused women.

The final absence in the Canadian decisions, perhaps the most startling, is the failure to mention any equivalent to the notion that, under the First Amendment, there is no such thing as a false idea. Perhaps under equality law, in some sense there is. When equality is recognized as a constitutional value and mandate, the idea that some people are inferior to others on the basis of group membership is authoritatively rejected as the basis for public policy. This does not mean that ideas to the contrary cannot be debated or expressed. It should mean, however, that social inferiority cannot be imposed through any means, including expressive ones.

Because society is made of language, distinguishing talk about inferiority from verbal imposition of inferiority may be complicated at the edges, but it is clear enough at the center with sexual and racial harassment, pornography, and hate propaganda. At the very least, when equality is taken seriously in expressive settings, such practices are not constitutionally insulated from regulation on the ground that the ideas they express cannot be regarded as false. Attempts to address them would not be prohibited—as they were in rejecting the Indianapolis pornography ordinance, for example— on the ground that, in taking a position in favor of equality, such attempts assume that the idea of human equality is true. The legal equality guarantee has already decided that. There is no requirement that the state remain neutral as between equality and inequality—quite the contrary. Equality is a "compelling state interest" that can already outweigh First Amendment rights in certain settings.[28] In other words, expressive means of practicing inequality can be prohibited.

This is not the place to spell out in detail all the policy implications of such a view. Suffice it to say that those who wish to keep materials that promote inequality from being imposed on students—such as academic books purporting to document women's biological inferiority to men, or arguing that slavery of Africans should return, or that Fourteenth Amendment equality should be repealed, or that reports of rape are routinely fabricated—especially without critical commentary, should not be legally precluded from trying on the grounds that the ideas contained in them cannot be assumed false. No teacher should be forced to teach falsehoods as if they must be considered provisionally true, just because bigots who have managed to get published have made their lies part of a debate. Teachers who wish to teach such materials should be prepared to explain what they are doing to avoid creating a hostile learning environment and to provide all students the equal benefit of an education. Wherever equality is mandated, racial and sexual epithets, vilification, and abuse should be able to be prohibited, unprotected by the First Amendment. The current legal distinction between screaming "go kill that nigger" and advocating the view that African-Americans should be eliminated from parts of the United States needs to be seriously reconsidered, if real equality is ever to be achieved. So, too, the current line separating pornography from hate speech and what is done to make pornography from the materials themselves.

Pornography, under current conditions, *is* largely its own context. Many believe that in settings that encourage critical distance, its showing does not damage women so much as it sensitizes viewers to the damage it does to women. My experience, as well as all the information available, makes me think that it is naive to believe that anything other words can do is as powerful as what pornography itself does. At the very least, pornography should never be imposed on a viewer who does not choose—then and there, without pressure of any kind—to be exposed to it. Tom Emerson said a long time ago that imposing what he called "erotic material" on individuals against their will is a form of action that "has all the characteristics of a physical assault."[29] Equality on campuses, in workplaces, everywhere, would be promoted if such assaults were actionable. Why any woman should have to attend school in a setting stacked against her equality by the showing of pornography—especially when authoritatively permitted by those who are legally obligated to take her equality seriously—is a question that those who support its showing should have to answer. The answer is not that she should have to wait for the resulting abuse or leave.

Where is all this leading? To a new model for freedom of expression in which the free speech position no longer supports social dominance, as it does now; in which free speech does not most readily protect the activities of Nazis, Klansmen, and pornographers, while doing nothing for their victims, as it does now; in which defending free speech is not speaking on behalf of a large pile of money in the hands of a small group of people, as it is now. In this new model, principle will be defined in terms of specific experiences, the particularity of history, substantively rather than abstractly. It will notice who is being hurt and never forget who they are. The state will have as great a role in providing relief from injury to equality through speech and in giving equal access to speech as it now has in disciplining its power to intervene in that speech that manages to get expressed.

In a society in which equality is a fact, not merely a word, words of racial or sexual assault and humiliation will be nonsense syllables. Sex between people and things, human beings and pieces of paper, real men and unreal women, will be a turn-off. Artifacts of these abuses will reside in a glass case next to the dinosaur skeletons in the Smithsonian. When this day comes, silence will be neither an act of power, as it is now for those who hide behind it, nor an experience of imposed powerlessness, as it is now for those who are submerged in it, but a context of repose into which thought can expand, an invitation that gives speech its shape, an opening to a new conversation.

Case Study: The Santa Rosa Junior College SOLO Case

In January 1992, Santa Rosa Junior College (SRJC) journalism professor Roger Karraker, faculty adviser to the editorial board of the SRJC student newspaper, *The Oak Leaf,* established a computer conferencing system as a campuswide educational resource. The system, Super Oak Leaf Online (SOLO), allowed participants to post messages to a host of online bulletin boards, called "conferences," on a wide variety of subjects and serving a wide range of interest groups. Most of the conferences were open to any member of the campus community. A few conferences, for example the conference serving the *Oak Leaf* editorial board, were restricted, or "private."

The next semester, students expressed interest in establishing "gender exclusive" SOLO conferencing for the discussion of "gender-sensitive issues." In March 1993, responding to these requests, Mr. Karraker established two new "private SOLO conferences," "Women Only" and "Men Only." A security system of pass codes and a confidentiality rule were established; and a student moderator was appointed for each of the new gender-exclusive conferences.

Meanwhile, also in March 1993, the *Oak Leaf* ran an advertisement for a local surf shop featuring a rear-view photograph of the torso of a young woman wearing a thong bikini bottom. Several students objected to the publication of the ad as promoting sexism. These women attempted first to convince the editorial board of the *Oak Leaf* to pull the ad from future publications, and when this attempt was frustrated (running into editorial resistance based on First Amendment considerations), they exercised their First Amendment rights to demonstrate publicly on campus in an attempt to organize a boycott of the *Oak Leaf* and its advertisers.

In the ensuing controversy numerous messages about the issue were posted to many of the SOLO conferences, including a series of messages posted to the Men Only conference containing anatomically explicit and sexually derogatory remarks about some of the women protestors. A subscriber to the Men Only conference leaked the contents of this series of messages to the women. The women went immediately to Mr. Karraker to complain. Mr. Karraker responded by immediately dismissing the moderator of the Men Only conference, closing down the Men Only conference, and suspending SOLO access privileges for the authors of the offending messages. The student who leaked the contents of the offending messages to the women protestors also lost his SOLO privileges (for having violated the confidentiality rule).

This was not the end of the matter. In June 1993, exercising their First Amendment right to petition their government for a redress of grievances, the two women students who had been the subjects of the offending messages and the student who had leaked the contents of those messages to them filed formal complaints with the United States Department of Education, Office of Civil Rights, claiming to have been victims of sexual harassment. Their specific grievances were as follows: they argued that the offending messages had been posted in a forum created and administered under the auspices and supervision of the college and had created a "hostile learning environment" for the two women students, and so constituted a violation of their rights to equal educational opportunity. The student who had leaked the contents of the offending messages argued that, in having had *his* access privileges to SOLO suspended, he had suffered retaliation for "whistle-blowing." To redress these grievances the three students called for the college to (1) take further disciplinary action against the authors of the offending messages and (2) establish policy to regulate standards of conduct for participants in college-sponsored electronic forums (in effect, regulating the content of messages posted to SOLO conferences) and provide for disciplinary action against possible future violations of these standards; they further sought (3) monetary damages from the college as well as (4) the resignation or dismissal of Mr. Karraker from the college faculty.

Imagine that you are an ombudsperson to the college. Your role is to moderate disputes and mediate conflicts that arise in the campus community, and to make recommendations toward resolutions and toward establishing policies designed to avoid unhealthy conflict. How would you advise the campus administration, the school paper's editorial board, the faculty member, and the students involved in this case?

2.3 SEXUAL HARASSMENT IN CYBERSPACE In the following selection, Leslie Regan Shade explores the Santa Rosa Junior College SOLO Case in light of the First Amendment and the 1996 Communications Decency Act, which was intended to restrict the access of minors to indecent and obscene material over the Internet. Her examination illustrates the many ethical considerations raised by concerns about confidentiality, free speech, discrimination, and empowerment in communications technology.

QUESTIONS FOR STUDY AND DISCUSSION

1. What was Professor Karraker's major reason for insisting upon confidentiality within the bulletin board system (BBS)?
2. What is the mission of the Office for Civil Rights (OCR)? Does this mission conflict with the primary mission of the BBS?
3. The OCR allows for the segregation of students by sex under certain conditions. What are some of these conditions? Why did the OCR consider the BBS segregation inappropriate? Do you agree?

4. Why have electronic media not enjoyed the same degree of free speech as print media?
5. Why is it so important to decide which metaphor—broadcast or print media—to apply to the BBS?
6. How might the Communications Decency Act lead to a "dumbing down" of the Internet?

THE SANTA ROSA CASE[30]

LESLIE REGAN SHADE

Overview of the SRJC Case

Roger Karraker, a journalism instructor at Santa Rosa Junior College (SRJC), started SOLO (Super Oak Leaf Online), a bulletin board system (BBS) using FirstClass, SoftArc's networking software client-server package for BBS's for the Journalism students who were working on SRJC's school newspaper, *The Oak Leaf.* At one time the BBS was so popular that there were more than 200 conferences on a variety of topics.

In early 1993, some students requested that Karraker set up a women-only conference. Karraker was not initially enthused by the idea, but eventually he set up both a women-only and a male-only conference. The following guidelines and conditions for participation in the single-sex conferences were disseminated by Karraker:

1. Private conferences, by definition, are NOT public. You gain admittance by sending e-mail to the conference moderator. Only persons of the appropriate gender may gain admittance.
2. To encourage frank, private discussion, persons who gain entrance to a conference agree that what is said there is private. It is a violation of the rules of these private conferences to show messages or discuss their contents (other than a general summary) with a non-member of that conference. If you can't abide by that rule, don't ask for admission to the conference. If you gain admittance, then later violate that rule, you will be summarily thrown out of the conference. If your indiscretion is grievous enough, you may be tossed off SOLO as well. Violating others' confidences is a major sin; don't do it.

Several months after the conferences were set up, students Lois Arata and Jennifer Branham complained that harassing and sexually demeaning remarks were made about them in the male-only conference. They learned of these comments from one of the male participants in the conference, Dylan Humphrey. Evidently, the comments concerning Arata were made over her public campaign protesting *The Oak Leaf's* decision to run a surfboard store ad she thought demeaning to women. The comments made about

Branham, an editor at *The Oak Leaf,* were made by a former boyfriend. All of the comments made in the male-only conference were of a rude, juvenile, locker-room mentality.

When he learned about the breach of confidentiality, Karraker suspended both conferences and took away Humphrey's SOLO privileges for failing to respect the confidentiality guidelines. Arata, Branham, and Humphrey then took their complaints to college administrators and the U.S. Department of Education's Office of Civil Rights (OCR) in San Francisco, claiming that they were subjected to sexual harassment, a "hostile learning environment," and retaliation. SRJC administrators put Karraker on leave from his duties as adviser to the newspaper.

The mission of the Office for Civil Rights . . . is to ensure equal access to education through the enforcement of several civil rights statutes. OCR had jurisdiction over the case through Title IX, which prohibits discrimination against students on the basis of sex in education programs or activities that receive federal financial assistance. Title IX of the Education Amendments of 1972 (20 U.S.C. sec. 1681 et. seq.) states that "No person in the United States shall, on the basis of sex, be excluded from participation in, be denied the benefits of, or be subjected to discrimination under any program or activity receiving federal financial assistance."

Under certain circumstances, segregation of students by sex is allowed. For instance, in music classes, schools may have requirements based on vocal range or quality, which may result in all-male or all-female choruses; portions of elementary and secondary classes that deal exclusively with human sexuality may

be conducted in separate sessions for boys and girls; and, students may be separated by sex in certain physical education classes or activities where the major purpose or activity involves bodily contact (i.e., wrestling, boxing, rugby, ice hockey, football, and basketball). In general, a school system that operates separate educational programs or activities for members of each sex must ensure that the separate course, services, and facilities are comparable for the members of the opposite sex.

OCR initially found the SOLO conferences amounted to sex discrimination in violation of Title IX. OCR ruled that the BBS was an educational program or activity under the meaning of Title IX; and that by restricting access to the system based on sex, a violation of Title IX had occurred.

OCR found that Arata and Branham had been subjected to a hostile learning environment because of retaliation against their complaints. They also found that Arata and Branham had been victims of sex discrimination because they had been barred from access to the male-only forum. It did not matter that there was both a male and a female separate-sex conference; what was discriminatory in OCR's viewpoint was that females did not have access to the male conference (and conceivably, the reversal would be true too). The comments made in the male-only conference were also considered to constitute sexual harassment. OCR also found that Humphrey was not subject to retaliation for disclosing the contents of the postings in the male-only conference.

In a controversial decision, OCR required that SRJC regulate all online communications to prohibit comments that could create a hostile environment for women or ethnic minorities. In effect, this decision by OCR stipulated that online communications represent a "limited public forum" and therefore do not enjoy the same First Amendment protections as a full public forum. OCR's proposed Remedial Action Plan read:

> SRJC (Santa Rosa Junior College) shall promulgate guidelines of appropriate conduct for users of the Super Oak Leaf Online (SOLO) computer network and any other computer networks or bulletin board established or operated by SRJC. The Guidelines shall also notify users of their right to be free from harassment on the basis of race, color, national origin, or disability and of their right to be free from retaliation for protesting such harassment. In particular, the SRJC proposed computing procedures shall be amended to read as follows:
> A. Paragraph 4 of the SRJC "Administrative Computing Procedures" shall be amended to read as follows:
>> The computing facilities at Santa Rosa Junior College are provided for the use of Santa Rosa Junior College students, faculty, and staff in support of the programs of the College. All students, faculty, and staff are responsible for seeing that these computing facilities are used in an effective, efficient, ethical, non-discriminatory, and lawful manner.
> B. A new paragraph 14.2 shall be added to the SRJC's Administrative Computing Procedures" to read as follows:
>> 14.2 Non-discrimination— All users have the right to be free from any conduct connected with the use of SRJC computing systems which discriminates against any person on the basis of race, color, national origin, sex, or disability. Discriminatory conduct includes, but is not limited to, written or graphic conduct that satisfies both the following conditions: (1) harasses, denigrates, or shows hostility or aversion toward an individual or group based on that person's gender, race, color, national origin, or disability, AND (2) has the purpose or effect of creating a hostile, intimidating, or offensive educational environment. "Harassing conduct" and "hostile educational environment" are defined below. . . .
>> "Harassing conduct" includes, but is not limited to, the following: epithets, slurs, negative stereotyping, or threatening, intimidating, or hostile acts that relate to race, color, national origin, gender, or disability. This includes acts that purport to be "jokes" or "pranks" but are hostile and demeaning. A "hostile educational environment" is established when harassing conduct is sufficiently severe, pervasive, or persistent so as to interfere with or limit the ability of an individual to participate in or benefit from the SRJC computing systems.

SRJC attorneys responded that some online services are forums for ideas and that OCR's proposed regulations would infringe on students' free speech as protected under the First Amendment.

The case continued to drag on, and, according to journalism professor Karraker, "On January 30, [1995], the U.S. Department of Education's Office for Civil Rights closed the case after making no findings, no determinations, and issuing no final report. Much like the U.S. Military in Vietnam, OCR declared victory and quietly decamped, making no public mention of its change of course."[31] (Karraker, 1995).

The three students (Arata, Branham, and Humphrey) were later awarded with a settlement of $15,000 each in return for releasing SRJC of any and all claims based on this incident.

The Santa Rosa case brings to the fore several prominent debates surrounding the use of the Internet:

What is the scope of permissible speech in online communications?

Is the First Amendment designed to protect offensive speech online?

What is the appropriate metaphor to use towards the regulation of BBS's: are they akin to libraries, bookstores, or newsstands, and thereby not to be held accountable for their content?

The SRJC case also sends a message to many college and university administrators and faculty in the U.S. who receive federal financial assistance that gender-segregated BBS's are a potential violation of civil rights laws.

Free Speech on the Internet
The CDA

What is the scope of permissible speech in online communications, and how should the First Amendment be interpreted for online communications? The First Amendment to the U.S. Constitu-

tion prohibits the government from "abridging the freedom of speech, or of the press," and guarantees freedom of association as well. Print media and public media have enjoyed a long and rich history of freedom from governmental interference, but the same degree of freedom has not been granted to electronic broadcasting, although the recent ruling in *ACLU* v. *Reno* (discussed below) provides some solid basis for granting First Amendment status to online communications.

The Federal Communications Commission (FCC) and Congress have long subjected radio and television communications to regulation and censorship. The Supreme Court believed that regulation was necessary to prevent interference among frequencies and to make sure that the scarce resources were allocated fairly, but even with the multiplicity of cable TV networks the Court and Congress have been reluctant to abandon such an outmoded approach. The Internet provides an opportunity for lawmakers and courts to remove the distinction between the print and electronic media and to extend First Amendment guarantees to all communications regardless of the medium. The recent uproars over the Communications Decency Act highlights the vociferous debates over Internet content and its First Amendment implications. In the U.S., Democrat Senator Exon's amendment to the telecommunications reform package, *The Communications Decency Act—CDA* . . . was proposed legislation as part of the joint House/Senate Conference Committee on Telecommunications Reform. The Telecommunications Act of 1996 (47 USC sec 254) was approved by Congress in February 1996.

The CDA provisions were intended to restrict the access of minors to indecent and obscene material on the Internet. As it read, the CDA legislation would impose the standard of "indecency" as used in broadcast media: "taken as a whole, appeals to the prurient interest in nudity, sex, or excretion; depicts, represents or describes in patently offensive ways, ultimate sexual acts, normal or perverted, actual or simulated sado-masochistic acts or abuse; or lewd exhibition of the genitals, pubic area, buttocks, or post-pubertal female breasts . . ." Examples of "indecency" could include passages from John Updike or Erica Jong novels, certain rock lyrics, and Dr. Ruth Westheimer's sexual-advice column. The proposed CDA legislation also made all individual Internet system operators (sysops) responsible for the content they carry and provide to their users. This would include anyone who "makes, creates, or solicits and initiates the transmission of, any comment, request, suggestion, proposal, image, or other communications which is obscene, lewd, lascivious, filthy, or indecent, with intent to annoy, abuse, threaten, or harass another person;" and anyone who "uses an interactive computer service to send directly to any person under 18 years of age, or to send to any interactive computer service for display in a manner available to a person under 18 years of age, any comment, request, suggestion, proposal, image, or other communication that is harmful to minors, regardless of whether the maker of such communication placed the call or initiated the communication." The CDA also asked that criminal penalties of 2 years imprisonment and $100,000 in fines be levied

upon the knowing transmission of offensive material to minors.

Critics contended that the CDA would lead to a "dumbing down" of the Internet. Under the CDA, it would be criminal to "knowingly" publish such material on the Internet unless children were affirmatively denied access to it. "It's as if the manager of a Barnes & Noble bookstore could be sent to jail simply because children were able to wander the store's aisles and search for the racy passages in a Judith Krantz or Harold Robbins novel. The CDA would also allow states to impose additional restrictions on non-commercial activities such as freenets, BBS's, and non-profit content providers. For instance, community networks could be liable for any "indecent" content their users post: they could be fined for $100,000; and Boards of Directors could face two-year prison sentences. Given that community networks are so far the only viable means for ensuring universal access, this proposed legislation had the potential to greatly curtail access to the Internet for many.[32]

A constitutional challenge to the *Communications Decency Act* was initiated by several public interest groups, including EPIC (The Electronic Privacy Information Center), the ALA (American Library Association), and the ACLU (American Civil Liberties Union). *ACLU* v. *Reno* was filed in federal court in Philadelphia in February 1996, seeking a declaration that the CDA statute was unconstitutional. In June 1996, the Philadelphia panel ruled that the *CDA* was an unconstitutional abridgement of rights protected by the First and Fifth Amendments. Since then, the Department of Justice has filed an appeal with the Supreme Court.

In *ACLU* v. *Reno* (United States District Court for the Eastern District of Pennsylvania, No.96-963) the Court wrote that

> Cutting through the acronyms and argot that littered the hearing testimony, the Internet may fairly be regarded as a never-ending worldwide conversation. The Government may not, through the CDA, interrupt that conversation. As the most participatory form of mass speech yet developed, the Internet deserves the highest protection from governmental intrusion.
>
> Just as the strength of the Internet is chaos, so the strength of our liberty depends upon the chaos and cacophony of the unfettered speech the First Amendment protects.[33]

. . . What is libelous in the electronic environment? Should computer bulletin boards be treated as common carriers, or are they analogous to newspapers, letters, magazines, and books? Are we talking about freedom of the press or freedom of expression? Who owns and is responsible for the content of the bulletin board? Is the responsibility of the individual poster, or the responsibility of the educational institution where the post originated?

What is the appropriate metaphor to use towards the regulation of BBS's and the Internet? Are they akin to libraries, bookstores, or newsstands, and thereby not to be held accountable for their content? Two different court decisions in the U.S. have attempted to grapple with the issue of liability on online content.

A court ruling treated the operator of an electronic information system (EIS) as a distributor rather than as a publisher, in order to assess liability at the state libel law level. *Cubby, Inc.* v. *CompuServe, Inc.* [1991] also set an important precedent by ruling that the system operator or EIS owner could not reasonably be held liable for the content of the message it carries, given the sheer volume and rapidity of the messages on computerized boards. . . .

In a later decision *(Stratton Oakmont* v. *Prodigy,* 1995), a New York state court judge ruled that Prodigy (a private online subscription service) could be held responsible for libelous statements placed on one of its discussion lists because of Prodigy's high-profile policy of editing and controlling the content of its service. Indeed, this feature of Prodigy (it has been described as being sanitized in the Disney mold) is what distinguishes Prodigy from other online services. Although Prodigy has retracted many of its earliest editorial policies and now maintains that it does not and cannot ensure that all publications and notices on its service are not obscene or libelous, the judge in *Stratton Oakmont* ruled that by taking editorial control of the items submitted for distribution, Prodigy was acting more like a publisher. This made Prodigy subject to liability for defamatory statements that it allows to be "broadcast," akin to a distributor of information. *Stratton Oakmont* was appealed by Prodigy, and settled with the issuance of an apology by Prodigy and a promise that they had "reformed their approach" to publication. This ruling distinguished it from the earlier *Cubby* ruling, yet also muddled the regulatory scene.

Sexual Harassment and Women-Only Forums on the Internet

Even though some educational programs are sex segregated (e.g., women's health and counseling clinics), the SRJC case sent a message to many college and university administrators and faculty in the U.S. who receive federal financial assistance that gender-segregated BBS's are a potential violation of civil rights laws. Given widespread measures to increase access to the Internet by women and the rush toward information infrastructure adoption and development in higher education the creation of women-only forums has been found to increase the level of comfort for women, who are often intimidated by the technology and the pervasiveness of what some see as a masculine computer culture, and, hence, the diffusion of Internet working technology by more women.[34]

The issue of what constitutes sexual harassment on the Internet is controversial. Many women complain that various Usenet newsgroups and networking environments are hostile towards women. Harassment has been alleged to take many forms: in both public forums and in private e-mail. It can be subtle, such as personal questions directed to a woman, or blatant, such as women receiving sexual propositions via e-mail. . . .

Several researchers have examined whether or not there are gender differences between the way men and women talk and participate online. . . .

> . . . male and female academic professionals do not participate equally in academic CMC [a linguistics electronic list]. Rather, a small male minority dominates the discourse both in terms of amount of talk, and rhetorically, through self-promotional and adversarial strategies. Moreover, when women do attempt to participate on a more equal basis, they risk being actively censored by the reactions of men who either ignore them or attempt to delegitimize their contributions. Because of social conditioning that makes women uncomfortable with direct conflict, women tend to be more intimidated by these practices and to avoid participating as a result . . . rather than being democratic, academic CMC is power-based and hierarchical. This state of affairs cannot however be attributed to the influence of computer communication technology; rather, it continues pre-existing patterns of hierarchy and male dominance in academia more generally, and in society as a whole.[35]

The Usenet newsgroup *soc.feminism* is open to all male and female participants interested in discussing feminist issues. But, according to Tittle Moore (1994) "*soc.feminism* attracts men who are disturbed by aspects of feminism and are willing to take the time to debate the issues (which is not exactly what many of the women reading *soc.feminism* want). The men who have no trouble with feminism, who are mainly hoping to learn more about feminism and exchange ideas with other feminists on what it means to them, I think are the least likely in some respects to have anything to do with *soc.feminism.*"

The idea of women-only lists and conferences has been suggested as a way to counteract harassment and monopolization of postings by men. Of course, given the relative insecurity of electronic identity, and the fact that electronic personas can be easily spoofed, such segregation is difficult to control. Several women-only conferences exist, including WOW (Women on the WELL); two private women-only conferences on Echo, including WIT (Women in Telecommunications), and another for WAC (the Women's Action Coalition); and Systers, a private, unmoderated, mailing list for female computer professionals in the commercial, academic, and government world, as well as female graduate and undergraduate computer science and computer engineering students.

Anita Borg, the founder and moderator of Systers, has often been asked to justify the exclusion of men from her list, particularly given that the list is not limited solely to discussion of women's issues, but deals in professional and technical concerns. As of 1993, Systers consisted of more than 1,500 members in seventeen countries. "The likelihood that an underpowered minority is keeping otherwise accessible information from the large empowered majority . . . seems small indeed," Borg contends. "Exclusively female forums, such as Systers are a particularly effective way to connect women in our field with each other. They also ultimately contribute to improved communication between women and men."[36] And, since women in computer sciences are geographically dispersed, and a "frequently individually isolated minority," they rarely have the chance to interact professionally with each other. Female-only forums thus can encourage mutual support and mentoring opportunities. . . .

Results of a survey conducted on Systers . . . confirmed this positive view of female-only forums. A broad range of questions was disseminated on Systers in 1993, asking participants about their experiences of electronic communication. The results showed that

> Overall, the Internet was perceived to be a male culture. This was reflected in the perception that there were more men online, as well as the dominance of a male interpersonal communication style online.
>
> Thirty-nine percent of respondents reported being harassed online, with harassment defined as a hostile and unwelcome environment, interpersonal confrontational styles including overt flaming, personal attack and hate mail. Nineteen percent of respondents reported having been sexually harassed on the Internet—defined as not just offers of sex, but as the creation of a hostile environment.
>
> Eighty-four percent of respondents said they felt women-only forums were necessary, with 68 percent stating that they felt more comfortable communicating in an all-women forum. Given the very personal information often exchanged on Systers, ethical guidelines posit that communication on Systers must not be taken offline.

Ethics and Community Norms

Participants in the WELL's WOW (Women on the WELL) conference must agree to a confidentiality statement prior to admittance to the private, women-only conference. The confidentiality statement came about because of breaches in the then-unstated ethical guidelines for WOW, namely, not to reveal the contents of WOW, participants' names, and other information to any source. The confidentiality statement says, in part, that

> This conference provides a private place for women to discuss ideas and experiences openly and candidly, in a way that some of us find awkward or difficult to do in the public conferences on the WELL. In order to encourage the flow of conversation in the direction of honesty and openness, participants' desire for confidentiality "must" be respected. WOW members agree not to quote, paraphrase, publish, broadcast, discuss, or otherwise reveal what is said in WOW to anyone who is not a member of WOW, unless the information is of an impersonal, general nature; the information is available elsewhere; or the poster of the information gives explicit permission to be quoted or paraphrased. Violation of this policy constitutes grounds for expulsion from the conference.

It should be noted that WELL also has a private men-only conference but whether there is a confidentiality statement for that venue is not known. Also, insofar as the ethics of revealing the contents of WOW, I could be in violation of this by quoting some of the confidentiality statement here.

Karraker's gender-specific SOLO conferences also had a confidentiality clause in it, and when that was widely violated by several students in question he immediately shut down the private conference. Thus, members of the online community were held accountable for their conduct offline, by revealing the online content.

Was OCR correct to require that SRJC regulate all online communications to prohibit comments that could create a hostile environment for women, or ethnic minorities? This stipulation that online communications represented a "limited public forum" and therefore are not accorded the same First Amendment protections as a full public forum, has been shown to be unconstitutional as per the *ACLU* v. *Reno* decision with respect to the CDA. There is also the sheer impossibility of monitoring online communication given the rapidity of messages, as well as assessing who should be liable for the content of the messages: the individual who writes and sends the messages? the system operators? the "owner" or moderator of the discussion group? the educational facility-computing center, administrators, faculty, individual programs of study?

Was SRJC correct in responding that some online services are forums for ideas and that OCR's proposed regulations would infringe on students' free speech as protected under the First Amendment? Certainly the CDA decision affirms SRJC's point, but under the current academic environment concerning hate speech and speech codes, SRJC's rationale could come under closer scrutiny.

. . . Given that some women perceive the Internet to be a threatening and hostile environment, women-only forums can provide a civilized opportunity for conversation, and, in many instances, a valuable professional and mentoring space. Additionally, sensitive topics such as issues surrounding sexuality, sexual harassment and abuse, workplace issues, professional ethics, etc., can be discussed in a safe and supportive environment. Women-only forums can also provide a conducive environment for women to experiment with new technol-ogy, and can eventually lead to a greater degree of gender equity in the use, design, and development of the Internet.

CASE STUDY: GENDER EQUITY

Shade and Borg suggest a case for women-only and minority-only bulletin boards that does not support men-only bulletin boards. What do you think? Can men show a comparable need for men-only forums?

CASE STUDY: INDUSTRY SELF-REGULATION

Prodigy was held responsible for comments posted on its bulletin board because it had committed itself to monitoring and editing postings. Prodigy had to become less like a publisher or broadcast medium and more like a library or a bookstore by modifying its editorial stance in order to avoid liability for libelous postings. Even libraries, however, do not routinely make hardcore printed pornography available on the shelves for patrons to stumble upon. In fact although most university libraries, like ours, carry *Playboy* and *Playgirl;* few probably carry *Penthouse, Screw,* or *Hustler.* University bookstores often carry similar selections. Given, then, that print media outlets make choices about what they offer patrons, under what conditions might a moral Internet provider block access to Internet sites? Notice that we need not think of children in this context. University students are not children. How about this example: The German government blocked access to a site devoted to the memory of Hitler to combat the renewal of anti-Semitism. Is that a good idea? Is it morally preferable to have such actions taken by corporations and not the government? America Online and CNN deleted postings and suspended users from chat rooms for anti-Semitic postings about Senator Joseph Lieberman prompted by his selection as a candidate for the vice presidency of the United States. Was that proper?

CASE STUDY: MEDIATION REVIEW

Champions of the Internet believe it facilitates learning and fosters the development of political, and other types, of community. Now review the recommendations you made as "ombudsperson to the college" prior to reading Shade's analysis of the case. Evaluate the actions of Professor Karraker; students Arata, Branham, and Humphrey; and the unnamed students who made sexist remarks on the male-only BBS in light of these moral goals (learning and community) of the Internet. Would you alter any of your recommendations based on further readings or reconsiderations?

Case Study: The Communications Decency Act

The Communications Decency Act is dead, but attempts to regulate the Internet in the interests of morality will continue. Check the Web sites of the Center for Democracy and Technology, the Electronic Frontier Foundation, and the Electronic Privacy Information Center for current cases. Their addresses appear at the end of this chapter under suggested readings.

Case Study: Suicide.net

A Dutch Internet site with an anonymous owner posted instructions on how to commit suicide. The site led some Dutch politicians to advocate government action against the site and increased government regulation of the Internet because the information was available to minors. The site included "Step-by-step instructions [to] guide the reader through wrist-slashing, sleeping pills, jumping off buildings, and the reasonably painless . . . death of carbon monoxide poisoning. The Pink Floyd song, "Goodbye Cruel World," can be heard on the home page, along with verses from the William Butler Yeats poem, "An Irish Airman Foresees His Death."[37]

This sounds like an Internet site that takes suicide less than seriously, but people interested in ending their life painlessly might find the site helpful. Is the government interest in protecting children sufficient to justify blocking or regulating suicide information? If you think so, how should the regulation be carried out and liability fixed? Should the Associated Press have carried the address of the suicide site in reporting the story?[38]

Suggested Readings:

Goffman, Erving. *Gender Advertisements.* Cambridge: Harvard University Press, 1979.
Keen, Sam. *Faces of the Enemy: Reflections of the Hostile Imagination on the Psychology of Enmity.* San Francisco: Harper and Row, 1986.
Lichtenberg, Judith. (Ed.). *Democracy and the Mass Media.* New York: Cambridge University Press, 1990.
The Center for Democracy and Technology. http://www.cdt.org
The Electronic Frontier Foundation. http://www.eff.org
The Electronic Privacy Information Center. http://epic.org

Notes

Media Values I: Freedom and Information

Free Speech for Me, But not for Thee

1. Pages 148–71, 251–7 from *Free Speech for Me, But Not for Thee,* by Nat Hentoff, Copyright © 1991 by Common Sense, Inc., Reprinted by permission of HarperCollins, Inc.

EQUALITY AND SPEECH

2. The Christian Gauss Memorial Lectures in Criticism, Princeton University, April 1992; published by Harvard University Press, 1993.

3. Reprinted by permission from *Only Words* by Catharine MacKinnon, Cambridge, MA: Harvard University Press, Copyright © 1993 by Catharine MacKinnon.

4. A further possible result is that escalations of hate propaganda and pornography, as for example in Eastern Europe, will be met with indifference or embraced as freedom under U.S.-style speech theory. As pornography and its defense as "speech" take over more of the world, pervading law and consciousness, desensitizing populations to inhumanity, and sexualizing inequality, there are grounds for concern that legal attempts to reverse rising racial, ethnic, and religious discrimination, harassment, and aggression will be disabled.

5. The origin of this notion appears to be "The best test of truth is the power of the thought to get itself accepted in the competition of the market." Abrams, 250 U.S. 616 at 630 (Holmes, J., dissenting).

6. John Milton, *Areopagitica 58* (Richard Jebb, Ed., 1918): "Let [Truth] and falsehood grapple; who ever knew Truth put to the worse, in a free and open encounter?"

7. The authoritative articulation of this notion is in a defamation case, *Gertz* v. *Robert Welch, Inc.,* 418 U.S. 323, 339–340 (1974): "Under the First Amendment there is no such thing as a false idea. However pernicious an opinion may seem, we depend for its correction not on the conscience of judges and juries but on the competition of other ideas."

8. *Cohen* v. *California,* 403 U.S. 15 (1971). "Offensive" is a word used to describe obscenity. *Paris Adult Theatre I* v. *Slaton,* 413 U.S. 49, 71 (1973) (Douglas, J., dissenting) (" 'Obscenity' at most is the expression of offensive ideas"). Indeed, "patently offensive" is an element of the obscenity test. *Miller* v. *California,* 413 U.S. 15, 24 (1973).

9. *New York Times Co.* v. *Sullivan,* 376 U.S. 254 (1964).

10. *Brown* v. *Board of Education,* 349 U.S. 294 (1955). *Brown's* invalidation of "separate but equal" education was unprincipled, according to Wechsler, because it was a new fact-driven doctrinal leap addressing a problem that was not really about inequality, but about a deprivation of freedom of association. Herbert Wechsler, "Toward Neutral Principles of Constitutional Law," 73 *Harvard Law Review* 1, 31–34 (1959). From a doctrinal perspective, the *Sullivan* argument that libel could raise First Amendment speech issues was *totally* new. Is libel more obviously speech than segregation is inequality? In the companion case to *Sullivan, Abernathy* v. *Sullivan,* 376 U.S. at 254, brought against the civil rights leaders themselves, those leaders did complain of the racism and denial of equal protection of aspects of their trial, but not of inequality problems in the speech arguments of the libel claim. *Abernathy* was not chosen by the Supreme Court as the flagship case for its First Amendment decision. For Wechsler's argument in *Sullivan,* see Brief for the Petitioner, *New York Times Co.* v. *Sullivan,* 376 U.S. 254 (1964) (No. 39).

11. Sullivan, 376 U.S. at 268–269 [discussing *Beauharnais* v. *Illinois,* 343 U.S. 250 (1952)].

12. Usually, they sound in tort. See the creative, audacious, and foundational article by Richard Delgado, "Words that Wound: A Tort Action for Racial Insults, Epithets, and Name-Calling," 17 *Harvard Civil Rights-Civil Liberties Law Review* 133 (1982). Sometimes, in international law or in other countries, hate propaganda laws are rendered as "antidiscrimination" provisions, but this is little discussed. The major exception, of course, is Canada. See below, and Catharine A. MacKinnon, "Pornography as Defamation and Discrimination," 71 *Boston University Law Review* 793, 806 n.33 (1991).

13. Harry Kalven Jr., *The Negro and the First Amendment* (1965), 35.

14. However, in defense of its statute, Illinois did argue that the speech of Beauharnais was unprotected because it led to discrimination in violation of Illinois's State Civil Rights Act. Respondent's Brief, *Beauharnais* v. *Illinois*, 343 U.S. 250 (1952) (No. 118) at 4. Such discrimination was argued to be a "substantive evil" that petitioner's publications may "directly tend to incite." ibid. at 5–6. Illinois also argued that prevention of riots and lynchings is a duty of government, and the history of Illinois was "stained with blood spilled from Negroes simply because they were Negroes." ibid. at 6. "Every riot has its incitement in words." ibid. Further worth noting, the ACLU argued for Beauharnais that since racial segregation did not violate the federal Civil Rights Act, and "we attorneys for the ACLU have never been so bold to make that invalid suggestion ourselves in our efforts to combat segregation," advocacy of segregation cannot violate the law either. Petitioner's Reply Brief, Beauharnais, 343 U.S. 250 (1952) (No. 118) at 5–6.

15. The most notable victory of this kind is *Pittsburgh Press Co.* v. *Comm'n on Human Relations*, 413 U.S. 376 (1973). Pornography regulation lost in *American Booksellers Ass'n, Inc.* v. *Hudnut*, 771 F.2d 323 (7th Cir. 1985), aff'd 475 U.S. 1001 (1986).

16. On campaign financing as speech, see *Buckley* v. *Valeo*, 424 U.S. 1 (1976).

17. *Young* v. *New York City Transit Authority*, 903 F.2d 146 (2d Cir. 1990), cert. Denied, 111 S. Ct. 516 (Restriction on begging and panhandling in some public transit does not violate First Amendment).

18. *Brandenburg* v. *Ohio*, 395 U.S. 444 (1969).

19. *NAACP* v. *Claiborne Hardware Co.*, 458 U.S. 886 (1982).

20. 42 U.S.C § 2000 (d) et seq. (1988) (Title VI, requiring racial equality in education); 20 U.S.C. § 1681 (1988)(Title IX, requiring sex equality in education).

21. *Kingsley Int'l Pictures Corp.* v. *Regents of the University of New York*, 360 U.S. 684 (1959). Cf. the litigation on *Deep Throat* as a clear example of the latter. See citations in Catharine A. MacKinnon, *Feminism Unmodified: Discourses on Life and Law* 34 n. 30 (1987).

22. ". . . above all else, the First Amendment means that the government has no power to restrict expression because of its message [or] ideas . . ." Hudnut, 771 F.2d at 328–329. Similar construction of nude dancing as public discourse occurs in the majority opinion in *Miller* v. *Civil City of South Bend*, 904 F.2d 1081, 1088 (7th Cir. 1990), invalidating a provision restricting nude dancing. The Supreme Court upheld the provision, reversing the Seventh Circuit in *Barnes* v. *Glen Theatre, Inc.*, 111 S. Ct. 2456 (1991).

23. *State* v. *Mitchell*, 485 N.W.2d at 820 (Babitch, J., dissenting). The Supreme Court of Oregon, siding with this dissent, upheld an Oregon hate crime statute against First Amendment attack, *Oregon* v. *Plowman*, 838 P.2d 558 (Or. 1992). The U.S. Supreme Court upheld the Wisconsin statute, *Wisconsin* v. *Mitchell*, 1993 U.S. LEXIS 4024 (June 11, 1993).

24. *I. Schiro* v. *Clark*, 963 F.2d 962 (7th Cir. 1992) at 973. The Seventh Circuit affirmed the penalty of death for Schiro on the legally unsatisfying conclusion that although pornographers could be held responsible for some rapes (!), *Hudnut* does not say "the rapist is not also culpable for his own conduct."

25. *Regina* v. *Keegstra*, [1991] 2 W.W.R. 1 (1990)(Can.).

26. *Butler* v. *Regina*, [1992] 2 W.W.R. 577 (Can.).

27. First Amendment law has long taken the position that the "sensibilities of readers" must be ignored in deciding whether a state has an interest in suppression of expression. *Simon and Schuster, Inc.* v. *Members of the New York Crime Victims Bd.*, 112 S. Ct. 501, 509 (1991). As the Court sees it, the offensiveness of an opinion goes to establishing its protection: "The fact that society may find speech offensive is not a sufficient reason for suppressing it. Indeed, if it is the speaker's opinion that gives offense, *that consequence* is a reason for according it constitutional protection." *FCC* v. *Pacifica Foundation*, 438 U.S.

726, 745 (1978) (emphasis added), quoted with approval in *Hustler Magazine, Inc.* v. *Falwell,* 485 U.S. 46, 55 (1988): "If there is a bedrock principle underlying the First Amendment, it is that the Government may not prohibit the expression of an idea simply because society finds the idea itself offensive or disagreeable." These authorities were found to support the view in *Simon and Schuster* that the Crime Board "does not assert any interest in limiting whatever anguish Henry Hill's victims may suffer from reliving their victimization," 112 S. Ct. at 509. *Hudnut* states that the role of pornography in perpetuating subordination "simply demonstrates the power of pornography as speech." 771 F.2d at 329. As distinguished from *Hudnut,* in *Simon and Schuster* it was not asserted that the crimes were committed to produce the accounts of the crimes, as women coerced into pornography assert; nor does *Simon and Schuster* bar civil recovery for damages either for mental anguish or to reputational or privacy interests. There was also no claim in that case that the portrayals of the crime victims were false, defamatory, placed them in a false light, or discriminated against them.

28. *Roberts* v. *U.S. Jaycees,* 468 U.S. 609, 623 (1984) holds that states have a "compelling interest in eradicating discrimination" on the basis of sex, which can outweigh the First Amendment right of association, as it did here. In ruling against the First Amendment challenge, and in favor of statutory sex equality, *Roberts* states that "acts of invidious discrimination in the distribution of goods, services, and other advantages cause unique evils that government has a compelling interest to prevent—wholly apart from the point of view such conduct may transmit. . . . Accordingly. . . such practices are entitled to no constitutional protection." ibid. at 628.

29. Thomas I. Emerson, *The System of Freedom of Expression* 496 (1970): "A communication of this [erotic] nature, imposed upon a person contrary to his wishes, has all the characteristics of a physical assault" and "can therefore realistically be classified as action." A comparison with his preliminary formulation in *Toward a General Theory of the First Amendment* 91 (1963) suggests that his view on this subject became stronger by his 1970 revisiting of the issue.

THE SANTA ROSA CASE

30. Reprinted From the *Journal of Information Ethics* vol. 6:2 © by permission of McFarland & Company, Inc., Box 611, Jefferson NC 28640.

31. Roger Karraker, "An Indictment of the OCR," *Proceedings of the Fifth Conference on Computers, Freedom, and Privacy,* Burlingame, CA, 28–31, March 1995.

32. The text of the CDA is available at URL: http://www.cdt.org/policy/freespeech/ 12-21.cda.html. See also the Electronic Frontier Foundation's Campaign to stop the Net Censorship Legislation at URL: http://www.eff.org/publ Alerts/s652_hr1555.alert.

33. URL: http://www.epic.org/cda/highlights.html

34. Leslie Regan Shade, "Wired in the Ivory Tower: Access and Copyright Issues Surrounding the Internet and Higher Education in North America," *Education for Information,* September 1995, 1–18.

35. Susan Herring, "Gender and Communication in Computer-Mediated Communication," *Electronic Journal of Communication* 3 (1993).

36. Anita Borg, "Why Systers?" *Computing Research News* (September, 1993).

37. Anthony Deutsch, "Suicide Web Site Sparks Controversy," Associated Press wire story, 31 January 2000.

38. http://huizen.dds.nl/~thisbe/verder. [The page has been removed.]

3

MEDIA VALUES II: ASSESSING MEDIA PERFORMANCE

*With regard to the press: one could only conclude that the
media had formed too cozy a relationship with those in
power, that they were helping to limit the policy debate
rather than reporting fairly on it. Whether such coziness is
purposeful, thoughtful, or inadvertent, it subverts the
fundamental principle that democracy only works when
there is an enlightened and informed electorate. Such a
state is achieved only when people have a shared basis of
reliable information, one in which all points of view
and approaches and options find expression and are
fairly reported.*

CONGRESSMAN RONALD V. DELLUMS

INTRODUCTION

Probably an analysis of the institutional functions of the press provides the best way
to begin to formulate standards for assessing press performance in a democratic society. In a democratic society such an analysis would presuppose, as discussed in
Chapter 2, the principles of freedom of speech and of the press. In a democracy, the
press ideally, first, provides the citizenry with information essential to rational deliberation of leadership and policy issues facing the nation. Second, the press provides
the citizenry with a forum in which leadership and policy issues facing the nation are
freely and openly debated. Third, the press monitors the workings of government and
the conduct of public servants in office. Finally, through the press the people can
organize among themselves for political purposes. Much of the professional ethics
of journalism, the responsibilities and liabilities of working journalists and of the

journalistic institutions for and within which they work, can be derived from these four functions.

For example, consider the concept of "newsworthiness." All news organizations, even the really big ones, have finite resources. They can send only so many reporters on assignments. There are only so many camera crews. A news organization, whether in print or broadcasting, must allocate a finite quantity of space or time to the news of the day. There is always much more going on in the world, in the nation, in a city, than the news section of the daily paper or a half-hour or one-hour newscast can cover. The press evaluates and reevaluates constantly what is worth covering, how much coverage a given story deserves, and how prominent the coverage should be. Thus what eventually gets reported as news reflects news reporters' and editors' judgments of the "newsworthiness" of the day's stories and potential stories. What factors influence these judgments? Which factors *ought* to influence these judgments? One reasonably good beginning would be to derive criteria of "newsworthiness" based on the category "information essential to rational deliberation of the leadership and policy issues facing the nation."

As important as what gets covered and what doesn't is the interpretation or "spin" put on coverage. News does not reach us as raw undigested information. It is analyzed and interpreted for us by reporters, editors, news analysts, commentators, editorial cartoonists, pundits, and so on. These interpretations play a deep and significant role in shaping our eventual understandings of the news and of the events covered in the news. People who are frequently in the news understand the importance of these interpretations, and so they often hire expert specialists, media consultants, or "spin doctors," to help with "spin control." Thus, we can also assess press performance in terms of criteria focused on interpretation—criteria such as independence, objectivity, balance, and bias.

If the press is to effectively monitor the workings of government and the conduct of public servants in office, the press must of course be independent of government or official control or influence. By the same token, government or official interest in leadership and policy issues facing the nation should not influence the public forum in which these issues are discussed and debated. This concept of "independence" is clear enough in theory; in practice it becomes problematic when, for example, the press depends on sources within the government for information. The situation is further complicated where corporate power and corporate interests become involved in the political process. In the same way, the press cannot effectively discharge its watchdog function over the workings of power if its independence of those in power is compromised. This is an important part of the rationale for public broadcasting services, and even more for locally controlled listener-sponsored broadcasting.

As a news value, objectivity derives from the subjective/objective dichotomy. What is "subjective" is inner and private, and may vary from person to person. What is "objective" is what's "out there" and public, available to other perceivers. Thus an event that takes place in front of several witnesses may be experienced differently by each of the witnesses. The event is "objective," but the various experiences of it are "subjective." In a sense, absolute objectivity is unattainable because it is impossible to report anything without introducing at least some subjective interpretive elements. Journalism is essentially a kind of storytelling. News is typically presented in narrative form, as a "story," and to tell a story requires interpretation. Hence the best that we can expect of a reporter is "relative" objectivity. To be absolutely objective, a reporter would have to refrain completely from commenting on or interpreting or introducing any private subjective element into a report of the event, and simply "let the facts speak for themselves." But facts don't speak for themselves, which is why we have reporters in the first place. Nevertheless, this understanding of objectivity underlies the distinction between editorializing and straight reporting, between the editorial and opinion pages of the newspaper and the news sections.

The concept of "balance" has evolved in an attempt to ensure fairness in the marketplace of ideas, to prevent putting ideas or positions contending for public support at an "unfair" disadvantage. The concept of balance can be seen operating in such regulations as the equal-time rules and the Fairness Doctrine incorporated by Congress into the Communications Act. These regulations require that broadcasters provide reasonable and fair opportunity for the discussion of conflicting views on issues of public importance. For example, if a broadcaster allows one candidate for office to make a statement, other qualified opponents must be granted equal time.

The concept of "bias" is used extensively throughout media criticism, meaning something like "coverage that departs from professional standards or norms of objectivity, or balance, or neutrality." Unfortunately, media watchdog groups occupying precisely opposite positions on the political spectrum regularly attack the very same coverage, one group claiming that the coverage is biased in one direction and the other claiming bias in the opposite direction. It begins to look like each group measures press performance according to its own set of standards and "bias" ends up meaning "a spin we disagree with." Professional journalists find this sort of disagreement convenient. Editors even use it to show how *un*biased their coverage is, based on the theory that if you're getting criticized from both directions you must be pretty well balanced.

Thus arises a problem. To what independent standards or norms can we appeal in order to identify and measure the direction and degree of bias? Just as with judgments of newsworthiness we might begin with the role of a free press in a democratic society. As noted earlier, one of the central functions of a free press in a democratic society is to provide the citizens a forum in which ideas can freely compete with one another for public support in vigorous and open debate. From this we might begin to derive professional standards of objectivity, neutrality, and balance.

One way to facilitate an open forum is for the press to accommodate a wide variety of partisan voices, each free to articulate and advocate its own position on the issues of the day as vigorously as it can and in whatever terms it chooses. Suppose every city had as many newspapers as it had significant distinct perspectives—a conservative newspaper, a liberal newspaper, a libertarian newspaper, a socialist newspaper, a communist newspaper, a radical feminist newspaper, a labor newspaper, a fundamentalist Christian newspaper, and so on. On this supposition the society could witness and participate in vigorous and open debate and all ideas would have access to the arena of debate. We could speak of a "free marketplace of ideas." As we shall see in the following readings, in some ways this reflects the state of the American press in the early post-colonial period and well into the nineteenth century. Notice that there's no need in such circumstances to criticize a given newspaper for having a conservative bias (or a liberal bias or a feminist bias or whatever). One expects a given newspaper to stand for something, and other newspapers to stand for something else. Newspapers are expected to advocate ideas—to argue against each other, and so "bias" in an individual instance or with an individual news organization is not a problem. However, as large corporate entities have come increasingly to dominate the news business, and as more and more massive audiences have been assembled nationally and globally, this model of a contentious marketplace of ideas has gradually been replaced by a blander and more monolithic model in which the press seems to speak with a single voice. And the professional values journalism uses to assess the performance of this voice are evolving accordingly.

In terms of democratic theory, it makes sense to ask how well these evolving news values serve the original purposes of a free press. The readings to follow will help us do that. As you explore the three readings in this chapter, keep the following general questions in mind: First, do you think the mass media currently do well in serving the needs and purposes of the democratic process? If not, what explanatory hypotheses best diagnose the problem? If you see a need for reform, how would you propose to accomplish such reform in keeping with First Amendment principles?

3.1 HOW MEDIA OWNERSHIP AFFECTS PRESS PERFORMANCE Ben
Bagdikian built a successful journalistic career as a newspaperman with the *Providence Journal,* where he served as foreign correspondent and Washington bureau chief, and the *Washington Post,* where he was assistant managing editor and won a Pulitzer Prize in 1973 for his role in the publication of the Pentagon Papers. After that, Bagdikian pursued a second career as a scholar and teacher of journalism at the University of California at Berkeley from which he retired as dean of the graduate school of journalism in 1990.

Bagdikian's most widely known scholarly work is his study of the trends and effects of proprietary concentration in the media. In *The Media Monopoly,* first published in 1983 and updated through five subsequent editions, Bagdikian has documented the trend toward greater corporate concentration of ownership of the businesses and institutions responsible for gathering and distributing public information. When the first edition was published in the early 1980s, some fifty corporations controlled most of the business in all the major media. By the time the second edition was published in 1987, that number had shrunk to twenty-nine. Two years later, Bagdikian wrote in the *Nation,*

> A handful of mammoth private organizations have begun to dominate the world's mass media. Most of them confidently announce that by the 1990s they—five to ten corporate giants—will control most of the world's important newspapers, magazines, books, broadcast stations, movies, recordings and videocassettes. Moreover,

each of these planetary corporations plans to gather under its control every step in the information process, from creation of "the product" to all the various means by which modern technology delivers media messages to the public. "The product" is news, information, ideas, entertainment, and popular culture; the public is the whole world.

In the following essay Bagdikian explains why such a trend should be alarming from the point of view of democracy. The United States presents a particularly vivid example of the need in a democracy for information presented in detail and in context. Compared to many other industrialized democracies, American democracy is especially localized. The representative legislative body of the central national government is distributed among fifty states (the Senate) and 435 districts (the House of Representatives). Below the federal level are the fifty state governments, similarly distributed. And below these, a very large portion of the decision making that determines Americans' quality of life is reserved to local institutions—cities, counties, transportation districts, school districts, and so on. Moreover, the two major political parties in the American system are ill-defined coalitional parties, with broadly overlapping political philosophies and agendas and only minimal discipline over the political judgment and action of individual elected representatives. Therefore policy options are not organized and packaged in American democracy along clearly demarcated partisan lines. Voting on a strictly partisan basis is of little use in expressing one's support for policy options on specific issues. Each citizen, to vote intelligently, must absorb an overwhelming amount of information about individual candidates and specific issues at all levels of political decision making—national, state, and local. Furthermore, quantity does not replace quality: the information must be framed within a context conducive to in-depth interpretive understanding—a context which would make it possible for the citizen to draw reasonable inferences relevant to the issues and decisions at hand. In his essay Bagdikian critiques many of the guiding principles and prevailing values of American journalism—professional norms such as "objectivity" and "neutrality"—as these have evolved over the course of the industrial age and now into the age of information.

QUESTIONS FOR STUDY AND DISCUSSION

1. According to Bagdikian, how do the contemporary professional standards of objectivity and neutrality function to impoverish American journalism?
2. Bagdikian considers and rejects several explanatory hypotheses in attempting to account for American journalism's trend toward "social neutralism." What are these hypotheses, and why does Bagdikian reject them?
3. According to Bagdikian the growth of which particular industry is primarily responsible for the growing social neutralism in American mass media? Explain the impact of this industry on the evolution of news coverage and the professional standards of performance in journalism.

4. According to Bagdikian what additional factors contribute to the growth of social neutralism in American mass media?

THE POLITICAL ECONOMY OF THE MASS MEDIA[1]

BEN BAGDIKIAN

At the turn of the century long before the human race had engaged in two global wars and created nuclear weapons and other self-destructive acts, Steven Crane wrote: "A man said to the universe, 'I exist.' 'However,' replied the universe, 'that fact in me has not created a sense of obligation.' " One continues to hope that this is a sobering thought: that in the vastness of the universe our species is an almost negligible ant-heap, and if in arrogance and pride we destroy ourselves, the galaxies will not weep, or worse not even notice. If we are to establish some viable relationship between ourselves and our planet it must come from our own thoughts and acts. Those saving thoughts need not be technological or scientific— our technological ingenuity has already brought us close to mutual annihilation. Our salvation lies in creating a humanistic climate that favors civilized survival.

There are many sources of a society's prescriptions of its needs. A major source and an increasingly important source is the mass media. Those relatively new mechanisms on the human scene— newspapers, magazines, radio, television, books, and movies. These both reflect mass culture and create it. And through their pervasiveness in the consciousness of almost every living person, as they legitimize and propagate some values more than others. The presence of these media in the American environment is impressive. We have 1,700 daily newspapers, 8,000 weeklies, 11,000 magazines, 9,000 radio stations, and 1,000 television stations. It is said that by the time an American child has left high school, he or she has spent 9,000 hours in the classroom and 18,000 hours before a television set, and has seen 350,000 television commercials.

The content of these media varies, of course. This content has creative and constructive elements and it has the opposite. I am not concerned in this paper with the aesthetic qualities of our various media, but with their range of social and political ideas and the nature of the framework for their presentation of public affairs and news. I suggest that this range is unusually narrow in the United States and in it has evolved a style that lacks coherence for the mass of impressions that inundates the average citizen. The resulting fragmentation into unrelated agglomerations of information minimizes the possibility of making intelligent inferences of social and political significance. Instead of diverse and competing ideas we have a somewhat homogenized, seemingly neutralist, social and political context in the large outpouring of our media information and popular culture. This is at odds with the diversity of culture and circumstances within the United States, and with this country's interaction with the rest of the world, which in our time is increasingly diverse and volatile.

In a world increasingly politicized, our media content has the appearance of being severely depoliticized. When perception of cause and effect often becomes urgent for managing a dynamic world, we tend to present facts and events as isolated physical phenomena. Without comparison, without analysis of cause and effect, without perceptions of relationships, there is minimal critical thinking and therefore minimal intelligent and moral choice. This does not mean that our mass media content does not propagate powerful values. It does. Neal Hurley, looking at American television from the standpoint of a foreign audience, has written: "Even a James Bond movie, a doctors or nurses TV serial, a space exploration adventure, or private eye mystery, inculcate the values and attitudes that reinforce the Western model of man as shaper of his own destiny, as one free of environmental determinism, and the heavy hand of the past, as a person capable of innovation and choice." "Interlarded with these values, however," he goes on, "are others that are not in the central tradition of the classical Western view of man. One discerns such dubious philosophies as nationalism, America *Uber Alles,* materialism (blind faith in an escalating standard of living), doctrinaire conservatism (social conformity and resistance to change), liberal progressivism (things get better all the time), and social Darwinism (survival of the fittest and might makes right). Clearly these values exist in the output of our newspapers, magazines, and broadcasting; but they are *implicit,* not *explicit.* They are subtly associative and not rational. And while one does not look to art and grammar for doctrinal utterances, much of popular information and entertainment including advertising is suffused either with self-serving emotional manipulation, or information detached from context.

An appalling quantity of media output, whether in entertainment or advertising, is expertly designed to condition behavior and attitude by deliberately discouraging thought. There has always been drama, ritual, and legend in human affairs, and they have been crucial in creating values. But never before have there been such powerful engines of projecting these into the daily lives of so many people, for narrow purposes of commerce, or for avoidance of political and social significance. I am not making the same complaint that over the years is made of news and entertainment by many intellectuals and specialists. These complaints often are against the lack of profundity and expertise, or reject the legitimacy of popular rather than elite entertainment. Too often these complaints do not accept or even understand the need for widespread information and art outside the particular needs and tastes of an elite. That is not my complaint today. Mine instead is that the average citizen, intellectual or not, aesthete or not, is served by the major media in such a bland and sterile way that very few people, intellectual or otherwise, can fit together these bits and pieces into a useful form for comparison, analysis, and application to one's own life.

Incoherent social and political information finds Americans peculiarly vulnerable, because Americans have an almost unique need for masses of political and social information. Unlike other industrialized democracies, the American political system retains a large portion of decision-making for central institutions at a local, almost personal level. Functions that in other countries are decided on a national centralized basis are decided in this country on a local community basis, like control of education, land use, policing, and so forth. Even the national government is highly localized, with 435 districts in the House of Representatives. To make the process even more complex, the United States does not have major ideological parties that have clear distinctions in political philosophy and programs. Instead it has two coalitional parties that have such a degree of overlap that voting strictly by party is only minimally useful in expressing support for either specific programs or political philosophy.

Finally, and perhaps most burdensome on the voters' struggle with information overload, the United States does not have a parliamentary system in which each political party designs national policy. Instead each elected representative is independent in his or her political action, and is not bound by party platform. Consequently, to vote intelligently, each citizen must learn a great deal about a large number of individual candidates. All of this must be applied not only to voting for President, Senate, and House, but various jurisdictions from 3,000 county governments, 19,000 municipalities, 17,000 townships, 15,000 school districts, and 30,000 other kinds of local governmental units that together form the fabric of American political life. The American voter is required to absorb vast quantities of information if the voter is to act in intelligent community and self-interest. In addition, corporate life is unusually influential in the American social and physical environment and being less closely related to

national policies than in other democracies introduces yet another variable in social decision-making. The question is not whether this is a good or a bad system; it has great strengths and it has disadvantages. My point is that it imposes on the average citizen enormous burdens of absorbing information and translating that information into personal analysis and decision-making.

The narrow range of ideas and analysis in our mass media and the avoidance of intelligent framework and context for so much of mass media output does more to worsen the citizen's problem of decision-making than it does to help. The way fragmented, depoliticized, and socially neutral information pours out of our media means that the high volume of this output becomes a curse, rather than a blessing. Fragmented unrelated masses of information, whether in the classroom or political and social life, can produce intolerable chaos and confusion, which results in rejection and demoralization. I believe we are seeing something of this sort in the contemporary American political scene.

In the reporting of news, in American journalism, there is a doctrine called objectivity, by which is meant that the facts should be presented without social or political interpretation being imposed by the writer. This has evolved to mean removing from the facts sufficient background and context to make clear their social and political significance. We have a high degree of monopoly in newspapers and oligopoly in broadcasting and while there are variations among the individual outlets they are alike in their deliberate avoidance of social and political context to their facts. Consequently, despite the very large numbers of outlets of individual newspapers, magazines, and broadcast stations, they are remarkably similar in their social and political content or lack of it. For newspapers and radio and television, the prevailing ethic is to assume that each is the only source of information for all the citizens.

So, each is under an assumed obligation to be neutral, to avoid partisanship, and in the evolution of these media, this has been accomplished by a technique of style and approach that strains out social and political context. It assumes that facts, data, and physically observed events remain more or less isolated phenomena that speak for themselves. There are attempts from time to time to offer causes and consequences for these events, but they are limited and superficial, since to go further requires an interpretation of social forces. To describe possible causes and consequences, or to analyze the social forces that create theories of facts and events is to enter the field of politics and intellectual ideas. These have become, in our media ethics, "biases to be avoided." A recent example of my point is the current spread of political violence and hostage-taking around the world. Despite tons of newsprint and hours of expensive television coverage, day after day, of the most intense and time-consuming kind, the American public received little or no comprehension of where this violence comes from, and therefore how it can be understood. The news coverage by itself created a national impulse for action yet withheld any context that would make that action rational.

There are thousands of journalistic observers in the United States and many of them have sufficient grounding in history, economics, and social science to have personal insights into the context of the news. But their personal views differ, and if they were to provide a fuller context for their surface observations, there would be conflicting interpretations. Some of these interpretations would inevitably lack sufficient knowledge and insight but many would have some historical and analytical validity, yet still differ one from the other even as these scholars also differ one from the other. And the existence of these differences would violate the contemporary norms of journalism that the only legitimate presentations are uniform presentations. There are strengths to these norms. They have eliminated most of the wild sensationalism and scurrilous partisanship of the previous century's journalism. They have been a standard that is important in creating a basic sense of obligation to be fair and balanced which is not a small matter. Given the prevalence of monopoly among printed voices in each city, these norms prevent gross and overwhelming partisanship. But they have done this by adopting a presentation of events largely detached from their social moorings. It is a standard of American journalism now called social responsibility, because it speaks to everyone evenhandedly without explicit partisanship or opinion.

The single neutral voice in the popular marketplace of ideas is a very different model from that envisioned by the framers of our Constitution and creators of our political system. They assumed that multiple voices, each of whom added ideas, opinions, and interpretations—distinctly different from the rival voices—would also be available to the citizenry. The freedom to speak and therefore to print without inhibition was important to the founding fathers because they had a sensitive awareness of censorship left behind in England, Europe, and the earlier colonies in America. They understood that political democracy was inextricable from freedom of expression. The arrogance of unaccountable government was expressed in 1680 by Roger LeStrange, licenser of the press in London, who attacked the press in these terms, "A newspaper makes the multitude too familiar with the actions and councils of their superiors and gives them not only an itch but a kind of colorable right and license to be meddling with the government." Modern democracy assumes that the itch to be meddling with the government should become permanent, sustained by the stimulus of free and competing ideas, and so it seemed to the creators of the republic.

The intellectual leaders of the revolution of 1776 were well-versed in the European philosophies of democracy, from scholarly works to the flaming rhetoric of Thomas Paine, but the rebels of 1776 became the rulers of 1796. John Adams, who signed the Constitution and the First Amendment, so hated and feared foreign influence in the rival party of Thomas Jefferson, that he enacted the Alien and Sedition Acts. They violated the Constitution, reinstituted seditious libel, and punished those who criticized the government. Fortunately, those acts contributed to the downfall of Adams' party and the success of Jefferson, who then became President. But philosophical commitment to free expression is meaningless, unless it can tolerate opposition and perceived error. Even the sainted Jefferson was vulnerable. Before he became President he made the statement

that is beatified by journalists, "Were it left to me to decide whether we should have a government without newspapers, or newspapers without government, I should not hesitate a moment to prefer the latter." After he entered the White House and suffered the printed malice of opponents, he wrote, "Nothing can now be believed which is seen in a newspaper." Yet, freedom of the press survived.

In the colonial and post-revolutionary period, newspapers were established mainly by printers who did it for commercial or political reasons. Nineteenth-century American newspapers were vigorous and varied, partisan sometimes to the point of scurrility. Their political content varied from monarchism to socialism, their style from the elegiac to rabble-rousing. Social dogmas were quickly adopted from Europe and applied to the growing nation. Profound issues energized, and at times tormented the society. Issues like slavery versus anti-slavery; states rights versus centralized government; ruralism versus urbanism; agriculture versus industry; populist economics versus laissez-faire capitalism; popular representative government versus elitist representation; and nativist power versus equality for immigrants. The marketplace of ideas at the time was rich. Sometimes it was violent. A free marketplace can not be limited to the voices seen as calm and rational, but inevitably will include some voices which will be seen as anti-social. But all were reflected in the media of the time.

It was during the later part of that century that the nature of American society began its transformation toward an urbanized industrial country. The mass media were part of this development. High-speed printing and growing affluence spread the printed daily word to growing masses of people, who were poorly educated and semi-literate, many of them immigrants. Previously the printed newspaper had been the media mainly of a minority who were educated and literate.

The new industrialism created severe problems, but it simultaneously created a new kind of newspaper that reacted to those problems. The rapid expansion of corporate life affected newspapers, and the first substantial chains were those of E. W. Scripps, William Randolph Hearst, and Joseph Pulitzer. Scripps and the early Hearst were socialists, and their papers reflected their views of the world. The editorials of the early Hearst articulated the Populist policies of redistribution of wealth, government assistance to the poor, government housing, better working conditions, and better health care. The news columns regularly exposed abuses of labor by management, and abuse of power by financial institutions. Scripps was just as vigorous in the same line. Pulitzer was a progressive reflecting mid-nineteenth-century German political thought. These papers filled a void in the new industrialism, because the older established papers like the *Sun* and *Tribune* were elite conservative papers, with little to say about the social demands of a society that was no longer ruralistic and no longer agricultural.

Our standard histories have accentuated the journalistic sins of Hearst and Pulitzer, which were many. The so-called yellow journalism of these publishers was sometimes sensational and sometimes false, but muted in our histories is the serious social and political content of these same papers—the content that made important contributions to

relevant policies in a changed society. Both Pulitzer and Scripps later demonstrated that social sensitivity and sensationalism did not have to go together though Hearst in his later years merely demonstrated that politically ambitious young men can become eccentric and embittered old men.

A similar addition to the marketplace of ideas occurred in magazines. During the muckraker period of 1900–1912, some of the country's most influential magazines, as well as a dozen new ones, became critics of the pathologies of the new industrialism and fed the reformist politics of Theodore Roosevelt. Without this new ingredient in the marketplace of ideas, it is unlikely that during this period we would have enacted the first legislation to attempt some balance between uninhibited concentration of private power, and the need for social responsibility throughout the whole society. This was the start of the national attempt to preserve livable space, to attempt to have safe working places, enact anti-trust laws, and care for the sick and the elderly. The fact that the popular marketplace also included racism and classism is the cost of an open arena of thought. It is also a test of the basic fabric of society. Societies that are fragile or close to collapse cannot withstand the internal pressure of contentious public discourse, but it is through this kind of discourse, that viable ways are found to prevent a society becoming fragile. The alternative is rigidity against change, and imposition of order by force.

World War I ended the period of rapid reform and change in the new industrial state. In this period there appeared the unmistakable signs of a basic change in the American marketplace of ideas.

There began the depoliticizing of the American press and with it a transformation of the earlier model—a marketplace of clearly competing ideas in the mass media. When broadcasting would appear on the scene in the 1920s, it would soon find itself growing in conformity to the new model of a single neutral-seeming voice. One reason this conformity and blandness began, I believe, is a change in the economics and structure of the mass media. The new model grew and became the ethos of the American media for the next seventy years, including the present, because it served perhaps by happenstance the purposes both of commercialism and established power.

Initially newspapers were the enterprises of individuals who were either commercial printers or editors or both. The entrepreneurs might be interested mainly in making a profit, in providing a glue in newly created communities, or in promoting causes and candidates. They were small and they were personal. Their popularity depended almost entirely on their ability to enlist the interest and loyalty of some group of readers. But as the country industrialized and centralized in its commercial institutions, so did the press. Powerful, even tyrannical editors like Scripps, Pulitzer, and Hearst found themselves directing large bureaucracies from distant places, and the nature of cities themselves changed.

In 1851 Horace Greeley, testifying before a committee of the British Parliament about American newspapers said, "[An American city of 15,000 has a daily newspaper.] . . . [S]ometimes that is the case when they have as few as 10,000. 15,000 can be stated as the average at which a daily paper commences. At 20,000 they have two and so on. In cen-

tral towns, they have from three to five daily journals." Why is it that in the 1850s most of our cities and towns would have daily newspapers, and now ninety percent of our cities and towns do not? There were competing daily papers in most cities but today there are competing papers in less than two percent of newspaper cities. For one thing, the country no longer consisted of small agricultural communities of the kind that Jefferson saw as the basic unit of democracy. Cities, huge and impersonal, took their place. Newspapers that served such cities were no longer quickly created or Quixotic. They became substantial financial and industrial enterprises. The modern newspaper became a complex factory whatever else it might be. This might account for the slowing of the process of new entries into the business. But it does not explain why a rapidly growing number of cities fell behind in the pattern of each having its own newspaper. As the number of cities and towns grew, the absolute number of daily newspapers declined. Nor would this explain the growing political and social blandness of content. The cities were filled with new tensions and experimental policies that spawned contending political and social groups.

Contending political and social groups had in the past always been the basis for new competing newspapers. Furthermore the change in the nature of cities does not by itself explain another curious change in the relationship between the reader and the newspaper. In 1900, the three-cent daily paper represented something like six percent of average daily per-capita disposable income. During ensuing decades the real income of the average citizen increased, yet today the 25-cent paper represents less than one percent of daily disposable income. Since newspaper proprietors are not loathe to charge what the traffic will bear, this must reflect a lowered loyalty of readers to their particular medium. And why is it that eighty years ago competing newspapers presented their news and views in clearly contending advocacies of policy and politicians, while today the news columns, by self-adopted ethical imperatives, are neutral and minimally concerned with social and economic context? Why has there been such a change in two generations, and what does this mean for the national, social, and political discourse?

One explanation might be that we now have such a high degree of national unity in politics and social goals, that there are no longer serious issues to debate. But that of course is not true—either of public opinion, or of unresolved social issues. We still have a high degree of structural poverty for an affluent economy. We still have bitter debates on the economy. Health care is almost an obsession in our society, but there is no agreement on a coherent national plan. On the basic issues of war and peace, nuclear annihilation, or survival, there is profound disparity, sometimes leading to violence. Yet where there have been grass roots movements on such issues, whether it is on race relations, poverty, war and peace, or Naderite consumer advocacy, these have arisen with remarkable media indifference, and usually with media rejection. Only dramatic and fairly widespread independent action as seen in race relations, the nuclear freeze movement, and the Anti-Vietnam War movement, have led to later reluctant treatment in the news media. Or one might suspect a con-

spiracy, that for two generations, has plotted to keep out of the media any significant reflection of political and social ideas that threaten the status quo, or the political values of media owners. That is a tempting theory because there are many documented instances of media owner intervention to kill disliked stories and ideas, and to emphasize owners political preferences. There are clearly lower thresholds into the news for basic economic ideas that conform to owners preferences, like Friedmanesque marketplace economics, and almost absolute resistance to normal treatment of socialist or Marxist economics, even though these are current in the mass media of other industrialized democracies. However, I do not believe that the present paucity of competing ideas and media treatment of news and public affairs is the result of an explicit conspiracy. I believe that owners exhibit acquiescence, albeit welcome acquiescence, to the neutralism that has happened for other reasons. The net result as between overt agreement among media owners and acquiescence to an evolved pattern, may not be different, but it is important to understand the dynamics of how this came about, not only as a matter of intellectual interest but also as a measure of the depths to which neutralism and passivity have become embedded in the national consciousness. Furthermore, a conspiracy would have a strong probability of creating an organized resistance. Instead the opposite has happened. This devotion to depoliticized public information has created ethical and organizational conventions which journalistic professionals with differing social and political values enthusiastically obey. Even owners with strong opinions and full proprietary powers adhere to these conventions of seeming neutrality, sometimes with private bitterness.

Nor can traditional anti-intellectualism in the press be the cause for this lack of intellectual and social content in the mass media. After World War II most of the anti-intellectualism in American journalism disappeared, especially after the Russian Sputnik stimulated a national commitment to academic skills, if not to intellectualism. Modern journalists, unlike those of the years before World War II, are overwhelmingly graduates of colleges, sometimes with graduate degrees, usually in the humanities.

I believe that there is a much more impersonal source for the conscious social neutralism in our mass media. I think it has been the complex consequence of the emergence of mass advertising in the United States. Advertising, for one thing, has been a major contributor to the growth of monopoly and all oligopoly in the media which itself creates pressures against open advocacy. The resulting model of a neutral media has been accepted because it resolves a serious personal and professional conflict within the media. The growth of advertising in the American economy during the twentieth century has been phenomenal. Advertising represents a larger proportion of the American gross national product than it does in any other country. The combination of mass production techniques, consumer goods, and national affluence, has created a surplus of goods and a mammoth proliferation of goods, for which mass advertising became the basic method of merchandising. The natural carriers for most of this new element in the economy

became the mass media, until today, advertising represents eighty percent of revenues for daily newspapers, fifty percent for magazines, and almost one hundred percent for broadcasting.

Advertising has profoundly influenced the character of the non-advertising content of newspapers, magazines, radio, and television. Some of that influence has been attributed to direct coercion by advertisers, which does occur, but is often exaggerated. Far more important is the understandable desire of both advertisers and media owners to maximize their separate revenues—a process of adaptation that permits each side to be rational and efficient in its goals but which over the years, has deeply affected the nature of popular news and entertainment in the United States. Part of that adaptation is the meagerness of social and political analysis and background in the media. Advertisers understandably wish to reach their most desirable targets, affluent consumers, as efficiently as possible. More than anything else advertising rates are based on how efficiently a medium reaches this desirable audience and how effectively this audience is influenced by the ads. Advertisers do not wish to pay for distribution of their promotion to people who predictably are not likely to buy the products, or at least not buy the products at a high rate. So, advertisers are extremely interested in the demographics of media audiences—in the economic and social characteristics of the audience of a particular newspaper, magazine, or broadcast program.

Over the decades, advertisers have become more sophisticated in analyzing those population characteristics that appear to support maximum buying of their products. On their side, the mass media have also developed expertise in analyzing their subscribers or listeners. All media promote themselves by using their gross distribution statistics, the circulation for newspapers and magazines, and ratings for radio and television. When they sit down with major advertisers, their principal argument is elaborate computer printouts showing the various permutations of their distribution among the desired target of affluent consumers between the ages of eighteen and forty-nine, the family formation years of maximum purchasing of consumer goods and services. Newspapers and magazines have some direct influence over the nature of their readership. They promote subscriptions in the more affluent neighborhoods and communities, but they are minimally interested in pursuing subscriptions in non-affluent areas or those populated by the elderly. Some magazines for example, do not send renewal notices to postal zones with low-income levels. Broadcasters cannot control their signal in such a precise way, so they depend on the vast easy reach of radio and television signals and the content of their programs, with which to harvest an acceptable absolute number of affluent consumers. This becomes a successful strategy because of the low cost of propagating a broadcast signal compared to the high cost of physical delivery of a printed message to each home. Thus, both argue that mass advertisers will not waste their money on a medium that reaches people who are not affluent, or who are too old.

Advertisers are interested not only in reaching the most desirable consumers, they are also interested in the attitude and mood of those consumers at the moment that they are exposed to the advertisement. They are interested in what the trade calls a "buying mood." Thus non-advertising content, the news and articles in our newspapers or the broadcast programs in which commercial spots appear is of extreme importance to the mass advertiser. An extreme but real example of buying mood concern would be that of an airline which does not wish its newspaper or magazine promotion to appear next to an article describing an airplane crash, or of a cigarette company not wanting its advertisement to appear next to an article on the tobacco causes of heart and lung disease. In effect, a broadcast program dealing with starvation in Africa would be considered inappropriate for juxtaposition with a commercial for a product promising to cause people to lose weight. Advertisers and major media organizations have used advanced social science and psychological techniques to learn how to maximize buying mood for particular kinds of products. Most consumer goods are advertised with a high degree of emotional association and a minimum of product information. In broadcasting, the emotional association is more pronounced because of the ephemeral nature of broadcasting impressions and the vividness of the human voice, of music, and associative imagery. Consequently, for most mass media, the more serious and analytical the editorial content, the less effective it is as an environment for consumer advertising.

It is no accident that most advertising in metropolitan newspapers does not appear in a section containing serious news. In the large expansion of average daily pages in the American newspaper, the least expansion has been in the sections carrying serious news. Nor is it an accident that programming on commercial television has a large degree of fantasy and euphoric endings. A case in point is the change in prime time television. In the early 1950s, the most popular programs were serious original dramas by playwrights like Paddy Chayevsky, and with actors like Paul Newman and directors like Sidney Lumet. The sponsors were major American corporations, as they are today, but these programs were sponsored by Philco Television, Goodyear, Kraft, U.S. Steel, Motorola, and so forth. The ads were institutional, promoting the general image of the corporation rather than pressing for the sale of specific items. Ratings of audiences were high, and profits for the network were high. But these programs were cancelled despite the large audiences and over the protests of the sponsors, because the networks, in the meantime, had discovered that commercial spots of ten, twenty, or thirty seconds in duration from several different advertisers and peppered throughout a program increased profits even more.

Serious basic programs produced the wrong frame of mind for a series of unconnected brief sales pitches based largely on fantasy. So, primetime American television and therefore world television, became dominated by light reviews, situation comedies, or purely physical conflicts with content that would not put the viewer in an analytical rational frame of mind.

Avoidance of seriousness and rational analysis in entertainment is one thing, even in skilled dramaturgy, but avoidance in news is quite another. The appeal of news as a commodity depends on its being current and compelling and there-fore cannot be devoted largely to fantasy. Nevertheless, serious news in the United States remains largely fragmented, without a framework of explanatory social consequences and context.

Every country's news media has variations of seriousness even in authoritarian states. Privileged information and serious events as isolated phenomena can be found in the news media everywhere. What is different in the United States is the pervasiveness of the avoidance of social and political context for news, and the narrow spectrum for commentary and analysis in even the most serious newspapers and the most serious broadcast news programs. News, unlike media entertainment, does not have a large portion of fantasy for which we may be grateful. Instead the major news media are excessively devoted to the strictly physical manifestations of human life, preferably violent manifestations, conflict and tragedy, crime and catastrophe are prominently displayed. Where there is conflict it tends to be depicted as personality even when it is clear that it is a confrontation of deep social forces. The graphic realism of the news, however, is merely the void filled by avoidance of social context—the bleaching out of the news, of causes and consequences, and of the framework that alone makes individual events comprehensible. While there is interpretation and background, occasionally, usually brief and thin, it seldom deviates from established centrist views. There is more tolerance in moving toward the right, where ideological interpretations do appear, but even there the level of social analysis is superficial. Consequently, the presentation of physical events is similar throughout the media and what little social and political context is provided is also similar and vague. It is this pattern of neutralist, and largely physical presentation of world events, that constitutes the new model of the media marketplace. And it is the homogeneous, non-controversial voice, in contrast to the earlier model of many diverse voices, that has become the prevailing voice of the media marketplace.

This narrow spectrum of expression in the news is directly related to the influence of mass advertising. That influence is not so much from direct intervention from advertisers, as it is from the profound impact of advertising on the structure and content of the non-advertising part of the media. Eighty years ago many newspapers were printed simultaneously in each city of any size because each paper appealed to a different social, economic, or ethnic constituency. Those constituencies paid most of the cost of the paper because this was a paper that represented a direction and events that touched their lives.

Advertising was a significant ingredient in those newspapers, but it was a secondary one. The primary goal of the paper was to win the loyalty of a large enough group. Where a significant group lacked the news or analysis of news that it most wanted there was a likelihood of a new entrepreneur to fill that need. But as advertising became a major element in most newspaper revenues, and one hundred percent in broadcasting, all major media began aiming for the same audience—the audience desired by advertisers. Partisanship that attracted the loyalty of some readers, might offend other readers, who regardless of their different loyalties were equally attractive

targets for advertising. As all daily papers began to aim consciously toward the same audience, it is not surprising that their content began to become similar and that partisanship in news selection and social analysis of the news, shrank in favor of unfocused information. Advertising unwittingly became the primary influence in creating monopoly in local newspapers and oligopoly in broadcasting.

As each paper reached out to the same large audience, the point of view and depth of treatment of particular subjects became less important than the more generalized qualities of personality, graphics, and physical excitement. If, by whatever means, one paper began to pull substantially ahead of its rivals, thanks to economies of scale, it could deliver ads for less cost per household than other papers, and advertising revenues would shift toward that paper, and the slide toward monopoly began. In broadcasting, somewhat the same process evolved with two differences. Broadcasting, especially television, became the most powerful merchandising mechanism in human history, creating new areas of spending and product proliferation. Ratings of audience sizes could be done with increasing rapidity until they are now done overnight. This means that there can now be a rapid adjustment of programming to overcome some momentary loss of competitive rating. And although this is done with a quality approaching hysteria, the quick and frequent changes make all broadcasting more uniform. There is enough volume of revenues to support several channels of this multiplication of uniform content, so that even the losers in ratings make extraordinary profits.

Monopolistic audiences by themselves created pressures for moderation of differences in content and political and social values. The desire not to offend significant members of the advertising audience naturally led to moderated political content. Eventually the doctrine called objectivity in news and public affairs evolved on the premise that ethical grounds militate against clear social values and analysis. But, when values are not explicit, and there are not commonly available comparisons of different viewpoints, the ability to analyze and to make meaningful choices declines. There are benefits for the public in this new moderation and uniformity. It ended sensationalism and the likelihood that separate groups would live with isolated views of the world. But it also has meant a dangerously uncritical assessment of established power, and a relatively insignificant set of criteria for granting political power. That is a threat to the continued vitality of any democracy. In a volatile world, it means that there will be an artificially induced impression, that there are no alternatives to existing power relationships within society. Thus, without conspiracy or conscious malice, the mass media become supportive of established power beyond anything that existed earlier in our history, and anything that exists today in most other industrialized democracies.

Within journalism, this new neutralism is accepted by both sides of the major elements in the profession. On one side are the owners that are overwhelmingly conservative, on the other side are professional journalists, who in general reflect the social and political characteristics of the rest of the population of their educational and income levels. Which is to say, a social and political pattern running from slightly right of center, to somewhat more left of center. Like the general population for example, more journalists identify with the Democratic party than with the Republican party. The proprietors, who are more conservative, have the power to hire and fire their journalist employees, but they tolerate them. Though they have the power to do so if they wish, most publishers and network owners do not insist on news that openly reflects their personal interests. They do it not so much out of a sense of social obligation, though that is how they now explain it. They did it originally and they do so now because an explicit doctrinal approach of their own ideas, which are minority ideas among the American public, would cost them most of their audience and most of their profits.

Journalists as a whole accept the idea of news without social and political context, because that also solves a profound problem for them. It keeps under control the owners' power to turn journalists work into open propaganda, with which most journalists would disagree. Nevertheless, ideas that are not made explicit in the news can be expressed implicitly by indirection, and ideas expressed only implicitly are more difficult to subject to rational analysis. Furthermore, in the moderation manifested by the news media with all its advantages, it is still true that some ideas are treated more moderately than others. Silence in the selection of news can be as effective as amplified sound. Ralph Nader, for example, has had a larger impact on his times than any single major corporate leader in the country, but any of those corporate leaders have easier access to the news media than Ralph Nader. Reporting on foreign policy is by now so oriented to official interpretation, that any departure from the official line is in danger of being characterized as unpatriotic, even if it may be documented by scholarly research or direct observation. Certain social ideas have become so subject to taboos or silence, that even when they are implemented out of sheer necessity, like a planned economy or income redistribution, they are not permitted to be called by their correct names. Ideas that are improperly labeled are in danger of being improperly thought about. So if the public has gained something from depoliticized news, it has lost something real in its ability to identify and therefore to influence social policy.

The contemporary media model presupposes that a single neutral observer has the effect of artificially ossifying the status quo. By remaining neutral, the media inevitably become undiscriminating conduits for the most powerful voices—official government and private corporate voices. But the idea of a single neutral voice does something more. This model has developed over the last eighty years. This means that two generations of Americans have lacked in experience, common to earlier generations, namely the experience of a marketplace of ideas, rich in diversity and rivalry. Lacking that for so long has created the feeling that a rich marketplace of ideas is improper and dangerous. It has made neutralism, including moral neutralism, close to the national norm. Timidity toward competing ideas makes the public more vulnerable to authoritarian arguments that

sanctify conformity, uniformity, and unthinking adherence to the official view.

The old model of competing voices was based largely on the perceived needs of a political democracy. The new model of a neutral uniform voice is based largely on commercial expediency without regard for the needs of the noncommercial interests of the population. Thus tax laws were enacted and adjudicated to encourage concentrated media power and giant units, instead of encouragement of new and diverse voices. The early national radio system was dismantled, and the widely popular, noncommercial stations operated by universities were taken away. This gave the best frequencies and power to the commercial operators who had just discovered the extraordinary profits in broadcast advertising. When television was established as a system after World War II, it too let pass the opportunities of the new and powerful system, in effect allowing it to be totally devoted to commerce without effectively mandating significant non-commercial access to the public and for public affairs. Where once there was easy access for the average citizen to a variety of ideas, which was seen as the only way to preserve a healthy democracy, there now seems to be an environment, in which only minor permutations of a homogenized single view are accepted in the mass media, and therefore the national discourse. If that kind of homogeneity has ever worked, it has been either in a secluded, stable state, or in an authoritarian one. It is not a reassuring prescription for a dynamic democracy in a changing world.

CASE STUDY: MEDIA WATCH GROUPS

Below are the Web site addresses for three media watchdog organizations. Each of these organizations is devoted to the assessment and critique of press performance. Fairness and Accuracy in Reporting (FAIR) publishes a bimonthly newsletter, *Extra,* "in an effort to correct bias and imbalance" in national media coverage. The Media Research Center (MRC) publishes a monthly newsletter, *MediaWatch,* to expose and correct what they consider a pervasive liberal bias in national media coverage. Accuracy in Media (AIM) publishes a bimonthly newsletter, the Aim Report, dedicated to "fairness, accuracy and balance in news reporting."

Visit and explore the following three Web sites. Compare, contrast, and evaluate the criticisms of the press you find there.

FAIR: http://www.fair.org

The Media Research Center: http://www.mediaresearch.org.

AIM: http://www.aim.org.

CASE STUDY: INDUSTRY SELF-ASSESSMENT

The Poynter Institute describes itself in its mission statement as a financially independent, nonprofit organization dedicated to teaching and inspiring journalists and media leaders. Visit and explore the Poynter Institute's Web site at http://www.poynter.org. What main differences do you notice between the media criticism you encounter here and that which you encountered at the three Web sites above?

CASE STUDY: PUBLIC BROADCASTING

According to Bagdikian's analysis, mass media corporate giants financed primarily by corporate advertising compromise the essential democratic functions of the press and degrade the political process. This underscores the rationale for public broadcasting. National Public Radio (NPR) and the Public Broadcasting System (PBS) are financed by viewer or listener support, subsidized with tax revenue, and underwritten by corporate sponsorship. Pacifica Radio depends almost entirely on listener subscriptions for its operating budgets. Visit and explore their Web sites at the following addresses.

Public Broadcasting System: http://www.pbs.org

National Public Radio: http://www.npr.org

Pacifica Radio: http://www.pacifica.org

More important: sample the programming of these broadcast services. Evaluate them as information service providers. Devise a scale on which to rate them and be prepared to explain its basis to your classmates. To what extent do you find these information services responsive to the information requirements of citizenship in a democracy?

CASE STUDY: PACIFICA RADIO

In 1999, coinciding with the fiftieth anniversary of listener-sponsored radio station KPFA, flagship station of the Pacifica network, a struggle erupted that pitted the network's national board of directors and management against KPFA's local station management, on-air staff, and listening audience. This confrontation provides a complex and fascinating case study of the forces, principles, and stakes involved in establishing and maintaining democratic information services.

According to the chronology of events published by the embattled KPFA staff,

On March 31st, 1999, the Pacifica Foundation's Executive Director Lynn Chadwick informed KPFA general manager Nicole Sawaya that her job with the station had been terminated, effective immediately. . . . The firing revealed an utter disregard for the first and most obvious rule of community radio: major policy decisions will be made in consultation with the community. Pacifica management talked to no one beyond its own inner circle before taking this drastic step. A strong, independent minded leader, Sawaya was very much liked by KPFA's staff and the larger community. Her ousting provoked a huge wave of protest from KPFA supporters across Northern California. That night KPFA's news department prepared a report for the listeners about the sad decision. To the astonishment of the staff, Pacifica told the station's news director not to run it. The story was broadcast in defiance of the order. Even before Sawaya's dismissal, however, Pacifica was clearly moving in an alarming direction. On February 28th, the Pacifica National Board met in Berkeley and decided to remove Local Advisory Board (LAB) members from its national governance board. Local advisory boards are the backbone of community input into Pacifica national policy. They meet once a month and hear the concerns of listeners, volunteers—whoever has something to say. Formal LAB member presence on the national board helps keep Pacifica accountable to the network's stations. Now that LAB members were gone, Pacifica's national board became a completely self-appointing body. KPFA's signature voice, Larry Bensky, appeared before the National board to argue against this decision. Bensky is a 30-year veteran of the Pacifica network, having won the Polk Award for his historic gavel-to-gavel coverage of the Iran-Contra hearings in 1986. Bensky warned the board that Pacifica's National Office was becoming unaccountable and top-heavy with staff. When Pacifica terminated Sawaya as general manager, Bensky became even more worried about a management style that had now become autocratic. He took his concerns to the listeners on his regular Sunday program. On April 9th, Pacifica responded by firing Bensky as well. The coup strategy was now obvious to anyone who cared to look: centralize your authority, remove from any position of governance those who seem like they might question you, and fire your critics. These actions came from an organization whose flagship daily public affairs program is called "Democracy Now," and, in its own literature, refers to Pacifica as "democratic communications."

On April 2, 1999, Pacifica Executive Director Lynn Chadwick went on the air over KPFA to respond as follows:

This is Lynn Chadwick, Executive Director of Pacifica, with a message for our listeners. Over the last several months, there has been a good deal of confusion and speculation about some changes made within the Pacifica organization. I had previously chosen not to go on air to discuss these matters for two reasons: First, internal Pacifica issues and management decisions are precisely that—internal. We have made decisions that reflect the best management practices for the organization, regardless of their popularity. As a nonprofit organization, we have a responsibility to our supporters to run the organization in the most efficient and cost-effective manner possible in accordance with our strategic plan, while striving to achieve our mission. Second, internal Pacifica issues and management decisions are not news. It is not appropriate for any media outlet, including KPFA, to use airtime to voice internal grievances, nor should a parent organization, such as Pacifica, use airtime to counter such grievances. This is not the purpose of community radio. Our journalists have a responsibility to report the news, not create it. They also have a responsibility to detach themselves and provide objectivity when making a determination as to what is and what is *not* news. KPFA has made two erroneous news reports in recent months, both regarding Pacifica staff. On Wednesday night's 6 o'clock news, KPFA reported the firing of station manager Nicole Sawaya. Let me make it perfectly clear that Nicole was *not* fired. Her contract expired on March 31 and we made a decision not to renew it. I also want to emphasize the fact that neither KPFA nor any other Pacifica station is for sale, nor do we have any intention of considering such measures. The second incorrect report was regarding Larry Bensky, host of "Sunday Salon." Again, KPFA reported the firing of Mr. Bensky late last year. Larry Bensky was not fired, nor did public outcry result in his new weekly show, "Sunday Salon." The legalities surrounding personnel issues and their confidentiality make it impossible for me to share the particulars of either situation with you. Finally, I am sad to report that someone performed an act of violence against the Pacifica national office Wednesday night. Gunshots were fired into our office, causing serious destruction to our property as well as disruption of our operations. It is an understatement to say we are grateful that no one was injured. The very name of our organization is derived from the word "pacifist," and I simply cannot understand how anyone could perpetrate an act of violence, especially against an organization whose mission is to achieve peace and tolerance among all people, a mission we continue to work towards.

Visit and explore the following Web sites of two interested parties to the ongoing struggle over KPFA and the Pacifica network: http://www.savepacifica.net, http://www.pacifica.org. Learn what you can about the struggle. What lessons can you draw from your observations of this struggle about the media and democracy?

3.2 THE PRESS AND "PUBLIC RELATIONS"   Born in 1889, Walter Lippmann studied philosophy at Harvard University with George Santayana as well as political science and economics. After graduating in 1910, he pursued an illustrious career in journalism, interrupted by World War I, during which he left private life to become assistant secretary of war. Following the war, he assisted in preparing data for the peace conference at Versailles. During stints as associate editor of the *New Republic* in its early days (1914–17) and as a syndicated columnist at the New York *Herald Tribune,* the Washington *Post,* and *Newsweek,* Lippmann won two Pulitzer Prizes and became perhaps the most influential political commentator of his time. He wrote several influential books on current events, political affairs, and political theory. His writings led the development of "public relations" as a political profession.

Probably the most important of Lippmann's writings in determining the course of American political science is his book *Public Opinion,* published in 1922. It was in this book that Lippmann coined the notion of "manufacturing or engineering consent." In the following selection from *Public Opinion* Lippmann argues first the metaphysical point that the "external world," including all public affairs, is distinct from and often quite different from the perceptions any of us have of it. He argues further the epistemological point that reality, including affairs of state, is too large and complex to be fully comprehended from any single vantage point. On the basis of these two premises he draws several striking conclusions about the construction and distribution of decision-making power and authority, and about the role of the press and other agencies of information, in a democracy.

Lippmann concludes that no individual citizen can ever be adequately informed about all leadership and policy issues that face a democratic nation, and therefore that responsible government must delegate decision-making authority to experts. Lippmann concludes further that the press's proper role in the political process is to assist in managing public opinion and engineering or manufacturing public consent to policies determined by leaders guided by advisers with specialized expertise.

QUESTIONS FOR STUDY AND DISCUSSION

1. This chapter begins with a quotation in which Congressman Ron Dellums echoes the Jeffersonian ideas that the *people* of a society ought to make the political decisions, and that in their own best interests they have the responsibility to be well informed. Lippmann argues against these central principles of democracy. What is Lippmann's argument?

2. What, according to Lippmann, is the underlying reason for the existence of press agents? Describe the role of the press agent, as Lippmann conceives it, in shaping the news.

3. Lippmann and Bagdikian share areas of substantial agreement regarding the citizen's need for information in the American political system, and yet they come to radically different conclusions about the press's role and responsibilities. Outline the areas of agreement and explain the points of disagreement.

4. What is Lippmann's definition of propaganda? What role does Lippmann assign to propaganda in the political process?

5. What does Lippmann mean when he says that public opinion must be organized *for* the press rather than *by* the press and that this organization is the task of political science functioning properly as formulator in advance of real decision making?

THE TRUTH, PUBLIC OPINION, AND THE NATURE OF NEWS[2]

WALTER LIPPMANN

There is an island in the ocean where in 1914 a few Englishmen, Frenchmen, and Germans lived. No cable reaches that island, and the British mail steamer comes but once in sixty days. In September it had not yet come, and the islanders were still talking about the latest newspaper. . . . [F]or over six weeks those of them who were English and those of them who were French had been fighting on behalf of the sanctity of treaties against those of them who were Germans. For six strange weeks they had acted as if they were friends, when in fact they were enemies. But their plight was not so different from that of most of the population of Europe. They had been mistaken for six weeks, on the continent the interval may have been only six days or six hours. There was an interval. There was a moment when the picture of Europe on which men were conducting their business as usual, did not in any way correspond to the Europe which was about to make a jumble of their lives. There was a time for each man when he was still adjusted to an environment that no longer existed. All over the world . . . men were making goods they would not be able to ship, buying goods they would not be able to import, careers were being planned, enterprises contemplated, hopes and expectations entertained, all in the belief that the world as known was the world as it was. Men were writing books describing that world. They trusted the picture in their heads. And then over four years later came the news

of an armistice, and people gave vent to their unutterable relief that the slaughter was over. Yet in the days before the real armistice came, though the end of the war had been celebrated, several thousand young men died on the battlefields.

Looking back we can see how indirectly we know the environment in which we nevertheless live. We can see that the news of it comes to us now fast, now slowly; but that whatever we believe to be a true picture, we treat as if it were the environment itself. It is harder to remember that about the beliefs upon which we are now acting, but in respect to other peoples and other ages we flatter ourselves that it is easy to see when they were in deadly earnest about ludicrous pictures of the world. We insist, because of our superior hindsight, that the world as they needed to know it, and the world as they did know it, were often two quite contradictory things. We can see too, that while they governed and fought, traded and reformed in the world as they imagined it to be, they produced results, or failed to produce any, in the world as it was. They started for the Indies and found America. They diagnosed evil and hanged old women. They thought they could grow rich by always selling and never buying. A caliph, obeying what he conceived to be the will of Allah, burned the library at Alexandria.

. . . Now in any society that is not completely self-contained and so small that everyone can know all about everything that happens, ideas deal with events that are out of sight and hard to grasp. [Someone] is aware that a war is raging in France and tries to conceive it. She has never been to France, and certainly she has never been along what is now the battlefront. Pictures of French and German soldiers she has seen, but it is impossible for her to imagine three million men. No one, in fact, can imagine them, and the professionals do not try. They think of them as, say, two hundred divisions. [She] has no access to the order of battle maps, and so if she is to think about the war, she fastens upon Joffre and the Kaiser as if they were engaged in a personal duel. Perhaps if you could see what she sees with her mind's eye, the image in its composition might be not unlike an eighteenth-century engraving of a great soldier. He stands there boldly unruffled and more than life size, with a shadowy army of tiny little figures winding off into the landscape behind. Nor it seems are great men oblivious to these expectations. . . .

The only feeling that anyone can have about an event he does not experience is the feeling aroused by his mental image of that event. That is why until we know what others think they know, we cannot truly understand their acts. I have seen a young girl, brought up in a Pennsylvania mining town, plunged suddenly from entire cheerfulness into a paroxysm of grief when a gust of wind cracked the kitchen window-pane. For hours she was inconsolable, and to me incomprehensible. But when she was able to talk, it transpired that if a window-pane broke it meant that a close relative had died. She was, therefore, mourning for her father, who had frightened her into running away from home. The father was, of course, quite thoroughly alive as a telegraphic inquiry

soon proved. But until the telegram came, the cracked glass was an authentic message to that girl. Why it was authentic only a prolonged investigation by a skilled psychiatrist could show. But even the most casual observer could see that the girl, enormously upset by her family troubles, had hallucinated a complete fiction out of one external fact, a remembered superstition, and a turmoil of remorse, and fear and love for her father.

Abnormality in these instances is only a matter of degree. When an attorney general, who has been frightened by a bomb exploded on his doorstep, convinces himself by the reading of revolutionary literature that a revolution is to happen on the first of May 1920, we recognize that much the same mechanism is at work. The war, of course, furnished many examples of this pattern: the casual fact, the creative imagination, the will to believe, and out of these three elements, a counterfeit of reality to which there was a violent instinctive response. For it is clear enough that under certain conditions men respond as powerfully to fictions as they do to realities, and that in many cases they help to create the very fictions to which they respond. . . .

By fictions I do not mean lies. I mean a representation of the environment which is in lesser or greater degree made by man himself. The range of fiction extends all the way from complete hallucination to the scientists' perfectly self-conscious use of a schematic model, or his decision that for his particular problem accuracy beyond a certain number of decimal places is not important. A work of fiction may have almost any degree of fidelity, and so long as the degree of fidelity can be taken into account, fiction is not misleading. In fact, human culture is very largely the selection, the rearrangement, the tracing of patterns upon, and the stylizing of, what William James called "the random irradiations and resettlements of our ideas."[3] The alternative to the use of fictions is direct exposure to the ebb and flow of sensation. That is not a real alternative, for however refreshing it is to see at times with a perfectly innocent eye, innocence itself is not wisdom, though a source and corrective of wisdom. . . . For the real environment is altogether too big, too complex, and too fleeting for direct acquaintance. We are not equipped to deal with so much subtlety, so much variety, so many permutations and combinations. And although we have to act in that environment, we have to reconstruct it on a simpler model before we can manage with it.

The analyst of public opinion must begin, then, by recognizing the triangular relationship between the scene of action, the human picture of that scene, and the human response to that picture working itself out upon the scene of action. . . . We shall assume that what each man does is based not on direct and certain knowledge, but on pictures made by himself or given to him. If his atlas tells him that the world is flat he will not sail near what he believes to be the edge of our planet for fear of falling off. If his maps include a fountain of youth, a Ponce de Leon will go in quest of it. If someone digs up yellow dirt that looks like gold, he will for a time act exactly as if he had found gold. The way in which the world is imagined determines at any particular moment what men will do. . . . But what is propaganda, if not the effort to alter the picture to which men respond, to substitute one social pattern for another?

The world that we have to deal with politically is out of reach, out of sight, out of mind. It has to be explored, reported, and imagined. Man is no Aristotelian god contemplating all existence at one glance. He is the creature of an evolution who can just about span a sufficient portion of reality to manage his survival, and snatch what on the scale of time are but a few moments of insight and happiness. Yet this same creature has invented ways of seeing what no naked eye could see, of hearing what no ear could hear, of weighing immense masses and infinitesimal ones, of counting and separating more items than he can individually remember. He is learning to see with his mind vast portions of the world that he could never see, touch, smell, hear, or remember. Gradually he makes for himself a trustworthy picture inside his head of the world beyond his reach.

I argue that representative government, either in what is ordinarily called politics, or in industry, cannot be worked successfully, no matter what the basis of election, unless there is an independent, expert organization for making the unseen facts intelligible to those who have to make the decisions. I argue that the serious acceptance of the principle that personal representation must be supplemented by representation of the unseen facts would alone permit a satisfactory decentralization, and allow us to escape from the intolerable and unworkable fiction that each of us must acquire a competent opinion about all public affairs. My conclusion is that public opinions must be organized for the press if they are to be sound, not by the press as is the case today. This organization I conceive to be in the first instance the task of political science that has won its proper place as formulator, in advance of real decision, instead of apologist, critic, or reporter after the decision has been made. . . .

The established leaders of any organization have great natural advantages. They are believed to have better sources of information. The books and papers are in their offices. They took part in the important conferences. They met the important people. They have responsibility. It is, therefore, easier for them to secure attention and to speak in a convincing tone. But also they have a very great deal of control over access to the facts. Every official is in some degree a censor. And since no one can suppress information, either by concealing it or forgetting to mention it, without some notion of what he wishes the public to know, every leader is in some degree a propagandist. Strategically placed, and compelled often to choose . . . between the equally cogent though conflicting ideals of safety for the institution, and candor to his public, the official finds himself deciding more and more consciously what facts, in what setting, in what guise he shall permit the public to know.

That the manufacture of consent is capable of great refinements no one, I think, denies . . . and the opportunities for manipulation open to anyone who understands the process [whereby public opinions arise] are plain enough. The creation of consent is not a new art. It is a very old one which was supposed to have died out with the appearance of democracy. But it has not died out. It has, in fact, improved enormously in technique, because it is now based on analysis rather than on rule of thumb. And so, as a result of psychological research, coupled with the modern means of communication, the practice of democracy has turned a corner. A revolution is taking place, infinitely more significant than any shifting of economic power.

Within the life of the generation now in control of affairs, persuasion has become a self-conscious art and a regular organ of popular government. None of us begins to understand the consequences, but it is no daring prophesy to say that the knowledge of how to create consent will alter every political calculation and modify every political premise. Under the impact of propaganda, not necessarily in the sinister meaning of the word alone, the old constants of our thinking have become variables. It is no longer possible, for example, to believe in the original dogma of democracy; that the knowledge needed for the management of human affairs comes up spontaneously from the human heart. Where we act on that theory we expose ourselves to self-deception, and to forms of persuasion that we cannot verify. It has been demonstrated that we cannot rely upon intuition, conscience, or the accidents of casual opinion if we are to deal with the world beyond our reach.

All the reporters in the world working all the hours of the day could not witness all the happenings in the world. There are not a great many reporters. And none of them has the power to be in more than one place at a time. Reporters are not clairvoyant, they do not gaze into a crystal ball and see the world at will, they are not assisted by thought-transference. Yet the range of subjects these comparatively few men manage to cover would be a miracle indeed, if it were not a standardized routine.

Newspapers do not try to keep an eye on all mankind. They have watchers stationed at certain places, like Police Headquarters, the Coroner's Office, the County Clerk's Office, City Hall, the White House, the Senate, House of Representatives, and so forth. They watch, or rather in the majority of cases they belong to associations which employ men who watch "a comparatively small number of places where it is made known when the life of anyone . . . departs from ordinary paths, or when events worth telling about occur. For example, John Smith, let it be supposed, becomes a broker. For ten years he pursues the even tenor of his way and, except for his customers and his friends, no one gives him a thought. To the newspapers he is as if he were not. But in the eleventh year he suffers heavy losses and, at last, his resources all gone, summons his lawyer and arranges for the making of an assignment. The lawyer posts off to the County Clerk's office, and a clerk there makes the necessary entries in the official docket. Here in step the newspapers. While the clerk is writing Smith's business obituary a reporter glances over his shoulder and a few minutes later the reporters know Smith's troubles and are as well informed concerning his business status as they would be had they kept a reporter at his door every day for over ten years."[4]

When Mr. Given says that the newspapers know "Smith's troubles" and "his business status," he does not mean that they know them as Smith knows them, or as Mr. Arnold Bennett would know them if he had made Smith the hero of a three-volume novel. The newspapers know only "in a few minutes" the bald facts which are recorded in the County Clerk's Office. That overt act "uncovers" the news about Smith. Whether the news

will be followed up or not is another matter. The point is that before a series of events become news they have usually to make themselves noticeable in some more or less overt act. Generally, too, in a crudely overt act. Smith's friends may have known for years that he was taking risks, rumors may even have reached the financial editor if Smith's friends were talkative. But apart from the fact that none of this could be published because it would be libel, there is in these rumors nothing definite on which to peg a story. Something definite must occur that has unmistakable form. It may be the act of going into bankruptcy, it may be a fire, a collision, an assault, a riot, an arrest, a denunciation, the introduction of a bill, a speech, a vote, a meeting, the expressed opinion of a well-known citizen, an editorial in a newspaper, a sale, a wage-schedule, a price change, the proposal to build a bridge. . . . There must be a manifestation. The course of events must assume a certain definable shape, and until it is in a phase where some aspect is an accomplished fact, news does not separate itself from the ocean of possible truth.

Naturally there is room for wide difference of opinion as to when events have a shape that can be reported. A good journalist will find news oftener than a hack. If he sees a building with a dangerous list, he does not have to wait until it falls into the street in order to recognize news. It was a great reporter who guessed the name of the next Indian Viceroy when he heard Lord So-and-So was inquiring about climates. There are luck shots, but the number of men who can make them is small. Usually it is the stereotyped shape assumed by an event at an obvious place that uncovers the run of the news. The most obvious place is where people's affairs touch public authority. It is at these places that marriages, births, deaths, contracts, failures, arrivals, departures, lawsuits, disorders, epidemics, and calamities are made known.

Whenever there is a good machinery of record, the modern news service works with great precision. There is one on the stock exchange, and the news of price movements is flashed over tickers with dependable accuracy. There is a machinery for election returns, and when the counting and tabulating are well done, the result of a national election is usually known on the night of the election. In civilized communities deaths, births, marriages, and divorces are recorded, and are known accurately except where there is concealment or neglect. The machinery exists for some, and only some aspects of industry and government, in varying degrees of precision for securities, money and staples, bank clearances, realty transactions, wage scales. It exists for imports and exports because they pass through a custom house and can be directly recorded. It exists in nothing like the same degree for internal trade, and especially for trade over the counter.

It will be found, I think, that there is a very direct relation between the certainty of news and the system of record. If you call to mind the topics which form the principal indictments by reformers against the press, you find they are subjects in which the newspaper occupies the position of the umpire in an unscored baseball game. All news about states of mind is of this character; so are all descriptions of personalities, of sincerity, aspiration, motive, intention, of mass feeling, of national feeling, of public opinion, the policies of foreign govern-

ments. So is much news about what is going to happen. So are questions turning on private profit, private income, wages, working conditions, the efficiency of labor, educational opportunity, unemployment, monotony, health, discrimination, unfairness, restraint of trade, waste, "backward peoples," conservatism, imperialism, radicalism, liberty, honor, righteousness. All involve data that are at best spasmodically recorded. The data may be hidden because of a censorship or a tradition of privacy, they may not exist because nobody thinks record important, because he thinks it red tape, or because nobody has yet invented an objective system of measurement. Then the news on these subjects is bound to be debatable, when it is not wholly neglected. The events which are not scored are reported either as personal and conventional opinions, or they are not news. They do not take shape until somebody protests, or somebody investigates, or somebody publicly makes an *issue* of them.

This is the underlying reason for the existence of the press agent. The enormous discretion as to what facts and what impressions shall be reported is steadily convincing every organized group of people that whether it wishes to secure publicity or to avoid it, the exercise of discretion cannot be left to the reporter. It is safer to hire a press agent who stands between the group and the newspapers. Having hired him, the temptation to exploit his strategic position is very great. [M]any of the direct channels to news have been closed and the information for the public is first filtered through publicity agents. The great corporations have them, the banks have them, the railroads have them, all the organizations of business and of social and political activity have them, and they are the media through which news comes. Even statesmen have them.

Were reporting the simple recovery of obvious facts, the press agent would be little more than a clerk. But since, in respect to most of the big topics of news, the facts are not simple, and not at all obvious, but subjects of choice and opinion, it is natural that everyone should wish to make his own choice of facts for the newspapers to print. The publicity man does that. And in doing it, he certainly saves the reporter much trouble, by presenting him a clear picture of a situation out of which he might otherwise make neither head nor tail. But it follows that the picture which the publicity man makes for the reporter is the one he wishes the public to see. He is censor and propagandist, responsible only to his employers, and to the whole truth responsible only as it accords with the employer's conception of his own interests.

The development of the publicity man is a clear sign that the facts of modern life do not spontaneously take a shape in which they can be known. They must be given a shape by somebody, and since in the daily routine reporters cannot give a shape to facts, and since there is little disinterested organization of intelligence, the need for some formulation is being met by the interested parties.

The good press agent understands that the virtues of his cause are not news, unless they are such strange virtues that they jut right out of the routine of life. So if the publicity man wishes free publicity he has to start something. He arranges a stunt: obstructs the traffic, teases the police, somehow manages to entangle his client or his cause with an event that is already news.

All the subtler and deeper truths are very unreliable truths. They involve judgments about standards of living, productivity, human rights that are endlessly debatable in the absence of exact record and quantitative analysis. And as long as these do not exist, the run of news will tend, as Emerson said, quoting from Isocrates, "to make of moles [*sic*] mountains, and of mountains moles [*sic*]." Where there is no constitutional procedure, and no expert sifting of evidence and the claims, the fact that is sensational to the reader is the fact that almost every journalist will seek. And so to try disputes by an appeal through the newspapers puts a burden upon newspapers and readers which they cannot and ought not to carry. As long as real law and order do not exist, the bulk of the news will, unless consciously and courageously corrected, work against those who have no lawful and orderly method of asserting themselves. The bulletins from the scene of action will note the trouble that arose from the assertion, rather than the reasons which led to it. The reasons are intangible.

Every newspaper when it reaches the reader is the result of a whole series of selections as to what items shall be printed, in what position they shall be printed, how much space each shall occupy, what emphasis each shall have. There are no objective standards here. There are conventions. Take two newspapers published in the same city on the same morning. The headline of one reads: "Britain pledges aid to Berlin against French aggression; France openly backs Poles." The headline of the second is "Mrs. Stillman's Other Love." Which you prefer is a matter of taste, but not entirely a matter of the editor's taste.

It is a matter of his judgment as to what will absorb the half hour's attention a certain set of readers will give to his newspaper. Now the problem of securing attention is by no means equivalent to displaying the news in the perspective laid down by religious teaching or by some form of ethical culture. It is a problem of provoking feeling in the reader, of inducing him to feel a sense of personal identification with the stories he is reading. News which does not offer this opportunity to introduce oneself into the struggle which it depicts cannot appeal to a wide audience. The audience must participate in the news, much as it participates in the drama, by personal identification. Just as everyone holds his breath when the heroine is in danger, as he helps Babe Ruth swing his bat, so in subtler form the reader enters into the news. In order that he shall enter he must find a familiar foothold in the story, and this is supplied to him by the use of stereotypes. They tell him that if an association of plumbers is called a "combine" it is appropriate to develop his hostility; if it is called a "group of leading business men" the cue is for favorable reaction.

It is in a combination of these elements that the power to create opinion resides. Editorials reinforce. Sometimes in a situation that on the news pages is too confusing to permit of identification, they give the reader a clue by means of which he engages himself. A clue he must have if, as most of us must, he is to seize the news in a hurry. A suggestion of some sort he demands, which tells him, so to speak, where he, a man conceiving himself to be such and such a person, shall integrate his feelings with the news he reads. This is the plight of the reader of the general news. If he is to read it at all he must be interested, that is

to say, he must enter into the situation and care about the outcome. But if he does that he cannot rest in a negative, and unless independent means of checking the lead given him by his newspaper exists, the very fact that he is interested may make it difficult to arrive at that balance of opinions which may most nearly approximate the truth. The more passionately involved he becomes, the more he will tend to resent not only a different view, but a disturbing bit of news. That is why many a newspaper finds that, having honestly evoked the partisanship of its readers, it can not easily, supposing the editor believes the facts warrant it, change position. If a change is necessary, the transition has to be managed with the utmost skill and delicacy. Usually a newspaper will not attempt so hazardous a performance. It is easier and safer to have the news of that subject taper off and disappear, thus putting out the fire by starving it.

As we begin to make more and more exact studies of the press, much will depend upon the hypothesis we hold. If we assume that news and truth are two words for the same thing, we shall, I believe, arrive nowhere. We shall prove that on this point the newspaper lied. We shall prove that on that point the critics of the press lied. We shall demonstrate that the critics of the press lied when they said that somebody lied, and that somebody lied when they said the critics of the press lied. We shall vent our feelings, but we shall vent them into air.

The hypothesis which seems to me the most fertile is that news and truth are not the same thing, and must be clearly distinguished. The function of news is to signalize an event, the function of truth is to bring to light the hidden facts, to set them into relation with each other, and make a picture of reality on which men can act. Only at those points, where social conditions take recognizable and measurable shape, do the body of truth and the body of news coincide. That is a comparatively small part of the whole field of human interest. In this sector, and only in this sector, the tests of the news are sufficiently exact to make the charges of perversion or suppression more than a partisan judgment. The absence of these exact tests accounts, I think, for the character of the profession, as no other explanation does. There is a very small body of exact knowledge, which it requires no outstanding ability or training to deal with. The rest is in the journalist's own discretion. Once he departs from the region where it is definitely recorded at the County Clerk's office that John Smith has gone into bankruptcy, all fixed standards disappear. The story of why John Smith failed, his human frailties, the analysis of the economic conditions on which he was shipwrecked, all of this can be told in a hundred different ways. There is no discipline in applied psychology, as there is a discipline in medicine, engineering, or even law, which has authority to direct the journalist's mind when he passes from the news to the vague realm of truth. There are no canons to direct his own mind, and no canons that coerce the reader's judgment or the publisher's. His version of the truth is only his version. And the more he understands his own weaknesses, the more ready he is to admit that where there is no objective test, his own opinion is in some vital measure constructed out of his own stereotypes, according to his own code, and by the urgency of his own interest. He knows that he is seeing the world through subjective lenses.

The press is not constituted to furnish from one edition to the next the amount of knowledge which the democratic theory of public opinion demands. . . . If the newspapers are to be charged with the duty of translating the whole public life of mankind, so that every adult can arrive at an opinion on every topic, they fail, they are bound to fail, in any future one can conceive they will continue to fail. It is not possible to assume that a world, carried on by division of labor and distribution of authority, can be governed by universal opinions in the whole population. Unconsciously the theory sets up the single reader as theoretically omni-competent, and puts upon the press the burden of accomplishing whatever representative government, industrial organization, and diplomacy have failed to accomplish. Acting upon everybody for thirty minutes in twenty-four hours, the press is asked to create a mystical force called Public Opinion that will take up the slack in public institutions. The press has often mistakenly pretended that it could do just that. It has at great moral cost to itself, encouraged a democracy, still bound to its original premises, to expect newspapers to supply spontaneously for every organ of government, for every social problem, the machinery of information which these do not normally supply themselves. Institutions, having failed to furnish themselves with instruments of knowledge, have become a bundle of "problems," which the population as a whole, reading the press as a whole, is supposed to solve.

The press, in other words, has come to be regarded as an organ of direct democracy, charged on a much wider scale, and from day to day, with the function often attributed to the initiative, referendum, and recall. The Court of

Public Opinion, open day and night, is to lay down the law for everything all the time. It is not workable. And when you consider the nature of news, it is not even thinkable. For the news, as we have seen, is precise in proportion to the precision with which the event is recorded. Unless the event is capable of being named, measured, given shape, made specific, it either fails to take on the character of news, or it is subject to the accidents and prejudices of observation.

Therefore, on the whole, the quality of the news about modern society is an index of its social organization. The better the institutions, the more all interests concerned are formally represented, the more issues are disentangled, the more objective criteria are introduced, the more perfectly an affair can be represented as news. At its best the press is a servant and guardian of institutions; at its worst it is a means by which a few exploit social disorganization to their own ends. In the degree to which institutions fail to function, the unscrupulous journalist can fish in troubled waters, and the conscientious one must gamble with uncertainties.

The press is no substitute for institutions. It is like the beam of a searchlight that moves restlessly about, bringing one episode and then another out of darkness into vision. Men cannot do the work of the world by this light alone. They cannot govern society by episodes, incidents, and eruptions. It is only when they work by a steady light of their own, that the press, when it is turned upon them, reveals a situation intelligible enough for a popular decision. The trouble lies deeper than the press, and so does the remedy. It lies in social organization based on a system of analysis and record, and in all the corollaries of that principle; in the abandonment of the theory of the omnicompetent citizen, in the decentralization of decision, in the coordination of decision by comparable record and analysis. If at the centers of management there is a running audit, which makes work intelligible to those who do it, and those who superintend it, issues when they arise are not the mere collisions of the blind. There too, the news is uncovered for the press by a system of intelligence that is also a check upon the press.

That is the radical way. For the troubles of the press, like the troubles of representative government, be it territorial or functional, like the troubles of industry, be it capitalist, cooperative, or communist, go back to a common source: to the failure of self-governing people to transcend their casual experience and their prejudice, by inventing, creating, and organizing a machinery of knowledge. It is because they are compelled to act without a reliable picture of the world, that governments, schools, newspapers, and churches make such small headway against the more obvious failings of democracy, against violent prejudice, apathy, preference for the curious trivial as against the dull important, and the hunger for sideshows and threelegged calves. This is the primary defect of popular government, a defect inherent in its traditions, and all its other defects can, I believe, be traced to this one.

EXERCISES

1. This exercise works well with a small group. Follow one story of national or international significance for a week or more in two or more major metropolitan or national dailies, such as the *New York Times, Washington Post, Los Angeles Times,* or *Wall Street Journal.* Note any areas of significant uniformity in the coverage. Note also any differences. Identify the sources of authoritative attribution. Who in other words, do the reporters quote or reference to establish facts? What significant patterns, if any, do you notice? What significance do you attach to such patterns?

2. According to some analyses and hypotheses, the Internet promises to revitalize democratic electoral politics. In order to evaluate this idea, we must examine how political causes and candidates are presented to the electorate over the Internet, as well as how easily the average citizen can find political information on the Internet. In this exercise, pick an issue or contest of local political significance and conduct an Internet search. What sort of information do you find? Do you believe the quantity and quality of information adequately informs you as a voter? How does Internet information compare with information available via other mass media? Repeat the exercise with an issue or contest of national political significance.

3.3 THE "FREE PRESS" AND PROPAGANDA Noam Chomsky is a unique figure in American intellectual life. He is known around the world for his revolutionary work in linguistics and as a philosopher of language. Much as Einstein's theory of relativity defined modern physics and Freud's theory of the unconscious defined modern psychology, Chomsky's theory—that all human languages are based on common deep structural regularities that all of us are naturally equipped to learn—is generally regarded as the defining point of departure for modern linguistics. In addition, over the course of his nearly fifty-year career, he has spoken out regularly on issues of global politics and power, becoming equally well known as one of the most tenacious and formidable public dissidents currently working anywhere in the world.

As an American citizen, Chomsky makes it his special responsibility to focus on American foreign policy. His work in this area has matured into a sustained and deeply coherent critical analysis of American power and its application in world affairs throughout the twentieth century. A crucial aspect of Chomsky's political work is his critique of press performance in the United States. In totalitarian regimes, where the state owns, operates, and otherwise controls the media, and where no constitutional guarantees of freedom of expression exist such as our First Amendment, we see the media function as an instrument of state propaganda. By contrast, in democratic societies such as ours, we generally see the media as an independent counterweight to official power. Surprisingly, Chomsky argues that in democratic societies such as ours the mass media function as a propaganda system—a sophisticated instrument of indoctrination that serves state power—indeed, a more subtle and effective system of indoctrination than dreamed of in even the most totalitarian regimes.

To summarize Chomsky's analysis, a totalitarian system can control the population by enforcing obedience through the threat and use of violence. An official ministry of truth will provide the only publicly available version of information. For all practical political purposes it won't matter whether you *believe* the official propaganda line or not, as long as you don't say anything against it in public; in a totalitarian framework you can pretty much *think* whatever you want *privately,* as long as you *behave publicly* in the prescribed manner—as long as you *do* as you're told. In a democracy, where people can't be punished for public dissent, the only way to control the population would be to control what people *think,* and that takes more sophisticated techniques of indoctrination than the brute force typical in repressive totalitarian regimes.

In democratic indoctrination, the media tacitly assume certain basic premises crucial to the interests of those in power. Vigorous debate is tolerated and even promoted in the media, but always within the framework of these basic assumptions. In effect, all *meaningful* dissent is confined within a framework defined by the interests in power. It becomes harder for people to notice that indoctrination is taking place because to do so they must think outside the framework of these basic assumptions. If you do happen to think outside the framework of these basic assumptions, you can express your ideas and your questions, but these ideas and questions get effectively marginalized, as "meaningless." They get left out of the current public debate in the media and are excluded from any actual policy-making deliberations, because of all the vigorous public debate going on *within* the framework of the basic assumptions.

Taking this as a working hypothesis, Chomsky's argument, sustained over a series of books, has been to apply it to representative cases and episodes of media coverage of foreign policy and international affairs, finding more and more confirmation as he goes. As an introduction to this argument, we've selected Chomsky's comparison of one such episode—one that took place in the Soviet press—with the patterns of U.S. press coverage of the Vietnam War.

QUESTIONS FOR STUDY AND DISCUSSION:

1. How would Chomsky rate the American press's performance in covering American foreign policy in terms of the functions prescribed for the press by Lippmann?

2. Formulate, either on your own or in discussion with your classmates, a well-focused general ethical principle on which Chomsky's critique of western "brainwashing under freedom" is based. On the basis of what simple ethical principle does Chomsky identify a "systematic bias" in American mainstream coverage of American foreign policy? Do you think Chomsky sets a fair and reasonable standard for American press performance?

3. Chomsky's critique of the American press sounds so "radical" that it makes immediate sense to try refuting it by example. See if you and your classmates can come up with a counter-example—in other words, an example in which American press performance has risen to meet the standard Chomsky sets.

1984: Orwell's and Ours[5]

NOAM CHOMSKY

[A]s far as I'm concerned the primary ethical question that arises with regard to the news media has to do, very simply, with the question of truth. That is, to what extent do the media present the world to us with factual accuracy, with comprehensiveness? What kind of selectivity is there? What sort of interpretation takes place? Is there analysis that is honest and free of subordination to external power? My main interest is international affairs. Here I think very serious questions arise, not about the accuracy of reporting what is observed, but rather about the selection, interpretation, and reshaping over the years. In this respect, I think we find a systematic bias which is sufficiently severe so as to call into question the very concept of a free press.

I think it's useful to have a standard of comparison for reference, and so, to begin with, I'd like to comment briefly on an example which is taken from a totalitarian state that does not even have a formal commitment to the concept of press freedom—namely, the Soviet Union. I'd like to recall to you a rather remarkable event of last May. A Soviet newscaster, Vladimir Danchev, denounced the Russian war in Afghanistan over Moscow state radio in five successive programs running over a week. He called on the rebels "not to lay down their arms," and to fight against the Soviet "invasion" of their country. Now the Western press was overwhelmed with admiration, and rightly so, for his startling departure from what the *New York Times* called "the official propaganda line." Another *Times* commentator wrote that Danchev had "revolted against the standards of doublethink and newspeak." In Paris, a prize was established in honor of Danchev to be given to "a journalist who fights for the right to be informed." Danchev was taken off the air after a week and sent to a psychiatric hospital. He was returned to work in December after psychiatric treatment, and a Russian official was quoted in the *Times* as saying "he was not punished, because a sick man cannot be punished." This event was widely covered here and is considered to have afforded a glimpse into the world of 1984. And Danchev's act was justly regarded as a triumph of the human spirit—a refusal to be cowed by totalitarian violence—which is perfectly correct.

What was remarkable about Danchev's action was not simply that he protested against the Russian invasion but that he referred to the Russian invasion as "an invasion." In Soviet theology there is no such event in history as the Russian invasion of Afghanistan. Rather what there is is a "Soviet defense of Afghanistan"—against "terrorists," "bandits," they call them, supported from abroad. The USSR protests that it was invited in, and in a certain technical sense that's true, but as the London *Economist* proclaimed grandly with respect to that claim: "An invader is an invader unless invited in by a government with some claim to legitimacy,"—which is fair enough. Only in Orwellian newspeak can one regard such aggression as defense against externally supported terrorism.

Implicit in the press coverage of the Danchev incident was a certain note of self-congratulation—that is, "it couldn't happen here." Certainly no Danchevs are sent to psychiatric hospitals in the United States for calling an invasion an "invasion." But we might ask a little further as to why exactly that's the case.

One possibility is that the question just doesn't arise, because, statistical error aside, there simply are no Danchevs here. That is, journalists and other intellectuals are so subservient to the doctrinal system that they can't even perceive that "an invader is an invader unless invited in by a government with a claim to legitimacy," when it's the United States that is an invader. If this were the case, it would be a stage beyond what Orwell imagined, a stage beyond what Soviet totalitarianism has achieved. Now the question I'd like to raise is whether this is merely an abstract possibility or an uncomfortably accurate assessment of our own world.

Well, consider the following facts. In 1961–62 the U.S. Air Force began a systematic heavy bombardment and defoliation of South Vietnam—the first direct attack by the United States against South Vietnam. This was part of a campaign to drive several million people into concentration camps, which we called "strategic hamlets," where they would be surrounded by barbed wire and armed guards and "protected," as we called it, from the guerrillas whom they were voluntarily supporting. They were protected, in other words, from what we called the "Vietcong," which was, as everyone recognized, the southern branch of the Vietminh—the anti-French resistance. Now, this is what we call "aggression"—an "invasion"—when it's conducted by some official enemy. The

American attack against South Vietnam at that point was directed against the rural population, about 85% of the population. We recognized, incidentally, that the "Vietcong" had *very* heavy support. Our own estimate was about 50% of the population, which is a good deal more than George Washington could have claimed. As to the GVN, the government that, theoretically invited us in, *that* was regarded by American government analysts as a creation of the United States. It had no legitimacy, and we recognized that it had virtually no popular support; in fact its leadership was regularly overthrown by U.S.-backed coups when it was feared that they might negotiate with the enemy. Before the outright U.S. invasion of 1962, there had been a very heavy attack against the South Vietnamese population carried out by what was in effect a U.S. mercenary army, which had about as much legitimacy as the Afghan army today. The United States invaders continued to block all efforts at negotiations and political settlement, regularly overthrowing the government that we had installed because it seemed to be moving towards negotiations. And in 1964 the invaders, the United States, began preparations for a vast escalation of the war against the South, and also, combined with it an attack against North Vietnam, at the same time beginning an invasion of Laos and later extending the war to Cambodia.

For the past 22 years now, I've been searching in vain for a single reference in mainstream journalism or scholarship to any such event as an "American invasion of South Vietnam," or American "aggression" in South Vietnam. In the American doctrinal system there is no such event. What there is, is a "defense of South Vietnam against terrorists supported from abroad." In other words, there simply is no Danchev in the United States, although in this case it took no courage at all to tell the truth, simply honesty. You wouldn't really be sent to a psychiatric hospital.

Even at the peak of opposition to the American war against South Vietnam and later the rest of Indochina, only a miniscule portion of the intelligentsia opposed the war on grounds of principle, that is, on grounds that aggression is wrong. Most came to oppose the war well after leading business circles did, and on the same grounds, namely, on what were called "pragmatic grounds"—that is, it just was costing too much. It's worth noting, incidentally, that popular attitudes were rather different. As recently as 1982, over 70% of the population, according to Gallup polls, regarded the war not simply as a mistake but as "fundamentally wrong and immoral." That's 72% of the general population. A much lower percentage of "opinion leaders" and virtually none of the articulate intelligentsia hold this view. Popular attitudes constitute a problem which has a technical name: it's called the "Vietnam syndrome" in American political discourse.

Now, facts such as these should give us pause, if we're interested in the press. How was such astonishing subservience to the doctrinal system achieved? And it *is* astonishing—22 years and we are unable to call an invasion an "invasion." No Danchev here.

We can begin to understand how it works by looking at the nature of the debate that was carried out between people called "doves" and "hawks" during the Vietnam war. The "hawks" were people like journalist Joseph Alsop, who thought that with sufficient dedication we could win. The "doves" were people like Arthur Schlesinger, who thought that we probably couldn't win even with sufficient dedication, but who added, in one of his dovish books, for which he was highly praised and regarded as an anti-war leader: "We all pray that Mr. Alsop is right." In other words, he took for granted that, of course if we *can* win in this attack against South Vietnam that's fine, but he felt that we probably couldn't. That makes him a "dove." Anthony Lake, who was such a critic of the war that he resigned from the government upon the Cambodia invasion and who is considered a leading dove, wrote recently that the doves considered the war "a hopeless cause"; that was his phrase. And everyone agrees that the war was "a failed crusade," undertaken for motives that were "noble" though "illusory," and with "the loftiest intentions." These are the words of Stanley Karnow in his recent best-selling companion volume to the PBS series, which is highly regarded for its critical candor.

Now, it's striking that there *is* a position that's omitted from the debate between the hawks and the doves—namely, the position of the peace movement, the position, in fact, which is held by 72% of the American people even today, and by more at that time. That's the position that aggression is wrong. You know, that maybe we could win but we didn't want to win. We wanted to prevent the victory, and, in fact, if you think about it for a minute, it's obvious that the peace movement position is eliminated from the debate between the hawks and the doves. If the peace movement thought that the war was a "hopeless cause," as the official doves claim, then what was the point of protesting? What was the point of protesting and in fact suffering the costs, which were not at all minimal? The consequences of that protest, the costs, were often severe. The fact is that the position of the peace movement, which in fact is the position of the majority of the population, was that the war was fundamentally wrong and immoral; not that it was a "hopeless cause." But that position doesn't enter into the debate as it's framed by the establishment media, and scholarship is exactly the same.

Now all of this illustrates the genius of what has sometimes been called "brainwashing under freedom." In a totalitarian state, it's required only that official doctrine be obeyed; but in a democratic system of thought control more is required. It's thought to be necessary to take over the entire spectrum of opinion, the entire spectrum of discussion, so that nothing can be thinkable apart from the party line, not just that it be obeyed, but that you can't even think anything else. The state propaganda is not expressed; it's rather implicit; it's presupposed. It provides the framework for discussion among people who are admitted into mainstream discussion. So the debate has been between the doves and the hawks—between the Alsops, who think that we can win, and the Schlesingers, who think we can't, though take for granted that if we *could*, that would be terrific. The position that the United States is engaged in aggression and that aggression is wrong, that has to remain unthinkable and unexpressed. The "responsible critics" make a major contribution to the cause and that's why they're tolerated, in fact, even honored.

The nature of Western systems of indoctrination was not understood by Orwell and is typically not understood by dictators who do not understand the utility for propaganda of a critical stance that incorporates the framework, the basic assumptions of official doctrine, and thereby marginalizes criticism: authentic and rational critical discussion is marginalized and eliminated. There is, incidentally, very rarely any departure from this. So, for example, I suppose the harshest critic of the war in mainstream journalism was Anthony Lewis, and he argued that the U.S. involvement began with what he called "blundering efforts to do good"; but by 1969, he says, it was clear that it was "a disastrous mistake." And 1969 was over a year after major sectors of American business turned against the war, incidentally. There were very few academic scholars who were more critical of U.S. policy than John King Fairbank of Harvard. He gave the presidential address to the American Historical Society in December 1968, a year after the Tet offensive. There he said that we entered the war in an "excess of righteousness and disinterested benevolence," but it was a mistake to do so, as events showed.

Now there are very few dictators who can boast such total conformity to higher truths, even in the most totalitarian states. The devices that are used to ensure this kind of obedience are effective and often not very subtle.

There are thousands of examples of this sort. I doubt that any story has ever received the coverage of the downing of the KAL Flight #007 last fall. This was sure proof that the Russians are the worst barbarians since Attila the Hun and that we, therefore, have to install missiles in Germany and step up the war against Nicaragua. Well, I took a look at the *New York Times'* very densely printed index. They have *seven full pages of the index* devoted to that story in September alone. I didn't check, but I doubt that even the outbreak of the Second World War had that much coverage. In the midst of all the furor over the KAL flight, the *Times* devoted one hundred words to the following fact: UNITA, who are the "freedom fighters" supported by the U.S. and South Africa, took credit for downing an Angolan civilian jet plane, with 126 people killed. Now there were no ambiguities there: nothing was off course; this was just plain premeditated mass murder. And that deserved a hundred words and no further comment. In October of 1976, a Cuban airliner was bombed by CIA-backed terrorists, killing seventy-three civilians. In 1973 Israel downed a civilian plane lost in a sandstorm over the Suez Canal with 110 people killed. There was no protest, only editorial comments about how "no useful purpose is served by an acrimonious debate over the assignment of blame." That's the *New York Times*. Well, one could offer thousands of such examples. In fact, I've done so. These are the ways in which history is shaped in the interests of those in power.

All of this falls under the rubric of what Walter Lippman, in 1921, called the "manufacture of consent." This he described as an art which is "capable of great refinements" and will lead to a "revolution" in the practice of democracy. This art has been very much admired in the American social sciences since. For example, Harold Lasswell, a well-known academic who worked on communication, wrote in 1933 that we must avoid "democratic dogmatisms" such as the belief that people are "the best judges of their own interests." Democracy permits the voice of the peo-ple to be heard, and therefore it's the task of the intellectuals, including the media, to ensure that this voice expresses the "right opinions," that is, approves of what far-sighted leaders determine to be the right course. Propaganda, he said, is to democracy as violence is to totalitarianism: namely, the device for ensuring that the leadership can do what it wants without difficulty, and the techniques have been honed to a high art—far beyond anything Orwell dreamt of. The device of "pretended dissent," which incorporates the doctrines of the state religion and eliminates critical, rational discussion is one of the more subtle means, though simple lying and suppression of fact and other crude techniques are also highly effective and are reasonably widespread in the media, as these few examples illustrate. And there are many more.

It should be noted, incidentally, that ideological control, what in the Soviet system is called "*Agitprop*," is far more important in the democracies than it is in states that rule by violence and, therefore, it's more refined and generally more effective. There simply are no Danchevs here except at the remote margins of political debate.

For people who are seriously concerned to achieve something that could honestly be called a free press, I don't think that there can be any more urgent task than to try to come to understand the mechanisms and the practices of indoctrination. These are very easy to perceive in the totalitarian societies, where they're overt and obvious. They're much less so in the system of "brainwashing under freedom," to which we are all subjected and which all too often we serve as willing or unwitting instruments.

CASE STUDY: PROJECT CENSORED

Since 1976 communications studies students at Sonoma State University have conducted Project Censored, an annual national research project to assess press performance in terms of "newsworthiness." Each year researchers in a mass media seminar select twenty-five stories from a list of several hundred nominated by journalists, educators, librarians, and the general public as stories of national significance that failed to receive due coverage in the mainstream of both print and broadcast journalism. A panel of professional journalists and media analysts review these stories to determine the ten most under-covered stories of the year. A parallel list of top "junk-food news" stories of the year—stories that received undue attention—is also tabulated. Visit the Web site for Project Censored at http://www.projectcensored.org. Review the lists of top-ten censored stories and the junk-food-news lists for the last several years. To what extent do they confirm Chomsky's critique?

CASE STUDY: ELIAN GONZALEZ

In November 1999, five-year-old Elian Gonzalez was one of three survivors rescued off the coast of Florida in a failed for-profit refugee smuggling attempt from Cuba. The young boy immediately became a cause célèbre in the Cuban refugee community in south Florida and the focus of an international child custody battle. Elian's parents had been separated and had shared custody of Elian. The boy's mother, Elizabeth Broton Rodriguez, was among the casualties in the ill-fated refugee smuggling attempt. The boy's father, Juan Miguel Gonzalez, with the support of the Cuban government, claimed custody and demanded that Elian be returned to Cuba. Other relatives in Miami initiated asylum proceedings and United States citizenship applications on Elian's behalf. The state and federal courts, the Immigration and Naturalization Service, and the attorney general all became quickly and deeply involved, and the story was of course widely and prominently reported in all the national media. To what extent does the American mass media coverage of Elian Gonzalez's story confirm Chomsky's critique of the American press? What simple hypothetical variation(s) in the story would one need to consider to determine this?

EXERCISE

Pick a significant local political issue, contest, or story, and compare it to the coverage of national and international affairs. To what extent do the analyses and critiques of the three authors in this chapter apply to local political journalism in your community? Do you notice any significant differences between coverage of local politics in your community and mass media coverage of national and international politics? How would you account for any differences you observe?

SUGGESTED READINGS:

Bagdikian, Ben. *The Media Monopoly.* Boston: Beacon Press, 2000.

Chomsky, Noam, and Edward M. Herman. *Manufacturing Consent.* New York: Pantheon, 1988.

McChesney, Robert W. *Rich Media, Poor Democracy.* Urbana and Chicago: University of Illinois Press, 1999.

NOTES

MEDIA VALUES II: ASSESSING MEDIA PERFORMANCE

THE POLITICAL ECONOMY OF THE MASS MEDIA

1. Copyright © Ben H. Bagdikian, author of *The Media Monopoly.* Transcribed from the proceedings of the 10th International Conference on Critical Thinking and Educational Reform at Sonoma State University, August, 1987, and published here for the first time by permission of the author.

THE TRUTH, PUBLIC OPINION, AND THE NATURE OF NEWS

2. Walter Lippmann, *Public Opinion* (New York: Free Press, 1922), 3–20, 214–30. Reprinted with the permission of Scribner, a Division of Simon & Schuster from *Public Opinion* by Walter Lippman. Copyright © 1922 by Walter Lippman, renewed 1950 by Walter Lippman.

3. William James, *Principles of Psychology*, vol. 2, 638.

4. John L. Given, *Making a Newspaper,* 57.

1984: ORWELL'S AND OURS

5. Transcribed from an address before the Northwest Broadcast News Association in Minneapolis, MN, February 24, 1984, published in *The Thoreau Quarterly* vol. 16, 1984. Copyright © 1984 by *The Thoreau Quarterly.* Reprinted by the kind permission of the University of Minnesota Department of Philosophy.

4

ETHICS AND ADVERTISING

*... the core tendencies of a profit-driven, advertising-
supported media system [are] hypercommercialism and
denigration of journalism and public service. It's a poison
pill for democracy.*

ROBERT W. MCCHESNEY

INTRODUCTION

Media ethics, as an area of applied ethics, began as an extension of journalism's professional ethics, for many years a course taught in graduate schools of journalism. Media ethics starts with the traditional concerns of journalism ethics—the responsibilities and liabilities of working journalists and of the journalistic institutions for and within which they work. The subject has expanded to include the wide variety of mass media through which journalism today is transmitted and received and all other programming—entertainment, the arts, advertising—communicated through these same mass media.

Thus far, we have explored the ethics of information within the conceptual framework of political theory—the nature, construction, and distribution of power in society. Journalism's crucial political role as an institution has led to the traditional assumption that journalism ethics, too, is best examined within the framework of political theory. As we now broaden the scope of our inquiry, we will also be broadening our conceptual framework to include economics—the nature, construction, and distribution of wealth. This broadening reflects the crucial role that business has played in the development of the mass media, which constitute the "delivery system" for journalism.

Wealth and power are, of course, closely related, but it is important—in theory and in practice—not to confuse or equate them. The central concept of freedom itself is subject to confusion based on its ambiguous usage. In the Western world of the

136

industrialized democracies, but especially in the United States of America, we are encouraged throughout public discourse to regard freedom as central and essential to both our political (democratic) and our economic (free-market) systems. This tends to obscure a fundamental distinction between democracy in political theory and free-market capitalism in economic theory. Remember that political theory is about power, and economics is about wealth.

Democracy says that power is held "by the people" *collectively as a group* and distributed or shared *equally* among them *as individuals.* One person, one vote. This distribution of power is designed to secure the maximum conditions of freedom, or liberty, to each individual, consistent with respect for the individual rights of others. This is precisely what our capitalist free-market economics *refuses* to say or even consider about wealth. Wealth is not to be held collectively by the people as a group. That would be "socialism." Rather, wealth is to be held privately and may be accumulated disproportionately. Free-market economic theory neither places an obligation nor even offers any encouragement to "share the wealth," certainly not equally among all members of society. This distinction is crucial for media ethics, because it allows us to recognize and consider the possibility that democratic principles that limit and distribute political power may be at cross purposes with and even subverted by familiar economic arrangements. If we failed to recognize the distinction between economics and democracy, many of the questions raised in this chapter would be unintelligible or at least deeply confusing.

Beyond this, indeed, it can be argued that what capitalism has made of the mass media—private sector, corporate, conglomerate, commercial, entertainment delivery systems—is fundamentally incompatible with the functional purposes of a free press in a democratic system.[1]

When we examine the evolution of mass media, we immediately confront advertising. As an institution, advertising has played a dominant role in shaping the mass media, from macro-levels of structure and size of the business concerns that control the media down to minute-by-minute levels of programming format, content, and composition. One important set of ethical issues has to do with the overall social utility of advertising's influence on the media—with whether advertising's role in shaping the mass media is beneficial or harmful to society. On the one hand, the business of advertising provides a level of financial support to the media, without which the media would be hard pressed to survive and function. This is the central claim in one of the standard utilitarian arguments in support of advertising as a positive social institution. On the other hand, the financial support comes with "strings attached," and so counterarguments tend to look critically at the trade-offs that the media in particular and society as a whole must make for this massive subsidy.

Besides advertising's influence on mass media behavior and content, advertising has become a large and significant programming category in its own right. Not only is there a lot of it, but some of it provides entertainment value that competes pretty successfully with regular programming. Some ads (for example, Budweiser beer's the Louis the Lizard ads) are at least as funny as a lot of the situation comedy shows on television in recent years. Entertaining or not, advertising certainly occupies a large share of public attention. However entertaining advertising may be, its primary intended function is to encourage commerce, so it is designed to function as persuasive discourse. In this connection another set of ethical issues arises, having to do with deception and manipulation. When we look closely and carefully, many advertising stratagems seem, from at least some vantage points, to be, . . . well, . . . less than completely forthright. By what moral and ethical standards should we measure and assess advertising strategies and tactics? And if some advertising strategies and tactics should turn out to be morally questionable, what sort of regulations ought to govern advertising? How might such regulations be enforced without threatening principles of free speech and expression? In this chapter's readings we will examine these questions.

4.1 THE SUBTEXT OF ADVERTISING We begin this chapter with an essay by an advertising critic. Just as Gene Siskel and Pauline Kael are movie critics, and Clement Greenberg and Arthur Danto are art critics, Leslie Savan is an advertising critic. She publishes a regular column, "Op Ad," in the *Village Voice*, for which she has twice been a finalist for a Pulitzer Prize in criticism. In 1994 she published a collection of her commentaries in a book entitled *The Sponsored Life: Ads, TV, and American Culture*. The following selection is from the introduction.

Because Savan writes as a critic and not as a philosopher, and writes for a general audience rather than an academic one, she does not explicitly theorize her critique of advertising. Her views about advertising ethics are in no way veiled or obscured, but her answers to the main ethical questions of central concern in this chapter are mostly implied in and by her commentary. To integrate this reading into an instructive exercise, we recommend the following as study and discussion questions:

QUESTIONS FOR STUDY AND DISCUSSION

1. One important set of ethical issues addresses whether and how much advertising's presence benefits and/or harms society. As you read the following essay, highlight Savan's indications of her answer. How would you summarize Savan's assessment of the overall social utility of advertising?
2. Another important set of ethical issues regards advertising strategies and tactics. As you read the following essay, highlight specific advertising strategies and tactics Savan identifies. How would you characterize her assessment of each of these strategies and tactics? On what criteria or basis of principle might she ground these assessments?

THE BRIBED SOUL[2]

L E S L I E   S A V A N

Television-watching Americans—that is, just about *all* Americans—see approximately 100 TV commercials a day. In that same 24 hours they also see a host of print ads, billboard signs, and other corporate messages slapped onto every available surface, from the fuselages of NASA rockets right down to the bottom of golf holes and the inside doors of restroom stalls. Studies estimate that, counting all the logos, labels, and announcements, some 16,000 ads flicker across an individual's consciousness daily.

Advertising now infects just about every organ of society, and wherever advertising gains a foothold it tends to slowly take over, like a vampire or a virus. When television broadcasting began about 50 years ago, the idea of a network that would air nothing but commercials was never seriously considered, not even when single-sponsor shows were produced straight out of the sponsor's ad agency. But today, by the grace of cable, we have several such channels, including MTV, stylistically the most advanced programming on the air, and FYI, a proposed new channel that would run only ads—infomercials, home-shopping shows, regular-length commercials, and, for a real treat, programs of "classic" ads. Similarly, product placement in the movies started small, with the occasional Tab showing up in a star's hand, but now it's grown big enough to eat the whole thing. In its 1993 futuristic thriller *Demolition Man,* Warner Brothers not only scattered the usual corporate logos throughout the sets, but it also rewrote the script so that the only fast-food chain to survive the "franchise wars" of the 20th century was Taco Bell—which, in return, promoted the movie in all its outlets.

Even older, far statelier cultural institutions have had their original values hollowed out and replaced by ad values, leaving behind the merest fossil of their founders' purpose. Modernist masters enjoy art museum blockbusters only when they can be prominently underwritten by an oil company or a telecommunications giant; new magazines are conceived not on the basis of their editorial content but on their ability to identify potential advertisers and groom their copy to fit marketing needs. In the process, the function of sponsored institutions is almost comically betrayed. The exotic bug exhibit at the Smithsonian Museum's new O. Orkin Insect Zoo, for example, opens with the red diamond logo of Orkin Pest Control and displays various little beasties, ever so subtly planting the suggestion that if they were to escape their glass cages you'd know who to call. Though the Smithsonian would never be so crass as to actually recommend Orkin's services, it is crass enough to never once mention in its exhibits the dangers of pesticides.

As for those television-watching Americans, hit on by those 16,000 paid (and tax-deductible) messages a day, they're even more vulnerable than their institutions. Most admakers understand that in order to sell to you they have to know your desires and dreams better than you may know them yourself, and they've tried to reduce that understanding to a science. Market research, in which psychologists, polling organizations, trends analysts, focus group leaders, "mall-intercept" interviewers, and the whole panoply of mass communications try to figure out what will make you buy, has become a $2.5 billion annual business growing at a healthy clip of about 4.2 percent a year (after adjustment for inflation). Yet this sophisticated program for the study of the individual consumer is only a starter kit for the technological advances that will sweep through the advertising-industrial complex in the 1990s. Today, the most we can do when another TV commercial comes on—and we are repeatedly told that this is our great freedom—is to switch channels. But soon technology will take even that tiny tantrum of resistance and make it "interactive," providing advertisers with information on the exact moment we became bored—vital data that can be crunched, analyzed, and processed into the next set of ads, the better to zap-proof *them.*

Impressive as such research may be, the real masterwork of advertising is the way it uses the techniques of art to seduce the human soul. Virtually all of modern experience now has a sponsor, or at least a sponsored accessory, and there is no human emotion or concern— love, lust, war, childhood innocence, social rebellion, spiritual enlightenment, even disgust with advertising—that cannot be reworked into a sales pitch. The transcendent look in a bride's eyes the moment before she kisses her groom turns into a promo for Du Pont. The teeth-gnashing humiliation of an office rival becomes an inducement to switch to AT&T.

In short, we're living the sponsored life. From Huggies to Maalox, the necessities and little luxuries of an American's passage through this world are provided and promoted by one advertiser or another. The sponsored life is born when commercial culture sells our own experiences back to us. It grows as those experiences are then reconstituted inside us, mixing the most intimate processes of individual thought with commercial values, rhythms, and expectations. It has often been said by television's critics that TV doesn't deliver products to viewers but that viewers themselves are the *real* product, one that TV delivers to its advertisers. True, but the symbiotic relationship between advertising and audience goes deeper than that. The viewer who lives the sponsored life— and that is most of us to one degree or the other—is slowly re-created in the ad's image.

Inside each "consumer," advertising's all-you-can-eat, all-the-time, all-dessert buffet produces a build-up of mass-produced stimuli, all hissing and sputtering to get out. Sometimes they burst out as sponsored speech, as when we talk in the cadences of sitcom one-liners, imitate Letterman, laugh uproariously at lines like "I've fallen and I can't get up," or mouth the words of familiar commercials, like the entranced high school student I met in a communication class who moved his lips with the voiceover of a Toyota spot. Sometime they slip out as sponsored dress, as when white suburban kids don the baggy pants and backward baseball caps they see on MTV rappers. Sometimes they simply come out as sponsored equations, as when we attribute "purity" and "honesty" to clear products like Crystal Pepsi or Ban's clear deodorant.

To lead the sponsored life you don't really have to do anything. You don't need to have a corporate sponsor as the museums or the movies do. You don't even have to buy anything—though it helps, and you will. You just have to live in America and share with the nation, or at least with your mall-intercept cohorts, certain paid-for expectations and values, rhythms and reflexes.

Despite advertising's enormous role in our lives, most of the media feel that, like hot dogs and military budgets, advertising goes down most easily when it's unexamined. They react this way, of course, because they are sponsored. Conveyors of commercial culture are free to question nearly all of modern life except their own life-support system. This conflict of interest means that unlike "official" cultural products—films, TV shows, books, paintings, and so on—advertising finds few regular critics in the mainstream press.

When the Center for the Study of Commercialism, a well-respected, Washington, D.C.-based nonprofit group, called a press conference in 1992 to announce the results of a study that showed the press repeatedly censoring itself under direct or anticipated advertiser pressure, not a single TV or radio reporter attended, and only a few papers even mentioned it. If journalism looks at ads at all, it usually settles for soft-shoe analysis, pieces that ask, essentially, "Does this ad work?" Most newspapers are pleased to do celebrity profiles of ad directors or agencies that have a few hits on their hands (possibly the agency will direct more ad dollars the paper's way, but more importantly over the long run, such stories prove that the publication offers a "positive environment" for advertisers). Ads are usually examined only when they make "news," through scandal, product failure, or superstar megadeals, like Madonna's or Michael Jackson's with Pepsi.

The chief expectation of the sponsored life is that there will and always should be regular blips of excitement and resolution, the frequency of which is determined by money. We begin to pulse to the beat, the one-two beat, that moves most ads: problem/solution, old/new, Brand X/hero brand, desire/gratification. In order to dance to the rhythm, we adjust other expectations a little here, a little there: Our notions of what's desirable behavior, our lust for novelty, even our visions of the perfect love affair or thrilling adventure adapt to the mass consensus coaxed out by marketing. Cultural forms that don't fit these patterns tend to fade away, and eventually *everything* is commercial culture—not just the 30-second spot but the drama, news segment, stage performance, novel, magazine layout—comes to share the same insipid insistence on canned excitement and neat resolution.

What's all the excitement about? Anything and nothing. You know you've entered the commercial zone when the excitement building in you is oddly incommensurate with the content dangled before you: does a sip of Diet Coke really warrant an expensive production number celebrating the rebel prowess of "ministers who surf," "insurance agents who speed," and "people who live their life as an exclamation not an explanation"?!? Of course not. Yet through the sympathetic magic of materialism we learn how to respond to excitement: It's less important that we purchase any particular product than that we come to expect resolution *in the form of* something buyable.

The way ads have of jacking up false excitement in the name of ultimately unsatisfying purchases has given Western societies a bad case of commercial blue balls. You're hit on, say, by yet another guy on TV hawking fabric whitener, but—wait a minute—he "can't be a man" because he packs a different brand of smokes. And maybe you moan, "I can't get no, no no no. . . ."

Anyway, that's how the Rolling Stones put it in that seminal semiotic text "(I Can't Get No) Satisfaction" back in 1965. Commercials are the tinny jingles in our heads that remind us of all we've abandoned in exchange for our materially comfortable lives—real extended families, real human empathy, real rebel prowess. The result of stale promises endlessly repeated is massive frustration.

But Mick Jagger is younger than that now: Long after "Satisfaction" had dropped off the charts, the Rolling Stones became the first major band to tour for a corporate sponsor, Jovan perfumes, in 1981. By then Jagger had become a symbol of the most popular postmodern response to advertising's dominant role in our culture: the ironic reflex.

Irony has become the hallmark of the sponsored life because it provides a certain distance from the frustration inherent in commercial correctness. For some time now the people raised on television, the baby boomers and the "Generation Xers" that followed, have mentally adjusted the set, as it were, in order to convince themselves that watching is cool. They may be doing exactly what their parents do—but they do it *differently*. They take in TV with a Lettermanesque wink, and they like it when it winks back. In many cases (as Mark Crispin Miller has described it so well in *Boxed In*), the winkers have enthusiastically embraced the artifice, even the manipulativeness, of advertising as an essential paradox of modern life, a paradox that is at the crux of their own identity.

The winkers believe that by rolling their collective eyes when they watch TV they can control *it*, rather than letting it control them. But unfortunately, as a defense against the power of advertising, irony is a leaky condom—in fact, it's the same old condom that advertising brings over every night. A lot of ads have learned that to break through to the all-important boomer and Xer markets they have to be as cool, hip, and ironic as the target audience likes to think of itself as being. That requires at least the pose of opposition to commercial values. The cool commercials—I'm thinking of Nike spots, some Reeboks, most 501s, certainly all MTV promos—flatter us by saying we're too cool to fall for commercial values, and therefore cool enough to want their product.

If irony is weak armor, how do we ward off the effect of billions of words and images from our sponsors? No perfect wolfsbane exists, but I can suggest some tactics to keep in mind:

When watching, watch out. Literally. Watch as an outsider, from as far a distance as you can muster (farther even than irony)—*especially* when watching ads that flatter you for being an outsider, as more and more are doing.

Big lie, little lie. All advertising tells lies, but there are little lies and there are big lies. Little lie: This beer tastes great. Not all ads tell little lies—they're more likely to be legally actionable (while big lies by definition aren't). And many products do live up to their modest material claims: This car runs. But all ads *must* tell big lies: This car will attract babes and make others slobber in envy. Don't be shocked that ads lie—that's their job. But do try to distinguish between the two kinds of lies.

Read the box. Look not just at whether an ad's claims are false or exaggerated, but try to figure out what portion of an ad is about the culture as opposed to the product. Read the contents as you would a cereal box's: Instead of how much sugar to wheat, consider how much style to information. Not that a high ratio of sugar to wheat is necessarily more malevolent than the other way around. But it's a sure sign that they're fattening you up for the shill.

Assume no relationship between a brand and its image. Marlboro was originally sold as a woman's cigarette, and its image was elegant, if not downright prissy. It wasn't until 1955 that the Marlboro Man was invented to ride herd on all that. The arbitrary relationship between a product and its ads becomes even clearer when you realize how much advertising is created to overcome "brand parity"—a plague more troubling to marketers than bodily odors. Brand parity means that there is little or no difference between competing brands and that the best a brand can do is hire a more appealing image. When advertising works at all, it's because the public more or less believes that something serious is going on between a product and its image, as if the latter reveals intrinsic qualities of the former. Peel image off item, and you too can have more of the freedom that ads are always promising. Likewise . . .

We don't buy products, we buy the world that presents them. Over the long run, whether you actually buy a particular product is less important than that you

buy the world that makes the products seem desirable. Not so long ago a BMW or a Mercedes was required if you seriously bought the worldview that their ads conveyed. Still, buying an attitude doesn't automatically translate into product purchase. If your income precluded a BMW, you might have bought instead a Ralph Lauren polo shirt or even a Dove bar (which is how yuppie snack foods positioned themselves—as achievable class). Sure, GE wants you to buy its bulbs, but even more it wants you to buy the paternalistic, everything's-under-control world that GE seems to rule. Buying *that* will result, GE is betting, not only in more appliance sales but also in more credibility when spokesmen insist that defrauding the Pentagon is not *really* what GE is all about. That is to say . . .

The promotional is the political. Each world that commercials use to sell things comes packed with biases: Entire classes, races, and genders may be excluded for the coddling of the sponsored one. Lee Jeans' world (circa 1989) is a place where young people are hip, sexual, and wear jeans, while old people are square, non-sexual, and wear uniforms. The class and age politics here is more powerful than the Young Republicans'. There is politics in all advertising (and, more obviously, advertising in all politics). It makes sense that these two professions call what they do "campaigns."

Advertising shepherds herds of individuals. When Monty Python's mistaken messiah in *The Life of Brian* exhorts the crowd of devotees to "Don't follow me! Don't follow anyone! Think for yourselves! . . . You are all individuals!" they reply in unison, "We are all individuals!" That is advertising in a nutshell.

Advertising's most basic paradox is to say: Join us and become unique. Advertisers learned long ago that individuality sells, like sex or patriotism. The urge toward individualism is a constant in America, with icons ranging from Thomas Jefferson's yeoman farmer to the kooky girl bouncing to the jingle "I like the Sprite in you!" Commercial nonconformity always operates in the service of . . . conformity. Our system of laws and our one-man-one-vote politics may be based on individualism, but successful marketing depends on the exact opposite: By identifying (through research) the ways we are alike, it hopes to convince the largest number of people that they need the exact same product. Furthermore, in modern pop culture, we construct our individuality by the unique combination of mass-produced goods and services we buy. I sip Evian, you slug Bud Light; I drive a Geo, you gun a Ford pickup; I kick sidewalk in cowboy boots, you bop in Reeboks. Individuality is a good angle for all advertising, but it's crucial for TV commercials. There you are sitting at home, not doing anything for hours on end, but then the very box you're staring at tells you that you are different, that you are vibrantly alive, that your quest for freedom—freedom of speech, freedom of movement, freedom to do whatever you damn well choose—will not be impeded! And you can do all that, says the box, without leaving your couch.

It's the real ad. The one question I'm most often asked is, Does advertising shape who we are and what we want, or does it merely reflect back to us our own emotions and desires? As with most nature-or-nurture questions, the answer is both. The real ad in any campaign is controlled neither by admakers nor adwatch-

ers; it exists somewhere between the TV set and the viewer, like a huge hairball, collecting bits of material and meaning from both. The real ad isn't even activated until viewers hand it their frustrations from work, the mood of their love life, their idiosyncratic misinterpretations, and most of all, I think, their everyday politics. On which class rung do they see themselves teetering? Do they ever so subtly flinch when a different race comes on TV? In this way, we all co-produce the ads we see. Agency people are often aghast that anyone would find offensive meanings in their ads because "that's not what we intended." Intention has little to do with it. Whatever they meant, once an ad hits the air it becomes public property. That, I think, is where criticism should aim—at the fluctuating, multi-meaning thing that floats over the country, reflecting us as we reflect it.

Follow the flattery. I use the word "flattery" a lot. When trying to understand what an ad's really up to, following the flattery is as useful as following the money. You'll find the ad's target market by asking who in any 30-second drama is being praised for qualities they probably don't possess. When a black teenager plays basketball with a white baby boomer for Canada Dry, it's not the black youth that's being pandered to. It's white boomers—the flattery being that they're cool enough to be accepted by blacks. Ads don't even have to put people on stage to toady up to them. Ads can flatter by style alone, as do all the spots that turn on hyper-quick cuts or obscure meanings, telling us—uh, *some* of us— that we're special enough to get it.

We participate in our own seduction. Once properly flattered, all that's left is to close the sale—and only we can do that. Not only do we co-produce the ads, but we're our own best voiceover—that little inner voice that ultimately decides to buy or not. The best ads tell us we're cool *coolly*—in the other meaning of the word. McLuhan used to say that a cool medium, like television, involves us more by not giving us everything; the very spaces between TV's flickering dots are filled in by our central nervous system. He refers to "the involvement of the viewer with the completion of 'closing' of the TV image." This is seduction: We're stirred to a state so that not only do we close the image but, given the right image at the right time, we open our wallet. All television is erotically engaged in this way, but commercials are TV's G-spot. The smart ads always hold back a little to get us to lean forward a little. Some ads have become caricatures of this tease, withholding the product's name until the last second to keep you wondering who could possibly be sponsoring such intrigue. The seduction may continue right to the cash register, where one last image is completed: you and product together at last. It'd be nice to say that now that you've consumed, you've climaxed, and everyone can relax. But sponsorship is a lifetime proposition that must be renewed every day.

EXERCISE: DECODING ADSPEAK

One of the most creative and witty people we know owns a small media production company and advertising agency. In his own promotional package he includes a list of advertising cliches complete with translations. Here is a portion of the list:

THIS CLICHÉ	MEANS
BEST KEPT SECRET IN TOWN!!!	business is lousy
...AND MUCH, MUCH MORE!!!	there must be some other interesting things to say, but we can't think of them
GRAND OPENING CELEBRATION!!	there'll be balloons!
SAVINGS OF UP TO 70%!!!	the big left-handed green paisley one is 70% off.
EXTRAVAGANZA!!!	there'll be balloons!!
FRIENDLY, COURTEOUS SERVICE	they'll talk to you.
PRICE-BUSTER SALE-ABRATION!!!!	there'll be balloons!!!
BUY NOW AND SAVE!	go figure
REGISTER TO WIN!	welcome to our mailing list

Now extend this list from your own experience. Look through the ads in your favorite magazine for examples of advertising clichés. For each example you find, using Savan's interpretive guidelines, figure out a suitable interpretation of what the ad really says.

4.2 ADVERTISING AND FREE-MARKET ECONOMICS We turn now to an in-depth analysis of the philosophical issues opened up by criticisms of advertising such as Savan's. The next selection is from an essay by philosopher Alan Goldman originally published in a collection entitled *Just Business: New Introductory Essays in Business Ethics.* Goldman sees ethical issues in advertising related to individual advertisers and their practices, but also to the industry as a whole. He takes the larger issues as theoretically basic, and so begins by exploring the rationalizations of advertising as an institution within the framework of free-market economics. As he does so, he goes on to consider what ethical restrictions, if any, on the conduct of individual advertisers flow logically from these rationalizations.

Fundamental to free-market economic theory is the conceptual apparatus of the eighteenth-century British utilitarian philosophers Jeremy Bentham and John Stuart Mill: first, the notion that there is the at least theoretical possibility of measuring the overall well-being of a social state of affairs ("social utility": the technical term in philosophy and economic theory for the overall well-being of a social state of affairs); second, the notion that social utility is measured by calculating—or at least estimating—the aggregate satisfactions and dissatisfactions of needs and wants of individual members of a society; and third, the notion that policies and courses of action can and should be evaluated morally by calculating and comparing the actual and probable future social utilities of competing policies and courses of action.

In this conceptual framework, then, the question of justifying an institution such as advertising boils down to this: Is society better or worse off in terms of the aggregate satisfactions and dissatisfactions of the needs and wants of the members of society as a result of there being advertising? Or, to put it in plain English: Are we happier or less happy than we would be if there were no advertising? This is, let us admit right away, not an easy question to answer. To answer it, we must figure out how many of our needs and wants are satisfied or left dissatisfied *as a result of the presence of advertising.* That's not all: we also must figure out how many of our needs and wants, whether satisfied or not, are *themselves the results of the presence of advertising.* This, then, is the central question of this chapter. (Actually, it's more a complex set of questions.) Bear in mind that although Goldman is willing to assume that advertising generates enough social utility to be "justified" in a free market, this central question remains open to debate.

Based on standard free-market arguments in support of the institution of advertising, Goldman develops ethical principles for the conduct of advertising as a business—particularly with regard to truthfulness and the use of nonrational persuasion tactics. He goes on to consider advertising as a form of speech or expression as understood in the First Amendment, and in this connection the distinction between commercial speech or expression on the one hand and political and artistic speech or expression on the other. On the basis of this distinction, and the Constitutional principle of congressional authority to regulate commerce, Goldman considers government regulation of commercial advertising and its possible effect in enforcing the proposed ethical principles.

QUESTIONS FOR STUDY AND DISCUSSION:

1. For the sake of argument, Goldman assumes that the theoretical model of the free market is a morally defensible economic system. What, according to Goldman, are the theoretical assumptions involved in the free-market economic model? What reasons can you find to challenge the assumption that the free market is a morally defensible economic system?
2. What theoretical assumptions underlie the free-market economic model, according to Goldman, and what moral constraints upon conduct of the business of advertising flow from these assumptions?
3. How do techniques of nonrational persuasion cohere within the framework of a free-market economic justification of advertising as an institution? How does Goldman defend strategies of nonrational persuasion against a general moral condemnation? Are the qualifications he proposes reasonable in your view?
4. One familiar economic justification for advertising invokes the indirect benefits advertising provides to society as a whole. What are these indirect benefits? Which of them do you consider genuinely beneficial and genuinely attributable to advertising?
5. According to Goldman, what differences between political or artistic speech and commercial discourse justify government regulation of advertising without compromising the principles of free speech and expression? How should these considerations apply to political advertising?

THE JUSTIFICATION OF ADVERTISING IN A MARKET ECONOMY[3]

ALAN GOLDMAN

The first virtue of a market economy is its efficiency in allocating economic resources, capital, and labor to satisfy collective needs and wants for products and services. In theory, maximum efficiency obtains given certain ideal conditions of pure competition. These conditions include: (1) competition within industries among firms, each of which is too small to dictate prices to the market; (2) fluidity of labor and capital; (3) perfect knowledge on the part of consumers of prices and features of various products and services; and (4) knowledge on the part of producers of consumer demand for various goods. Given such conditions, the market, through its price mechanisms, guides profit seeking producers to allocate economic resources in ways that optimize the aggregate satisfaction of demand—that is, the sum total of wants in society. Goods are distributed in turn to those with greatest demand, the degree of demand being measured by willingness to pay. The result approximates to maximization of utility, understood as the greatest sum of the satisfaction of wants over the whole society. Those goods are produced and distributed that yield the greatest surplus of value over economic costs.

The market mechanism theoretically underlying efficiency of resource allocation was first described by Adam Smith. When a certain good is under-supplied in relation to the demand for it, its price is bid upward. Consumers are willing to pay more for a product they want when it is in short supply, and pro-ducers can improve their profits by sell-ing the limited supply at a higher price. The possibility of higher profits will at-tract new resources (that is, capital and labor) to the industry, until supply is in-creased and the margin of profit falls again to approximate that of other indus-tries. Thus supply adjusts to demand. Conversely, oversupply of a good means that some of it will have to be sold at a loss, driving resources from the industry and adjusting the production downward. The tendency is toward an equilibrium at which the marginal value of all goods is equal and, taken collectively, maximal in relation to the relative social demand for the various goods.

This process is dynamic and progres-sive. At the same time as optimal effi-ciency is achieved in allocating resources so as to satisfy particular wants at partic-ular times, competition generates progress through improvement of pro-ductive techniques and processes. Each competitor is motivated to modernize production so as to increase volume and cut unit costs of products. The price a producer pays for obsolescence is being undersold by the more efficient competi-tion and thereby driven out of business. Thus the free market is theoretically effi-cient over time. It guarantees not only the most efficient use of resources in the pre-sent, but the production of more and more goods and services in the future.

A further virtue of the competitive market economy, given ideal conditions, is its maximization of individual free-doms. All transactions within this econ-omy are to be voluntary. Individuals are free to choose their occupations, in-vestors to invest where they like, and consumers to buy or refuse what is of-fered for sale. For a transaction to take place, given the ideal condition of full knowledge of its features and alterna-tives, it must be perceived as mutually beneficial to the parties involved.

If we accept this model as a morally defensible economic system, where in it can we find a place for the institution of advertising? The ideal requires relevant knowledge on the part of consumers of the existence, quality, and prices of prod-ucts, and it is unclear that advertising, at least as we know it, accomplishes this goal. Second, the model also assumes that consumer demands are given and judges the efficiency of the market by the extent to which they are satisfied. Advertising, however, sometimes aims to *create* desires in the consuming pub-lic, and it is unclear whether the satisfac-tion of these desires should likewise be counted as a gain in utility or social value. An even more fundamental diffi-culty may be explained as follows. Our model assumes that consumer demand for a product dictates prices to individual firms, which then manufacture goods until the marginal costs equal the price (that is, until no more profit can be made from additional units). But some econo-mists have argued that advertising con-tributes to conditions in which producers can control prices, by creating demand to match planned levels of supply at fixed prices. Similarly, advertising often seeks to create *consumer loyalty,* which arguably makes it more difficult for new competitors to enter the market—specifically, more expensive, since it requires extensive advertising campaigns to overcome consumer loyalty. Brand loyalty may also be inefficient in itself, since it leads consumers to perceive differences among products when there may be no real differences in quality, which might cause them to forgo savings in price among identical products, (for example chemically identical aspirin tablets), thereby diminishing maximum utility.

More recently, however, economists have taken the opposite stand on this issue. Some have argued that advertising actually facilitates entry of new competitors by allowing them to publicize their products and lure customers away from established firms.[4] The purpose of ad campaigns, it is now said, is to create brand *dis*loyalty. Campaigns are typically directed not at those who already are customers, but at potential new customers. In response to the claim that ads lead consumers to make ungrounded and costly product differentiations, it is pointed out that brand recognition and even brand loyalty create benefits for consumers as well. When shoppers can identify products and their manufacturers, the latter are pressured to maintain quality. At the same time comparison shopping is facilitated among retailers, so that they must sell within price limits.

In assessing this debate, it appears that the claims of the opposing sides may all be true, showing only that advertising produces *both* positive *and* negative effects upon competition and prices for consumers. It seems clear, first, that there have been successful advertising campaigns of both sorts, those that reinforce brand loyalty and help to retain a clientele (perhaps by reinforcing a favorable image of the brand in consumers' minds), and those that lure new customers away from established brands. Furthermore, while brand loyalty may raise successful entry costs, advertising may simultaneously ease entry for those with the capital to mount extensive campaigns. Finally, while ads may create the illusion of product differences where none exist and hence prevent choice of cheaper alternatives, brand recognition, achieved through exposure to ads, does facilitate comparison shopping among retailers. In the absence of data weighing these opposing tendencies across many industries, it seems impossible to justify or condemn advertising by its effects on the degree of competition in various product markets. There is no good reason at present, in short, for believing that advertising is inconsistent with the free market's aims of eliminating monopolies and encouraging competition.

To defend the institution of advertising against the charge that it fosters monopolistic control of particular industries is only to show that the institution *could* find a place within a free market economy, not that it *does* so, and there are any number of arguments that have been given against its place in a free market. One criticism claims that advertising is wasteful of economic resources, even when not directly harmful. If advertising does waste resources that could be used to more benefit elsewhere, perhaps the main ethical imperative for advertisers would be to do as little of it as possible or seek other professions. Of course it may be that corporations, like individuals, have a right to waste their time and energies if they so choose. It may also be that what is wasteful for the economy as a whole is not so for individual corporations seeking to gain competitive advantages. There is another answer available here as well. It is that the encouragement of product differentiation, which underlies claims of differences even when none exist, also motivates genuine changes in products and product features. While some of these too may be trivial or meaningless, cumulatively they may add up to real progress in product design. In rewarding innovation, advertising cannot help but bring about some useless changes along with beneficial ones, but the incentive it provides aims in the right economic direction in speeding progress. In allowing innovation to pay off more quickly, it also encourages investment in new techniques and products.

A different criticism is that advertising is wasteful in raising the costs and adding to the prices of products without adding value to the products themselves. This charge applies especially to "defensive strategies," in which large firms increase advertising expenditures when their competitors do so, until a standoff in overall effect is achieved. Advertising generally increases prices, one might argue, because the costs of the ad campaigns must be absorbed by consumers. But this point ignores the fact that, as an effective means of marketing or selling, advertising can lower unit costs and prices by increasing volume and speeding turnover in retail outlets. Thus once again we find opposing tendencies in the overall effects under consideration: advertising can raise prices because its costs are added to products and because it creates brand loyalty and hence fosters monopoly-like conditions; it can lower prices as a cost-effective means of marketing that can

also ease seasonal fluctuations, and because it facilitates comparison shopping by price. Some recent empirical studies indicate generally lower prices in industries after the introduction of extensive advertising.[5] This is predictable in those markets in which advertising is introduced or permitted for the first time, for products such as eyeglasses or services of professionals, for example. For most products the truth is probably that advertising, like other capital outlays, can cut unit costs by increasing volume up to a certain level of expenditure, and after that it will increase costs.

In judging the wastefulness of advertising, it must be compared to other methods of marketing goods, for example direct selling. One must keep in mind, too, that there are different forms of advertising in different contexts, some more or less wasteful than others. Defensive ad campaigns by large and well-established brands may involve less efficient use of resources than campaigns to inform consumers of genuinely new products or features. Finally, we should recognize in this context that use of resources that may be inefficient in the context of our economy operating at full capacity may not be so in contexts of less than full employment and use of other resources.

To defend the consistency of advertising with free-market competition or to answer the charge of wastefulness is only to show that the institution *could be* justified, given the free-market approach, not that it *is* justified. To show the latter one must show what social benefits derive from having the institution. Principal among the direct benefits claimed to result from advertising is the benefit of consumers' having relevant knowledge of the existence, quality, and price of products. How well advertising provides this benefit will concern us shortly. First, though, let us consider an indirect social benefit attributed to the institution of advertising: namely, that it subsidizes the media. Commercial radio and television, as well as most newspapers and magazines, could not survive without this subsidy, certainly not in the forms we know them and at the prices we are used to paying. It can be argued, then, that since these media themselves add much to the social environment in the way of information and entertainment, the institution of advertising is indirectly but importantly valuable in making this possible.

Once again, however, one must recognize as well the negative influence of advertising, especially upon the broadcast media. The main problem, of course, is the desire of the stations, pressured by the sponsors, to appeal to the largest possible audience with every show. The result is the reduction of content and style to the lowest common denominator of taste. Commercial television can be held responsible for debasing American taste, certainly for failing to elevate it and contribute culturally and aesthetically as it could. Advertising sponsors are the main culprits. Not only the "highbrow," but also the innovative, daring, or controversial is shunned as possibly offensive, when sponsors exercise effective censorship over programming. This is true not only of cultural and entertainment shows, but perhaps more seriously, sometimes of news and information programs as well.

Apologists can respond that condemnation of television on aesthetic grounds is a matter of purely subjective judgment. It can be argued that such aesthetic condemnations are purely subjective, and that intellectuals have no right in any case to impose their taste on the majority, and further that sponsors and programs merely reflect cultural preferences, rather than dictate them. But this is too simple.

First, we now know that the medium in public, cable, and pay-per-view formats can be more sensitive to the tastes and preferences of various cultural minorities. Second, subsidizing television and offering it free to the public makes good economic sense only if the benefits of watching exceed the value of the resources used to produce programs, and if direct payments for those benefits are impracticable or involve high transaction costs. Free provision of a good tends to create over-consumption of that good in relation to its true value comparative to other goods. Free television junk is in fact over-consumed in relation to other forms of cultural enrichment and entertainment. Furthermore, the advertiser offers only a package deal to the public: programs together with ads often viewed as an irritating nuisance. The increasing popularity of alternative television funding bears witness that this package is not always of maximum benefit to the consuming public.

Thus once more we find a mixed blessing at best in the social effect of advertising. Here we can begin to draw some morals for advertisers. The service provided by advertising in subsidizing the media seems clearly preferable when sponsors do not act as censors. When commercial considerations come first, this priority is clearly detrimental to the aesthetic value of programs. This may be even more clearly true of the informative value of news and information programming. Very large audiences can be expected to be attracted only to the familiar and aesthetically un-innovative. But the judgment of artistic merit, as well as that of newsworthiness, ought to be made on intrinsic grounds by those with some expertise, rather than on strictly commercial grounds, if the media are to realize their potential for educating and not simply tranquilizing the public. In order to accomplish this, self-restraint, sometimes at the expense of the short-term self-interest of particular advertisers and their business clients, is required.

If advertising is to be ethically justified, given the free-market approach, it is not enough to argue for its consistency in a free-market economy, or that it is not wasteful of economic resources, or even that it provides certain indirect social benefits. The positive justification must include the direct benefit that allegedly accrues from this institution: namely, the provision of relevant information. Maximal value can be obtained by consumers only if they know all the alternative ways of satisfying their desires and the costs of doing so. For any beneficial transaction to occur, people must be acquainted with products available. Advertising so informs them, also often providing data on product features, changes, and prices. Such information must be continuously provided because of the arrival of new consumers, new products, and new product features. So advertising seems justified in a free market as a valuable source of information. Even when it attempts mainly to persuade rather than to inform directly, it will tell of a product's availability and perhaps of its prominent features.

However, some critics of advertising claim that the information provided by advertisers is neither the most desirable nor the most useful to the rational consumer. That information would consist in full and objective appraisals of products, including negative features, by neutral investigators. There are very few industries or product lines where consumers could make intelligent choices among alternatives based on the information provided by advertisers. Given the bias of commercials, there are sources of information for consumers far better than advertising. These include private consumer research groups such as Consumers Union and government-subsidized studies, such as those sponsored by the Food and Drug Administration. Despite the transaction costs involved, one must ask whether, all things considered, private, independent consumer groups are economically sounder as sources of information than advertisers. Those who want and benefit from the information provided by such groups can pay for it without having others bear costs locked into the prices of products. It is economically more efficient to have people pay directly for the benefits they seek. This weakens the positive justification of advertising as a source of information for consumers. On the other hand, advertising does appear to be a relatively efficient means of providing information and facilitating transactions because of the large number of people it can reach, as opposed to more direct person-to-person methods of selling. In addition, from at least one perspective it appears to be efficient for the seller to provide the information in this form free of direct cost to the consumer. Because of the number of people a single ad can reach, and because the seller has both the resources and motivation to provide this information to the public at large, advertising appears to involve fewer and lower transaction costs than would the provision of information by direct sale to individual consumers.

Certain moral demands appear to follow quite obviously from this justification. If advertisements are to be justified as sources of information for consumers then they ought to be truthful and avoid deception. If, in the area of consumer decisions, free choice is most likely to satisfy genuine desires and maximize welfare, then lies in the marketplace tend to subvert the entire rationale of the free-market economy. If consumers are misled, they will no longer be free in their choices and will no longer be maximizing utility; the virtues of the free market will be lost.

A central function of much advertising is to persuade people to buy products. One method of persuading someone to buy something is simply to inform him of its features and availability. This suffices when the object is known to satisfy some pre-existing desire. A slightly more complex method that better fits our usual concept of persuasion consists in showing someone that he *should* desire something because it is a means to achieve something else that he desires. This is still a typical form of rational persuasion—one provides reasons for desiring that are to be consciously weighed by the person addressed.

A more controversial method of persuasion bypasses reason and even conscious thought processes, attempting rather to create an association in the consumer's mind between the product and some image that expresses a subconscious wish or desire. A possibly more sinister variation on this persuasive strategy seeks to establish an association between the lack or absence of the product and some unconscious fear or anxiety.

The consumer is then to choose the product as a way of fulfilling his unconscious wish or avoiding the object of his unconscious anxiety.

The psychological theory behind typical variations on this method is eclectic, a mixture of Freudian ideas and behavioral conditioning methods. Notions of subconscious wishes, fears, and sublimations combine with techniques to induce association by conditioning. Methods of advertising (like simple repetition of a brand name or slogan) that make little sense if we think of them as means of providing information become intelligible under this alternative analysis. But though economically successful at least some of the time, such advertising might be condemned on moral grounds. Why?

Persuasion by rational means respects the right of the intended object of persuasion to free and informed choice. But when the influence is intended to be subconscious, the persuasion appears similar to deception. The method appears then to violate a central requirement of at least one major moral tradition, the imperative to treat other persons as equals and to respect their rationality and freedom of choice. It also seems to contradict a major justification of the free economic market: that the system permits all economic transactions to be voluntary. A consumer's decision to buy is not voluntary, it can be argued, when he has been unduly influenced in this way.

Suppose we grant that there is a right to advertise. Businesses have the right to promote their products and services, and advertisers have the right to provide this service to them. Advertising is a form of speech, and as such it seems to require no further justification than appeal to the right of free expression. There remains a constitutionally supported distinction between commercial and other relevant forms of speech, that is, political and literary. Congress is granted the right to control commerce, but not to abridge other forms of speech. Granted that certain economic freedoms are central—for example, the freedom of individuals to work, invest, and consume as they choose—even in these areas there are limitations to protect others as well as the agents themselves. One cannot buy dangerous explosives or work on certain jobs without wearing safety equipment; one cannot invest in the heroin trade. In the realm of speech, the right to advertise does not include a right to defraud, or moral license to mislead people into buying harmful products. Legally, the Federal Trade Commission requires that advertisements be truthful and that their factual claims be substantiated. Such requirements, of course, would not be tolerated in other realms of discourse. We would not trust the government to prohibit political speech it judges to be untrue or literary works it holds misleading or even subversive. Lying by politicians or by private citizens generally is not illegal; nor should it be. Yet the regulation of advertising is morally justified. Again, how can we justify this distinction?

There are differences between politics and advertising that explain why we have greater trust in the clash of political debate to produce rational choices. Individuals are more easily deceived about the nature of products for sale than about political ideas. Defects in commercial products are more easily verified by expert researchers, even though the defects may be technologically complex and thus hidden from average consumers. It is therefore reasonable to require pre-market tests of products by experts. The position of the government also differs in the two contexts. Whereas the interest of the government in power renders it unreliable in regulating political speech, it can more easily serve as a neutral third party in protecting consumers against abuse. The objective verification of fraud and potential harm in products as opposed to political ideals and literary works, and the greater probability of neutrality on the part of government in the realm of commerce, sufficiently distinguishes the two contexts. Government regulation of political speech inhibits rational choice in the long run; regulations requiring truth in advertising can facilitate it.

In endorsing regulation of advertising we must recognize certain negative consequences. First, strict scrutiny of factual claims may lead advertisers to reduce their content, relying instead upon nonrational methods of persuasion. One could argue that the net result is less information to consumers. We can reply that less information is better than false or misleading information. In addition, information that gives good reasons to prefer the product remains valuable for use in ads. The public can still recognize substantiated claims of superiority in product features, and such claims are likely to be more persuasive than meaningless jingles, with less repetition required. Second, it has been argued that regulation makes ads more believable in the eyes of the public, which only makes it easier for the less scrupulous to deceive. But to argue in that way against holding advertisers to the truth suggests more generally that we ought not to encourage honesty, since honesty as a rule makes deception in particular cases easier. This argument is absurd.

We must recognize, secondly, that not all morally objectionable practices on the part of advertisers can be made illegal or regulated. Fair regulation requires objectively verifiable criteria on which to base enforcement. It must therefore center on fraud and deception in factual claims and upon limiting promotion of obviously harmful products such as cigarettes. Non-rational persuasion that creates false associations or insecurities, or that encourages pretentious and unfulfilling patterns of consumption and lifestyles, cannot be prohibited, since enforcement of the prohibitions could not be fair and non-controversial. Such practices nevertheless remain morally objectionable. On the question of irritation and aesthetic pollution of the environment, regulators must be limited to restrictions on amounts of advertising permissible in various media, without judging aesthetic merit. It is reasonable, for example, to prohibit the complete obfuscation of our landscape by billboards, but not to prohibit specific ads as too irritating. It nevertheless remains wrong for advertisers to irritate or harass us in order to gain our attention.

Despite the limitations on regulation, then, it is clear that the right to advertise does not include a moral right to deceive, mislead, or harass, or to create or foster insecurities or self-defeating values. The legal right to advertise is narrower than the corresponding right to free non-commercial speech. The moral right to engage in specific advertising practices is narrower still, not including certain activities that cannot be legally sanctioned (because of the costs involved). That there is a right to advertise as part of a broader right of speech and expression means that advertisers need not justify their profession by demonstrating its overall positive effects. Nevertheless advertisers may feel comfortable with the fact that they do provide valuable information to consumers in some ads and of course provide economic benefits to their business clients. But justification of the institution of advertising, insofar as it appeals either to the contribution advertising makes to overall social utility, or to rights, depends upon advertisers' obeying the following moral demands.

The social effect of advertising subsidies to print and broadcast media is optimized when sponsors restrain their inclinations to censor program material in order to appeal to uniformly large audiences and avoid offending them. Only uncensored media can educate public taste rather than accommodating to its lowest common denominator. Here is the first case of a moral demand that may run counter to the profit-maximizing motive of the advertiser and his client. The injunction against censorship is a genuinely moral requirement, since the social effect of commercial censors seems no less pernicious than that of government censors.

A function more intrinsic to advertisements themselves is the provision of information to consumers enabling them to make more rational choices among products so as to better satisfy their desires. The performance of this function requires that advertisements be truthful and verifiable in their explicit and implied factual claims. "Puffery" or hyperbole must be clearly distinguishable from factual claims by the audience, this requirement becoming broader and stricter when the product is potentially harmful and the intended audience less worldly wise (for example, children). While the advertiser is not morally required to aim at providing complete information, material omitted must not negate claims made or implied, or relate to probable harm from the product.

Moral demands upon advertisers in their role as persuaders or creators of demand are somewhat more subtle and less subject to legal sanction, but nonetheless real. The basic principle regarding effects of persuasion is that advertisers ought not to create desires whose fulfillment would be more harmful than beneficial to consumers. More broadly, the principle we propose would prohibit encouraging irrational desires. Desires are irrational if their targets are falsely believed to be means to ends sought, if their satisfaction blocks that of other more important desires, or if the costs of their satisfaction are too high. Proscribed are desires for specific products known by the advertiser to be harmful, as well as yearnings for a lifestyle out of reach or ultimately low in overall satisfaction. The advertiser's ignorance of the harmfulness of the product he advocates is normally no excuse. Since he shares responsibility for the consumer's buying the product, he must share the blame for the harm that results. To avoid such blame he is obligated to find out, within reasonable limits, the nature of the products he sells.

Especially in regard to the rationality of lifestyles idealized in the advertiser's images, questions may arise for our principle concerning the relevant point of view. What is fulfilling for one person may not be for another; hence the rationality of desires can and does vary from individual to individual. The advertiser must rely here upon his own values and his knowledge of the audience he addresses. While he may without impropri-

ety advocate products and even lifestyles he does not find personally appealing, he should not become a spokesman for what he considers harmful or irrational from the point of view of his typical audience.

Turning to the methods of non-rational persuasion, important moral considerations include the resistibility of the appeal to the audience, that is, whether the choices under its influence remain free, and the importance of the choices at stake. The former is especially relevant in the case of children, where the advertiser must exercise extreme caution and restraint. The latter is most relevant in the political arena, where the advertiser's influence may be most pernicious. At the same time, however, restrictions on the promotion of political candidates are not only difficult to enforce legally, but also difficult to specify on moral grounds. Persuasion, as we have said, is an essential part of the democratic process, and a right to persuade is included in a right to free speech. Ideally persuasion should consist in rational argument. But the merchandizing of political candidates by ad campaigns in the media has become a major part of the persuasive process in our political arena. We have by now grown accustomed to the emphasis upon the personalities, appearances, and speech mannerisms of the candidates. Not only public relations and advertising professionals, but also reporters and media journalists have encouraged this emphasis, minutely analyzing after each television debate whether this candidate smiled at the right time or that one sounded firm enough. Image-building can no longer be realistically prohibited, although political promoters ideally ought to emphasize substantive issues. One hopes that voters will retain rational control over decisions and the ability to separate political views from images. Perhaps here the clash of competing ad campaigns can cancel out much of the effect from image-building, if limitations are placed upon cost. If, instead, non-rational persuasion continues to increase its influence on election outcomes, we can expect the gap between appearance and substance to continue to widen in our highest office holders.

Weaker moral demands relate also to the aesthetics of advertising. The advertiser ought not to harass or irritate us intentionally or pollute our natural or aesthetic environments in order to get our attention. Such injunctions become moral (although not major) when the ads are difficult to avoid. When one can choose whether to read or view material, its content is a matter of taste alone, and the only relevant moral principle specifies a right of free expression. But when the material intrudes upon our sensibilities without being sought out, as so much advertising does, we have the right not to be unreasonably offended or harassed, and the advertiser ought to honor that right according to his own sincere aesthetic appraisal.

CASE STUDY: PENTACOM

The following passage is part of a letter sent to fifty magazines by the Chrysler Corporation's ad agency, PentaCom, a division of BBDO North America. First, do you believe the letter presents a coercive threat to induce the editors to submit to censorship (explain, and be specific)? If so, what would you, as a member of the editorial board of one of these magazines, recommend in response?

> In an effort to avoid potential conflicts, it is required that Chrysler Corporation be alerted in advance of any and all editorial content that encompasses sexual, political, social issues or any editorial that might be construed as provocative or offensive. Each and every issue that carries Chrysler advertising requires a written summary outlining major theme/articles appearing in upcoming issues. These summaries are to be forwarded to PentaCom prior to closing an order to give Chrysler ample time to review and reschedule if desired. . . . As acknowledgment of this letter we ask that you or a representative from the publication sign below and return to us no later than February 15.

CASE STUDY: NETZERO

Reflecting on advertising's role in shaping the media of newspapers, magazines, radio, and television leads to studying advertising's impact on development of the world's latest and fastest growing medium: the Internet. Such a study can choose its focus from an endless array of examples, and a useful comparison requires several in order to carry out reasonable speculations and evaluate hypotheses about trends and innovations. We recommend using the Internet as a source of information, for reasons that should be obvious. We have chosen one case to illustrate some examples of analysis that adapt fairly easily to individual or small-groups projects: the Internet Service Provider (ISP) NetZero.

NetZero promoted itself in 2000 with a large, aggressive, and costly national advertising campaign, including sponsoring nationally televised coverage of National Basketball Association playoffs and finals halftime segments using the slogans "Defenders of the Free World" and "Free Internet Access and Free e-mail Forever!" The television ads, shot in black and white and presented in "letterbox format" with red borders (reminiscent of IBM's Internet Business Solutions campaign with blue borders), portray a series of young NetZero corporate representatives, all of whom would fit right into a typical 1950s television sitcom or drama, testifying before a Congressional committee. The committee members are all grouchy old men who impatiently harass the NetZero representatives with questions using exaggerated regional accents (the gentleman from Rhode Island? Kentucky? Iowa?). The accusatory questions all clearly and deliberately invoke the specter of McCarthyism by implying that NetZero's business practices are "un-American!" The NetZero representatives refuse to be intimidated and proudly proclaim their ongoing commitment to the cause of free access to the Internet and free e-mail forever. The ads encourage viewers to visit the NetZero Web site by frequent repetition of its increasingly memorable address fragment: NetZero.com.

Logging on to the NetZero.com Web site activates a window that invites the visitor to enter a "Surf4Cash Sweepstakes." The view goes no farther until the window is deactivated. Even so, the viewer can gather a considerable amount of information about NetZero from which to sketch out a reasonably detailed business profile.

For example, in its posted "Privacy Policy" NetZero tells you that when you participate in a contest or promotion (such as the Surf4Cash Sweepstakes) NetZero obtains "contact information (your e-mail address) and demographic information (like your zip code, age, income level) in order to administer the contest and notify winners." It is unclear how your income level would be relevant to *these* purposes.

Addressing itself to potential investors, NetZero also posts an "Online Investor Kit," where we learn that NetZero Inc.—whose stock is traded on the NASDAQ exchange—is

> a leading provider of advertising and commerce-supported Internet access offering a broad range of interactive marketing, research, and measurement solutions. NetZero offers consumers free access to the Internet, free e-mail and customizable navigation tools that provide 'speed dial' to key sites on the Internet. Serving more than 4 million registered users in 2,500 cities across the United States, using proprietary technologies, NetZero offers advertisers unique targeting capabilities through numerous online advertising and sponsorship channels. The company's CyberTarget division offers marketers and advertisers mass-scale, online market research and measurement services.

And here is some of what NetZero offers to potential advertisers:

> Subscribers to NetZero provide basic demographic and geographic information along with data on their hobbies and interests. Based upon this NetZero Profile, sponsors are able to precisely target the exact consumers they want to reach. This win-win situation enables both our sponsors and our members to benefit from ads

that have been designed with the members' specific interests in mind. And, since our precision zCAST™ tracking technology records the user's movement around the Internet, sponsors can send messages that address what's most relevant to someone at exactly the right moment. When members visit a site, it suggests their interest in a specific product. NetZero sponsors can meet them there instantly via the ZeroPort. Since the ZeroPort is the Internet traveler's constant companion and link to NetZero, it enables sponsors to display customized messages the entire time the member is online. When members see an ad that interests them, just one click takes them directly to the sponsor's site. Quite simply, we turn millions of NetZero members into individuals. NetZero offers one-to-one marketing in its truest form, unavailable in any other medium.

NetZero offers its sponsors specific advertising strategies:

"Marquee Banner" ad placement   (A fairly standard device. The sponsor secures a priority presentation position in a viewer's online session on a monthly basis. Viewers are selected by geographic, demographic, and "psychographic" profile).

"Keyword" ad placement   (The sponsor "buys" a keyword covering all searches conducted over the NetZero search engine).

The "Ad Missile"   (An innovation. The sponsor is able to "immediately target a member who is visiting a competitor's site").

The "Anti-Ad Missile Defense Shield"   (These guys have evidently been brainwashed by defense contractors. The sponsor is able to advertise over its own protected site to block out competitors' ad missiles).

"LazerMail"   (They call this a "permission-based, opt-in e-mail marketing solution." Evidently, it encourages members to sign up for electronic junk mail).

"Zero-Out"   (In their own words: "Prime branding opportunity with click-thru to sponsor's site. Shows sponsor's compelling products or promotional messages every time a member exits the service for an entire month. Members can click-thru to sponsor's site and stay online. Zero-Out leaves strong impression since it's the last message the member sees." You get the picture).

Consider the various audiences NetZero is speaking to in its promotional materials. Develop an analysis of each audience in terms of its interests. Where do the interests of the audiences overlap or coincide? Where do the interests of the audiences diverge? Where you find divergent audience interests, are these interests nevertheless complementary or compatible, or do they conflict? Which of these audiences are revenue generating for the corporation? Based on these considerations, now assess the claims made by NetZero in its promotional materials. Where do you find the most revealing and truthful claims? Explain.

4.3 ADVERTISING IN THE PUBLIC SPHERE: ARE THERE LIMITS?   We turn now to a controversy in which issues of freedom of expression and the legitimacy of commercial advertising meet issues of restraint of trade. As we have just seen, a standard economic argument in support of advertising is based on the indirect benefits advertising contributes to society in the form of subsidies to other socially

useful institutions. The next reading explores a specific instance of this argument. In this case the socially useful institution is education. Should the public schools accept subsidies, in the form of equipment or instructional materials, in exchange for the opportunity to present commercial advertising messages to students?

One way to frame this controversy would be in terms of corporate influence on education, and "good corporate citizenship." Are the goals and objectives of public education at odds with the interests of business? Some will argue that they are. Public education is fundamentally concerned with preparing students for citizenship, while the business community is interested in commerce. Business interests in educating students will have to do, in the final analysis, with preparing "human resources" (that is, a trained labor force) and "consumers" (that is, market development). On the other hand, the interests of the business community and the citizenry are not mutually exclusive. After all, many citizens are business people, most citizens work, and all citizens are consumers. The business community's involvement in civic affairs generally, and in public education policy making in particular, might be regarded as a healthy manifestation of democracy. Certainly members of the business community have the same rights to represent their interests and to advocate policies and programs as any other citizen. And, similarly, just as parents and community groups have an interest in well-run public education and are welcome as voluntary contributors to their school programs, so individual members of the business community and the business community at large have interests in well-run public education, and they certainly have valuable resources to contribute. Shouldn't the schools welcome the business community's contributions when these contributions genuinely enhance educational programs? Why should the business community's vision of advancing its own interests by such means stand in the way? Aren't win/win arrangements possible? And if so, shouldn't they be developed and encouraged?

A proposal of just this sort is examined in the following essay, written by one of the editors of your textbook. The proposal, to supply public schools with commercially sponsored current affairs television programming and related technology, has proven a relatively successful business model, more recently emulated for Internet materials and technology. This essay, which opposes the proposal, was part of a symposium on corporate influence in education published in *Educational Leadership,* in 1990.

QUESTIONS FOR STUDY AND DISCUSSION

1. What distinction does Rudinow make between textbooks and other potential vehicles for placing advertising in public schools? What ethical difference does this distinction make?
2. Explain the two distinctive innovations Whittle Communications has made in advertising delivery systems.
3. According to Rudinow, what significant benefits does the Whittle proposal offer the public schools? According to Rudinow, what significant benefits

does the Whittle proposal offer the sponsor? From public education's point of view, do you consider this a reasonable trade-off? In your view, should the fact that significant benefits flow to the sponsor under the plan count against public schools accepting the Whittle offer, as Rudinow suggests? Explain why or why not.

4. What, if any, alterations in the Whittle proposal do you think would render it acceptable to a critic such as Rudinow?

WHITTLING AWAY AT EDUCATION[6]

JOEL RUDINOW

If It Sounds Too Good to Be True . . .

In March of 1989, American magazine entrepreneur Chris Whittle of Tennessee-based Whittle Communications launched *Channel One,* a pilot venture billed as a "new kind of partnership between business and education." What Whittle proposed to provide to the six secondary school districts chosen to participate in the nationwide test of the program was impressive indeed. The project would deliver to each district $50,000 worth of TV monitors, VCRs, and satellite dish hardware, along with news and information programming produced in a television format specifically designed for secondary school students. If the initial test of the project proved successful, the project would be expanded in the following year to 8,000 schools nationwide, each to receive a similar package of technology and programming at an estimated total cost of $80 million annually.

The education establishment, and the public at large, were strongly encouraged, through a series of advertisements, news releases, editorials, and op-ed pieces (including one in the *New York Times* by Whittle himself, subtitled "Business Can Aid Starved Schools"[7]), to understand the project fundamentally in terms of the pressing needs of education and against a backdrop of national educational crisis. Quoting strategically from the Bennett/Bloom/Hirsch school of education criticism, Whittle's promotional campaign literature points to stunning, even comical, instances of political and cultural illiteracy—high school students confidently reporting that Chernobyl is Cher's full name or that the District of Columbia is a Central American country. But demonstrating a level of public relations savvy well above that of most of the "Nation at Risk" crowd, Whittle quickly added that neither the schools themselves nor the teachers were entirely to blame. American schools and teachers continue to be, according to the Whittle literature "over-burdened and under-funded," so that their performance, however abysmal, is at least understandable under the circumstances. What the schools need are the kind of contemporary technological and informational resources which public funding is increasingly hard pressed to provide. Thus at the outset, in his statement of the social problem to which the project is ostensibly addressed, Whittle is already able to work a minor miracle by quoting in the same breath not only from Bennett and Hirsch but from Albert Shanker and Mary Hatwood Futrell, the presidents of the two national teachers unions.

How would Whittle propose to deliver such a massive golden egg to American public schools? By soliciting corporate sponsorship for the news and information programming. In each of the twenty-five twelve-minute segments of *Channel One* produced for the initial pilot series, two minutes would be set aside for commercial messages from the corporate sponsors, whose fees would underwrite the project.

On the face of it this looks like another triumph of the American entrepreneurial spirit. What initially seems an impossible collision of forces and interests, a growing crisis in public education in a period of unavoidable fiscal constraints, yields to a remarkably simple idea. Once again American ingenuity turns crisis and conflict into a win/win situation, making money in the bargain. The schools get high technology, the teachers get lesson plans, the students get information in an entertaining format, the districts (hopefully) get results, Whittle gets a cash cow, and the sponsors get . . .

A Captive Audience

The obvious issue which was immediately raised against *Channel One* was over the appropriateness of commercial advertising in school curricula. Critics immediately protested that what Whittle was proposing would be like placing advertisements in school textbooks. And

they raised the specter of Saturday morning children's television programming, in which the commercials—an overwhelming barrage of bad taste aimed at badgering six-year-olds into craving a lot of useless junk—cannot be clearly distinguished from the programming itself. Was Whittle really about to bribe school administrators into handing their students over to Pepsi and McDonalds for more of the same?

Whittle anticipates these criticisms, but his responses are at best ambiguous. He points out that the *Channel One* audience will be comprised not of impressionable six-year-olds but of "TV-savvy teenagers" who see an average of one hundred perfectly similar TV commercials a day, and that the programming in this case will be "network quality news." He argues that there's nothing special about the "captivity" of the *Channel One* audience, since teenagers have the ability to "tune out" whatever they are disinterested in, for example standard textbooks and lessons. He points out further that commercial advertising is already tolerated in the public school environment, for instance on athletic scoreboards. In other words, Whittle's answer appears to be "Yes, we are indeed proposing that the schools hand over their students to our commercial sponsors. But there's nothing essentially wrong with that, given established precedents concerning advertising in the public schools, given the inherent educational value of the surrounding programming and its superiority in terms of interest to the run-of-the-mill of existing curricula, and given that the students, sophisticated television viewers that they are, will be able to take the commercials easily in stride." And finally, he cautions that critics of the proposal should withhold their criticisms pending the results of initial trials of the program in the six pilot schools.

To the extent that they work at all, these responses succeed only in dodging and blurring the issues, while at the same time hustling the project. First of all, the fact that the *Channel One* audience is already well seasoned through extensive exposure to television and its commercials does not mean that it is not an impressionable audience. If it were not an impressionable audience, if it were not presumably susceptible to the influence of advertising, Whittle could scarcely hope to attract sponsors for *Channel One*. Secondly, the underlying assumption that network quality news has significant educational value which would distinguish it as suitable material for the secondary school curriculum is dubious to say the very least. (We'll return to this matter momentarily.) Finally, there is the crucial difference between the placement of commercial messages in the public school environment, in such places as on soft drink cups and athletic scoreboards for example, and the inclusion of commercial messages in curricula, in material to which students are required to give their attention as part of their compulsory educational experience—in other words in course content, required readings and viewings, and so on. Even if it were agreed that the presence of commercial advertising in the public school environment is tolerable or (more likely) unavoidable, the question would remain as to whether including commercial advertising within the required curriculum wouldn't thoroughly compromise the integrity of public education. Thus the one analogy with any relevance, the analogy

between *Channel One* and ads in textbooks, is the one Whittle studiously avoids. As for withholding criticism and suspending judgment, in June of 1989, not even a full semester into the trials, Whittle announced the "results" of the five-week pilot project as well as plans to go nationwide in 1990 with a three-channel educational network.

What were these "results"? Whittle claimed in the June press releases that students who had watched *Channel One* did about 20% better than the control group on about 80% of the test questions which concerned current world and national affairs and some of which were focused on information presented only on *Channel One*. Persistent attempts since the June press releases to obtain copies of the instruments used in Whittle's educational impact study and of the raw data generated have to date net this writer nothing but evasive responses. One can only speculate. In addition, I submit that the results of short answer assessment instruments administered immediately after exposure to the material can't possibly indicate anything in the important areas of lasting recall and authentic understanding. Besides there are conflicting studies. In an experiment conducted for the *Columbia Journalism Review* students who had been exposed to *Channel One* and those who had not achieved identically unimpressive 55% scores on current affairs tests.[8]

All in all, the *Channel One* proposal adds up to little more than a remarkably audacious example of hypocrisy in which the public rationale of support to struggling institutions of public education barely masks the patently obvious real agenda of penetrating one of the few remaining preserves in contemporary

American society and harvesting it as an advertising market.

The Real Whittle Agenda

Though Whittle was honored in 1984 by *Adweek* and the Magazine Publishers' Association as Publisher of the Year, Whittle is not a publisher of periodicals in the normal or conventional sense of the term, though even that is shifting under the influence of innovators such as Whittle. Though it is by now a commonplace in publishing wherever advertising revenue is the primary source of funding that circulation and advertising sales exert a powerful influence on editorial policy, periodicals publishing nevertheless is rooted in a tradition in which editorial policy is the fundamental and central consideration—circulation and advertising being at least originally subordinate as means to ends. And generally speaking editorial policy can at least theoretically and to some extent also in practice be separated from considerations of circulation and advertising sales. Not so at Whittle Communications. Whittle is in the business of creating efficient vehicles for advertising pure and simple. Thus Whittle accounts for his company's remarkable growth and success precisely in terms of the innovations he has introduced to streamline his advertising clients' access to specifically targeted audiences.

Whittle's fundamental insight was that advertisers might be less than fully satisfied with traditional mass media as vehicles for their messages. First of all, traditional mass media generally reach a large, but therefore needlessly diverse audience for the purposes of many advertisers, whose products are often de-signed to appeal to a much narrower market. The efficiency trick in advertising is to match the audience as closely as possible demographically to the target market for the product. Secondly, traditional mass media accept advertising from one's competition. Thus Whittle's two major innovations are what he calls "target specific media" or media "custom-made" for the target market, and the "single-sponsor concept" or "the proprietary vehicle." For example *GO!* (Girls Only!) is targeted at girls in their pre- and early teens and carries the ads of the Personal Products Corporation (makers of a line of feminine hygiene products) exclusively. It should be fairly obvious that editorial policy and therefore content in this sort of context are going to be entirely subservient to the corporate agenda, in this case establishing habits of consumption and product loyalty at the onset of menstruation. (*GO!* is distributed three times annually free of charge through the schools.) It's like an airline in-flight magazine, where the columns and features have no substance whatsoever other than the bare and trivial minimum required to promote travel consumerism. Indeed they barely resemble editorial policy and content. Literally nothing that detracts from the purpose of the vehicle, namely that of delivering a specific category of potential consumers to the advertiser in a mood receptive to the advertiser's message, will appear in the pages of such a vehicle. Media analysts have coined the term "advertorial" to describe this new post-modern range of phenomena, which interestingly enough has aroused sufficient concern among magazine editors that the American Society of Magazine Editors recently adopted a set of guidelines intended to reinforce the distinction between editorial content and advertising.[9] What goes for Whittle and publishing goes double for Whittle and education. If the "advertorial" worries magazine editors, how much more concerned should educators be over the advent of "advercation"?

In assessing the *Channel One* proposal educators who may initially be bowled over by the promise of thousands of dollars worth of high technology should first of all be aware of the strings attached to the offer. First, the offer is not available to schools with less than 500 students, in other words, to schools which do not represent a large enough share of this advertising market to count as cost-effective. Second, participating schools would be obligated under this arrangement to show the *Channel One* program in its entirety, with the commercials intact, on a daily basis, with only very limited discretion. Third, participating schools would be further obligated *not* to show any other broadcast news service for the three-year period of the contract. This final restriction is secured in part by means of a limitation built into the satellite dish itself: the dish is "locked onto" one particular communications satellite (the one on which Whittle has rented channels) and not equipped so as to be able to "tune in" others.

Educators should also look very carefully at what this package offers the sponsor. Ordinarily, harvesting the attention of an audience of potential consumers on a large enough scale to interest a major advertising sponsor involves considerable risk. Programming is produced for which the audience can at best be merely "projected." Often audiences behave in ways that audience estimators

utterly fail to predict or understand. The commercially sponsored entertainment industry is thus characterized over time by occasional surprise "hits" and rather more frequent big-budget flops. With *Channel One* the risk is for practical purposes entirely eliminated. *Channel One* sponsors know to a degree of certainty unmatched by virtually any other form of advertising what the size and demographic makeup of their audience will be. From the point of view of the advertising buyer, *Channel One* will deliver an audience of significant size and stability. And an audience with considerable spending power and extremely malleable but predictable consumer interests and preferences to boot. This is what leads such advertising buyers as Dan Chew, marketing manager for Levi Strauss to view *Channel One* as a "very efficient and cutting edge" way of reaching his target market. As Peggy Charren, president of Boston-based Action for Children's Television, an advocacy group concerned particularly with television commercials aimed at children, puts it, "When you have a captive audience of every tenth grader in the country, you have reached advertising Valhalla."

Whittle has been successfully targeting the schools for years with a total of six properties reaching students in elementary schools, junior high schools, high schools, and colleges. For example, Whittle's wall-magazine *Connections* is posted in some 5,000 high schools and claims to reach more than half of the nation's high school students. [Whittle's large poster-size "wall media" format combines a magazine approach with the impact of a billboard.] With *Channel One,* however, the presence and impact of advertising within education would be magnified several times over. The most obvious factor is the medium of television, whose superiority as a delivery system for advertising is universally recognized. A less obvious, but ultimately more significant, factor is the movement of advertising from the peripheral social environment within the schools—the bulletin board, the pages of the school newspaper, and so on—into the curriculum itself.

The Compatibility Argument

Whittle is quick to argue that there is no necessary incompatibility between the goals of education and those of profitable business or commercial advertising, and therefore that genuinely educational material might indeed be a suitable context for effective advertising, and that the presence of effective advertising needn't detract from the educational value of the surrounding material. It's a clever argument. Interpreted theoretically the premise is plausible. Why not? After all, entertainment can be educational, and education entertaining.

However, in practice, where it counts, advertising and education are at cross purposes. Educators and advertisers alike recognize this. The active, alert, engaged, inquisitive, creative, skeptical, reflective, critically self-reliant habits of mind that education both depends on—and at its best aims to encourage—are hardly optimal for the reception of advertising from the point of view of the sponsor. What you want as an advertiser is an audience which is passive, unreflective, credulous, susceptible to the dictates of external authority. The interesting ambiguity about entertainment—

which the compatibility argument is all too happy to exploit—is that it can be used to foster *both* casts of mind: that of the educated thinking individual and that of the couch potato. Thus the most potent explanatory hypothesis to account for the dismal level of most commercially sponsored television programming: namely, it is produced precisely to prepare an audience to receive advertising. As media analyst Ben Bagdikian put it recently, years of experimentation with various kinds of programming during the early decades of television have by now produced a basic formula for maintaining receptive second-by-second audience attention: "constant violence, gratuitous sex and deliberate manipulation of split-second change of images and sounds to make an emotional and sensory impact that leaves no time for reflection."[10]

In short, advertising homogenizes and degrades whatever it touches. This goes not only for predictable prime-time-crime-slime and Saturday-morning-drek-and-drool. It goes not only for silly sitcoms, stupid soaps, trivial talk shows and vacuous-consumer-fantasy-game-shows like *Wheel of Fortune*. It goes also for "network quality news," which as even the casual viewer can easily ascertain, likewise follows the formula. Thus, Whittle's stress on the distinction between the norm of children's television and *Channel One* as "network quality news" and what additional reassurances he has to offer regarding *Channel One's* editorial independence and educator input into its production are not very soothing.

Initial suspicions concerning *Channel One's* depth and educational value are quickly confirmed on viewing any of the pilot programs. MTV production values predominate throughout. This means of course that the emphasis is on superficial polish and lightning fast pace. The three main program segments (separated by the commercial breaks), averaging roughly three minutes in length, are sub-divided into story-packages averaging a minute or less each. Transitions are accomplished via ten- and twenty-second "Fast Fact," "Pop Quiz," and "Flash-back" spots. Subtract the show's opening billboard, the "teases" for upcoming segments and for tomorrow's program, and the closing segment's obligatory piece of "human interest" fluff, and what's left? It is scarcely an exaggeration to say that each of the commercials makes a heavier, and a thirty seconds longer, demand on the viewer's attention than any of the "news and information" items—just what one would expect.

Self-Censorship

This connection between commercial advertising and the degradation of intellectual substance, formulated here as a general rule, is not absolute, but neither is it accidental. There are occasional exceptions to the rule, but the rule expresses pressures which, though they are certainly not irresistible, are nevertheless very real, tangible, powerful, and understood at least implicitly by everyone who works in advertising and the media. The relationship between a corporate sponsor and the producers of the programming or other material that carries the sponsor's message has an asymmetry a lot like that between landlord and tenant. It tends to engender a pattern of self-censorship re-sponsive to the interests of the corporate sponsor.

In his new book *Culture Inc.: The Corporate Takeover of Public Expression,*[11] communications scholar Herbert I. Schiller of the University of California describes this tendency as manifested in the arts, as museums and other arts institutions become increasingly dependant upon corporate benefactors for support. Like prime-time television, popular music, and the like, major metropolitan museums are gradually but increasingly getting seduced, through lucrative corporate grants and "charitable contributions," into playing a role in the organized pursuit of the corporate public relations agenda—what Schiller describes as "the consciousness industry." Thus under the prominently displayed banners and logos of the corporate sponsors, major arts institutions are tending more and more to mount performances and exhibits designed to maximize the museum equivalents of audience-share ratings and up-scale demographics, shows which celebrate centrist values, de-emphasize cultural diversity, and avoid controversy, particularly anything that might call into question the social distribution of wealth and power, with the predictable result that public awareness of social and political reality is diminished. Schiller's analysis suggests that what he calls "the consciousness industry" might better be described as "the UNconsciousness industry." Again, this underscores the difficulty of maintaining uncompromising editorial independence in capital intensive productions such as *Channel One*, when they are underwritten by powerful corporate interests with agendas of their own.

Channel One and The Global Media Market

There is a further item on the real Whittle agenda to which educators need to give due consideration in their assessments of the *Channel One* proposal. As an entrepreneur, as a builder of a business, Whittle is understandably interested in maximizing the value of his company as a business asset in the increasingly "hot" world media market. Thus Whittle proudly charts the company's performance from its inception as a student venture to its position as a $152 million concern with annual revenues of $105 million, a ten-year annual growth rate of 30%, and projected annual revenues of $500 million. In less than twenty years, Whittle had become a major player in the world media market, significant enough to have been listed among thirty-seven media innovators in a special issue of *U.S. News and World Report* entitled "Who Runs America: The New American Establishment."

It is important to understand the dimensions of this new world media market and the financial opportunities it presents, as well as the sociopolitical hazards of the exploitation of these financial opportunities. The prospects of developing the burgeoning populations and emerging economies around the world as markets for consumer goods and services supplied by major multinational corporations, the huge advertising revenues associated with such development, and the emergence of new instantaneous global communications technologies such as satellite systems and fiber optics making such development feasible, have opened world communications as a new field for magnificently profitable enterprise of immense scale. This is reflected in a sharp increase in the level of spectacular merger and takeover activity in the field in recent years. This process has produced a shrinking number of stunningly huge market leaders which, by virtue of their shared and overlapping interests and their interrelationships with other major multinational concerns, represent an alarming centralization of control of the global information environment largely beyond the scope and regulatory reach of existing political structures, all of which has been very clearly summarized over the years by Ben Bagdikian:

> A handful of mammoth private organizations have begun to dominate the world's mass media. Most of them confidently announce that by the 1990s they—five to ten corporate giants—will control most of the world's important newspapers, magazines, books, broadcast stations, movies, recordings, and videocassettes. Moreover, each of these planetary corporations plans to gather under its control every step in the information process, from creation of "the product" to all the various means by which modern technology delivers media messages to the public. "The product" is news, information, ideas, entertainment, and popular culture; the public is the whole world. . . . In 1979 the largest media merger in history was the Gannett newspaper chain's purchase of a billboard and television company for $362 million. Nine years later, Rupert Murdoch bought *TV Guide* from Walter Annenberg's Triangle Publications for $3 billion. Only seven months later, the merger of Time Inc. and Warner Communications Inc.

created the world's largest media firm, worth $18 billion. On April 9, Gulf Western (Simon and Schuster books and Paramount Pictures), once the country's most diversified conglomerate, announced that it was entering the global race by selling all its nonmedia industries in order to concentrate on the new gold mine of planetary media, and changing its name to Paramount Communications Inc.[12]

In October 1988, Time, Inc., acquired 50% of Whittle Communications for $185 million, making Whittle Communications part of what promises to be the world's largest media conglomerate. Thus what is perhaps the most dangerous, though least discussed, of the implications of Whittle's *Channel One* proposal: namely the substantial transfer of control over curriculum and content from locally responsible individuals and institutions—from teachers, school boards, and parent groups—to a remote corporate hierarchy.

An Idea Whose Time Has Come?

The ominous and horrible idea of commercially sponsored television in the schools is probably not going to go away soon. To hear Whittle tell it, *Channel One* is unstoppable. It has everything going for it, though it does have its critics and detractors, some of whom occupy positions of no mean influence in education. For a while, former California State Superintendent of Public Schools Bill Honig, withheld funding on a pro-rata basis from California public schools for each minute of class time devoted to Whittle material, a gesture which probably had as much symbolic

as financial impact. But such gestures also carry political risks. Honig was immediately blasted for taking this position in editorials in quite a few California newspapers. In the present American climate of public opinion, proposals like Whittle's do have a lot going for them. Whittle is, if nothing else, a persuasive salesman, and the general public is all too easily sold on this sort of thing. A Gallup public opinion poll (commissioned by Whittle) shows parents and school-age youngsters to be quite receptive to the *Channel One* idea, and Whittle has been remarkably successful in obtaining favorable press coverage, editorial and op-ed support, and most important, enthusiastic reception from local school administrators and teachers. With an obliqueness *almost* polite, Whittle characterizes *Channel One's* critics and detractors as out of step with the times and . . . well, grouchy. The *Channel One* press kit includes a sheet entitled "Reactions to New Ideas"—a compendium of pronouncements which history has managed to embarrass such as "When the Paris Exhibition closes, the electric light will close with it and no more will be heard of it." (Oxford University Professor Erasmus Wilson, 1878); "It's an amazing invention, but who would ever want to use one of them?" (President Rutherford B. Hayes, speaking of the telephone in 1876); "Radio has no future" (Lord Kelvin, 1897); "Video won't be able to hold onto any market after the first six months. People will soon get tired of staring at a plywood box every night." (20th Century Fox President Darryl F. Zanuck, 1946). To all outward appearances, Whittle is nowhere near ready to give up on *Channel One*.

But even if Whittle eventually were to abandon the project, other media tycoons wait in the wings. Ted Turner has already entered the arena with a proposed educational television service for the schools which, though it is not to be directly supported by commercials, nevertheless embodies a number of the problematic dimensions mentioned above. The Turner proposal, which was initially announced as intended "to compete with *Channel One* in the potentially lucrative school market," was initially planned to function on the basis of "substantial revenues" to be derived from corporations who would be allowed to insert "public service announcements." Turner, who now says that he isn't sure precisely where he will derive funding for his service, has apparently backed away from what has by now proven to be the main sticking point in the Whittle proposal, at least as far as public reaction is concerned. Nevertheless, it remains clear that media giants are falling all over each other in a rush to stake out territory in the schools. There is only one plausible explanation for this intense interest, given the present economic structure of American mass media, and that is the financial (that is, commercial) value of the market. If its value cannot be harvested presently, then it's the market's future value that Whittle and Turner want to corner. The last ditch of defense against *Channel One* and similar proposals will have to be organized, informed, and most of all sustained resistance on the part of educators, particularly classroom teachers.

CASE STUDY: ZAPME!

To continue reflecting on advertising's role in shaping the newspaper, magazine, radio, and television media, and now the Internet, consider a business venture called ZapMe!, following the model illustrated above with NetZero. To begin with, read the following statement assembled from the ZapMe! Web site. For more complete background information you may visit the site at www.Zapme.com. As you examine this material, notice similarities as well as differences between the business profiles of ZapMe! and NetZero and Whittle Communications as discussed in the last reading. Imagine that you are a parent of children in high school or middle school and that your local district school board is considering installing the ZapMe! system. What course of action would you advocate at the school board meeting?

ZapMe! Corporate Backgrounder

Providing Free High-Speed Internet Computers to Schools

Most schools are ill-equipped for the digital information age. They are short of money, have outdated PCs, want Internet access, and are looking for low-cost computer solutions that are easy to implement. Both teachers and parents want the best possible learning tools for their students (and children).

The call to action is clear. Vice President Al Gore says let's connect all Americans to the information highway, and equip every classroom with modern multimedia computers that can access the Internet. It's about time all kids have this opportunity to realize their full potential and to prepare for an increasingly competitive future in our digital world.

ZapMe! Corporation sees a clear mandate for all schools to provide students with multimedia computers delivering high speed Internet access. The information age demands it, and the ZapMe!™ netspace provides this—at no cost to the schools. The multimedia educational content and the cool personalization and communication tools help educators engage the diverse personalities of all students, from the impatient and uninspired to the fast-track students.

ZapMe!, the leading provider of quality technology and online educational content to schools and communities nationwide, has built America's largest Internet media network specializing in education.

ZapMe! is dedicated to bridging the digital divide and closing the technology gap in schools by providing students with access to the latest technology and educational resources they need to succeed in the digital age. High-performance computer labs with satellite broadband capabilities provide safe, high-speed delivery of aggregated educational Web content—including 13,000 pre-selected, indexed educational sites—and make the ZapMe!™ netspace the premier interactive educational medium and provide a powerful learning experience to middle and high school students, educators, and parents across the country.

If your teenager is a student in a ZapMe! school, they can access more than 13,000 educational Web sites cached on their school's ZapMe! network server. These sites are pre-selected for their relevance and appropriateness for school curriculum by a select board of editors, and indexed into content categories for easy use by teachers and students. And students can keep up on current events by accessing school, local, national, and world news and current events from the My Yahoo @ ZapMe! home page and CNN.

When ZapMe! provides your school with the latest computer hardware, it's complete, ready-to-use and absolutely free of charge. That means ZapMe! and its technology partners install a network of 15 state-of-the-art multimedia desktop computer systems, a high-speed "broadband" rooftop satellite for Internet connectivity, a high-performance Internet server, and a laser printer.

Every computer is fully outfitted for immediate use. A custom Web browser with Internet filtering and monitoring software enables students to conduct research, chat and exchange e-mail, accomplish classroom tasks and even play games. All this within a safer, education-appropriate environment in accordance with your schools' Internet usage policies. And ZapMe!'s support doesn't stop there. Training for teachers and students, and maintenance and upgrades are provided by ZapMe!—again at no cost to your school.

ZapMe! serves our nation's secondary school system. It's a huge audience, reaching over 23 million students, as well as parents, and educators. It is also a system in need of help. Open almost any newspaper today and you'll find an article or editorial lamenting that our educational system—great as it is—is failing our students in important ways. Chief among these is the failure to fully harness the power of technology to enhance the educational process, and to prepare students for the digital future. Unfortunately, even in times of great prosperity there simply aren't funds available to provide all of our schools—the wealthiest and the poorest—with the necessary hardware, software, and technology expertise. Bridging this "digital divide" is perhaps the most critical challenge facing our educational system, and one that ZapMe! is committed to overcoming.

One of our most important goals is making the ZapMe! experience as convenient as possible for our users. Our network helps achieve this goal by incorporating broadband connectivity over a satellite delivery system. This means we can simultaneously multicast data, including audio and full-motion video. The resulting speed of this design allows ZapMe! to offer our users fast access to graphic-oriented Internet content and new bandwidth-intensive multimedia applications.

The Internet holds enormous potential for improving the educational process by bringing a galaxy of information to every classroom in the world. Even students in the poorest, most isolated schools can have access to the same information as students in the wealthiest districts—provided they have the necessary hardware, software, and network connection. This is where ZapMe! can make a difference. In partnership with companies like Dell, Gilat, GE Spacenet, NEC, and Toshiba, we are installing networked computer labs at no cost to the schools. This is possible through support from corporate sponsors, whose names and brand images are displayed within the ZapMe! netspace. We believe that our sponsorship model is the most effective way to bring the richness of the Internet to every student. In fact, the dissemination of free and accurate information, whether through a newspaper, magazine, or televised news program, is virtually always made possible by advertising. Likewise, free content on the Internet is only feasible because of banner ads and other forms of electronic sponsorship. In this light, the ZapMe! model is firmly in the tradition of American journalism—and the "right to free speech" that we all cherish. We are keenly aware that bringing the Internet to our nation's youth carries a great responsibility. We are firmly committed to maintaining the privacy of our users through one of the strictest privacy policies on the Internet. In particular, we accept only sponsorships that we feel are appropriate to a student audience. And we carefully screen the content of our netspace, in concert with educators, to ensure that it is educationally appropriate.

The Internet enables information to be delivered in many different formats, including text, audio, video, and interactive versions of all three. With our high-speed satellite connection, unique local caching technology, and state-of-the-art hardware, ZapMe! brings all the richness of new media to students, parents, and educators— and brings it to them fast. Today's students grew up with MTV, 100-channel cable television, video games, and movies with dazzling special effects. They expect and deserve a network experience that is not only educational but innovative, interactive, and engaging. We believe ZapMe! delivers just such an experience. Our netspace attempts to harness all the power and potential of new media to add excitement and relevance to the learning process.

Above all, we're a network. Secondary education has traditionally been a locally run system, and for many very good reasons. ZapMe! is committed to supporting local control while providing the significant advantages of a national network. For example, when a student at any ZapMe! school requests a piece of information—on a recent news event, say, or college admissions trends—that piece of information is loaded into the ZapMe! cache server in that student's school. It is thus made available at local network speeds to every user throughout the network. Students and teachers can use our network to compile educational resources that apply to students and teachers everywhere. As the largest education-based broadband Internet media network, we have built something far more valuable than "virtual real estate" on the Internet. We have attempted to integrate the hardware and software and the satellite connection that brings the entire education community together, regardless of geography. We believe owning our network is a great business proposition—and that we're here to stay! More importantly, ownership enables us to create a vibrant online community. Our users constitute perhaps the most committed, highly motivated affinity group in the world. Because students, parents, and educators care deeply about education, they are very active participants in the ZapMe! community. They contribute their ideas, their concerns, their passion—and the ZapMe! network connects them all together. And that's great for all of us who care about the future of education.

SUGGESTED READINGS:

Herman, Edward S., and Robert W. McChesney. *The Global Media: The New Missionaries of Corporate Capitalism.* London: Cassell, 1997.

Klein, Naomi. *No Logo.* New York: Picador, 1999.

Schiller, Herbert I. *Culture Inc.: The Corporate Takeover of Public Expression.* Oxford: Oxford University Press, 1989.

NOTES

ETHICS AND ADVERTISING

1. This argument can easily be extrapolated from the work of Ben Bagdikian (see Chapter 3). See also Robert W. McChesney, *Rich Media, Poor Democracy: Communication Politics in Dubious Times* (Urbana: University of Illinois Press, 1999).

THE BRIBED SOUL

2. Reprinted from *The Sponsored Life* by permission of Don Congdon Associates, Inc. Copyright © 1994 by Leslie Savan.

THE JUSTIFICATION OF ADVERTISING IN A MARKET ECONOMY

3. Alan Goldman, "The Justification of Advertising in a Market Economy," from *Just Business: New Introductory Essays in Business Ethics,* ed. Tom Regan (New York: Random House, 1983), 235–70. Reprinted by permission of McGraw-Hill Companies.
4. See Jules Blackman, *Advertising and Competition* (New York: New York University Press, 1967).
5. See for example Robert Steiner, "Does Advertising Lower Consumer Prices?" *Journal of Marketing,* 37 (1973).

WHITTLING AWAY AT EDUCATION

6. Joel Rudinow, "Channel One Whittles Away at Education" *Educational Leadership* 47 (December 1989/January 1990), 70–3. Reprinted with permission from ASCD. All rights reserved.
7. "Commercials Plus Education: Business Can Aid Starved Schools," *New York Times,* 1 March 1989.
8. Cassandra Tate, "Opinion: On Chris Whittle's School-news Scheme" *Columbia Journalism Review,* May–June, 1989, 52.
9. Jonathan Alter, "The Era of the Big Blur," *Newsweek,* 22 May 1989, 73–6.
10. Ben H. Bagdikian, "Cornering Hearts and Minds: The Lords of the Global Village," *Nation,* 12 June 1989, 819.
11. Herbert I. Schiller, *Culture Inc.: The Corporate Takeover of Public Expression* (Oxford, England: Oxford University Press, 1989).
12. Bagdikian, 805.

5

ETHICS AND ENTERTAINMENT I: HUMOR AND COMEDY

Humor and offensiveness are two different things. It's telling them apart that's sometimes hard.

ROY BLOUNT JR.

If you're going to tell the truth, you'd better make it funny. Otherwise they'll try to kill you.

WILL ROGERS

INTRODUCTION

As we saw in Chapter 4 on advertising, the dominant role advertising has assumed in the economy of mass communications has a profound effect on the content of mass media programming. Especially notable is the prevalence of entertainment and entertainment values in mass media programming generally. To understand this correlation it is useful to consider that in essence entertainment *is* what entertainment *does*—and what entertainment does is hold attention agreeably. Of course in essence this is what the producers and sponsors of commercial advertising want: an audience held agreeably at attention. Notice that this analysis of entertainment's essential function does not require the entertainment itself to always be "agreeable," in the sense of being "pleasant to attend to." Horror movies and thrill rides and shock radio all serve entertainment's essential function, or they wouldn't be commercially successful. In this and the next chapter, we will explore two important categories of entertainment and some ethical issues connected with them—beginning in this chapter with humor and comedy.

We live in an age of heightened sensitivity where conflicts can easily arise over humor and offensiveness, pressing issues of freedom of expression to the forefront of public policy debate. Enough gravity surrounds the issue of levity to call for serious

175

philosophical consideration. In this chapter on the ethics of humor and comedy, we will set aside questions of how to reconcile freedom of expression with conflicting moral and ethical demands (explored in Chapter 2). We will concentrate instead on a shifting set of philosophical problems at the frontiers of the "unfunny" (where, as it turns out, a lot of hard philosophical work remains to be accomplished).

Typically, moral or ethical objections lodged against a joke or joke type find expression in claims that the joke or joke type is NOT FUNNY. Jokes are almost never thought funny but (morally or ethically) objectionable. The objection seems to destroy the humor, at least for the objector, and often for others as well. One set of philosophical issues has to do with *why* this is so, and whether it should be.

Similarly, in response to such objections one often hears the reply, "What's the matter? Can't you take a joke? Where's your sense of humor?" And so, further philosophical issues arise: Does the recognition that humor can be objectionable on moral or ethical grounds necessarily come at the expense of one's capacity to enjoy humor? Are feminists, for example, who find dumb blonde jokes unfunny, humorless? At what point does sensitivity become hypersensitivity? Or is all of this just in the funny bone of the beholder?

People's senses of humor do vary considerably. We've all heard of cases where two people have such divergent senses of humor that relationships are strained. One person finds Garrison Keillor amusing. Another cracks up at the Three Stooges. Both people "get" all the jokes. The problem is that what the one person finds amusing, the other does not. They just have different senses of humor. Even so, this commonplace truth fails to free us from the philosophical labyrinth. What if the jokes you find most amusing happen to be the ones that others find most offensive? What do you think of people who enjoy and circulate jokes that offend you? Is something wrong with *their* sense of humor or *yours?* And if someone is offended by what you call innocent humor—same philosophical problem.

Humor is *inter*active. Humor always presupposes a joke-teller (or writer or presenter) and an audience. Accordingly, we can approach this philosophical tangle of ethical issues that revolve around jokes and joking from the vantage point of either an audience member or a joke-teller. From the audience member's vantage point the issues have primarily to do with articulating the nature of the offense in offensive humor. In philosophical terms, this means giving a theoretically coherent and defensible account of what it is that makes a joke morally objectionable. And this takes us immediately into several deeply interesting areas of philosophical intrigue at once.

First we confront the questions of what in essence humor is and how it works—philosophical issues also of interest from the point of view of making or telling jokes. Of course we have a range of philosophical theories to consider here.[1] Plato, Aristotle, Thomas Hobbes, and others seem to have held that humor is mostly based on feelings of superiority, that laughter and amusement are expressions or manifestations of such feelings, and that jokes and other forms of humor are devices for arousing or activating such feelings. This could be called the "superiority theory" of humor. It is fairly easy to see how, on this theory, one might begin to account for the nature of the offense found in morally offensive humor. On this theory, humor already sounds basically unsavory, or morally suspect. Sigmund Freud held that humor allows us to express repressed or forbidden urges. One could call this the "relief theory" of humor. Again, this theory might begin to account for the nature of the offense found in morally offensive humor. On this theory, although humor itself avoids already sounding unsavory or morally suspect, the urges it allows us to express do. The German philosophers Immanuel Kant and Arthur Schopenhauer held that humor was essentially a response or reaction to a certain kind of surprise that we tend to experience when confronted with an incongruity. It is not immediately apparent how this "incongruity theory" of humor alone might account for the nature of the offense found in morally offensive humor.

A second area of philosophical intrigue has to do with the nature of the harm or injury involved in morally offensive humor. Even if it is settled, as Catharine MacKinnon argues in Chapter 2, that words have the power to cause actual injury to people and that speech is a form of action for which people may legitimately be held accountable, it still remains a philosophically intriguing puzzle to identify the precise nature of the particular harm or injury caused by morally offensive *humor*— and even to identify the victim of the harm or sufferer of the injury. Is the harm caused by morally offensive humor a direct consequence of the telling of an offensive joke, or a less direct consequence of traffic in such humor? Is the harm just the "hurt feelings" or "offended sensibilities" of the audience member who finds the humor offensive, or is it something more lasting or more far-reaching? Is the injury confined to the audience alone, or might it extend to some third party—or to the joke teller himself?

This brings us around once again to the other vantage point from which this tangle of ethical issues can be approached. From the joke-telling vantage point the issues primarily concern assessing and managing the risk of offense. People who pursue their livelihoods in comedy confront this set of problems constantly in their work. Consider the situation from the point of view of a working or aspiring comedian or comic writer, and you can appreciate that these problems are no less philosophical, but they are immediate, inevitable, and most of all *practical*. Try writing three minutes of stand-up comic material, and you'll soon see what we mean. This vantage point offers valuable insights. For example, we might reflect for a moment on the special value of humor as a healing agent. If humor is a healing agent, then presumably there are wounds to be healed. This might help considerably in understanding the sensitivities that people often exhibit in connection with humor—especially when they have occasion to recognize themselves and their own situations implicated in the jokes.

5.1 THE ETHICS OF SLAPSTICK COMEDY Robert C. Solomon is Quincy Lee Centennial Professor of Business and Philosophy at the University of Texas, and around the world one of the most widely known and respected contemporary American philosophers. He is the author of many articles and books on a wide variety of philosophical topics and is also a fan of the post-vaudevillian, neo-*commedia dell'arte* group known as the Three Stooges. Among his many published works is a collection of popular essays, written over a twenty-year period and published in 1992, entitled *Entertaining Ideas.* This collection is based on the assumptions that (1) philosophy is—or ought to be—fun, and (2) philosophy is for anyone and everyone, not just for the recluse or the professional. The following selection is taken from this collection. In it Solomon considers the humor of the Three Stooges, particularly in response to the widespread sentiment that indeed the Stooges are *not* funny, or, at any rate, that their humor is juvenile, and appeals to adolescent boys more than it does either to adults generally or females generally.

The most obvious reason for this is that the Stooges practice a genre of humor often neglected by philosophical and literary theorists: so-called slapstick comedy. Typically, slapstick exemplifies the superiority theory of humor. It depends upon amusement at the expense of some "inferior beings," because of the stupidity—or other defects such as stubbornness, greed, gluttony, and so on—attributed to them. Solomon argues that this does not fairly represent the Stooges. Instead, Solomon argues that the Stooges exemplify a rather more virtuous attitude, which he calls "upward contempt." This targets the "mighty," the "elite," the "upper classes" and so on for humiliation—an attitude made even more virtuous by the fact that the Stooges make great and constant fun of themselves. Along with this interpretation of the Stooges, Solomon considers several ethical questions about humor in general. First, whether such humor ought to be enjoyed without guilt, for the very notion of laughing *at* (as opposed to laughing *with*) someone—even if they fully intend to be laughed at—raises certain ethical doubts. Next comes a much-neglected question in ethics—Why is it so important (much-touted advantages of health and conviviality aside) to have a good sense of humor? And finally, the question with which this entire chapter is concerned: Does laughing at the Stooges indicate a good sense of humor, or the contrary? Are the girls right after all?

QUESTIONS FOR STUDY AND DISCUSSION

1. How does Solomon counter the criticism that the Three Stooges' humor is too violent? Do you find his defense persuasive?
2. Explain the "Superiority Theory of Humor" and why Solomon thinks it inadequate in accounting for the humor in the Three Stooges.
3. Explain the "Relief Theory of Humor" and why Solomon thinks it inadequate in accounting for the humor in the Three Stooges.
4. Explain the "Incongruity Theory of Humor" and why Solomon thinks it inadequate in accounting for the humor in the Three Stooges.
5. What is Solomon's "Inferiority Theory of Humor" and how is it meant to solve the problems posed by the humor of the Three Stooges?

ARE THE THREE STOOGES FUNNY? SOITAINLY!

(OR WHEN IS IT OK TO LAUGH?)[2]

ROBERT C. SOLOMON

*Everything is funny so long as it happens to
someone else.*

WILL ROGERS

"Rire est le propre de l'homme" ("to laugh is fitting to man"), wrote Rabelais. Of course he never saw the Three Stooges. Would they have given him second thoughts? Can you imagine raunchy Rabelais watching Curly or Shemp doing the dying chicken? Trying to appreciate bowl-coiffured Moe pulling Larry's rag mop of hair, slapping him down while calling him a moron? Of course, Rabelais' countrymen today think that Jerry Lewis is the funniest thing since the invention of the baguette, so there is reason to suppose that an appreciation of idiocy is well settled into the Gallic gene pool. But these are also the people who elevated *logique* to the status of an art, and the juxtaposition is instructive. Although philosophers have long made much of the supposed fact that human beings are the only creatures who "reason," it seems to be just as plausible (with some of the same exceptions) to insist that we are just as unique in our silliness. We are fundamentally creatures who laugh, and these two familiar human functions, reason and humor, are intimately tied together. The bridge between them, as Mark Twain once suggested, is embarrassment.

The Three Stooges have caused considerable embarrassment in their fifty years of success and popularity. Their humor is chastised as being childish, violent, vulgar, and anti-feminist. (Their first film, by way of evidence, was entitled *Women Haters.*) Consequently, relatively few women find them funny, perhaps because their older brothers acted out one too many Stooges antics at their expense. Stooge appreciation also takes time, the time to convert idiotic madness into familiar ritual. Educators, rarely Stooge fans themselves, pontificate about their bad influence. The Soviets once wanted to use the shows "to show how Americans had been brutalized . . . in the name of fun." Few adults in their chosen professions would dare attempt a Stooges gesture when the door closes and the boss is out of view. I only hesitate to suggest that it is one of the most basic bonds between men, and it is far more elemental than the mere phrase "a sense of humor" could ever suggest.

Impropriety is the soul of wit, according to Somerset Maugham, and few wits since the Romans have ever been more improper than the Stooges. But the comedy of the Three Stooges is not just rudeness personified. The comedian John Candy says of the Stooges that "the magic was their subtlety." Film critic Leonard Maltin insists that "their art was artlessness." The Stooges were ideal for television, and that was where they made their mark. Their films were originally made and distributed as "shorts" to precede feature-length movies, but the Stooges found and still find their largest audience on the small screen. There is nothing special about television humor except, perhaps, that it is so condensed and concise, and it is shared by so many people, across generations and social classes. It lacks, of course, the audience participation that one might enjoy or suffer in a live theatrical or vaudeville performance. There is a drop in the intensity of humor in the conversion of live stage to television screen (e.g., the televised sessions of "Evening at the Improv") which cannot be explained by appeal to censorship alone. It is, however, that loss of the immediacy that allows stand-up comics to be intimate that allows the Stooges to be safely sealed, like miniatures in a box from whom the audience is safely protected. Within their little box, the Stooges are the heirs of ancient forms of humor, from the theater of Aristophanes and Plautus to the *commedia dell'arte* and then modern vaudeville, where they started, with their unique combination of wit, slapstick, insult, skill, tomfoolery, and stupidity. But their humor and their message, drawn from those ancient sources, are refreshingly up-to-date, primarily aimed at puncturing the pretensions of the rich and powerful.

The humor of the Stooges is the humor of the underdog, the humor of the common man. As the Stooges make fools of themselves and each other, they ridicule every profession and the world of the wealthy in particular by their very presence within it. Doctors, plumbers, tailors, soldiers, used chariot salesmen,

Nazis, or millionaires, no one is safe from Stoogery. No one is without pretensions, and pretensions are set-ups for slapstick. It is slapstick, not the pun, that is the lowest form of humor, although the Stooges made ample use of both. Slapstick humiliates, simply and directly, and the difference between the Stooges and (most of) their unhappy targets is that the Stooges humiliate themselves and beat the world to the punch. In their self-inflicted nonsense, there is dignity, the dignity of the unpretentious. This makes us uncomfortable, but it is also something we recognize and admire. This is not "high" humor, nor could it be. The witty comeback line, the deft put-down, the subtle revenge—these are not for the Stooges. Their answer to humiliation is a shriek, a "whoop," a little dance, a slap, or belly-punch in return. Isn't that how we all sometimes feel like reacting, despite our fragile veneers of respectability? (Can you really trust anyone who is never willing to make a Stooge-like sound?)

Slapstick is the ultimate prick of pretension, so long as it is evenly inflicted and suffered in turn as well. "Some things just aren't funny," the critics have always complained (though some of them catch themselves laughing nevertheless). But why not? Enjoying slapstick does not require a college education, much less skill or wisdom or philosophical sophistication. There is very little to understand, and that, perhaps, is why so many people find it "beneath" them. Indeed, nothing undermines a philosophical argument so quickly as a belly-laugh, and that, perhaps, is why intellectual life has for so long been suspicious of laughter. It is not the belly-laugh but rather the attempt to elevate humor to some level of sophistication that is and ought to be suspicious, however. That Shakespeare's puns seem sophisticated to us now is perhaps because only sophisticated people now read Shakespeare, and some of the language in which he punned now sounds almost foreign to us. His own view was that the pun is as low as one can go, and Shakespeare's humor was often as bawdy as one can imagine, far beyond what is routinely censored from adult television today. So, too, we should remind ourselves that classic Italian opera and much of Mozart are typically riotous, and despite their status in "high culture" today, most of those operas were originally street fare and popular extravaganzas, the low art of their day. One did not (and did not need to) take them seriously.

There is, of course, the accusation of violence. Never mind that no one ever gets hurt in a Three Stooges comedy. And apart from the unseen Dearly Departed who may set up the plot with an oddly worded will, no one ever dies. Never mind that the average television cop show, not to mention the latest *Teenage Mutant Ninja Turtles* movie, has a body count far exceeding the number of thumps, dumps, and pokes of a Stooges film. It is argued that kids will imitate what they see, but do these critics think that kids are idiots? It is one thing to glorify the use of handguns and other firearms, with their lethal noise, slick mechanism, and abstract ability to kill at a distance. It is something else to use as slapstick just those gestures and minor brutalities that kids routinely inflict on one another and full well recognize for the minor hurts they cause. In the context of what little boys try to do to one another, the typical Stooge routine, even the infamous eye-poke and familiar slap-

ping, is harmless. Luckily they lack the strength and coordination. The critical problem here is a failure, particularly on the part of TV "violent incident" counters, to distinguish between violence and slapstick. Slapstick is meant to be funny, and it is funny just because the "slap" in question is so obviously an act that one person would not normally do it to another. Of course, all TV violence is pretend violence, except for contact sports and live police and war broadcasts, but its violence pretends to be real. Slapstick does not, even when it is real, as when one Stooge hits another with a pie.[3] One of the charms of the Stooges is that their "artlessness" makes their pretending and their feigning so much more obvious, so that what kids imitate is not the violence nor even the imitation of violence. There are no moral lessons in slapstick, but nothing to be afraid of either. The violence critics should rather stick to Dirty Harry. Indeed, in these days when six-to-ten-year-olds carry guns to elementary school (and occasionally use them) there is much to be said for the more innocent nonsense of the Stooges. The world will still be full of insults and outrages, but the Stooges teach that the most effective response is humor, not violence. Humor is not "giving in" and it is not weakness. It is a special kind of strength, harmony conceived in foolishness.

Humor is a species of vicarious emotion. Caesar gets stabbed, not once but twenty times, even by his best friend. The audience watches with vicarious horror. They have seen it many times before, this betrayal and multiple stabbing of Caesar. In another theater Othello strangles his struggling but innocent wife. This is called tragedy. (No one laughs.) Nor does anyone comment that the actor playing Caesar isn't really bleeding, or that Desdemona will go out for a cappuccino after the performance. The "willing suspension of disbelief," as Coleridge famously coined it, is alive and well here. No one is "really" hurt so we can allow our emotions their free "make believe" reign. Why, then, is the equally feigned petty violence of the Three Stooges in question as comedy? Perhaps because it wildens the kids, but then, doesn't everything? But it is not the word "violence" that best captures the Stooges mutual abuse of their various foils and of each other. It rather falls into the category of ritual humiliation. The Stooges' humor is the humor of humiliation, taking it as well as dishing it out, but one misses the point if he or she sees humiliation as the end in itself. It is humiliation to end all humiliation, for once one accepts oneself as a Stooge, the slings and arrows of outrageous fortune are nothing but fodder for another joke or gesture.

Laughter may indeed be the "best medicine" as one of our more prestigious periodicals proclaims, but laughter at what? We make a rather harsh distinction (at least in polite discourse) between "laughing *at*" and "laughing *with,*" and rule number one of our ethic of humor is not to laugh at the misfortune of others. And yet, most of what we find funny in the Stooges is just that, a foolish or frustrated Curly carrying a block of ice up fifteen flights on a hot summer day, Moe wearing a mask of paint or flour, an innocent bystander deprived of his wig, a customer who leaves the shop with a gigantic hole in his pants, a room full of sophisticated diners hit by a battery of pies and, even worse, allowing themselves to join in. And then, of course, there is the usual: Moe's ritualized double eye-poke, Curly's equally practiced hand block, and Moe's counter-feign. Then Curly's cry and hyperkinetic dance of pain and indignation. (One should not underestimate the importance of sound in undermining the seriousness of the Stooges' violence: the kettledrum stomach punch, the violin pluck eye-poke, and the ratchet ear twist.) "That's not funny," decry the righteous, but they're wrong.

Henri Bergson hypothesized that humor blocks normal emotion, but I think that the opposite is true. It is the sympathetic laughter we enjoy at the Stooges' alleged expense that makes us aware of our own best and least pretentious emotions. Pride, envy, and anger all disappear. That sense of status that defines so much of our self-image dissolves. Accordingly, Plato urged censorship of humor as well as poetry to preserve the good judgment and virtue of the guardians of the republic. I would argue to the contrary that laughter opens up the emotions and it is good humor that makes good judgment possible.

The philosophy of humor is a subject that itself tends to be all-too humorless. But that is perhaps because it does not appreciate the extent to which it is itself a ludicrous topic, and my basic belief in these matters is that the basic meaning of humor and "a sense of humor" is ultimately laughter *at oneself.* But for this to be meaningful the laughter will have to be "low humor" and folly rather than wit and learned cleverness that are the hallmark of humor, quite the contrary of those examples preferred by the most contemporary theorists. Philosophers, in particular, appreciate cleverness, preferably based on some profound linguistic or ontological insight. Freud, by contrast, preferred elephant and fart jokes, but then he was looking for a diagnosis rather than a good laugh (Did Freud chuckle as he was writing his *Wit and Its Relation to the Unconscious?* Or did he rather insist on maintaining that famous stone face of disapproval, even in the solitude of his study?) The Stooges, by contrast again, were always laughing at themselves, and they invited us to do so, too, with the understanding that we were laughing at ourselves as well. Their shorts are often cited as paradigms of bad taste but have nevertheless dominated television from its earliest days and continue to influence and be imitated by the most talented comedians today. They are not particularly clever or chauvinist or brutal but they provide a mirror for our own silliness—if only in our laughing at them.

But why are the Stooges funny? They would seem to provide an obvious case of *laughing at.* Watching the Three Stooges, what we seem to experience is what the Germans (wonderfully humorous people) describe as *schadenfreude*—the enjoyment of other people's pain and suffering, deserved or undeserved. Are we really so cruel? We might note here with some wonder that it is so easy to be funny when there is something to laugh at but hard to be funny when praising or admiring. Critic John Simon is hopeless when (rarely) he likes something. His reviews are memorable when they are offensive. Why? It does not seem to matter whether or not they are deserved. If they are deserved, of course, we can have a clear conscience in laughing, but we find ourselves laughing at insults even when they are not fair. The Stooges, on this easy account, set themselves up to be ridiculed. Their humor is a gift, allowing us to feel wittily superior.

Since ancient times, according to John Morreall in his book on laughter,[4] one can discern three dominant conceptions of humor. First, there is the *superiority* theory, assumed by Plato and Aristotle, in which laughter expresses one's feeling of sophistication, wisdom, and superiority over the poor slob who would get himself entrapped in such a situation. Obviously such humor would be appealing in aristocratic societies or any society that has a more or less clearly delineated inferior class. According to Albert Rapp, in his *Origins of Wit and Humor,* the original laugh was probably a roar of triumph for the victor in a fight. Roger Scruton, who is not unsympathetic to aristocratic thinking, has hypothesized that humor involves devaluation.

The Three Stooges would seem to fit perfectly into this conception of humor, for what losers have ever made themselves more lowly, more ridiculous, more prone to ridicule? In a world in which everyone has the right not to be offended and where everything is becoming offensive, humor by way of superiority is too often inappropriate, "politically incorrect." Laughing at the Stooges, however, is OK. The problem, however, is that we do not just laugh at the Stooges, and much of their humor depends on the humiliation of others. Superiority theory doesn't quite work. One doesn't walk away from the Stooges feeling superior, but, rather, released and relieved.

The second conception might be called the *relief* theory. It was most famously advocated by Freud, and it renders laughter akin to sport in safely expressing violence and, of course, forbidden sexual impulses. If you can't *do it,* in other words, at least you can laugh about it. But such laughter, so understood, is not just laughing at; it is also a vicarious form of activity, "the word as play." We laugh because the Stooges do what we would like to do, act as we would like to act, not sexually to be sure but as fools, clowns beyond humiliation, humiliating those whom we would also love to humiliate: e.g., pompous doctors, overbearing matrons, "tough" bosses, and crooked politicians. Humor thus becomes a devious expression of *resentment,* and the release and relief we feel is nothing less than the catharsis of one of our most poisonous emotions. There is something suspicious, however, about a theory that makes laughter out of a weakness, a leak in one's psyche, so to speak, and directs itself mainly to one's hostile or immoral thoughts of others. One cannot disprove such a theory, of course, but we should be very cautious about accepting it. Three Stooges' humor does not feel particularly vicious, and those who complain that it seems so are easily dismissed as those who have not allowed themselves to "get into it."

Finally, there is the *incongruity* theory, defended by Kant and Schopenhauer among others and described by the Danish existentialist Kierkegaard as "comedy as painless contradiction." What makes this theory attractive is that it dispenses with any notion of "laughing at" and looks to the language and the humorous situation as such for a clue to the humor. Humor is our reaction to things that don't fit together. We laugh at stupidity not because we feel superior to it but because the juxtaposition of actions and events surprises us. Linguistic incongruity, for example, is, of course, the favorite conception of humor in academia, where facility with language is a special virtue and puns, wordplay, and cleverness are readily appreciated. Similarly, John Morreall suggests that humor involves a "pleasant psychological shift," such as when one is caught off guard. There are, to be sure, any number of unexpected and unusual psychological shifts required to follow the typical Stooges plot, and incongruity is central to much of their humor. But the incongruity theory does not explain why the Stooges get better and better with repetitive viewing, and why imitation is part and parcel of Stooges spectatorship. It also sells the Stooges short, prettifies their humor, and ignores or denies its bite. The humor of the Stooges is the humor of mutual humiliation, not mere incongruity or surprise, but neither is it merely relief of our own frustrations or the sense of superiority that comes from laughing at someone else.

No one, to my knowledge, has advocated what we might call the *inferiority* theory of humor, laughter as the great leveler, beyond contempt or indignation, antithetical to pretension and pomp. Sitting on the sofa watching *Malice in the Palace* for the twenty-seventh time, we allow ourselves to fall into a world of miniature mayhem in which we feel as foolish as they are. We enjoy these petty plots of ambition, ire, and revenge, and not because we feel superior to them or use them for our own catharsis much less because, on the twenty-seventh viewing, we are in any way surprised. Why should we not? Do we still have to pretend with the critics that our own natures are not similarly petty, vengeful, and, viewed from the outside, uproariously slapstick? Larry, Moe, Shemp, and Curly capture the silly side of human nature just as surely as Macbeth and Hamlet represent the tragic side, but we can easily understand why the critics would prefer to ennoble themselves with the latter while rejecting the former. Satire and parody may be much more effective for developing individual thought than tragedy and self-righteousness, and in order to avoid the supposed bad taste of enjoying the Three Stooges we encounter the much greater danger of taking ourselves too seriously.

Voltaire once commented that, to combat human misery, we require hope and sleep. It was the moralist Immanuel Kant, of all people, who corrected Voltaire by suggesting that in addition to hope and sleep as palliatives for human misery we should also count laughter. But Kant, I presume, would not have found Moe's eye-poke or Curly's clucking chicken to be laughable, and Kant's idea of a good joke would no doubt fall flat on television today. Kant, like most intellectuals, thought that a joke should be profound. For the Stooges and their fans, repetitive, mindless silliness was the way to humor. Philosophers, as people of reason, have always found laughter and humor suspicious. As far back as the *Philebus,* Plato warned against the dangers of humor as he had chastised the falsification of poetry in the *Republic,* and he urged censorship to protect the guardians of the republic from the distortions and distractions of laughter. Aristotle—despite his lost treatise on comedy, which provides the theme of Umberto Eco's *The Name of the Rose*—shared many of Plato's reservations about comedy. And despite the proliferation of comedy among the "low arts" throughout the ages, comedy as such was never held in high regard. Humor

and *commedia dell'arte* were strictly the province of the masses, the *hoi polloi.* The most famous "comedy" of the Middle Ages, appropriately, was a thoroughly somber poetic journey through Heaven and Hell, neither place known for its humor.

Among many faults recently raised against the "Western tradition" since Plato—its sexism, racism, Eurocentrism, scientism, technophilia and obsession with control, hyper-rationality, myopic universality, asexuality and denial of the body, ecological mean-spiritedness and wastefulness—surely must be included its lack of humor, its utterly solemn seriousness. Recent defenses of that tradition, e.g., in the fighting words of Allan Bloom, only make that fault even more glaring, and Third World and feminist critics, however right on the money, seem only to make it worse, more humorless, more deadly serious, more depressing. Socrates was, first of all, a stooge, a clown, a champion of intellectual slapstick. (Aristophanes gets it right in *Clouds.*) By contrast, Wittgenstein suggested that an entire philosophy could be written entirely in jokes, although he himself seemed incapable of telling one. Perhaps the most successful if controversial philosopher joking today, Jacques Derrida, makes his best points with puns, historical wisecracks, and self-deprecating humor (charms often lacking in his traditionally serious, even pugnacious students, who take Derrida's well-aimed jokes as a serious "methodology"). Against the wisdom of the age, I would say that humor, not rationality, is the key to tolerance and peace. Nothing is so important in philosophy or anywhere else as not taking oneself too seriously.

> *Rebukes are easily endured, but it is intolerable to be*
> *laughed at. We are quite willing to be wicked, but we do not*
> *want to be ridiculous.*
>
> MOLIERE

CASE STUDY: CARTOON CULTURE

At the close of the twentieth century a trend in televised "cartoons for grownups" led to what some cultural critics might describe as a "race to the bottom" in the promotion of social values. Fox Network's *The Simpsons,* MTV's *Beavis and Butthead,* and Comedy Central's *South Park* each broke established standards for television content and pushed the thresholds of public acceptability in television fare. These cartoon programs are still widely accessible in video format. Review a sample of any one (or more) of these cartoon series. What specific transgressions against conventional moral values can you find in your viewing selection? To what extent can you defend these transgressions—in "aesthetic" (artistic) terms; in ethical terms?

CASE STUDY: CARTOON VIOLENCE

In footnote number three to the essay you have just read—in the process of slashing through the general critique of media violence as applied to the Three Stooges— Professor Solomon briefly alludes to a "special problem" presented by cartoon violence. A challenging but rewarding exercise would be to compose a detailed analysis of this "special problem." What, precisely, is the "special problem" with cartoon violence? How would you propose to resolve it?

5.2 THE ETHICS OF SEXIST HUMOR In the next essay, Merrie Bergmann, who taught in the philosophy department at Dartmouth College in the 1970s, offers an explanation of the essential nature of sexist humor—the kind feminists find offensive—and the offense feminists find in it. Bergmann subscribes to the "incongruity" theory of humor. She defines humor as anything that is both funny and produced with the intention that it be recognized and appreciated as funny. And she holds that incongruity makes "funny" things funny. Funny things are incongruities that we attend to in fun. Other elements—for instance, feelings of superiority, or relief—may enhance the fun, but they're not essential to it in Bergmann's view. This makes her task more difficult, because, as we explained above, unlike the superiority or relief theories of humor, the incongruity theory does not immediately support an intuitively plausible account for the nature of the offense found in morally offensive humor. But Bergmann identifies several "humor-defeating conditions"— circumstances that interfere with or defeat funniness in situations or episodes that otherwise would qualify as funny, and on this basis she accounts for the offense in morally offensive humor.

Returning to "sexist humor," Bergmann argues that the offense in sexist humor is a real offense committed by the person who finds fun in sexist humor. Bergmann defines "sexist humor" as humor that requires either holding sexist beliefs, attitudes, and/or norms in order to perceive the crucial incongruity or using them to add to the fun effect of the incongruity. What makes such humor offensive is that tellers and appreciators of sexist humor either are or ought to be aware of relevant and applicable humor-defeating conditions, yet persist in finding the humor funny. It is the same sort of offense as would arise in the case of a practical joke gone wrong with tragically harmful consequences if someone were nevertheless to persist in finding the practical joke funny.

QUESTIONS FOR STUDY AND DISCUSSION

1. Of the four theories of humor mentioned in Solomon's essay on the Three Stooges, which one is central to Bergmann's account of sexist humor?
2. What "humor-defeating conditions" does Bergmann think interfere with or defeat funniness in situations or episodes that otherwise would qualify as "funny"? Do you agree with Bergmann that such conditions undermine humor? Can you think of any instances in your own experience that either confirm or disconfirm Bergmann's claims about these limitations on funniness?
3. What are the five ways Bergmann identifies for sexist beliefs to play a role in generating humor?
4. Bergmann considers what we might call the "only-joking defense" against objections to offensive sexist humor. What is that defense and what does Bergmann think is wrong with it?

HOW MANY FEMINISTS DOES IT TAKE TO MAKE A JOKE?

MERRIE BERGMANN

Sexist Humor and What's Wrong with It[5]

For anyone who refers to feminists as "women's libbers" or, better yet, as "ladies' libbers," it typically takes only one feminist to make a joke. In fact, she is the joke. The joke is complex, for she is both a woman and a person committed to a particular point of view. Women are traditional objects of humor in our culture (and in numerous other cultures). We have countless jokes about dumb blondes, scatter-brained redheads, myopic wives, mothers, mothers-in-law, lady drivers, and college coeds. Because she is a woman, a feminist is an amusing creature indeed.

The complexity of the joke enters precisely where the feminist distinguishes herself from non-feminist women. For while she is unwilling to accept the stereotypes of women's ignorance, irrationality, irresponsibility, and so on, or to accept the fate ordained by such stereotypes, she is still a woman and hence subsumed under those stereotypes in the eyes of many beholders. Her challenge to the stereotypes then merits serious consideration only if she can demonstrate that she is an *exception* to the stereotypes, that is, only if she can demonstrate that the challenge does not come from ignorant, irrational, and irresponsible quarters. There are rich sources for humor here. I shall describe three.

First, if the feminist does establish herself as an exception to the stereotypes, she may be laughable (funny, ridiculous) for just that reason. Kant said that

> [a] woman who has a head full of Greek, like Mme. Dacier, or carries on fundamental controversies about mechanics, like the Marquise de Chatelet, might as well even have a beard—for perhaps that would express more obviously the mien of profundity for which she strives."[6]

It is a small step from Kant's astute premise to Nietzsche's conclusion that

> [i]t betrays a corruption of the instincts—quite apart from the fact that it displays bad taste—when a woman adduces Madame Roland or Madame de Stael or Monsieur George Sand, of all people, as if they proved anything *in favor* of "woman as such." Among men these three are the three *comical* women as such—nothing more!— and precisely the best involuntary *counterargument* against emancipation and feminine vainglory[7]

Here, a woman is laughable for not living up to the stereotypes.

Second, the stereotypes may be confused for fact rather than the norms that they are, and the feminist now becomes laughable by virtue of having the ironically stupid notion that she is knowledgeable, the irrational notion that she is rational, and so on, when these beliefs are so obviously false. At the beginning of my first term of residence as a graduate student, a fellow student (male, I will add) laughed at me when I told him that I intended to specialize in logic. We do laugh at stupidity that manifests itself in the face of the obvious, and the woman who supposes herself to have certain virtues when in fact she has the corresponding defects is a case in point.

Third, there is the syllogism: everything that a feminist does is something that a woman does; everything that a woman does is trivial or ridiculous; therefore, everything that a feminist does is trivial or ridiculous. Thus, consciousness-raising turns out to be a fancy name for women's gossip and babble; a feminist is a frustrated woman who couldn't catch her fellow; and we are assured that there is indeed a generic use of the word "man" that applies to females, as well as to males, on the strength of the formula "Man embraces woman." Here the fun is in deflating specific feminist views and practices, as if they did not merit serious consideration in their own right.[8]

The feminist who does not smile when faced with this plethora of humor may be dubbed a "killjoy" or worse. And what reply is adequate to attempts at appeasement like: "What's the matter? Can't you take a joke?" or: "It's all in fun. Where's your sense of humor?" It used to be said that women have no sense of humor. More recently, the target has been refined: *feminists* have no sense of humor. But ingenious empirical research has disproved both claims.[9] Nevertheless, despite her excellent sense of humor, the feminist still isn't laughing. She, along with many people who do not identify themselves as feminists, thinks that all this humor is a serious matter. It is that thought that motivates the questions I am concerned with in this paper, namely: What is sexist humor, the humor about women that the feminist objects to? and What is the nature of the offense in sexist humor?

Because there can be no adequate account of sexist humor, nor a fair estimation of its offense, without a prior account of humor, the project of this section is to provide such an account. I use "humor" to denote episodes—situations, objects, words, statements, and stories—that are funny and that are produced with the intention that they be funny.

What makes for funniness? There is a family of theories of humor that state that the source of funniness in a humorous episode is the incongruous, and I believe that this claim is correct. Although incongruity is explicated differently from theory to theory, John Morreall has neatly summed up incongruity theories as follows:

> The basic idea . . . is very simple. We live in an orderly world where we have come to expect certain patterns among things, properties, events, etc. when we experience something that doesn't fit these patterns, that violates our expectations, we laugh.[10]

On my account, an episode or element of an episode is incongruous if it is contraindicated by our beliefs, attitudes,

and/or norms. (I'll refer to this cluster as "our beliefs.") Contraindication by our beliefs is not simply a matter of something that our beliefs have not prepared us for. It is a matter of something that our beliefs prohibit: something that we believe is absurd, improbable, or implausible, something that just doesn't make sense to us, or something that we believe is clearly inappropriate. Whether there is incongruity in an episode depends upon the perceiver. Some incongruities will be incongruities for a whole community, while others will be found only by a subgroup of that community or by an idiosyncratic individual.

The seventh page of a book that is called *A Book* is headed "Contents," and it contains a list that begins: "Words, numerals, punctuation, diacritical marks, artwork (a trace), paper, glue, ink. . . ."[11] That is an incongruous list—it is inappropriate to list *those* contents on the contents page of a book. It is also funny. In general, an episode is funny to us if it presents us with an incongruity that we attend to in fun. We are interested, but we are amused rather than puzzled or concerned, entertained rather than insulted. Many incongruity theories demand more than incongruity in funny episodes, but I believe that this is due to a confusion. Advocates of these theories mistake the various methods by which humorists get us to attend to incongruities, and methods that are conducive to our having fun in doing so, for necessary ingredients in funny episodes. For example:

Consider simple nonsense humor: "No gnus is good gnus" or "Is this Picadilly or is it Thursday?" What makes these bits of nonsense funny, while other bits of nonsense—like "No lamb chops eat good apples"—are not? According to "hidden sense" theories, the first two sentences have the *appearance* of sense while the third does not, and it is this appearance that makes for funniness in the former cases.[12] The first owes the appearance of sense to the phonetic similarity of "gnus" and "news," the second to the fact that the sentence would be one of a sort that we run across every day if another name such as "Kensington" were substituted for "Thursday" at the end of the sentence. Hidden sense incongruity theories claim that in all humor we will find either some apparent sense in or behind the incongruity, or some element that makes the incongruity plausible. Thus, the apparent sense behind the incongruity in *A Book* is that words, diacritical marks, etc., are, in some sense of the expression "contents" of the book. Or consider Dick Gregory's story: "On the first day of integration a black man gets on a bus and sits on a front seat. The driver is so angry he drives around town backwards."[13] Driving around town backwards is the incongruity here. The apparent sense comes as we realize that the driver has ensured that, as in the old days, the black will still be the last to arrive.

However there are incongruous episodes that we find funny but that do not have the appearance of "sense." We laugh when, after searching for a hat for a few minutes, we discover that it is on our head, or when someone who has just completed careful installation of a burglar alarm turns and accidentally sets off the alarm. Overlooking the obvious is a type of incongruity—since anything obvious is something no one could miss. Hence there is incongruity in such cases to account for the funniness. But where is the apparent sense?

In attempting to answer this question, hidden sense incongruity theorists grade off into "hidden moral" theorists.[14] Hidden moral incongruity theories maintain that behind the incongruity in a funny episode, there is always a moral—a point to the joke. The moral in cases of overlooking the obvious—or when anyone does something inept or stupid—is that the person in question *is* inept or stupid. When we laugh at ourselves in cases where *we* have done something inept or stupid, we are taking the stance of an observer who concludes that, after all, we are what we appear to be. In Gregory's story, the moral concerns the stupidity of rednecks. Much humor does seem to have a point or hidden moral. Consider the following story: a little boy was

> . . . left in the playroom of a department store while his parents shopped. When they were ready to go, he refused to get off the rocking horse on which he was mounted. It was time for the store to close, but he still would not leave. His parents, the floor walkers, the managing director, cajoled and bribed him, but in vain. Finally a young man in the crowd said to the child's father "May I try? I have made a special study of child psychology." "Please do," said the father. Whereupon the young man stepped forward and whispered in the child's ear. The boy immediately slid off the horse and said, quietly: "Take me home please, Daddy." Afterwards the young man was asked if he would mind revealing the magic formula. "Not at all," he said, "I just said: "Get off that horse, you little ——————— or I'll knock your head off!"[15]

The young man's method was certainly incongruous, given his self-description. But this story also leaves us with a moral about the various schools of psychology.

With a little work, we can attribute the fun even in nonsense humor to hidden morals. Perhaps we have just shown our stupidity or gullibility by consuming the nonsense. Or we may attribute stupidity to the implied author of the nonsense. There are incongruity theories of humor that maintain that disparagement is necessary to humor.[16] However, neither the hidden moral theory nor a disparagement theory can account for the funniness in the following story.

> Jones, seated in a movie house, could not help being aware that the man immediately in front of him had his arm around the neck of a large dog which occupied the seat next to him. The dog was clearly observing the picture with understanding, for he snarled softly when the villain spoke, yelped joyously at the funny remarks, and so on. Jones leaned forward and tapped the man in front of him on the shoulder. He said, "Pardon me, sir, but I can't get over your dog's behavior." The man turned around and said, "Frankly, it surprises me too. He hated the book."[17]

There is no hidden moral to the story, nor is either man—nor the implied author nor the audience—belittled.

Neither the appearance of sense, nor a hidden moral nor disparagement, is necessary to our finding funniness, but each of these may help us to do so, by enhancing the fun in attending to an incongruity; and so humorists, in their attempts to amuse us, may rely on one or more of these devices. The appearance of sense in nonsense may interest us in the nonsense—catch our fancy—long enough for us to be amused. Discovering an apparent sense in an incongruity, as in the case of Gregory's story, may add to the amusement or fun. It is like puzzle-solving. Discovering a hidden moral may similarly be fun, if we like the moral. And all of us enjoy harmless disparagement—even if we are the target. There are other methods that humorists may use to add to our fun in contemplating incongruities, e.g., telling us jokes about one of our favorite "naughty" topics like sex or sacrilege. Although allowing us one or more of these satisfactions adds to the *fun* in humor, however, none is necessary to humor. All that is necessary is that we contemplate, or attend to, an incongruity in fun.

Where the humor succeeds, we do attend to the incongruity in fun. Of course, this does not always happen. For example, many humor theorists have noted that our moods may affect our receptivity to humor. If we are melancholy, say, we may be unable to accept anything in fun. (Although we may still be able to say sincerely: "I see that the story was funny; I'm just not in the mood for jokes.") But regardless of our mood as the humor begins, even the methods of humorists may fail to achieve the goal of our attending to the incongruous in fun if our engagement with the incongruity is not detached, in the following ways.

The incongruity must not be a source of pain to us. We do not find it funny when a man who slips on a banana peel is obviously hurt—unless we desire him to be hurt, or are indifferent to his suffering, or believe that he deserved it. We may also laugh afterwards in recollecting the banana peel episode, even if the man was hurt and this concerned us at the time. But when we laugh in this case, we recollect the episode in isolation from his pain, as if there were no painful outcome. We can do so, say, if the man is fully recovered, no longer has vivid recollections of his pain, and hence can laugh along with us.

Nor do we find it funny when we see the incongruous as a serious challenge to our beliefs or norms. Philosophers may find it funny when they are told that "philosophy is systematic abuse of a terminology specially invented for that purpose,"[18] but not if they discern behind those words a grave question about their discipline. On the home front, our own stupid or inept actions are funny to us only if we are not puzzled by our having so acted, that is, only if we do not seriously wonder how or why we could ever have done such a thing. In short, our confrontation with the incongruous, if we are to find it funny, must not simultaneously be the cause of serious or painful concerns.[19]

With that account in hand, it is a simple matter to characterize sexist humor. Sexist humor is humor in which sexist beliefs, attitudes, and/or norms either must be held in order to perceive an incongruity or are used to add to the fun effect of the incongruity. In the latter case, sexist beliefs may allow someone to uncover an apparent sense behind an incongruity, to discover hidden morals, to enjoy disparagement, or to treat certain topics as "naughty." (I am not going to give a criterion that tells us which beliefs are sexist. The examples that follow

are, I believe, straightforward.) I shall illustrate these different ways in which sexist beliefs can play a role in generating humor.

1. *Incongruities generated by sexist beliefs.* The funniness my fellow student found when I told him that I intended to specialize in logic came from his perception of an incongruity based on a sexist belief: women do not think logically. Humorists can rely on shared sexist beliefs to generate perceptions of incongruity. Here is a description of a comic postcard: "Hyper-active female sunbathing with a newspaper across her midriff. Headline reads, 'Today's Sport.' "[20]

Perceiving an incongruity here depends upon having a sexist attitude toward women.[21] In our culture, there is nothing incongruous in a newspaper resting on the body of a sunbather. Nor is there anything incongruous in a newspaper's having a page headed "Today's Sport." What *is* incongruous is that the newspaper headline should refer to, or label, the body that is shaded by the paper, that is that "Today's Sport" is the female's body as a sex object. I use "body" deliberately, for it is clearly not the person who is labeled in this case, and that is what is sexist in seeing women as sex objects. (In this example, as well as in the examples that follow, the fun effect may be heightened by virtue of certain sexist beliefs beyond the ones that I point out. For example, it may add to the fun if it is thought that the woman is a typical dumb blonde who didn't notice that she was labeling herself.)

2. *Apparent sense or plausibility generated by sexist beliefs.* Most examples of sexist humor that I have seen or heard

are sexist in their reliance on sexist beliefs to generate the appearance of sense behind an incongruity. This is not surprising. Typically feminine foibles are well known: women are spendthrifts, can't see the forest for the trees, are sentimental, are illogical. The chuckles attending "You think just like a woman" depend on drawing our attention to something incongruous that a woman has just said, in a way that simultaneously "explains" why she said it. Hence the heightened fun in a cartoon showing a middle-aged woman standing before a group of the same, with the caption "I just wanted to say that I'm perfectly willing to serve as treasurer, provided every penny doesn't have to come out exactly even."[22] That is an incongruous thing to come out of the mouth of a candidate for treasurer, but it "makes sense" (is plausible or quite understandable), given common sexist beliefs about women and money.

Much of the fun in the following lines from a student newspaper is also due to the "sense" that can be made of an incongruity on the basis of a sexist belief:

> Margaret Trudeau goes to visit the hockey team. When she emerges she complains that she has been gang-raped. Wishful thinking.

The last comment is certainly incongruous, since it is inappropriate to the experience allegedly reported by Trudeau in this story. But in this case, the incongruity should be a source of concern to anyone who is sensitive to the seriousness of rape. The hidden sense comes from the belief that Trudeau is sexually promiscuous (not in itself a sexist belief) and that "rape is just a

variant form of sexual intercourse."[23] The last belief is clearly sexist.

3. *Hidden morals generated by sexist beliefs*. Hidden sense, when it hinges on sexist beliefs, may often be turned into a hidden moral. What goes into "making sense" of the episode is at once confirmed by the episode. The laughs provoked by "Women will be women" and the eye-rolls accompanying "Ah, the ladies" typically depend on the belief that something a woman has just said or done is incongruous combined with the view that the episode is another confirmation of women's ignorance, irrationality, and irresponsibility.

This means that humor in which sexist beliefs are not necessary for perceiving an incongruity, or for finding apparent sense behind an incongruity, may nevertheless be sexist because it confirms sexist stereotypes or beliefs. A joke about a particular woman's stupidity can at once be taken as a joke with a point about women in general. A woman says:

> "Gee, did I fool that fellow. Imagine trying to make me pay him $5,000 for a fur coat."
> "But I saw you sign the check."
> "I know, but he'll never be able to cash it."
> "Why not?"
> "I didn't fill in the amount!"[24]

There are jokes about stupid men, but for effect they typically characterize the men as morons, as car mechanics, as politicians, or as members of an ethnic group of which stupidity is part of the current stereotype. The fur coat joke— by virtue of the incongruity and the apparent sense in the check-writer's reasoning—may be funny no matter who is writing the check, but the fun is heightened if the episode confirms a popular stereotype. In this case, the dumb woman is everywoman—and the moral is not to trust her with a checkbook.

4. *Disparagement enjoyed because of sexist beliefs.* The statement, "A feminist is a woman who couldn't catch a man," is incongruous, given the real motivations for feminism. The statement is, for that very reason, also disparaging to feminists. Many quips about feminist goals or activities are similarly disparaging. But it is not only feminists who suffer disparagement because of sexist beliefs.

For example, some people believe that the typical woman who reports a rape has not been forced to have sexual intercourse against her will. If she reports rape, then, she does so in order to retaliate against a man with whom she has just quarreled or, say, to relieve her own guilt after sexual intercourse. According to this view, the alleged rapist is the real victim. Anyone who holds such a belief may find satisfaction in an episode that makes a fool of a woman who reports rape:

> Lawyer inquires of a hefty woman how she could possibly be raped by the diminutive accused. "Well, your Honor," she answers, "I stooped a bit."[25]

5. *Sense of "naughtiness" generated by sexist beliefs.* Something is "naughty" for adults when they believe it to be forbidden, prohibited, or not spoken of and they also think that indulging in it or alluding to it is harmful fun. For many people, premarital heterosexual sexual relations are naughty, but extramarital or homosexual sexual relations are simply wrong. Jokes about the former are then fun because they are naughty, while jokes about the latter are fun because they are disparaging or convey a hidden moral. The prevalence of rape jokes in our culture may be due, in part, to the aura of naughtiness surrounding rape for many people: it is prohibited, but harmless fun.

I believe that a sense of naughtiness is needed to explain the fun reported in the following story:

> . . . a Tri Kap brother decided to tell me the nickname of the female mannequin that hung by a noose from a moose. . . . "Her nickname," he said with a twinkle in his eye, "is 'The Bitch Said No.' " My silence and glare stilled the laughter that threatened to bubble up from his belly. "Aww, Maria," his frustration was not masked, "the trouble with you being a feminist is you have no sense of humor!"[26]

There are two incongruities in this episode: nicknames are typically names, not declarative sentences, and the fate of the woman-mannequin is inappropriate to the "offense" of saying "no."

We have to fill in a little here: the occasion for saying "no" was some sexual advance from a young man. Unfortunately, some young men seem to believe that a woman is not entitled to say "no" under certain circumstances, for example, if she has gone to a man's dormitory room or if she and a man have been necking. She is responsible for having led him on and turned him on, and she is consequently obligated to satisfy his sexual demands. If he forces himself on her he is being "naughty"—he has done something that is prohibited (she has said "no"), but nonetheless harmless fun (as in "She knew what she was getting into," "She probably enjoyed it," "Chicks like to be fucked"). This same attitude of harmless fun is needed to deflect any serious, painful concern in contemplating the idea of hanging a woman who says "no." The air of propriety in the mannequin's nickname is then just an exaggeration or parody of the naughtiness of young men in less dramatic episodes. And that sense of "naughtiness," which makes the incongruity fun, depends on ignoring or denying the integrity of the woman.

Sexist beliefs, then, can play different roles in humor. When they play the roles described above, the humor that results is sexist. I want to stress that not all humor that incorporates sexist beliefs is sexist—in fact, much feminist humor uses sexist beliefs. A feminist cartoon contains frames of a woman in reflexive repose, with the running caption

> If all women secretly want to be raped, you're not a real woman if you don't want to be raped. But since you always get what you really want, if I haven't been raped, maybe I secretly don't want to be a woman [The woman sits up.] I've got to find a shrink to help me get raped.[27]

That final statement is funny—it is incongruous, and the reasoning that "leads" to the conclusion adds to the fun. The sexist belief that all women secretly want to be raped plays a role in generating the humor, but not by being one of the background beliefs *assumed* by the humorist. In fact, the moral to be drawn is that this particular belief is stupid. The

humor here is about a sexist belief, while sexist humor presupposes sexist beliefs on the part of the audience.

Being aware of a sexist belief is not the same as holding it. Because a feminist is aware of sexist beliefs, she may see why particular episodes are thought to be funny yet nevertheless not find them funny herself. But when we do not find a particular bit of humor funny, our stance is often one of indifference. Feminists and sympathizers alike believe that sexist humor is offensive. In this section I examine the nature of the offense.

Here is the sort of discussion that often follows laughter at a sexist joke. A feminist who is present objects to the joke. The joke-teller or a laughing member of the group (I'll use 'he' to refer to either) says, "What's the matter? Where's your sense of humor?" She says, "That wasn't funny. It's offensive to women." He says, "but it was only a joke. No offense intended." She says, "It's *not* only a joke—you are having fun at women's expense." He says, "Come on, there are jokes about men too." She says, "Yes, but they don't belittle men." He says, "*Of course* they do. Haven't you heard the one about the big shot lawyer who puts his foot in his mouth?! I'm a lawyer, too, and I'm a man, but I can still laugh at that joke."

This discussion has not gotten to the heart of the matter, namely: What is it about sexist humor that is offensive? And it won't get to the heart of the matter if the man goes on to make the point that we're all the butt of a joke at some time or other and asks why it is that only feminists don't laugh when *they're* the butt of the joke. The question is rhetorical, for he has an answer: feminists are too sensitive. They take offense at everything, even when no offense is intended. This brings the discussion full circle. She is offended; he maintains that no offense is intended.

Yet it appears that along the way, the man has raised a legitimate question. Anyone of us can be the butt of a friendly joke, and we are expected to accept the fun in the joke in good nature. We do not have much patience or sympathy for the person who takes offense whenever she or he is teased or is the butt of a friendly joke. Why are feminists so different?[28] I stress the word "friendly" here, for it seems that whether sexist humor *can* be friendly may be the point at issue between the feminist and that man.

In an article entitled "Why We Aren't Laughing . . . Anymore," Naomi Weisstein explains the feminist's position as follows.

> It is . . . extraordinarily difficult to *understand* what it means to be out of power when you aren't there. . . . It is very difficult for someone not under personal or physical threat to understand why someone else is so nervous, so jumpy, so dumb, so slow moving, so "dizzy." . . . It is a commonplace in the Women's Movement to tell men that if they really want to understand what we mean by our total oppression, they should "pass" for women for a day and see what happens. Ignored in conversation, patronized at work, hello-babied by strangers, ogled in the street, followed into buildings, fondled in crowded buses, attacked in elevators; objects of ridicule and contempt, even the most neutral transaction is usually accompanied by abuse: "Hey, Dutch, she says do we have any pork chops? Lady, what's your *problem*? Can't you see that we don't have any pork chops?"

> As women, we live in a coercive, threatening, unpleasant world; a world which tolerates us only when we are very young or very beautiful. If we become stupid or slow, jumpy or fast, dizzy or high pitched, we are simply expressing the pathology of our social position. So when we hear jokes against women, and we are asked why we don't laugh at them, the answer is easy, simple, and short. Of course, we're not laughing . . . Nobody laughs at the sight of their own blood.[29]

To the feminist who constantly and continuously encounters situations in which she feels oppressed, belittled, and harmed because of social attitudes towards her as a woman, sexist humor does not seem that friendly at all. A man who is not a member of a target ethnic group can typically accept friendly teasing or ridicule as just that, for he knows that it will end momentarily. On the other hand, teased or ridiculed; it is rather one instance among many in which women are belittled or disparaged.[30]

However, this only explains why the feminist *feels* offended by sexist humor. What if a person who finds fun in sexist humor makes it absolutely clear that when she or he enjoys it, no offense is intended? What if that person argues that the humor is merely intended as friendly teasing or ridicule, that there is no hidden message of belittlement or disparagement? It seems that the ends do not quite meet here, if the feminist's position is that sexist humor *is* offensive and not merely that it is *felt* to be offensive. That is, in any situation in which sexist humor is shared, it can be made clear by parties to the humor that it is only a matter of a joke. And if this is so, there should be no offense felt in such cases. If a feminist does feel offended, it is not the humor that is responsible for the offense. Rather, she is offended because she is psychologically unable to separate what goes on in the parlor room from what she experiences outside the parlor room.

I shall argue for a stronger conclusion. The offense felt in sexist humor is not simply a by-product of the feminist's psychological inability to compartmentalize different segments of her social life or to distinguish between friends and enemies. The offense is a real offense committed by the person who finds fun in sexist humor.

Consider the claim that a particular bit of humor is *only* a joke, that no offense is intended. Saying "it's only a joke" is a common way of begging off responsibility for something that we have said or done, even if it was not originally intended as a joke. In the case where we say "it's only a joke" *of* a joke, what we mean is something like: "I don't really believe that so-and-so is as dumb as she or he is made out to be in the joke." We are begging off responsibility for any hidden morals or disparagement that others may find in the joke. We are not, however, denying that there is fun in the joke; we are merely trying to confine the fun within respectable limits.

This maneuver of begging off responsibility for offense still leaves the offense in sexist humor, precisely because sexist humor is offensive in what it takes to be *fair grounds* for fun. Sexist humor does not just incidentally incorporate sexist beliefs—it depends upon those beliefs

for the fun. The "Today's sport" cartoon is funny only if women's bodies count as sport; the story about Trudeau is funny only if rape is desirable to women; etc.[31]

Is the offense of sexist humor, then, merely the offense of sexism? Certainly, having sexist beliefs is requisite to finding the fun in sexist humor. But put this way, it looks as if sexist humor is merely a symptom of which sexism is the cause, and as if sexist humor is offensive only because it evinces sexist beliefs. I do not believe that this is the whole story. The offense of sexist humor is not just the offense of sexism. Sexist humor adds an offense that is additional to the offense of sexist beliefs, attitudes, and norms.

As Weinstein's illustrations show, sexist beliefs hurt. They are painful to feminists and like-minded people. They are also the motivating factor behind many painful and harmful situations that women encounter every day in the social and political sphere. Sexist humor, in taking sexist beliefs as fair grounds for generating fun, adds insult to the injury of sexism. To understand the nature of the insult clearly, let us return to the banana peel.

Recall that if a man slipping on a banana peel were obviously hurt, there were still several alternative conditions under which we could find fun in the episode. Each condition required our detachment from serious concern, or if we were, we could still later appreciate the fun by recalling the episode *in isolation* from his pain. But now suppose that we had contributed to the episode, say, by intentionally dropping that banana peel on the sidewalk, and that the man were seriously injured. The episode is no longer funny to us unless we just are not seriously concerned about his injury. We can no longer view the episode in isolation from his pain and our responsibility for that pain. (Here I am making an empirical claim about psychologically healthy human beings.) If we try to find fun in that episode, it is an insult to the man we have injured.

The insult of finding fun in sexist humor is very much like this insult, although it is not quite the same. First, let me draw out the parallel. The person who finds fun in sexist humor is like the person who deliberately places the banana peel on the walk; both contribute to the stage-setting for the fun. In the latter case, the person contributes the banana peel that is a necessary condition for the fun. In the case of sexist humor, the contribution is simply having the requisite sexist beliefs. Short of those beliefs, there is no fun in sexist humor. Moreover, the item contributed in each case is a source of pain. But when we ask "Whose pain?" a disanalogy emerges. The pain of the banana peel episode is the pain of a participant in that episode. But the pain caused by sexist beliefs need not be the pain of any character in the episodes portrayed by sexist humor. Those characters are by and large fictional, while the pains caused by sexist beliefs are the pains of real people outside of those episodes.

Consider, then, the case of creating a funny episode that ends up causing injury to someone other than the participants in the episode. A professor comments that he would like to live the life of Socrates; the next day a student presents the professor with a bottle of hemlock. The professor finds this funny, as the student had intended, and, chuck-ling, carries the hemlock home. The following morning he discovers that his young daughter has crept into his study and drunk the hemlock. In this case, it would be an insult to the child (to put it mildly), if the student, after hearing the news and offering sympathy, were to slap a classmate on the back and say, with a belly laugh, "Still, it was funny that I thought of giving him that hemlock, wasn't it?" It would also be an insult if the classmate laughed along.

The insult of finding fun in sexist humor is formally the same. It is the insult of finding fun in an episode when part of the stage-setting that we have contributed to the episode, and that is necessary to the fun, hurts someone. I offer the hemlock example as a magnifying glass through which the insult in sexist humor comes out in relief. Sexist beliefs are not just harmless props for jokes. Whenever somebody tells or laughs at a sexist joke it is an insult to those people who have been hurt and who will be hurt by sexist beliefs, whether the insult is intended or not.[32] This insult is the special offense of sexism.

Here the argument of the paper draws to an end. But it is clear that the argument depends upon another. Although I have claimed that the offense of sexist humor is not just the offense of sexism, it is clear that the offense of sexist humor is parasitic on the offense of sexism. Any person who still does not believe that sexist beliefs hurt will not be convinced by my argument that there *is* an offense in finding fun in humor that relies upon those beliefs. In full appreciation of this point, I conclude with the epilogue: How Many Feminists Does It Take?

CASE STUDY: LENNY BRUCE AND "THE 'N'-WORD"

Lenny Bruce is the "father" of improvisational stand-up comedy. He may not have been absolutely the *first improvisational* stand-up comic, but he took improvisation the furthest and made it famous. During the 1950s, the early years of the cold war, a new movement emerged in politically relevant stand-up comedy. The new "political satirists"—Mort Sahl, Dick Gregory, and above all Lenny Bruce—departed from the neutrality and detachment of the Bob Hope, Milton Berle generation of comics. Most important, the new political satirists, particularly Lenny Bruce, broke longstanding cabaret taboos by doing jokes about politics, religion, race, sex, and by using "forbidden words." In 1961, Lenny Bruce was busted on the second night of his engagement at San Francisco's Jazz Workshop for violating the California Obscenity Code on his opening night—specifically, for referring to the exposure of male genitalia, doing "impressions" of couples vainly trying to achieve orgasm, and using a vernacular word for fellatio.

Lenny Bruce's comedy was marked, in part, by a commitment to "authenticity" or "honesty"; more precisely a crusade *against* hypocrisy in all its forms (false modesty, pious pretense, and so on). This is a main reason why he refused to obey laws forbidding the use of certain words in public performance. Here is another one of Lenny Bruce's famous controversial comic bits involving a forbidden word. It is interesting that this bit would not likely have gotten him into trouble as far as the California Obscenity Code was concerned. In its day (the early 1960s), and in public, however, this was indeed *daring*. As you read the following, imagine witnessing it in performance in a comedy club. What are the risks inherent in giving such a performance today? How do you imagine the risks have evolved since Lenny Bruce first performed it?

> The reason I don't get hung up with, well, say, integration, is that by the time Bob Newhart is integrated, I'm bigoted. And anyway, Martin Luther King, Bayard Rustin are geniuses; the battle's won. By the way, are there any niggers here tonight?
>
> [*outraged whisper*] *"What did he say?* 'Are there any *niggers* here tonight?' Jesus Christ! Is that *cruel*. Does he have to get that low for laughs? Wow! Have I ever talked about the *schwarzes* when the *schwarzes* had gone home? Or spoken about the Moulonjohns when they'd left? Or placated some Southerner by absence of voice when he ranted about *nigger nigger nigger?"*
>
> Are there any niggers here tonight? I know that one nigger who works here, I see him back there. Oh, there's two niggers, customers, and, ah, *aha!* Between those two niggers sits one kike—man, thank God for the kike!
>
> Uh, two kikes. That's two kikes, and three niggers, and one spic. One spic—two three spics. One mick. One mick, one spic, one hick, thick, funky, spunky boogey. And there's another kike. Three kikes. Three kikes, one guinea, one greaseball. Three greaseballs, two guineas. Two guineas, one hunky funky lace-curtain Irish mick. That mick spic hunky funky boogey.
>
> Two guineas plus three greaseballs and four boogeys makes usually three spics. Minus two Yid spic Polack funky spunky Polacks.
>
> AUCTIONEER: Five more niggers! Five more niggers!

GAMBLER: I pass with six niggers and eight micks and four spics.

The point? That the word's suppression gives it the power, the violence, the viciousness. If President Kennedy got on television and said, "Tonight I'd like to introduce the niggers in my cabinet," and he yelled "niggerniggerniggernigger-niggerniggernigger" at every nigger he saw, "boogeyboogeyboogeyboogeyboogey, niggerniggerniggernigger" till "nigger" didn't mean anything anymore, till "nigger" lost its meaning—you'd never make any four-year-old nigger cry when he came home from school.

Screw "Negro!" Oh, it's so good to say, "Nigger!" Boy![33]

5.3 HUMOR AND "BAD TASTE"   Ted Cohen is a professor of philosophy at the University of Chicago, past president of the American Society for Aesthetics, an avid joke teller and joke collector, and, in the estimation of many of his colleagues, one of the best "stand-up philosophers" of our generation. As a philosopher, Ted Cohen is one of those rare individuals who has achieved a widespread reputation as a sharp and deep thinker with a style of philosophizing uniquely his own—on the basis of a relatively small body of published work. He is also one of those rare philosophers who has been able to lead the profession of philosophy into neglected areas of interest by addressing his talents to topics outside the professional mainstream with results that other professional philosophers find insightful and worth studying. Photocopied and mimeographed copies of an early Cohen paper on jokes were in wide private circulation for many years prior to its eventual publication in the 1980s. That paper eventually grew into a short book entitled *Jokes: Philosophical Thoughts on Joking Matters,* published in 1999 by the University of Chicago Press, from which the following selection is excerpted.

In *Jokes* Cohen develops the theory that jokes, like works of art more generally, function crucially as means to the achievement of intimacy—more precisely, that joke *telling* is a social activity whose central purpose is the establishment of a community based on a shared experience of understanding and appreciating the joke. Within this theoretical framework, Cohen points out that often the joke teller's identity, and the identities of intended and *un*intended audiences, determine a great deal about whether a given joke will work—whether, and how, it will be understood how well it will be appreciated, whether it will be received as amusing—and even about what the joke means.

In the end, Cohen reaches what will strike many a reader as a surprising and somewhat frustrating—maybe even baffling—resolution to the issues raised in this chapter. Cohen eventually abandons all hope of resting any moral judgment concerning the propriety or impropriety of jokes or joking on any theoretical foundation whatever. And yet, strangely enough, he does not think that this undermines the passing of moral judgment upon the propriety or impropriety of jokes or joking.

Questions for Study and Discussion

1. What does Cohen mean by "hermetic" as applied to jokes? On what basis would Cohen classify a joke as hermetic? Can you illustrate this with an example of your own (perhaps from your own joke collection)?

2. Cohen considers the conceptual device of the "impartial observer" (sometimes called "the ideal observer") as a possible means of determining which jokes are truly objectionable, but quickly abandons it as ineffective. What is this conceptual device, and on what grounds does Cohen abandon it?

3. In the end, Cohen relinquishes hope of a theoretical foundation for moral judgments concerning the propriety or impropriety of jokes or joking. Even so, this, to him, does not undermine the passing of moral judgment upon the propriety or impropriety of jokes or joking. Do you find these two views consistent? If so, explain. If not, see if you can explain how Cohen might hope to reconcile these views.

TASTE, MORALITY, AND THE PROPRIETY OF JOKING[34]

TED COHEN

When I first wrote about jokes, I thought of dividing them into the pure ones and the conditional ones. A conditional joke is one that can work only with certain audiences, and typically is meant only for those audiences. The audience must supply something in order either to get the joke or to be amused by it. That something is the *condition* on which the success of the joke depends. It is a vital feature of much joking that only a suitably qualified audience—one that can meet the condition—can receive the joke, and the audience often derives an additional satisfaction from knowing this about itself. A pure joke would be universal, would get through to everyone, because it presupposed nothing in the audience.

It now seems clear to me that there is no such thing as a pure joke. It is a kind of ideal, but it doesn't exist. At the very least, the audience will have to understand the language of the joke, and probably much more. But even if all jokes are conditional, it is still useful to note just how strongly conditional a particular joke is, and just what kind of condition is presupposed.

When the background condition involves knowledge or belief, I call the joke *hermetic*. Perhaps all you need to understand my joke is a working knowledge of the English language. But you may need a good bit more, as the background information becomes ever more specific and arcane. Some of the most strongly conditional hermetic jokes are ones involving the topics and jargon of a profession. Some such jokes are not actually *within* the profession. For instance, this doctor joke:

> Four doctors went duck hunting together. Together in the duck blind, they decided that instead of all shooting away at the same time, they would take turns as each duck came by. The first to have a shot would be the general practitioner, next would be the internist, then the surgeon, and finally the pathologist.
>
> When the first bird flew over, the general practitioner lifted his shotgun, but never fired, saying, "I'm not sure that was a duck."

The second bird was the internist's. He aimed and followed the bird in his sights, saying "It looks like a duck, it flies like a duck, it sounds like a duck . . ." but then the bird was out of range and the internist didn't take a shot.

As soon as the third bird appeared, flying up out of the water only a few feet from the blind, the surgeon blasted away, emptying his pump gun and blowing the bird to smithereens. Turning to the pathologist, the surgeon said, "Go see whether that was a duck."

Or this philosopher joke:

The president of a small college desires to improve his school's academic reputation. He is told that the best way to do this is to create at least a few first-rate departments. It would be good to work on the mathematics department, he is told, because that would not be too expensive. Mathematicians do not require laboratories or even much equipment. All they need are pencils, paper, and wastebaskets. It might be even better to work on the philosophy department. The philosophers don't need wastebaskets.

You don't need to be a doctor or a mathematician or a philosopher to appreciate these jokes, nor even know much at all about doctoring, mathematics, or philosophy. At most you need some acquaintance with the presumed proclivity of surgeons to cut first and then diagnose, and of philosophers' professional license to say anything they want because there is no way to prove them wrong, and so they are permitted to do anything they can get away with (like writing a book about jokes).

With some hermetic jokes what is required is not knowledge, or belief, in the first instance, but an awareness of what might be called "commonplaces."

A young Catholic woman told her friend, "I told my husband to buy all the Viagra he can find."

Her Jewish friend replied, "I told my husband to buy all the stock in Pfizer he can find."

It is not required that the audience (or the teller) actually *believe* that Jewish women are more interested in money than in sex, but he must be acquainted with this idea. When jokes play upon commonplaces—which may or may not be believed—they often do it by exaggeration. Typical examples are clergymen jokes. For instance,

Three rabbis, one Orthodox, one Conservative, and one Reform, are accustomed to playing golf together every Sunday. On one particular Sunday their play is going very slowly because the foursome ahead of them is playing very slowly. In annoyance, the rabbis send one of their caddies ahead to speed things up, to tell the foursome ahead to play faster or to let the rabbis play through.

When the caddie returns he looks crestfallen, and he says, "I am so ashamed. The foursome ahead is playing slowly because all four of them are blind. Blind golfers have to play slowly. They must wait while their caddies find their balls and then align them to swing in the right direction. And there I was complaining. As soon as I learned, I was so embarrassed. I apologized and left."

"Oh my," says the Orthodox rabbi. "I am humiliated."

"Me, too," says the Conservative rabbi. "I think we should pray for those less fortunate and remind ourselves, as the Torah says, not to put obstacles in the path of the blind."

"Right," says the Reform rabbi. "Yeah, fine. Why the hell don't they play at night?"

Jokes like these, besides being caustic and possibly unflattering, sometimes incorporate genuine profundity. For instance,

After many days of hard continuous rain, the river is in danger of flooding, and word goes out that people may have to abandon their homes. When the river crests, water pours through the town, inundating houses, and it continues to rise. Firemen are sent in a small motorboat to go through the streets to make sure everyone is leaving. When they come to the house of the rabbi, they find him standing knee-deep in water on his front porch.

"Come on, Rabbi," say the firemen. "The river will go much higher, and you should leave with us."

"No," says the rabbi. "God will protect me." And he sends them away.

The river rises higher, the rabbi is forced to go up to the second floor of his house, and now the police come in a motor launch.

"Come on, Rabbi," say the police. "There isn't much time."

"No," insists the rabbi. "I will stay right here. God will look after me." And he sends them away.

Now the river rises so high that the rabbi is forced to stand on the roof of his house. When the National Guard arrive in a large boat,

telling him that the river is sure to go even higher, the rabbi says, "All my life I have been a man of faith, and I will stay now, and trust in God," and sends them away.

The river rises, the rabbi is swept away, and the rabbi drowns.

Forthwith the rabbi appears in heaven, where he angrily approaches the throne of God, demanding, "How can You have let this happen to me? For all my life I have kept Your *mitzvot*. I have done what You asked, and trusted in You. Why?"

A voice resounds from the throne: "You schmuck. I sent three boats."

I suppose some hearers might find these jokes unflattering, but I doubt that the jokes are found very offensive. I doubt that New Yorkers or citizens of New Jersey object to either of these:

A family from Nebraska went to New York City for the first time on a week's vacation. After being battered by New York and its citizens for the first few days, the entire family felt exhausted and humiliated, and they were nearly ready to cut their vacation short, but the father insisted on trying once more to have an agreeable vacation in New York. The family walked out of their hotel in the morning, and the father went up to a traffic policeman and inquired, "Officer, would you tell me the way to the United Nations building, or should I just go fuck myself?"

How is the alphabet recited in New Jersey?

"Fuckin' A, fuckin' B, fuckin' C, . . ."

It is difficult to say just when such jokes become genuinely offensive. What do you make of this one?

> What does it say on the bottom of a Polish Coke bottle?
> "Open other end."

Should we be laughing at the fact of death? Death is a bleak topic. Jokes about death can be bleak. But apart from all that bleakness, joke-telling about death has a special dark side, which it shares with much joke-telling. I am one of those who believe jokes and joke-telling are wonderful and can be very serious, but I am also aware of the danger in too much joke-telling and joke-telling when it is out of place. Whether joking is in place or out of place may depend upon who is telling jokes to whom. In this regard, at least in America, or at least in my part of America, there seems to be a difference between men and women. Although it is not true uniformly and universally, men are much more likely to tell jokes to one another than are women to tell jokes to one another. Men are probably joke-tellers more than women, and when women do tell jokes, they are more likely to tell them to men than to women. Why is that? Perhaps women have other conversational devices for establishing and maintaining intimacy, while for at least some men, joke-telling is a primary device of this kind. But joking is almost always out of place when it is a kind of avoidance. Telling a joke about death can be a way of dealing with death, even of grappling with it; but sometimes the only proper way to think about death is to try looking it straight in its morbid, mordant eye, and on those occasions telling a joke is exactly the wrong thing to do because it is a way of avoiding the real issue. People like me who tell too many jokes, and tell them too often and in too many kinds of situations, usually get away with it because the laughter and ostensible humor are taken to be good things, things worth having even at the cost of other things. But we shouldn't get away with it, because a laugh is not always worth it, not if it is a deflection from something else that needs to be done. Mark Twain knew a very great deal about these matters, but when he said "Against the assault of laughter nothing can stand," he neglected to note that some things should remain standing.

When is it in order to joke about death, and when not? I cannot say. No one can say. There is no rule here. It is up to you every time, it is up to you and your own moral sensibility (which includes concern for the sensibilities of others) to decide whether to tell a joke or to get serious, or whether, perhaps, telling a joke is a way of getting serious. This is a fact about all joke-telling, whether the jokes are about death or about anything else.

Here are two principles: One, jokes cannot be the entire human response to death, or to anything else; two, any total response to death that does not include the possibility of jokes is less than a totally human response.

Sometimes a joke is exactly the wrong response, the wrong overture to make. But when is this? If those jokes about New York and New Jersey are acceptable and are not seriously offensive, this one is a bit different.

> When God was creating the world, when He finished Europe He realized that France had come out perfect, which was not His plan. So He made Frenchmen.

However you feel about these jokes yourself, I think you know this: it would be surprising if New Yorkers or New Jerseyites were upset about the man from Nebraska or the recitation of the alphabet. But it would not be surprising if Frenchmen (and maybe others) were annoyed by this joke. But what is the difference? If, as I think, there is no formula to tell us which jokes are offensive or when it is the wrong time to put forth a particular joke, it may be possible to say something about just what goes wrong when these transgressions occur. To start, it will be useful to take a look at almost everyone's favorite example of jokes that shouldn't be told, "ethnic jokes."

In one kind of so-called ethnic joke, the ethnicity of the characters is not essential to the joke, because identifying someone as a Pole, or a Sikh, or an Iowa legislator is simply to stipulate that the character is inept or stupid or benighted. There is no doubt considerable significance in the fact of just which groups are chosen to be used in this way, and there may be moral, political, or social objections to using these groups in this way, but their ethnicity itself does not function in the joke. In other jokes, also deservedly called ethnic jokes, the ethnicity itself (or the religion or nationality) is a substantial element in the joke. Here is an Irish joke (which is also an English joke, to a degree):

> An out-of-work Irishman went walking around London until he found a construction site with a sign announcing that workmen were being hired. When he applied for the job it was his bad luck that the foreman in charge was an Englishman with a dismal view of the Irish.

> "So, Paddy, you think you can do the work?" asked the foreman.
> "Oh yes," said the Irishman. "I've been doin' construction for thirty years."
> "Then you really understand construction?" asked the foreman.
> "Of course," said the Irishman. "I can do it all—the plumbin', the electric, the carpentry."
> "Then you wouldn't mind if I gave you a bit of a test?" asked the foreman.
> "No, no. Test away."
> "Then tell me, Paddy, what is the difference between a joist and a girder?"
> "It's too easy," said the Irishman. "'Twas the former wrote *Ulysses*, whilst the latter wrote *Faust*."

And here is a Polish joke (which is also a Russian joke, to a degree):

> In the days of the cold war, long before the collapse of the Soviet Union, a Polish man let it be known to his friends that he kept his life savings, one hundred thousand zlotys, in his bed, under the mattress.

> In horror one of his friends objected, "It isn't safe there. You must put it in the bank."
> "Oh?" said the man, "and what if the bank fails?"
> "How could the bank fail? It is supported by the Polish government."
> "Oh?" said the man, "and what if the Polish government fails?"
> "How could our government fail? It is kept in place by the Soviet Union."
> "Oh?" said the man, "and what if the Soviet Union collapses? Wouldn't that be worth 100,000 zlotys?"

In jokes like these, the relevant ethnicities are essential. Commonplaces about the Irish (that they are exceedingly and excessively literary), about the English (that they don't care much for the Irish), and about the Poles (that they are given to marvelously intricate subtleties and indirections of logic, and that they don't like Russians) are relatively very specific—quite different from just a generalized presumption that they are smart or stupid or venal. And in fact even if it were wrong it would not be unreasonable to believe that these commonplaces are in fact truths, whereas it is unreasonable to the point of utter ignorance to believe that Poles or Sikhs or students at Texas A&M are stupid.

An intermediate example is the joke in which an Englishman hears a joke about a monkey and a martini.

A man told this joke to a group of acquaintances, including an Englishman.

"A man walked into a saloon, sat at the bar, and ordered a martini. When the drink had been put in front of him, before he could touch it, a monkey that had been sitting on the bar a few yards away walked over to the drink, straddled it, and bent until his genitals were in the drink. In horror the patron said to the bartender, 'Did you see that?'

"'Oh yes,' replied the bartender, 'that was one of the worst things I've seen in this bar.'

"'Well, what are you going to do about it?' demanded the patron.

"'I'm afraid I can't do anything,' said the bartender, 'the monkey belongs to the piano player.'

"The patron immediately strode to the piano and said to the piano player, 'Do you know your monkey dipped his balls in my martini?'

"'No,' said the piano player, 'but if you can hum a few bars I'll pick it up.'

When the joke was finished, all laughed except the Englishman. When he was asked why he didn't like the joke, he replied that he had not understood it. It was then explained to him that the expression "Do you know. . . ?" has a special significance for musicians, and then he laughed considerably.

"So now that you understand it, you think it's pretty good?" he was asked.

"Oh my, yes," he replied, "but you do have to know the tune."

Of course it is not true that the English have no sense of humor or appreciation of jokes, but it is nevertheless a kind of commonplace about them, and so the appreciation of the joke requires knowing this relatively specific commonplace.

I confess to a fondness for the structurally simplest kind of ethnic jokes, like:

This year's Polish science prize went to an engineer in Warsaw who has developed a solar powered flashlight.

But I have a deeper appreciation for ethnic jokes in which the ethnicity is used, even if as slightly as in this:

A Polish man walks up to a counter and says, "I want to buy some sausage."

"You want Polish sausage?" asks the clerk. "Kielbasa?"

"Why do you think I want Polish sausage?" replies the man indignantly. "Why wouldn't I want Italian sausage, or Jewish sausage? Do I look Polish? What makes you think I'm Polish?"

The clerk responds, "This is a hardware store."

Here there is at least a reliance on the fact that there is such a thing as Polish sausage, even if the main presumption of the joke is the artificially given obtuseness of some group.

Sometimes the established presumption is not that the principal character is stupid or inept, but that he is disagreeable—mean, nasty, vicious. And sometimes that is all there is to the presumption, as in a number of jokes about agents and lawyers. For instance,

> A man walked angrily into a crowded bar, ordered a drink, and then said to the bartender, "All agents are assholes."
>
> From the end of the bar a man spoke up, saying, "Just a minute. I resent that."
>
> "Why? Are you an agent?"
>
> "No, I'm an asshole."

In that joke nothing whatever is made of what might be disagreeable about agents as such, nor is anything made of lawyers in this joke:

> You find yourself trapped in a locked room with a murderer, a rapist, and a lawyer. Your only hope is a revolver you have, with two bullets left. What do you do?
>
> Shoot the lawyer. Twice.

Some jokes of this kind manage to involve something at least slightly more specific, as in:

> One summer noontime two lawyers were walking together over the Michigan Avenue bridge when they passed a particularly good-looking young woman in a thin summer dress walking the other way.
>
> "Man, I'd like to screw her," said one of the lawyers.
>
> His companion answered, "Yeah? Out of what?"

This joke suggests at least that lawyers' main interest is in taking advantage of people, and that that ambition supercedes any other interest they might take in human beings. It is possible, however, for such jokes, ones that presume to take an ethnically or professionally or otherwise identified character as the principal focus to make much more of the putative characteristics of the person. I have a preference for jokes that do this, that make more of the presumed profession or ethnicity, and so I think that ethnic jokes like the one about the Irish workman who knows his Joyce and Goethe are, if not better, at least richer and subtler, and they are devices for achieving considerably greater intimacy. One reason is the same as the reason why I think color movies are better when the color is used for something, large-scale orchestral music is better when the extra instruments are used for more than simply increasing the volume, and fiction is better when all the characters have something to do with the story and are not added only as filler. I tend to have a better opinion of works of art, and to be further moved by them, when all their parts seem relevant. If the only point in making a character in a joke Polish is to signal that he will be inept, I have the feeling that some potential "material" in the joke has gone unused, and this seems somehow a waste.

Another reason for preferring a Polish or Irish joke in which it really matters that the character is Polish or Irish, is that such jokes require more of the hearer, involve him more intimately, and give him greater opportunity for self-congratulation in his appreciation of the joke. They involve a bigger and richer contribution from the hearer. It is one thing to know, simply, that there are jokes in which Polish characters are found to do misguided things, even though such jokes can be very funny, and it is another thing, a more substantial thing, to know that Poles have a long-standing, historical distrust of Russia.

All of these jokes, the simpler and the more complex ones, feel innocuous, but they carry a hint of something unsavory.

It is a very widespread conviction, shared by me, that some jokes on some occasions, and maybe some jokes on all occasions, are, as we say, "in bad taste," and should be thought of as morally objectionable. But it is very, very difficult to say just what this moral defect is. First is the problem of finding a basis for any moral judgment passed upon fiction, and then there is the problem of establishing the impropriety of laughing at something, especially when the something is fictional. Fiction itself might be objectionable as such, for instance when one puts it forth in hopes of inducing a belief in something false, but surely this is not characteristic of jokes. I say this to you:

> A man was told by his doctor that to improve his health he should take up jogging, and he should run two miles every day. After a couple of weeks the man was to call the doctor to tell him how he was feeling. Two weeks later the man called the doctor asked, "So how are you doing?"

> "I feel pretty good," said the man, "but I'm twenty-eight miles from home."

Would you object, and be angry with me because I had told you a falsehood? Ridiculous. (Of course even if there were such a misguided jogger, you might just find that funny.) Consider again this exquisite children's joke:

> What do Alexander the Great and Winnie the Pooh have in common?
> They have the same middle name.

Would you object to this that it is not true, that the word 'the' is not the middle name of either character, and, furthermore, that there is no such creature as Winnie the Pooh? Ridiculous. It cannot be an objection solely that the joke contains falsehoods. In fact, in many cases the entire joke is a falsehood. Actually, it is a *fiction*, and a fiction is not—simply—a falsehood. (And a joke is not—simply—a fiction.) Of course a fiction might be taken as a statement of fact, but the fiction is not itself accountable for that. And yet something disturbing appears in some jokes. Some people are bothered by this joke:

> A man calls home from his office one day, and his phone is answered by the maid, Maria. "Maria," says the man, "I'd like to speak to my wife."
> "I'm sorry *señor*, but she cannot come to the phone. She is making love to a man in the master bedroom."
> "My God. Maria. Can that be true?"
> "Yes, *señor*. I am *muy* sorry."
> "Maria, I must ask a favor. You have been with me many years,

and now I need something from you."

"Yes, *señor*. What is it?"

"Maria, are you in my study?"

"*Si, señor.*"

"In the upper right drawer of the desk you will find a loaded revolver. Take it to the bedroom and shoot them both."

The phone goes dead for a few minutes, and then Maria's voice comes through. "It is done, *señor.*"

"Good, Maria. I am in your debt. Now take the revolver, wipe off the handle, and throw it into the swimming pool."

"*Señor?* We have no swimming pool."

"Is this 555-4694?"

And, probably, more people are bothered by this one:

This year's annual prize for Polish medicine went to a surgeon in Krakow who performed the world's first appendix transplant.

But many more people are bothered by this one:

How did a passerby stop a group of black men from committing a gang rape?

He threw them a basketball.

Exactly what is wrong with any of these three jokes, and why is the last one so much more disturbing? The first one is from a short-lived genre of "Maria jokes" that came from Southern California, I think (all such jokes involving a Mexican maid named Maria); the second is a Polish joke, so called; and the third is a black joke (although the category seems to me less well defined).

Each joke says that something happened, and in fact it didn't. There was no man who called home for his wife, got the wrong number without knowing it, and commissioned the murder of two strangers. There is no annual prize for Polish medicine, and no Polish surgeon performed an appendix transplant. No group of black men was distracted from a criminal sexual assault by being given an opportunity to play basketball.

But none of the jokes says that these things really happened. The jokes are short stories, fictions, perhaps, although of a very peculiar kind, and one can no more sensibly object to them as falsehoods than one might object to *Hamlet* that in fact there never was a prince of Denmark who had a couple of friends named Rosencrantz and Guildenstern.

Is it that the jokes say that Mexican maids are obtusely obedient even to the point of murder, that Poles are so stupid that they do not understand the point in organ transplant, that black men are sexually violent and mindlessly committed to playing basketball?

But the jokes don't say those things, any more than they say anything at all. Do they somehow purvey stereotypes, and disagreeable ones at that? Do those who respond to these jokes either believe in advance or come to believe nonsense about Mexican maids, Polish scientists, and black men? I doubt this. And I doubt that one could show any connection between traffic in such jokes and negative beliefs about these groups of people. Even if there is such a connection, I have myself been amused by all three jokes, and I do not myself believe any of those generalizations about the relevant characters, and yet these jokes disturb me, especially the last one, the one about criminal black basketball players. Why?

There are two questions. First I would like to know just why these jokes disturb me, and then I wonder whether my personal discomfort and objection can be generalized and rendered "objective" so that a negative assessment might be made about the jokes themselves. It may be that my personal dislike is just that—personal. This does not mean that it is unreal, that you should persist in telling me such jokes on the ground that it is only a personal, subjective matter that they do not agree with me, but it would mean that my complaint that such jokes are in bad taste or unwholesome comes to nothing more than my wish to be free of them. That is pretty much how it is for me, for instance, with regard to the music of Wagner and some of Eliot's poetry. I do not claim that these works are poor or corrupt, but only that I do not care for them; and if you do care for them, then this may mark a significant difference between you and me, but it signals nothing I am prepared to say about the works in themselves.

Why am I made uneasy about the joke about the black men? I think it is because I am made uneasy by the idea that black men are criminals and mindless basketball players. But how can an *idea* do that to me? Is it that I think the idea is false, or that it would lead to a false proposition if one believed it? But I think that almost all the statements and ideas presented in almost all the jokes I know are false in the sense that they would lead to false propositions if one believed them. Is there something especially disagreeable or obnoxious in this particular idea's being believed? Yes, I think so. If I, or others, believed in this idea, then I and others might well treat people badly. But so what? As a matter of fact I don't be-

lieve this idea, and don't think that your telling me this joke leads either of us to believe this idea, nor does it suggest that either of us already believes it.

It is possible that the existence of such jokes and commerce in them are symptoms of pernicious attitudes and beliefs, and perhaps the jokes even are causes of the perniciousness. If that were true, then of course that would be the basis for a moral objection to the jokes. I do not know that this is true, and I do not know that it is false. And neither does anyone else know about this, nor does anyone have any idea how to discover whether it is true. But this question—the question of what role such jokes may play in bad behavior—might be set aside, if we could agree on how to answer a different question.

If jokes about the uncontrolled animalism of black men or about the venality of Jews could be shown to have no effect whatever on people's beliefs about black men and Jews, then would the jokes cease to be troublesome? I think the jokes would still be disturbing. Why? And need there be an answer to this question? Let me restart this little moral inquiry by asking, again, just what is disturbing in these jokes, as well as in certain works of art.

I do not like the portrayal of the Jewish nightclub-owners in Spike Lee's *Mo Better Blues,* and I do not like the ridiculous portrayal of Jews in Edith Wharton's novel *House of Mirth.* No doubt this is at least partly because I am Jewish, but neither do I like the portrayal of black men in D. W. Griffith's movie *Birth of a Nation.* And why don't I like those portrayals? Because they are inaccurate? Because they are stereotypes? These seem lame answers to me.

I am not much bothered by the portrayal of WASPs in the movie *Auntie Mame,* although that portrayal is at least as inaccurate and unflattering as the others. It must be relevant that I do not regard WASPs as vulnerable, not in the way that Jews and blacks seem vulnerable. Is it that I am worried that people will think that Jews and blacks are in fact as they are portrayed in these works, and that I have no worry on behalf of the WASPs? It is not that I have no concern for the WASPs; it is that I think they have nothing to worry about. But is that true? Are they not as entitled as anyone to object to stereotypical representations of themselves? Incidentally, stereotypes can be annoying, just as such, without regard to whether they are negative. In "Concerning the Jews," Mark Twain offers an exceedingly flattering characterization of Jews, and it troubles me almost as much as the negative portraits offered by T. S. Eliot and Edith Wharton. A stereotype can rob you of your particularity just as surely if it is flattering as if it is negative. What about the stereotype of young black men in that basketball joke?

The fact that this joke works is a fact only because of some genuine truths—not truths about black men, but truths about how black men are thought of. These truths are, for instance, that young black men are associated with basketball, and they are thought to have a passion for basketball that takes them away, for instance, from learning mathematics or learning to read; and that is what is being insinuated in a joke in which they give up even violent sex—another of their putative passions—for the chance of a slam-dunk. I know all that, that these are associations that go with young

black men, and it is only because I know all that that I am able to respond to the joke. Do I, perhaps, dislike it in myself that I know these things? And do I then dislike my own laughter at the joke? Is the joke working its magical establishment of intimacy by forcing me to acknowledge something I don't care for in myself? Would I rather that I did not know these things? Of course I wish that these were not things to be known, but is it my fault that they are, and that I know them?

If I were to offer some resounding moral condemnation of this joke, no doubt I would have to invoke some "moral theory," and then show that an implication of the theory is that this joke is Bad. I will not do that. I think it can't be done.

A common, sometimes useful device in analytical, conceptual moral theory is the idea of an ideal creature, sometimes called an ideal observer, or an impartial spectator, or a person of practical wisdom. First, such a creature is characterized (perhaps as being completely informed, disinterested, and so on), and then it is supposed that the right way to act, or to feel, or to judge, is to act, feel, or judge as this ideal creature would. Try thinking up such a person, and then ask whether this person would disapprove of these jokes, whether he would tell them or laugh at them, and how he would feel about anyone who tells them. What do you think? Would he damn these jokes? I don't know, and neither, I think, do you.

Among contemporary normative theories of morality, most would require that it be shown that traffic in these jokes produces genuine harm to someone, or at least that it reduces the moral character of those who traffic in them. It seems to me preposterous to suppose that anyone could show that either of these consequences obtains. One of the more ponderous and depressing features of large-scale moral theories is that they tell you what makes things right or wrong, good or bad, and then leave it to you to take a case about whose morality you feel strongly and try to outfit it with the theory's sanctioned reasons. Thus someone who hates that joke about the black basketball players is forced to give his reasons for declaring it morally disagreeable. It may be that a mammoth raft of literature, propaganda, fiction, poetry, religious writing and preaching, and casual conversation can produce or sustain a general opinion of things, including an opinion of kinds of people—surely it would be foolish to deny that; but it is far fetched to indict a movie or a novel or a joke on those grounds. And worse: when it turns out that you can find no convincing evidence to support this claim about the effects of such jokes you seem obliged to give up your moral complaint. And you shouldn't do that.

Here is some friendly advice: When you feel strongly that some joke (or anything else) is no damned good, and especially when you don't like having that joke told, and it seems to you that the thing—or the telling of it—is morally defective, hold on to that feeling, and continue to express the feeling in terms of moral condemnation. When someone demands a moral-theoretical reason for your condemnation, ask them why they think you need one. You don't have to prove that a joke is funny, or that it is unfunny (good thing, too, because you couldn't do it), and surely you don't have to prove that it seems to you to be immoral. Do you have to prove that it is

immoral? I don't think so. If your opponent thinks so, then ask him to supply the theory, the apparatus that would allow a claim that something is morally objectionable. When he does, then either you will be able to fit this joke to his theory, or you won't. If you can't make the theory work in support of your conviction, then try telling your philosophical opponent that you now have good reason to disbelieve his theory, namely that it can't account for the immoral character of this joke you hate. But before you do that, perhaps you should expand your categories. Not everything you dislike is illegal, or should be. Not everything you dislike is immoral. But something's being legal and morally acceptable doesn't mean you have to think it is OK. Nor does it mean you have to put up with it.

Don't like it, and don't put up with it when someone commits murder. Or when someone commits adultery. Or when young men don't give up their seats to burdened women standing on the bus. Or when someone picks his nose. Or when people don't write thank-you notes for parties you have given or gifts you have sent. You don't have to put up with any of these. But don't suppose that there should be laws forbidding them, at least not all of them. And don't imagine that your dislike must be grounded in some stupefying Moral Theory.

You can avoid people who tell jokes you hate, or at least insist that they not tell them to you or when you are present. You can tell strong young men that they should give up their seats to pregnant women (although before doing this, you might well consider just what bus you are riding on).

Clarify these matters for yourself, and choose your words carefully—and above all be sure that they are *your words*—when you express your disapproval. This requires asking yourself persistently *why* you don't like something, as I tried to discover why I don't like the one about the black basketball players. Then notice whether you have felt a need for moral vocabulary.

I wish you good luck in thus maintaining your feeling of disgust—moral disgust, if that's how it feels to you—at the joke, but I insist that you not let your conviction that a joke is in bad taste, or downright immoral, blind you to whether you find it funny.

When an obnoxious portrayal is in a joke, it is likely to be upsetting in a special regard. Jokes are humorous, amusing, fun. It is ponderous and obtuse to object to the fun. The offended person who takes issue with a joke finds himself doubly assaulted, first by the offensive portrayal in the joke, and then again by the implicit accusation that he is humorless. But the offended person may make the reflexive mistake of denying that the joke is funny. More than once someone has demanded of me that I explain exactly why anti-Semitic jokes are not funny. I have come to realize that if there is a problem with such jokes, the problem is compounded exactly by the fact that they *are* funny. Face that fact. And then let us talk about it.

A young earnest white college student confesses his guilt at his own reactions when walking big-city streets after dark. He finds that he is more worried when a stranger appears on the street when that stranger is black than he is when the stranger is white. He feels guilty for having this feeling, and he wishes he didn't feel this way. He is right to wish he didn't feel this way, if that is a wish that the

world were different, but he is not wrong to have the feeling. Given the world as it is, there is nothing wrong with having the feeling, and it might well be a practical error not to have the feeling. As a matter of fact, given the neighborhood he walks in, it is enormously more likely that he will be set upon by a black stranger than by a white one. And that is a God-damned shame. But it is a fact. By all means, wish that it were not a fact. Weep because it is a fact. Try to change the world so that it will cease to be a fact. But don't turn away from the fact, don't force yourself to deny it.

Wish that there were no mean jokes. Try remaking the world so that such jokes will have no place, will not arise. But do not deny that they are funny. That denial is a pretense that will help nothing. And it is at least possible, sometimes, that the jokes themselves do help something. Perhaps they help us to bear unbearable affronts like crude racism and stubborn prejudice by letting us laugh while we take a breather.

What do you think of this joke?

> The Secret service has an opening in its ranks, needing to recruit someone to join those who guard the president of the United States. They post a notice in bulletins for government workers, and soon they receive three applications, one from an FBI man, one from an agent from the Bureau of Alcohol, Tobacco, and Firearms, and a third from a Chicago city policeman. Each of the three is given a qualifying examination, beginning with the FBI man.
>
> The FBI man is given a revolver and told to go into the adjacent room and shoot whomever he finds there. When he has been gone

only a few minutes, the FBI man returns, saying, "You must be out of your minds! That's my wife. I'm not shooting her."

"Fine," say the examiners. "You must be a good family man, but you're not cut out for the Secret Service."

Next the ATF agent is sent in with the revolver, with the same instructions to shoot whomever he finds in the next room. He too returns in minutes exclaiming, "That's the mother of my children, you lunatics."

"Good for you," say the examiners. "Enjoy your career in the bureau and continue looking after your wife; but we can't use you in the Secret Service."

Finally, the Chicago policeman is given the same test. When he has been in the adjacent room for about ten minutes, sounds are heard, the sounds of struggle and muffled groaning. A few minutes later the cop reappears, looking somewhat mussed, and says, "Some moron put blanks in the gun; I had to strangle her."

Now consider this: this marvelous story was told to me by my wife. She learned it from a Chicago policeman. I do not know where the policeman came by it, but I do know that he and his fellow officers have had a good time telling it to one another. Do you think that is a bad thing? I don't. I don't know just what to make of it, but I do know that the dynamics of joking—including the intimacy sought and achieved, the relief gained from unpleasantness, and the moral dimensions of all this—depend absolutely upon who tells the joke and who hears it. Do you think this story says something about Chicago cops? If it does, it may well not be the same thing said when cops tell the joke to one another as it is when civilians exchange this joke. I think that Chicago cops' telling this joke to one another is a very good thing, a hopeful sign in a difficult world.

EXERCISE: THREE-MINUTE STAND-UP—WITH SIX RULES OF THUMB, AN "ETIQUETTE FOR JOKERS"

In the introduction to this chapter, we encouraged you to consider the issues discussed here from the point of view of a working or aspiring comedian or comic writer. We also suggested, as a means of understanding how immediate, inevitable, and practical these philosophical issues can be, that you might try writing three minutes of stand-up comic material. Go ahead. Write three minutes of material, as though you were going to do a three-minute stand-up monologue for your class. To help you keep the issues of this chapter clearly in view while you practice the art of comedy, we have adapted the following "Etiquette for Jokers," from a set of guidelines originally published in the *New Republic* in 1987.

1. There is a "sliding scale" of sensitivity based on the current and shifting state of political affairs. Some groups are more subject to unfair and unequal treatment than others. The risk of causing offense in telling a given joke goes up or down depending upon which group the joke teller belongs to and which group the joke is about.

2. It's better to tell jokes on your own group. Even if all such humor is based on some stereotype or other, the fact that one tells the joke "on oneself" tends to undermine, rather than promote, the stereotype.
3. If the joke is about some other group, a rough and ready test is whether you would be embarrassed to tell the joke in the presence of a friend who is a member of that group. If so, that's a pretty good sign that the joke is over the line.
4. There is a sliding scale of stereotypes based on the mutability or perceived mutability of the characteristic attributed to the group in the stereotype. For example, jokes about physical characteristics are more offensive than jokes about bad table manners.
5. If you are going to tell a joke, make sure the joke is funny. This is a surprisingly important reminder, and it serves as a test of one's motives in telling a joke on a given occasion. Watch yourself to make sure that your aim is to amuse and not to express contempt.
6. Finally, if you hear a joke that you find funny, feel free to laugh. Examine your conscience later. It's healthier that way.

SUGGESTED READINGS:

Morreall, John. *Taking Laughter Seriously.* Albany: State University of New York Press, 1983.
Morreall, John, ed. *The Philosophy of Laughter and Humor.* Albany: State University of New York Press, 1986.

NOTES

ETHICS AND ENTERTAINMENT I: HUMOR AND COMEDY

1. See John Morreall, *Taking Laughter Seriously* (Albany: State University of New York Press, 1983).

ARE THE THREE STOOGES FUNNY? SOITAINLY!

2. This essay was prepared for a symposium on the Three Stooges at the Toronto meeting of the Society for Popular Culture, November of 1990, and published in Robert C. Solomon, *Entertaining Ideas: Popular Philosophical Essays: 1970–1990* (Buffalo, NY: Prometheus Books, 1992), 139–47. Copyright © Robert C. Solomon. Reprinted with the kind permission of the author.
3. A special problem arises here with cartoon violence, where the acts depicted are lethal despite the fact that the recipient quickly recovers. But the very frame of the cartoon, including cartoons juxtaposed on flesh-and-blood characters, presents the violence as assuredly make-believe and aimed wholly at humor.
4. See John Morreall, *Taking Laughter Seriously* (Albany: State University of New York Press, 1983).

HOW MANY FEMINISTS DOES IT TAKE TO MAKE A JOKE?

5. Merrie Bergmann, "How Many Feminists Does It Take to Make a Joke?" *Hypatia* 1 (1986): 63–82. Reprinted with the permission of Indiana University Press.

6. Immanuel Kant, *Observations on the Feeling of the Beautiful and the Sublime*, trans. John T. Goldthwait (Los Angeles: University of California Press, 1960) 78.

7. Friedrich Nietszche, *Beyond Good and Evil*. Quoted in Carolyn Korsmeyer, "The Hidden Joke: Generic Uses of Masculine Terminology," in *Feminism and Philosophy*. eds. Mary Vetterling-Nraggin, Frederick H. Elliston, and Jane English (Totwaw, NJ: Littlefield, Adams, & Co., 1977), 141.

8. The last example is from Casey Miller and Kate Swift, *Words and Women* (Garden City, NJ: Anchor/Doubleday, 1977), 19. Roberta Salper noted in 1973 that "the feminist movement has the distinction of being the only major social movement in the history of the United States that is regarded by its opponent as a joke" (*Introduction to Female Liberation*) quoted in Korsmeyer, *op. cit.* 152.

9. See the chapter on "Joking Matters" in Cheris Kramarae, *Women and Men Speaking* (Rowley, MA: Newbury House, 1981).

10. John Morreall, "A New Theory of Laughter," *Philosophical Studies* 42 (1982): 244-5.

11. Cromwell Kent, *A Book* (Scarborough, Ontario: The Vanity Press, 1970).

12. "Hidden sense" incongruity theorists include D. H. Monro, *Argument of Laughter* (Victoria: Melbourne University Press, 1951) and Arthur Koestler, *The Act of Creation* (London: Pan Books, 1975).

13. Quoted in Charles R. Gruner, *Understanding Laughter* (Chicago: Nelson Hall, 1978), 13).

14. The arguments of Monro *op. cit.,* vacillate between these two kinds of incongruity theory.

15. Monro, *op. cit.,* 250.

16. These include "superiority theories," of which Thomas Hobbes is the best-known proponent. Monro contains several excellent chapters on these theories.

17. Isaac Asimov, *A Treasury of Humor*, quoted in George M. Robinson, *Towards a Cognitive Model of Humor* (Smith College, Manuscript, 1980), 6.

18. Arthur Koestler, *op. cit.,* 89.

19. Bergson said that "to produce the whole of its effect . . . the comic demands something like a momentary anesthesia of the heart." See Henri Bergson, *Laughter, in Comedy*, edited by Wylie Sypher (Baltimore: Johns Hopkins University Press, 1956), 64. The point that detachment is necessary to finding something funny has been made, in different ways, by many humor theorists. Morreall sums up situations in which we laugh (including those in which the stimulus is not funny) with the formula: "Laughter results from a pleasant psychological shift" (*op. cit.* 249). It follows that in situations in which we are pained or puzzled, we will not laugh at an incongruity. Conversely, positive affective involvement with an incongruous episode, as in the case where we desire that someone be hurt, will enhance our laughter.

20. Anthony J. Chapman and Nicholas J. Gadfield, "Is Sexist Humor Sexist?" *Journal of Communication* 26 (1976): 144.

21. I distinguish between *perceiving* an incongruity and *seeing* an incongruity. When from our point of view an episode *is* incongruous, we perceive the incongruity. When we descern a point of view from which an episode *would be* incongruous, we see the incongruity. I can *see* the incongruity in this cartoon; but I do not *perceive* the incongruity.

22. Helen Hopkinson, *The New Yorker* (1942). Reprinted in Naomi Weisstein, "Why We Aren't Laughing . . . Anymore" *Ms.* 2 (1973): 50.

23. The turn of phrase is from Ronald de Sousa, "The Ethics of Laughter," (University of Toronto manuscript, 1981). De Sousa's paper is my source for the story about Trudeau (he found it in the University of Torontos's Engineering School newspaper). De Sousa also claims that the joke is funny only if certain sexist beliefs are held. It is one of a class of jokes that require that we share certain beliefs, if we are to find them funny; we cannot "hypothetically assume" these beliefs and expect to find the fun.

    I am pleased to report that many people with whom I have discussed this particular joke have been unable to see what is supposed to be funny about it. I offer the following sitcom-type story, where the incongruity is parallel in structure, to show why adoption of the beliefs noted in the text might make the Trudeau joke funny.

    John's wealthy spinster aunt gave him an extraordinarily ugly painting, saying that it was one of her favorites. And that she knew he would appreciate it and that it would look marvelous in her favorite nephew's den. Not wishing to lose his future inheritance, John reluctantly hung the painting in the den.

    The day before the aunt comes to visit, John enters his den and discovers that the painting has disappeared. He runs to his wife, exclaiming in a pained voice, "The painting— the one my aunt gave me—it's been stolen!" Whereupon the butler appears and calmly says, "Wishful thinking. The maid removed it for a cleaning."

    The butler's comment, "Wishful thinking," is an incongruous reply to a report of theft, but it makes sense on the assumption that it would be a good thing if the painting were stolen.

24. David Freeman, quoted in Max Eastman, *The Enjoyment of Laughter* (London: Hamish Hamilton, 1937), 308.

25. Chapman and Garfield *op. cit.* 144.

26. "Maria" (unpublished surname), "Do Feminists Laugh?" *Open Forum*, Dartmouth College, November 1, 1981, 8.

27. Cartoon by Ellen Levine, in Gloria Kaufman and Kay Blakely, eds. *Pulling Our Own Strings* (Bloomington: Indiana University Press, 1982), 105.

28. There is a special sting in the claim that feminists have no sense of humor; it is not merely a descriptive statement but a critical one. I have long thought that the accusation is not simply one of oversensitivity, but that it is also one of dogmatism. Peter Jones—in "Laughter," *Proceedings of the Aristotelian Society* Supplementary Volume 61 (1982)— points out that fanatics are characteristically humorless and explains why. Thanks to Jones's discussion, I now realize that the special sting in the claim is that it is an accusation of fanaticism.

29. Weisstein 1973, 51 and 58.

30. A variation of this explanation of the feminist's position maintains that women have been the butt of jokes for so long that it is impossible for them to take these jokes as "friendly teasing." Too many jokes add up to the message that the jokes are quite serious in their ridicule, or disparagement, of women. The conclusions I draw about this variation are the same as the conclusion I shall draw about the position presented in the text.

31. Actually, this is not true of some of the humor I have labeled "sexist." For example, I pointed out that the fur coat joke could still be funny if the check-writer were a man. If a hidden moral about women is not drawn from the joke, it no longer counts as sexist. In the argument that immediately follows, I concentrate on humor that will not be found funny at all in the absence of the requisite sexist beliefs. I shall return to "ambiguously" sexist humor, like the fur coat joke, in the next note.

32. There is also the fact the laughing at sexist humor may suggest to others that it is *acceptable* to hold the beliefs that are presupposed by the humor, that those beliefs are just harm-

less stage props for the fun of the moment. Hence a person who indulges in "ambiguously" sexist humor (see previous note) can commit an offense even if that person does not her- or himself draw any hidden moral concerning women, *as long as* she or he is aware that others might draw such conclusions to enhance fun. The social functions of humor have been widely studied, particularly insofar as humor can foster a sense of community of belief and values. Humor that communicates certain values, in the sense that holding those values enhances or is itself responsible for the fun in the humor, can serve the function of reinforcing those values. This has often been pointed out in connection with sexist, racist, and ethnic humor: such humor reinforces sexist beliefs, racist beliefs, or unfair stereotyping of ethnic groups and is on that count objectionable. Thus Korsmeyer states in connection with ridicule of women and of feminism: "Laughter, [Bergson} claims, occurs in situations where the spectators are relatively uninvolved, at least temporarily, with the subject of their mirth. . . . Whether or not all instances of laughter follow this design, certainly this is a component of the ridicule that serves a political purpose in the chivalrous resistance to "women's lib." It keeps sympathy at a distance and allows one to dismiss the subject of laughter as not deserving consideration" (Korsmeyer, 148). Korsmeyer's claim applies directly to the examples of humor discussed early in this paper. For further discussion of the fostering of community through shared humor, see de Sousa, Morreall, and Ted Cohen (the next selection in this book). Wayne Booth's discussion of the achievement of community through the use of irony is also applicable to humor. See his *A Rhetoric of Irony* (Chicago: University of Chicago Press, 1974), 27–31, 39–44.

33. "Blacks," in *The Essential Lenny Bruce,* ed. John Cohen (New York: Bell, 1967), 11–12.

TASTE, MORALITY, AND THE PROPRIETY OF JOKING

34. Ted Cohen, *Jokes* (University of Chicago Press, 1999), 12–21, 69–86. Copyright © 1999 by the University of Chicago. Reprinted by permission of the author and the University of Chicago Press.

6

ETHICS AND ENTERTAINMENT II: SEX AND VIOLENCE

*There's a great illusion that we now have more freedom
merely because people say 'fuck' more often. . . . The
language in movies and on TV has gotten raunchier, the
subject matter has gotten sexier and more explicit—but
there's no content to it. . . . It's all jack-off jokes and
narcissistic references to bodily functions. There's
practically no real political satire or social
commentary. . . . When we were censored it wasn't
four-letter words we were fighting for. It was ideas. We were
censored for talking about the war, about voter registration,
about Martin Luther King. If we were on the air right now
we'd be talking about how our government is up for sale to
the highest bidder . . . how all these politicians, busy
playing the money game, have turned America into the
most corrupt country on the
planet . . . how American arrogance has damaged country
after country, all around the world. We sure wouldn't waste
what 'freedom of speech' we have trying to pass off a few
four-letter words.*

TOMMY SMOTHERS,
SONOMA COUNTY INDEPENDENT, 23–9 SEPTEMBER 1999

INTRODUCTION

For the sake of simplicity we may reasonably sort the actual content of mass media programming into three broad categories. First, let's say that journalism—the news and public affairs programming—is intended primarily to perform the essentially

219

political and public service functions discussed in Chapter 2. Second, advertising is programming designed to serve the essentially commercial functions discussed in Chapter 4. Finally, arts and entertainment programming is everything else. In some borderline cases, programming seems to straddle two or more of these categories—MTV comes to mind. Indeed some prominent media critics have argued that the boundaries between commercial advertising and the entertainment programming that traditionally surrounded it, as well as between entertainment programming and journalism, have gotten more and more blurry in recent years. Tommy Smothers, in the above epigram, indicates that the *Smothers Brothers' Variety Hour,* essentially a comedy show, also frequently had a public affairs agenda. Still, we can fairly easily identify clear examples of each of these general categories of programming for purposes of analysis and discussion.

When we think of mass media in this connection, we're of course not confining ourselves to television, but rather thinking comprehensively to include all the media through which an audience receives any of these categories of material. We're thinking of radio, television, movies, books, magazines, sound recordings, video games, the Internet, and so on—*all* the mass media. Taken together, these add up to a pervasive and powerfully influential social force.

A tradition stretching as far back as Plato's *Republic* sees the moral character of the individual citizen and of the society at large reflected in each other as mutual influences. According to this tradition, a morally well-ordered society both consists of and tends to foster morally well-ordered individual citizens. Similarly, social and personal corruption go hand in hand. The same tradition sees the stories and myths used in the society to educate the youth and to cultivate character as a crucial element in determining the moral character of both the individual citizen and the society at large. Plato's *Republic* includes a famous elaborate discussion of the "censorship" of both the content and the style, and even of the musical elements—the rhythms and harmonies—of the poems to be used in grooming the young for leadership in the model city. In contemporary terms, many see the development of the moral character of each individual citizen and of the society at large as inextricably intertwined. And moral and ethical concerns about the social impact of the mass media are raised, because the mass media are understood to play a crucial role in determining the course of this process of development. What we see on TV and at the cinema, and hear on the radio—the news, the music, the video games we play, the Web sites we visit, the commercials we are exposed to—all have an impact on the development of our personal and shared values.

Such concerns over the impact of mass media on character development and social values formation surface whenever moral crises either erupt or appear to erupt and threaten social stability and a shared sense of social well being. (We are considering both real and apparent moral crises because whether the moral crisis facing society is real or only apparent, both social stability and a shared sense of social well being are threatened and concerns are raised about the impact of mass media. So, one pertinent question to ask when the mass media are singled out as a cause of social decay or collapse is whether the moral crisis facing society is real or only imagined—or exaggerated). Such concerns intensify when the moral crisis of the moment involves young people. For example, in 1999, a shooting spree at Columbine High School in Littleton, Colorado, brought an apparent increase in the incidence and severity of violent behavior among young people into the center of public attention. For the moment, let us suppose this to be a real (not merely an imagined) moral crisis for society. Much public concern rightly focused on the issue of regulating access to firearms. At the same time, a great deal of concern addressed the violent content of entertainment material produced for and distributed to adolescent audiences by the mass media in the form of movies, music videos, video games, and so on. It was argued that mass media entertainment contributed significantly to a social climate in which violent behavior had become more readily accepted and more easily resorted to, and in which the value of human life was depreciating.

In the ancient philosophical tradition on the role of what we now call mass media in the formation of social values, the development of moral "character" is a central concept, as are the concepts of "virtue" and "vice." The word *virtue* means essentially "a *good* character trait," or a disposition to behave in a morally good way. A virtuous person is a person who is generally disposed to act in morally good ways. So, for example, honesty is a virtue. An honest person has a general disposition to tell the truth. "Vice" means the opposite: "a *bad* character trait," a tendency or disposition to behave in a morally bad way. So, for example, dishonesty is a vice. A dishonest person lies. In contemporary usage, the word *vice* (more so than the word *virtue*) has evolved to embrace some broader, though closely related, applications. For instance, a vice can be a weakness of moral character, a susceptibility to one or another kind of temptation; or a vice can be an activity or a habit which tends to weaken one's moral character, like gambling; finally, by extension of this, a vice can be just a bad habit, like smoking, (which threatens one's *health* more than one's moral character). As we turn from the individual to the society as a whole, we can see how reasonable it is to suppose that, for example, a society consisting of mostly honest people will tend to produce honest leaders and will tend to develop and maintain trustworthy social institutions. Whereas similarly, the leadership and social institutions of a society consisting of mostly corrupt individuals will tend to be corrupt as well.

Turning back to the mass media and their social impact, our concern naturally focuses on programming content and the degree to which it may promote or foster the development of morally virtuous or vicious and corrupt character traits. In theoretical terms, all of this seems quite plausible and even relatively simple. A plausible theory of learning says that we learn by imitating the role models presented to us in the stories and legends we encounter over the course of our lives, especially during our "formative years." Monkey see, monkey do. And no doubt in plenty of real-world examples this traditional understanding seems to apply in practice in a simple and plausible way. Perhaps we can all agree, for example, that the kind of programming produced by the Children's Television Workshop is on the whole better for children to watch than the Teenage Mutant Ninja Turtles. Perhaps we can all agree that the kinds of characters and dramatic scenarios presented these days by the World Wrestling Federation are pretty worthless—and that any viewers who take that stuff at all seriously, do so to the general detriment of their moral development.

But beyond that, actual definitions become pretty messy pretty quickly, because debate flourishes over precisely how various kinds of programming influence viewers and also over what in specific detail constitutes good character. For example, when the cartoon series *The Simpsons* was first broadcast, numerous moralistic school principals condemned the program, going so far as to ban Bart T-shirts and other *Simpsons* paraphernalia from school premises, on the grounds that school children were imitating Bart's "antisocial" behavior ("Like, don't have a cow, man!"). Does Bart's characteristic disrespect for authority, especially school authority, encourage mischief among his young fans? Probably; but does the fact that they watch the *Simpsons* and express their mischievous tendencies a la Bart Simpson, make them any more mischievous than they would be anyway? And are we so sure that a certain tendency toward mischief isn't a healthy characteristic in young people? Should children be prevented from reading *The Adventures of Huckleberry Finn,* lest they find in that book something mischievous to imitate?

Then, too, there's the element of parody, a slippery literary device that lends itself to misunderstanding. The more subtle the parody, the more likely it is to be misunderstood. Homer Simpson is an oaf. His character is a parody of, among other things, inept parenting. You're not supposed to find in him a worthy and attractive role model as a father or head of household. And yet, when the cartoon series *Beavis and Butthead,* a parody of brain-dead latchkey teenagers, was first broadcast, quite a few brain-dead teenagers seemed to find—of all things—personal validation in the parody. This raises what will turn out to be a crucial issue of responsibility. If someone produces programming that is misunderstood by some segment of its audience whose moral development is thereby retarded or misdirected, where does the responsibility for that sad state of affairs really lie?

When we generalize this issue of responsibility we come to a knot at the crux of our concern over the social impact of mass media. Where does the responsibility lie for however general trends in mass media programming turn out? Suppose we decide that mass media programming is generally too violent, or too materialistic, or too sexy. To whom do we assign ultimate responsibility for this state of affairs: the producers of the programming, or the sponsors of the programming, or the viewing audience itself? The producers do produce the programming, and the sponsors do pay for it, but it can be and often is argued that, in the final analysis, all of this answers to audience preferences. If people weren't tuning in, the programming wouldn't be what it is. Corollary to the responsibility knot is the equally knotty remedy question. Again, suppose we decide that mass media programming is generally too violent, or too materialistic, or too sexy. Now, suppose further that this state of affairs arises out of the interaction among large businesses pursuing legitimate interests coupled with free entertainment choices made by huge numbers of individuals, all reinforcing each other. Where should we direct our efforts to alter this state of affairs?

In the following section we will confine ourselves to two characteristic themes of mass media programming most frequently cited as problematic for the development of moral character and the formation of social values: sex and violence. The two have important differences. Unlike violence, sex is not intrinsically wrong or even problematic. In and of itself, sex is natural, functional, beautiful, meaningful. At its best, sex is a sacrament, a mutual expression of love, something to be savored and celebrated with reverence. As such it would surely seem to be a suitable subject for appropriate treatment in literature and art. But the needs and desires that sex gratifies are so fundamental, profound, and strong in us that sexual expression is easily perverted from its ideal, and just as easily exploited, which is what tends to happen in the mass media generally. This in turn gives rise to perennial efforts to repress or at least regulate sexuality as it is expressed in mass media, which brings us to consider once again the issue of pornography, discussed by Catharine MacKinnon in Chapter 2. Violence, on the other hand, though it too may be "natural" at least in the sense that we seem as humans to have a natural *capacity* for violence, is at least problematic in and of itself. Violence inherently threatens much of what is essential to well being and happiness, including life itself. No doubt this is also a main reason why violence is so fascinating, why it so powerfully attracts our attention, why we slow down and rubberneck at roadside wrecks, and why fist fights draw crowds. In this section we will consider violence in the context of journalism as we explore the responsibilities and liabilities of working journalists who cover violence in the news. We will also consider violence in the context of entertainment and the arts as we explore themes of violence and misogyny in rap music.

6.1 PORNOGRAPHY AND LIBERALISM Joel Feinberg is professor emeritus of philosophy at the University of Arizona and a preeminent authority in philosophy of law. His book *Freedom and Responsibility* is widely used as a textbook in philosophy of law. The following essay was originally published in the *University of Pittsburgh Law Review* (40.4, Summer 1979), and later formed the basis of a chapter in *The Moral Limits of the Criminal Law* (New York: Oxford University Press, 1983).

In this essay, Feinberg reviews the history of jurisprudence in obscenity law as applied especially to pornography. He argues that it is based fundamentally on a confusion between the concepts "obscene" and "erotic," and a misguided effort to prevent by means of legislation and enforcement the kinds of perversion and exploitation to which human sexuality may be, as we suggested above, naturally prone. He suggests a simpler, more plausible, and more coherent way of resolving conflicts over pornography and its regulation: an approach based on the law of nuisances. According to this approach, the private possession of pornography, or the possession for sale and distribution of pornography to willing adult consumers, would not be appropriately subject to legislative restriction or to punishment under the law. Pornography would become a legitimate issue for legislation and enforcement only where it was imposed on unwilling audiences or children. As he puts it, "Only patently offensive exhibitions to captive audiences in public places or to children would be prohibited."

Questions for Study and Discussion

1. What, according to Feinberg, do nuisance laws have to do with "privacy"?
2. What is the "law of torts"?
3. What, according to Feinberg, are the defining characteristics of the philosophical position known as liberalism? What implications does this position hold for legal approaches to regulating sexual and violent media material? Is Catharine MacKinnon's support for criminal sanctions against pornography consistent with Feinberg's understanding of liberalism?
4. What is the *Hicklin* formula? What three objections to it are found in the *Roth* decision written by Justice Brennan?
5. Feinberg distinguishes between defining a term (for example, "obscenity") and stating the criteria or tests for the presence of obscenity. Can you explain in detail this distinction and why it is an *important* one to understand?

Pornography and the Criminal Law[1]

JOEL FEINBERG

When the possession, use, or display of sexually explicit materials is prohibited by law, and violations are punished by fine or imprisonment, many thousands of persons are prevented from doing what they would otherwise freely choose to do. Such forceful interference in private affairs seems morally outrageous, unless, of course, it is supported by special justifying reasons. In the absence of appropriate reasons, the coercive use of government power, based ultimately on guns and clubs, is merely arbitrary and as such is always morally illegitimate. Criminal prohibitions, or course, are sometimes backed by appropriate reasons, and when that is the case, they are not morally illicit uses of force but rather reasonable regulations of our social activities.

What then are "appropriate reasons" for criminal prohibitions? Surely the need to prevent harm or injury to persons other than the one interfered with is one kind of legitimate reason. Some actions, however, while harmless in themselves, are great nuisances to those who are affected by them, and the law from time immemorial has provided remedies, some civil and some criminal, for actions in this category. So a second kind of legitimate reason for prohibiting conduct is the need to protect others from certain sorts of offensive, irritating, or inconveniencing experiences. Extreme nuisances can actually reach the threshold of harm, as when noises from the house next door prevent a student from studying at all on the evening before an examination, or when an obstructed road causes a person to be late for an important appointment. But we are not very happy with nuisances even when they do not harm our interests, but only cause irritations to our senses, or inconvenient detours from our normal course. The offending conduct produces unpleasant or uncomfortable experiences—affronts to sense or sensibility, disgust, shock, shame, embarrassment, annoyance, boredom, anger, or humiliation—from which one cannot escape without unreasonable inconvenience or even harm.

We demand protection from nuisances when we think of ourselves as *trapped* by them, and we think it unfair that we should pay the cost in inconvenience that is required to escape them. In extreme cases, the offending conduct commandeers our attention from the outside, forcing us to relinquish control of our inner states, and drop what we were doing in order to cope, when it is greatly inconvenient to do so. That is why laws prohibiting nuisances are sometimes said to protect our interest in "privacy."

What distinguishes the "liberal" position on this question is the insistence that the need to prevent harm to others and the need to prevent nuisances to others between them exhaust all the types of reasons which may appropriately support criminal prosecution. Insofar as a criminal statute is unsupported by reasons of either of these two kinds, it tends to be arbitrary and hence morally illicit. In this respect certain commonly proffered reasons are no better than no reasons at all. The need to protect either the interests or the character of the actor himself from his own folly, does not, according to the liberal, confer moral legitimacy on a criminal statute, nor does the need to prevent inherently sinful or immoral conduct as such. Liberalism so construed does not purport to be a guide to useful public policy for the utilitarian legislator, nor does it claim to provide a

key to the interpretation of the American, or any other, constitution. (It is entirely possible that the moral restrictions liberalism would place on legislative discretion are not always socially useful, and also that the Constitution itself allows some morally illegitimate statutes to remain as valid laws.) Instead liberalism purports to indicate to the legislator where the moral limits to government coercion are located.

Let me state from the outset that I am a committed liberal, in this sense, on the question of the legal regulation of pornography. I believe that pornography, at its worst, is not so much a menace as a nuisance, and that the moral right of legislatures to restrict it derives from, and is limited by, the same principles that morally entitle the state to command owners of howling dogs to stop their racket, to punish owners of fertilizing plants for letting odors escape over a whole town, to prohibit indecent exposure and public defecation, and so on. It is absurd to punish nuisances as severely as harmful or injurious conduct, however, and unless certain well-understood conditions are satisfied, it may be illegitimate to punish a given nuisance at all. For that reason it may be useful, before looking at the pornography problem, to examine the restrictions recognized by legislatures and courts on the proper regulation of harmless but offensive nuisances.

The most interesting aspect of the law of nuisances is its version of the unavoidable legal balancing act. Both legislatures, when they formulate statutes that define public nuisances, and courts, when they adjudicate conflicts between neighboring landowners in "private nuisance" cases, must weigh opposing considerations. Establishing that one person's conduct is or would be a nuisance to someone else is by no means sufficient to warrant legal interference. First one must compare carefully the magnitude of the nuisance to the one against the reasonableness of the conduct of the other, and the necessity "that all may get on together." Practically all human activities, unless carried on in a wilderness, interfere to some extent with others or involve some risk of interference, and these interferences range from mere trifling annoyances to serious harms. It is an obvious truth that each individual in a community must put up with a certain amount of annoyance, inconvenience, and interference, and must take a certain amount of risk in order that all may get on together. The very existence of organized society depends upon the principle of "give and take, live and let live," and therefore the law of torts does not attempt to impose liability or shift the loss in every case where one person's conduct has some detrimental effect on another. Liability is imposed only in those cases where the harm or risk [or inconvenience or offense] to one is greater than he ought to be required to bear under the circumstances. According to Prosser's *Handbook of the Law of Torts* the magnitude of the nuisance to the plaintiff in a private nuisance action depends upon (1) the extent, duration, and character of the interference, (2) the social value of the use the plaintiff makes of his land, and (3) the extent to which the plaintiff can, without undue burden of hardship, avoid the offense by taking precautions against it. These three factors yield the weight to be assigned to the seriousness of the inconvenience. They must be weighed against the reasonableness of the defendant's conduct, which is determined by (1) "the social value of its ultimate purpose, (2) the motive of the defendant [in particular its character as innocent or spiteful], and (3) whether the defendant by taking reasonable steps can avoid or reduce the inconvenience to the plaintiff without undue burden or inconvenience to himself." Finally, we are to throw on to the scale the interests of the "public at large," in particular its interest in "the nature of the locality" where the nuisance occurred—to "what paramount use it is already devoted"—and given that background, "the suitability of the use made of the land by both plaintiff and defendant."[2] In sum, the more extended, durable, and severe the inconvenience to the plaintiff, and the greater the social value of the land uses interfered with, then the greater is the magnitude of the nuisance, while the greater the ease with which the plaintiff can avoid the nuisance, the smaller its magnitude. Similarly, the greater the social value of the defendant's conduct and the freer his motives of spite toward the plaintiff, the more reasonable is his conduct, despite its inconvenience to the plaintiff, while the easier it is for him to achieve his goals by means that do not inconvenience the plaintiff, the less reasonable is his offending conduct. Finally, the prevalent character of the neighborhood weighs heavily, so that a householder who takes up residence in a manufacturing district cannot complain, as a plaintiff in a private nuisance suit, of the noise, dust, or vibration, whereas the same amount of disturbance caused by a factory in a primarily residential district, will be declared a nuisance to the landowners in its vicinity.

If, as I recommend, we think of pornographic exhibitions and publications as nuisances which may properly be controlled by the law under certain very strict conditions, we shall have to posit a similar set of conflicting considerations to be weighed carefully, not only by juries in private tort suits, but also by legislatures in their deliberations over the wording of criminal statutes designed to prohibit and punish pornography. Let me suggest that legislators who are impressed by the model of "public nuisance" should weigh, in the case of each main category and context of pornography, the seriousness of the offense caused to unwilling witnesses against the reasonableness of the offender's conduct. The magnitude of the offensiveness would be determined by (1) the intensity and durability of the repugnance the material produces, and the extent to which repugnance could be anticipated to be the general reaction of strangers to the conduct displayed or represented (conduct offensive only to persons with an abnormal susceptibility to offense would not count as *very* offensive), (2) the ease with which unwilling witnesses can avoid the offensive displays, and (3) whether or not the witnesses have willingly assumed the risk of being offended either through curiosity or the anticipation of pleasure. (The maxim *volenti non fit injuria*[3] applies to offense as well as to harm.) We can refer to these norms, in order, as the "extent of the offense standard" (with its "exclusion of the abnormal susceptibility corollary"), the "reasonable avoidability standard," and the "*volenti* standard."

These factors would be weighed as a group against the reasonableness of the pornographers' conduct as determined by (1) its personal importance to the exhibitors themselves and its social value generally, remembering always the enormous social utility of unhampered expression (in those cases where expression is involved), (2) the availability of alternative times and places where the conduct in question would cause less offense, (3) the extent if any to which the offense is caused by spiteful motives. In addition, the legislature would examine the prior established character of various neighborhoods, and consider establishing licensed zones in areas where the conduct in question is known to be already prevalent, so that people inclined to be offended are not likely to stumble on it to their surprise.

A legislature, of course, does not concern itself with judging specific actions and specific offended states after they have occurred. Rather its eyes are to the future, and it must weigh against one another, or authorize courts to weigh against one another, generalized *types* of conduct and offense. In hard cases this balancing procedure can be very complex and uncertain, but there are some cases that fall clearly within one or another standard in such a way as to leave no doubt how they must be decided. Thus, the *volenti* standard, for example, preempts all the others when it clearly applies. Film exhibitors cannot reasonably be charged with criminally offensive conduct when they have seen to it that the only people who witness their films are those adults who voluntarily purchased tickets to do so, knowing full well what sort of film they were about to see. One cannot be *wrongfully* offended by that to which one fully consents. Similarly bans on *books* must fail to be morally legitimate in view of the ease with which offense at printed passages can be avoided. Since potential readers are not "captive audiences," here the reasonable avoidability standard is preemptive. So also do inoffensively expressed political or theological opinions fail to qualify as "criminal nuisances," by virtue of their personal and social importance as "free expression." On the other hand, purely spiteful motives in the offender can be a preemptive consideration weighting the balance scale decisively on the side of unreasonableness. In some cases, no one standard is preemptive, but nevertheless all applicable standards pull together towards one inevitable decision.

One final preliminary matter: to what are we referring when we use the terms "pornographic" and "obscene"? There is no more unfortunate mistake in the discussion of obscenity than simply to identify that concept, either in meaning or in scope of designation, with pornography. To call something obscene, in the standard uses of that term, is to condemn that thing as blatantly disgusting, for the word "obscene," like the word "funny," is used to claim that a given response (in this case disgust, in the other amusement) is likely to be the general one, and/or to endorse that response as appropriate. The corresponding term "pornographic," on the other hand, is purely descriptive, referring to sexually explicit writing and pictures designed entirely and plausibly to induce sexual excitement in the reader or observer. To use the terms "obscene" and "pornographic" interchangeably, then, as if they referred to precisely the same things, is to beg the essentially controversial question of whether any or all (or only) pornographic materials really are obscene. Surely, to those thousands of persons

who delight in pornographic books, pictures, and films, the objects of their attachment do not seem disgusting or obscene. If these materials are nevertheless "truly obscene," they are not so merely by virtue of the definitions of the terms "obscene" and "pornography," but rather by virtue of their blatant violation of some relevant standards, and to establish their obscenity requires serious argument and persuasion. In short, whether any given acknowledged bit of pornography is *really* obscene is a logically open question to be settled by argument, not by definitional fiat.

The United States Supreme Court has committed itself to a different usage. In searching for definitions and tests of what it calls "obscenity," it has clearly had on its collective mind only pornography: not expressive oaths and intensifiers, not abusive curses and epithets, not profanity, (usually) not scatology, nor any other impolite language for which the term "obscene" is a conventional label; not objects disgusting to the senses, or non-sexual conduct and materials that offend the higher sensibilities; but *only* verbal, pictorial, and dramatic materials and exhibitions *designed effectively to be instruments of erotic arousal.* "Obscene" came to *mean* "pornographic" in the Court's parlance. Justice Harlan quite explicitly underwrote this usage in *Cohen* v. *California* in 1971. Paul Robert Cohen had been convicted in a county court of disturbing the peace by wearing a jacket emblazoned on its back with the words "Fuck the draft." When the Supreme Court considered his appeal, Harlan wrote:

> This is not . . . an obscenity case. Whatever else may be necessary to give rise to the State's broader

power to prohibit obscene expression, such expression must be, in some significant way, erotic. It cannot plausibly be maintained that this vulgar allusion to the Selective Service System would conjure up such psychic stimulation in anyone likely to be confronted with Cohen's crudely defaced jacket.[4]

Whatever the word "obscene" might mean to the world at large, within the chambers of the Supreme Court, it has a narrow meaning indeed. Nothing can be "obscene" in the Court's primary usage unless it tends to cause erotic states in the mind of the beholder, and anything that does tend to produce that kind of "psychic stimulation" is a likely candidate for the obscenity label whether or not the induced states are offensive to the person who has them or to anyone else who may be aware of them. As we shall see, the court has occasionally departed from this narrow usage when it labels quite anti-erotic materials "obscene" because of the extreme and universal disgust they produce. On these occasions the Court has recalled its liberal function to protect unwilling audiences from offensive nuisances. But on many other occasions the Court has spoken as if "prurient interest," offensive or not, is its real enemy, as if its tests of obscenity were intended to prevent and punish inherently evil mental states (invoking the illiberal principle of "legal moralism") or else to "protect" adults from the corruption of their own characters even when that corruption is produced by their own voluntary conduct and threatens neither harm nor offense to others (invoking a moralistic version of "legal paternalism"). The simple liberal approach would have been to ascribe to

the word "obscene" the same meaning in the law that it has in ordinary usage, namely "blatantly disgusting," and to interpret anti-obscenity laws as having the traditional liberal function of preventing offensive nuisances, subject of course to the usual balancing tests. Instead the Court chose to *mean* by "obscene," "lust inducing," and to attribute to anti-obscenity statutes the quite illiberal functions of preventing sexy states of mind as an end in itself, and protecting autonomous adult citizens from moral corruption. I shall suggest that these two related mistakes—that of misdefining "obscene," and that of endorsing as constitutional the principles of moralism and paternalism—have led the Court to its present uncomfortable impasse in the law of obscenity.

Although this is not an essay in American constitutional law, it will be interesting to cast a quick glance at some extraordinary recent decisions of the Supreme court about the permissibility of pornography, and in particular the various judicial formulae the Court has produced for dealing with the problem. Even a hasty survey will reveal, I think, that the Court has moved back and forth among our various legitimizing principles, applying now a liberal offense principle mediated by balancing tests and later a thinly disguised moralism, here flirting with paternalism, there sniffing for subtle public harms, and never quite distinguishing with any clarity among them. Moral philosophers, of course, have different objectives from courts of law. My purpose is to determine which governmental restrictions and suppressions are morally legitimate; the Supreme Court aims to establish which restrictions are permitted by the Constitution, especially the First Amendment. Still a third kind of concern, to be sharply distinguished from both of the others, is that of federal and state legislators who must decide which restrictions from among those that are consistent both with the Constitution and with principles of moral legitimacy it would be good public policy to write into law. Despite these different concerns, it should be possible to interpret each crucial formula in various leading court decisions in the terms of our own recommended liberal standards (derived in part from nuisance law), and to criticize the deviations. Where the Court's standards depart from our own, we can conclude either that the Court has misread the Constitution or that the Constitution itself fails to satisfy our ideal prescriptions. We need not opt for one of these verdicts or the other, since this is not an essay in philosophical jurisprudence. A "legal positivist" no doubt would argue that the Constitution, for better or worse, is the law of the land, and that if it falls short of our moral ideals we should work for its amendment. A "natural law" theorist, on the other hand, would insist that all valid moral ideals are tacitly incorporated by the Constitution, so that any interpretation that ascribes to it moral ideals of an inferior or defective kind must be mistaken. Fortunately, my limited purposes in this paper enable me to evade this vexatious jurisprudential issue.

When one approaches the problem of obscenity from within a First Amendment framework, the distinction between action and expression is vitally important. Offensive conduct, as such, poses no particular constitutional problem. American legislatures are perfectly free to employ the offense principle as medi-

ated by the standards we have recommended in prohibiting loud, raucous conduct, brazenly indecent conduct, public nudity, lewdness, offensive solicitation, and the like. But when the only "conduct" involved is the expression of some proposition, attitude, or feeling in speech or writing, or of whatever it is that gets "expressed" in art, music, drama, or film, then restrictive legislation would seem to contravene the explicit guarantees of the First Amendment. And when the "conduct" in question is the mere possession of protected symbolic or expressive materials like books, pictures, tapes, or films, or the distribution or exhibition of such materials to willing recipients or observers, then its prohibition would also seem to violate the First Amendment's strictures since it would render dangerous the creation of such materials and have a "chilling effect" on the spontaneity and freedom of expression generally. Moreover, expression is rarely valued or valuable in itself but only as a part of the process of communication, and that process requires an audience. It follows that to deprive a symbol-user of his willing audience is to interfere with the "expression," and that is precisely what the First Amendment forbids. The problem that presents itself to the Supreme Court then is this: how, if at all, can statutes that forbid and punish offensive obscenity be reconciled with the First Amendment's "free speech" and "free press" guarantees, when the offensiveness of the prohibited conduct resides in spoken or printed words, in pictures, plays, or films?

Until the 1950s, the United States Supreme Court had never taken a clear stand on the question of whether "obscene" (i.e., "sexy," "lust-inducing," "erotic," etc.) materials and actions are protected by the First Amendment's ban on statutes that "abridge the freedom of speech, or the press." By that time, both the federal government and virtually every state had enacted criminal statutes prohibiting obscenity, and more and more convictions were being appealed on the ground that these statutes were unconstitutional as violating freedom of expression. At the time the Court first decided to hear some of these appeals it might have appeared (as it does now to our privileged hindsight) that there were two broad alternative courses open to it:

It could hold that explicitly erotic materials, or the act of distributing or exhibiting them, do qualify as "speech" or expression, and hence for protection under the First Amendment. In that case, obscene expressions, like every other use of "speech," cannot be banned because of their expressive content (the proposition, opinion, feeling, or attitude that they express) but at most, only because of the manner in which they are expressed in the circumstances. Just as speech that is ordinarily free might be punishable if it is defamatory or fraudulent, or if it is solicitation, or incitement to crime, so obscene speech, while ordinarily free, might be prohibited if in its circumstances it is a public nuisance or falls under some other recognized heading of exception. Under this alternative, the exceptive headings that include defamation, fraud, and the like do *not* include "obscenity" (in the Supreme Court's sense) as such.

Even if the Court took this first course it could allow that statutes prohibiting obscenity might nevertheless be constitutional if they are drawn with sufficient care. Statutes might, for example, prohibit public showings of obscene matter on the grounds that such materials are extremely offensive, but in that case, one would think that the Constitution would require satisfaction of something like our proposed balancing tests for the offense principle. That is to say that even admittedly "obscene" (that is, erotic) material cannot be prohibited if the offense is only moderate or sporadic, or if it is reasonably avoidable, or if its risk is voluntarily assumed, etc. One could easily imagine what a constitutional statute controlling pornography (sexual "obscenity") would be like. Only patently offensive exhibitions to captive audiences in public places or to children would be prohibited. In short, on this first alternative course, either there would be no statutes prohibiting "obscenity," or else the statutes would all be of the kind that control public nuisances and are legitimized by a properly mediated offense principle.

A model for this first interpretation of the constitutional status of obscenity can be found in the long sequence of Supreme Court decisions interpreting the "free exercise of religion" clause of the First Amendment. Normally, any conduct that is an essential part of what is recognizably a religious service or observance, or is required by a moral rule of a recognizably religious sect, is protected. Nevertheless, such conduct can be punished if it should happen to satisfy the definition of a crime, such as ritual human sacrifice, or incitement to crime in a sermon read from the pulpit. Given that the First Amendment explicitly recognizes the distinctively important value of religious freedom, we can infer that there is a proportionately greater burden on those who would criminalize any conduct that is part of a religious observance. The more important a part of the religious observance is the conduct in question, the more important must be the "state's interest" (i.e., the harm, offense, or other evil for the aversion of which the prohibition is necessary). Thus, balancing tests of the sort we have found in nuisance law and then built into the offense principle are an essential element in the application of the First Amendment to statutes that restrict religious liberty.The Court could hold, alternatively, that purely pornographic materials do not qualify as speech or artistic expression, that in terms of the values enshrined in the First Amendment, they are utterly without worth or significance. This is by no means a wildly implausible or "illiberal" alternative. It would be more implausible to interpret most works of pornography as expressions of "ideas," and while the line between erotic realism in drama or literature, on the one hand, and pure pornography on the other, is obscure, at least the clear cases of pornography are easily distinguished from any kind of expressive art. So-called "filthy pictures" and hard-core pornographic "tales" are simply devices meant to titillate the sex organs *via* the mediation of symbols. They are designed exclusively to perform that function and are valued by their users only insofar as they succeed in that limited aim. For the pure cases (if only they could always be identified!) it would be absurd to think of them as speech or art as it would to think of "French ticklers," and other mechanical devices made solely to stimulate erotic feelings, in the same fashion.

This second alternative course for the Court then would be to deny pornography the protection of the First Amendment on the ground that it is not "speech" in the requisite sense. It does not follow, however, that pornography is not protected by any part of the Constitution just because it is not protected by the First Amendment; nor would it follow from the fact that it stands beyond the scope of the whole Constitution that it is morally legitimate to prohibit it unconditionally. If legislatures are free to bar individuals from wholly private and harmless indulgences just on the ground that they are "obscene" (sexually stimulating), then the exercise of that legislative freedom in many cases will lead to an invasion of the "privacy" of individuals, or (avoiding that troublesome word) of their liberty to control their own sexual experiences in any way they like short of harming or offending others. Unqualified prohibition of pornography may well be in this way a violation of individual rights even though, *ex hypothesi*, it does not violate First Amendment rights.

Faced with this morally repugnant consequence, the Supreme Court following this second alternative might respond in either of two ways. It could look, if it were so disposed, elsewhere in the Constitution for an implicit right that is violated by the prohibition of private, consensual, harmless conduct in so basic a department of human experience as sexuality. In *Griswold* v. *Connecticut,* for example, the Court discovered in the interstices of the First, Fourth, Fifth, Ninth, and Fourteenth Amendments a hitherto unnoticed "right to privacy," which would perhaps be less misleadingly described as a right to personal *autonomy* in self-regarding and peculiarly intimate affairs. In *Griswold* the right to privacy was invoked to defend the sanctity of the marriage bed against laws that would prohibit the use of contraceptives. The same right was extended to unmarried persons in *Eisenstadt* v. *Baird,* and to the viewing of pornographic films in one's own home in *Stanley* v. *Georgia.* Once more the same right was invoked in *Roe* v. *Wade* to strike down statutes that would deny to women the opportunity to have abortions and thus violate their "privacy," that is, their autonomy in respect to what is done to their own bodies. It may be stretching things a bit to use one label, "the right to privacy," for such a diversity of rights, except to indicate that there is a realm (or a number of realms) of human conduct that are simply nobody's business except that of the actors, and *a fortiori* are beyond the legitimate attention of the criminal law. Graham Hughes was encouraged by the trend of the Supreme Court "privacy" decisions to speak cautiously of "the maturing constitutional freedom to engage in discreet sexual stimulation or gratification." What provides coherence to those motley decisions as a group, he suggests, "must be that there is something special about erotic activity that entitles a person to protection from the law unless the activity is being offensively thrust before members of the public."

The second possible approach of the Court, if it were to exclude pornography from the scope of the First Amendment, would be to conclude that there is no protection to be found anywhere in the Constitution for "obscene materials" even when they are used discreetly and restricted to adults. In that case, a judge might personally regret that the properly mediated offense principle is not written

into the Constitution and urge legislatures to initiate the amendment process. Or he might advocate that those anti-obscenity statutes that can be legitimized only by paternalistic or moralistic principles be modified or repealed. But as a justice sworn to uphold the Constitution as he understands it, he would not be free arbitrarily to strike down the offending statutes, odiously unfair though they may be.

The two generic alternative courses sketched above will not always be as distinct as they first appear, for they will overlap in mixed cases of pornography-cum-art-or-opinion, and in instances of erotic materials that are borderline-expressive. One would think that the chief need of the Court in these cases would be not for a criterion of "obscenity" but for a criterion of "protectible expression," for where such expression is present *and* there is no captive audience or children involved, then it doesn't matter how lurid, tawdry, provocative, or unseemly the expression is; it cannot be proscribed. The point is not that explicit sexiness per se is prohibitable if only we can learn how to recognize and define it; but rather that expression per se is not prohibitable (except where it is a nuisance), so we had better learn how to recognize and define *it.*

Until the United States Supreme Court took its first close look at the problem of obscenity in 1957, the leading judicial precedent in the field was an English one. In the famous case of *Regina* v. *Hicklin,* Lord Cockburn formulated a test for obscenity that was widely accepted in the American courts well into the twentieth century. Between 1868 and 1957 American appellate courts commonly applied the *Hicklin* test in judging appeals of convictions under vaguely worded federal and state statutes against obscenity. Lord Cockburn's words were quoted over and over again during that period: "I think the test of obscenity is this, whether the tendency of the matter charged as obscenity is to deprave and corrupt those whose minds are open to such immoral influences, and into whose hands a publication of this sort may fall."

The first thing to notice about the *Hicklin* formula is that it is a test of obscenity, not a definition of the word "obscenity." Lord Cockburn apparently means by "obscenity" something like "objectionable treatment of sexual materials," so his "test" tells us how to determine whether a given treatment of sex in writing or pictures is sufficiently objectionable to be banned by statutes that forbid "obscenity."

It is important to notice next that Lord Cockburn's test appeals in no way to an offense principle but rather to certain speculative harms that might be produced by exposure to erotic materials. Reading dirty books and leering at filthy pictures can "deprave and corrupt" persons who might otherwise remain innocent and pure. Virgins will become libertines and harlots; virtuous men will become rakes and lechers. Even if the skeptical view of former New York mayor Jimmy Walker is correct ("No nice girl was ever ruined by a book") and pornography does not cause virtuous people to commit sexual sins, it may yet strengthen the habit to dwell on one's sexual thoughts, and be absorbed in one's sexual fantasies short of actual conduct. That too might be a form of "corruption" or "depravity" by Victorian standards. The ultimate (and tacit)

justification of the *Hicklin* test might have been derived from the harm principle, if Lord Cockburn had in mind "social harms" like the weakening of the social fabric that would come about if people generally abandoned themselves to lives of debauchery. There was no doubt an element of moralism involved too, since we can suppose that Lord Cockburn held lustful states of mind to be inherent evils whether or not they issue in harmful conduct. More likely still, the ultimate rationale is a blend of moralism and paternalism. Potential viewers of pornography need to be protected from "moral harm"; that is, harm to their characters. No matter that they voluntarily run the risk of corruption; they need to be protected from themselves. The Victorian justification for keeping pornography from adults, on this interpretation of motives, is precisely the same as our own noncontroversial rationale for keeping it away from children. Nowhere does Lord Cockburn express concern for the captive observer who might be caused offense; he is much too preoccupied with the danger to "those whose minds are open to such immoral influences" to worry about offenses to the sensibilities of those not in moral jeopardy.

There would appear to be more than a hint of the traditional British patronizing of the lower classes in Lord Cockburn's concern for those "into whose hands a publication of this sort may fall." Educated gentlemen no doubt can read pornographic books without fear of serious corruption, or corruption beyond that which motivates them in the first place, but what if the dirty book should just happen to fall into the hands of their servants, and be disseminated among ordinary workers and others (not to mention their own wives) who may be more susceptible to such influences? Perhaps Lord Cockburn's models for those "whose minds are open to such immoral influences" were alcoholics who can't hold their liquor and can't leave it alone. Perhaps he suspected that there is a similar class of "sex-addicts" who can get "hooked" on pornography and need ever greater stimulation to satisfy their growing needs, so that in the end mere pornography won't do, and illicit sexual conduct in ever greater frequency takes its place. Such would not be the normal reaction to dirty books, of course, but only the response of those unnamed susceptibles "whose minds are open to such immoral influences."

Mr. Justice Brennan, when he came to write his groundbreaking majority opinion in *Roth* v. *United States* in 1957, rightly found the *Hicklin* formula (as it had come to be interpreted) objectionable on three grounds: (1) it permitted books to be judged obscene on the basis of isolated passages read out of context; (2) it allowed the obscenity of a work to be determined by its likely effects on unusually susceptible persons; (3) it posited fixed standards of propriety regardless of time, place, and circumstances. These three objectionable features had made it possible for courts in Massachusetts to uphold the ban of Dreiser's *American Tragedy,* Lillian Smith's *Strange Fruit,* and Erskine Caldwell's *God's Little Acre,* and for federal prosecutors to attempt (unsuccessfully) to ban Joyce's *Ulysses.* The "isolated passage" and "culturally invariant standard" part of the *Hicklin* test now seem to be simple mistakes, but the "susceptible person" standard seems especially

wrongheaded in the light of our discussion of the mediating standards for determining the gravity of a nuisance which minimizes the seriousness of offenses to abnormally susceptible individuals. *Hicklin's* concentration on the abnormally vulnerable moral character invites comparison with laws that would impose civil liability for frightening unusually skittish horses or laws that would ban the use of table salt on the grounds that some persons are allergic to it. Whatever else Brennan would put into the new test for obscenity in his *Roth* opinion, he would certainly correct the three errors of *Hicklin,* and that he did. Henceforth, he decreed, a book can be judged obscene only if "the dominant theme of the material taken as a whole" is so judged; and only if it is the likely effect of the materials on "the average person" (and not the especially susceptible person) that is taken into account, and only if "contemporary community standards" (and not eternally fixed Victorian upper class standards) are applied to the work. The three key expressions—"dominant theme of the material taken as a whole," "average person," and "contemporary community standards"—became a fixed part of subsequent court formulations of an obscenity test, and while their vagueness did breed some mischief, they were clearly distinct improvements over *Hicklin.* Brennan had made a good start.

Unfortunately the rest of the *Roth* opinion caused a good deal of confusion, much of which remains to this day. Some of the trouble stems from the locutions "utterly without redeeming social importance" and "appealing to prurient interest," which are of course the fourth and fifth famous phrases of the *Roth* opinion. It is possible that Brennan intended his statement that obscenity is utterly without redeeming social importance to be a "synthetic judgment" giving low grades to some class of objects that can be independently identified and defined. But I suspect that his statement functions more naturally in his argument as part of the stipulation of a new legal *definition* of "obscenity." The other part of the definition is constituted by the "appeal to prurient interest" clause. So interpreted, he is saying: This is what we shall henceforth *mean* by "obscene," namely "whatever is produced for the sole purpose of arousing lustful thoughts and thus has no expressive value or function that is protected by the First Amendment." Risqué novels are still literature, and the First Amendment protects *all* literature. But pure pornography, whether it uses words or pictures, or both, is no kind of literature or art at all, good or bad, but rather some quite different kind of thing, properly classifiable with chemical aphrodisiacs and mechanical sex aids rather than with poems, plays, and the like. Radical opinions advocating more sexual liberty are expressions of opinion about sexual titillation, and, as such, they too are protected, even if they should happen themselves to be intended to titillate. "Mixed cases" of art-cum-pornography (if there are any such cases when one judges "dominant themes" of "whole works") are also to be treated as protectible expression. When you add "no value" to "small value" you get a diluted value, but even diluted values must be protected.

This interpretation finds some support in a subsequent paragraph of the *Roth* opinion where what looks like a formal definition of "obscenity" is presented: "Obscene material is material which deals with sex [genus] in a manner appealing to prurient interest [difference]," in other words, pornography. The generic part of the definition makes clear that it is the realm of the erotic only which is on the Court's mind; the phrase "appealing to prurient interest" serves to rule out various non-pornographic ways of portraying sex, "for example, in art, literature, and scientific works." The whole definition says simply that legal obscenity is pornography; then the "utterly without importance" clause adds "and nothing but pornography." The complete definition thus identifies legal obscenity, in effect, with *pure* pornography.

What remains vague is the meaning of "appealing to." Does it mean "intended to excite such interest" or "having the function, intended or not, of exciting such interest?" Very likely, intention and probable effect are each necessary and are jointly sufficient for a work to qualify as pornography. We must embrace this interpretation if we are to handle plausibly the case of the inept pornographer who tries to earn a living selling photographs of embarrassed and heavily garbed middle-aged relatives, under the mistaken impression that they will "turn on" lustful customers. His appeal to prurience is genuine enough, just as the appeal to the mercy or charity of a hard-hearted skinflint might be genuine enough, but in neither case does it seem to be the sort of appeal that could hit its mark. The inept pornographer tried to make pornography but failed despite his evil intentions. So an "appeal," in the sense of simple intention, to the prurience of one's audience is not enough to constitute pornography. In addition the effort must be of a general character that can plausibly be expected to strike a responsive chord . . . in whom? "In the average person in one's own contemporary community," say the earlier clauses about the "average person" and "community standards," thus filling out the definition.

If we are right about the Court's definition of "obscenity," what then is its test for determining obscenity? A chemist can tell us what he means by the word "acid" by citing a feature of the molecular structure of acids, for example that they contain hydrogen as a positive radical, or by mentioning other essential characteristics of all acids. But then when we ask him how we can go about telling an acid when we see one, he will give us answers of a different kind, theoretically less interesting, but more useful for our purposes, for example that acids are soluble in water, sour in taste, and turn litmus paper red. Similarly, a dictionary can explain the meaning of "drunk" and a physiologist can enumerate the biochemical characteristics that underlie all instances of drunkenness, but if we wish a useful and precise test of drunkenness, then we need something like a drunkometer machine (e.g., a "breathalyser") and a metric criterion. The old *Hicklin* formula had not been meant to be a definition of "obscene," but to be more like a litmus test or drunkometer test for determining when obscenity is present. Just as the one test says that drunkenness is present when there is a certain percentage of alcohol in the blood, so the other test says that materials are obscene when they are capable of producing a certain effect on susceptible persons. Actually, the analogy is much closer to a test for determining when a substance is intoxicating than to a test for determining when a person is intoxicated. In each case what is being tested is the capacity of an object to produce effects of some measurable kind on a precisely defined class of subjects. Obviously the *Hicklin* test fails totally to do its assigned job in a satisfactory way. Does *Roth* provide a test that does any better?

Probably the best way of interpreting *Roth* is to conclude that it doesn't even attempt to supplement its definition of "obscenity" (as pornography) and its analysis of pornography (as non-expressive) with a practical test for determining the presence of obscenity. More likely the Court, both in *Roth* and its numerous *sequalia,* never even attempted to provide identifying tests of obscenity. The difficulty of doing so, in fact, filled it with collective despair, most piquantly expressed by Mr. Justice Stewart in *Jacobellis v. Ohio* who said that he would not try to specify a criterion of "hard-core pornography," and "perhaps I could never succeed in intelligibly doing so. But I know it when I see it. . . ." It may be that no litmus test of "obscenity" is needed since pure unredeemed and unsupplemented pornography is indeed accurately characterized in general descriptive formulae and is easily recognized by the ordinary men and women who sit in juries. Once we have it that a given book, for example, is pornographic, the only test that is needed is whether, "taken as a whole," it is also literature or opinion, that is, protectible expression. Pure pornography is easy to recognize; what are hard to spot are the "redeeming" units or aspects of expression in such impure admixtures as artfully pornographic films and erotic realism in novels.

When all five famous phrases are combined in the *Roth* opinion, there emerges, nevertheless, a formula that bears the superficial appearance of an identifying test. It is one of the predominant confusions of the Court in those subsequent decisions in which the *Roth* formula is refined, that it is unclear whether or not the Court intended the formula to provide a practical litmus test. Indeed, Mr. Justice Brennan refers to the standard as a "substituted test" for *Hicklin* in the very sentence in which he formulates it. ". . . this test: whether to the average person, applying contemporary community standards, the dominant theme of the material taken as a whole appeals to prurient interest." The central source of the confusion in this formula, however, is not its obscure status or its imprecision as a test; it does no worse, surely than *Hicklin* on those counts. Rather the confusion stems from the fact that it is not really a "substitute" for *Hicklin* so much as a mere modification of *Hicklin*: "average person" is substituted for unusually susceptible persons, "contemporary community standards" for eternally fixed Victorian standards, "the material as a whole" for isolated passages. These substitutions suggest that the *Roth* formula shares starting points, purposes, and initial assumptions with the *Hicklin* test, but just does its common job more carefully, avoiding undesirable side effects.

But in fact the *Hicklin* test judges that sexual materials are sufficiently objectionable to be denominated "obscene" when they are capable of producing effects of a certain kind. Those effects are taken to be so evil in themselves that even responsible adults can be protected from their own choices and not permitted to run the risk of infection. The ultimate principles appealed to are,

as we have seen, moralistic and paternalistic; the idea of offensive nuisance is not used or mentioned even implicitly. Can we believe that Mr. Justice Brennan, one of the Supreme Court's staunchest liberals, really intended to incorporate moralistic paternalism as a principle of constitutional jurisprudence? Can we believe that he thought that the state has a right to protect "the average person" from morally deleterious mental states ("itches") induced in him by materials he has freely chosen precisely because he wished to experience such states, when there is no clear and present danger of public harm and no third parties to be offended? The only answer to these questions, I think, is that Mr. Justice Brennan may not quite have understood what he was saying.

His confusions come out most strikingly in his use of the phrase regarding the "average person, applying . . . standards," Standards of what? And who, exactly, applies them: the average person or later, the court? There are at least three possible answers to these questions. First of all, if *Roth* really is but a small modification of *Hicklin,* the "standards" in question are norms for determining when materials have sufficient capacity to cause corruption or depravity. (The analogous question is when a beverage has sufficient capacity to cause intoxication in the "average person.") In that case the standards are not applied *by* the average person (as suggested by Brennan's syntax) but rather by the court *to* the average person. The Court's task, according to this interpretation, is to determine whether the likely effect of the materials on the average person would be a change in his character which, according to the standards of his (our?)

community, would be corrupting or depraving. In effect, the plural term "standards," on this view, refers to two distinct standards: one for determining what the causal effects of the materials on the average person would be, and one for evaluating those effects as morally corrupting. The former standard would come from the social sciences, the latter from " the contemporary community."

Still, it is hard to believe, especially in light of the opinions in later obscenity cases, that standards of offensiveness were not lurking somewhere in the penumbra of Brennan's opinion in *Roth*. These standards too vary from place to place, and change from time to time. On a second interpretation of *Roth* they too are among the "standards" that must be "applied." Quite apart from, or in addition to, their desirable or undesirable effects on traits of character, would the materials be likely to *shock* the average person? To answer this question about offensiveness, we must look to the standards of decorum in a given historical community that are held by its "average member" in such a way that their violation causes him shock of disgust (quite apart from the speculative effect on his own character).

The actual wording of the *Roth* formula, however, suggests a third interpretation, that the relevant "standards" are to guide yet another determination, namely whether the materials in question can be expected to *excite* ("appeal to") the average person's lustful thoughts ("prurient interests"). These standards too vary from community to community and from one culture to another. These standards too are in gradual constant change within one community over extended periods of time. With changes in

the norms determining permissible conduct and dress come concomitant changes in the customary effects of different styles of dress and deportment on observers. Grandpa was excited even by bare ankles, dad by flesh above the knee, grandson only by flimsy bikinis. According to this third interpretation, a court must look at a contemporary community and decide what it takes then and there to excite the average person to a certain level of lust, and that will depend, in part, on what the average person is accustomed to see, to do, to experience.

Which of these three interpretations of the *Roth* formula is correct? My conclusion is that the court simply hadn't thought these matters out, that there is some plausibility in each interpretation, that ambiguities in judicial language here reflect uncertainties and conflicts in judicial thought. If the first interpretation is the correct one, then Mr. Justice Brennan, like Lord Cockburn before him, was basically a moralistic paternalist, endorsing the propriety and constitutionality of legislative efforts to protect citizens from harm to their own characters, quite apart from other consequences. Since it is difficult to believe that Mr. Justice Brennan, of all people, held such a view, the first interpretation is perhaps not very convincing. On the second interpretation, the Court was applying the offense or nuisance principle to the question of obscene materials, but—astonishingly—without the mediating maxims that would protect the privacy of willing consumers. The third interpretation is perhaps the one closest to the Court's conscious intentions, because it understands the *Roth* formula to be a test of when something is pornographic, hence "obscene" in the Court's sense, quite apart from further questions about its effects on sensibility and character. On this interpretation, as on the other two, the concept of obscenity is a relative one, varying on this reading with the average person's susceptibility to lustful feelings. In a way, this interpretation of the formula makes it even more disappointing to the liberal than the others. In the Court's view, so understood, there is no question about a legislature's right to ban lust-inducing materials, and no explanation why "obscenity" defined in this way (as pornography) and determined by these varying standards may be prohibited. The unwritten assumption apparently is that if legislatures think lustful states of mind are inherently evil (quite apart from harm or offense), that is sufficient.

From the language of the majority opinion in *Roth* it would appear that the offensiveness of materials has nothing to do with the question of whether they are obscene or properly subject to legislative ban. Obscenity *means* pornography, and pure pornography without redeeming literary or scientific admixture totally lacks qualification for First Amendment protection. What then is the test of whether a given set of materials—a book or a film—is truly pornographic? Whether a court, applying prevailing community standards to the average person finds that "the dominant theme of the materials taken as a whole appeals to prurient interests." Not a word about whether they are repulsive, abhorrent, disgusting, or shocking to anyone. Not a suggestion that the state's legal interest in their regulation might derive from their character as nuisances.

Five years later, however, in *Manual Enterprises* v. *Day* the Court recalled the concept of offensiveness, and added it,

as a kind of afterthought to the *Roth* formula. The Post Office Department had barred from the mails on the grounds of obscenity three magazines *(Manual, Trim,* and *Grecian Guild Pictorial)* that specialized in photographs of nude or nearly nude male models. Manual Enterprises, the publisher of all three, appealed to the Supreme Court objecting that, among other things, the publications were "body-building magazines" and therefore not obscene. Justice Harlan, the author of one of the two opinions supporting the petitioner in this case, sidestepped the question of whether the materials could be judged obscene on the grounds that they appealed to the prurient interests of the average (male) homosexual rather than the "average person" (the question of relevant audience that was finally settled in *Mishkin* v. *New York* in 1966), and gave emphasis instead to the question of offensiveness: "These magazines cannot be deemed so offensive on their face as to affront current community standards of decency— a quality that we shall hereafter refer to as 'patent offensiveness' or 'indecency.' " Mr. Justice Harlan then went on to spell out a "twofold concept of obscenity" according to which "patent offensiveness" and "appeal to prurient interest" are each necessary and jointly sufficient for obscenity. Only one of these "distinct elements" (at most) was present in the body-building magazines; hence they were not obscene, however much they may have excited homosexual lust. The presence of both elements is determined by the application of community standards; offensiveness by standards of decorum or "customary limits of candor," prurience presumably by standards of average susceptibility. "In most obscenity cases," Harlan rushed to reassure us, "the elements tend to coalesce," and what obviously appeals to prurience will on that account alone be "patently offensive."

The next steps in the evolution of the *Roth* formula occurred on one strange day in 1966 when the Court handed down decisions in *Ginzburg* v. *United States, Mishkin* v. *New York,* and *A Book Named "John Cleland's Memoirs of a Woman of Pleasure"* v. *Attorney General of Massachusetts* (*"Memoirs"* v. *Massachusetts,* for short). The *Mishkin* case makes the best transition from *Enterprises* v. *Day,* so I shall begin with it. This case settled the problem of relevant audience which Mr. Justice Harlan had put aside in *Enterprises.* Mishkin was appealing a conviction and a sentence of three years in jail and a $12,000 fine for violation of a New York state criminal statute prohibiting publication, possession, and distribution for sale of obscene materials. The books in question described sadomasochistic sexual acts, fetishisms, lesbianism, and male homosexuality. It was clear that the "average person" would be repelled rather than aroused by such materials and that the books, therefore, made no appeal to the prurience of the "average person" at all. In a 6-3 decision, the Supreme Court upheld Mishkin's conviction anyway, and reformulated the *Roth* criteria at the same time: "Where the material is designed for and primarily disseminated to a clearly defined deviant sexual group, rather than the public at large, the prurient-appeal requirement of the *Roth* test is satisfied if the dominant theme of the material taken as a whole appeals to the prurient interest in sex of the members of that group." Thus were the equal rights of sadomasochists, fetishists, and homosexuals to be free from stimulants to their own kind of lustfulness vindicated in the highest court. Apparently, "patent offensiveness" is determined by the standards of the "average person" (even when no average person is in fact offended), while the prurient interest test is applied to the special audience at which the materials are aimed.

One would think, that as a general rule, the more special the audience addressed, the greater the offensiveness as measured by the standards of the general public. The average person is more offended (shocked, disgusted) by homosexuality than by heterosexuality, more repelled by bestiality than even by human homosexuality, etc. On the other hand, as a general rule one would expect that the more special the audience addressed, the smaller the total amount of lustfulness induced. It would follow then that the more fully the offending materials satisfy the "patent offensiveness" test, the smaller the amount of prurience they actually produce in the community as a whole—at least for the more familiar sorts of sexual deviance. In a limiting case, the offensiveness might be extreme but the lust actually stimulated so minuscule as to be insignificant, in which case the materials would satisfy only one of the two necessary conditions for obscenity. Apparently, however, the Court recognizes no lower limit to the amount of prurience that must be stimulated by a book in order for it to be judged obscene. Given satisfaction of the "patent offensiveness" standard, any increase in the net amount of prurience is an evil that a legislature is entitled to prevent. Where offensiveness is extreme, then, the appeal to the prurient interest standard hardly seems necessary at all. In fact, sale or display of the offending materials might be prohibitable as nuisances anyway in that case; minimal appeal to prurience is necessary only if the prohibition is made on the grounds of "obscenity." But what importance is there in a mere name?

The addition of the "patent offensiveness" component to the *Roth* formula saves the Court from another kind of severe embarrassment that would result from the applications to certain hypothetical cases, at least, of a test for obscenity that makes no reference to offensiveness at all. Without the offensiveness component, the *Roth-Mishkin* criteria would require only that socially valueless materials appeal to the prurient interest of some audience, no matter how special or small, in order to be judged obscene. In that case, if there are seventeen people in the entire United States who achieve their sexual gratification primarily by fondling stones, then a magazine aimed directly at them which publishes lurid color photographs of rocks and pebbles would be obscene. As it is, the Courts is saved from such an absurdity by Mr. Justice Harlan's afterthought of offensiveness. Since the *Mishkin* decision, a sex magazine for rock fetishists would qualify as obscene only if it published, for example, pictures of naked people rubbing up against a variety of sandstone, limestone, basalt, and marble rocks in various erotic postures suggesting abandonment to ecstasy. Then no doubt the deviant cultish magazine would be fully obscene by both the "prurient interest" standard (minimally satisfied) and the "patent offensiveness" standard, though it might yet be "redeemed" by scientifically serious articles about geology interspersed among the photographs.

United States v. *Ginzburg* decided the same day as *Mishkin*, took a wholly unexpected new path for which *Roth* had not prepared observers of the Court. That path led the Court into a thicket from which it subsequently retreated, and it led Ralph Ginzburg, to his astonishment and despair, to prison for a five-year term. Ginzburg had been convicted of violating the federal statute against obscenity by publishing among other things the magazine *Eros* and the book, *The Housewife's Handbook on Selective Promiscuity*. He appealed, and the Supreme Court spent most of its time during oral argument trying to apply the newly interpreted "three pronged" *Roth* formula to the publications to determine whether they were truly obscene. To be obscene, a majority agreed, the materials must appeal to their audience's prurient interests, be patently offensive by community standards of decorum, and be "utterly without redeeming social importance." Ginzburg's lawyers were especially concerned to argue that respectable literary and journalistic materials were intermixed with the avowedly pornographic materials, thus establishing some redeeming social value in the materials taken as a whole. But none of this mattered, according to the decision which the Court dropped like a bomb shell on March 21, 1966. Justice Brennan argued in his majority opinion that Ginzburg's publications could be found obscene because of the "leer of the sensualist" that permeated the *advertising* for the publications. If the Court had considered it solely on the basis of the *content* of the publications, he admitted this would have been a close and difficult case, but the emphasis of Ginzburg's advertising made all the difference.

A close examination of Mr. Justice Brennan's decision reveals the usual uncritical mixture of appeals to moralism, paternalism, and the oddly unmediated offense principle. Mr. Justice Brennan, employing his own *Roth* formula (at that time in *Memoirs* the three-pronged test), must first decide whether the materials are pornographic. Do they "appeal" to the prurient interests of prospective readers? Well, of course they do; their own advertising explicitly makes such an appeal. The materials are "openly advertised to appeal to the erotic interest of their customers." To be sure, in court Ginzburg's lawyers had argued that some of the articles and stories conferred a redeeming social importance to the publications taken as a whole, but this doubtful claim, Brennan argues, is belied by Ginzburg's own sales pitch where his "appeal" is made. The advertising is "relevant to determining whether social importance claimed for material in the courtroom was, in the circumstances, pretense or reality— whether it was the basis upon which it was traded in the marketplace or a spurious claim for litigation purposes." And it must be admitted that there was not a single mention of literary values, scientific studies, or moral-political advocacy in Ginzburg's advertising; "[T]he purveyor's sole emphasis is on the sexually provocative aspects of his publications. . . ." This then is Brennan's first argument: In "close cases" the advertising for publications may be used as evidence of whether or not the materials appeal exclusively to prurient interest, that is, are purely pornographic, meaning legally obscene. When in doubt, judges should take the defendant's own words into account as evidence of the obscene

content of his publications. This last-minute rationalization that could not possibly have been anticipated at the time of the criminal conduct sent poor Ginzburg to prison for five years. Subsequent publishers of pornography took warning. Their advertisements used euphemisms and code words like "adult books" and "erotic literature," but their books were as "dirty" as ever. This decision sent one man to prison, but changed little else.

Mr. Justice Brennan's opinion did pay some homage to the offense principle, as indeed it had to, since "patent offensiveness" was now one of the three prongs of the revised *Roth* formula. But his words are very sparse on this subject: "The deliberate representation of petitioners' publications as erotically arousing . . . would tend to force public confrontation with the potentially offensive aspects of the work; the brazenness of such an appeal heightens the offensiveness of the publications to those who are offended by such material." Perhaps these cryptic words do make a good point. An unavoidable sign in large red letters on a billboard in a crowded place that shrieks "FILTHY PICTURES FOR SALE" will be predictably offensive to anyone who would be offended by the filthy pictures themselves, and no doubt also to a great many who would not be offended by a private perusal of the advertised products. Still, the advertisement for the filthy pictures could hardly be as offensive as the filthy pictures themselves would be if *they* were on the public billboard. In comparison with the latter impropriety, the shrill advertising is a mere peccadillo. In any case, advertising can be regulated by explicit statutes that put advertisers on warning. No such statutes were violated by Ginzburg's advertisements; he was jailed, in effect, for conduct that he could not have known to be criminal.

The final argument in Brennan's opinion for the relevance of advertising to the determination of obscenity is a moralistic-paternalistic one. *"Eros* was created, represented, and sold solely as a claimed instrument of the sexual stimulation it would bring. Like the other publications, its pervasive treatment of sex and sexual matters rendered it available to *exploitation by those who would make a business of pandering to 'the widespread weakness for titillation by pornography.'* " The latter phrase is especially revealing. It is not pornography and erotic stimulation as such that are the object of Brennan's wrath, but rather "the sordid business of pandering—'the business of purveying textual or graphic matter openly advertised to appeal to the erotic interest of their customers.' " Brennan here follows the Model Penal Code in taking an "oblique approach" to the problem of obscenity. That approach is well explained by Louis B. Schwarz:

> The meretricious "appeal" of a book or picture is essentially a question of the attractiveness of the merchandise from a certain point of view: what makes it sell. Thus, the prohibition of obscenity takes on an aspect of regulation of unfair business or competitive practices. Just as merchants may be prohibited from selling their wares by appeal to the public's weakness for gambling, so they may be restrained from purveying books, movies, or other commercial exhibition by exploiting the well-nigh universal weakness for a look behind the curtain of modesty.[5]

Customers, in short, need protection from the state from enticing advertisements that "exploit their weaknesses," whether the weakness be for erotic fantasy, gambling, or whatever. (But why not then also for cigarettes, sweets, and fried foods?)

In treating the desire for titillation by pornography as a "weakness," Brennan seems to be making a contestable moral judgment that permits him in effect to incorporate part of the conventional sexual morality into the law. Suppose that a regular customer for pornographic materials were to deny that his need and taste is a weakness? "I don't think of the titillation I crave as a temptation to do something evil by my own standards," he might say. "Rather it is an appetite like any other, entirely innocent in my eyes. I seek it in good conscience, and find it patronizing indeed to be told that my moral sense needs correction, or that my moral resolution needs reinforcement by the law." Another user might have moral reservations. He might admit that he is sometimes ashamed of his pornographic indulgences, but deny vehemently that his moral struggles are anyone else's business. Certainly, he will say, they are not the law's business. Both of these users might admit that they have a need for erotic titillation, while denying that every need is a "weakness" that renders them incapable of governing themselves without outside help.

The reasonableness of these replies to Mr. Justice Brennan is underscored by the contrast between the taste for titillation and the genuine weakness of the alcoholic for whiskey, the drug addict for heroin, or the cigarette smoker for nicotine. An advertising sales pitch aimed directly at alcoholics encouraging them to strengthen their habit would be unfair not only to one's more scrupulous competitors in the liquor business (one of Schwarz's prime concerns) but also to the poor wretches one is trying to exploit. Their addiction is a weakness in the sense that it is something they regret and try to resist themselves, something that is objectively bad for them, as they would be the first to admit. Similarly cigarette advertisements aimed directly at teenagers can fix a fatal habit on unsuspecting innocents from which many will find relief only in a painful and premature death. But these analogies fail to provide convincing models for the willing customer of pornography. The tenability of the principle of moralistic paternalism is a matter to which justice cannot be fully done here. It suffices to point out that Brennan's final argument for the relevance of advertising to determinations of obscenity tacitly invokes that principle.

We need not linger long over the last of the three obscenity cases decided by the Supreme Court in March 1966. *John Cleland's Memoirs of a Woman of Pleasure* was much more widely known by the name of its central character, *Fanny Hill*. The book, first distributed in England in 1750, was published anew in the United States in 1963. Obscenity charges were promptly brought against it by the Commonwealth of Massachusetts whose Supreme Court, in a 4-3 decision, officially declared it obscene. Many expert witnesses, including distinguished professors of English and history, testified that the book was not utterly without redeeming value, although its similarity to more recent works of pure hard-core pornography was marked. The sole issue in the case according to Mr. Justice

Brennan's majority opinion, was whether the book actually is obscene as determined by the *Roth* formula, and he decided that it was not. The main significance of the opinion stems from Brennan's explicit endorsement of the "three-pronged test"—appeal to prurient interest, patent offensiveness, and utter absence of redeeming social value—as the proper criterion of obscenity, naturally evolved from his own *Roth* formula laid down nine years earlier. That criterion came to be called "the *Memoirs* criterion," or "the Fanny Hill test" more commonly than "the *Roth* formula" in the years following.

The next landmark obscenity decision left the formula for obscenity unchanged, but was important for its judgment on another matter. *Stanley* v. *Georgia* raised the issue whether mere possession in one's own home of an admittedly obscene film, where there is no attempt to sell it or distribute it further, could be grounds for prosecution. In a resounding 9-0 decision the Court emphatically denied that it could. Mr. Justice Marshall derived the right to possess obscene materials from a more general right to privacy implicitly guaranteed, he claimed, by the First and Fourteenth Amendments, and made explicit in *Griswold* v. *Connecticut*. Civil libertarians applauded the result, as well they should have, but in a cooler hour many of them had some misgivings about Mr. Justice Marshall's reasoning, for the privacy Marshall invoked was not so much a personal privacy as a set of rights derived from the "sanctity of the home." The appellant, Marshall wrote, "is asserting . . . the right to satisfy his intellectual and emotional needs in the *privacy of his own home*. He is asserting the right to be free from state inquiry into the contents of *his library*. . . . If the First Amendment means anything, it means that a State has no business telling a man, sitting alone *in his own house,* what books he may read or what films he may watch." But though the state has no business investigating the contents of a person's library or bedroom, there is nothing in the Marshall opinion to deny that the state has business inquiring into the contents of a person's boat or automobile, or luggage, or his pockets, briefcase, or wallet. The confines of one's home can make very narrow boundaries for the area of one's privacy.

The next important day in the history of the Supreme Court's struggle with the riddles of obscenity, and the last important day to this date, was June 21, 1973, when the Court decided both *Miller* v. *California* and *Paris Adult Theatre I* v. *Slaton.* By that time the membership of the court had undergone a new change and a "conservative" majority had emerged under the leadership of Chief Justice Warren Burger. There had been a great outcry in the country against pornography and excessively "permissive" Supreme Court decisions. Chief Justice Burger and his conservative colleagues clearly wished to tighten legal controls on obscenity to help "stem the tide," but they also felt bound to honor the Court's own precedents and particularly the *Memoirs* formula. The result was a pair of 5-4 decisions in which the opinion of the Court delivered by Chief Justice Burger gave some lip service to the *Memoirs* test while modifying each of its three prongs. Henceforth: (1) whether materials appeal to prurient interest is to be determined by the application of local community standards rather

than a national standard; (2) the use or display of sexually explicit materials may be deemed patently offensive even when it involves only willing adult observers in a commercial theatre (nor can the privacy of the home be equated "with a 'zone' of 'privacy' that follows a distributor or a consumer of obscene materials wherever he goes." Furthermore, not all conduct directly involving "consenting adults" only has a claim to constitutional protection.); (3) a finding of obscenity requires not that the materials be utterly without redeeming social value but only that they lack "serious literary, artistic, political, or scientific value."

The intended consequence of this decision clearly was to permit more aggressive prosecutions of pornographers while maintaining continuity with earlier Court tests for obscenity. Recourse to a local community norm rather than a national standard for applying the "prurient interest" test permits local courts to find persons guilty for distributing materials that could not plausibly be found obscene in other, more sophisticated, jurisdictions. In denying that there is a movable zone of privacy that follows a person wherever he goes and that private transactions between consenting adults cannot be patently offensive, the Court permits local authorities to prevent the display of pornographic films in public theatres no matter how discreetly they are advertised, no matter how effectively customers are forewarned, no matter how successfully children are denied admittance. By insisting that a book with sexual themes must have serious literary, artistic, political, or scientific value if it is to qualify for the First Amendment protection, the Court allows successful prosecutions of such borderline works as *Fanny Hill,* which had a certain elegance of language and an incidental interest to critics and scholars of history and sociology, although it was basically pornographic in intention. *Fanny Hill* admittedly was not *utterly* without social value, but it could hardly be said to have *serious* literary value.

Burger then did achieve his double goal. He tightened the screws on obscenity and maintained fidelity to the Court's basic *Roth-Memoirs* approach. In so doing, however, he reduced that approach to something approaching absurdity. The substitution of local community standards in effect makes it difficult to publish anywhere materials that would violate the most puritanical standards in the country. Publishers will have to screen out-of-state orders more carefully than Larry C. Flynt did when he routinely mailed a copy of his publication *Hustler* to a person who had ordered it by mail from a town in Ohio. He was subsequently tried for violation of the Ohio obscenity statutes and sentenced to 7–25 years in prison! How can a national publisher or film producer hope to distribute his book or film nationally when he might misjudge the "community standards" of one small town somewhere and thereby end up in jail? Publication will be commercially feasible only when the materials are unchallengeable anywhere in the country. Willard Gaylin describes these absurdities and inequities well when he writes that

> The principle established by the Supreme Court . . . was intended to let local communities set their own standards, allowing diversity to flourish as the people of each area

wished. Instead . . . what community control does is to set the limits for nationally distributed literature and television at the level of the bluest-nosed small town critic.[6]

The Burger Court's second modification of the *Memoirs* formula is, from the moral point of view, even more absurd, for at a stroke it restricts personal privacy arbitrarily to the confines of one's home and denies constitutional recognition of the *volenti* maxim. (But of course it is always possible that it is the Constitution that is absurd, not the five-man majority of the Supreme Court.) The third "modification" is more than a mere tightening or adjustment of the *Roth* "utterly without redeeming social value" formula; it completely guts the theory of the First Amendment that Mr. Justice Brennan had employed when he formulated that clause. That people should be free to make serious efforts to produce works of art and literature, political and moral judgments, and scientific discoveries; that they should be free to innovate and experiment, to depart from or defend orthodoxies; that they should be free to fail and thus to produce bad art or to be in error, if that's what it comes to, as they themselves choose and see fit: *that* is what has "social value" and is defended by the First Amendment.

The Burger "modification" seems to limit constitutional protection to good novels and films, seriously valuable political commentaries, and importantly correct scientific reports and theories. If future courts take his words seriously, they shall have to strip protection from most novels that deal with sexual themes, since assuredly most of them, like most other novels, lack "serious literary importance." The Court's message to writers is a discouraging one: If you plan to write a novel that contains explicitly sexual scenes that an average person in a remote community would judge to be titillating or shocking, you had better make sure that it has important literary value; if it turns out to be merely mediocre on literary grounds, your publisher may end up in jail. How could anyone seriously believe that this is the way the First Amendment protects the enterprise of literature?

Mr. Justice Brennan, whose opinion in *Roth* sixteen years earlier had set the Court on the serpentine path that led to *Miller* and *Paris Adult Theatre,* lost his patience finally with that basic approach, and in a ringing dissent to *Paris Adult Theatre* urged a new beginning. Chief Justice Burger's majority opinion, Brennan wrote, was not a "veering sharply away from the *Roth* concept," but rather simply a new "interpretation of *Roth.*" The *Paris Adult Theatre* decision, while ostensibly tougher on pornographers, nevertheless shares in equal degree the primary defects of the earlier decisions. First, Justice Brennan argued, these cases rely on essentially obscure formulas that fail to "provide adequate notice to persons who are engaged in the type of conduct that [obscenity statutes] could be thought to proscribe." "The underlying principle," as Chief Justice Warren had written earlier, "is that no man shall be held criminally responsible for conduct which he could not reasonably understand to be proscribed." No one now can predict how the Supreme Court is going to decide close obscenity cases, of which there are in principle an endless number, and the resulting uncertainty not only makes "bookselling . . . a hazardous profession" but also "invites arbitrary

and erratic enforcement of the law." Secondly, it creates a chilling effect on all writing that deals candidly with sexual matters, since at any point the wavering and uncertain line that separates permissible from impermissible expression may veer suddenly and leave a writer unprotected on the wrong side of the line. Finally, Brennan concluded, constant need to apply obscure formulas to materials was amounting to a kind of "institutional strain." Brennan is therefore forced to conclude that no amount of tinkering with the *Roth-Memoirs-Paris Adult Theatre* formulas will ever lead to definitions of obscenity sufficiently clear and specific to avoid these unfortunate by-products.

How then can the Court find a new approach? Brennan suggests a strategy. "Given these inevitable side-effects of state efforts to suppress what is assumed to be *unprotected* speech, we must scrutinize with care the state interest that is asserted to justify the suppression. For in the absence of some very substantial interest in suppressing such speech, we can hardly condone the ill effects that seem to flow inevitably from the effort." What is the alleged "state interest" that makes the unobtrusive and willing enjoyment of pornographic materials the state's business to control and prevent? That interest could not be the prevention of harm to persons caused by other persons, since the conduct at issue is freely consented to, and that kind of private harm is excluded by the *volenti* maxim. It cannot be the protection of children, since there is no controversy about the state's right to prevent dissemination of obscene materials to juveniles, and the fact that the Paris Adult Theatre had effectively excluded children from its performances had been deemed irrelevant by the Georgia Supreme Court in its ruling that was upheld by the Burger majority opinion. It cannot be the prevention of offensive nuisances, since the materials in *Paris Adult Theatre* had not been obtruded on unwilling witnesses nor advertised in luridly offensive ways. "The justification for the suppression must be found, therefore, in some independent interest in regulating the reading and viewing habits of consenting adults."

The implicit rationale for such regulation is not hard to find, and it has been present all along in the background of *Roth* as well as *Hicklin,* in *Memoirs* as well as in *Paris Adult Theatre.* Even when some lip service is paid to the requirement of offensiveness, the ultimate appeal has been to the principle of *moralistic paternalism.* How else can we explain why the Court recognizes a state interest in proscribing pornography *as such,* even when privately and unobtrusively used by willing adults? Moralistic paternalism, however, is extremely difficult to reconcile with the Constitution, which the Court has interpreted in other cases to permit responsible adults to go to Hell morally in their own way provided only that they don't drag others unwillingly along with them. "In *Stanley,*" writes Brennan, "we rejected as 'wholly inconsistent with the philosophy of the First Amendment' the notion that there is a legitimate state concern in the 'control [of] the moral content of a person's thoughts.'" Brennan concludes then that there is no legitimate state concern in preventing the enjoyment of pornography as such, but that there may be valid state interests in regulating the "manner of distribution of sexually oriented materials," these being, presumably, prevention of the corruption of children, protection of captive audiences from offense, and the preservation of neighborhoods from aesthetic decay. Brennan thus ends up precisely where years earlier he could have begun: with a concept of pornography as a potential source of public nuisance subject to control by statutes that satisfy the provisions of a properly mediated offense principle. Where pornography is not a nuisance, then it can be none of the state's business.

CASE STUDY: THE CHILD PORNOGRAPHY PREVENTION ACT AND "VIRTUAL CHILD PORNOGRAPHY"

It should be quite clear by this point in your studies that defining pornography in the law presents a considerable philosophical challenge. However, the courts have historically had little difficulty disposing of one category of pornography: child pornography. The main reason that no legal and philosophical issues have arisen around the category of child pornography is that in order to produce *child* pornography (however pornography itself is defined), someone, presumably, must actively engage in corrupting and otherwise harming a child. So, given the clarity of the harm and the vulnerability of the victim, there has been little doubt about the status of child pornography as morally and legally impermissible, that is, until recently. Suddenly now—in the age of video gaming, high-powered computer animation, and virtual reality—it is *technically easy* to produce child pornography without harming, at least *directly*, any actual child.

The next argument is that child pornography, however it may be produced, *indirectly* harms many actual children—the victims of sex offenders inspired or influenced by the pornographic material—and harms children in general by raising the risk of such victimization. So now it becomes much more important, but also much less obvious, how we ought to define "*child* pornography" in law.

There are, and probably always have been, a few artful ways around the obstacle of producing child pornography without directly harming any child. If one were determined to produce or gain access to believable material in which children are portrayed in sexually explicit poses or acts, one might *describe* such things, in a work of literature for instance (Nabokov's *Lolita*). Or one might use adult actors to portray minors in sexually suggestive poses (the Calvin Klein jeans ads of 1995). But again it is argued that child pornography, however it may be produced, harms children *indirectly*. Thus, in 1996, the federal Child Pornography Prevention Act broadened the definition of "child pornography" to include "any visual depiction . . . that *appears to be* of a minor, . . . or is advertised, promoted, presented, described, or distributed in such a manner that it *conveys the impression of* a minor engaging in sexually explicit conduct."

Research the history of this piece of legislation. What can you find out about the goals and objectives and political motivations behind the Child Pornography Prevention Act? What can you find out about the legal challenges to the legislation, the goals and objectives and political motivations behind these challenges, and how these challenges have fared in the courts? How do you think Feinberg and MacKinnon would argue on this issue? How would you argue on this issue?

Exercise

In light of Feinberg's interpretation and assessment of obscenity law history as it applies to pornography, go back and review Catharine MacKinnon's discussion of obscenity law and pornography. Do you see any common ground between Feinberg and MacKinnon? How satisfactory would someone like MacKinnon find Feinberg's proposed legal model for dealing with pornography (nuisance law)? What arguments do you imagine MacKinnon would have with Feinberg's approach? How do you imagine Feinberg would respond to MacKinnon's position and arguments? Which of the two positions do you find more reasonable and why?

6.2 CRIMES OF VIOLENCE AND MASS MEDIA COVERAGE We turn now to an issue facing working journalists. Violence does occur in society, and much of it is legitimately newsworthy, and not simply because it grabs attention—which of course it does. In any case, working journalists are often assigned to cover or to edit stories involving violence: stories like the siege of the Branch Davidian compound at Waco, Texas; or the Oklahoma City bombing; or the Columbine High School shootings. What social impact accompanies the coverage such stories receive in the mass media? This is a variation of the crucial "responsibility knot" we mentioned in the introduction to this chapter. Can the coverage reach such a pitch of volume and/or intensity that it begins to have harmful effects on society at large? Can there be "too much" coverage? Or suppose that some deranged reader of a news report on some such event is provoked to take violent revenge, or to perpetrate a copycat act. How far does the responsibility of the reporter or the editor extend for the influence her coverage may have on the behavior of her readers?

In the following essay, Clayton Cramer analyzes news coverage of mass murders in national news magazines over a seven-year period. He finds evidence of disproportionate, and perhaps politically motivated coverage of certain categories of mass murder, some of which he finds evidentally linked causally to subsequent acts of violence.

Clayton Cramer wrote this essay as an undergraduate studying history and political science at Sonoma State University. The essay was originally written as a term project for a course in media ethics taught by one of the authors of this book. It was awarded the 1993 Prize for an Undergraduate Essay in the Carol Burnett/AEJMC (Association for Ethics in Journalism and Mass Communication) Ethics Competition and later appeared in the *Journal of Mass Media Ethics* (vol. 9.1, 1994).

QUESTIONS FOR STUDY AND DISCUSSION

1. Cramer acknowledges that news organizations covering a violent crime cannot in general be held responsible for what a deranged reader might be inspired or provoked to do as a result of reading such coverage, even if some such risks are foreseeable. Why not?
2. Given that a news organization cannot *in general* be held responsible for what a deranged reader might be inspired or provoked to do by reading its coverage of a violent crime, how *can* a news organization be held responsible for what a deranged reader might be inspired or provoked to do as a result of reading such coverage?
3. What is Cramer's evidence that the coverage of mass murders involving firearms has been disproportionate?

ETHICAL PROBLEMS OF MASS MURDER COVERAGE IN THE MASS MEDIA[7]

CLAYTON CRAMER

On January 17, 1989, a homosexual prostitute and drug addict with a long history of criminal offenses and mental disturbance, Patrick Purdy, drove up to Cleveland Elementary School in Stockton, California. He firebombed his car, entered a playground during recess carrying a Chinese-made AKS (a semi-automatic version of the full automatic AK-47), shot to death five children, wounded 29 other children and a teacher, then shot himself in the head with a 9mm handgun.

Initial coverage of Purdy's crime was relatively restrained and only the essential details were reported. *Time* gave Purdy only part of a page in the first issue after the crime.[8] *Newsweek* gave a page to "Death on the Playground,"[9] and pointed to four prior attacks on school children, starting with Laurie Dann. Purdy's photograph was included in the *Newsweek* article. *Newsweek's* article quoted the authors of a book on mass murder. "There's a copycat element that cannot be denied."

But a week later, Patrick Purdy's name continued to receive press attention, and consequently, his fame increased. The front cover of *Time* showed an AK-47 and an AR-15 crossed, beneath an outline of the United States stylized into a jawless skull, entitled, "Armed America." Inside, Church, Shannon, and Woodbury's "The Other Arms Race,"[10] which occupied slightly more than six pages, opened with Patrick Purdy's name. Articles referencing Purdy or his crime continued to appear in both *Newsweek* and *Time* for many months.

On September 14, 1989, Joseph Wesbecker, a disabled employee of Standard Gravure Co. in Kentucky, entered the printing plant carrying an AKS and a 9mm handgun. How profoundly similar Wesbecker's actions were to Purdy's was shortly detailed by United Press International wire service stories, such as Inman's "Wesbecker's rampage is boon to gun dealers":

> When Joseph Wesbecker, a mental patient, read about the destructive power of Patrick Purdy's weapon

> in a . . . schoolyard massacre in January, Wesbecker knew he'd have to have the gun. So he bought an AK-47. . . . He used a picture to describe the gun to a local dealer, who ordered it through the mail. Wesbecker, police say, was already planning a massacre of his own— one which killed eight Thursday and wounded 13. He used an AK-47 on all victims but himself. He committed suicide with a pistol. In the same way Wesbecker's interest was peaked [sic]—he had clipped out a February *Time* magazine article on some of Purdy's exploits— gun dealers expect a renewed blaze of interest in the big gun. "With all the media attention since then," said Ray Yeager, owner of Ray's Gun Shop in Louisville, "and all the anti-gunner's attempts to ban (assault rifles), the result has been massive sales."[11]

How important was the news coverage of Purdy's crime in influencing Wesbecker's actions, above and beyond identifying the weapon of choice for such an act of savagery?

> Police now believe Wesbecker had begun plotting the suicide rampage for at least seven months. Searching Wesbecker's house, police found a copy of a February 6 *Time* magazine detailing mass murders in California, Oklahoma, Texas, and elsewhere. A headline underlined by Wesbecker read Calendar of Senseless Shootings.

> The major gun purchases were made between February and May. Initially police thought Wesbecker was an ardent gun handler or paramilitary buff, but evidence indicates his interest in guns was relatively young.

"We have no information indicating he had a collection of guns, or was even interested in them before last year," said Lt. Jeff Moody, homicide investigator. "As far as we know he had no formal training in weapon use."[12]

This disturbing information about the connection between the *Time* article and Wesbecker's actions didn't make it into *Time, Newsweek,* or many newspapers' coverage of this tragedy. For this study I selected two of the leading "newspapers of record" serving major media markets on the East and West coasts: the *New York Times,* and the *Los Angeles Times,* and also followed the coverage in our own media market, using the San Francisco *Chronicle* and the Santa Rosa (CA) *Press Democrat* as representative examples. All of the newspapers in our sample left this embarrassing detail, at least embarrassing to *Time,* out of their coverage. It wasn't a lack of space that was responsible for this omission, for this was a front-page story in the *Los Angeles Times* and the *Press Democrat.*

Nor was it that no one in the media saw a connection between Wesbecker's reading material and the crime. The *Los Angeles Times,* the *Press Democrat,* and the *New York Times* all suggested a connection between Wesbecker's actions and *Soldier of Fortune* magazine. Wesbecker had taken to reading *Soldier of Fortune,* but none of the articles indicate that *Soldier of Fortune* had been found in such an incriminating position as the *Time* article.[13] Apparently, *Soldier of Fortune*'s mere presence in Wesbecker's home was an important piece of news, while the marked-up copy of *Time,* left open, wasn't important enough to merit coverage; only the San Francisco

Chronicle included the disturbing connection between *Time's* coverage and the crime:

> At Wesbecker's home, police found manuals on weapons and a February 6 issue of *Time* magazine devoted to mass killers, including Robert Sherrill, who slaughtered 14 people in an Oklahoma post office three years ago, and Patrick Purdy, who killed five children with an AK-47 assault rifle in Stockton, CA, in January. An AK-47 was the main weapon used by Wesbecker.[14]

Clearly, Joseph Wesbecker was not a healthy, well-adjusted person driven to commit his crime simply because of the sensational news coverage. To argue this would deny Joseph Wesbecker's personal responsibility for his actions. As tempting as it might be to hold *Time* responsible for having indirectly caused this horrible crime, this temptation must be resisted. The editors of *Time* might have foreseen the possibility of their coverage promoting "copycat" crimes, but to use this as a principle of law would make it impossible to ever write a factual account of a serious crime, without fear of being hauled into a court to answer for the actions of a deranged reader. Indeed, even this discussion of the ethical problems could be considered inflammatory by such a standard.

However, even absent a notion of legal responsibility, sensitivity to notions of some moral responsibility, and awareness of a causal relationship should provoke concern among journalists. Joseph Wesbecker, without question, was headed toward some sort of unpleasant ending to his life. Yet in the absence of the February 6 coverage by *Time,* would he have chosen this particular method of getting attention? Wesbecker was under psychiatric care at the time, and had already made three suicide attempts.[15] Did *Time's* sensational coverage, transforming the short unhappy life of Patrick Purdy from obscurity to permanent notoriety, encourage Wesbecker to transform the end of his life from, at most, a local news story of a suicide, into a story that would be carried from coast to coast?

In this paper, I shall argue that *Newsweek* and especially *Time,* perhaps for reasons of circulation, perhaps for political reasons, have published coverage of mass murder in the United States which can be questioned on ethical grounds. The coverage can be implicated as a major cause of the murder of seven people in 1989, and may have played a role in the murders of others in recent years. The coverage in question provides a concrete example of a problem in media ethics that is at least two centuries old: How much and what type of coverage should the press give to violent crime? There are three related problems to consider:

1. The level of coverage given by *Time* and *Newsweek* (and perhaps by other news media) to certain great crimes appears to encourage unbalanced people, seeking a lasting fame, to copy these crimes—as apparently happened in Joseph Wesbecker's 1989 homicidal rampage.
2. The quantity of press coverage given to mass murder suggests that political motivations may have influenced *Newsweek* and especially *Time* to give undue attention to a particular type of

mass murder, ultimately to the detriment of public safety.
3. The coverage given to murder by *Newsweek* and *Time* gives the electorate a very distorted notion of the nature of murder in the United States, almost certainly in the interests of promoting a particular political agenda.

Fame and infamy are in an ethical sense opposites. Functionally, they are nearly identical. Imagine an alien civilization that does not share our notions of good and evil studying the expanding shell of television signals emanating from our planet. To such extraterrestrials, Winston Churchill and Adolph Hitler are both "famous"; without an ability to appreciate the vituperation our civilization uses to describe Hitler, they might conclude that both were "great men." Indeed, they might assume that Hitler was the "greater" of the two, because there has certainly been more broadcast about Hitler than about Churchill. The human need to celebrate human nobility, and to denounce human depravity, has caused us to devote tremendous attention, both scholarly and popular, to portraying the polar opposites of good and evil.

The pursuit of fame can lead people to acts of great courage and nobility. It can also lead to acts of great savagery. The Italian immigrant Simon Rodia, builder of Los Angeles' Watts Towers, once explained that his artistic effort was the result of an ordinary person's desire for fame, because "A man has to be good-good or bad-bad to be remembered."[16] But, for most people, fame isn't as easy as building towers of steel, concrete, and pottery. Unfortunately, being "bad-bad" is easier than being "good-good," as history amply demonstrates.

In 356 B.C., an otherwise unremarkable Greek named Herostratus burned the Temple of Artemis at Ephesus in an effort to immortalize his name. That we remember the name of this arsonist, the destroyer of one of the Seven Wonders of the World, shows that great crimes can achieve lasting fame. Fisher Ames, a Massachusetts Federalist who sat in the House of Representatives from 1789 to 1800, expressed his concerns about this very subject in the October 1801 issue of the *Palladium.*

> Some of the shocking articles in the papers raise simple, and very simple, wonder; some terror; and some horror and disgust. Now what instruction is there in these endless wonders? Who is the wiser or happier for reading the accounts of them? On the contrary, do they not shock tender minds, and addle shallow brains? . . . Worse than this happens; for some eccentric minds are turned to mischief by such accounts as they receive of troops of incendiaries burning our cities; the spirit of imitation is contagious; and boys are found unaccountably bent to do as men do. . . . Every horrid story in a newspaper produces a shock; but, after some time, this shock lessens.[17]

The problem that concerned Representative Ames remains with us today as the two 1989 mass murders discussed above, linked by this "spirit of imitation" demonstrate.

Mass murder isn't new to America (or anywhere else) nor is the popular horror and interest in such crimes. Consider the following children's doggerel about the

1892 murders in Fall River, Massachusetts: "Lizzie Borden took an axe and gave her mother forty whacks. When she saw what she had done, she gave her father forty-one."

As a child growing up in the 1960s, I remember vividly the horror at, but also widespread coverage of, the crimes of Richard Speck, Charles Manson and friends, and the Zodiac killer. In the mid-1960s, when I must have been old enough to have seen newspaper coverage of it (though it made no conscious impression on me), Charles Whitman engaged in a murderous rampage from a university tower in Texas, killing 16 people with a rifle.

In the 1980s, there were a number of mass murders in the United States, and yet the quantity of press coverage for these crimes varied widely. All other things being equal, when mass murder is committed in this country, we should expect the coverage to be generally proportionate to the number of victims. How do we measure the quantity of press coverage for a major crime? The more remote a newspaper is from a crime, the less extensive the coverage we should expect. As a result, it would not be a meaningful measure of the quantity of press coverage to examine any sort of local or even regional newspaper coverage; the coverage of a West coast crime in California newspapers will doubtless be far greater than coverage of a similar crime that took place on the East coast. A more meaningful measurement is the press coverage given by the national news magazines, such as *Time* and *Newsweek.*

An analysis of articles in *Time* and *Newsweek*—America's mass circulation news magazines—shows some interesting characteristics of how mass murder in America is covered. For the purposes of this essay, any story which mentioned a mass murderer, even by referring to his specific criminal act, was considered to be "fame" in the sense we defined earlier. Even if the story was primarily about some related subject, if the mass murderer was mentioned, the entire story was considered as adding to that killer's "fame."

Why the entire story? Because a potential mass murderer will consider any future story that mentions him to be "publicity." Wesbecker demonstrated this by leaving open in his room the February 6 *Time* article. Although the article was primarily about gun control and mass murder, it included Purdy's name and crime as part of the introduction.

Attempting to locate stories that refer to these mass murderers is difficult, because many of these articles cannot be located by keyword search. In the case of mass murderers who used guns, I looked through all the articles during the period 1984 to 1991 that were about gun control or mass murder, and included only those that referenced the murderers or their crimes. For arson murders, I looked up pieces about arson and fire hazards. Stories purely about gun control or fire hazards that failed to mention these mass murderers by name or action were not included in the analysis. For mass murders committed with other weapons, I looked up appropriate articles about the weapon used, as well as articles about mass murder.

The criticism could be made that even a brief mention of a mass murderer's actions in a larger story will tend to exaggerate the level of coverage given to that crime. This is a valid concern, but as long as all categories of mass murder receive identical treatment, the results should be roughly equivalent. Where an article contained no mention of the mass murderer or his actions, and a sidebar article did, only the sidebar article was included in the computation of the space given.

What constitutes mass murder? This is important, because by manipulative definition of "mass murder," one can prove nearly anything about the news coverage. Clearly, there is a difference between serial murderers and mass murderers, and a difference that makes them non-comparable from the standpoint of analyzing the news coverage. The difference is that serial murderers commit their crimes over a relatively long period of time, and so each murder is, by itself, a story. Also, because serial murderers sometimes are successful in making the remains of the victim disappear, the only news story is when that serial murderer's actions are finally noticed. For these reasons, and for the purposes of this essay, a mass murder has two distinguishing characteristics:

1. Actions intentionally taken, with the expectation that great loss of life will result, or where any reasonable person would recognize that great loss of life will result. The component of expecting loss of life, of course, is a fundamental part of the question of whether publicity plays a role in promoting such crimes. For this reason, I have excluded such tragedies as Larry Mahoney's drunken driving motor vehicle wreck that caused 27 deaths in May of 1988. Mahoney was convicted of manslaughter, so the essential element of pre-meditation

was lacking, except in the sense that getting drunk and operating a motor vehicle is *potentially* quite dangerous. However, including crimes like Mahoney's in this study would tend to strengthen my argument that *Time* and *Newsweek* give special treatment to firearms mass murderers, since Mahoney received no press in *Newsweek,* and only 0.15 square inches per victim in *Time.*

2. The actions causing the loss of life all take place within a 24-hour time frame, or the deaths are all discovered within 24 hours. This is an arbitrary period of time, of course. It could have been extended to 48 hours, or 72 hours, however, without significantly widening the bloody pool of crimes whose coverage will be studied here.

Many people are quite surprised to find out that there are mass murderers who kill with weapons other than guns. They are even more surprised when they find out that arson mass murder victims in the last few years have outnumbered gun mass murders. Why is this a surprise? The reason is that press coverage of non-firearms mass murders is almost non-existent. As Table 1 shows, arson mass murderers and knife mass murderers receive relatively little attention from *Time* and *Newsweek.* As should be obvious, there is a very large discrepancy between the amount of coverage given to arson mass murders, and mass murderers involving guns exclusively. Almost nine times as much coverage was given to exclusive firearms mass murderers, as to arson mass murderers.

A large part of this discrepancy, however, is the many articles that mentioned Patrick Purdy's crime. Yet, even excluding all coverage of Patrick Purdy's crimes (a charitable assumption for *Time* and *Newsweek,* considering the centrality of *Time's* coverage to Wesbecker's actions), the square inches per dead body for firearms mass murderers is still 4.75 times the coverage for the arson mass murderers. Mass murder coverage rose dramatically with the crimes of Laurie Wasserman Dann and Patrick Purdy and suddenly dived back to the pre-Dann levels with the Wesbecker incident. *Time,* more prone to covering firearms mass murders before Dann and Purdy, was the more noticeably restrained of the two magazines in its coverage of mass murders after Wesbecker. Did someone at *Time* see the connection between their coverage of Purdy and Wesbecker's bloody rampage?

Was Wesbecker just one amazing case? Although considerable energy has been devoted by the academic community to research on the effects of violent entertainment on aggression, a search of the available literature suggests that the influence of news coverage on aggression has not been examined. The only work even remotely related to this topic is Cairns's study of how television news coverage of political violence influenced children's perceptions of the level of political violence in Northern Ireland.[18] The study made no attempt to determine what effect, if any, this news coverage had on levels of violence or aggression among the children themselves.

In the area of entertainment violence, a rich scientific literature exists, but serious questions exist as to its applicability to the effect of news coverage on adults.

TABLE 1 **Square Inches of New Coverage Per Dead Body**

Murderer	Month/Year	Dead	Time Sq. In.	Time Sq. In./Dead	Newsweek Sq. In.	Newsweek Sq. In./Dead	Total Sq. In./Dead
James Hubert	Jul 84	22	109.63	4.98	157.50	7.16	12.14
Sylvia Seegrist	Nov 85	2	20.75	10.38	00.00	0.00	10.38
William B. Cruse	Apr 87	6	33.06	5.51	00.00	0.00	5.51
David Burke	Dec 87	43	52.50	1.22	57.75	1.34	2.56
Robert Dreesman	Dec 87	7	105.00	15.00	00.00	0.00	15.00
Ronald G. Simmons	Dec 87	16	15.94	1.00	78.75	4.92	5.92
Laurie W. Dann	May 88	2	107.63	53.81	54.00	27.00	134.63
Patrick Purdy	Jan 89	6	720.00	120.00	370.34	61.72	181.72
Joseph Wesbecker	Sep 89	8	19.69	2.46	52.50	6.56	9.02
James Pough	Jun 90	9	00.00	00.00	00.00	0.00	00.00
George Hennard	Oct 91	24	225.00	9.38	78.75	3.28	12.66
Firearms Murders		**152**	**1420.44**	**225.35**	**849.59**	**111.98**	**337.33**
Firearms Murders Excluding Purdy		**146**	**700.44**	**105.35**	**479.25**	**50.26**	**115.61**
Ramon Salcido	Apr 89	7	78.75	11.25	00.00	0.00	11.25
Knife/Gun Murders		**7**	**78.75**	**11.25**	**00.00**	**0.00**	**11.25**
Hector Escudero	Dec 87	96	155.63	1.62	78.75	0.82	2.44
Julio Gonzalez	Apr 90	87	76.63	0.88	00.00	0.00	0.88
Arson Murders		**183**	**232.26**	**2.50**	**78.75**	**0.82**	**3.32**

Those studies that attempted to evaluate the effects of regular televised entertainment violence either explicitly excluded special news programs that appeared in prime time,[19] or implied that only entertainment programs were rated for violence.[20]

The applicability to adults of the research that has been done regarding violent entertainment's effect on children is also a troubling question. Wood, Wong, and Chachere (1991) summarized the existing research on children, aggression, and media violence and concluded that the results demonstrated a statistically significant relationship between media violence and subsequent aggressive behavior, but also admitted:

> All of our studies were conducted with children and adolescents, and our results may be peculiar to young samples. Children are sometimes characterized as especially susceptible to media impact (cf. Wartella, 1988). However, the relation between age and impact may be complex. Hearold (1986) found a decline in media effect on physical aggression with age for girls but not for boys.[21]

Similarly, Harris explains that one of the reasons for her research with college students was that "much of the research has been done with children and young adolescents . . . rather than adults. . . ." Harris' work found that the violence of television shows watched "was weakly but significantly correlated with aggression against males . . . and total aggression . . ." as measured by surveys of the test subjects. A deficiency of this study is that the 416 test subjects were all college students and, therefore, possibly excludes those members of the population who are sufficiently antisocial to have already become involved in the criminal subculture.

More troubling about these studies is that a critical reading suggests the researchers approached the problems with a goal to prove a particular point, and assumptions so heavily loaded as to prevent an accurate assessment of the significance or validity of information. One rather obvious example is Lester's study, "Media Violence and Suicide and Homicide Rates."[22] This one-page article summarizes two reports from the National Coalition on TV Violence. The first report asserted a negative correlation between suicide and violent, top 10 best-selling books (apparently in the United States) from 1933 to 1984 and a positive correlation to homicide during that same period. The second report asserted similar, but not statistically significant relationships between best-attended films and suicide and homicide. That the National Coalition on TV Violence is a less than objective source on this topic should be obvious, but this does not preclude it being a valid source. Unfortunately, Lester made no attempt to analyze the methods used or critically evaluate the significance of these reports.

There are serious problems proving or disproving a causal relationship between television entertainment and violent behavior, and there is no reason to assume that television news provides any easier opportunity for such research. But, even though we cannot prove that the coverage of Purdy's crime provoked Wesbecker, the evidence found in Wesbecker's home should make managing editors ask themselves, "What should we do about this?" The editors of *Time* should especially ask themselves,

"Would less sensational coverage of Patrick Purdy have prevented the massacre at Standard Gravure? What if we hadn't run the February 6 article?"

The ethical issues here are more than just how coverage of one crime causes a copycat crime. Not only did both *Time* and *Newsweek* give disproportionate coverage to firearms mass murder (relative to other types of mass murder), but even relative to other types of murder, mass murder is grossly over-represented in the news magazines. In the years 1987 to 1991, a total of 96,666 people were murdered in the United States. Mass murder victims from our sampled articles during this period totaled 318. *Time* and *Newsweek,* in order to give equivalent coverage to the other 96,348 murders, would have needed 693,657.12 square inches, or more than 42 pages per week between them!

There are reasons why mass murders are given exceptional coverage relative to other murders. The most obvious is that in many ordinary murders, there is insufficient information to determine who did it, or even who might have done it. In 1991, 34% of the murders were a complete mystery to the police. The tawdry little details of tens of thousands of murders would be mind-numbingly boring, especially without an explanation of who did it and why; a news magazine that fails to entertain, fails to keep subscribers. (A less cynical explanation is that reporters simply don't consider these "little" murders to be newsworthy.)

An example of this approach is *Time*'s "Seven Deadly Days."[23] In this article, *Time* obtained photographs and details of every person killed by a gun in the week May 1 to 7, 1989. This included not only murders, but also justifiable homicides (both police and civilian), suicides, and accidents. Although this could have been a useful mechanism for providing the sort of balance needed to obtain a more complete picture of murder in the United States, because it excluded the one-third of murders committed with other weapons, the effect was severely unbalanced. That the intent was to promote restrictive gun control laws was made clear in the article that followed, "Suicides: The Gun Factor."[24]

It should be obvious that this problem of balance cannot be solved practically by expanding coverage of the "little" murders. But how can a news magazine achieve coverage that conveys the reality of murder in the United States? One way would be to either reduce coverage of these very atypical firearms mass murders, or dramatically enlarge their coverage of more typical murders. In looking through the *Reader's Guide to Periodical Literature* for the years 1984 to 1991, it became obvious that murders involving guns were deemed worthy of coverage in *Time* and *Newsweek,* whereas murders of equally minor importance to the nation committed with other weapons were simply not covered. In spite of the 17,489 murders committed with knives and other "cutting instruments" in the years 1897 to 1991 (about 18% of the total murders), notices of these crimes are almost non-existent in *Time* and *Newsweek.* The same is true for the murders committed with blunt objects, hands, fists, and feet (11,088 in 1987 to 1991, or 11% of the total murders).

The net result is a very misleading understanding of what sort of murders are committed in the United States. My experience over the years, when engaged in discussions with journalists, elected public officials, and ordinary citizens, is that they are usually quite surprised to find that firearms mass murder is a rare event and are even more surprised to find that more than one-third of U.S. murders involve weapons other than firearms. This misunderstanding doubtless plays a part in the widespread support for restrictive gun control laws, and the relatively relaxed attitude about more general solutions to the problem of violent crime of all sorts.

This problem is not limited to the subject of murder and firearms. Meyer pointed to the problem of how unbalanced reporting of health and safety issues in the popular media causes wildly inaccurate notions of the relative risks of various causes of death. As an example, a surveyed group greatly underestimated deaths caused by emphysema, relative to deaths by homicide. Meyer described a study done by researchers at the University of Oregon, which found "the pictures inside the heads of the people they talked to were more like the spooky, violent world of newspaper content than they were like the real world."[25]

It is important that we recognize that this misleading portrayal of the real world is not only an artifact of popular morbid curiosity, which newspapers must satisfy or lose circulation. It may also reflect what Meyer (1987) called, "the distorting effect of perceptual models."[26] In brief, journalists (like the rest of the human race) bring certain assumptions to their work. Facts that do not fit into the journalist's perceptual model tend to be downgraded in importance or ignored. When the facts include statistical analysis, at even the most basic

level, the primarily liberal arts orientation of many journalists comes to the forefront, and the perceptual model takes precedence. Especially because of the deadline pressure of daily or weekly journalism, the opportunity for careful reflection about the validity of these perceptual models may not exist.

How should the news media respond? First of all, let us be clear on what is not appropriate: the government taking any action to regulate or limit news coverage. Even ignoring the First Amendment guarantee of a free press, there are sound pragmatic arguments against giving this sort of power to the government. This essay asks only ethical questions, not political or legal questions.

Governmental power to decide the "appropriateness" of news coverage of violent crime would almost certainly become a tool for manipulation in favor of the agenda of the moment. A government that sought to whip the populace into a frenzy of support for (depending on ideology) restrictive gun control laws, reduced protections of civil liberties, or even something as mundane as higher pay for police, could, and almost certainly would, use its power over press coverage of crime to achieve these goals.

The same power, of course, can be used by the news media. *Time* and *Newsweek* engaged in exactly this sort of manipulative coverage in 1988 and 1989, attempting to get restrictive gun control laws passed, by exaggerating the significance of firearms mass murders. What would be the practical difference between a system in which the government used regulatory authority in this way and the current system?

The difference is that, even within the current system, diversity does still exist.

Although three of the four newspapers sampled chose not to cover the instructional influence of *Time* on Wesbecker's killing spree, at least the fourth newspaper let its readers know that there was more to the problem of mass murder in America than just the availability of guns. In a system in which the government held this power and shared the clear goal of *Time* and *Newsweek,* all four newspapers would have agreed with *Time* and *Newsweek's* coverage of this event.

Violent crime as entertainment serves no apparent public interest. As art or simply as entertainment, amusements that portray violence can perhaps be justified. But we must remember that entertainment in the United States is a big business, and however much someone may seek to justify slasher movies as "art," the main reason for their being produced is profit. In the film *Grand Canyon,* Steve Martin plays a director of "action" movies that contain violence, bloodshed, and lots of weaponry. Early in the movie, we see the director watching the studio's cut of his new film. He complains that they have cut out an essential piece of the scene: "The bus driver's head, brains on the window, viscera on the visor shot." Later in the film, after the director is shot and seriously injured by a robber, he concludes that his "art" is part of what cheapens and brutalizes life in modern America, and he decides that he would rather make quality films that promote humanistic values, instead of violent films that degrade the viewer. But by the end of the film, the director is reminded by his accountant that his "action" movies are very profitable, and the sort of films he wants to make won't support him in the

sybaritic manner to which he has become accustomed. As a consequence, he again defends his films as "art," and resumes making bloody, gratuitously violent "action" movies. Clearly, the writer and director of *Grand Canyon* were expressing their opinion about how profit corrupts people and that violence on the screen helps to create violence on the street. (This sort of criticism of the current system from Hollywood insiders is especially telling.) Although it is tempting to blame the producers of films that glorify violence, it is important to recognize that what makes violent entertainment profitable is that the audience for such films is very large. We have only to recall the popularity of the gladiatorial contests in the Circus Maximus to see that the purveyors of such violent films are, to some extent, captives of popular taste, and there is no reason to believe that these tastes are recently degraded. However, news coverage of violent crimes does serve the public interest. How much coverage is necessary? Is it necessary to cover every violent crime in the same level of detail?

In balance, coverage of crimes in our society can be a valuable tool for decision making. In the political realm, the electorate and their representatives may make rational governmental decisions based on news coverage. Individuals, properly informed, can make rational decisions about their personal safety. However when the population has been misled, intentionally or not, about the nature of the crimes in a society and the rarity or commonality of those crimes, their decision making will be anything but rational. When the coverage is simply endless repetition of apparently meaningless tragedies, the numbing effect described by representative Ames above undoubtedly takes its toll on the population. Such is the situation today.

Although the public interest may be the justification for the coverage of mass murders, profit is almost certainly the real motivation because the mass media are in the business of making money. Should the mass media ignore mass murders? No, because the news media are in grave danger of losing credibility if they simply pretend that bad things are not going on out there. To the extent that our mass media play a part in acting as a watchdog of governmental actions, it is necessary that they be a Doberman, not a basset hound. Ignoring mass murder would quickly destroy their credibility, simply because mass murder, especially in recent years, seems to be an increasing part of Western culture. (This problem, unfortunately, is not limited to the United States; Canada, Britain, France, Australia, and Switzerland have all experienced such incidents recently, in spite of considerably stricter laws regulating firearms ownership in most of these countries.)

The problem of unintentionally promoting mass murder is a serious one. How should the mass media determine what is an appropriate level of coverage? Is it necessary to cover every such crime? Are there ways of managing the coverage of such episodes, so as to more effectively discourage potential copycats? Unfortunately, this problem has not been adequately addressed in existing works on media ethics. A review of a number of established works in this field suggests that while the general problem of psychological and economic harm caused by inaccurate or unethical reporting has been considered in great depth,

this very severe form of harm, unintentionally encouraging mass murder, has not been specifically discussed.

Klaidman and Beauchamp discuss the issue of journalistic-induced harm, but only with respect to damaged reputations and business losses. Although Klaidman and Beauchamp also pointed to the problems of news organizations that create news events, including the problems of international terrorism, the possibility that a journalist's efforts might play a part in causing a specific murder is not discussed.[27] Lambeth, while providing a very thorough theoretical model for addressing the ethical issues of journalism, failed to address this specific problem of media-induced harm.[28] Hulteng sampled the ethical codes of a number of American newspapers; he also reprinted the complete text of the codes of ethics for the Associated Press Managing Editors, the American Society of Newspaper Editors, and the Society of Professional Journalists.[29] Although all addressed the issue of harm and balance in a general way, none directly discussed how coverage of a particular criminal act can lead to copycat crimes.

Can the news media satisfy both the obligation to accurately inform the public about the nature of America's murder problem and the obligation to stockholders to keep circulation up, or does the inevitable public boredom with coverage of the tens of thousands of meaningless "little" murders make this an impossible balancing act? The tradition of covering some murders in a sensational manner is not new. Editors will doubtlessly continue to justify this time-honored (or time-worn) tradition based on economic considerations. But in light of the major role that the disproportionate coverage of Patrick Purdy's crimes played in the bloody way that Joseph Wesbecker chose to end his life, editors need to ask themselves: "How many innocent lives will we sacrifice to boost circulation or promote a political agenda?"

Can we develop a code of ethics that resolves this problem? Let us consider the following as a first draft of such a standard: A crime of violence should be given attention proportionate to its size, relative to other crimes of violence, and relative to the importance of its victim. Violent crimes of all types should be given attention, relative to other causes of suffering, proportionate to its social costs. We must develop a strategy for dealing with this problem before another disturbed person decides to claim his 15 minutes of fame.

Epilogue

Unfortunately, it happened again. As this essay was being revised for publication, Gian Luigi Ferri entered a San Francisco law office, murdered eight people, and wounded six others. When it became apparent that he would not escape the building alive, he killed himself. In his briefcase he had the names and ad-

dresses of more than a dozen TV shows, including *Oprah Winfrey, Phil Donahue,* and even *Washington Week in Review.* Ferri apparently believed that this infamous crime would provide him a platform from which to describe his "victimization" by lawyers, real estate firms, and the manufacturers of mono-sodium glutamate. When we consider the sort of characters interviewed on the afternoon talk shows (sometimes characterized as "freak of the week"), it is only slightly absurd that Ferri thought this brutal act would provide him with a national soap box. Local coverage of the crime and its aftermath was dramatic, continuous, and heart-rending.

Two weeks later, in Antioch, California, a suburb of San Francisco, Joel Souza murdered his children, then killed himself as an act of revenge against his estranged wife. When police searched a van that Souza had rented, they found a copy of a July 4 newspaper with headlines about Ferri's crime. Was the presence of the newspaper a coincidence? Apparently not; the newspaper was already a week old when Souza rented the van. Souza had been holding on to this reminder of Ferri's fame when he made the decision to murder.[30]

Case Study: Violence in Sports

Considerable evidence indicates an increase in the level of violence in professional sports. Harvard law professor Arthur Miller writes

> An influence often cited is the intense media coverage, particularly by television, which tends to focus on the more violent aspects of the game, either because these elements are more photogenic, or because they will appeal to the largest audience. Often it's the crunching tackle or the bone-rattling fore check that gets emphasized by the television commentators and the replay technology, rather than the perfectly run pass pattern or the superb display of skating. By giving so much attention to

what is only one part of the game, the media impose a subtle pressure on players, coaches, and owners to live up to the violent image of their sport.[31]

Hockey, football, basketball, and even baseball have seen numerous outbreaks of violence involving players, coaches, and even fans. League officials often impose fines and other penalties on players and other personnel involved. This shows some concern among league officials in maintaining a positive public image for the sports they manage based in part on some at least halfway admirable model of sportsmanship. This becomes increasingly difficult in part because every time a fight breaks out after the play has been blown dead, or a batter charges the mound after being brushed back by a pitch, guess what makes the highlight reel!

Imagine that you are the sports anchor for one of the network affiliated television stations in your media market. Today's game, involving the NBA franchise in your market region was marred by a bench-clearing brawl, apparently started when the trash-talking "bad-boy" star of the home team (your team) threw an opposing player to the floor. The officials take five minutes to restore order, during which time several members of each team are ejected. The game is eventually decided in overtime by a series of free throws. You have a five-minute segment toward the end of the late night newscast, with three ten-second promotional "teases." How do you handle the story? What additional information would you want as you approach this first question? In other words, what additional variables would affect your decision, and how would these additional variables play into your reasoning?

6.3 VIOLENCE AND MISOGYNY IN RAP MUSIC Finally in this chapter, we turn to what has proven to be among the most baffling and, to some observers at least, disturbing developments in the arts and the entertainment industry in quite a long time: hip hop culture and rap music. To those outside hip hop culture, rap music often seems incomprehensible—noise mostly, not even music. The performers' dress and body language—the posture and gestures—add to the overall effect of insolence and belligerence. Few of the words are even intelligible, and most of those are familiar epithets used so regularly that they may seem to the uninitiated to function as abusive punctuation marks. Once past the dialect and unfamiliar idioms, the actual lyrical content reveals what frequently seem like disturbing themes and sentiments of violence and misogyny. Add to this the fact that leaders of rival rap styles and regions (Tupac Shakur and Biggie Smalls) have been shot to death in what appear to be gang-related vendettas, and it is not hard to understand why outsiders to the culture might be baffled and disturbed. And yet hip hop and rap are now immensely popular global phenomena, and have effectively eclipsed rock and roll as the basis of pop music at the turn of the millennium. In the following essay, philosopher Crispin Sartwell explores these themes in rap music, arguing that they are part of an artistic strategy of resistance against persistent racism in which the racial stereotypes most hated and feared by white society are used subversively to tell the truth about racial stereotyping.

Crispin Sartwell is an associate professor of humanities and philosophy at Pennsylvania State University, Harrisburg. He is the author of *The Art of Living:*

Aesthetics of the Ordinary in World Spiritual Traditions, and several other works in philosophy of art. The following essay was adapted from his book *Act Like You Know: African-American Autobiography and White Identity.*

Questions for Study and Discussion

1. In his essay on jokes in Chapter 5, Ted Cohen argued that the very *meaning* of the joke depends upon who tells it to whom and under what circumstances. How does this principle apply to Sartwell's analysis of rap music's lyrical content?

2. What, according to Sartwell, are the claims to "truth" and "reality" made by white academic culture and by hip hop culture on behalf of blacks, and how do these claims contrast and compete against each other?

3. What role, according to Sartwell, do generality and particularity play in the contrast between black and white conceptions of truth and reality? (See question 2 above.)

4. According to Sartwell's analysis, rap's deliberate use of stereotypes of black criminality for example have deeper meanings that in effect undermine those stereotypes. Given that the stereotypes are *repeated* in the lyrics and imagery of rap music and music videos, can you explain how this can be understood to subvert or undermine them?

Rap Music and the Uses of Stereotype[32]

CRISPIN SARTWELL

Black folks are supposed to be musical, and the aesthetic products of black culture that have been known best and appropriated most by white culture have been black musical forms. Like a lot of white folks, I have been fascinated or even obsessed with black music since I was a child. It should be noted, however, that rap is also, in the age of music video, to some extent a visual art form. And it is an incredibly dense semiotic textual art form. In fact, the first criticism of rap by those who hate it (mostly white people, in my experience) is that it isn't music at all, because it is not sufficiently melodic. Rather it is held to be a kind of declamation or speechifying. That criticism is wrong—much rap is intensely melodic—but it contains a grain of truth: In rap, the text (which must be understood as a spoken and recorded form, not as a written form) is central.

Rap is, among other things, music, poetry, fiction, autobiography, advertising, philosophy, commodified spectacle. As philosophy, rap is simultaneously assertion and demonstration, theory and enactment. As autobiography, it is description, but also performative self-creation; it remakes the life that is described, as the rapper tells us what she is doing right now as she raps (smokin suckaz wit logic, perhaps). Rap as auto-biography and as fiction takes up experi-ence into narrative, but it also transforms the life that is being narrated. And it in-terrupts or transgresses narrative with what exceeds narrative. As spectacle, it both participates in and alters the racial-izing transaction of ejected asceticism by seizing power at key points in the struc-ture of exchange and the circulation of commodities.

The music that underlies rap—hip hop—is a quintessential postmodern form; it consists of snatches of appropri-ated songs. Hip hop takes up the songs it samples and uses them, but also transfig-ures them, or reduces them to single, es-sential gesture, or ridicules them, or turns them against themselves. The en-tire history of recorded sound is avail-able to be sampled; in a sense, the instrument of hip hop is the history of recorded sound. Rap as poetry drives rhythm into speech, investing the act of speaking with a very pure power. One thing that is inevitably missing from a written discussion of rap is that recorded or performed rap is presented as spoken (usually) by the voice that composes it; it is not primarily a written form. Thus it relies on, indeed is inconceivable with-out, the dissemination of sound on vinyl record, audio tape, compact disk. Any written discussion of rap needs to ac-knowledge that the form must be heard as recorded, and that transcriptions of rap inevitably lose much of its artistic power.

Rap does not speak with one voice. It is tenaciously multi-vocal, often within the same song. The early rappers—The Furious Five, The Sugarhill Gang, and later Run DMC and Whodini, for example—rapped in crews or tag teams,

each voice as identifiable by its preoccu-pations as by its timbre. Albums such as Dr. Dre's *The Chronic* or Notorious B.I.G.'s *Ready to Die* are sprawling col-laborations of voices; male and female, tough and tender, violent and mellow. The musical styles appropriated on these disks—soul, jazz, advertising jingles, funk, rock—reflect a similar diversity, as do the lyric themes in rap generally: everything from the politically charged philosophy of Public Enemy to the evo-cations of sex and violence by the Los Angeles Gangsters, the out-front femi-nism of Queen Latifah, and the celebra-tory bawdiness of Salt 'n Pepa or Positive K. There are regional differ-ences and identifications: from the stac-cato attack of New York to the slow melodic groove of L.A., the Southern rural orientation of Arrested Develop-ment, and Fesu's tales of Houston hous-ing projects. Thus if there are generalizations in what follows, I warn you in advance to take them with a grain of salt.

Rap is, often enough, precisely about power. But the content of that "about" is of interest. Rap often asserts superiority: the superiority of black over white, man over woman (or woman over man), or the personal superiority of the rapper over other rappers, or other people in general. But as a rapper describes the su-periority of her skills, she does so by dis-playing those very skills. Rap, then, becomes a very particular sort of speech act; it has a ceremonial force. It effects power by incantation. The fact that my voice is coming out of your speakers shows that there is a particular power in what I am doing, and that very voice as it comes out of your speakers is telling you that there's a particular power in what

I am doing. If rap asserts the superiority of black over white culture, it mounts a demonstration precisely within that assertion. Another common assertion of power is the rapper's claim to move the bodies of the audience, to produce words and rhythms that *possess* the listeners' bodies, making them dance. The creativity of the slang and word play, the profundity of the poetry, the engagement of the body by the beat: these are aspects of this particular African-American cultural production that show you, as they tell you, that black culture has power. Thus, the rap speech act aspires to, asserts, but also enacts a reversal of cultural and personal domination. . . .

The assertion of fame in rap, repeated over and over, requires that to *know*, listeners must take those rappers on their own terms. Being known as a rapper precisely inverts the relations between agency, power, and knowledge present in, say, case histories of prisoners. This knowledge is not supposed to be extracted from bodies or lives, but rather bubbles up through word of mouth and radio play. Being "known" in rap terms means having your neighborhood's attention and loyalty, means having fame and fans, means *setting the terms* of representation through the power to be heard. MC Lyte *makes* you know what she *wants* you to know, and in the process takes your twenty bucks. And if you *don't* know, you better *act like* you know; if you're ignorant, you're going to be roundly abused.

Likewise, there is a constant cultural aggression in rap, an assertion of the *reality* or *truth* of black culture in the face of white domination. This aspect connects rap with the African-American response to oppression that stretches back to the slave narratives. As do leading African-American academic intellectuals (for example Houston Baker and Henry Louis Gates), Ice T, in his book *The Ice Opinion,* connects rap to African-American traditions:

> The main interpretation and misunderstanding of rap is in the dialogue—in the ghetto talk and machismo, even in the basic body language. From the nasty tales of Stagolee in the 1800s to H. Rap Brown in the '60s, most of rap is nothing more than straight-up black bravado. . . . In the ghetto, a black man will say, "I'll take my dick and wrap it around this room three times and fuck yo' mama." Now this man cannot wrap his dick around the room three times and probably doesn't want to fuck your mother, but this is how he's gonna talk to another brother.[33]

Notice that this both confirms and contextualizes the material of stereotype; aggressiveness and sexuality are put *in play* here in a way that is typical of rap. We have a celebration of black traditions (playing the dozens, for example) that is related to an Afrocentric self-construction of the sort that Malcolm X put forward and to the African-American aesthetic enunciated and enacted by Zora Neale Hurston. African-American linguistic codes and cultural traditions are centralized and their meanings explained without excuse. But here it is precisely the elements of African-American culture that are despised and feared by white culture (also by some elements within black culture: the Reverend Calvin Butts springs to mind) that are simultaneously thematized and enacted. This was Hurston's strategy in, for example, *Mules and Men* and "Characteristics of Negro Expression." Rather than asserting that African-American culture is a "high" culture by European standards, there is here an expression and demonstration of a power whelming from below.

As expressed in rap, this aesthetic has one criterion of quality: reality. An alternative formulation of the same standard is this: blackness. KRS One (Knowledge Reigns Supreme Over Nearly Everyone), for example, raps, "Let me show whose ass is the blackest." To assert that his ass is the blackest is for him to assert precisely that his stuff is real, authentic, hard-core rap. . . .

The association of reality with blackness implies by contrast that whiteness (culturally) is constructed out of an imaginary ejection of the concrete, the embodied, the real, and that it aims toward or makes a supreme value out of unreality. A "real" hard-core rap is an extremely black rap, and that means bass-heavy, gritty, completely embodied, completely intrinsic in its own enactment. White culture makes competing and contrasting claims of its own regarding knowledge, reality, and truth. Notice that, in the construction of whiteness, we white folks associate knowledge, and science and comprehension with ourselves and expel you from them. But notice too that comprehension also *falsifies,* that in ranging the particular fact under the general category, we must erase the jagged edges of that fact, its massed idiosyncrasies. This abandons by ejection an entire realm of truths to those who are left in the realm (or behind the veil) of the particular. To speak of *reality* [as rap does] is a powerful way of reasserting these truths; one might say that

all that is left out of a [comprehensive, scientistic] Theory of Everything is . . . reality: grit, jaggedness, immediacy, violence. If rappers know what they are talking about, then (white) sociologists haven't a clue. If rap is real, white culture has got to be "unreal."

Ice T puts it this way: "I rap about my life, and I rap about it in the hardest, most blatant sense. I consider what I say as real. This is the way the world I come from is. This is the way I talk and live. This is the only way I can be."[34] In rap, then, discourse materializes, becomes a hard, solid thing. The discourse of white science, of ejected asceticism, is material as well, but systematically hides that materiality and denies its effects; in rap the materiality of discourse is explicitly thematized. Rap brings the particular truth in a particular embodiment to bear directly on the racial situation, enacts it and slaps you with it. The particular truth of rap is put forward by and in a particular voice. The truth is transformed into art, but the reality of the art itself becomes a mode of resistance. Just as the slave narrative made the slave's truth a possession and a weapon, asserting the slave's ownership of his truth, rap, too, is an assertion of ownership of the truth or of the reality. The predominant mode of aesthetic evaluation of rap is not, say, beauty, but precisely reality (blackness) and the authority to present it.

It is often asserted that rap glorifies violence. That may occasionally be true (though far less frequently, I think, than is commonly supposed), and when it *is* true, one of its functions is, of course, the reassertion of what has been excluded; rap music is, among other things, a confrontation of white culture with its ejection of the body. Violence as transgression *interrupts* the operation of the machinery by which dualisms are enforced. But, as I say, this is occasional, and the bald general assertion that rap glorifies violence makes me wonder what these people have been listening to, if anything. . . .

In fact, there is a whole genre of rap videos that depict gang funerals, or in which the dead or injured are mourned and avenged. One thing such works do *not* do is make death an entertaining game; the pain is palpable. . . .

These lyrics do not glorify violence, unless you take the position that to *notice* violence linguistically, to admit that it exists, is to glorify it. Rather they tell about violence, mourn it, object to it, and rage against the conditions that make violence a day-to-day reality. . . .

Rap yields narratives, including narratives about violence and death. But narrative is also containment, and hence threat. Narrative has been a weapon of white culture. It has been used, as Derrida puts it, as "white mythology," above all in the scientific *explanation* of the object which is ejected in the self-construction that make science possible and that set up the material world, including the human body, as an object for study. Narrative containment is how we explain you to ourselves, and thus us to ourselves, while simultaneously removing ourselves from the scene of description by our objectivity. Our story about ourselves is that our histories are not stories, but sciences. In someone like Hegel, for instance, our story of progress becomes the entire inner truth of History and Being (significantly, as Kobena Mercer points out, Africa gets left out of history, or rather is on principle excluded).[35] Of course, this is only one

possible form of narrative, even in the modern West. There are counter-narratives: not only those that sweep unnarrated materials into the dominant narrative structures, but those that display different forms and possibilities for narrative. For example, there are African models of narration, that admit a plurality of narratives without trying to gather them all into a coherent structure. And rap definitely uses non-Western or not-only-Western modes of narration in constructing a discourse of resistance that asserts the other as other and is more than the assertion of the other as other.

There is, however, an even more radical excess available here, and available precisely out of the forms and concretions of oppression; for there are experiences that resist being swept into narrative altogether, and some of those experiences are signs or nodes of oppression itself. Thus what stands in excess to narrative can be gestured toward precisely in narrative. There is a white mythology that gives the sociological story, for example, of the underclass, with its substance abuse, its poverty, its violence, and its transgression of "our" values. These very experiences, however, are constant challenges to narrative in general. There can be narratives of acts of violence, but violence as it is experienced shatters narrative structures; violence might be defined precisely as what exceeds and destroys the coherence of narrative. The "slave narrative," for example, is both narrative and an interruption of narrative; the sheer intensity of the violence depicted cannot be smoothly incorporated in a story; its intensity disturbs the experience of the narrative as story. William Andrews points out that some slave narrators "lamented the inadequacy of language itself to represent the horrors of slavery or the depth of their feelings as they reflected on their sufferings. In some cases black narrators doubted their white readers' ability to translate the words necessary to a full rendering of their experience and feeling."[36]

To narrate one's own death, for example—as do Snoop and Biggie Smalls—is to make oneself impossible as a narrator in our ordinary reality. Ice T says this:

> Gangs have been able to get away with so much killing it just continues. The capability of violence in these kids is unimaginable. Last year, five of my buddies died. I don't even go to the funerals anymore. It's just so crazy. There are just so many people dying out there. Sometimes I sit up with my friends and think, "There will never be another time on earth where we'll all be together again." . . . You get hard after a while. You get hard. People on the outside say, "These kids are stone-faced; they don't show any remorse or any emotion." It's because they are . . . conditioned, like soldiers in war, to deal with death. You just don't know what it's like until you've been around it.[37]

Death exceeds story. Living with the constant threat of death and the constant capacity to kill is "unimaginable." It cannot be told; to be understood, it must be lived. And yet rap confronts you with its results, or with the situations in which life in the face of death is the only possible life. The gesture in narrative to those forms of experience is one way that rap connects with its intended audience: It gestures toward forms of experience that

are not really describable, but the gestures are understood by those whose lives are punctuated by such experiences. Likewise, to shoot up heroin or to get stone drunk are ways of being sucked into oblivion, an oblivion that interrupts and attacks narrative coherence. Ultimately, in such experiences, one must *let go* of narrative; to allow oneself to sink into oblivion is to let go of one's story of oneself, and to overflow and escape from other people's stories.

White culture is obsessed with the talk of constructing a narrative of black culture, an "explanation." It does this partly in various attempts at self-absolution, self-abasement, or self-accusation. But in all cases it allocates to itself the right to tell the story of African-American culture, perhaps as a preliminary step in "solving its problems" for it. Rap insists that African-Americans are, and must be, telling their own stories.

Even more profoundly, rap often indicates that African-American experience (like all experience, finally) cannot be contained in stories and psychological structures. . . .

Substance abuse, violence, sex, death, love, and hatred are ways of falling off the deep end, tumbling into the abyss; they are calls to oblivion and ecstasy. . . .

Oblivion and ecstasy (and there is hardly a distinction), pull narrative apart by making it particular and then inserting into it a condition that abrogates it. The experience described is a "going under." This is one reason why rap is continually asserted by its practitioners to be "real" or "true": it refuses containment in the fantasy structures of narrative, insists on particularity, and pulls toward a letting go. Violence in this sense is used, first, as a weapon against white people, and second, as a weapon against white scientific and narrative structures, as an attempt at the deepest level to undermine white art, white sociology, white pathologization of blackness and African-American culture—in short every gesture of containment.

Rap constantly enacts transgression. It flouts the law; it flouts taboos about what words to use and taboos about racial signifiers; it flouts sexual mores, and drug prohibitions, and polite language. Violence is transgression *per se:* a sheer violation. No story contains or captures violence; no story expresses the oblivion out of which it emerges or the oblivion it imposes. Violence is the Kantian thing in itself about which we can say nothing positively or wholly true. Even violence that fits into the most recognizable stories of white culture does so uneasily, and there is a penumbra of excess about it. Violence is something into which we are forced, or into which we are seduced; thus violence calls to the self for its oblivion. Often it makes this call precisely through an intensification of self to the point of collapse, shooting someone is an assertion of self, indeed the most pointed and extreme assertion of self, but it pulls the self by vertigo into a vortex. Violence is a destroyer of selves, and hence of every attempt to contain or explain the self.

Rap music has been criticized by black leaders for reinforcing racial stereotypes. The widespread use of words such as "bitch," "ho," and "nigger" is taken as an expression of self-hatred now extended into hatred of whatever resembles oneself. And rap has even been criticized for the same reason by some rappers. Sister Souljah, who is both a rapper and a community activist, writes the following in her autobiography, *No Disrespect:*

> Racism has turned our communities into war zones where we are dying every day. It is black-on-black hate, created by racism and white supremacy, that is killing us. Black people killing black people. Can African male-female relationships survive in America? Not if black-on-black love is dead. . . . Not if our young men continue to refer to young women as "bitches," or our young women refer to young men as "motherfuckers," or all of us refer to each other as "niggas." It is a sad measure of our profound contempt for each other and of our thoroughgoing self-loathing that we continue to persist in this ugly practice.[38]

Souljah's book is essentially about the difficulties of heterosexual love in a shattered community, a community, for example, where more of the young men are in jail than in college. Some rap takes that issue up in a very "positive" way. Heavy D, for example, says "black coffee, no sugar, no cream: that's the kind of girl I want down with my team." Salt 'n Pepa's "Whatta Man" is a celebration of black male beauty. Coolio's song "Mama I'm in Love With a Gangsta," by a stunning shift of view, portrays the pain of loving a man who is in jail through the eyes of his female lover, with Coolio portraying the incarcerated man. The late Tupac Shakur's "Black Pearl" is a celebration of the strength of black womanhood (though that celebration appeared more than a trifle ironic after Tupac's conviction for sexual abuse).

But the style called "gangsta rap" shows the force of Souljah's charge. Da

Brat, for example, refers to herself as a "bitch" and a "ho." It is sometimes said that rap denigrates education, celebrates violence and substance abuse, and confirms white America's image of African-Americans as ignorant, threatening crackheads (or whatever the latest drug of choice happens to be). If this were offered as a general critique of rap, it would be, as we have seen, ridiculously overgeneralized. But it is not without force.

Sherley Anne Williams gives a quite typical argument:

> Black people have to ask ourselves why so much [rap] has become so vehemently misogynistic, violent, and sexually explicit, so soaked in black self-hatred? Why, given that we are so ready to jump on Hollywood, the Man, the Media, and black women writers for negative and distorted portrayals of black people, have black academics, critics, and intellectuals been so willing to talk about the brilliant and innovative form of rap? Proclaiming rap's connection to traditional wells of black creativity and thus viewing even its most pornographic levels as "art," intellectuals have been slow to analyze and critique rap's content. We have, by and large, refused to call that content, where appropriate, pathological, anti-social, and anti-community. And by our silence, we have allowed what used to be permissible only in the locker room or at stag parties, among consenting adults, to become the norm among our children.[39]

Now I have quite a hostile response to this passage, which is notable above all for its prissiness, for its unquestioning

assumption that what is art cannot be obscene, and for its assumption that *describing* the realities of some black lives amounts to self-hatred. But again, it is obvious that the criticism has bite in that it refers to the actual content of many raps.

The charge of misogyny, for example, is hardly misplaced. Here is Claude Brown on the term "bitch":

> Johnny was always telling about bitches. To Johnny, every chick was a bitch. Of course, there were some nice bitches, but they were still bitches. And a man had to be a dog in order to handle a bitch.
>
> Johnny said once, "If a bitch ever tells you she's only got a penny to buy the baby some milk, take it. You take it, 'cause she's gon git some more. Bitches can always git some money." He really knew about bitches.
>
> Cats would say, "I saw your sister today, and she is a fine bitch." Nobody was offended by it. That's just the way things were. It was easy to see all women as bitches.[40]

Here the use of the term "bitch" is related directly to predation on women by men, a predominant theme of *Manchild in the Promised Land*. So the last thing I want to do is simply suggest that such speech is not problematic.

But one question that remains is, Problematic to whom? A common bromide of some sorts of feminist discourse is that the animal metaphors used for the genders are differentially inflected: a man is "cock of the walk" or a "dog" for instance, while a woman is a "bitch," a "cow," a "shrew." It is taken as obvious that those words *must* be valorizing of men and derogatory to women. And certainly in the history of white gender discourse they are derogatory. But is it obvious that such words must always, wherever they are used, mean just that? Or do some listeners assume that the comparison of a woman to a dog *must* be a derogatory metaphor, even when those using it claim otherwise? I do not want to answer this question definitively here, but only to point out that to assume that the meanings of words are set by one particular history of meaning encodes a certain cultural assumption of superiority. No matter what you claim to mean by certain terms, or what those terms mean in your community in practice, cultural commentators are likely to dismiss your claim about meaning in the name of what the words *really* mean— that is, what they would mean in the white community and what practices they support in the white community. As I explore this, I want you to understand that I take seriously the fact that black figures like Sister Souljah, Queen Latifah, and Sherley Anne Williams also attack such forms of words. It is worth mentioning that the term "bitch" is a particularly unstable one in the current scene of changing gender politics. A feminist friend of mine was called a bitch by a male objector to the feminist discourse in which they were speaking. Another, older feminist told her not to worry about it, but to be proud of it; "bitch," she said, is just what men call women when women don't go along with male preferences and definitions, and thus is a badge of honor. Ice T, in an interview on National Public Radio in which the interviewer sought to confront him with his "misogynistic" use of the word "bitch," tried to show her that it could be used as a term of affection, in a talk that started out, "Say you were *my* bitch," and finished off with, "Oh baby, quit trippin. You know I love you. But you're still my bitch." This reduced the interviewer to silence, though I suspect to enraged silence. And of course, had the interviewer been a man, Ice T could not have reduced him to silence in just this way. The question of *who gets to say what words mean,* however, is central to the possibility of a discourse that resists white hegemony of the sign. And typically, in white discourse, it is words themselves as abstract objects that are supposed to be the holders of power, as if the sheer phonemes in "bitch" or "nigger" carried the same meaning whenever, or wherever, or by whomever they are uttered—as if to expunge them from the language would actually be concretely to remedy sexist or racist oppression.

I am going to try, however, to give an analysis of the sort Williams demands. Seizing upon and turning around stereotypes is a weapon of subversion. In his memoir, *Colored People,* Henry Louis Gates writes:

> I used to reserve my special scorn for those Negroes who were always being embarrassed by someone else in the race. Someone too dark, too "loud," someone too "wrong." Someone who dared to wear red in public. Loud and wrong: we used to say that to each other. Nigger is loud and wrong. "Loud" carried a triple meaning: speaking too loudly, dressing too loudly, and just *being* too loudly.
>
> I do know that, when I was a boy, many Negroes would have been the first to censure other Negroes once they were admitted into all-white neighborhoods or schools

or clubs. "An embarrassment to the race"—phrases of that sort were bandied about. Accordingly, many of us in our generation engaged in strange antics to flout those strictures. Like eating watermelon in public, eating it loudly and merrily and spitting the seeds into the middle of the street, red juice running down the sides of our cheeks, collecting under our chins.[41]

Where assimilation may be a form of cultural erasure and where a culture resists assimilation by its loudness, where integration means the production of the appearance of whiteness and hence the minting of double consciousness, where the non-assimilated culture is constructed by stereotype—there the stereotype becomes a weapon of resistance to hegemonic power. Nigger is loud and wrong, hence dangerous and recalcitrant. Gates says that he eventually tried to stop telling people how to be black. But meanwhile being *extremely* black precisely by the standards of the stereotype is a way of asserting cultural existence and cultural difference.

It is one thing for a white moviemaker to portray black men as dangerous, violent addicts; it is quite another for Spike Lee to present such characters (as he did, for example, in *Mo Better Blues* and *Clockers*). Even if the portrayals coincided precisely (and they do not), they have exactly opposite positions in the power structure. One way to try to destroy the power of stereotype is to defy it, to go get a Ph.D., for example. This has its advantages, and of course it is not only a strategy for racial empowerment but for personal development. But *as* a strategy for racial empowerment, it has its disadvantages as well. First,

stereotypes stand up remarkably well to "exceptions"; stereotypes are not really generalizations, even bad generalizations, but rather templates through which we interpret experience. It is very easy for me to see a black professor as a racial anomaly; worse, the blackness of the black professor is in danger of disappearing in my eyes; he may walk like me and talk like me, and perhaps I can make of him an honorary white guy. And notice, too, that the Ph.D. may be seen by African-Americans as being purchased at the price of racial identification; it may be seen as a racial betrayal; one may be told to "stay black." I am certain that this is a maddening thing to be told, particularly in a situation such as academia, which is fraught with racial tensions and in which the color of the professor is not, ultimately, forgettable. It is, I am sure, a maddening thing to be told to stay black when there is really no choice in the matter. Nevertheless, the black professor at Harvard or wherever is operating in the white-dominated world, and may be doing so in part by creating a white surface. This compromises stereotypes, but only locally, and it also raises the threat of cultural annihilation by assimilation (an issue that is also vividly present in the Jewish community, where it focuses around intermarriage).

Academia is one perfect node of white self-construction; we professor types are pure minds, and we are notoriously physically inept and badly dressed because we have forgotten our bodies. To be a professor is to be very, very white, though there are also transgressive ways of taking up this or any other role. This is one reason that academia resists integration, and one reason why the forms of integration practiced in academia are particularly insistent in demanding a white surface from those by whom it is integrated. Yet the integration of this space is particularly needful and particularly fecund; as figures such as Cornel West, bell hooks, Henry Louis Gates, Houston Baker, and Patricia Williams strive to make a black authorship in the academic culture, they strive to operate within that culture while simultaneously throwing into question its most basic underpinnings in race. If we could be confronted with the minds of our pure bodies, we might watch a collapse of our own self-image. It goes without saying, however, that we white academics take extraordinary measures, unconscious to ourselves, to avoid that confrontation.

Another strategy is to use the stereotype in profound acts of self-empowerment: "If you think this is what I am, I'll give it to you (so to speak) in spades." And notice the potential of the stereotype, particularly of the black man, as a weapon against the power that creates it: Black guys are, according to the stereotype, animalistic, armed, violent, out of control. Rap's reply: "Hell yes we are, so get the fuck out of the way." Ice T says:

> Crime is an equal opportunity employer. It never discriminates. Anybody can enter the field. You don't need a college education. You don't need a G.E.D. You don't have to be any special color. You don't need white people to like you. You're self-employed. As a result, criminals are very independent people. They don't like to take orders. That's why they get into this business. There are no applications to fill out, no special dress codes. In crime you need only one thing: heart.[42]

This is something of an explanation. But it is also a demonstration of the power of transgression, a demonstration of how transgression becomes a form of economic and characterological resistance. It confirms the stereotype, but with a self- and other-awareness that are incompatible with the supposed neutrality of the values that make and enforce the stereotype, and with a skill and self-consciousness that are incompatible with the stereotype itself. It says, "*This* is what you have made by stereotype." People are *trapped* in a situation of violence, and the claustrophobia that accompanies the description of violence in rap is palpable.

Furthermore, it leads to a heightened romanticism of black culture by whites: every confirmation that black people are earthy, ignorant, violent, criminal, sexy, or drunk calls up both a greater fear and a greater yearning toward that culture on the part of people whose lives have been designed to omit or simply fail to acknowledge these things. So white parents find their children listening to and dressing like Snoop (and maybe sipping on gin and juice or smoking chronic [a kind of marijuana]), and they face a racial situation that has been to some extent transformed. One runs across a similar strategy in certain strands of feminism ("eco-feminism," for instance), where the image of woman as intuitive or instinctive mammalian nurturer is not derided as a stereotype but intensified into a mode of subversion. "Bitch" animalizes the person to whom it is applied. "Ho" sexualizes, or equates person with sexual body. "Nigger" carries with it the weight of the entire white cultural construction of black people as savages. There's no doubt that such terms are "degrading," and so forth. But there is, equally, no doubt of the capacity for reversal and subversion that lies in those terms when they are appropriated by black people and shoved at or sold to white people.

In the marketing of rap to white folks, we see something very like the erotics of interracial sex. And let me make clear my own positioning with regard to that erotics. I *identify* with figures such as Ice T or Snoop: they're my "ego ideal." These guys are my *heroes.* Of course, in yearning to be them, I am yearning to be what I am not, or yearning to be what I have excluded from myself; I am yearning to become my other. And yet, somewhere at the point where Ice T is on the lecture circuit and I'm at the rap show, our lives are actually running together in certain ways precisely out of the strength of our mutual exclusions and the concomitant desires. I not only *want* what I'm *not supposed to want* (black women), I want to *be* what I'm *not supposed to be* (a black man). Now this is not to say that if I actually woke up tomorrow in a black body I could remain happy about that for very long; I'd then have to deal with all the shit that goes along with that position. And yet when I'm watching a rap video, I'm identifying more intensely with the star than when I'm watching a Woody Allen or Clint Eastwood movie (to take two poles of white masculinity). This erotics of identification is of course intensified precisely by its transgressiveness, and by the fact that the black man is, for us white guys, very close to a pure sign of transgression. I yearn to be a pure body, a pure violence; but what I yearn for most of all is to *use* that status strategically, intelligently in an attack on white

culture, the way Ice T does. This essay (you may have noticed) is just such an attack on Western culture, but I would like it if this attack took the form of a rebellion against those who oppressed me, and hence generated a pride in myself and my culture, rather than the form of a rebellion against my apparent peers that generates only a measure of relief from self-loathing.

In rap music, by a magical reversal, the instrument of oppression, the stereotype, becomes—in the hands of those against whom it is used—an instrument of resistance. My criticism of white culture is not the same as Ice T's; it would not be the same criticism even if we used the same words. The words are not the same when different voices speak them for different ends. Critics who read rap as a manifestation of self-hatred are supposing that the words and images *must* mean what they *would* mean if they proceeded from white mouths, under the auspices of white authority. But the shift in voice and authority fundamentally changes the speech act. It is not too much to say that rap, by a sort of alchemy, converts oppression itself into resistance. Like a martial art, it turns the attacker's energy against him and threatens him with his own violence.

This is appropriate to the particular mode of oppression in which we white folks are now engaged. For we have become invisible as oppressors; we have learned not to say the wrong words. Our oppression has become continually more subtle until it is maddeningly elusive; as the oppressed turn their thoughts to resistance, they find it difficult to finger any particular individual as directly responsible. (There are, of course, exceptions to this, such as certain members of the

LAPD.) Racism seems to be a matter of fudged vocabularies and implicit standards, a sort of linguistic log-jam of domination assignable to nobody's act or control. But rap has invented a manner of resistance that employs the submerged energy of oppression that still flows palpably in the direction of African-Americans; rap hijacks the language of oppression itself and both attacks and uses the constructions of its imaginary locations. Tupac Shakur said "I'm not a gangster; I'm a thug." He had "Thug Life" tattooed on his stomach. Then the oppressor feels threatened even if he is not aware that he *is* an oppressor.

The stereotype is a mode of ejection, an attempt to insulate the culture from aspects of its own humanity that it perceives as threatening or bizarre. The stereotype in this sense is conceptual segregation. It functions the same way in individuals: Bigotry is an attempt to eject aspects of oneself that one finds intolerable. For such reasons, bigotry has been at its most explicit in segments of white culture that are in fact closest to black culture: in poor southern whites, for example. Here the conceptual exclusion of the other is at its most tenuous, and so extreme methods of insulation must be developed. With regard to rap, this ejection has been quite explicit and quite extreme; rap is continually censored. Many artists make one version of their songs for CD and another for radio and television. Words such as "nigger," "bitch," and "ho" are emitted, bleeped, or replaced. This has its ironies, since Queen Latifah cannot say, on the radio, that you shouldn't call women bitches. This is not the problem of *equality of language* reappearing; even the oppressed cannot use the words to say,

"Don't call me that." It is as though words had meanings outside purposes for which and contexts in which they are spoken. This is an important *strategy* for disclaiming responsibility, and for repressing speech mechanically. The fact that you can't say "nigger" in polite white society does nothing to combat racism; it intensifies racism because it renders it invisible. (Unbelievably, during the O. J. Simpson trial "nigger" was referred to by the white-dominated press as "the 'N'-word." People, please: Let's get real.) But it is supposed to follow from that prohibition that black folks shouldn't say "nigger" either.

Tupac, who before his death in the second hail of bullets directed at his body had been consistently censored, as well as legally hounded (perhaps for good reasons), samples Dan Quayle on "Pac's Theme." Quayle says, over and over, "It has no place in society," a perfect call to cultural ejection; Tupac's equally perfect reply: "I'm a product of this society." Ice T, who was forced to remove the song "Cop Killer" from one of his CDs when prosecutors in a murder trial claimed (wrongly) that the song had motivated a young Texas man to kill a policeman, writes, "I realized a long time ago that censorship is as American a tradition as apple pie." And he adds,

> We made the album *Rhyme Pays*, and then Warner Brothers came to me at the label and said they wanted to put a sticker on the record. I asked why. They explained it was to inform the public some material on the album might offend listeners.
>
> I said, "Fine, that's cool." Then they explained to me the organization behind the stickering was

called the Parent's Music Resource Center—the PMRC. I thought, "What a nice organization, what a nice name." Little did I know that it was founded and headed by this crazed bitch named Tipper Gore, who made it her job to put down nearly every artist in the music industry for saying what's on their minds. Gore and the PMRC are wholeheartedly against information exchange. Tipper Gore is the only woman I ever directly called a bitch on any of my records, and I meant that in the most negative sense of the word.[43]

The modes of ejection and marginalization that white culture practices against black culture could not be clearer than they are in the case of rap. The operations of the PMRC echo the censorship of Queen Latifah's feminist anthem. Since white people don't need the word "nigger" anymore to keep the machinery of racism humming, it now becomes forbidden for anyone to say the word, even those to whom its use is essential in describing the history of their oppression. "Nigger" reminds white people too uncomfortably of their very recent past, and suggests (unthinkably!) that the situation is not so very different now just because the word is out of style.

White identity could not be more perfectly visible than it is in these cases of ejection and marginalization. As Tipper defends our children, she does so in the blandest, most boring way; she appears in her pure whiteness. She becomes a pale spokeslady for pale "family values," the neutral ethical centerpoint on which we are all supposed to be agreed. She even claims a kind of nice appreciation for sixties black music, nice party dance music: We normal matrons aren't racist.

We like black music, as long as it stays apolitical and doesn't offend us and corrupt our children. Whereas the people she attacks are relentlessly particularized, she, in her matronly outfit, is relentlessly generalized into a defender of "our" values, "our" children, "our" culture from the bizarre forces of obscenity, transgression, and violation. She is protecting us from those who *say the wrong words* and thus compromise our culture as a *white* culture. White culture, in the person of Tipper Gore, can consume and enjoy black cultural production as long as it stays in its place.

What must be rejected or expunged are the parts of oneself one finds intolerable (above all, violence and desire, the violence of desire, the desire for violence). The content of the stereotype, thus, is *per se* what threatens the self-image of the bigot and, more widely, what threatens the image that white culture makes of itself. So the stereotype can be utilized as an absolutely precise weapon against the dominant culture: what we've tried to make of you is precisely what compromises us most deeply. The oversexed and overdrugged black gangster is the perfect "shadow" self of white culture, its absolutely intolerable negative image. Thus the stereotype is invested with a preternatural power to threaten white culture and white personality; it can be used as a weapon.

Our fear of the figure that Tupac Shakur explicitly invoked is the product in part of our shaping of that figure and applying it to people who look like Tupac. It is a position we manufactured, a composite of our ejections and oppressions, and it is beginning to speak in its own voice, and use the very power we have ascribed to it. What we do not understand is that this violence is our own violence, returning to us from the ghetto into which we sought to confine it. Our lack of self-knowledge makes this threat incredibly intense, gives it an air of something surreal; in making ourselves what we are, we have made this violence, returned upon us, incomprehensible to ourselves. And since our self-construction is precisely a comprehension, we are threatened *at our core* by a violence we cannot understand or contain. It is for precisely that reason that rap is censored. Bizarrely, for example, MTV blanks out all guns from rap videos, and bleeps out words that refer to guns. But of course guns are ubiquitous on television in general; the policy applies *only* to black popular music. Violence and its signifiers are permissible in the "right" hands, and those hands belong to Sylvester Stallone, not to Doctor Dre.

Ice Cube's "What Can I Do?" turns the stereotype around on a dime.[44] The song starts with a PBS narrator saying this:

> In any country, prison is where society sends its failures. But in this country society itself is failing.

Cube then proceeds to describe, in the first person, the life of a drug dealer which proceeds from wealth to prison to working at McDonald's. . . . The person whose story Cube tells in his own voice is a stereotype. The rich, black drug dealer with his bitches and mobile phone could be straight out of a police profile. In prison, he opts for body-building over books, a choice with economic consequences that raise the specter of a black man with sixteen-inch arms and an ax to

grind. White folks have tried to eject their criminality into the "black underclass"; black disrespect for order is supposed to be mirrored by our effortless respect for it. White self-constructions congratulate themselves on abiding by an order white culture has *made*. Law, whether conceptual, scientific, or governmental, is at the center of our self-constructions; we are the people who order ourselves and one another. The making of that order, the one we follow and you proverbially break, has also been the history of oppression, of the breaking of bodies and the subjugation of peoples. The fact that we have imaginatively excluded criminality, transgression, from ourselves allows us to ignore the most obvious facts about ourselves. It allows us, in fact, to practice criminality on a huge, generalized, worldwide scale while seeming to ourselves to be law-abiding citizens. As KRS One puts it in "Sound of Da Police," "Your laws are minimal/Cause you won't even think about looking at the real criminal." This is a particularly sharp formulation because it makes the matter turn on visibility. What we seek to make visible in black folks by an amazingly elaborate and publicly conducted process of enforcement is precisely what we seek to make invisible in ourselves; to see the real criminal, we'd have to look in the mirror. In fact, Cube's conviction of "the white man" is exactly right; because though relatively few of us are criminals as defined by the legal system, we all together constitute a criminal capable of robbing the world and practicing modes of exclusion that verge on annihilation. This amazing work is typical of the African-American tradition in many ways. It makes philosophy out of personal experience. In the tradition of Frederick Douglass, the charge is hypocrisy; the cure, truth.

CASE STUDY: WHAT IS VIOLENCE?

Socialist political theorist James W. Messerschmidt writes:

> Public perception of what serious violent crime is—and who the violent criminals are—is determined first by what the state defines as violent and the types of violence it overlooks. . . . [45]

Before reading any further, make a list of examples of violent crimes that would exemplify the "official definition" of violent crime as described by Messerschmidt. Make a second list of examples of violent offenses that the "official definition" of violence overlooks. Can you generalize in any meaningful way over the two lists? What characteristics do you see as common to the examples on each of your two lists? What differences do you see between the two lists? Call this generalization your "Interpretive Hypothesis as to the Class-Biased Definition of Violence." Next, read Messerschmidt's own interpretive hypothesis below for comparison. How closely does your interpretive hypothesis come to his? Where they do not coincide, can you defend yours?

> The criminal law defines only certain kinds of violence as criminal—namely, one-on-one forms of murder, assault, and robbery, which are the types of violence young marginalized minority males primarily engage in. The criminal law excludes certain types of avoidable killings, injuries, and thefts engaged in by powerful white males, such as maintaining hazardous working conditions or producing unsafe products. [46]

CASE STUDY: FALSE PROPHETS

Rapper KRS-One has written:

> Since the invasion of educational rap on a militant revolutionary level, others have desperately tried to swing their careers in that mode. I believe that it is good and healthy to have people in communications communicating uplifting messages to the masses of people. However I've witnessed the frauds of revolution stand up and take a false stand. In one breath they call themselves the teachers and in another breath they're gangster pop star pimps acting the way the government wants black people to act. These are false prophets and they should be pointed out immediately. The true revolution will unite humanity not Black or White or Asian or Indian, all races. And when you rise up for humanity you'll notice that you'll fall right in place with Africa if you're a Black African or Asia if you're an Asian or Indian etc., etc., etc. The enemy is not the masses of people worldwide, it's the masses of demonic governments worldwide. When these demonic people are wiped out and a new human consciousness arises every race will get their due respect. Forward ever, backwards never,

prepare for whatever and always stay clever, in any endeavor intelligence is better and be on guard for false prophets in leather.

[Boogie Down Productions, *Edutainment,* (Jive/Zomba, 1990)]

Who do you think are KRS-One's "false prophets"?

SUGGESTED READINGS:

Bok, Sissela. *Mayhem: Violence as Public Entertainment.* Reading, MA: Addison-Wesley, 1998.

Rose, Tricia. *Black Noise: Rap Music and Black Culture in Contemporary America.* Hanover, NH: Wesleyan University Press, 1994.

Copp, David, and Susan Wendell, eds. *Pornography and Censorship.* New York: Prometheus, 1983.

Walser, Robert. *Running With the Devil: Power, Gender, and Madness in Heavy Metal Music.* Hanover, NH: Wesleyan University Press, 1993. Chapter 5.

NOTES

ETHICS AND ENTERTAINMENT II: SEX AND VIOLENCE

PORNOGRAPHY AND THE CRIMINAL LAW

1. Joel Feinberg, *Pornography and the Criminal Law* 40 U. PITT. L. REV. 567 (1979). Reprinted by permission of the *University of Pittsburgh Law Review.*
2. W. Prosser, *Handbook of the Law of Torts 597* (4th ed., 1971), 597–600.
3. "The volunteer suffers no wrong"; no legal wrong is done to the person who consents. In tort law, this means that you cannot usually claim damages when you consent to the activity that caused the damages.
4. 403 U.S. 15 (1971), at 20.
5. Louis B. Schwarz, *Morals Offenses and the Model Penal Code* 63 Column. L. Rev. 669,678 (1963).
6. Willard Gaylin, "Obscenity," *Washington Post,* 20 February 1977, Outlook Section, 1.

ETHICAL PROBLEMS OF MASS MURDER COVERAGE IN THE MASS MEDIA

7. Reprinted from the *Journal of Mass Media Ethics* 9.1 (1994) by permission of the author and Lawrence Erlbaum Associates, Inc.
8. "Slaughter in a School Yard," *Time* (January 30, 1989): 29.
9. J. Baker, N. Joseph, and G. Cerio, "Death on the Playground," *Newsweek* (January 30, 1989): 35.
10. G. Church, J. Beaty, E. Shannon, and R. Woodbury, "The Other Arms Race," *Time* (February 6, 1989): 20–26.
11. W. Inman, "Wesbecker's Rampage is Boon to Gun Dealers," United Press International, September 16, 1989.

12. W. Inman, "Gunman's Assault Weapon Ordered Through the Mail at $349," United Press International, September 16, 1989.

13. E. Harrison, "Gunman Kills Seven and Himself at Kentucky Plant." *Los Angeles Times,* September 15, 1989, A1.

14. "Kentucky Killer's Weird Collection," *San Francisco Chronicle,* September 16, 1989, A2.

15. Inman, "Gunman's Assault Weapon Ordered Through the Mail at $349," United Press International, September 16, 1989.

16. "Simon Rodia, 90, Tower Builder," *New York Times,* July 20, 1965, 20.

17. W. Allen, ed. *The Works of Fisher Ames* (Indianapolis: Liberty Classics, 1983), 14–15.

18. E. Cairns, "Impact of Television News Exposure on Children's Perceptions of Violence in Northern Ireland," *Journal of Social Psychology* 130 (1990): 447–52.

19. J. Price, E. Merrill, and M. Clause. "The Depiction of Guns on Prime Time Television," *Journal of School Health* 62 (1992): 15–18.

20. W. Wood, F. Wong, and J. Chachere, "Effects of Media Violence on Viewers' Aggression in Unconstrained Social Interaction," *Psychological Bulletin* 109 (1991): 380.

21. M. Harris, "Television Viewing, Aggression, and Ethnicity," *Psychological Reports* 70 (1992): 137–8.

22. D. Lester "Media Violence and Suicide and Homicide Rates." *Perceptual and Motor Skills* 69 (1989): 894.

23. E. Magnuson, J. Leviton, and M. Riley, "Seven Deadly Days," *Time* (July 17 1989): 30–60.

24. E. Magnuson, J. Leviton, and M. Riley, "Suicides: The Gun Factor," *Time* (July 17, 1989): 61.

25. P. Meyer, *Ethical Journalism.* (New York: Longman, 1987).

26. *Ibid.,* 48–50.

27. S. Klaidman and T. Beauchamp, *The Virtuous Journalist* (New York: Oxford University Press, 1987).

28. E. Lambeth, *Committed Journalism: An Ethic for the Profession.* (Bloomington, IN: Indiana University Press, 1986).

29. J. Hulteng, *Playing it Straight* (Chester, CT: Globe Pequot, 1981).

30. E. Hallissy, "Behind Killer Dad's Deadly Rampage," *San Francisco Chronicle* July 13, 1993, A18.

31. Arthur R. Miller, *Miller's Court* (Boston: Houghton Mifflin, 1982), 109–10.

RAP MUSIC AND THE USES OF STEREOTYPE

32. Excerpted from Chapter 5 of *Act Like You Know: African-American Autobiography and White Identity* by Crispin Sartwell, (Chicago: University of Chicago Press, 1998). Copyright © 1998 by the University of Chicago. Reprinted by permission of the author and the University of Chicago Press.

33. Ice T, as told to Heidi Siegmund, *The Ice Opinion: Who Gives a Fuck?* (New York: St. Martin's, 1994), 94.

34. *Ice Opinion,* 97.

35. Kobena Mercer, *Welcome to the Jungle: New Perspectives in Black Cultural Studies* (New York: Routledge, 1994), 109.

36. William L. Andrews, *To Tell a Free Story* (Urbana: University of Illinois Press, 1986), 9.

37. *Ice Opnion,* 31.

38. Sister Souljah, *No Disrespect* (New York: Random House, 1994), 350.

39. Sherley Anne Williams, "Two Words on Music: Black Community," in *Black Popular Culture,* ed. Gina Dent (Seattle: Bay Press, 1992), 167–68.

40. Claude Brown, *Manchild in the Promised Land* (New York: Macmillan, 1965), 109.
41. Henry Louis Gates, *Colored People* (New York: Knopf, 1994), xiii–xiv.
42. *Ice Opinion*, 53.
43. *Ice Opinion*, 98.
44. Ice Cube, "What Can I Do?" *Lethal Injection* (Priority Records, 1993).
45. James W. Messerschmidt, *Capitalism, Patriarchy and Crime: Toward a Socialist Feminist Criminology* (Savage, MD: Rowman and Littlefield, 1986), 52.
46. Ibid.

7

INFORMATION ACCESS I: PRIVACY

Has the Information Super-Highway become the
Information Super-Spy-way?
JOHN MCCHESNEY, (NATIONAL PUBLIC RADIO)

INTRODUCTION

Most of us have had the experience of anticipating that someone was about to tell us something and wishing that person would withhold the revelation. Unwelcome intimacy is not as common as purposeful withholding of information to maintain privacy or distance from another, but it happens. The desire to preserve one's own privacy and that of others also asserts itself on the Internet.

DotComGuy is not the only person to have placed his life on the Web. A recent talk show featured three young women whose sorority house had installed cameras for Internet broadcasting. The studio audience expressed curiosity about the extent of the activities carried live on the Net and gasped when one woman revealed that a camera in the bathroom partially showed the toilet. Clearly even a television talk show audience believes that some activities should remain private.

Most Internet users have e-mail access at more than one location. Universities offer free access to the university server to students, faculty, and staff from both on and off campus. One benefit to the university is that employees are accessible to administrators, colleagues, and students while off campus. In one sense, this access is convenient. Employees read and process the morning e-mail before leaving for work. But do most people really want to integrate their home with their workplace to that extent? Each of us must address and answer this question in light of our feelings about our workplace and our ability to ignore work when other interests and duties call us. Many people protect privacy by establishing (and paying for) a second e-mail address and Internet connection available only to friends and family. In this manner they reconstruct the separation of office from home in the virtual world.

This example deals primarily with the desire to keep some places private, but privacy is also a matter of access to information. As teachers of ethics, we sometimes receive papers from students that stray from evaluation of a social choice or selection of a behavior into autobiography. Reading such papers can produce that feeling of wishing someone would not reveal something. As instructors of ethics we need not know whether a student had an abortion in order to grade a paper about abortion. People use such information to distance relationships or foster greater intimacy. But sometimes we assert privacy for even more trivial interests. The Internet carries abundant free software and shareware for download. Usually the price of shareware is your name and an e-mail address. The e-mail address is for notification of updates and offers of other software for sale. For such interactions it is useful to have a third e-mail address with, say, Hotmail, a free Web-based e-mail. All such offers can go to that account and be quickly deleted. This tactic protects the virtual home or virtual place of business from invasive advertising. Free services such as Hotmail, of course, have their price. Users must provide an economic profile and mailing address. This generates more e-mail advertising, which, fortunately, all goes to that address.

Some search engines include the option of searching Usenet groups instead of Web pages. The search engine does not discriminate about where it finds fields. If you search Usenet groups for "John Rocker" you will receive both posts about him and by him. The search engine allows you to read the Usenet postings of your coworkers, neighbors, and anyone else who uses their own name or whose e-mail identification you know. Likewise, whatever you post to a newsgroup under your own name is open to the public.

Search engines do not search regular e-mail, but other privacy concerns arise. Most employers claim ownership of all e-mail sent and received through the employer's server. It does not matter if you use a workplace computer provided by the employer or a privately purchased at-home computer. The mail you send through your employer's server belongs to your employer and may be read. Employers routinely archive e-mail. About twenty percent of all United States–based companies routinely sample e-mail. In addition, e-mail communications are frequently subpoenaed in court cases. Perhaps the search device most susceptible to misuse is *Lexis Nexis*. This tool is quite expensive and generally used only by law firms. It is a great source for court decisions at all levels of the judicial system. Universities often receive discounted promotional access as a means of marketing the tool to future professionals. On one California campus, faculty reportedly used it to investigate the background of an administrator whom several instructors did not particularly like. The faculty found an embarrassing no-contest plea to a criminal charge in the administrator's past. Somehow this knowledge found its way to a local newspaper. Obviously, *Lexis Nexis* provides information about the criminal activities of friends and neighbors. It can satisfy curiosity about the financial situation of someone you heard filed bankruptcy.

Philosophers generally regard rights as trumps that are overridden by consideration of consequences only in extreme cases. The law is more inclined to speak of balancing rights against other rights and against state interests and social consequences. Think of rights as valid claims with a presumption in favor of recognition by others. If you are inclined to think that the sorority women should not place cameras in the toilet no matter what the financial benefits, or that students should not reveal personal information to give a paper more validity, you probably believe not only in a right to privacy but also that the right is inalienable. Inalienable rights are rights so integral to the meaning of being human that humans have no right to waive them. We recognize at least two types of privacy rights—a right to *place* privacy (for example, in the home) and a right to govern access to information (*access* privacy)— regardless of whether you are at home or at the office. The stronger the presumption you grant to privacy the more you will be inclined to see it as a right to be left alone. After all, the company that provides shareware free of charge has an interest in selling the advanced MP3 player to users who download the shareware version. Anyone who sends the company's advertisements to the trashcan without even reading them says implicitly, if not explicitly, that the right to be left alone should override the company's economic interest.

It is tempting to see the right to privacy as a property right. The bestowal and withholding of information bears a superficial resemblance to gift giving. Gifts are a bestowal of property on another, and the type of gift indicates the degree of real or desired intimacy. Privacy allows the accumulation of a kind of information capital that the owner exchanges for intimacy, friendship, or shareware. In a landmark essay on the right to privacy United States Supreme Court Justices Louis Brandeis and Samuel Warren argued that the right to privacy was based in the right to life.

Brandeis and Warren saw law as evolving toward a fuller recognition of the extent of moral rights. Originally the right to life only protected citizens from physical assault. But ". . . there came a recognition of man's spiritual nature, of his feeling and intellect." The scope of law broadened in recognition that the right to life includes the right to enjoy life; and that includes being left alone. Brandeis and Warren remarked that the law came to recognize the value of sensations as a logical extension of the value of being free from physical assault.[1] They saw the individual's right to determine to what extent thoughts, feelings, and sensations were expressed to others reflected in common law. Most importantly, they remarked that "the same protection is accorded to a casual letter or an entry in a diary as to the most valuable poem or essay, to a botch or daub and to a masterpiece."[2] It is not in the value of the informational property, but in the human stake in being left alone to enjoy life that Brandeis and Warren find the source of the right to privacy.

7.1 PRIVACY IN THE INFORMATION AGE   Ethicists disagree about whether to approach the professions as distinct areas of moral inquiry or as areas in which to apply general ethical theories to specific problems. For instance, the morality of telling a lie does not change if the lie is directed to your parents, the Internal Revenue Service, a telemarketer, or a business rival. On such an approach information ethics would be no more than the application of ethical theory to new and perhaps interesting problems. The challenging work of developing a hierarchy of rights and values would already have been completed. James Moor, a leading information ethicist, calls this approach to information ethics "routine ethics." The alternative proposed by cultural relativists, that the ethics of each society should be reflected on the Web, is equally unhelpful. Moor points out that the Web cannot honor all views on censorship or privacy. The Web is a global electronic village incapable of being divided up into regions that respect the different ethics of different geographic areas.

Moor views computer information ethics as having two components: study of the social impact of the new technology and formulation of policies in response to moral issues in a context that has been *informationalized*. Information technology leads to information enrichment of social practices and causes a shift in the core meaning of informationalized practices. Two examples of such practices are warfare and finance. Moor points out the importance of disrupting Iraqi communications and the role of the stealth bomber in the Gulf War as instances of the importance of information in changing the conduct of warfare.[3] And certainly computer technological advances are an essential part of the technology that makes it possible to consider winning a war from a distance.

The war against Yugoslavia brought us media advocates of the new and old ways of waging war. NATO successfully avoided the use of ground troops against an opponent that sought to eventually win through waging a drawn-out ground war and inflicting a level of casualties that would erode popular support for the NATO commitment. At times the Yugoslavian side communicated the opinion that an air war was somewhat dishonorable. The same opinion came from supporters of the NATO campaign who thought that the air war would not be sufficient or successful soon enough. Substantial disagreement also arose over the bombing of television transmitters over the proper definition of military target. These sorts of changes in the nature of war, brought about by information technology, call for the formulation of ethical policy sensitive to informationalization.

Moor approaches information ethics with a sensitivity to the core values found in every human society. He believes that humans who expressed no core moral values would be irrational.

> Life and happiness are two of the most obvious of such values. At the very least people want to avoid pain and death for themselves. . . . Other core values (or core goods) for humans include ability, freedom, knowledge, resources, and security. . . . Core values are articulated in a multitude of delightful ways but they also constrain the realm of possibilities.[4]

Moral agents go beyond this minimal rationality and show respect for others and for the core values of others. This means that policies for the Internet may lead to disagreement over relative priorities of various human values, but recognition of core human values such as privacy and security will also lead us to brand some policies as unacceptable and others as at least reasonable compromises. In the following reading Moor applies the core-value approach to privacy.

QUESTIONS FOR STUDY AND DISCUSSION

1. What determines whether something has instrumental value or intrinsic value? Give an example of each.
2. Why does Moor not consider privacy a core human value?
3. Was Moor's privacy invaded by the pizza company?
4. Has the information age led to a change in the priority of place and informational access privacy? What would Moor say?
5. Make sure you can state the three principles Moor introduces at the end of the article.
6. Moor advocates privacy zones and not place privacy or even the privacy of information. This approach suggests that no information can be withheld absolutely by an individual. Any item of information has a zone in which access by another is justified. What do you think? Does any information belong to the individual alone?

TOWARD A THEORY OF PRIVACY IN THE INFORMATION AGE[5]

JAMES MOOR

Greased Data

When we think of ethical problems involving computing probably none is more paradigmatic than the issue of privacy. Given the ability of computers to manipulate information—to store endlessly, to sort efficiently, and to locate effortlessly—we are justifiably concerned that in a computerized society our privacy may be invaded and that information harmful to us will be revealed. Of course, we are reluctant to give up the advantages of speedy and convenient computerized information. We appreciate the easy access to computerized data when making reservations, using automatic teller machines, buying new products on the Web, or investigating topics in computer databases. Our challenge is to take advantage of computing without allowing computing to take advantage of us. When information is computerized, it is *greased* to slide easily and quickly to many ports of call. This makes information retrieval quick and convenient, but legitimate concerns about privacy arise when this speed and convenience lead to the improper exposure of information. Greased information is information that moves like lightning and is hard to hold onto.

Consider, for example, listed telephone numbers which have been routinely available through a telephone operator and a telephone book but which now are available along with address information in giant electronic phone books on the Internet. The Hanover, New Hampshire, telephone book (the telephone book for where I live) is rather hard to locate in most places in the world, but now anyone in the world with access to the Internet can easily find out my phone number, who my wife is, and where I live. One can even retrieve a map of my residential area. I don't consider this to be a breach of privacy, but I use it to point out how the same information, which has technically been public for a long time, can dramatically change levels of accessibility practically speaking when put into electronic form on computer networks. It is ironic that my name may be hard to find in the Internet phone book in that it is listed there anachronistically in an abbreviated form. "James" is abbreviated as "Jas," an abbreviation I never use and have seen only in old print phone books, presumably introduced to save print space but mindlessly copied when put on the Internet. Don't tell anyone.

The greasing of information makes information so easy to access that it can be used again and again. Computers have elephant memories—big, accurate, and long term. The ability of computers to remember so well for so long undercuts a human frailty that assists privacy. We, humans, forget most things. Most short term memories don't even make it to long term memory. Every time I go to a busy supermarket I am a new customer. Who can remember what I bought the last time I was there? Actually, a computer does. Most of the time I shop at a cooperative food store that gives a rebate at the end of the year. When I buy food, I give the checkout person my account number (I can remember at least that most days). The checkout person scans my purchases which appear on a screen by the name of the item and its price. This information is definitely greased. It appears as quickly as the checker can move the items across the barcode reader. Then my total is displayed and the information is added to my grand total of purchases on which I get a certain percentage back each year. Notice that in addition to the total of my purchases the

market also has information about what I have purchased. It helps the market keep track of its inventory. But, it also means that the store has a profile on my buying habits. They know how much wine I purchase, my fondness for Raisin Bran cereal, and the kind of vegetables I prefer. In principle, such evidence could be subpoenaed if my eating habits were relevant to a court case. Does this accumulation of information violate my privacy? I suppose not, but it is greased so that it moves easily and is more accessible over a longer period of time than ever before. Practically speaking, the information is never forgotten. A documented history of purchases generates the possibility for an invasion of privacy that does not exist without it.

In the case of my food shopping the collection of information is obvious to me. I can see my eating habits and my limited willpower flash on the display screen as the calories tumble by on the conveyor. But information about us can be collected subtly when we don't realize it. The greasing of information allows other computers to capture and manipulate information in ways we do not expect. Consider a final personal example to illustrate this. Not long ago I lived for a few months in Edinburgh. On days I didn't feel like cooking, I would sometimes order pizza. The pizza was delivered to my apartment and hence was a convenient way to get a quick meal. However, I was somewhat taken aback the second time I phoned the pizza establishment. Without my placing an order the pizza makers already seemed to know my address and my favorite pizza. Did I want to have another medium pepperoni and mushroom delivered? I hadn't been in Edinburgh very long. How could they possibly know my taste (or lack of taste) so quickly? The answer, of course, was their use of caller ID. No mystery here. I had called before and given information about my pizza preference and my delivery address, and they had linked it with my phone number. When I called the second time, my phone number was captured electronically by the pizza parlor and used to select the other information from my first call. Had my privacy been invaded? Probably not, but I confess that I initially felt some mild indignation that my pizza profile had been stored away without my knowing it. If I were a frequent customer in a fine restaurant and the waiter had memorized my tastes, I would feel complimented that he remembered me. But, as efficient as the caller ID/computer system was, I found no gain in self worth by having a pizza parlor computer recall my intake of pepperoni and mushroom pizza.

I mention these three examples, the Internet phone book, the supermarket refund policy based on bar code data, and the pizza parlor caller ID, not because they represent some deep treachery but because they are perfectly ordinary activities and illustrate how effortlessly information is collected and transmitted without any of us giving it a second thought. Once information is captured electronically for whatever purpose, it is greased and ready to go for *any* purpose. In a computerized world we leave electronic footprints everywhere and data collected for one purpose can be resurrected and used elsewhere. The problem of computer privacy is to keep proper vigilance on where such information can and should go.

For the most part the need for privacy is like good art, you know it when you see it. But sometimes our intuitions can be misleading and it is important to become as clear as possible what privacy is, how it is justified, and how it is applied in ethical situations. In this paper I will assemble pieces of an overall theory of privacy and try to defend it. In the computer age during a period when information technology is growing rapidly and its consequences are difficult to predict more than a few days in advance, if at all, it is more important than ever to determine how privacy should be understood and guarded.

Grounding Privacy

From the point of view of ethical theory, privacy is a curious value. On the one hand, it seems to be something of very great importance and something vital to defend, and, on the other hand, privacy seems to be a matter of individual preference, culturally relative, and difficult to justify in general. Is privacy a primary value? How can we justify or ground the importance of privacy?

I will discuss two standard ways of justifying privacy, both of which I have used before, and describe the limitations of these two approaches. Then I will present a third way to justify the importance of privacy which I now find more defensible. Philosophers frequently distinguish between instrumental values and intrinsic values. Instrumental values are those values which are good because they lead to something else which is good. Intrinsic values are values which are good in themselves. Instrumental values are good as means; intrinsic values are good as ends. My computer is good as a means to help me write papers, send e-mail, and calculate my taxes. My computer has instrumental value. However, the joy I gain from using my computer is good in itself. Joy doesn't have to lead to anything to have value. Joy has intrinsic value. And, as philosophers since Aristotle have pointed out, some things, such as health, have both instrumental and intrinsic value. This familiar philosophical distinction between instrumental and intrinsic values suggests two common ways to attempt to justify privacy.

Almost everyone would agree that privacy has instrumental value. This is its most common justification. Privacy offers us protection against harm. For example, in some cases if a person's medical condition were publicly known, then that person would risk discrimination. If the person tests HIV+, an employer might be reluctant to hire him and an insurance company might be reluctant to insure him. Examples of this nature are well known and we need not amass examples further to make a convincing case that privacy has instrumental value. But, so do toothpicks. To justify the high instrumental value of privacy we need to show that not only does privacy have instrumental value but that it leads to something very important. One of the best known attempts to do this has been given by James Rachels. Rachels suggests that privacy is valuable because it enables us to form varied relationships with other people.[6] Privacy does enable us to form intimate bonds with other people that might be difficult to form and maintain in public. But the need to relate to others differently may not ground privacy securely because not everyone may want to form varied relationships and those who do may not need privacy to do it. Some people simply do not care how they are perceived by others.

The justification of privacy would be more secure if we could show that it has intrinsic value. Deborah Johnson has suggested a clever way of doing this. Johnson proposes that we regard "privacy as an essential aspect of autonomy."[7] So, assuming that autonomy is intrinsically valuable and privacy is a necessary condition for autonomy we have the strong and attractive claim that privacy is a necessary condition for an intrinsic good. If privacy is not an intrinsic good itself, it is the next best thing. But, is it true that "autonomy is inconceivable without privacy"?

I have proposed a thought experiment about Tom, an electronic eavesdropper, which, I believe, shows Johnson's claim to be incorrect.[8] In this thought experiment Tom is very good with computers and electronics and has a real fondness for knowing about you—all about you. Tom uses computers secretly to search your financial records, your medical records, and your criminal records. He knows about your late mortgage payments, your persistent hemorrhoids, and that driving while intoxicated charge that you thought was long forgotten. Tom is so fascinated with your life that he has clandestine cameras installed which record your every movement. You know nothing about any of this, but Tom really enjoys watching you, especially those instant replays. "For Tom, watching your life is like following a soap opera—The Days of Your Life." I think most of us will agree that there is something repugnant about Tom's peeping. But what is it? It is not that he is directly harming you. He doesn't use any of this information to hurt you. He doesn't share the information with anyone else or take advantage of you in any way whatsoever. Moreover, you have complete autonomy, just no privacy. Thus, it follows that privacy is not an essential condition for autonomy. It is conceivable to have autonomy without privacy. Nevertheless, I would agree that some people, including myself, regard privacy as intrinsically valuable, not merely instrumentally valuable.

Now let me consider a third approach to justifying the importance of privacy. I wish to maintain that there is a set of values, which I call the "core values," which are shared and fundamental to human evaluation. The test for a core value is that it is a value that is found in all human cultures. Here is the list of some of the values that I believe are at the core: *life, happiness, freedom, knowledge, ability, resources,* and *security.* My claim is an empirical one. I am claiming that all sustainable human cultures will exhibit these values. I am not suggesting for a moment that all cultures are moral or that these goods are fairly distributed in every culture. Regrettably, they almost never are. (An ethical theory requires an account of fairness as well as an account of the core values.) What I am claiming is that every viable culture will exhibit a preference for these values. Consider the most primitive, immoral culture you can imagine. As barbaric and repulsive as it is, its members must find nourishment and raise their young if the culture is to survive. These activities require at least implicit acknowledgment of the core values. To abandon the core values completely is to abandon existence.

Is privacy a core value? I wish it were. It would make the justification of privacy so much easier. But, upon reflec-

tion it is clear that it is not in the core. One can easily imagine sustainable and flourishing human cultures that place no value on privacy. Consider a man and a woman who live together but give each other no privacy and who could care less about privacy. Presumably, many couples live this way and have no trouble existing. Now imagine a family or a small tribe with equal disinterest in privacy. Everybody in the group can know as much as they want about everybody else. They might believe that their society functions better without secrets. An anti-Rachelsean in the society might maintain that they have better and more varied human relationships just because they can know everything about everybody! The concept of privacy has a distinctly cultural aspect which goes beyond the core values. Some cultures may value privacy and some may not.

How then should we justify privacy? How is it grounded? Let me propose a justification of privacy by using the core values. The core values are the values that all normal humans and cultures need for survival. Knowledge, for example, is crucial for the ongoing survival of individuals and cultures. The transmission of culture from one generation to the next by definition involves the transmission of knowledge. I emphasize the core values because they provide a common value framework, a set of standards, by which we can assess the activities of different people and different cultures. The core values allow us to make transcultural judgments. The core values are the values we have in common as human beings. To focus on the core is to focus on similarities. But, now let's focus on the differences. Individuals and cultures articulate the core values differently depending on environment and circumstances. The transmission of knowledge is essential for the survival of every culture, but it is not the same knowledge that must be transmitted. Resources such as food are essential for everyone, but not everyone must prefer the same kind of food. So, though there is a common framework of values, there is also room for much individual and cultural variation within the framework. Let's call the articulation of a core value for an individual or a culture the "expression of a core value."

Although privacy is not a core value per se, it is the expression of a core value, viz., the value of security. Without protection, species and cultures don't survive and flourish. All cultures need security of some kind, but not all need privacy. As societies become larger, highly interactive, but less intimate, privacy becomes a natural expression of the need for security. We seek protection from strangers who may have goals antithetical to our own. In particular, in a large, highly computerized culture in which lots of personal information is greased it is almost inevitable that privacy will emerge as an expression of the core value, security.

Consider once again the dichotomy between instrumental and intrinsic values. Because privacy is instrumental in support of all the core values, it is instrumental for important matters; and because privacy is a necessary means of support in a highly computerized culture, privacy is instrumentally well grounded for our society. Moreover, because privacy is an expression of the core value of security, it is a plausible candidate for an intrinsic good in the context of a highly populated, computerized society. Tom,

the electronic eavesdropper, who doesn't harm his subject when he spies, nevertheless, seems to be doing something wrong intrinsically. The subject's security is being violated by Tom even if no other harm befalls the person. People have a basic right to be protected, which from the point of view of our computerized culture, includes privacy protection.

I have argued that using the core value framework privacy can be grounded both instrumentally and intrinsically—instrumentally, as a support of all the core values, and, intrinsically, as an expression of security. I am, however, concerned that the traditional instrumental/intrinsic understanding may be misleading. Traditionally, instrumental/intrinsic analyses push us in the direction of a search for a *summum bonum,* a greatest good. We try to find the one thing to which all other things lead. In the core value approach that I am advocating some values may be more important than others; but there is not a *summum bonum.* Rather the model is one of an intersupporting framework. The core values, as the beams of a truss, are in support of each other. Asking whether a core value or the expression of a core value is instrumental or intrinsic is like asking whether a beam of a truss is supporting or supported. It is essentially both. The core values for all of us are mutually supporting. Some people will emphasize some values more than others. An athlete will emphasize ability, a businessperson will emphasize resources, a soldier will emphasize security, a scholar will emphasize knowledge, and so forth. However, everyone and every culture needs all of the core values to exist and flourish. Privacy, as an expression of security, is a critical, interlocking member in our systems of values in our increasingly computerized culture.

The Nature of Privacy

Understanding privacy as the expression of the core value of security has the advantage of explaining the changing conception of privacy over time. Privacy is not mentioned explicitly either in the United States Declaration of Independence or in its Constitution.[9] It is strange that a value that seems so important to us now was not even mentioned by the revolutionary leaders and statesmen who were so impressed with the ideals of individual freedoms. The concept of privacy has been evolving in the U.S. from a concept of non-intrusion (e.g., the Fourth Amendment to the U.S. Constitution offering protection against unreasonable governmental searches and seizures), to a concept of noninterference (e.g., the *Roe v. Wade* decision giving a woman the right to choose to have an abortion), to limited information access (e.g., Privacy Act of 1974 restricting the collection, use, and distribution of information by federal agencies). Privacy is a concept that has been dramatically stretched over time as it [is]. In our computer age the notion of privacy has become stretched even further. Now the concept privacy has become so informationally enriched that "privacy" in contemporary use typically refers to informational privacy though, of course, other aspects of the concept remain important.

Consider a useful distinction that helps to avoid some misunderstandings about the nature of privacy. The term "privacy" is sometimes used to designate a situation in which people are protected from intrusion or observation by natural or physical circumstances. Someone spelunking by herself would be in a naturally private (and probably dangerous) situation. Nobody can see her in the cave she is exploring. In addition to natural privacy there is normative privacy. A normatively private situation is a situation protected by ethical, legal, or conventional norms. Consultations with a lawyer or doctor would be normatively private situations. Obviously, many normatively private situations are naturally private as well. We send mail in sealed envelopes. When an unauthorized entry is made into a normatively private situation, privacy has not only been lost, it has been breached or invaded.

Now if we put the evolving conceptions of privacy together with distinction between normative and natural privacy we get a useful account of the nature of privacy.

> An individual or group has normative privacy in a situation with regard to others if and only if in that situation the individual or group is normatively protected from intrusion, interference, and information access by others.[10]

I use the general term "situation" deliberately because it is broad enough to cover any kinds of privacy: private *locations* such as one's diary in a computer file, private *relationships* such as e-mail to one's pharmacy, and private *activities* such as the utilization of computerized credit histories.

The situations which are normatively private can vary significantly from culture to culture, place to place, and time to time. This doesn't show that the privacy standards are arbitrary or unjustified, they are just different. For example, at a private college faculty salaries are kept confidential, but at some state colleges faculty salaries, at least salaries above a certain level, are published. Presumably, the private colleges believe that protecting salary information will reduce squabbling and embarrassment; whereas state colleges (or the state legislatures) believe that the taxpayers who support the institution have the right to know how much faculty members are being paid. These are different but defensible policies for protecting and releasing information.

Clearly some personal information is very sensitive and should be protected. We need to create zones of privacy, a variety of private situations, so that people can ensure that information about themselves which might be damaging if generally released will be protected. With different zones of privacy one can decide how much personal information to keep private and how much to make public. Notice that on my account the notion of privacy really attaches to a situation or zone and not to the information itself. For instance, if an Internal Revenue Service employee uses a computer to call up and process a movie star's income tax return, then the employee is not invading the star's privacy. He is allowed in this situation to investigate the star's tax return. However, if that same employee were to call up that same star's tax return on his computer after hours just to browse around, then the employee would be violating the star's privacy although the employee may gain no new information! The employee has legitimate access in the first situation but not the second.

The theory I am proposing is a version of the restricted access view of privacy. The major opposing view is the control theory of privacy. One proponent of this view, Charles Fried, writes, "Privacy is not simply an absence of information about us in the minds of others, rather it is the *control* we have over information about ourselves."[11] I agree that it is highly desirable that we control information about ourselves. However, in a highly computerized culture this is simply impossible. We don't control vast amounts of information about ourselves. Personal information about us is well greased and slides rapidly through computer systems around the world, around the clock. Therefore, to protect ourselves we need to make sure the right people and only the right people have *access* to relevant information at the right time. Hence, the restricted access view puts the focus on what we should be considering when developing policies for protecting privacy. However, the restricted access account, at least in the form I am proposing it, has all of the advantages of the control theory for one of the goals in setting policies to give individuals as much control (informed consent) over personal data as realistically possible. For this reason I will label my account as a "control/restricted access" theory of privacy.

The control/restricted access conception of privacy has the advantage that policies for privacy can be fine tuned. Different people may be given different levels of access for different kinds of information at different times. A good example occurs in a modern, computerized hospital. Physicians are allowed access to online medical information which secretaries are not. However, physicians are generally not allowed to see all the information about a patient that a hospital possesses. For example, they don't have access to most billing records. In some hospitals some medical information such as psychiatric interviews may be accessible to some physicians and not others. Rather than regarding privacy as an all or nothing proposition—either only I know or everybody knows—it is better to regard it as a complex of situations in which information is authorized to flow to some people some of the time. Ideally, those who need to know do, those who don't, don't.

The control/restricted access also explains some anomalies about private situations. Usually, when we consider privacy, we are thinking about situations in which individuals possess possibly damaging personal information they want to keep others from knowing. But situations can be private in other circumstances. Imagine a situation in a restaurant with scores of people dining. A couple begin to argue loudly and eventually each shouts to the other about a marital problem they are having. They go into excruciating detail about various kinds of sexual dysfunction and bodily needs. Everyone can hear them and many patrons of the restaurant feel uncomfortable as they proceed with their meal. Finally, the waiter, who thinks he can help, cannot stand it anymore. He walks over to the couple and asks whether they would like his advice. The couple in unison tell him, "No, it's a private matter."

As ironic as their comment may be, it does make sense on several levels. In private situations the access to information can be blocked in both directions. This couple did not want to allow information from the waiter although they themselves had been indiscreet in revealing details to the entire population of the restaurant. Moreover, in our culture some activities are required to be done in private. Discussions of one's intimate marital problems may be one of them. Privacy is a form of protection and it can protect the general population as well as individuals.

Setting and Adjusting Policies for Private Situations

So far I have commented on the greasing effect computerization has on information and the potential problems for privacy computerization poses. I have proposed a justification for privacy as an expression of one of the core values and as an essential member of the central framework of values for a computerized society. I have characterized the nature of privacy as an evolving concept which has become informationally enriched with the development of computing. And I have argued that privacy is best understood in terms of a control/restricted access account. Now it is time to focus on practical policies for the protection of privacy. An example I will use is information gathered from genetic testing. This is an interesting case because, practically speaking, genetic testing would not be possible without information technology and with information technology genetic testing is one of the greatest potential threats to our individual privacy. Improper disclosure of our genetic information may be the ultimate violation of our privacy.

Suppose a patient decides to have herself tested for a breast cancer gene. She does not have breast cancer, but breast cancer runs in her family and she wants to know whether she is genetically disposed to have breast cancer. She goes to the hospital for tests for the gene and the results are positive. The results are put in her medical record so that the information is available to physicians to encourage aggressive testing for the disease in the future. The information will be computerized, which means that many health care providers throughout the state may have access to the information. The patient's health insurance company will also have access to it. Information of this kind could be detrimental to the patient when obtaining life insurance or future health insurance, and eventually, if the information slides through enough computer networks, it could be detrimental to the patient's children when obtaining insurance and applying for employment though they have shown no signs of the disease and have never been tested.

In formulating policies we should try to minimize excess harm and risk. In cases like this, it may be hard to do. Clearly, the medical records should be treated confidentially but that may not be enough to protect the patient. Because the records are computerized, and hence well-greased, information will be sent rapidly along networks and gathered by third parties who may find their own self-interested uses for it. New legal policies might be helpful here including the passage of statutes protecting patients from discrimination on the basis of genetic testing. Also, the hospital might consider setting up a zone of privacy for patients who want only predictive testing done. There is a difference between predictive genetic testing in which the patient is tested for genetic information that may be indicative of future disease and diagnostic testing in which the

patient is tested for genetic information that may confirm a diagnosis of an existing disease. The hospital could establish a private situation for predictive testing so that the patient's records were not incorporated into the regular medical file. These records would be computerized but not accessible to all of those have access to the general medical record. This is a way of adjusting the access conditions to increase the level of privacy for the patient. Of course, the patient should be told what will happen to the test information. The patient might prefer to have the information included in her medical record.

One of the principles that should guide the establishment of policies for privacy is the Publicity Principle.

The Publicity Principle: Rules and conditions governing private situations should be clear and known to the persons affected by them.

In effect, we can plan to protect our privacy better if we know where the zones of privacy are and under what conditions and to whom information will be given. If an employer can read one's e-mail, then applying for a new job is done more discreetly by not using e-mail. The publicity principle encourages informed consent and rational decision making.

Once policies are established and known circumstances sometimes arise which invite us to breach the policy. Obviously, policy breaches should be avoided as much as possible as they undermine confidence in the policy. However, sometimes truly exceptional circumstance occur. Suppose that after some predictive genetic tests are run, new information about the consequences of the test results are uncovered. New scientific evidence in combination with the rest results show that the patient surely must have transmitted a devastating disease to her offspring but that the disease can be treated effectively if caught in time. In such circumstances it would seem that the hospital should notify not only the patient but also her adult offspring even though that was not part of the original agreement. The harm caused by the disclosure will be so much less than the harm prevented that the breach is justified.

The Justification of Exceptions Principle: A breach of a private situation is justified if and only if there is a great likelihood that the harm caused by the disclosure will be so much less than the harm prevented that an impartial person would permit a breach in this and in morally similar situations.

These exceptional circumstances should not be kept secret from future users of the policy. Hence, we need a principle for disclosure and adjustment in the policy statement itself.

The Adjustment Principle: If special circumstances justify a change in the parameters of a private situation, then the alteration should become an explicit and public part of the rules and conditions governing the private situation.

In this example those who continued to have predictive genetic testing would know what information would be released in the stated exceptional circum-stances. They would know the possible consequences of their decision to have predictive genetic testing and could plan accordingly. The control/restricted access theory can give individuals as much personal choice as possible while still being concerned about information flow beyond individual control.

Conclusion

In a computerized society information is greased. It moves like lightning and will have applications and reapplications that are impossible to imagine when initially entered into a computer. In a computerized society the concern for privacy is legitimate and well grounded. Privacy is one of our expressions of the core value of security. Individuals and societies that are not secure do not flourish and do not exist for long. It is, therefore, imperative that we create zones of privacy that allow citizens to rationally plan their lives without fear. The zones of privacy will contain private situations with different kinds and levels of access for different individuals. It is important to think of privacy in terms of a control/restricted access account, because this conception encourages informed consent as much as possible and fosters the development of practical, fine grained, and sensitive policies for protecting privacy when it is not.

CASE STUDY: MONITORING EMPLOYEE E-MAIL

Texas Health Resources is a major hospital chain in the Southwest of the United States. The company uses software than scans employee e-mail for keywords that may indicate inappropriate content such as pornography or offensive jokes. Flagged messages are investigated further by specially designated employees. Another major corporation, American Telephone and Telegraph, uses software that rejects incoming messages indicated as having offensive content. Do either of these companies violate employee privacy rights? Is it important that companies inform employees before installing such programs?

CASE STUDY: OOPS

Sometimes the postman puts mail in the wrong mailbox. It happens often enough that most people have received a neighbor's mail. Most people never purposely open someone else's mail but take it immediately to the proper box. Often enough people make mistakes with the e-mail address book and send mail to the wrong address. Perhaps your address book includes several Kenneths, and in a distracted moment you might select the wrong one. Suppose while at work you received an e-mail intended for someone else and it contained racist, sexist, or otherwise offensive jokes. Would you be violating the privacy of either the sender or intended recipient if you made the e-mail available to the company's human resources department?

7.2 E-MAIL PRIVACY Dr. Richard A. Spinello is an associate research professor in the Carroll School of Management at Boston College. He has written two books on computer ethics, *Ethical Aspects of Information Technology* and *Case Studies in Information and Computer Ethics,* and he is the coauthor of a book on knowledge management, *Corporate Instinct: Building a Knowing Enterprise for the 21st Century.* He has also written numerous articles and scholarly papers on ethics and information technology.

In this paper Spinello rejects the common viewpoint that monitoring employee e-mail is morally acceptable. Instead he contends that an individual has a *prima facie* (conditional) right to the confidentiality of his or her e-mail communications. This right must be carefully balanced with the corporation's information requirements and its "need to know." One way to achieve this balance is to insist that corporations seek only *relevant* knowledge about their workers using *ordinary* means of inquiry. E-mail monitoring, however, is an extraordinary method of acquiring information and, like other extraordinary methods, it is intrusive and offensive. Although some circumstances might legitimize this surveillance, in general employee communications should be free from routine monitoring because it represents such an impertinent interference in their affairs. This prohibition implies that employees do have at least a conditional right to the confidentiality of their e-mail communications. A strong presumption must be given to privacy rights in the workplace. Failure to do so manifests disrespect for the dignity and intrinsic worth of human beings that derives from their capacity for rational self-determination. Such capacity is severely curtailed when the cloak of privacy is removed.

The case study following this reading (p. 312) includes a sample e-mail policy. If you have never read an institutional e-mail policy you might want to read it before you read Spinello's selection.

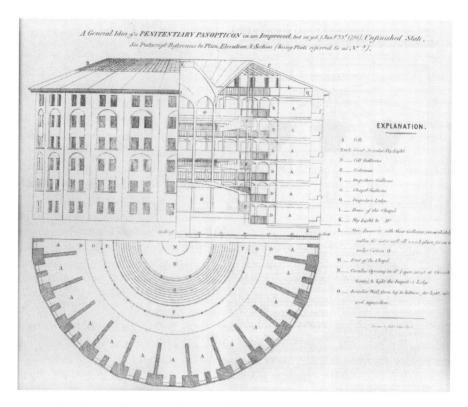

*Figure 7.1   Jeremy Bentham's drawing of the panopticon, a utopian prison.
Reprinted by permission of University College, London, from the Bentham Collection
within the archives of University College, London.*

QUESTIONS FOR STUDY AND DISCUSSION

1. The concept of the panopticon, a utopian prison, was reintroduced into contemporary philosophical discussions by Michel Foucault, but it was first formulated by the father of utilitarianism, Jeremy Bentham. One of Bentham's drawings appears in Figure 7.1. Consult Foucault's analysis of the Panopticon in his book *Discipline and Punish: The Birth of the Prison.*[12] How Does Bentham's architectural design serve the essential functions of a prison?

2. Why does Spinello consider privacy essential to autonomy?

3. What is the relevance of employer-employee reciprocity to privacy rights?

4. What does Kant mean by a categorical imperative? Do you agree that privacy is essential to human dignity? Why?

5. Does Fromm's view that *can* has come to imply *ought* amount to saying that morally problematic technology will be accepted and rationalized as long as its application is useful to business and government?

ELECTRONIC MAIL AND PANOPTIC POWER IN THE WORKPLACE[13]

RICHARD A. SPINELLO

Introduction

It is not uncommon these days to find articles and books with ominous titles such as "The End of Privacy," "What Happened to Privacy?" or *Privacy for Sale*. The problem of privacy erosion is a pervasive one but it is becoming especially acute in the workplace. Thanks to computerized surveillance, workers' behavior is more transparent than ever before, and this has allowed employers to markedly increase their oversight and control.

One striking example of how the omniscient organization operates is the commonly accepted practice of reading employee e-mail or monitoring voice mail systems. A growing number of companies such as Pillsbury, UPS, and Intel Corporation have adopted policies that allow them to routinely inspect the e-mail messages of their employees. Some of these companies let their employees know quite explicitly about this practice, while others are more covert.

Kmart Corporation, for example, has adopted a policy that allows its managers to review all e-mail messages, and every employee is informed of this policy at orientation meetings.[14] A typical policy will inform employees under what circumstances their e-mail messages may be examined, and identify those in the organization who might be inspecting these messages.

Many of the companies that have embraced a formal e-mail policy seem to believe that this goes a long way to legitimizing the archiving and random inspection of e-mail messages. There is a general sentiment in the business community that as long as employees are informed of this policy it is morally permissible to inspect their e-mail.

In this paper we reject this common but misguided viewpoint. Rather, we contend that an individual has a *prima facie* right to some level of confidentiality of his or her e-mail communications that at least includes protection from systematic monitoring.

We begin our defense of this position with a cursory overview of the legal status of e-mail privacy. We will then discuss the critical importance of privacy as a condition for personal autonomy and explicate why there should be privacy rights in the workplace. Obviously this right must be carefully balanced with the corporation's information requirements and its "need to know." One way to achieve this balance is to insist that corporations seek only *relevant* knowledge about their workers using *ordinary* means of inquiry. We contend that e-mail monitoring or surveillance is an extraordinary and unnecessary method of acquiring information. To support this contention we will demonstrate that like other extraordinary methods this type of surveillance is intrusive and offensive. Although there may be circumstances where a just cause legitimizes this surveillance, we argue that in general employee communications should not be subject to routine monitoring since it represents such an impertinent interference in their affairs. This prohibition against arbitrary e-mail monitoring implies that employees have a *prima facie* or conditional right to the confidentiality of their e-mail communications.

Our underlying assumption throughout this presentation is that a strong presumption must be given to privacy rights in the workplace. Failure to do so is a manifestation of disrespect for the dignity and intrinsic worth of human beings that derives from their capacity for rational self-determination which is severely curtailed when the cloak of privacy is removed.

Legal Status of E-Mail Privacy

The Fourth Amendment of the Constitution protects written communications from "unreasonable searches and seizures." In *Katz* v. *United States* (1967) the Supreme Court reversed an earlier decision and ruled that telephone calls are included in this Fourth Amendment protection since the caller has a "reasonable expectation of privacy." Hence phones cannot be tapped without a warrant. At the present time, however, e-mail and other forms of electronic communications are not protected by the Fourth Amendment, though this could certainly change in future years.[15]

Part of the confusion and controversy about electronic mail stems from the distinctive features of this medium. E-mail has the same immediacy and transitoriness as a phone conversation, yet it has the permanence of the written word since these messages can be easily saved on the user's personal system or archived by the system administrator. This distinctiveness has led the Court to regard e-mail as a unique form of communication that does not deserve the same Fourth Amendment protection as phone calls and written documents.

Furthermore, recent court rulings have reaffirmed that employers can read with impunity electronic mail sent or received over their computer systems, even if employees are uninformed of this policy. Although a number of employee lawsuits have challenged this prerogative, we will review the salient facts of two cases that have become especially prominent. In the case of *Shoars* v. *Epson America* (1991), the e-mail administrator, Alana Shoars, maintained that she was fired after she complained that her manager, Roger Hillseth, was routinely intercepting and printing out all of the company's MCI e-mail. Shoars contended that she and her colleagues had assumed that their e-mail was private, since they were never informed that it would be monitored. She filed suit against the company claiming an invasion of privacy under section 631 of California state law. But the court ruled in favor of Epson recognizing its legal prerogative to monitor its e-mail system without any restrictions or any need to inform employees of its intentions.

In another precedent-setting case in 1996 the U.S. District Court in Pennsylvania ruled that Pillsbury Co. could fire a manager who had referred to his bosses as "backstabbing bastards" in an e-mail message. In his defense the manager claimed that he was given the explicit impression at Pillsbury that his e-mail messages were completely confidential. The judge ruled, however, that even if the company had made a promise of confidentiality, Pillsbury's actions did not "tortuously invade the plaintiff's privacy." The rationale advanced by the court was that "the company's interest in preventing inappropriate and unprofessional comments" took precedence over an employee's privacy rights.

In summary, then, electronic mail confidentiality in private networks is clearly not protected by the Fourth Amendment or any other federal laws such as the Electronic Communications Privacy Act (ECPA) which pertains only to public networks. Further, recent case law has confirmed that the employer has complete control over communications facilities such as e-mail systems. Thus, at the present time corporations have every *legal right* to monitor the e-mail of their employees even if they do not inform them of their intentions to do so.

Civil Liberties in the Workplace

The absence of any legal right to e-mail privacy does not necessarily preclude a moral right or entitlement to protection from e-mail surveillance. However, before we address whether or not there is such a right it would be instructive to put this discussion in some context and briefly review the history of civil liberties in the workplace.

Up until the 1960s there was scant attention paid to such rights. Prior to this time the dominant philosophy was known as Employment at Will (EAW): employers were free to hire, promote, or fire, at will, and if employees were unhappy with corporate personnel practices they were free to leave and look for work elsewhere. The employment relationship was a contingent one based on the agent-principal model where the employees were the agents who owed obedience and loyalty to their employer. There was no recognition of privacy rights and there were few limitations on the

employer's right to document and control the activities of its workers.

The emergence of large, hierarchically structured corporations was accompanied by the development of professional managers who often saw their function in terms of authoritarian control. Further, they were fully supported by the law which up to this point did not interfere in the "private" matters of hiring and firing workers. For example in the early 20th century a California court upheld the "arbitrary right of the employer to employ or discharge labor, with or without regard to actuating motives."[16]

This began to change in the mid- to late 1960s when public policy attention was focused on this neglected area of workplace rights. The Civil Rights Act of 1964 along with subsequent legislation made discrimination on the basis of race, sex, age, and religious belief illegal. Also, much was being written about the need to extend civil liberties to the workplace, and this prompted conscientious corporations to regard some of these rights more seriously. Business writers such as Ewing and philosophers like Werhane argued vigorously for a broad spectrum of workplace rights including privacy and the even more dubious ones such as "meaningful work."[17] As a result of all this, employee relationships became more valued as reflected in many corporate codes of conduct such as the well-known Credo of Johnson and Johnson:

> We are responsible to our employees, the men and women who work with us throughout the world.
> Everyone must be considered as an individual.
> We must respect their sense of dignity and recognize their merit.

But thanks in part to technological advancements and other pressures we seem to be entering a new era where there is a diminished respect for these basic rights. There appear to be several factors accounting for this change. Intense global competition and the exodus of American jobs to foreign countries with low labor costs has strengthened the position of many corporations while it has simultaneously weakened the bargaining leverage of once powerful unions. In our more litigious society there is also a greater threat of liability hanging over the corporate world. For example, corporations can now be held liable for negligent hiring if they fail to adequately check the background of their employees. And, of course, sophisticated surveillance technologies create the opportunity to exercise control in an unprecedented fashion. All of this has been especially perilous for rights like privacy which, as we have seen, are not well protected in the law. Thus, technology seems to be spurring a regression from the recognition and respect for workplace rights that had become more typical of many corporate environments. However, as we will argue here, a reasonable and balanced right to privacy must be sustained in spite of technology and the opportunities for surveillance which it creates.

The Importance of Privacy

In order to appreciate why employees should have some sort of privacy rights in the workplace, we must first understand the nature and importance of privacy. Privacy is not a simple concept that can be easily defined. Perhaps the most basic and inclusive definition dates back to a seminal *Harvard Law Review* article written by Samuel Warren and Louis Brandeis in 1890. They differentiated the right to privacy from other legal rights and defined it as the right to be left alone, that is, the right to some measure of solitude in one's life.

This general definition is a good starting point but it is obviously inadequate, since the "right to be left alone" is rather broad. Perhaps a more suitable but still comprehensive definition is Gavison's.[18] She defined privacy as the limitation of others' access to an individual with three key elements: secrecy, anonymity, and solitude. Anonymity refers to the protection from undesired attention; solitude is the lack of physical proximity to others; and secrecy is equivalent to confidentiality since it involves limiting knowledge about oneself. For our purposes anonymity and secrecy are especially germane for e-mail privacy.

Although philosophers in different traditions have long held that we must all have a right to privacy, they have disagreed on how this right can be grounded or justified. The most compelling approach regards the right to privacy as derived from other basic rights such as property, bodily security, and freedom. A primary moral foundation for the value of privacy is its role as a condition of freedom (or autonomy): a shield of privacy is absolutely essential if one is to freely pursue his or her projects or cultivate intimate social relationships. The lack of a proper "privacy zone" can thwart our autonomy, our basic capacity for making choices and directing our lives without outside interference.

According to Reiman, without privacy there are two ways in which our freedom can be appreciably attenuated.[19]

First, there is the risk of an extrinsic loss of freedom, since the lack of privacy often makes individuals vulnerable to having their behavior controlled by others. Sensitive information collected without one's permission and knowledge can be a potent weapon in the hands of those in positions of authority. Such information might be used to deprive individuals of certain rewards and opportunities such as job promotions or transfers or even membership in certain groups. As Gould has observed, "privacy is a protection against unwanted imposition or coercion by others and thus a protection of one's freedom of action."[20]

There is also the risk of an intrinsic loss of freedom. It is common knowledge that most people will behave differently when they are being watched or monitored by others. In these circumstances it is normal to feel more inhibited and tentative about one's activities. As Wasserstrom puts it, without privacy life is often "less spontaneous and more measured."[21]

In summary, then, without the benefit of privacy we are more subject to the manipulation and control by others and we are more inhibited and timid about the pursuit of our goals and activities. This is precisely the "panoptic effect" which most prison systems seek to achieve whereby the inmate feels that he is in a "state of conscious and permanent visibility that assures the automatic functioning of power."[22] But do we really want to establish such a demoralizing and indecent environment in our factories and offices?

Privacy in the Workplace

Even if we admit that all human beings have a basic right to privacy, does this right extend to the workplace? Indeed do employees have *any* rights in the workplace, or must they abandon their civil liberties when they cross the corporate threshold? This normative question is a highly controversial one which cannot be fully treated in this discussion. A convincing case for workplace rights has been made by many philosophers such as Werhane. Suffice it to say that without any rights in their respective workplaces, human beings would be extremely vulnerable. They would find the work environment to be an oppressive and hostile place, and in the long run this would surely undermine important economic goals such as efficiency and productivity.

Kant sums up the essence of an individual's moral obligation to others as *respect,* which entails treating the other as an end and not merely as a means. If corporations as moral agents aspire to live up to this obligation they must respect the basic human rights of their workers, though the scope and nature of those rights in the work environment can certainly be debated.

If there are workplace rights, privacy must surely be one of them, given its great importance as noted above. There are several cogent arguments supporting workplace privacy rights, but we will focus on one line of reasoning which seems especially pertinent and tenable. The argument centers on each person's fundamental right to autonomy, to make choices freely and direct one's activities. As we argued above, privacy is a critical prerequisite for the exercise of one's autonomy. Without privacy, autonomy will be consistently threatened and enervated. Moreover, autonomy is a basic aspect of one's humanity according to moral common sense and most philosophical traditions. The Kantian conception of personhood, for example, links the moral worth of persons to "the supreme value of their rational capacities for normative self-determination."[23] All normal persons have an innate capacity to determine and pursue their own conception of the "good life" and to respect that same capacity in others.

Kantian self-determination is protected in our society by the civil liberties guaranteed by our Constitution, and this protection should not be discarded in a corporate environment. Managers do not have some sort of moral immunity simply because they are interfering with the autonomy of *their* employees. Respect for the autonomy of others is a moral imperative that cannot be arbitrarily jettisoned or overridden for the sake of economic expediency. As Werhane has argued, disrespecting the right to autonomy in the workplace "is equivalent to disrespecting employees as persons."[24] And since privacy is a necessary condition of autonomous behavior, it follows that workers must have some sort of privacy rights.

Of course, this does not imply that employees have complete freedom in the workplace environment, since they are accountable to their employers for fulfilling the normal demands of their jobs. Autonomy and privacy must be circumscribed appropriately and circumspectly to help meet those demands. It does mean, however, that unless there is a *legitimate "need to know"* employers should not be gathering information about their employees that needlessly erodes their privacy and thereby threatens their basic autonomy.

The vast majority of employers would probably agree with all this, at least from a theoretical point of view. They do not deny that their workers are entitled to *some* level of privacy protection. Most employers, for example, do recognize that they should not spy on their workers at home or pry too deeply into the irrelevant details of their personal lives. Their tendency, however, is to acknowledge a narrow right to privacy, while civil libertarians would argue for a more robust right. There is also disagreement over the propriety of methods used to collect information about employees. Some corporations have employed questionable methods such as polygraph tests, psychological testing, and covert surveillance cameras to acquire data about their workers.

Given these disagreements, how do we achieve a reasonable balance between worker's privacy rights and the corporation's need for information? There seem to be at least two important guidelines that can help us to delineate the appropriate privacy zone for employees. First, employers should only gather *relevant* information about their employees. For prospective employees this will undoubtedly include job history and other important background information, while for employees already on the job it will include data related to job performance or the furtherance of corporate objectives. For instance if a bank manager is evaluating the performance of a commercial loan officer he or she must be able to assess the quality of loans that have been made, the efforts expended by the loan officer to open new accounts, expense reports associated with these activities, and so forth. Second, according to Velasquez, an employer should only utilize *ordinary* and common methods of acquiring information, that is, "the supervisory activities that are normally used to oversee employees' work."[25] Employers should not routinely use extraordinary data collection methods, which include the deployment of hidden surveillance devices, secret cameras, wiretaps, polygraph testing, and so forth. Like Velasquez, DesJardins argues that extraordinary means of data collection such as "blanket surveillance of all employees" are illegitimate because they are so intrusive and potentially harmful.[26] Hence they should not be adopted "unless the circumstances themselves are extraordinary."[27] For instance, suspicion that trade secrets were being pilfered would certainly justify the use of extraordinary measures to ensure their protection. In some cases certain extraordinary methods may also be necessary for quality control purposes. For instance, if monitoring is the only way to really determine whether customers are being serviced appropriately over the phone or through the medium of e-mail, one could make a case that an exception should be made provided of course that employees are fully informed of this policy and the reasons for it.

Beyond any doubt, monitoring and reading electronic mail in a systematic fashion is a form of surveillance and hence falls under the classification of extraordinary data collection methods. Clarke defines surveillance as the "systematic investigation or monitoring of the actions or communications of one or more persons."[28] When an employer decides to print out and scrutinize every e-mail message as in the Epson case or to routinely read an employee's incoming and outgoing electronic mail on a regular basis, we are most definitely talking about a modified version of surveillance, since the employer is engaged in systematically monitoring the communications of its employees.

Problems with E-Mail Surveillance

Even if one concedes that monitoring e-mail is a form of surveillance and is an extraordinary means of inquiry into employee activities, it may not be immediately apparent that *this* type of surveillance is really impertinent or harmful. It is instructive to consider, therefore, precisely how the extraordinary data collection method of e-mail monitoring is an intrusive invasion of one's privacy.

Clearly, when one's electronic mail messages are randomly inspected, one's privacy is violated since confidentiality (or secrecy) and anonymity are lost. Recall that these are two key elements of Gavison's definition of privacy. The information in the message is no longer confidential since it is read by a third party (a systems administrator or a manager) and the names of the sender and receiver are exposed so both lose their anonymity.[29]

But in what ways could this be officious and harmful? To begin with, many interactions in the workplace intersperse business and personal information; this often happens inadvertently when workers allude to certain aspects of their personal lives as they conduct business. It seems untenable and unrealistic to demand that workers refrain from doing this at all times. Also, employees who regularly work from 9 a.m. to 5 p.m. (and in many cases for much longer hours) often have no choice but to conduct some personal business affairs from their offices.

As a result, those companies which routinely inspect e-mail will sometimes become privy to an employee's business affairs or to sensitive details about an employee's personal life. For example, if

Manager X inspects e-mail correspondence between Joe and Marie he may discover things about Joe's personal life that could affect Joe's relationship with Manager X, including Joe's future in the firm. Perhaps in the midst of an exchange of electronic messages Joe has confided in Marie a few details about his personal affairs, since they explain why he has been tardy in completing an assignment at work. Joe's autonomy has then become potentially impaired since his future plans and aspirations in the firm may be unduly interfered with in certain ways by Manager X who has become privy to this personal information without Joe's knowledge or consent. Further the loss of *anonymity* could be consequential in some situations. For example, the correspondence between Joe and Marie might be perfectly innocuous and professional, but Marie's manager might draw an unwarranted inference from the frequency of those communications or it may be referenced out of context. This too might affect her future position in this company.

In addition, even if the communication between Joe and Marie is strictly business-related it may still contain sensitive corporate information meant only for specific individuals within the organization. Perhaps in a matrix-like organizational structure, Joe reports to Manager Y as well as Manager X and the communication with Marie involves information that pertains to Manager Y's domain but is of no concern to Manager X. If Manager X routinely inspects Joe's e-mail he is apt to gain access to this information which he shouldn't have. Here again Joe's autonomy could be compromised since Manager X may interfere directly or indirectly in Joe's activities involving Manager Y.

These fictional but realistic scenarios demonstrate why e-mail surveillance is so intrusive: exposing a person's communications (such as e-mail) for others to see clearly magnifies the risk of an extrinsic loss of freedom. Under usual circumstances, therefore, normal workplace communications should not be subject to these blanket surveillance techniques which are equivalent to a classic "fishing expedition." This prohibition on employers to refrain from this type of monitoring implies a moral, *prima facie* right to e-mail privacy. By safeguarding e-mail privacy a corporation preserves and protects an employee's autonomy or power of normative self-determination which is in jeopardy when privacy rights are infringed upon.

In summary then our basic argument supporting a right to e-mail privacy is as follows:

1. In order to balance employee privacy rights with the information needs of corporations, employers should acquire *relevant* information by *ordinary* and customary means.
2. Blanket surveillance techniques are a prime example of extraordinary means of inquiry which should not be employed unless there are tenable reasons because they are so obtrusive and harmful.
3. Monitoring employee e-mail is a form of such blanket surveillance.
4. Therefore unless there is a just cause or a genuine business necessity employers should be prohibited from using this extraordinary means of inquiry, and this implies that the employee has a *prima facie* right to some level of

e-mail privacy, which at a minimum includes a right not to be subjected to the systematic monitoring of his or her e-mail communications.

The Property Argument and Other Considerations

As a rebuttal to our essential argument corporations may contend that this type of surveillance is necessary not so much to acquire relevant information but to protect their assets, that is, in order to ensure that their computer resources, including electronic mail software, are being used exclusively for work-related matters. Doesn't the property owner have the prerogative to monitor how his or her property is being utilized in order to prevent the threat of abuse? This would appear to legitimize the use of surveillance cameras to prevent theft or the use of e-mail monitoring systems. To some extent, then, this disagreement over the propriety of e-mail monitoring can be reduced to a conflict between property rights and privacy rights. A corporation asserts that its property rights must take priority, while workers contend that their privacy rights ought to come first. How do we decide which of these conflicting claims takes precedence?

To be sure, property rights cannot be casually dismissed or ignored in the debate about e-mail privacy. Corporations must have the capacity to use reasonable means to protect their valuable resources from waste and misuse. I would submit, however, that at least when it comes to e-mail this can normally be accomplished with less intrusive methods than e-mail surveillance. When most organizations want to make sure that telephone communications are not being misused for expensive personal long distance

calls, they routinely compile and check the phone numbers called by their employees looking for patterns of abuse. A similar procedure can be done with electronic mail—it is simple enough to check the addresses to which e-mail is sent or from which it is received. This may signal the possibility of misuse without the need of reading the contents of the messages themselves. If this procedure does raise legitimate suspicions there may very well be a just cause to engage in e-mail surveillance. But the use of this extraordinary method should be the exception and not the norm. The privacy of innocent persons should not be violated based on the pretext of general suspicions of misuse, especially when there are less intrusive ways to safeguard one's assets.

One last word on this: Can it be reasonably argued that there is something distinctive about e-mail that justifies monitoring? Does e-mail abuse constitute a more serious threat to corporate security than other media? Most companies that do monitor electronic mail seem to implicitly make this assumption, since they do not listen in on their employees' phone calls or open up their interoffice mail. Why not monitor all interoffice phone calls to make sure that personal matters are not being discussed? What accounts for the different treatment? Employees use e-mail as a substitute for phone calls and interoffice mail, so why should it be singled out for special treatment?

The point is that there is nothing qualitatively different about the medium of electronic mail. The use of an e-mail system does not increase a corporation's vulnerability by making it easier for employees to indulge in excessive personal communications or to disseminate trade secrets—the phone, fax machine, and the regular mail can also be used for these same purposes. In my view, corporations would be hard pressed to substantiate the claim that their information assets are exposed to greater risk because of electronic mail.

But unlike these other forms of communication e-mail technology provides an easy means of saving and inspecting messages for many years. This is not as easy with other forms of communication in the workplace. There is no permanent record of a fax or a phone call. The opportunity, therefore, is too tempting for many managers who cannot resist using this technology for monitoring their workers. Moreover, they rationalize corporate policy to fit this opportunity. According to Fromm's perspective, this would represent an example of how a technological capability, or "can," implies an "ought," that is, how "technological development becomes the foundation of ethics."[30] Since corporations *can* efficiently monitor e-mail, they believe they have every right to do so.

Summary

In this paper we have sought to present a plausible case for a *prima facie* right to e-mail privacy. We have assumed that there should be civil liberties in the workplace and that privacy must be among them because of its significance and its role as a condition for the exercise of personal autonomy. We fully recognize that such privacy rights must be carefully balanced with the corporation's information needs and its own property rights. As a means of achieving this precarious balance we have followed the lead of many business ethicians and proposed that the employer should only

gather relevant information using ordinary means of inquiry. This precludes arbitrary blanket e-mail surveillance.

Throughout this analysis our ultimate point of reference is a conception of humanity that is well grounded in the philosophical tradition but is particularly explicit in Kant's moral philosophy. We have been at pains to insist here that privacy is indispensable for the exercise of freedom, and philosophers like Kant have demonstrated that freedom is intimately connected with our dignity as human beings. All human beings have a special dignity or intrinsic worth because they are free rational agents capable of making decisions, setting goals, pursuing projects, and guiding their ethical conduct. This capacity for rational self-determination is one basis for the respect that is due to all persons.

It follows then that the suspension or attenuation of privacy rights cannot be done arbitrarily or for insubstantial reasons, since to do so is to devalue at least indirectly the intrinsic worth of human beings. The workplace as panopticon, as a place where privacy and autonomy are routinely and even casually restricted, is an affront to basic human dignity. Instead we claim that there must be a strong presumption in favor of privacy rights in the workplace. The burden of proof is on the organization to make the case that a particular situation warrants the use of extraordinary methods of inquiry such as e-mail surveillance. If there is no just cause, if a case cannot be made that would satisfy a reasonable, objective person, then there is no justification for using these extreme methods, and the employee's *prima facie* right to e-mail privacy must be safeguarded.

CASE STUDY: A UNIVERSITY E-MAIL POLICY

The information policy reproduced below is from a university and is directed primarily at undergraduate and graduate students. It is a fairly reasonable policy that tries to balance concern for privacy, the university's educational mission, and adherence to relevant law. As you read the policy, look for recognition of the ethical values important to the various concepts of privacy discussed in this chapter. You might use the policy as the subject of an essay on how the policy could be improved or as a model in constructing a policy of your own. If you work for an institution with a different mission, read your employer's mission statement (or develop one) and replace the university's concern with education with one appropriate to your employer. Here are a few additional questions to ponder and discuss as you consider this policy statement and its adaptations:

1. James Moor urged the acceptance of three principles conducive to the establishment of computing policies that respect privacy. Does the CSU, Chico, policy satisfy these principles?
2. Does the policy treat reading of electronic communication by appropriate administrators as an exceptional act?
3. Does the policy treat user privacy as an intrinsic value or as one of highly instrumental value? Would Spinello agree that privacy is given its proper value and that users are respected as rational creatures?
4. Is e-mail sent from a user's home via a computer attached to the Chico ISP the property of the user, the recipient, or the university?
5. Look at the incident involving the download of a large video file described in exercise 1 on page 317 below. Did the administrator in that case act in accordance with the Chico policy?
6. What does the Chico policy mean by "reasonable cause for suspicion"?
7. Such policies are updated regularly. Here is the Web address for the Chico policy: http://www.csuchico.edu/computing/netpolicy.html.

POLICY ON THE USE OF COMPUTING
AND COMMUNICATIONS
TECHNOLOGY[31]

Definitions:

Computing and communications—These terms include voice, data, and video networks, switches, routers, and storage devices and any and all forms of computer-related equipment, tools, and intellectual property, including computer/communications systems, personal computers, and all forms of software, firmware, operating software, and application software which is owned by the University or is in the University's possession, custody, or control.

Electronic communications—This term refers to the use of computers and communications facilities in the communicating or posting of information or material by way of electronic mail, bulletin boards, or other such electronic tools.

Policy Scope:

This policy includes all systems/resources for both local departmental and central university wide facilities and applies only to institutional data and/or equipment.

This policy does not apply to computing equipment that is the property of faculty, staff, and students except that the use of personal equipment linked to university facilities (e.g., a personally owned microcomputer linked to the campus network) will be subject to applicable provisions. In all cases, applicable statutes and regulations that guarantee either protection or accessibility of institutional records will take precedence over this policy.

Purpose:

The purpose for computing and communications systems, services, and facilities at California State University, Chico is to support the educational and service mission of the University. This policy sets forth users' rights and responsibilities and is designed to address related access, use, and privacy issues in a way that meets the University's legal responsibilities, assures the maintenance of the campus network systems, and treats the campus community with respect. This policy assumes as a condition of use the exercise of common sense, common courtesy, and a respect for the rights and property of the University and other users.

Access:

Access to the university's computing and communications facilities and resources is a privilege granted for the purpose of educational use and legitimate university-related business to university faculty, staff, currently registered students, and to individuals or organizations outside the University who are actively involved in research, development, or other projects sponsored by a department, college, or the institution. Retired faculty and staff will be granted continued access to computing and communications facilities, but such access under certain circumstances may require modifications due to limited resources. Faculty and staff whose employment status has been terminated will not retain any form of access.

Legal Basis:

Use of the university's computing and communications facilities and resources is governed by all applicable CSU system and university policies and procedures, as well as by all applicable federal, state, and local laws and statutes. Material accessible to the CSU, Chico community through networks and material disseminated from CSU, Chico should not be restricted on the basis of its content nor because of the origin, background, or views of those contributing to its creation. University administrators, faculty, and staff should challenge any attempts to censor electronic information resources.

Privacy and Ownership (Disclaimers):

The University supports each individual's right to private communication and will take reasonable steps to ensure security of the network. However, messages on university computing resources are potentially accessible to others through normal system administration activities and to the public through public records laws. Hence, the University cannot guarantee absolute privacy of electronic communication.

The University supports each individual's right to privacy of personal files. However, in the normal course of system administration, the administrator may have to examine user files to gather information to diagnose and correct problems. Additionally, with *reasonable cause for suspicion*[32] and appropriate administrative authority, files may be examined by system personnel to determine if a user is acting in violation of the policies set forth in this document, other university policies, and state or federal statutes. The University cannot guarantee that, in all instances, copies of critical data will be retained on university systems. It is ultimately the responsibility of computer users to obtain secure, backup copies of essential files for disaster recovery.

The University will normally treat all e-mail messages, personal files, and personal data as private and confidential and will normally examine or disclose the contents only when authorized by the affected computer user(s). Requests for access to private messages/data for any other purpose than technical problem resolution will be approved by the senior Academic Affairs Officer or his/her designee, except as necessary to protect the integrity, security, and effective operation of the university's computing and communications facilities or as required by local, state, or federal law.

To protect the integrity, security, and effective operations of the university's computing and communications facilities and the users thereof against unauthorized or improper use of these facilities, the University reserves the right, without notice, to limit or restrict any individual's use of any computing and communications facility or resource and to inspect, copy, remove, or otherwise alter any data, file, or system resource which may undermine security, integrity, or the effective operation of the university's computing and communications facilities. The University disclaims responsibility for loss of data or interference with files resulting from its efforts to maintain the privacy and security of computing and communications facilities.

Caution:

Having open access to computing and communications facilities implies some risk. The University cherishes the diversity of values and perspectives endemic in an academic institution and is respectful of freedom of expression. Therefore, it does not condone censorship nor does it endorse the inspection of files other than on an exceptional basis. As a result, the University cannot protect individuals against the existence or receipt of material that may be offensive to them. Reasonable expectations of privacy are diminished once electronic communications are sent to other users or posted on public systems.

Like a written communication, an e-mail message received by an individual will be considered the prerogative of the recipient to dispose of (copy, delete, save, send to others, etc.) as he/she desires. An electronic message should be accorded care and courtesy similar to that accorded a written communication. University-purchased, -owned, or -maintained software for individual workstations and site licenses, data, and custom applications programs are the exclusive property of the University and shall be used by faculty, staff, and registered students only in the conduct of university business.

User Responsibilities and Acceptable Use:

Each faculty, staff, and student user of CSU, Chico's computer communications systems is responsible for the material that he or she chooses to send or display using the campus computing/communications resources. Acceptable use of computing and communications facilities and resources at CSU, Chico includes:

> Respect for the legal protections provided by copyright and licenses to programs and data as well as university contractual agreements.
>
> Respect for the rights of others by complying with all university policies regarding intellectual property.
>
> Using accurate identification in all electronic communications to avoid deliberately misrepresenting any user's identity. . . .

The University has subscribed to the statement on software and intellectual rights distributed by EDUCOM, the nonprofit consortium of colleges and universities committed to the use and management of information technology in higher education, and ITAA, the Information Technology Association of America, a computer software and services industry association:

> Respect for intellectual labor and creativity is vital to academic discourse and enterprise. This principle applies to work of all authors and publishers in all media. It encompasses respect for the right to acknowledgment, right to privacy, and right to determine the form, manner, and terms of publication

and distribution. Because electronic information is volatile and easily reproduced, respect for the work and personal expression of others is especially critical in computer environments. Violations of authorial integrity, including plagiarism, invasion of privacy, unauthorized access, and trade secret and copyright violations, may be grounds for sanctions against members of the academic community.

The following guidelines further pertain to the appropriate use of campus computing and network services.

1. Threats, Harassment*. Users may not use campus computing or network services to threaten, harass, defame, or otherwise interfere with the legal rights of others. (*Harassment is defined as the creation of an intimidating, hostile, or offensive working or educational environment.)

2. Respect for Privacy. Users must respect the privacy of other users. Examples of lack of respect for the privacy of others include reading their mail, accessing their files, or using their computer account or electronic mail address (except as may be required in the case of university employees for the purpose of facilitating official university business).

3. Sharing of Account. Users may not share their password with others or let others use their account (except as may be required in the case of university employees for the purpose of facilitating official university business).

4. Academic Honesty. Users must respect the intellectual property of

others and adhere to university standards of academic honesty. Examples of academic dishonesty include accessing or using the files of others without their permission, altering or destroying their files or messages, violating standard citation requirements for information accessible electronically, or using copyrighted software in violation of the copyright agreement.

5. Illegal/Incompatible Uses. Users may not use computing and network services for uses that are inconsistent, incompatible, or in conflict with state or federal law, CSU policy, or university policy.

6. System Disruption. Users must not intentionally disrupt the campus computing system or obstruct the work of other users, such as by interfering with the accounts of others, introducing or spreading viruses or other destructive programs on computers or the network, sending chain letters or blanket e-mail messages, or knowingly consuming inordinately large amounts of system resources.

7. Operational Procedures. Users must respect the University's operational procedures for computing and network services. Users are responsible for knowing and abiding by posted computer lab and network procedures. Generally, operational procedures prohibit printing multiple copies of documents on networked printers and playing games in labs when others are waiting for systems. Finally, as instructional use is paramount, users must leave a lab when it is needed by a class that has reserved the room in advance.

Colleges, departments, and other areas within the University are responsible for seeing that their communities are aware of this policy and its acceptable use provisions.

Sanctions and Disciplinary Actions:

University faculty, staff, and students who violate any of the above policy may be subject to disciplinary action following established university channels for disciplinary matters. Individuals who violate U.S. copyright law and software licensing agreements also may be subject to criminal or civil action by the copyright or license owners. Actions that are illegal or against university policy will be referred to the appropriate officials regardless of whether or not a computer was involved in their commission.

The University may track user activities and access any files or information in the course of performing normal system and network maintenance or while investigating violations of policy or statute. Anyone using CSU, Chico's resources expressly consents to such tracking and is advised if such tracking reveals possible evidence of criminal activity the University will provide the evidence to law enforcement officials. . . .

Notification:

The University will disclose this policy to new users at the time of their initial connection to the network by providing them with a copy of this document. It is the responsibility of the user to read and comply with this policy.

EXERCISES

1. Two Connecticut state employees were suspended for three weeks and incurred permanent salary reductions for accessing pornography from the Internet while on the job. The first case came to the attention of administrators when systems personnel investigated a complaint of poor system performance from a user. In looking into the performance degradation the systems administrator discovered that large video files had been downloaded. Such files tax the capacity of most computer servers. Further investigation uncovered the pornographic contents of the files. The second employee's activities came to light from a random inspection of a log of the Internet activities of all employees that is generated on a daily basis.

Does either method of monitoring activities seem morally superior to you? In other words, is the publicly announced random inspection of all Internet activities of different moral worth than inspection based only on a complaint of system degradation or some other significant job related factor? If you think a cause should exist for investigating e-mail and other Internet activities of employees, do you also think that investigation of the first employee's activity should have stopped when the cause was discovered and not extended into the contents of the downloads?[33]

2. It is increasingly common to find individuals willing to exchange personal information for free products or discounts. Even supermarkets exchange significant discounts to club members shopping with a special coded card. Internet search engines have the capacity to capture user e-mail identifications, which could be valuable data to various marketing companies. For instance, insurance companies might want information about who has recently searched a disease word. Do you think that the owners of major search engines such as Lycos, Infoseek, and AltaVista should have the legal right to sell data gathered from users of their search engines to interested third parties?

SUGGESTED READINGS:

Brandeis, Louis, and Samuel Warren. "The Right to Privacy." *Harvard Law Review* 4 (1890). Reprinted in *The Curse of Bigness,* ed. Osmond E. Fraenkel, 289–315. Port Washington, N.Y.: Kennikat Press, 1965.

Costello, Mark, et al. "The Searchable Soul: Privacy in the Age of Information Technology." *Harper's* (January 2000): 57–68.

Fried, Charles. *Right and Wrong.* Cambridge, Mass.: Harvard University Press, 1978.

Moor, James Helen. "Reason, Relativity, and Responsibility in Computer Ethics." *Computers and Society* (March 1998): 14–21.

Nissenbaum, H. "Protecting Privacy in an Information Age: The Problem of Privacy in Public." *Law and Philosophy* 17 (1998): 559–96.

Rachels, James H. "Why Is Privacy Important?" *Philosophy and Public Affairs* 4 (1975): 323–33.

Wallace, Kathleen. "Anonymity." *Ethics and Information Technology* 1 (1999): 23–35.

NOTES

INFORMATION ACCESS I: PRIVACY

1. Louis Brandeis and Samuel Warren, "The Right to Privacy," *Harvard Law Review* 4 (1890). Reprinted in *The Curse of Bigness,* ed. Osmond E. Fraenkel (Port Washington, NY: Kennikat Press, 1965), 289.
2. Ibid., 295.

PRIVACY IN THE INFORMATION AGE

3. James H. Moor, "Reason, Relativity, and Responsibility in Computer Ethics," *Computers and Society* (March 1998): 14–16.
4. Ibid., 19–20.

TOWARD A THEORY OF PRIVACY IN THE INFORMATION AGE

5. James Moor, "Toward a Theory of Privacy in the Information Age," *Computers and Society* (September 1997): 27–32. © Copyright James H. Moor 1997. Reprinted with the kind permission of the author.
6. James Rachels, "Why is Privacy Important?" *Philosophy and Public Affairs* 4 (1975): 323.
7. Deborah G. Johnson, *Computer Ethics* (Englewood Cliffs: Prentice Hall, 1994), 89.
8. "How to Invade and Protect Privacy with Computers," in *The Information Web,* ed. Carol C. Gould, (Boulder, CO: Westview Press, 1989): 61–2.
9. James Moor, "Ethics of Privacy Protection," *Library Trends* 39 (1990): 69–82.
10. Charles Culver, et. al., "Privacy," *Professional Ethics* 3 (1994): 6.
11. Charles Fried, "Privacy," in *Philosophical Dimensions of Privacy,* ed. F. D. Schoeman (New York: Cambridge University Press, 1984), 209.

E-MAIL PRIVACY

12. Michel Foucault, *Discipline and Punish: The Birth of the Prison* (New York: Vintage Books, 1979).

ELECTRONIC MAIL AND PANOPTIC POWER IN THE WORKPLACE

13. Richard A. Spinello, "Electronic Mail and Panoptic Power in the Workplace." Copyright 1998 by Richard A. Spinello. Printed with the kind permission of the author.
14. P. Samuels, "Who's Reading Your E-Mail? Maybe the Boss," *New York Times,* 12 May 1996, F11.
15. F. M. Tuerkheirmer, "The Underpinnings of Privacy Protection," *Communications of the ACM* 36 (1993): 69–73.
16. W. Shaw and V. Barry, *Moral Issues in Business* (Belmont, CA: Wadsworth, 1989), 233.
17. D. Ewing, *Do It my Way or You're Fired* (New York: Wiley, 1982); Patricia Werhane, *Persons, Rights, and Corporations* (Englewood Cliffs, NJ: Prentice Hall, 1985).
18. Ruth Gavison, "Privacy and the Limits of the Law," *Yale Law Journal* 89 (1984): 421–71.
19. J. Reiman, "Driving the Panopticon: A Philosophical Exploration of the Risks to Privacy Posed by the Highway Technology of the Future." *Santa Clara Computer and High Technology Law Journal* 1 (1995) 27–44.

20. Carol Gould, *The Information Web: Ethical and Social Implications of Computer Networking* (Boulder, CO: Westview Press, 1989), 23
21. Richard Wasserstrom, "Privacy: Some Arguments and Assumptions," *Philosophical Dimensions of Privacy* (New York: Cambridge University Press, 1984), 325.
22. Michel Foucault, *Dicipline and Punish: The Birth of the Prison* (New York: Vintage Books, 1979), 200.
23. Gerald Doppelt, "Beyond Liberalism and Communitarianism: Towards a Critical Theory of Social Justice," *Philosophy and Social Criticism* 14 (1988): 278.
24. Patricia Werhane, *Persons, Rights, and Corporations* (Englewood Cliffs, NJ: Prentice-Hall, 1985), 94.
25. M. Velasquez, *Business Ethics: Concepts and Cases*, 3rd ed., (Englewood Cliffs, NJ: Prentice Hall, 1992), 400.
26. J. DesJardins, *Contemporary Issues in Business Ethics* (Belmont, CA: Wadsworth, 1985) 226.
27. Velasquez 400.
28. R. Clarke, "Information Technology and Dataveillance," *Communications of the ACM* 31 (1988) 499.
29. Erni and Michael Loui Doss, "Ethics and the Privacy of Electronic Mail," *Information Society* 11 (1995), 223–35.
30. Erich Fromm, *The Revolution of Hope: Toward A Humanized Technology* (New York: Bantam Books, 1968), 34.

POLICY ON THE USE OF COMPUTING AND COMMUNICATIONS TECHNOLOGY

31. Executive Memorandum 97–18, (1997). Used with permission of California State University, Chico.
32. Emphasis added.
33. Reuters Wire Service, "Connecticut Raps Workers for Viewing Internet Porn," 23 December 1997.

8

INFORMATION ACCESS II:
SECRECY AND CONFIDENTIALITY

Don't ask; don't tell. . . .
WILLIAM JEFFERSON CLINTON

INTRODUCTION

If someone were to ask whether we know right from wrong, most of us would answer without the slightest hesitation that we do, and rightly so. And, when faced with a moral decision, most of us, under most normal circumstances, make up our minds what to do without recourse to a philosopher or a philosophy book. We make moral decisions "intuitively." Most of the time, this intuitive approach to moral decision making works well enough, but we can all recognize occasions when our moral intuitions seem less than reliable. For example, different people may have conflicting intuitions about what is morally right or wrong in a given situation. We may even experience conflicting intuitions in ourselves individually on some occasions. Nor do our intuitions, even when they are strong and unequivocal, help us much if we are called on to explain our judgments in any depth. These are the sorts of perplexities that give rise to philosophy. One of the major functions of ethics or moral philosophy is to provide clarification, guidance, and support to our intuitive moral judgments, for example by attempting to *define* with precision, but without oversimplification or excessive abstraction or obscurity, crucial moral terms and concepts.

Here is a good example: Every reader of this book presumably knows and uses the following three terms. Chances are you can use any of them or understand them in a sentence without looking them up:

privacy (or *private*);
secrecy (or *secret*);
confidentiality (or *confidential*)

However, you'd probably find it a surprising challenge to *define* these words in such a way as to make clear how each of these three concepts differs from and yet relates to the other two. Try it! This is philosophy.

In case you think this challenge can be easily met by simply looking the words up in a dictionary, think again. Dictionaries are useful tools, full of information both interesting and potentially relevant to philosophy, but generally speaking they leave most of the real philosophical work undone. For example, here is what the *American Heritage Dictionary of the English Language* gives as the definition of "*privacy*":

> **pri•va•cy** (pri've-se) *n., pl.* **–cies. 1.** The condition of being secluded or isolated from the view of, or from contact with, others. **2.** Concealment, secrecy.[1]

Notice that the first definition does little to clarify the status of privacy *as a right,* while the second definition simply equates privacy with secrecy, which, as we shall see shortly, proves confusing. The dictionary may be correct insofar as it reports the current usage of the terms involved, but that means only that these terms are not conventionally used with sufficient care and precision. And there some philosophical work remains to be done. Many people may find it convenient to use *privacy* and *secrecy* as (roughly) synonymous; but really they're not. Much is kept secret that is not in any sense "private." For example, a radio station might run a contest in which the lucky winner's name is kept secret until a certain date and time (when it is finally announced with great fanfare—and then the winner has 9 minutes and 35 seconds to phone in and claim the prize). Similarly, quite a few private matters are not secret. For example, the annual income of each of the authors of this book is a private matter, but no secret. These figures are known to our employers, our tax accountants, the Internal Revenue Service, various financial institutions with which we do business, and so on. So, clearly the two concepts are distinct; and one useful contribution philosophy might make would be to clarify the distinction. Now, here's the main point about philosophy and dictionaries: the kind of challenge posed by this sort of work— the work of clarifying concepts and distinctions—is more of a "figure-it-out" challenge than a "look-it-up" challenge. In this chapter we will help you figure these things out.

For a start, let us notice that all three concepts—privacy, secrecy, and confidentiality—involve controlling access to information. In other words, they each concern the "security" of information against unwelcome or unauthorized access. This point, by the way, helps explain why the three concepts might seem initially difficult to distinguish, and why in practice they tend to be muddled together. Another commonality among the three concepts is what we might call "moral relevance" or "moral weight." That is, privacy, secrecy, and confidentiality each have some moral significance or "weight" attached to them. Designating something as "private"—or as "secret," or as "confidential"—will in each case carry with it some moral implications, although not necessarily precisely the *same* moral implications. This point, by the way, suggests a way to begin to clarify the distinctions among them. In this chapter you also will gain some experience in weighing these concepts against each other in realistic situations. As a basic theoretical approach to the entire family of concepts covered in Chapters 7 through 10, we recommend thinking in terms of an ongoing struggle over access to information.

8.1 THE CONCEPT OF SECRECY The first reading in this chapter begins by working on the definition of "secrecy" and distinguishes the concept of secrecy from several closely associated concepts. Its author, Sissela Bok, is Distinguished Fellow at the Harvard Center for Population and Development Studies. She holds a B.A. and M.A. in clinical psychology from George Washington University, and a Ph.D. in philosophy from Harvard University. She has pursued a distinguished career as a pioneer in what is now known as "Applied Ethics." Her major works include *Lying: Moral Choice in Public and Private Life; Mayhem: Violence as Public Entertainment; A Strategy for Peace: Human Values and the Threat of War;* and *Secrets: On the Ethics of Concealment and Revelation,* from which the following selection was excerpted.

Bok begins by comparing and contrasting secrecy and lying. Both concern concealing or obscuring the truth. In practice secrecy and lying are often connected; people often have to lie in order to keep secrets, and secrecy is often useful or required in order to perpetuate a lie. But an important conceptual difference exists between the two. Lying is *prima facie* wrong. This means that lying always requires a "justification"—otherwise it's morally wrong. Sometimes circumstances are such that a lie is justifiable, but every case holds a negative moral presumption against lying, and some such extraordinary justifying set of considerations is required in order to overturn the presumption. Secrecy, on the other hand, is a little bit different and more difficult to categorize. Secrecy often enough involves deception, and in such cases it seems close to lying. It may be justifiable, but still it *calls for* justification. In other instances, secrecy may be closer to modesty and call for no justification beyond the simple truth that one may keep certain things to oneself because they are no one else's business and to disclose them would make one needlessly vulnerable or uncomfortable. In such cases there doesn't seem to be even a moral presumption against secrecy, perhaps even a moral presumption in favor of it. So, where lying is presumptively wrong, the most that can be said about the presumptive moral status of secrecy is that it is morally "problematic." This raises the question of how we determine what presumptions, if any, attach to different kinds of secrecy in different circumstances. Bok presents definitions of both "secrecy" and "privacy," and on this basis discusses the distinctions and relations between them. She goes on to consider differences between secrecy at the individual level of persons, at the collective level within groups, and at the larger organizational level—administrative and corporate secrecy, and how these differences may affect the moral weight that attaches to instances and practices of secrecy.

QUESTIONS FOR STUDY AND DISCUSSION

1. As we said above, designating something as "private," or as "secret," or as "confidential" in each case carries with it some moral implications, although not necessarily precisely the *same* moral implications. As you read Bok's essay, watch for helpful hints regarding the distinctive moral

implications for each of the three concepts. See how clearly you can spell out the distinctions in your own words and using examples from your own experience and imagination.

2. What is Bok's definition of "secrecy"? What does she mean when she describes her definition as a "neutral" one? What additional connotations are associated with secrecy and how do they interfere with the neutrality of our understanding of secrecy's essential nature?

3. What is Bok's definition of "privacy"? How, on this basis, does Bok relate privacy and secrecy and distinguish them from each other? Why is it important, in Bok's view, to be skeptical of the use of metaphors of privacy to describe and defend practices of large-scale governmental and corporate secrecy?

4. Bok arrives at the conclusion that we cannot begin an inquiry into the ethics of secrecy with a moral presumption either in favor of or against secrecy. What two presumptions *does* Bok begin with? Do these two presumptions apply equally to cases of secrecy at the individual level and at the collective level?

DEFINING SECRECY—SOME CRUCIAL DISTINCTIONS[2]

SISSELA BOK

Lying and secrecy intertwine and overlap. Lies are part of the arsenal used to guard and to invade secrecy; and secrecy allows lies to go undiscovered and to build up. Lying and secrecy differ, however, in one important respect. Whereas I take lying to be *prima facie* wrong, with a negative presumption against it from the outset, secrecy need not be. Whereas every lie stands in need of justification, all secrets do not. Secrecy may accompany the most innocent as well as the most lethal acts; it is needed for human survival, yet it enhances every form of abuse. The same is true of efforts to uncover or invade secrets.

A path, a riddle, a jewel, an oath—anything can be secret so long as it is kept intentionally hidden, set apart in the mind of its keeper as requiring conceal-

ment. It may be shared with no one, or confided on condition that it go no farther; at times it may be known to all but one or two from whom it is kept. To keep a secret from someone, then, is to block information about it or evidence of it from reaching that person, and to do so intentionally; to prevent him from learning it, and thus from possessing it, making use of it, or revealing it. The word "secrecy" refers to the resulting concealment. It also denotes the methods used to conceal, such as codes or disguises or camouflage, and the practices of concealment, as in trade secrecy or professional confidentiality. Accordingly I shall take concealment, or hiding, to be the defining trait of secrecy. It presupposes separation, a setting apart of the secret from the non-secret, and of keepers of a secret from those excluded. The Latin *secretum* carries this meaning of something hidden, set apart. It derives from *secernere,* which originally meant to sift apart, to separate, as with a sieve.[3] It bespeaks discernment, the ability to make distinctions, to sort out and draw lines: a capacity that underlies not only secrecy but all thinking, all intention and choice. The separation between insider and outsider is inherent in secrecy; and to think something secret is already to envisage potential conflict between what insiders conceal and outsiders want to inspect and lay bare.

Several other strands have joined with this defining trait to form our concept of secrecy. Although they are not always present in every secret or every practice of secrecy, the concepts of sacredness, intimacy, privacy, silence, prohibition, furtiveness, and deception influence the way we think about secrecy. They intertwine and sometimes conflict, yet they come together in our experience of secrecy and give it depth.

Too exclusive an emphasis on the links between the secret and the sacred can lead one to see all secrecy as inherently valuable. And those who think primarily of the links between secrecy and privacy or intimacy, and of secrets as personal confidences, have regarded them as something one has a duty to conceal. Negative views of secrecy are even more common. Why should you conceal something, many ask, if you are not afraid to have it known? The aspects of secrecy that have to do with stealth and furtiveness, lying and denial, predominate in such a view. We must retain a neutral definition of secrecy, rather than one that assumes from the outset that secrets are guilty or threatening, or on the

contrary, awesome and worthy of respect. A degree of concealment or openness accompanies all that human beings do or say. We must determine what is and is not discreditable by examining particular practices of secrecy, rather than by assuming an initial evaluative stance.

It is equally important to keep the distinction between secrecy and privacy from being engulfed at the definitional stage.[4] The two are closely linked, and their relationship is central. In order to maintain the distinction, however, it is important first to ask how they are related and wherein they differ. Having defined secrecy as intentional concealment, I obviously cannot take it as identical with privacy. I shall define privacy as the condition of being protected from unwanted access by others—either physical access, attention, or access to personal information. Claims to privacy are claims to control access to what one takes to be one's personal domain.

Privacy and secrecy overlap whenever the efforts at such control rely on hiding. But privacy need not hide; and secrecy hides far more than what is private. A private garden need not be a secret garden; a private life is rarely a secret life. Conversely, secret diplomacy rarely concerns what is private, any more than do arrangements for a surprise party or for choosing prize winners.[5]

Why then are privacy and secrecy so often equated? In part, this is so because privacy is such a central part of what secrecy protects that it can easily be seen as the whole. People claim privacy for differing amounts of what they are and do and own; if need be, they seek the added protection of secrecy. In each case, their purpose is to become less vulnerable, more in control. When do secrecy and privacy most clearly overlap? They do so most immediately in the private lives of individuals, where secrecy guards against unwanted access by others—against their coming too near, learning too much, observing too closely. Secrecy guards, then, the central aspects of identity, and if necessary, also plans and property. It serves as an additional shield in case the protection of privacy should fail or be broken down. Thus you may assume that no one will read your diary; but you can also hide it, or write it in code, as did William Blake, or lock it up. Secret codes, bank accounts, and retreats, secret thoughts never voiced aloud, personal objects hidden against intruders: all testify to the felt need for additional protection.

Similarly, groups can create a joint space within which they keep secrets, surrounded by an aura of mystery. Perhaps the most complete overlap of privacy and secrecy in groups is that exemplified in certain secret societies. The members of some of these societies undergo such experiences that their own sense of privacy blends with an enlarged private space of the group. The societies then have identities and boundaries of their own. They come into being like living organisms, vulnerable; they undergo growth and transformation, and eventually pass away.

It is harder to say whether privacy and secrecy overlap in practices of large-scale collective secrecy, such as trade or military secrecy. Claims of privacy are often made for such practices, and the metaphors of personal space are stretched to apply to them. To be sure, such practices are automatically private in one sense so long as they are not public. But the use of the language of privacy, with its metaphors of personal space, spheres, sanctuaries, and boundaries, to personalize collective enterprises should not go unchallenged. Such usage can be sentimental, and distort our understanding of the role of these enterprises.

The obsessive, conflict-ridden invocation of privacy in Western society has increased the occasions for such expanded uses of the metaphors of privacy; so has the corresponding formalization of the professional practices of secrecy and openness.[6] At times the shield of privacy is held up to protect abuses, such as corporate tax fraud or legislative corruption, that are in no manner personal.

While secrecy often guards what is private, therefore, it need not be so, and it has many uses outside the private sphere. To see all secrecy as privacy is as limiting as to assume that it is invariably deceptive or that it conceals primarily what is discreditable. We must retain the definition of secrecy as intentional concealment, and resist the pressure to force the concept into a narrower definitional mold by insisting that privacy, deceit, or shame always accompanies it. But at the same time we must strive to keep in mind these aspects of our underlying experience of secrecy, along with the others—the sacred, the silent, the forbidden, and the stealthy.

Secrecy is as indispensable to human beings as fire, and as greatly feared. Both enhance and protect life, yet both can stifle, lay waste, spread out of all control. Both may be used to guard intimacy or to invade it, to nurture or to consume. And each can be turned against itself; barriers of secrecy are set up to guard against secret plots and surreptitious prying, just as fire is used to fight fire.

Conflicts over secrecy—between state and citizen, or parent and child, or in journalism or business or law—are conflicts over power: the power that comes through controlling the flow of information. To be able to hold back some information about oneself or to channel it and thus influence how one is seen by others gives power; so does the capacity to penetrate similar defenses and strategies when used by others. To have no capacity for secrecy is to be out of control over how others see one; it leaves one open to coercion. To have no insight into what others conceal is to lack power as well.

In seeking some control over secrecy and openness, and the power it makes possible, human beings attempt to guard and to promote not only their autonomy but ultimately their sanity and survival itself. The claims in defense of this control, however, are not always articulated. Some take them to be so self-evident as to need no articulation; others subsume them under more general arguments about liberty or privacy. But it is important for the purposes of considering the ethics of secrecy to set forth these claims. The claims in defense of some control over secrecy and openness invoke four different, though in practice inseparable, elements of human autonomy: identity, plans, action, and property. They concern protection of what we are, what we intend, what we do, and what we own. Some capacity for keeping secrets and for choosing when to reveal them, and some access to the underlying experience of secrecy and depth, are indispensable for an enduring sense of identity, for the ability to plan and to act, and for essential belongings. With no control over secrecy and openness, human beings could not remain either sane or free.

Against every claim to secrecy stands, however, the awareness of its dangers. Secrecy can harm those who make use of it in several ways. It can debilitate judgment, first of all, whenever it shuts out criticism and feedback. The danger of secrecy goes far beyond risks to those who keep secrets. Because it bypasses inspection and eludes interference, secrecy is central to the planning of every form of injury to human beings. It cloaks the execution of these plans and wipes out all traces afterward. It enters into all prying and intrusion that cannot be carried out openly. While not all that is secret is meant to deceive—as jury deliberations, for instance are not—all deceit does rely on keeping something secret. And while not all secrets are discreditable, all that is discreditable and all wrongdoing seek out secrecy (unless they can be carried out openly without interference).

Given both the legitimacy of some control over secrecy and openness, and the dangers this control carries for all involved, there can be no presumption either for or against secrecy in general. Secrecy differs in this respect from lying, promise breaking, violence, and other practices for which the burden of proof rests on those who would defend them. Conversely, secrecy differs from truthfulness, friendship, and other practices carrying a favorable presumption. The resulting challenge for ethical inquiry into the aims and methods of secrecy is great. Not only must we reject definitions of secrecy that invite approval or disapproval; we cannot even begin with a moral presumption in either direction. This is not to say, however, that there can be none for particular practices, nor that these practices are usually morally neutral.

I shall rely on two presumptions that flow from the needs and dangers of secrecy that I have set forth. The first is one of *equality*. Whatever control over secrecy and openness we conclude is legitimate for some individuals should, in the absence of special considerations, be legitimate for all. My second presumption is in favor of *partial individual control* over the degree of secrecy or openness about personal matters—those most indisputably in the private realm. Without a premise supporting a measure of individual control over personal matters, it would be impossible to preserve the indispensable respect for identity, plans, action, and belongings that all of us need and should legitimately be able to claim. Such individual control should extend, moreover, to what people choose to share with one another about themselves—in families, for example, or with friends and colleagues. Without the intimacy that such sharing makes possible, human relationships would be impossible. At the same time, however, it is important to avoid any presumption in favor of *full* control over such matters for individuals. Such full control is not necessary for the needs that I have discussed, and would aggravate the dangers. It would force us to disregard the legitimate claims of those persons who might be injured, betrayed, or ignored as a result of secrets inappropriately kept or revealed.

CASE STUDY: WHISTLEBLOWING: THE PENTAGON PAPERS

The term "whistleblower" is a relatively recent coinage referring to those who expose secret information from inside organizations within which they work. A whistleblower typically wants to call outside attention to—and thereby halt or cause some change in—policies or practices she opposes. The whistleblower's opposition to the policy or practice she wishes to expose may be more or less principled, more or less public-spirited, more or less foolhardy. The whistleblower may be motivated by a genuine concern to expose corruption or culpable negligence, or by vengeance or paranoia. However, generally speaking, because the whistleblower elects to act outside of the "channels of communication" provided within the organization, she places herself at considerable risk of retaliation from within the authoritative structure in which she works. By the same token, the whistleblower undertakes an inherent moral risk. Having taken up a position within an organization, the whistleblower assumes certain obligations to that organization and to those working within it. As Bok describes it,

> The whistleblower hopes to stop the game, but since he is neither referee nor coach, and since he blows the whistle on his own team, his act is seen as a violation of loyalty.[7]

Over recent decades numerous heroic cases of whistleblowing have occurred, some quite well known, even dramatized on film: for example, Karen Silkwood's martyred attempt to expose unsafe working conditions and environmental hazards in the nuclear power industry; and Dr. Jeffrey Wigand's *exposé* of the tobacco industry. Others have been rather more disgraceful betrayals of institutional and personal loyalty (think of Linda Tripp). Thus the risks—practical, prudential, and moral—of blowing the whistle must be carefully assessed both by the whistleblower and by those whose attention is called to some "scandal" by means of whistleblowing.

Let us examine a short synopsis of one of the most important and famous cases of whistleblowing in United States history: The Pentagon Papers Case.[8] As you read through the following chronology of events, take note of the practical, prudential, and moral risks faced by those involved, especially by the whistleblower, Daniel Ellsberg. Discuss with your classmates the wisdom and propriety of Ellsberg's course of action.

By June of 1967 considerable controversy and division of opinion had already arisen both inside and outside the government over the Vietnam War. United States Secretary of Defense Robert S. McNamara commissioned an extensive historical review of the government's Vietnam policy-making processes. The result was a forty-seven volume top-secret document, *United States–Vietnam Relations 1945–1967,* more popularly known as "the Pentagon Papers."

Dr. Morton S. Halperin, a former Harvard University professor then serving as deputy assistant secretary of defense, was placed in charge of the project. Assisting him was a task force headed by Dr. Leslie Gelb, also a faculty member at Harvard and Wesleyan Universities, but then working in the Defense Department. A team was assembled to write the narrative that included military officers on active duty, as well as researchers and scholars attached to various academic and governmental institutions and agencies. Several participants were drawn from the Rand Corporation, a privately owned think tank originally working primarily for the Air Force. Among the Rand Corporation personnel was Dr. Daniel Ellsberg, a former Marine Corps officer who had also held high level appointments in both the Department of Defense and the State Department. In 1969 the Rand Corporation commissioned Ellsberg to produce a study on the "lessons of Vietnam" and for this purpose obtained authorization for Ellsberg to have access to and to read the "top secret" *United States–Vietnam Relations 1945–1967.*

When Ellsberg had read the documents he concluded that they recorded a history of duplicity by officials in the executive branch of the government and that it was in the best interest of the United States that the Congress and the public be informed of this history. He undertook to present the material to Senator J. William Fulbright, then chairman of the Senate Foreign Relations Committee. Apparently reluctant to make the materials public without Defense Department authorization, Fulbright requested that the full forty-seven volume report be made available to him. These requests were rejected. In effect, the Defense Department invoked a notion of "executive privilege," declining to reveal classified documents to the Congress for purposes presumably of Congressional oversight.

In 1971 Ellsberg offered the documents to Senator George McGovern, one of the Senate's more outspoken critics of the Vietnam War. McGovern declined to accept them, but urged him to take them to the press. Ellsberg did make the materials available to the *New York Times*, which began publishing them in June of 1971. The *Washington Post* also began to cover the story. The executive branch of the government sought and obtained injunctions against the *New York Times* and the *Washington Post* to block the publication of the Pentagon Papers, claiming that their publication compromised national security. These injunctions were soon overturned by the Supreme Court on the grounds that they violated the First Amendment principle prohibiting "prior restraint." Two days before the Supreme Court decision, Ellsberg was indicted in federal court on charges of espionage and theft of government property. The case was eventually dismissed.[9]

EXERCISES

1. Bok makes the point that although secrecy is sometimes essential to maintaining healthy human relationships and institutions, it is also dangerous. Based on her definition and analysis of secrecy and other closely related concepts, and on the moral presumptions she makes about secrecy, construct a more detailed "Ethic of Secrecy." In particular develop guidelines and policies to guard against the danger posed by the combination of secrecy and political power. Think about the differences between individual and collective decision making and how they might affect the ethics of secrecy. What are the differences between individual and collective secret keeping and how are they liable to affect the ethics of secrecy? Under what circumstances, if any, and under what sorts of safeguards should the government or its agents be permitted to keep secrets?

2. Apply the results of your deliberations in exercise 1 to the political institutions under which you live. For example, in the United States, you might focus on the Freedom of Information Act. Does the United States' Freedom of Information Act adequately determine the level of the government's ability to "classify" information and keep secrets?

3. Compare your deliberations with Bok's. To do so, consult the book from which the present reading was excerpted. In particular, you will want to look at Chapters 8, 12, and 13; and perhaps also at Chapters 14, 16, and 17.

8.2 CRYPTOGRAPHY AND THE NATIONAL SECURITY AGENCY We turn now to a situation involving government investigative surveillance and government secrecy, and the intriguing area of cryptography. *Cryptography* refers to the art of communicating in code. The word is part of an entire family of terms including *cryptic*, which means mysterious or obscure; *encryption*, which refers to putting something into code; *decryption*, which refers to decoding; and *cryptanalysis*, which refers to the art of cracking or breaking codes. All derive from the Greek word *kryptos*, meaning "hidden or secret" and relate to a fascinating area of human interaction: secret communication.

In her analysis of secrecy, Sissela Bok pointed out how secrecy always makes a distinction between insiders (those "in the know"—with whom the information is to be shared) and outsiders (those from whom the information is kept secret). Cryptography, the art of communicating in code, is especially pertinent whenever insiders and outsiders are, or might possibly be, in each other's presence. Whenever the actual communication cannot be carried on in a "secure" environment, safe against the intrusion or observation of any outsider, there arises a need for communicative strategies that can successfully transmit messages to insiders and at the same time keep those same messages from being understood by outsiders. Abundant examples of this sort of situation arise in all areas of human interaction. In warfare, one of the most obvious examples, the military command structures on both sides must keep communications secret from the enemy, who may be expected to engage in spying. Thus the central importance of codes and code-breaking to military intelligence and counter-intelligence practices worldwide throughout history. Crime is another obvious example. Criminals obviously want to avoid being caught and punished, so they will try to keep their sensitive communications secret. Meanwhile law enforcement officers try to intercept communications among suspected criminals, and of course they try to keep their efforts at such surveillance secret as well. In baseball, to take a more innocent example, players communicate fielding, base-running, batting, and pitching strategies on the field in sign language for much the same sorts of tactical reasons. For related, though slightly different sorts of reasons, parents sometimes use secret signals and code words that children aren't meant to understand.

The digital age has produced sharpening interest in cryptography and cryptanalysis, especially in industries and institutions and among individual households and persons that have anything to do with high-speed computerized telecommunications and the Internet. The growth of the Internet and the ever-increasing digitization of information have radically altered the communications infrastructure, posing new and in some ways unprecedented threats to personal security and privacy. More and more sensitive information—telephone conversations, faxes, e-mail, fund transfers, sales and acquisitions of securities, credit card transactions, trade secrets, health records—now circulates in electronic form through "cyberspace," where it is more vulnerable than ever to interception by governments, business competitors, nosy neighbors, hackers, thieves. The more we come to rely on digital information and communications technologies in our personal lives, the more crucial it becomes that we have means and mechanisms of maintaining personal security and privacy. This is where electronic encryption is of interest.

Computers transmit information in digital form, that is, in strings of 1's and 0's. In this form the information is almost always completely unintelligible to anyone without a digital device such as a computer. When you log on to your Internet service via a modem, that strange high-pitched "snoring" noise you hear is digital information. You can't tell what the information is by listening to it, can you? Even if it were printed out it would be just a string of numbers—something like this:

11111111100100001000000001111010101010000100001000010000001000000011...

Your computer converts it back into something you can understand. *But,* and this is where the concern over security and privacy comes in, *anyone* with a suitable digital device who can tap into your stream of digital information can read and understand it, *unless* it is somehow encrypted. This, too, can be accomplished electronically.

Here is how electronic encryption works. Encryption programs scramble these strings of numbers using an algorithm or mathematical formula that can be reconverted only with the correct formula or the "key." Thus, only an authorized person with the secret key can convert a scrambled string of numbers back into its original sequential order. The "strength" of an encryption program—that is, the level of security it provides against interception and conversion by unauthorized recipients—depends basically on the length (measured in bits) of the formula or key needed to decrypt the data. The longer the key, the stronger the encryption. For example, a 56-bit key is considered weak because computers can scroll through a vast number of formulae at incredibly high speed, and so it might take only a matter of minutes for an experienced hacker to identify the key. On the other hand, because the number of possible combinations increases exponentially with length, a 128-bit key might take the same hacker with the same technology a lifetime to break. So strengthening encryption is technically a simple matter of elongating the formulae ahead of the speed curve of computer-processing technology.

The problems surrounding electronic encryption are therefore neither technical nor technological. Rather they are policy problems with crucial ethical dimensions. Debate over electronic encryption has become one of the high-tech hot-button issues in Washington as well as other world capitols, where the main opposition to the development and dissemination of encryption technology has come from intelligence and law enforcement institutions. Their concern has been that the same data-scrambling technology that allows us to send credit card information over the Internet without worry also makes it harder for authorities to foil terrorist plots and catch cyber-criminals.

The conflicts between considerations of personal security, personal privacy, and other civil liberties on the one hand and on the other the capability of authorities to enforce national security and the law are not new, though they are evolving with the technology. Nearly a century ago, with law enforcement agencies pressing for expanded authority to eavesdrop on telephone conversations, Justice Louis Brandeis drew attention to an important difference between the new telephone technology and the earlier systems of communication it superceded. Surveillance of communications over the new, more powerful technology would tend to be more indiscriminate, and harder to confine within Constitutional limits. Brandeis wrote:

> The evil incident to invasion of the privacy of the telephone is far greater than that involved in tampering with the mails. Whenever a telephone line is tapped, the privacy of the persons at both ends of the line is invaded, and all conversations between them upon any subject, and although proper, confidential, and privileged, may be overheard. Moreover, the tapping of one man's telephone line involves the tapping of the telephone of every other person whom he may call, or who may call him. As a means of espionage, writs of assistance and general warrants are but puny instruments of tyranny and oppression when compared with wire tapping.[10]

We may assume that Justice Brandeis' point remains relevant to the current debate. Similarly, however, the advent of the Internet adds further complexity to the issues. The Internet, being global, takes the issues outside of the confines of any particular nation's legislative or Constitutional ambit. This means that the issues must ultimately find resolution on an international level and must therefore appeal ultimately to "global" principles. An excellent overview of these issues in a global perspective may be found at the Web site of the Electronic Privacy Information Center (EPIC), http://www.epic.org.

Our next reading, by John Perry Barlow and originally published in *Communications of the Association for Computing Machinery* (July, 1992), explores these issues in the American political context. John Perry Barlow is a retired cattle rancher who wrote song lyrics for The Grateful Dead and co-founded the Electronic Frontier Foundation, of which he is vice chair. The Electronic Frontier Foundation is a nonprofit, nonpartisan organization working in the public interest to protect fundamental civil liberties, including privacy and freedom of expression in the arena of computers and the Internet. They are an excellent source of information on these and other related issues. Visit them at http://www.eff.org.

QUESTION FOR STUDY AND DISCUSSION

As you read "Decrypting the Puzzle Palace," keep in mind the points and principles developed by Sissela Bok in the previous reading. Make a list of Bok's relevant points and principles as they come up. For each point of contact that you notice, explain in specific detail how Bok's analysis of the ethics of secrecy applies to Barlow's discussion of the National Security Agency and Internet surveillance.

DECRYPTING THE PUZZLE PALACE[11]

JOHN PERRY BARLOW

A little sunlight is the best disinfectant.
JUSTICE LOUIS BRANDEIS

Over a year ago, in a condition of giddier innocence than I enjoy today, I wrote the following about the discovery of Cyberspace:

Imagine discovering a continent so vast that it may have no other side. Imagine a new world with more resources than all our future greed might exhaust, more opportunities than there will ever be entrepreneurs enough to exploit, and a peculiar kind of real estate which expands with development.

One less felicitous feature of this terrain which I hadn't noticed at the time was a long-encamped and immense army of occupation. This army represents interests which are difficult to define. It guards the area against unidentified enemies. It meticulously observes almost every activity undertaken there, and continuously prevents most who inhabit its domain from drawing any blinds against such observation. This army marshals at least 40,000 troops, owns the most advanced computing resources in the world, and uses funds the dispersal of which does not fall under any democratic review. Imagining this force won't require the inventive powers of a William Gibson. The American Occupation Army of Cyberspace exists. Its name is the National Security Agency [NSA].

It can be argued that this peculiar institution inhibits free trade, has damaged American competitiveness, and poses a threat to liberty anywhere people communicate with electrons. Its principal function, as my colleague John Gilmore puts it, is "wire-tapping the world." It is free to do this without a warrant from any judge. It is legally constrained from domestic surveillance, but precious few people are in a good position to watch what, how, or whom the NSA watches. Those who are tend to be temperamentally sympathetic to its objectives and methods. They like power, and power understands the importance of keeping its own secrets and learning everyone else's.

Whether it is meticulously ignoring every American byte or not, the NSA is certainly pursuing policies which will render our domestic affairs transparent to anyone who can afford big digital hardware. Such policies could have profound consequences on our liberty and privacy. More to point, the role of the NSA in the area of domestic privacy needs to be assessed in the light of other recent federal initiatives which seem aimed at permanently denying privacy to the inhabitants of Cyberspace, whether foreign or American. Finally it seems an opportune time, directly following our disorienting victory in the Cold War, to ask if the

threats from which the NSA purportedly protects Americans are as significant as the hazards the NSA's activities present.

Like most Americans I'd never given much thought to the NSA until recently. (Indeed its very existence was a secret for much of my life. Beltway types used to joke that NSA stood for "No Such Agency.") I vaguely knew that the NSA was one of the twelve or so shadowy federal spook houses erected shortly after the creation of the Iron Curtain with the purpose of stopping its advance.

The NSA originated in response to a memorandum sent by Harry Truman on October 24, 1952, to Secretary of State Dean Acheson and Defense Secretary Robert Lovatt. This memo, the very existence of which remained secret for almost 40 years, created the NSA, placed it under the authority of the Secretary of Defense, and charged it with monitoring and decoding any signal transmission relevant to the security of the United States.

Even after I started noticing the NSA, my natural immunity to paranoia combined with a belief in the incompetence of all bureaucracies continued to mute any sense of alarm. This was before I began to understand the subterranean battles raging over data encryption and the NSA's role in them. Lately, I'm less sanguine. Encryption may be the only reliable method for securing privacy in the inherently public domain of Cyberspace. I certainly trust it more than privacy protection laws. Relying on government to protect your privacy is like asking a peeping tom to install your window blinds.

In fact, we already have a strong-sounding federal law protecting our electronic privacy, the Electronic Communications Privacy Act or ECPA. But this law is not very effective in those areas where electronic eavesdropping is technically easy. This is especially true in the area of cellular phone conversations, which, under the current analog transmission standard, are easily accessible to anyone from the FBI to you.

The degree of present-day law enforcement apprehension over secure cellular encryption provides evidence of how seriously they've been taking ECPA. Law enforcement organizations are moving on a variety of fronts to see that robust electronic privacy protection systems don't become generally available to the public. Indeed, the current administration may be so determined to achieve this end they may be willing to paralyze progress in America's most promising technologies rather than yield. Push is coming to shove in two areas of communications technology: digital transmission of heretofore analog signals, and the encryption of transmitted data.

As the communications service providers move to packet switching, fiber optic transmission lines, digital wireless, ISDN, and other advanced techniques, what have been discrete channels of continuous electrical impulses, voices audible to anyone with alligator clips on the right wires, are now becoming chaotic blasts of data packets, readily intelligible only to the sender and receiver. This development effectively forecloses traditional wire-tapping techniques, even as it provides new and different opportunities for electronic surveillance. It is in the latter area where the NSA knows its stuff. A fair percentage of the digital signals dispatched on planet Earth must pass at some point through the NSA's big sieve in Fort Meade, Maryland, 12 underground acres of the heaviest hardware in the computing world. There, unless these packets are also encrypted with a particularly knotty algorithm, sorting them back into their original continuity is not very difficult.

In 1991, alarmed at a future in which it would have to sort through an endless fruit salad of encrypted bits, the FBI persuaded Senator Joseph Biden to include certain language in Senate Bill 266. The new language in the bill required electronic communications services and those who created communications devices to implement only such encryption methods as would assure government's ability to extract the plain text of any voice or data communications in which it took a legal interest. It was as if the government had responded to a technological leap in lock design by requiring all building contractors to supply it with skeleton keys to every door in America. The provision raised wide-spread concern in the computer community, which was better equipped to understand its implications than the general public. In August of last year, the Electronic Frontier Foundation, in cooperation with Computer Professionals for Social Responsibility and other industry groups, successfully lobbied to have it removed from the bill. Our celebration was restrained. We knew we hadn't seen the last of it. For one thing, the movement to digital communications does create some serious obstacles to traditional wire-tapping procedures. I fully expected that law enforcement would be back with new proposals, which I hoped might be ones we could support. But what I didn't understand then, and am only now beginning to appreciate, was the extent to which this issue had already been engaged by the NSA in the obscure area of export controls over data encryption algorithms. Encryption algorithms, despite their purely defensive characteristics, have been regarded by the government of this country as weapons of war for many years. If they are to be employed for privacy (as opposed to authentication) and they are any good at all, their export is licensed under State Department's International Traffic in Arms Regulations or ITAR.

The encryption watchdog is the NSA. It has been enforcing a policy, neither debated nor even admitted to, which holds that if a device or program contains an encryption scheme which the NSA can't break fairly easily, it will not be licensed for international sale. Aside from marveling at the silliness of trying to embargo algorithms, a practice about as pragmatic as restricting the export of wind, I didn't pay much attention to the implications of NSA encryption policies until February of this year. It was then that I learned about the deliberations of an obscure group of cellular industry representatives called the Ad Hoc Authentication Task Force, TR45.3, and of the influence which the NSA has apparently exercised over their findings. In the stately fashion characteristic of standard-setting bodies, this group has been working for several years on a standard for digital cellular transmission, authentication, and privacy protection. This standard is known by the characteristically whimsical telco moniker IS-54B.

In February they met near Giants Stadium in East Rutherford, NJ. At that meeting, they recommended, and agreed not to publish, an encryption scheme for American-made digital cellular systems which many sophisticated observers

believe to be intentionally vulnerable. It was further thought by many observers that this "dumbing down" had been done in direct cooperation with the NSA. Given the secret nature of the new algorithm, its actual merits were difficult to assess. But many cryptologists believe there is enough in the published portions of the standard to confirm that it isn't any good. One cryptographic expert, who asked not to be identified lest the NSA take reprisals against his company, said: "The voice privacy scheme, as opposed to the authentication scheme, is pitifully easy to break. It involves the generation of two 'voice privacy masks' each 260 bits long. They are generated as a by-product of the authentication algorithm and remain fixed for the duration of a call. The voice privacy masks are exclusive_ORed with each frame of data from the vocoder at the transmitter. The receiver XORs the same mask with the incoming data frame to recover the original plain text. Anyone familiar with the fundamentals of cryptanalysis can easily see how weak this scheme is." And indeed, Whitfield Diffie, co-inventor of Public Key cryptography and arguably the dean of this obscure field, told me this about the fixed masks: "Given that description of the encryption process, there is no need for the opponents to know how the masks were generated. Routine cryptanalytic operations will quickly determine the masks and remove them."

Some on the committee claimed that possible NSA refusal of export licensing had no bearing on the algorithm they chose. But their decision not to publish the entire method and expose it to cryptanalytical abuse (not to mention ANSI certification) was accompanied by the following convoluted justification:

It is the belief of the majority of the Ad Hoc Group, based on our current understanding of the export requirements, that a published algorithm would facilitate the cracking of the algorithm to the extent that its fundamental purpose is defeated or compromised.

Now this is a weird paragraph any way you parse it, but its most singular quality is the sudden, incongruous appearance of export requirements in a paragraph otherwise devoted to algorithmic integrity. In fact, this paragraph is itself code, the plain text of which goes something like this: "We're adopting this algorithm because, if we don't, the NSA will slam an export embargo on all domestically manufactured digital cellular phones."

Obviously, the cellular phone system manufacturers and providers are not going to produce one model for overseas sale and another for domestic production. Thus, a primary effect of NSA-driven efforts to deny some unnamed foreign enemy secure cellular communications is on domestic security. The wireless channels available to Americans will be cloaked in a mathematical veil so thin that, as one crypto-expert put it, "Any county sheriff with the right PC-based black box will be able to monitor your cellular conversations." When I heard him say that, it suddenly became clear to me that, whether consciously undertaken with that goal or not, the most important result of the NSA's encryption embargoes has been the future convenience of domestic law enforcement. Thanks to NSA export policies, they will be assured that, as more Americans protect their privacy with encryption, it will be of a sort easily penetrated by

authority. I find it increasingly hard to imagine this is not their real objective as well. Surely, the NSA must be aware of how ineffectual their efforts have been in keeping good encryption out of inimical military possession. An algorithm is somewhat less easily stopped at the border than, say, a nuclear reactor. As William Neukom, head of Microsoft Legal puts it, "The notion that you can control this technology is comical."

I became further persuaded that this was the case upon hearing, from a couple of sources, that the Russians have been using the possibly uncrackable (and American) RSA algorithm in their missile launch codes for the last ten years and that, for as little as five bucks, one can get a software package called Crypto II on the streets of Saint Petersburg which includes both RSA and DES encryption systems. Nevertheless, the NSA has been willing to cost American business a lot of revenue rather than allow domestic products with strong encryption into the global market. While it's impossible to set a credible figure on what that loss might add up to, it's high. Jim Bidzos, whose RSA Data Security licenses RSA, points to one major Swiss bid in which a hundred-million-dollar contract for financial computer terminals went to a European vendor after American companies were prohibited by the NSA from exporting a truly secure network.

The list of export software containing intentionally broken encryption is also long. Lotus Notes ships in two versions. Don't count on much protection from the encryption in the export version. Both Microsoft and Novell have been thwarted in their efforts to include RSA in their international networking software, despite frequent publication of the entire RSA algorithm in technical journals all over the world. With hardware, the job has been easier. NSA levied against the inclusion of a DES chip in the AS/390 series IBM mainframes in late 1990 despite the fact that, by this time, DES was in widespread use around the world, including semi-official adoption by our official enemy, the USSR. I now realize that the Soviets have not been the NSA's main concern at any time lately. Naively hoping that, with the collapse of the Evil Empire, the NSA might be out of work, I learned that, given their own vigorous crypto systems and their long use of some embargoed products, the Russians could not have been the threat from whom this forbidden knowledge was to be kept. Who has the enemy been then? I started to ask around. Cited again and again as the real object of the embargoes were Third-World countries, terrorists and . . . criminals. Criminals, most generally drug-flavored, kept coming up, and nobody seemed concerned that some of their operations might be located in areas supposedly off-limits to NSA scrutiny.

Presumably the NSA is restricted from conducting American surveillance by both the Foreign Intelligence Surveillance Act of 1978 (FISA) and a series of presidential directives, beginning with one issued by President Ford following Richard Nixon's bold misuse of the NSA, in which he explicitly directed the NSA to conduct widespread domestic surveillance of political dissidents and drug users. But whether or not FISA has actually limited the NSA's abilities to conduct domestic surveillance seemed less relevant the more I thought about it. A better question to ask was, "Who is best served by the NSA's encryption export policies?" The answer is clear: domestic law enforcement. Was this the result of some plot between NSA and, say, the Department of Justice? Not necessarily. Certainly in the case of the digital cellular standard, cultural congruity between foreign intelligence, domestic law enforcement, and what somebody referred to as "spook wannabes on the TR45.3 committee" might have a lot more to do with the its eventual flavor than any actual whisperings along the Potomac.

Unable to get anyone presently employed by the NSA to comment on this or any other matter, I approached a couple of old hands for a highly distilled sample of intelligence culture. I called Admirals Stansfield Turner and Bobby Ray Inman. Their Carter administration positions as, respectively, CIA and NSA directors, had endowed them with considerable experience in such matters. In addition, both are generally regarded to be somewhat more sensitive to the limits of democratic power than their successors. And their successors seemed unlikely to return my calls. My phone conversations with Turner and Inman were amiable enough, but they didn't ease my gathering sense that the NSA takes an active interest in areas beyond its authorized field of scrutiny. Turner started out by saying he was in no position to confirm or deny any suspicions about direct NSA–FBI cooperation on encryption. Still, he didn't think I was being irrational in raising the question. In fact, he genially encouraged me to investigate the matter further. He also said that while a *sub rosa* arrangement between the NSA and the Department of Justice to compromise domestic encryption would be "injudicious," he could think of no law, including FISA (which he helped design), which would prevent it.

Alarmingly, this gentleman who has written eloquently on the hazards of surveillance in a democracy did not seem terribly concerned that our digital shelters are being rendered permanently translucent by and to the government. He said, "A threat could develop . . . terrorism, narcotics, whatever . . . where the public would be pleased that all electronic traffic was open to decryption. You can't legislate something which forecloses the possibility of meeting that kind of emergency." Admiral Inman had even more enthusiasm for assertive governmental supervision. Although he admitted no real knowledge of the events behind the new cellular encryption standard, he wasn't disturbed to hear it might be purposely flawed. And, despite the fact that his responsibilities as NSA director had been restricted to foreign intelligence, he seemed a lot more comfortable talking about threats on the home front. "The Department of Justice," Inman began, "has a very legitimate worry. The major weapon against white collar crime has been the court-ordered wiretap. If the criminal elements go to using a high quality cipher, the principal defense against narcotics traffic is gone." This didn't sound like a guy who, were he still head of NSA, would rebuff FBI attempts to get a little help from his agency. He brushed off my concerns about the weakness of the cellular encryption standard. "If all you're seeking is personal privacy, you can get that with a very minimal amount of encipherment." Well, I wondered, Privacy from whom?

Inman seemed to regard real, virile encryption to be something rather like a Saturday Night Special. "My answer," he said, "would be legislation which would make it a criminal offense to use encrypted communication to conceal criminal activity." Wouldn't that render all encrypted traffic automatically suspect? I asked.

"Well," he said, "you could have a registry of institutions which can legally use ciphers. If you get somebody using one who isn't registered, then you go after him." You can have my encryption algorithm, I thought to myself, when you pry my cold dead fingers from its private key.

It wasn't a big sample, but it was enough to gain an appreciation of the cultural climate of the intelligence community. And these guys are the liberals. What legal efficiencies might their Republican successors be willing to employ to protect the American Way? Without the familiar presence of the Soviets, we can expect a sharp increase in over-rated bogeymen and virtual states of emergency. This is already well under way. I think we can expect our drifting and confused hard-liners to burn the Reichstag repeatedly until they have managed to extract from our induced alarm the sort of government which makes them feel safe. This process has been under way for some time. One sees it in the war on terrorism, against which pursuit "no liberty is absolute," as Admiral Turner put it. This, despite the fact that, during the last year for which I have a solid figure, 1987, only 7 Americans succumbed to terrorism.

You can also see it clearly under way in the War on Some Drugs. The Fourth Amendment to the Constitution has largely disappeared in this civil war. And among the people I spoke with, it seemed a common canon that drugs (by which one does not mean Jim Beam, Marlboros, Folger's, or Halcion) were a sufficient evil to merit the government's holding any keys it wanted.

One individual close to the committee said that at least some of the aforementioned "spook wannabes" on the committee were interested in weak cellular encryption because they considered warrants not "practical" when it came to pursuing drug dealers and other criminals using cellular phones.

In a fearful America, where the people cry for shorter chains and smaller cages, such privileges as secure personal communications are increasingly regarded as expendable luxuries. As Whitfield Diffie put it, "From the consistent way in which Americans seem to put security ahead of freedom, I fear that most would prefer that all electronic traffic was open to government decryption." In any event, while I found no proof of an NSA–FBI conspiracy to gut the American cellular phone encryption standard, it seemed clear to me that none was needed. The same results can be delivered by a cultural "auto-conspiracy" between like-minded hard-liners and cellular companies who will care about privacy only when their customers do. You don't have to be a hand-wringing libertarian like me to worry about the domestic consequences of the NSA's encryption embargoes. They are also, as stated previously, bad for business. Unless, of course, the business of America is no longer business but, as sometimes seems the case these days, crime control. As Ron Rivest (the "R" in RSA) said to me, "We have the largest information-based economy

in the world. We have lots of reasons for wanting to protect information, and weakening our encryption systems for the convenience of law enforcement doesn't serve the national interest." But by early March, it was clear that this "business-oriented" administration had made a clear choice to favor cops over commerce even if the costs to the American economy were to become extremely high.

A sense of White House seriousness in this regard could be taken from their response to the first serious effort by Congress to bring the NSA to task for its encryption embargoes. Rep. Mel Levine (D-Calif.) proposed an amendment to the Export Administration Act to transfer mass market software controls to the Commerce Department, which would relax the rules. The administration responded by saying that they would veto the entire bill if the Levine amendment remained attached to it. Even though it appeared the NSA had little to fear from Congress, the Levine amendment may have been part of what placed the agency in a bargaining mood for the first time. They entered into discussions with the Software Publishers Association who, acting primarily on behalf of Microsoft and Lotus, got them to agree "in principle" to a streamlined process for export licensing of encryption which might provide for more robust standards than previously allowed. But the negotiations between the NSA and the SPA were being conducted behind closed doors. The NSA imposed an understanding that any agreement would be set forth only in a "confidential" letter to Congress. As in the case of the digital cellular standard, this would eliminate the public scrutiny by cryptography researchers. Furthermore, some cryptographers worried that the encryption key lengths to which the SPA appeared willing to restrict its members might be too short for the sorts of brute-force decryption assaults which advances in processor technology will yield in the near future. And brute-force decryption has always been the NSA's strong suit. The impression engendered by the style of the NSA–SPA negotiations did not inspire confidence. The lack of confidence will operate to the continued advantage of foreign manufacturers in an era when more and more institutions are going to be concerned about the privacy of their digital communications. But the economic damage which the NSA–SPA agreement might cause would be minor compared to what would result from a startling new federal initiative, the Department of Justice's proposed legislation on digital telephony. If you're wondering what happened to the snooping provisions which were in Senate Bill 266, look no further. They're back—bigger and bolder than before. They are contained in a sweeping proposal by the Justice Department to the Senate Commerce Committee. It proposes legislation which would "require providers of electronic communications services and private branch exchanges to ensure that the Government's ability to lawfully intercept communications is unimpeded by the introduction of advanced digital telecommunications technology or any other telecommunications technology."

This really means what it says: before any advance in telecommunications technology can be deployed, the service providers and manufacturers must assure the cops that they can tap into it. In other words, development in digital communications technology must come to a screeching halt until the Department of Justice can be assured that it will be able to grab and examine data packets with the same facility they have long enjoyed with analog wire-tapping.

It gets worse. The initiative also provides that, if requested by the attorney general, "any Commission proceeding concerning regulations, standards, or registrations issued or to be issued under authority of this section shall be closed to the public." This essentially places the attorney general in a position to shut down any telecommunications advance without benefit of public hearing. When I first heard of the digital telephony proposal, I assumed it was a kind of bargaining chip. I couldn't imagine it was serious. But it now appears they are going to the mattresses on this one.

Taken together with NSA's continued assertion of its authority over encryption, a pattern becomes clear. The government of the United States is so determined to maintain law enforcement's traditional wire-tapping abilities in the digital age that it is willing to cripple the American economy. This may sound hyperbolic, but I believe it is not.

The greatest technological advantages this country presently enjoys are in the areas of software and telecommunications. Furthermore, thanks in large part to the Internet, much of America is already wired for bytes. This is as significant an economic edge in the Information Age as the existence of a railroad system was for England one hundred fifty years ago. If we continue to permit the NSA to cripple our software and further convey to the Department of Justice the right to stop development of the Net without public input, we are sacrificing both our economic future and our liberties. And all in the name of combating terrorism and drugs.

This has now gone far enough. I have always been inclined to view the American government as fairly benign as such creatures go. I am generally the least paranoid person I know, but there is something scary about a government which cares more about putting its nose in your business than it does about keeping that business healthy. As I write this, a new ad hoc working group on digital privacy, coordinated by the Electronic Frontier Foundation, is scrambling to meet the challenge. The group includes representatives from organizations like AT&T, the Regional Bells, IBM, Microsoft, the Electronic Mail Association, and about thirty other companies and public interest groups. Under the direction of Jerry Berman, EFF's Washington office director, and John Podesta, a capable lobbyist and privacy specialist who helped draft the ECPA, this group intends to stop the provisions in digital telephony proposal from entering the statute books. We intend to work with federal law enforcement officials to address their legitimate concerns. We don't dispute their need to conduct some electronic surveillance, but we believe this can be assured by more restrained methods than they're proposing. We are also preparing a thorough examination of the NSA's encryption export policies and looking into the constitutional implications of those policies. Rather than negotiating behind closed doors, as the SPA has been attempting to do, America's digital industries have a strong self-interest in banding together to bring the NSA's procedures and objectives into the sunlight of public discussion.

Finally, we are hoping to open a dialog with the NSA. We need to develop a better understanding of their perception of the world and its threats. Who are they guarding us against and how does encryption fit into that endeavor? Despite our opposition to their policies on encryption export, we assume that NSA operations have some merit. But we would like to be able to rationally balance the merits against the costs. The legal right to express oneself is meaningless if there is no secure medium through which that expression may travel. By the same token, the right to hold unpopular opinions is forfeited unless one can discuss those opinions with others of like mind without the government listening in. Even if you trust the current American government, as I am still inclined to, there is a kind of corrupting power in the ability to create public policy in secret while assuring that the public will have little secrecy of its own.

In its secrecy and technological might, the NSA already occupies a very powerful position. And conveying to the Department of Justice what amounts to licensing authority for all communications technology would give it a control of information distribution rarely asserted over English-speaking people since Oliver Cromwell's Star Chamber Proceedings.

Are there threats, foreign or domestic, which are sufficiently grave to merit the conveyance of such vast legal and technological might? And even if the NSA and FBI may be trusted with such power today, will they always be trustworthy? Will we be able to do anything about it if they aren't? Senator Frank Church said of NSA technology in 1975 words which are more urgent today:

That capability at any time could be turned around on the American people and no American would have any privacy left. There would be no place to hide. If this government ever became a tyranny, the technological capacity that the intelligence community has given the government could enable it to impose total tyranny. There would be no way to fight back, because the most careful effort to combine together in resistance to the government, no matter how privately it was done, is within the reach of the government to know. Such is the capacity of this technology.

Case Study: Balancing Law Enforcement and Civil Liberties

The age-old conflict between the state's ability to enforce the laws and the civil liberties of citizens is arguably beyond firm and final resolution, and is rather destined to be with us as a site of dynamic struggle for as long as people live together in large social groups. If so, perhaps the most sensible way to approach this conflict is to think up as many ways as we can of compromising between the two conflicting sets of values. With enough persistence and imagination, perhaps we can find a mechanism or a model that would allow the state's security and law enforcement services to accomplish their legitimate purposes while still preserving the individual civil liberties of citizens. It's hard to imagine a more suitable context for such "thought experimentation" than within the framework of the challenges posed by digital electronic, global, networked communications. To explore some possibilities, form a small- or medium-sized group of classmates and imagine yourselves to be a legislative committee or perhaps a special-interest group seeking to influence the legislative process.

For starters, consider the following short list of models and mechanisms already formulated and to some extent implemented and tried by various governmental authorities around the world. Evaluate each of the models. For each model draw up a list of pro- and con- considerations, using questions like these: How effective is the model as a means of facilitating the legitimate purposes of law enforcement? How damaging is the model to individual civil liberties? What alterations or variations on the model would enhance or improve it?

Legislative Prohibition of Encryption Technology. In some countries the citizens are prohibited by law from possessing firearms, and only the duly constituted authorities—the police and the military—are permitted to use them. Given that encryption technology is so serviceable to the aims of criminal conspiracies both domestic and international, the development, dissemination, possession, and or use of such technology could be made punishable by law.

Import/Export Controls. A closely related approach—somewhat less direct, but much more widely relied on by governments as a means of generally retarding the development and dissemination of strong encryption—has been to restrict international commerce in encryption technology by outlawing its exportation and/or importation (see above discussion by Barlow). These mechanisms offer governments a political advantage in that they do not directly threaten individual civil liberties. They have rather far-reaching effects, however, in reducing the general availability of strong encryption in internationally used and widely distributed common programs or program bundles (operating systems like Windows, or word processors, or e-mail systems), and in retarding the development of international encryption standards.

Key Escrow.   In this concept, promoted by the United States government, individuals and organizations could use strong encryption technology in their systems, while a third party such as a government agency or a specially authorized private organization would hold decryption keys "in escrow" and provide them to government authorities when requested.

Lawful Access.   A new approach being considered by several governments would set up mechanisms whereby encryption keys can be lawfully subpoenaed. Individuals and organizations might be compelled by law to surrender encryption keys under certain circumstances, just as they can be compelled to submit to searches.

Free Access.   Let anyone or any group who wishes to develop strong encryption technology do so. Let anyone or any group who wishes to offer strong encryption technology for sale or exchange or for free do so. Let anyone or any group who wishes to acquire or use strong encryption technology do so. Let law enforcement authorities develop other appropriate methods of investigating criminal activities and apprehending and prosecuting criminals as needed, so long as such methods do not unduly infringe on the civil liberties of individual citizens.

We recommend your group try this exercise at first using only your own combined intelligence, imagination, and information already at your disposal. After you've deliberated in this manner for a while, you might find it interesting to consult the report of the Electronic Privacy Information Center (EPIC) entitled *Cryptology 2000* at the following Internet address: http://www2.epic.org/reports/crypto2000/. Finally, when you have deliberated on *this* basis, see if you can come up with any new and innovative models or mechanisms of your own.

8.3 TRUST AND CONFIDENTIALITY IN JOURNALISM   We began this chapter with the philosophical challenge of distinguishing three closely related concepts: privacy, secrecy, and confidentiality. Suppose we say, following Bok, that "privacy" is the condition of being protected from unwanted access by others. The right to privacy, then, is the right to control access to information about oneself—and "private" refers basically to those places and to those areas of personal information to which one has a basic human right to control access. Our earlier distinction between two types of privacy rights—privacy of place, and privacy of access to information—can be reduced as follows. Privacy of access to information is basic, and privacy of place derives from it. One's private places or "domains" are the more or less precisely defined physical zones (for example, one's household, or one's office, or one's own room) within which one's claim to privacy of access to information is inherently presumed to hold. And suppose we say, following Bok, that "secrecy" is intentional concealment. Secrecy, then, is one of the means to secure privacy; and the right to privacy is one of those considerations that can justify secrecy.

What, then, is "confidentiality," and how does it relate to privacy and to secrecy? Suppose we tell you something "in confidence," or "confidentially." What this means is that we are sharing some information with you, but we do so with the understanding that you will not be sharing it with others. In effect, we are offering to disclose information and at the same time asking you to agree to keep the information secret. Confidentiality is an important adjunct to privacy, because even though, as Bok explained, privacy is essential to human well being, so is social contact. We each need our measure of privacy and solitude in order to sustain our individual identities, to form and carry out our intentions, and so on. And yet we cannot survive and flourish in complete isolation. We also need to interact and collaborate with others; and the only way to accomplish this while at the same time maintaining any measure of privacy is to take people into our "confidence," to "confide" in them. Confidentiality, then, essentially involves an obligation to keep something secret. Such obligations can arise out of an occasional informal agreement such as we just described; or out of a more formal agreement—a contract, stated or implied; or out of a professional relationship governed by an understood set of professional ethical guidelines—as in law, medicine, the clergy, and therapeutic counseling; or more generally out of a relationship of trust.

In this next selection, Stephen Klaidman and Tom Beauchamp explore issues of trust and confidentiality in the professional practice of journalism, where, of course, concealment and disclosure of information are routine crucial concerns. Stephen Klaidman is a Senior Research Fellow at the Kennedy Institute of Ethics, Georgetown University. A distinguished career journalist, he has reported from Europe, the Middle East, Latin America, and Washington, as well as many other cities in the United States for the *New York Times, Washington Post,* and *International Herald Tribune.* Tom L. Beauchamp is a professor of philosophy at Georgetown University and is Senior Research Scholar at the Kennedy Institute of Ethics. The following selection is excerpted from Chapter 6 of their 1987 book *The Virtuous Journalist.*

QUESTIONS FOR STUDY AND DISCUSSION

1. What important difference, relevant to confidentiality, exists between the typical reporter–source relationship and the typical lawyer–client relationship or the typical doctor–patient relationship? How does it affect confidentiality in journalism?
2. How does the case of the *Tribune* story about Mayor Harold Washington illustrate the above crucial difference between source confidentiality in journalism and client or patient confidentiality in law or medicine?
3. In discussing a controversial story that arose out of the coverage of Jesse Jackson's 1984 bid for the Democratic presidential nomination, the authors refer to an argument by columnist Meg Greenfield about the relationship between "off the record" statements and the *real historical record.* What is Greenfield's argument? What are the moral questions it raises? How would you resolve these moral questions?

Trust, Trustworthiness, and the Relationship between Journalists and Sources[12]

Stephen Klaidman and Tom Beauchamp

Given the importance of trust for social cooperation generally, literature on its nature is surprisingly thin.[13] We use the term here to refer to an attitude of confidence, reliance, and approval placed in persons, institutions, statements, or even objects such as computers or automobiles. Usually trust is based on the expectation that persons, institutions, and so on will act as anticipated.

Because trust is an attitude, it can exist with little actual evidence of real trustworthiness to support it. Trustworthiness, however, is a virtue, and persons can be trustworthy even if no one places trust in them. Trustworthiness is the quality or character trait of reliability. A trustworthy person or institution must deserve the confidence that underlies trust, not merely have another's trust. Trustworthiness is also closely associated with fidelity and loyalty. A trustworthy person may be given a responsibility without having to investigate his or her credentials and without undue concern about the consequences (beyond inherent risks).

Certain forms of skepticism about how persons and institutions will act are logically incompatible with trust, but it is not illogical to trust persons in some respects while remaining skeptical about them in others. Competent journalism calls for a judicious blend of skepticism and trust. Sophisticated consumers of news also understand that, because of the constraints of journalism, uncritical trust in news reports is unjustified.

Of all the relationships in journalism there is perhaps none in which trust plays a more central role than the reporter–source relationship. If reporters cannot trust sources to be candid—not only to tell the truth, albeit from the source's perspective, and not to deceive them (except on rare occasions)—the sources are virtually unusable. Similarly, if sources cannot trust reporters to accurately convey their information to the public and to keep confidences, the sources will cease to be sources.

Confidentiality is at the heart of trust in regular reporter–source relationships. But relationships of confidentiality between reporters and sources are different from those found in other professional settings such as between lawyers and clients, physicians and patients, and clergy and parishioners. In these relationships, the right of confidentiality exists to protect privacy and to encourage the openness that is required to guarantee the client, patient, or parishioner the full benefit of the professional's services. In the case of reporters and sources, by contrast, there are non-fiduciary and even adversarial elements in the relationship, with the reporter angling to learn more than the source wants to tell and the source trying to promote a particular view; and, of course, from the standpoint of the journalist, the public's interest, not the source's, should be paramount.

David Shaw, the thoughtful media reporter and critic for the *Los Angeles*

Times, has pointed out that the failure to name sources is one way the press has run afoul of the public's trust. He says, "Reporters who write stories based on statements they do not identify for their readers are, in effect, asking their readers to trust them, to assume that the reporters (and their editors) have evaluated the source's credentials and credibility. Good reporters from good newspapers figure they have earned that trust."[14] Shaw has also called attention to the sometimes mindless abuse of the privileges of confidentiality and anonymity, saying that journalists should recognize that the names of sources are often an important part of the story and essential to maintaining broad public trust. Editors such as A. M. Rosenthal of the *New York Times* and Benjamin C. Bradlee of the *Washington Post* have consistently, and properly, pressed their reporters to find ways to persuade their sources to speak "on the record" as often as possible, and *USA Today* has argued in a lead editorial that the public trust depends, in important respects, on the naming of sources.[15]

Many other editors have criticized journalists for substantially the same flaw. Gene Foreman, managing editor of the *Philadelphia Inquirer*, notes: "By the very act of taking someone else into our confidence, we strain the confidence our readers have in us. . . . A few readers may readily give us [trust], most, I fear, resent being asked. Just as our profession has matured and become more sophisticated in the last generation, so, too, has our readership. There is skepticism, even cynicism, among our readers. We invite their wrath when we keep secrets from them, when we tell them 'Trust us.' "[16] Eugene Patterson, president and editor of the *St. Petersburg Times,* adds that many

editors think a reduction in the use of unnamed sources might help "rebuild that valued trust."[17]

Despite these criticisms, we are persuaded that if reporters could not provide a limited guarantee of confidentiality, much important news would never be reported. Reporters who break the trust put in them by sources are rare, even though a clash of values may sometimes justify doing so. We will discuss such a case later, but first consider two cases involving problems of confidentiality and trustworthiness.

The case of *New York Times* reporter Myron Farber and Dr. Mario Jascalevich is now something of a classic in the literature of free press versus fair trial, but the case is also instructive about trustworthiness and confidentiality. Farber and the *Times* led authorities to reopen a legal case against Jascalevich, who was eventually accused of having murdered five patients in 1965 and 1966 by injecting them with the powerful muscle relaxant curare. The lawyer for the defense requested that the judge order Farber to turn over his files and notes, to ensure that Jascalevich received a fair trial. Farber refused, on grounds that his confidential sources would be compromised.

Farber and the *Times* argued that their duty to protect their sources and thereby the principle of confidentiality outweighed any duty they might have had to Jascalevich, to the criminal justice system, or to any specific law, and that it was their right—guaranteed by the First Amendment—to make that determination. The defense countered that not to turn the files over would deny a citizen his right to a fair trial, as guaranteed by the Sixth Amendment.[18] The underlying argument by Farber and the *Times* was that a breach of confidence in this case would undermine all reporter–source confidential relationships, which are based on trust, and thereby undermine an institution without which a free press cannot survive.

Jascalevich's indictment resulted from a series of articles written by Farber ten years after the purported murders. During the trial Judge W. J. Arnold ordered Farber's notes to be submitted for the judge's private inspection. Farber refused; he was cited for contempt and fined $2,000. Eventually Farber went to jail and the *Times* paid substantial fines. Jascalevich was acquitted, while Farber and the *Times*—both of whom had been found guilty of criminal contempt— were subsequently pardoned by Governor Brendan Byrne of New Jersey.

Is the *Times'* and Farber's claim that sources will dry up if judges are allowed to review confidential information valid? To some degree, almost certainly. But trust entails an element of risk of disclosure; if there were no risk there would be no need for trust. And there are times when a competing value overrides an obligation such as confidentiality that is based on trust. The inability to promise absolute confidentiality should not undermine trust. Rather, it should alert sources to the rules of the game. There can be no pledge of confidentiality that carries an unconditional guarantee. All a reporter can guarantee is that a promise of confidentiality will be broken only for morally overriding reasons that are extraordinarily compelling. There will be cases, especially those involving potential prosecution, in which certain sources will refuse to talk to certain reporters for fear that they will be identified. But good reporters will generally be able to offer important sources adequate protection from the risk of identification so that

a high level of trust will be maintained. Even if a few sources evaporate, journalism as we know it will survive.

Consider this case, as recounted by James D. Squires, editor of the *Chicago Tribune:*

> It all started when a friendly but not too well-intentioned political operative dropped into the eager hands of an unsuspecting *Tribune* columnist a tape recording of a meeting between Mayor Harold Washington and two minor political figures. The mayor, the source whispered, had made some unflattering and potentially explosive comments about one of his political allies, a controversial alderwoman.
>
> Instinctively, as too many reporters are apt to do, the columnist promised confidentiality to the source. And that was the second mistake. The first was accepting the tape without knowing the circumstances under which it was obtained. Unlike most states, Illinois makes the taping of anyone without their knowing a crime.[19]

Squires said that he had no difficulty in deciding how to handle the story. He called Washington to find out if he knew he was being taped; when the mayor said he did not, the editor had his lead. He included in the story the unflattering remarks about the alderwoman and also a promise by the mayor of a city job to an opponent if he dropped out of the race. But, Squires said:

> [The story] also acknowledged high and unequivocally that the tape had been deliberately leaked to the *Tribune* by the opposing political camp in hopes of embarrassing the mayor on the eve of a special aldermanic election. Failure

to include the motivation of the leaker would have misled the reader, left the story in an incomplete if not erroneous perspective desired by the leaker, and further abused the system of protecting anonymous sources.

Squires said that the principle of confidentiality of sources "remains critical to the conduct of complete and responsible reporting," and that the *Tribune*, "even in this case," did what it could to honor the reporter's commitment. But, Squires continued:

> [The] time has long since passed when the pledge of an individual reporter can bind and incapacitate a news organization to [a] point where it supersedes all other ethical considerations. Readers deserve honesty as much as sources deserve loyalty. And there is no greater editor's responsibility than the life and credibility of the newspaper.

Squires correctly sees that the competing values are loyalty to a source and the public's need for information about the source. In this case, the source provided the information for partisan purposes, not to benefit the public, so the argument for protecting that source is less compelling than for protecting, for example, a whistle-blower who acts at risk to himself or herself and in the public interest. As Squires noted, the only way the *Tribune* could fulfill its public trust was to report on the motivation of the source, an obligation that seems weightier than any obligation to protect the source's interests by obscuring or suppressing his motives. There is also little risk that a decision like the one Squires made will undermine the principle of trust between sources and

reporters, but even if it should, it is a risk worth taking.

We affirm, of course, that trust is essential for the reporter–source relationship to flourish and that every such arrangement of trust involves an implicit contract whose terms express an arrangement of cooperation and confidence. However, if the terms are violated by either party, the other party's obligations are nullified. The source may legitimately have motives beyond the provision of information to the public, but the implied contract between the reporter and the source is that the source will not grossly deceive or mislead the reporter to further political, bureaucratic, career, ideological, or other goals at the reporter's expense. Similarly, the reporter is obliged to keep confidentiality and promises, as well as to exercise sufficient care to ensure that the source's information is not misrepresented in print or on the air.

As most reporters, sources, and editors agree, if the press is to provide the public with vital information that it needs and to which it is entitled, there is no practical alternative to the existing system. Which sometimes entails not identifying sources to the public. The point is not to dispense with these "contracts" and protections, but to present them to sources and to the public for what they are, which takes us to a perplexing case where a problem of this kind turned out to be more difficult to resolve than those discussed so far.

This case involved a journalist's decision that the public's right to a particular piece of information took precedence over an understanding of confidentiality with his source. Milton Coleman, a national reporter covering politics for the *Washington Post,* had a conversation with

Jesse Jackson during the 1984 presidential campaign when Jackson was seeking the democratic nomination. During this private conversation, Jackson referred to Jews as "Hymies" and to New York as "Hymietown." Coleman later wrote that Jackson said, "'Let's talk black talk,'" which Coleman understood to mean talk "on background," or not for direct attribution. Coleman signaled Jackson to proceed. According to Coleman:

> Jackson then talked about the preoccupation of some [Jews] with Israel. He said something to the effect of the following: "That's all Hymie wants to talk about is Israel; every time you go to Hymietown, that's all they want to talk about." The conversation was not tape recorded and I did not take notes. But I am certain of the thrust of his remarks and the use of the words "Hymie" and "Hymietown." I had not heard him use them before. I made a mental note of the conversation.[20]

Coleman did not use the material in one of his stories. Instead, he turned it over to another *Post* reporter, Rick Atkinson, who was assigned to do a story about, in Coleman's words, "Jesse and the Jews."[21] This story appeared on page one of the *Post* on February 13, 1984. It was fifty-two paragraphs long, and in paragraph 37 it said that Jackson referred to Jews as "Hymies" and to New York as "Hymietown" in private conversations with reporters. The thirty-eighth paragraph contained a denial by Jackson, but Jackson subsequently acknowledged making the remarks.

The issue of immediate interest is whether Coleman was justified in breaking an implicit but nonetheless acknowledged agreement of confidentiality with

Jackson, thereby potentially shattering a relationship based on trust that was of value to the *Post* and its readers. We will not concern ourselves here with the subsequent deplorable treatment of Coleman by Jackson and Louis Farrakhan—the latter of whom allegedly threatened the reporter's life[22]—or with the fact that many blacks perceived Coleman's reporting of Jackson's remarks as breaking trust with a black brother. We are concerned, rather, with a perspective on public trust advanced on the *Post* op-ed page by Meg Greenfield, which said in effect that the real record is usually "off the record," while the so-called record the media publish and broadcast is often little more than a manipulation of the public:

> What we call the record often tends to be the precise opposite of a record. It is, rather, the artifice, the cooked-up part, the image that the politician, with our connivance, hopes to convey and generally does. The off-the-record part is where the reality and authenticity are to be found and where they are generally supposed to remain forever obscure. . . .
>
> I don't think we contribute nearly enough to making the real record available, the one people need to see if they are to make a genuine choice. Forgive me if I can't get sufficiently exercised about the ground rules under which Jesse Jackson uttered his remarks. Those remarks were *part of the actual record.* I think they also *belonged on the one we put out for public consumption.*[23]

Greenfield's proposal is similar to Squires' assertion that violating accepted guidelines regarding confidentiality "is precisely what newspaper editors and reporters should have been doing for a long time—refusing to be duped and manipulated into the kind of irresponsible journalism that has caused a lot of our credibility problems."[24]

Greenfield's argument raises profoundly important questions. What is it, after all, that the public has a need and right to know? Should a reporter enter into blanket contracts of confidentiality with presidential candidates, public officials, and public figures that allow them to manage what filters through to the public in an attempt to manipulate the public's perception? Should the trust of a source be violated if it is essential for the "actual record" to be published or broadcast? If a politician is manipulating a reporter by selectively releasing information, does the reporter have any obligation of trust? How should journalists resolve conflicts between a source's rights and the public interest?

Much more is morally at stake in these questions than trust between reporters and their sources. Coleman's dilemma concerns the public's entitlement to relevant information as much as the bounds of confidentiality and the conditions of its possibility. Greenfield says she cannot get too exercised over violating the ground rules in such cases, but she does not elaborate beyond the quotation above. One possible argument is that what Jackson said was nasty enough to justify voiding the normal duty to fulfill a commitment of confidentiality. Another is that the casual way in which these commitments are entered into represents a poor service to the public, and therefore they need not always be honored. In some circumstances we would accept both rationales. But cases of this kind are comparatively rare, and they often involve exceptions to the moral principles that sustain relationships of confidentiality and trust.

To find an acceptable balance of the values in conflict in this thorny case is unusually difficult. Jackson's anti-Semitic remarks provide a clear-cut example of the kind of information a journalist is obligated to report to the public. Nevertheless, Coleman did promise confidentiality, and it is rarely acceptable to achieve a desirable goal by the morally perilous means of breaking a promise. Coleman's justification was that Jackson was intentionally concealing revealing and relevant information and thereby manipulating the public. The question, then, is whether it is justifiable to break a promise because a political candidate has made racist remarks in your presence (in circumstances, we note, where the candidate clearly has no chance to win). Is it not the reporter's moral obligation to keep promises to honor attribution agreements with politicians, no matter what the politicians say?

Syndicated columnist Carl Rowan wrote a column that only deepened the dilemma presented to Coleman when he questioned whether any moral rule applies to this case:

> I have had senators, Supreme Court justices, top White House officials say things at my luncheon or dinner tables that, if written, would have embarrassed them terribly. The Rev. Jackson has said things to me in telephone calls that I knew were private and "off the record." But when a reporter covers a candidate for the presidency, *there is no clear rule* that says "this is reportable" or "this I shall swallow and forget."[25]

Rowan is saying, in effect, that the rules for covering a presidential campaign are different from the rules normally understood to be in effect between reporters and sources. However, in twenty-four years in daily journalism, one of the present authors never heard anyone voice such a view, in private or in public, nor do reporters conventionally act on such a premise. In most circumstances, other journalists challenge a reporter's right to break promises that stand to endanger the prospects for trust in the future. Some would also question Greenfield's argument that Jackson's remarks were "part of the actual record" and therefore provide a sufficient reason for breaking promises and damaging relationships of trust. Greenfield herself points out that much of the "actual record" is regularly concealed from the public. Even if one takes the view that reporters should exercise more discretion in granting confidentiality, that viewpoint does not justify a leap to the proposition that promises of this kind, once made, may be broken because the source has provided juicier information than expected.

There are also practical drawbacks to breaking a promise, some with moral implications. Identifying a confidential source could shut down that particular fount of information, thereby depriving the public of other important news. It might also taint the reporter in the community of sources, resulting in a reputation for the reporter and even his or her publishing or broadcasting outlet as untrustworthy. The taint could spread beyond the paper or network, turning off sources for other reporters. These are serious concerns, and they strongly support the view that a source should not be compromised by breaching confidential-

ity except with powerful justification. Coleman's commitment to Jackson, therefore, should have been judiciously balanced against the importance of the information and the strength of the public's need for that information.

The case *for* Coleman's action is as follows: Jackson's comment was outside the realm of morally acceptable political discourse, and it showed an unbecoming side of his character that it was important for readers to know. It also had an indirect bearing on his views in an important policy area. Its coarseness and general relevance tend to undermine any moral claim on its concealment that Jackson might make. Coleman knew that Jackson wanted to talk on background because it would be politically damaging if he were publicly identified with anti-Semitic language and views. The public's need to know and the nature of the information therefore provided a clear and in some respects very compelling reason for Coleman's decision to allow the information to be used.

Nonetheless, we do not find Coleman's case totally compelling. We acknowledge the force and truth of Greenfield's and Squires' observations that the press too often aids and abets public officials in their manipulation of the public, but we cannot agree with Rowan that the rules are loose and different in a presidential campaign. True, the stakes are often higher in presidential politics by comparison to other contexts, and citizens need to know more than in most situations. But, granting that premise, trust between journalists and sources remains an exceptionally important value. Should it have been treated with more respect by Coleman than it was? We admire his courage and recognize his legal right to choose the course of disclosure, and we acknowledge the immorality of Jackson's comment. But Coleman's decision still casts some doubt on his trustworthiness in reporter–source relationships, and it is difficult to estimate the consequences of the skepticism that naturally arises as a result. In the short term, the public utility was undoubtedly served by Coleman's disclosure. But public service is not always an overriding moral value, and the long-term judgment is more difficult to make.

We could persevere in this vein, but the fact is that in this particular case, we—the two authors of this essay—agree on the principles but disagree on the decision. Disagreement in cases even when there is agreement on principles will occur occasionally, because the moral machinery for balancing conflicting reasons operates with less than perfect precision. Even careful moral reflection will not always yield an outcome free of hesitancy or uncertainty.

Case Study: Confidentiality

Someone may be under an obligation to keep certain information in confidence, yet fail to do so "by accident." Is a person who unintentionally divulges confidential information guilty of a breach of trust? If you answer either yes or no, explain your answer. If you answer that it depends, answer the question "On what?"

Consider the following scenario. The receptionist ushers you into the mayor's spacious and elegantly appointed office. In addition to the large executive desk and chair you see an ensemble of comfortable chairs and couches arranged around a small coffee table. A freshly brewed pot of coffee smells warm and inviting. The receptionist pours you a cup and asks, "How do you take your coffee?" "Oh, black is perfect," you reply. Sounds of other arrivals in the reception area are heard. The receptionist leaves you saying, "The mayor is just wrapping up his weekly press conference. He will be with you shortly." Five minutes go by. You have been admiring the décor—the pictures of the mayor shaking hands with Nelson Mandela, riding in a golf cart with Tiger Woods, being kissed on the cheek by Dolly Parton—when you notice on the mayor's desk, facing away from you, a file clearly marked "Confidential." Are you tempted to look? What stops you? If you were an investigative reporter, would you look? Maybe just close enough to see what or whose name is typed on the file tab?

Case Study: The Private Lives of Public Figures

Consider the following scenario, designed for discussion in groups of five:

Last season, Fairmont College, a small undergraduate liberal arts institution, surprised the nation by making it to the Final Four (in the NCAA post-season basketball tournament) largely on the strength of the play of sophomore Jason Israel. Jason turned out for basketball tryouts as a walk-on in his freshman year, not unusual at

Fairmont, which has never really had a nationally ranked team and has no major recruitment program. During his freshman year, Jason underwent a six-inch growth spurt, and by the end of his sophomore year he had blossomed into a world-class power forward. At six-foot-nine with a three-and-one-half-foot vertical leap, Jason led his team to a 25/2 won/lost record in the regular season, upsetting seven top-twenty teams, winning a league championship, and earning an invitation to the NCAA Tournament. The team advanced to the final four before being eliminated in the first round by the Duke Blue Devils, who went on to win the national crown. With two more years of eligibility, Jason has become a national attraction. A steady stream of NBA scouts have made pilgrimages to Fairmont to watch Jason play throughout summer basketball camp, fall scrimmages, and the early season. Three major athletic shoe companies have made attractive sponsorship offers to the coach and athletic director. All is not well, though. During a routine physical Jason tested HIV positive. Though he does not yet manifest any symptoms of AIDS and poses no appreciable health risks to his teammates or other competitors, his physicians have advised him and his parents (Jason is still a minor) that, for his own safety, it is best not to compete. The family has notified the coach, the athletic director, and other officials at Fairmont of Jason's condition with the understanding that it be kept strictly confidential. An official press release stating simply that Jason Israel has been placed on indefinite injured reserve went out through the office of the vice president for public affairs, the college's chief public relations officer. Still, rumors have been circulating and one ESPN commentator has already speculated that Jason has AIDS. Local fans have written letters to the local daily newspapers inquiring whether there is any truth to this rumor. A meeting with the coach and the athletic director has been arranged. Present are the columnists from both of the major dailies in the area and the vice president for public affairs.

The following paragraphs contain descriptions of the characters (roles) of the individuals who will be attending the meeting. In groups of five students, select roles with which each student feels comfortable and conduct a half-hour discussion. After that, step out of your "roles" and meet with other members of the class to discuss pressures you felt while you were playing your roles and how you dealt with those pressures.

Basketball Coach: You are the varsity basketball coach of the Fairmont Flames. You played point guard for a mediocre Ivy League team whose best record during your four years of eligibility was 6/10. With a masters degree in history, you hoped to coach at the junior college level. Five years ago, you were offered a position as assistant coach at Fairmont. You assumed the position as head coach two years ago when the then head coach accepted a position at a larger school. At the age of 42, your coaching career suddenly advanced to national prominence when Jason Israel showed up, grew a half foot, and people began comparing him to Scottie Pippen. The basketball program at Fairmont suddenly looked like it could become a real money maker for the school. Several heavily recruited high school seniors from around the state had already signed letters of intent to enroll at Fairmont just for the chance to play on Jason's team. For a moment you had visions of becoming the next

Al McGuire. Without Jason in the lineup, the Flames are unlikely to repeat as league champions, let alone make it to the NCAA tournament, and you can forget about that shoe contract. When NBA scouts started sniffing around last year you made a special effort to consult closely with Jason and his family. You recommended an agent whom you knew personally as someone who could be trusted to work out a deal that would be in Jason's long-term best interests. You counseled him to complete his college degree before turning pro. You have developed a close and trusting relationship with Jason and his family. Indeed you regard him almost as though he were your own son.

Athletic Director: Your background is in educational administration. In college you played intramural sports (swimming and tennis). Your last administrative position was dean of student affairs. You have the authority to hire and fire the basketball coach.

Sports Columnist (male):   You played football for a small state university in Division II. You went into sports coverage when one of your teammates got picked in the third round of the NFL draft by the defending Super Bowl Champion San Francisco 49ers. You signed on with your local daily and wrote a series of in-depth behind the scenes reports from training camp and on through the preseason, covering the trials and triumphs of the local hero. You're a good sportswriter, and it was a good story, so you got noticed. Now you cover college hoops for the *San Francisco Chronicle.*

Sports Columnist (female):   You are breaking the gender barrier as the first female basketball columnist at a major market daily newspaper in your state. You publish a weekly column on college basketball in the *San Francisco Examiner.* Last year you nearly lost your professional composure, not to mention your job, when the paper cut your story on the Stanford women's team and their third national title by half to make room for a Men's Wearhouse ad.

Vice President for Public Affairs: As the chief public relations officer you report directly to the president of Fairmont College and bear primary responsibility for protecting the college's reputation as a prestigious private undergraduate liberal arts college. Your office issued the carefully worded press release about Jason's "injured reserve status." For the past week your office phones have been ringing off the hook. Not just local but national media are pursuing the story. You're concerned that the story will get out of hand if the college does not respond to the media in some way. You have called this meeting in the hope of controlling damage.

Suggested Reading:

Gross, Larry P. *Contested Closets: The Politics and Ethics of Outing.* Minneapolis: University of Minnesota Press, 1993.

NOTES

INFORMATION ACCESS II: SECRECY AND CONFIDENTIALITY

1. *American Heritage Dictionary of the English Language* (New York: American Heritage/Houghton Mifflin, 1970), 1,042.

DEFINING SECRECY—SOME CRUCIAL DISTINCTIONS

2. From *Secrets: On the Ethics of Concealment and Revelation* by Sissela Bok, Copyright © 1982 by Sissela Bok. Reprinted by permission of Pantheon Books, a division of Random House, Inc.

3. The concepts of "discernment" and "secret," however different, are closely related etymologically. Both *discerner,* from which we have "discernment," and *secerner,* from which "secret" derives, have the same meaning of separating out. "Discernment" (as well as "discretion") comes from the active form of the first; "secret," from the passive form of the second. Discerning, correspondingly, is the activity of separating out; the secret, something that has been thus set apart.

4. The word "private" comes from the Latin *privatus,* meaning withdrawn from public life, and in turn from *privare,* meaning to bereave and deprive. For a history of the word "private" in English, see Raymond Williams, *Keywords* (New York, Oxford University Press, 1976), 203–4.

5. For a discussion of the treatment of privacy in philosophy and law, see J. Roland Pennock and John W. Chapman, eds., *Privacy* (New York, Atherton Press, 1971). Those who have compared secrecy and privacy have held widely divergent views. For a searching and provocative analysis of preconceptions about privacy, see Stanley Cavell *The Claim of Reason* (New York, Oxford University Press, 1979), pt. 4.

6. In the United States the impetus for the development of a law of privacy came in an impassioned and influential article published in 1890, in which Samuel Warren and Louis Brandeis affirmed that the time had come to recognize a separate legal right to privacy: "The Right to Privacy," *Harvard Law Review* 4 (1890): 193–220. They argued that the previously separate offenses of eavesdropping, publishing private matters, breaches of confidentiality, copying private letters, and illegal search and seizure are fundamentally similar: they are all violations of the right to privacy—"the right to be let alone"—and not merely discrete offenses against trust, property, or bodily integrity. Thus were the doors opened, in the United States, to litigation claiming invasion of privacy. The authors could perhaps not have foreseen how far their principle would be carried, but the seeds of the present confusion are discernible in their basing this right on an intuitive and undeveloped view of the nature of privacy.

7. Sissela Bok, "Whistleblowing and Professional Responsibilities," in Joan C. Callahan, ed., *Ethical Issues in Professional Life* (New York: Oxford University Press, 1988), 333; see also her Chapter 14 of *Secrets.*

8. This chronology is based on Leonard B. Boudin's in "The Ellsberg Case: Citizen Disclosure" in Thomas M. Franck and Edward Weisband, eds., *Secrecy and Foreign Policy* (New York: Oxford University Press, 1974), 291–311.

9. For more on Daniel Ellsberg and the Pentagon Papers, see Daniel Ellsberg, *Papers on the War* (New York: Simon and Schuster, 1972); Peter A. French, *Conscientious Actions: the Revelation of the Pentagon Papers* (Cambridge, Mass: Schenkman, 1974); Peter Schrag,

Test of Loyalty: Daniel Ellsberg and the Rituals of Secret Government (New York: Simon and Schuster, 1974); Sanford J. Ungar, *The Papers & the Papers; an Account of the Legal and Political Battle over the Pentagon Papers,* (New York: Dutton, 1972).

CRYPTOGRAPHY AND THE NATIONAL SECURITY AGENCY

10. *Olmstead* v. *United States*, 277 U.S. 438 (1928).

DECRYPTING THE PUZZLE PALACE

11. John Perry Barlow, "Decrypting the Puzzle Palace," *Communications of the ACM* 35.7 (1992): 25–31. Copyright © by John Perry Barlow. Reprinted with the kind permission of the author.

TRUST, TRUSTWORTHINESS, AND THE RELATIONSHIP BETWEEN JOURNALISM AND SOURCES

12. From *The Virtuous Journalist* by Tom L. Beauchamp and Stephen Klaidman, copyright © 1987 by Tom L. Beauchamp and Stephen Klaidman. Used by permission of Oxford University Press.
13. But see Virginia Held, *Rights and Goods, Justifying Social Action* (New York: FreePress, 1984), 62–85; Sissela Bok, *Lying: Moral Choice in Public and Private Life* (New York: Pantheon, 1978), 17–32; Bernard Barber, *The Logic and Limits of Trust* (New Brunswick: Rutgers University Press, 1983).
14. David Shaw, *Press Watch* (New York: Macmillan, 1984), 60.
15. Ibid., 59, 63–64; editorial "News Credibility," *USA Today,* 12 April 1985, 12A.
16. Gene Foreman, "Confidential Sources: Testing the Reader's Confidence," in *Social Responsibility: Business, Journalism, Law, Medicine,* ed. Louis W. Hodges (Lexington, Va.: Washington and Lee University Press, 1984), 24.
17. Quoted in Shaw, 60.
18. See Ronald Dworkin, "The Rights of Myron Farber," *New York Review of Books,* 26 October 1978, 34–35.
19. James D. Squires, "When Confidentiality Itself Is Source of Contention," in *Journalism Ethics Report* (Sigma Delta Chi, 1985–86), 7.
20. Milton Coleman, "18 Words, Seven Weeks Later," *Washington Post,* 8 April 1984, C8. Commonly, "off the record" means not for any kind of attribution; "on deep background" refers to a general form of attribution such as "a source close to the negotiations"; and "let's talk black talk" is Jackson's way of saying to black reporters, "on background," which means the source may not be named, and the attribution may be something like "a senior State Department official."
21. Rick Atkinson, "Peace with American Jews Eludes Jackson," *Washington Post,* 13 February 1984, A1.
22. See Sam Zagoria, "Reporting on Louis Farrakhan," *Washington Post,* 2 October 1985, A24.
23. Meg Greenfield, "Must Reality Be Off the Record," *Washington Post,* 11 April 1984, A21, emphasis added.
24. Squires, 7.
25. Carl Rowan, "A Threat to a Reporter—And to All Blacks," *Washington Post,* 4 April 1984, A23.

9

INFORMATION ACCESS III: INTELLECTUAL PROPERTY

It's our music. . . .
LARS ULRICH (DRUMMER, *METALLICA*)

INTRODUCTION

Private property is a major component of free enterprise or *laissez faire* capitalism, the economic system associated with democracy. A discussion of how property rights should be applied to intellectual and cultural products might seem to assume the validity of individual property rights and exclude nondemocracies, but even societies with only the slightest tendency toward capitalism recognize some degree of individual property right. Discussions of intellectual property rights often involve claims not of individuals but of nations, societies, or ethnicities to compensation for an appropriated good. It may be unclear just who owns the last piece of cake in the refrigerator; but it belongs to someone in the family. Blues is an art form in which practitioners freely borrow from each other without bothering too much with crediting a source. Yet many blues people believe that the blues belongs primarily to African Americans and that members of other ethnic and racial groups ought not to borrow as freely from the blues. In such ways questions of intellectual property rights are as likely to involve collective as individual ownership.

One often-overlooked aspect of the right to property is that it involves more than a priority in possession and enjoyment of a good or what the good can buy. The freedom to own property also encompasses the freedom to decide what to do with the property. Recent discussion of inheritance taxes in the United States has focused on whether it is fair, or even "American," for people to inherit great wealth. One writer cited Bill Gates as an example of a wealthy person who is going to limit each of his children's inheritance to a paltry ten million dollars. But it is one thing for Bill Gates to decide to whom he leaves money and another for the government to decide how an individual should distribute property. Whatever one thinks about inheritance taxes, property rights involve both the right to own property and the right to determine how the property is transferred.

The justifying factors behind property rights are surprisingly diverse. One often-cited factor is that an owner has worked for the property, or for some other good, or money to purchase the property. In this light, inheritance might look suspect; Bill Gates's children did not work to earn becoming Gates's children. Even if they cut his lawn and rake his leaves every weekend they will never be able to earn the wealth they will inherit. The labor theory is easy enough to understand on the practical level. Those are my tomatoes because I rototilled the soil, planted the seeds, watered regularly, and picked them. But not just any work justifies ownership. Perhaps I stole the seeds and borrowed the rototiller from my neighbor's shed when she was on vacation. Likewise, burglars, drug dealers, and recording industry pirates work hard but cannot be said to morally own the profits from their labor. In fact, governmental authorities feel justified not only in destroying their products but also in confiscating other property such as houses, automobiles, and computers used in the production of these goods. So, while work may be a major justification in acquiring a right to an item of property, both the purposes of the product and the prior just acquisition to use an item of property such as the seeds and the rototiller are significant also.

Inheritance, property acquired without work, could be regarded as a gift; it is an instance of property right being transferred voluntarily by a previous owner who satisfied some other criteria sufficient for just acquisition. The beneficiary does not earn the gift. Then it would be wages and not a gift. Yet the beneficiary justly takes possession of what another has acquired without force or fraud and now freely transfers. This is just one instance of how a right to property is entwined with a right to distribute the property. Yet the arguments over just amounts of inheritance suggest an intuition that some amount is appropriate and some other amount is not. In other words, all of us might agree that Bill Gates is not depriving his children by limiting their inheritances to ten million dollars. Still, at some lower figure we would begin to think that Gates was being stingy with the children, even if he planned to give the rest of the money to HIV research. This intuition suggests a natural right to inheritance, that natural relations have a *prima facie* claim to some degree of recognition. If this is a valid intuition then at least one other path of just property transfer and acquisition exists besides the labor theory.

John Locke argued for two important constraints on private ownership. Here is the classic passage from Locke:

> Though the earth and all inferior creatures be common to all men, yet every man has a property in his own person; this nobody has any right to but himself. The labour of his body and the work of his hands we may say are properly his. Whatsoever, then, he removes out of the state that nature has provided and left it in, he hath mixed his labour with, and joined it to something which is his own, and thereby made it his property. It being by him removed from the common state nature placed it in, it hath by this labour something annexed to it that excludes the common right of other men.

For this labour being the unquestionable property of the labourer, no man but he can have a right to what that is once joined to, at least where there is enough, and as good left in common for others.[1]

One constraint responded to the recognition that some goods could not be made private without seriously disadvantaging others. Allowing one individual absolute ownership of a river, or a road as in Heinrich von Kleist's *Der Rebell-Michael Kohlhaas,* seriously affects others' ability to earn a living. In doing so, private ownership conflicts with the most important right, the right to life. Therefore, the first constraint determined that some goods must remain in the commons. Locke was convinced that Nature had been beneficently constructed so that all human beings could earn a living and provide for themselves adequately if each took from nature only as much as they could consume without waste or spoilage. This second constraint applied to goods that could be made private and required limits to consumption that respected the right of others, including future generations, to have an opportunity to work for a living. Locke wrote, "For he that leaves as much as another can make use of, does as good as take nothing at all."[2] You need not accept Locke's view of a beneficent Nature to recognize that over consumption of a good in a world of finite resources places others at a disadvantage. Discussions of intellectual property reflect a concern to reward past labor but also to give the public reasonable access to the products of labor.

Private property is, therefore, a complex social institution that recognizes an individual's contribution to society through work and creativity, provides individual incentives through rewards such as money via patents, and respects the legitimate interests of others, including future generations, in access to intellectual and cultural products. For many people, a right to private property is limited by other moral concerns. Prostitution and selling body parts are not generally considered moral uses of our bodies, even for good causes.

9.1 PROPERTY RIGHTS AND COMPUTER SOFTWARE Deborah C. Johnson is a prominent computer ethicist. The following reading is from her book *Computer Ethics,* in which Professor Johnson addresses a variety of important topics in computer ethics and ethics of technology including privacy, hacker ethics, and professional codes of conduct.

Johnson points out three forms of legal protection available to software manufacturers.[3] Copyright treats a computer program as a literary work, and copyright holders can sue suppliers of programs that bear a striking enough resemblance to their own product to suggest the strong possibility that copying has occurred. In the absence of such a resemblance the copyright holder must show that a competitor relied on the original program and made no significant innovations. Trade secrecy allows a company to keep information secret, but it is difficult to maintain trade secrecy and sell a product to the public. Firms pursue trade secrecy in two ways. One is by receiving pledges from employees not to reveal details of software or copy software for personal use. Another approach is to license a software product with conditions designed to protect the product from competitors. Johnson notes that software companies will often license products rather than sell them and require that the licensee contract with the supplier for maintenance. Finally, patent is the form of protection most desired by software manufacturers because it confers a monopoly for a minimum of seventeen years. With copyright protection a competitor might still independently develop a comparable product. Patents are hard to come by because the degree of economic protection they foster effectively eliminates competition, whereas the other two forms of protection merely make competition more difficult.

Now, it might seem puzzling why anyone would write a program and try to keep it secret. These forms of protection are designed to provide a framework that encourages invention that will benefit the public. Capitalism believes that receiving financial benefits from inventions encourages further innovations. Software developers are rewarded primarily to encourage further development by holding out the hope of additional profit in the future. This does not entirely discount the developer's work in establishing a property right; but it establishes priorities in benefit to the public. And this perspective, the utilitarian benefit of a product to society, helps us understand that the more original the product the more protection it warrants.

These are just a few concerns related to intellectual property rights. Other important questions include what can be protected and what must remain primarily in the commons.

QUESTIONS FOR STUDY AND DISCUSSION

1. What does Johnson mean by the claim that property right is not a natural right but a right created by law?
2. What are the major reasons for creating a right to profit?
3. What is the natural-rights argument against ownership of software?
4. How is computer software like a literary work?
5. What are the major differences between copyright and patent?
6. If no natural right to property exists, why should other nations respect property rights instituted by the United States?

INTELLECTUAL PROPERTY RIGHTS AND COMPUTER SOFTWARE[4]

DEBORAH C. JOHNSON

The Philosophical Basis of Property

Property is by no means a simple notion. Property is created by law. Laws specify what can and cannot be owned, how things may be acquired and transferred.

Laws define what counts as property and create different kinds of property. The laws regulating ownership of an automobile, for example, are quite different from those regulating ownership of land. In the case of land, there are rules about how far the land goes down into the ground and how far up into the air space above, about what can and cannot be constructed on the land, when the land may be confiscated by the government, and so on. With automobiles, the laws are quite different. You may have to show proof of insurance in order to buy a car, and even if you own one, you cannot drive it on public roads unless you have a license. Thus, how you come to own something and what it means to own something are rather complex matters.

. . . [S]oftware has challenged our traditional notions of ownership in that the system of laws created specifically to deal with invention in the useful arts and sciences in the U.S. does not seem to grant property rights in software that are comparable to the property rights of inventors in other fields. In discussing this situation we often implicitly or explicitly make assumptions about or argue for moral (and not just legal) rights in property. These assumptions and arguments need to be fully articulated and critically examined. . . .

The reasoning behind both the patent and copyright systems is consequentialist in that the system's primary aim is to create property rights which will have good effects. Invention is encouraged and facilitated so that new products and processes will be made available. Nevertheless, many discussions of property rights assume that property is not a matter of social utility, but rather a matter of justice or natural right. We will consider this approach first, as it applies to the ownership of software.

Natural Rights Arguments

The strongest natural rights argument that can be made for private ownership of software is based on the idea that a person has a natural (and, therefore, moral) right to what he or she produces and this natural right ought to be protected by law. John Locke's labor theory of property bases the natural right of ownership on the labor one puts into a thing in creating it.

According to this theory, a person acquires a right of ownership in something by mixing his labor with it. Thus, in a state of nature (that is, before laws and civilized society), *if* an individual were to come upon a piece of land that looked suitable for cultivation, and *if* this person were to cultivate the land by planting seed, tending to the crops daily, nourishing them and so on, *then* the crops would belong to the person. The person has a strong claim to the crops because his labor produced them and they would not exist without this labor. It would be wrong for someone else to come along and take the crops. The intruder would, in effect, be confiscating the creator's labor.

On the face of it, this Lockean account seems plausible. Locke's theory is tied to the notion of individual sovereignty. A person cannot be owned by another and since a person's labor is an extension of her body, it cannot be owned by another. If an individual puts her labor in something and then someone else takes it, the laborer has been rendered a slave.

Using a Lockean theory of property, a software developer could argue that the program she developed is rightfully "hers" because she created it with her labor. . . .

Critique of moral rights in software. Now, while this argument seems plausible, it can be countered in several ways. First, we can imagine a just world in which we did not acquire rights to what we created. To be sure, it would be unjust if others acquired rights to what we created, but if there were no property rights whatsoever, then there would be no injustice. Those who created things would simply create things. If one mixed one's labor with something, one would simply lose one's labor. Robert Nozick alludes to the possibility of such an arrangement when he questions Locke's theory in *Anarchy, State and Utopia:*

> Why does mixing one's labor with something make one the owner of it? Perhaps because one owns one's labor, and so one comes to own a previously unowned thing that becomes permeated with what one owns. Ownership seeps over into the rest. But why isn't mixing what I own with what I don't own a way of losing what I own rather than a way of gaining what I don't? If I own a can of tomato juice and spill it in the sea so that its molecules (made radioactive, so I can check this) mingle evenly throughout the sea, do I thereby come to own the sea, or have I foolishly dissipated my tomato juice?[5]

A second counter to the Lockean theory applies only to intellectual or nontangible things, such as computer software. Though software's primary function is for use in computers, software is intelligible as a nontangible entity. The software designer can describe how the software works and what it does. Another person can comprehend, and even use this information as instructions—without the software ever being put into a machine.

The point is that with intellectual things, many people can "have" or use them at the same time. If a second person eats or sells food that I have grown, I have lost the products of my labor altogether. But one can continue to have and use software when others have and use it. So, when a person copies a program that I have created, she has not taken it from me. I am not deprived of it by her act. Rather, what is usually the case is that by copying my program, the person has taken my *capacity to profit from my creation,* either by making it difficult for me to sell it (since it becomes available at no cost), or by taking my competitive advantage in using the program (since my competitors can now also use it).

Once this difference between intellectual and tangible things is recognized, the natural rights argument appears much weaker than at first sight. The claim of software developers turns out *not* to be a claim to their creations (this they still have when others have their software), but a claim to a right to profit from their creations. However, to show that a person has a right to profit from his creation requires more than showing that he has created it. If he ever has a right to profit, it would seem that such a right would be socially created. It would be defined by an economic system with laws about what can be owned, what can be put into the marketplace, under what conditions, and so on. In other words, the right would derive from a complex set of rules structuring commercial activity.

The natural rights argument is, therefore, not convincing on its own. To be sure, there is a moral issue when it comes to confiscation for profit. It is unfair for one person (or company) to take a program written by someone else, and sell it. However, from a moral point of view software need never enter the commercial realm. It might be declared unownable or public property.

So, the claims of software developers must be understood not to be claims to a natural or moral right, but rather to a social right. Deciding whether or not such a social right should be created is a consequentialist issue. In a moment we will explore the consequentialist reasons for creating property rights in software, as already suggested by the rationale of the patent and copyright. For now it may be useful to point out that a natural rights argument could be made against private ownership of software.

Against ownership.   Some of the early legal literature on ownership of programs and some of the court cases focused on the idea that a patent on a program might violate "the doctrine of mental steps." This doctrine states that a series of mental operations like addition or subtraction cannot be owned. Discussion of the doctrine was based on the possibility that computers, in effect, perform, or at least duplicate, mental steps. It is acknowledged that the operations are performed quickly on the machine so that in a short time a large number of steps can take place. Still, it might be argued, the operations performed by the computer are in principle capable of being performed by a person. If this is so, then ownership of programs could be extremely dangerous for it might interfere with freedom of thought. Those who had patents on programs would have a monopoly on mental operations and might be able to stop others from performing those operations in their heads.

If this is right, then we have the basis of a natural rights argument against ownership of computer software. The argument would be that individuals have a natural right to freedom of thought, and ownership of software will interfere with that right. The argument is worthy of

further reflection, especially in light of research in artificial intelligence. . . .

Consequentialist Arguments

As suggested earlier the claims of software developers make most sense as arguments for a social right to ownership. They can and do claim that good consequences result from ownership and bad consequences result when there is no or inadequate protection. Unless individuals and companies have some proprietary rights in what they create, they will not invest the time, energy, and resources needed to develop and market software. Without protection, they can never make money at producing software. Why develop a new program if the moment you introduce it, others will copy it, produce it more cheaply, and yours will not sell? If we, as a society, want software developed, we will have to give those who develop it the protection they need; otherwise society will lose because the great promise of computers will not be realized. There must be an incentive to create programs and that incentive is profit—so the argument goes.

Objections can be made to this very important argument. In particular, we can argue that there are incentives other than profit to create software. For one thing, people will create software because they need it for their own purposes: they can use it and make it available to others or keep it to themselves, as they choose.

Another possibility is that we could create a credit system similar to what we have now with scientific publications, in which individuals are given credit and recognition for new knowledge they create when they publish it and make it available to others. (Admittedly, credit may not be enough of an incentive to encourage the development of expensive and elaborate programs, and it may lead to more secrecy.)

Along these lines, we might consider how "shareware" has fared and/or how to improve the environment for proliferation of shareware. Shareware is software that is made readily available. You are encouraged to make copies for yourself. Often it is distributed on networks or electronic bulletin boards. The developers of such software try to make money by encouraging users, if they like the software, to voluntarily pay a small price. Sometimes the developer offers to support the software and provide printed documentation to those who register and pay a fee. A fair amount of shareware is now available, though some argue that the quality is generally not as good as commercial software.

Another possible incentive on which we might rely, if software were not ownable, would be the incentive of hardware companies to create software to make their computers marketable. A company's computers are useless without good software to go with them. Indeed, the better the software available for a type of computer, the better the computer is likely to do in the marketplace.

The point is that if ownership of software were disallowed, software development would not come to a complete standstill. There would be other incentives for creating software. So, while the consequentialist argument for ownership is a good argument—ownership does encourage development—it is not such an overwhelming argument that we should reject all other considerations.

Indeed, as already explained, both the copyright and the patent system recognize reasons for limiting ownership. Both recognize that the very thing we want to encourage—development of the technological arts and sciences—will be impeded if we fail to limit ownership. Both the copyright and patent systems recognize that invention will be retarded if ideas and other building blocks of science and technology are owned.

This gets us to the dilemmas that we presently face in both copyright and patent law: How can we draw a line between what can and cannot be owned so that software developers can own something of value but not something which will interfere, in the long run, with development in the field?

This is no easy dilemma. It is precisely the same dilemma that leads to tough and related questions about the benefits and disadvantages of standardization in the computer industry. Up until recently the field of computing was wide open for new invention. More recently, it has begun to appear that in the realm of personal computers, the market has selected essentially two types, IBM or IBM compatible and Apple or Apple compatible. There is some indication that we may even be moving in the direction of compatibility between these two types. On the one hand, standardization will have great advantages for computer users; with some basic skills they will be able to use any computer and run any software. The debate about the ownership of look and feel is related to this. If look and feel is not ownable then a good deal of software might come to employ the same interface (possibly with continuous improvement). Consumers would benefit from this in that they would not have to learn a new system each time they bought new software.

On the other hand, standardization reduces innovation because once standardization takes place, there is greater resistance to change. Creative new computers and computer systems are still possible, but it takes much more to convince users to spend the money and take the time to learn a whole new way of doing things.

Conclusions from the Philosophical Analysis of Property

The preceding philosophical analysis of property rights in software supports a consequentialist framework for analyzing the property rights issues surrounding software (and not a natural rights framework). The consequentialist framework puts the focus on deciding ownership issues in terms of effects on continued creativity and development in the field of software. This framework suggests that we will have to delicately draw a line between what is ownable and what is not ownable when it comes to software, along the lines already delineated in patent and copyright law.

A number of authors have suggested that we might develop a special form of legal protection specifically applicable (*sui generous*) to software and software related inventions. While this is an idea worth considering, the preceding analysis would seem to suggest that any form of legal protection will have to draw distinctions in different aspects of software, and will have to decide which aspects should be ownable and which not, in terms of the long-term effects. Removing the process from the context of patent

and copyright law may not make this any easier to do.

Is It Wrong to Copy Proprietary Software?

We must now turn our attention to the individual moral issue: Is it wrong for an individual to make a copy of a proprietary piece of software? You will see that the answer to this question is somewhat connected to the preceding discussion of policy issues.

To begin, it will be helpful to clarify the domain of discussion. First, making a backup copy of a piece of software, which you have purchased, for your own protection is generally not illegal, and is, in any case, not at issue here. Second, while I have labeled this the "individual" moral issue, it is not just an issue for individuals but applies as well to collective units such as companies, agencies, and institutions. The typical case is the case in which you borrow a piece of software from someone who has purchased it and make a copy for your own use. . . . This case does not differ significantly from the case in which a company buys a single copy of a piece of software and makes multiple copies for use within the company in order to avoid purchasing more.

We can begin with the intuition (which many individuals seem to have) that copying a piece of software is *not wrong* (that it is morally permissible). This intuition seems understandable enough at first glance. After all, making a copy of a piece of software is easy, and seems harmless, and the laws aimed at preventing it seem ill-suited for doing the job. Nevertheless, when we examine the arguments that can be made to support this intuition, they are not very compelling. Indeed, after analysis, it seems difficult to deny that it is morally wrong to make an illegal copy of a piece of software. The key issue here has little to do with software per se and everything to do with the relationship between law and morality.

Perhaps the best way to begin is by laying out what seem to be the strongest arguments for the moral permissibility of individual copying. The strongest arguments claim (1) the laws protecting computer software are bad, and either (2a) making a copy of a piece of software is not intrinsically wrong, or (2b) making a copy of a piece of software does no harm, or (2c) *not* making a copy of a piece of software actually does some harm.

. . . [I]t is important to be clear on what could be claimed in Premise (1). Here are some of the possibilities: (1a) All property law in America is unjust and the software laws are part of this; (1b) all intellectual property laws are unjust and software laws are part of this; (1c) most property law in America is just, but the laws surrounding computer software are not; and (1d) while the laws surrounding the ownership of software are not unjust, they could be a lot better. The list could go on and just which position one holds makes much of the difference in the copying argument.

We will not be able to analyze each of the possibilities here, but it should be clear . . . that I believe that the system of intellectual property rights in America (in particular patent, trade secrecy, and copyright laws) may not be the best of all possible laws in every detail but they are roughly just. That is, copyright and patent laws aim at a utilitarian system of property rights and aim essentially to draw the right kind of line between what can and cannot be owned. I recognize that there are problems in extending these laws to software, and I recognize the system could be improved. Nevertheless, I do not believe that the system is blatantly unjust or wholly inappropriate for software.

Now, the next step in my argument is to claim that an individual has a *prima facie* obligation to obey the law of a roughly just system of laws. (*Prima facie* means "unless there are overriding reasons.") The *prima facie* obligation to obey the law can be overridden by higher-order obligations or by special circumstances that justify disobedience. Higher-order obligations will override when, for example, obeying the law will lead to greater harm than disobeying. Higher-order obligations may even require civil disobedience—that is, if the law is immoral, then disobedience is morally obligatory. Special circumstances can justify disobedience to an otherwise good law when harm will come from obeying the law this one time. For example, the law prohibiting us from driving on the left side of the road is a good law but we would be justified in breaking it in order to avoid hitting someone.

So I am not claiming that people always have an obligation to obey the law; I claim only that the burden of proof is on those who would disobey roughly good laws. Given that extant laws regarding computer software are roughly good and given that a person has a *prima facie* obligation to obey roughly good laws, the second premise carries the weight of the argument for the moral permissibility of copying. In other words, the second premise must provide a reason for disobeying roughly just laws.

Premises (2a)–(2c) must, then, be examined carefully. Premise (2a) to the effect that there is nothing intrinsically wrong with making a copy of a piece of software is true, but it doesn't make the argument. The claim is true in the sense that if there were no laws against copying, the act of copying would not be wrong. Indeed, I argued earlier that property rights are not natural or moral in themselves but a matter of social utility. They acquire moral significance only when they are created by law and only in relatively just systems of law. Still, premise (2a) does not support copying because copying has been made illegal and as such is prima facie wrong: There have to be overriding reasons or special conditions to justify breaking the law.

According to premise (2b), making a copy of a piece of software for personal use harms no one. If we think of copying taking place in a state of nature, this premise is probably true; no one is harmed. However, once we are in a society of laws, the laws create legal rights, and it seems that a person harms another by depriving him of his legal right. When a person makes a copy of a piece of *proprietary* software, she deprives the owner of his legal right to control use of that software and to require payment in exchange for the use of the software. This is a harm. (Those who think this is not a harm should think of small software companies or individual entrepreneurs who have gone into the business of developing software, invested time and money, only to be squeezed out of business by customers who would buy one copy and make others instead of buying more.) So premise (2b) is false. Making

a copy of a piece of proprietary software in our society harms someone.

Premise (2c) has the most promise as an argument for copying in that if it were true that one was doing harm by obeying the law, then we would have a moral reason for overriding the law, even if it were relatively good. Richard Stallman[6] and Helen Nissenbaum[7] have both made arguments of this kind. Both argue that there are circumstances in which not making a copy or not making a copy *and* providing it to a friend does some harm. However, in their arguments, the harm referred to does not seem of the kind to counterbalance the effects of a relatively just system of property rights. Both give examples of how an individual might be able to help a friend out by providing her with an illegal copy of a piece of proprietary software. Both argue that laws against copying have the effect of discouraging altruism.

Still, this argument ignores the harm to the copyright or patent holder. Even if we were to grant that not providing a copy to a friend does harm, we have to compare that harm to the harm to the owner and choose the lesser.

Given what I said above about the *prima facie* obligation to obey the law, it follows that there may be some situations in which copying will be justified, namely when some fairly serious harm can only be prevented by making an illegal copy of a piece of proprietary software and using it. In most cases, however, the claims of the software owner to her legal rights would seem to be much stronger than the claims of someone who needs a copy to make her life easier.

If the position I have just sketched seems odd, consider an analogy with a different sort of property. Suppose I own a private swimming pool and I make a living by renting the use of it to others. I do not rent the pool every day and you figure out how to break in undetected and use the pool when it is not opened and I am not around. The act of swimming is not intrinsically wrong, and swimming in the pool does no obvious harm to me (the owner) or anyone else. Nevertheless, you are using my property without my permission. It would hardly seem a justification for ignoring my property rights if you claimed that you were hot and the swim in my pool made your life easier. The same would be true, if you argued that you had a friend who was very uncomfortable in the heat and you, having the knowledge of how to break into the pool, thought it would be selfish not to use that knowledge to help your friend out.

Of course, there are circumstances under which your illegal entry into my pool might be justified. For example, if someone else had broken in, was swimming, and began to drown, and you were innocently walking by, saw the person drowning, broke in, and jumped in the pool in order to save the other. Here the circumstances justify overriding my legal rights.

There seems no moral difference between breaking into the pool and making a copy of a proprietary piece of software. Both acts violate the legal rights of the owner—legal rights created by reasonably good laws. I will grant that these laws do prevent others from acting altruistically, but this, I believe, is inherent to private property. Private property is individualistic, exclusionary, and, perhaps,

selfish. So, if Stallman and Nissenbaum want to launch an attack on all private property laws, I am in sympathy with their claims. However, I would press them to explain why they had picked out computer software law when private ownership of other things, such as natural resources or corporate conglomerates, seems much more menacing.

I conclude that it is *prima facie* wrong to make an illegal copy of a piece of proprietary software because to do so is to deprive someone (the owner) of their legal rights, and this is to harm them.

A Final Note

The issues discussed in this chapter are among the most fascinating and important. Our ideas about property are tied to deeply ingrained notions of rights and justice—economic justice. Law and public policy on the ownership of various aspects of computer software will structure the environment for software development and, thereby, shape its future development. The issue of the permissibility of making personal copies of proprietary software is also fascinating and important but for different reasons. Here we are forced to clarify what makes an action right or wrong. We are forced to come to grips with our moral intuitions and to extend these to entities with unique characteristics.

The thrust of this chapter has been to move discussion of property rights in computer software away from the idea that property rights are given in nature, and towards the idea that we can and should develop property rights which serve us all.

Case Study: What's Gnu?

Most computer users have heard of Napster, the free computer software that allows users to search for, copy, and store music files in MP3 format. A similar program, Gnutella, also free, allows its users direct access to each others' hard drives. Users can download whatever other Gnutella users offer in the designated share files. This includes games, DVDs, music CDs, software, videos—anything that can be copied to a hard drive. The Internet already had sites that offered disk space in which users could place files that could be accessed from various computers. This is an interesting and useful idea for users who want to be able to work on a file from various locations but do not wish to keep making multiple copies for different computers. Shared-disk-space sites also allowed multiple users with passwords to share files, such as music files. But Gnutella is more innovative than free shared-disk-space or Napster because it can be used independently of a public Web address.

Gnutella, named after the chocolate and hazelnut spread Nutella, links users and eliminates searching for the address of a Web site with shared disk space or MP3 files. Because it works independently of Web sites, Gnutella cannot be disabled as easily as Napster by server administrators who can block user access to Web addresses.

Someone had to write Gnutella and make the software available. It may have been written by programmers at Nullsoft and posted briefly on that company's Web site without permission. And, of course, once a program has been posted as freeware on the Internet it will remain available from different, shifting sites.

What do you think of the ethics of writing and posting Gnutella? Napster allows users to copy MP3 files. MP3 files are inferior to WAV files, which also store music and are downloaded with Gnutella. Having an MP3 file is not incompatible with having an incentive to buy the original on CD. Does this make Napster less objectionable than Gnutella?[8]

What is your reaction to the owner of a Web site that offers Gnutella for free download and says that what users do with the program is not his responsibility? What about the story itself? The wire report included Web addresses where readers could find Gnutella and Napster. If you were the editor of a newspaper carrying this story would you think it obligatory to omit those addresses?

Case Study: Richard Stallman and the Free Software Movement

The free software philosophy can be found on the Web at www.gnu.org, the site of the Gnu Foundation. Here is a selection from the free software philosophy drawn from the GNU Manifesto written by Richard Stallman. Visit the GNU site for a fuller understanding of the free software project. What do you think of this ethical argument offered for free software?

> I consider that the golden rule requires that if I like a program I must share it with other people who like it. Software sellers want to divide the users and conquer them, making each user agree not to share with others. I refuse to break solidarity with

other users in this way. I cannot in good conscience sign a nondisclosure agreement or a software license agreement. For years I worked within the Artificial Intelligence Lab to resist such tendencies and other inhospitalities, but eventually they had gone too far: I could not remain in an institution where such things are done for me against my will.

So that I can continue to use computers without dishonor, I have decided to put together a sufficient body of free software so that I will be able to get along without any software that is not free. I have resigned from the AI lab to deny MIT any legal excuse to prevent me from giving GNU away. . . .

GNU is not in the public domain. Everyone will be permitted to modify and redistribute GNU, but no distributor will be allowed to restrict its further redistribution. That is to say, proprietary modifications will not be allowed. I want to make sure that all versions of GNU remain free.[9]

What do you think of Stallman's effort to keep GNU from being modified into a proprietary version? What is the moral basis of that effort?

9.2 THE ROMANTIC AUTHOR   James Boyle is a law professor at American University in Washington D.C. His book, *Shamans, Software, and Spleens* demonstrates how the concept of romantic authorship is embodied in decision making about a wide variety of property rights claims. He calls our attention to how much our intuitions about morality and legal decisions are guided by an idea of authorship with a contingent, historical origination. This helps us see that a moral notion that appears natural has a social foundation. His approach also demonstrates how ethical issues such as the ownership of body parts have become informationalized. (See case study on page 382.)

Boyle uses important legal cases to demonstrate that thinking about property rights mixes rights frameworks with utilitarian concerns. The notion that rights theory and utility can be mixed is more common in law where interests and rights tend to be used interchangeably and decisions are made by balancing rights with rights and rights with state interests. But Boyle does not see law as separate from morality. Rather law is where a society embodies its developing and shifting moral concepts. This allows Boyle's thinking about intellectual property to be relatively unhampered by ethical theory as something objective, universal, and prior to actual human deliberations and conversations about justice. His analysis not only uncovers a notion governing intuitions and legal decisions about property, but also fosters the questioning of this notion in light of social utilities. Boyle concludes that our society, guided by the notion of romantic authorship, confers too many property rights and often confers them on the wrong persons.

Questions for Study and Discussion

1. Boyle thinks that the concept of romantic authorship is the key to understanding most of current law dealing with intellectual property. What is this concept? What alternative concepts does Boyle mention?

2. What is a public good and why are public goods underproduced?
3. How does "liberal political theory" conflict with patenting of software?
4. "No one can appropriate thoughts without altering the form of the thoughts." Do you agree? What is the importance of this claim?
5. What is the idea/expression distinction? How does it separate intellectual from other forms of labor?

AUTHORS ARE SPECIAL[10]

J A M E S   B O Y L E

Consciously and unconsciously, we are already developing the language of entitlement for a world in which information—genetic, electronic, proprietary—is one of the main sources and forms of wealth. We think about issues of entitlement using the vocabularies of classical liberalism, market, family, and property rights. ("Because it's my right." "Because it's efficient." "Because it protects family values." "Because it's *mine.")* Each of those ways of thinking makes assumptions about the relevance of information—whether to the well-functioning state, the efficient market, or the realm of personal privacy and individual ownership. How might those assumptions influence and in turn be changed by an information economy? If there are no fresh starts in history, if the future is made from fragments of the past, then the discourse of entitlement in an information society will draw on images of information that were produced in a society where information bore a very different relationship to technology, to power, to wealth, a different relationship even to our own bodies. To put it another way, if history is collage, then we need to look at the available pictures, scissors, and paste. That is what I have tried to do here, using law and the surrounding discourses on which legal analysis draws, from aesthetics to economics, as my raw material.

Although law is my starting place, I have tried to go beyond the style of legal writing best described as Jetson's Jurisprudence—a listing of technological marvels in the hope they will make a related set of legal rules alluringly futuristic by association. My main focus is on the way our society conceives of information, and on the paradoxical results that conception may entail. To use the jargon, this is an analysis of the social construction of reality. Unlike many such analyses, however, it has a practical intent. Thus I offer not only analysis and structure, but a conclusion—one much qualified in the pages that follow, but a conclusion nonetheless.

The conclusion is that—for a set of complicated reasons traced out in the pages that follow—we are driven to confer property rights in information on those who come closest to the image of the romantic author, those whose contributions to information production are most easily seen as original and transformative. I argue that this is a bad thing for reasons of both efficiency and justice; it leads us to have *too many* intellectual property rights, to confer them on the *wrong people,* and dramatically to undervalue the interests of both the *sources of* and *audiences for* the information we commodify. If I am right, this unconscious use of the author paradigm has wide-ranging negative effects, with costs in areas ranging from biodiversity and the production of new drugs to the shape of the international economy and the structure of the computer industry. As one Orwellian case study here reveals, it may even threaten our control over the genetic information in our own bodies.

Why should we believe that the idea of authorship would assume more importance in an information economy, let alone that it might produce the negative consequences I describe here? The argument is a complicated one with a simple conclusion. In law and ideology as in other more prosaic realms, things that seem to "work" tend to be used. Information presents special problems; the idea of authorship seems (wrongly) to solve or at least defer those problems.

But what does it mean to say that information presents special problems? I do not mean that the regulation, ownership, and control of information presents special *technical* or *functional* difficulties, though that is sometimes true. The "problems" I refer to are problems in the realm of ideas, paradoxes, or tensions in our assumptions, brought to the surface when the subject is information. To put it more specifically, as a form of wealth, a focus of production, and a conception of value, information is a problematic category within our most basic ways of thinking about markets, property, politics, and self-definition.

In market terms, information has significant "public good" qualities; it is often expensive to create or generate but cheap to copy. Economic theory tells us that "public goods" will be underproduced because there will be too little

incentive to create them. Suppose I spend two years and fifty thousand dollars creating a software program that can be copied for the price of a diskette. Alternatively, to use a nonelectronic example, suppose I spend the same time and money testing a thousand substances to find out which are valuable drugs— drugs that someone else can produce for pennies once the information about their properties is known. I sell one copy of my program, one dose of my drug, and then find the market has disappeared. Who would spend the time to write the program or test the drug in the first place? The obvious answer to these problems is the creation of "intellectual" property rights. Give inventors, scientists, programmers, and genetic engineers some kind of legal monopoly— a protection against copying. But information also has significant "efficiency" qualities; the more costly and restricted the access to information, the more inefficient the market, scientific research community, computer industry, or what have you. Is there a balance between incentive and efficiency? If so, how do we know where to strike it?

Information is problematic in other ways. Liberal political theory sees free access to and transmission of information as the lifeblood of the public sphere. The First Amendment is only the most famous of the many incarnations of this ideal. It is already hard—if not impossible—for us to square this tradition with two others: our strong idea of intellectual property rights on the one hand, and our vision of individual privacy on the other. In a world where "information" was the dominant form of wealth, the problem could only be magnified. I could go on but the basic point is simple. Information presents special problems and the discourse of authorship *seems* to solve those problems. (Actually, it merely assumes them away in a particularly unfortunate manner.) The discourse of authorship premises a grant of a limited monopoly (most familiarly, an intellectual property right) on a transformative originality more often assumed than proved. The author stands between the public and private realms, giving new ideas to the society at large and being granted in return a limited right of private property in the artifact he or she has created—or at least assembled from the parts provided by our common store of ideas, language, and genre. Precisely because of the way it couples romantic appeal and *apparent* efficacy, I would argue that this way of thinking—with its corresponding suppression of the claims of "sources" and "audience"—will be the default mode for dealing with issues of ownership and control of information.

The importance of the structure of thought I outline here goes beyond the negative effects of any particular rule or set of rules. The notion of the author does for information, for the knowledge-value revolution, what the Divine Right of Kings did for the monarchy, what classical economists' notion of the justice of "natural" unregulated markets did for the economic relations of the industrial revolution. This then is the story of the *imperial author* and the role that *the ideology of authorship* might play in an information society.

The author-vision conjures up a new political economy of wealth supported, and reflexively constituted, by a particular ideology of entitlement. At the bottom of the pyramid would be those whose lives, bodies, and natural environments provide the raw materials, or those who themselves are the ultimate "audience,"

for the products of an information economy. At the top of the pyramid of entitlement claims—at least in theory—would be those who gather and shape information amid information products. More important, perhaps, is the fact that the bureaucratic and corporate actors who *employ* the manipulators of information can justify their own, derivative intellectual property rights through the rhetoric of individualism and original genius. In fact, a striking feature of the language of romantic authorship is the way it is used to support sweeping intellectual property rights for large corporate entities. Sony, Pfizer, and Microsoft tend to lack the appeal of Byron and Alexander Fleming.

Actual "authors"—writers, inventors, genetic and software engineers—often lose out under the kind of regime I describe here. It is not merely that they find their work belongs to their employers. There are justifications for such a result, albeit ones that are currently invoked too widely. The true irony comes when we find that large companies can use the idea of the independent entrepreneurial creator to justify intellectual property rights *so* expansive that they make it much harder for future independent creators actually to create. The expansion of intellectual property inhibits the very process on which the expansionists premise their arguments. This irony has not gone entirely unnoticed. For example, recent years have seen the development of a fascinating set of protests in the software industry. People who owe their fame, and in some cases their fortunes, to their status as innovators—Mitch Kapor, creator of Lotus 1-2-3, Richard Stallman, the creator of GNU Emacs—have begun to argue that contemporary intellectual property rights are so broad as to *slow* the rate of innovation.[11]

The structure of thought I describe here does not make an equivalent social pyramid inevitable, anything but. Nor does it mean that struggling authors, inventors, and computer programmers are going to reap the rewards of the information society. How should we understand it then?

I am not imagining a conspiracy of the software designers or the genetic engineers; a real-life revenge of the nerds. Quite the contrary. My claim is that—for a number of reasons—the author vision exercises a strange fascination over our conceptions of the commodification of information, so that it is hard *even to imagine an alternative system*. There is nothing inevitable in all of this, however. No World Spirit stands ready to chide us if we stray from the path I sketch here. No executive committee of the ruling class or unbreakable consortium of multinationals dictates such a result. For one thing, the author paradigm—when played out in the way I describe here—produces effects that are not only unjust, but unprofitable in the long term. As the Bellagio Declaration points out, "At present, drugs drawn from the rain forest or from indigenous pharmacopoeias do not economically support the protection of either. Traditional patterns and dances can be taken without permission or recompense, perhaps diminishing the chance that the culture that originated them will survive."[12] Even a conventional economic analysis supports the idea that it is in the interest of those who are exploiting a "commons" to make sure that the commons continues to exist. The author vision blinds us to the importance of the commons—to the importance of the raw material from which information products are constructed. But precisely because of that blindness, there is some space for intervention by scholars, citizens, and activists of various stripes—before the information society's assumptions about entitlement rigidify in an inegalitarian and ultimately self-defeating pattern.

When I began this project, I found I was working largely without maps. There have been few attempts to produce a critical social theory of the information society. Most newspaper coverage has concentrated on a few narrow issues, generally defined by the technology to which they relate—the information superhighway, computer privacy, the Clipper chip. This is useful, but it doesn't get us far. An analogy might help to illustrate the point. Imagine a group of feudal serfs gathered around a newly invented power loom, wondering whether the lord of the manor will now increase the tithes. With the easy arrogance of hindsight, we find the picture ridiculous. How silly it would be to assume that all social arrangements, all hierarchies, all ideologies of entitlement, will remain exactly as they are and only the technology of production will change! Yet this is exactly the assumption made by most discussions of the *information* society.

Copyright and the Invention of Authorship

So far I have argued that, because of the contradictions and tensions described here, there are certain structural pressures on the way that a liberal society deals with information. When we turn to the area of law conventionally recognized as dealing with information—intellectual property law, and in this case copyright law—I claim that we will find a pattern, a conceptual strategy which attempts to resolve the tensions and contradictions in the liberal view of information. On one level, understanding this pattern will help us to make sense (if not coherence) of the otherwise apparently chaotic world of copyright. On another level, I claim that the conceptual strategy developed in copyright is important to understand, because parts of it can also be found in most, if not all, of the areas where we deal with information— even if those areas are conventionally understood to have nothing to do with copyright.

From what I have argued previously, it should be apparent that although intellectual property has long been said to present insuperable conceptual difficulties, it actually presents exactly the same problems as the liberal concept of property generally. It merely does so in a more obvious way and in a way which is given a particular spin by our fascination with information. All systems of property are both rights-oriented and utilitarian, rely on antinomian conceptions of public and private, present insuperable conceptual difficulties when reduced to mere physicalist relations but when conceived of in a more abstract and technically sophisticated way, immediately begin to dissolve back into the conflicting policies to which they give a temporary and unstable form. In personal or real property, however, one can at least point to a pair of sneakers or a house, say "I own that," and have some sense of confidence that the statement means something. As the *LeRoy Fibre*[13] case shows, of course, it is not at all clear that such confidence is justified, but at least property presents itself as an *apparently* coherent feature of social reality, and this is a fact of

considerable ideological and political significance. In intellectual property, the response to the claim "I own that" might be "what do you mean?"

As Martha Woodmansee discovered, this point was made with startling clarity in the debates over copyright in Germany in the eighteenth century. Encouraged by an enormous reading public, several apocryphal tales of writers who were household names, yet still living in poverty, and a new, more romantic vision of authorship, writers began to demand greater economic returns from their labors. One obvious strategy was to lobby for some kind of legal right in the text—the right that we would call copyright. To many participants in the debate, the idea was ludicrous. Christian Sigmund Krause, writing in 1783, expressed the point pungently.

> "But the ideas, the content! that which actually constitutes a book! which only the author can sell or communicate!"—Once expressed, it is impossible for it to remain the author's property. . . . It is precisely for the purpose of using the ideas that most people buy books— pepper dealers, fishwives, and the like and literary pirates excepted. . . . Over and over again it comes back to the same question: I can read the contents of a book, learn, abridge, expand, teach, and translate it, write about it, laugh over it, find fault with it, deride it, use it poorly or well—in short, do with it whatever I will. But the one thing I should be prohibited from doing is copying or reprinting it? . . . A published book is a secret divulged. With what justification would a preacher forbid the printing of his homilies, since he cannot

prevent any of his listeners from transcribing his sermons? Would it not be just as ludicrous for a professor to demand that his students refrain from using some new proposition he had taught them as for him to demand the same of book dealers with regard to a new book? *No, no it is too obvious that the concept of intellectual property is useless. My property must be exclusively mine; I must be able to dispose of it and retrieve it unconditionally.* Let someone explain to me how that is possible in the present case. Just let someone try taking back the ideas he has originated once they have been communicated so that they are, as before, nowhere to be found. All the money in the world could not make that possible.[14]

Along with this problem go two other, more fundamental ones. The first is the recurrent question of how we can give property rights in intellectual products and yet still have the inventiveness and free flow of information which liberal social theory demands. I shall return to this question in a moment. The second problem is the more fundamental one. On what grounds should we give the author this kind of unprecedented property right at all, even if the conceptual problems could be overcome? We do not think it is necessary to give car workers residual property rights in the cars that they produce—wage labor is thought to work perfectly well. Surely, an author is merely taking public goods—language, ideas, culture, humor, genre—and converting them to his or her own use? Where is the moral or utilitarian justification for the existence of this property right in the first place? The most obvious

answer is that authors are special, but why? And since when?

Even the most cursory historical study reveals that our notion of "authorship" is a concept of relatively recent provenance. Medieval church writers actively disapproved of the elements of originality and creativeness which we think of as an essential component of authorship: "They valued extant old books more highly than any recent elucubrations *and they put the work of the scribe and the copyist above that of the authors.* The real task of the scholar was not the vain excogitation of novelties but a discovery of great old books, their multiplication, and the placing of copies where they would be accessible to future generations of readers."[15]

Martha Woodmansee quotes a wonderful definition of "Book" from a mid–eighteenth-century dictionary that merely lists the writer as one mouth among many—"the scholar, . . . the papermaker, the type-founder and setter, the proof-reader, the publisher and bookbinder, sometimes even the gilder and brass worker"—all of whom are "fed by this branch of manufacture."[16] Other studies show that authors seen as craftsmen—an appellation which Shakespeare might not have rejected—or at their most exalted, as the crossroads where learned tradition met external divine inspiration. But since the tradition was mere craft and the glory of the divine inspiration should be offered to God rather than to the vessel he had chosen, where was the justification for preferential treatment in the creation of property rights? As authors ceased to think of themselves as either craftsmen, gentlemen, or amanuenses for the Divine spirit, a recognizably different, more romantic vision of authorship began to emerge. At first, it was found mainly in self-serving tracts, but little by little it spread through the culture so that by the middle of the eighteenth century it had come to be seen as a "universal truth about art."

Woodmansee explains how the decline of the craft-inspiration model of writing and the elevation of the romantic author both presented and seemed to solve the question of property rights in intellectual products: "Eighteenth-century theorists departed from this compound model of writing in two significant ways. They minimized the element of craftsmanship (in some instances they simply discarded it) in favor of the element of inspiration, and they internalized the source of that inspiration. That is, inspiration came to be regarded as emanating not from outside or above, but from within the writer himself. 'Inspiration' came to be explicated in terms of *original genius* with the consequence that the inspired work was made peculiarly and distinctively the product—and the property—of the writer."[17]

In this vision, the author was not the journeyman who learned a craft and then hoped to be well paid for it. The romantic author was defined not by the mastery of a prior set of rules, but instead by the transformation of genre, the revision of form. Originality became the watchword of artistry and the warrant for property rights. To see how complete a revision this is, one need only examine Shakespeare's wholesale lifting of plot, scene, and language from other writers, both ancient and contemporary. To an Elizabethan playwright, the phrase "imitation is the sincerest form of flattery" might have seemed entirely without irony. "Not only were Englishmen from 1500 to 1625 without any feeling analogous to the modern attitude toward plagiarism; they even lacked the word until the very end of that period." To the theorists and polemicists of romantic authorship, however, the reproduction of orthodoxy would have been proof they were not the unique and transcendent spirits they imagined themselves to be.

It is the *originality* of the author, the novelty which he or she adds to the raw materials provided by culture and the common pool, which "justifies" the property right and at the same time offers a strategy for resolving the basic conceptual problem pointed out by Krause—what concept of property would allow the author to retain some property rights in the work but not others? In the German debates, the best answer was provided by the great idealist Fichte. In a manner that is now familiar to lawyers trained in legal realism and Hohfeldian analysis, but that must have seemed remarkable at the time, Fichte disaggregated the concept of property in books. The buyer gets the physical thing and the ideas contained in it. *Precisely because the originality of his spirit was converted into an originality of form*, the author retains the right to the form in which those ideas were expressed: "Each writer must give his own thoughts a certain form, and he can give them no other form than his own because he has no other. But neither can he be willing to hand over this form in making his thoughts public, for no one can *appropriate* his thoughts without thereby *altering their form*. This latter thus remains forever his exclusive property."[18]

A similar theme is struck in American copyright law. In the famous case of

Bleistein v. *Donaldson Lithographing Company,* concerning the copyrightability of a circus poster, Oliver Wendell Holmes was still determined to claim that the work could become the subject of an intellectual property right because it was the original creation of a unique individual spirit.[19] Holmes's opinion shows us both the advantages and the disadvantages of a rhetoric which bases property rights on "originality." As a hook on which to hang a property right, "originality" seems to have at least a promise of formal realizability. It connects nicely to the romantic vision of authorship which I described earlier and to which I will return. It also seems to limit a potentially expansive principle, the principle that those who create may be entitled to retain some legally protected interest in the objects they make—even after those objects have been conveyed through the marketplace. But while the idea that an original spirit conveys its uniqueness to worked matter seems intuitively plausible when applied to Shakespeare or Dante, it has less obvious relevance to a more humdrum act of creation by a less credibly romantic creator—a commercial artist in a shopping mall, say. The tension between the rhetoric of Wordsworth and the reality of suburban corporate capitalism is one that continues to bedevil intellectual property discourse today. In *Bleistein,* this particular original spirit had only managed to rough out a picture of energetic-looking individuals performing unlikely acts on bicycles, but to Holmes the principle was the same. "The copy is the personal reaction of an individual upon nature. *Personality always contains something unique.* It expresses its singularity even in handwriting, and a very modest grade of art has in it something irreducible,

which is one man's alone. That something he may copyright."[20]

This quality of "uniqueness," recognized first in great spirits, then in creative spirits, and finally in advertising executives, expresses itself in originality of form, of expression. Earlier I quoted a passage from Jessica Litman which bears repeating here:

> Why is it that copyright does not protect ideas? Some writers have echoed the justification for failing to protect facts by suggesting that ideas have their origin in the public domain. Others have implied that "mere ideas" may not be worthy of the status of private property. Some authors have suggested that ideas are not protected because of the strictures imposed on copyright by the first amendment. The task of distinguishing ideas from expression in order to explain why private ownership is inappropriate for one but desirable for the other, however, remains elusive.[21]

I would say that we find the answer to this question in the romantic vision of authorship, of the genius whose style forever expresses a single unique persona. The rise of this powerful (and historically contingent) stereotype provided the necessary raw material to fashion some convincing mediation of the tension between the imagery of "public" and "private" in information production.

To sum up, then, if our starting place is the romantic idea of authorship, then the idea/expression division which has so fascinated and puzzled copyright scholars apparently manages, at a stroke, to do four things:

First, it provides a *conceptual basis* for partial, limited property rights, without completely collapsing the notion of property into the idea of a temporary, limited, utilitarian state grant, revocable at will. The property right still seems to be based on something real—on a distinction which sounds formally realizable, even if, on closer analysis, it turns out to be impossible to maintain.

Second, this division provides a *moral and philosophical justification* for fencing in the commons, giving the author property in something built from the resources of the public domain—language, culture, genre, scientific community, or what have you. If one makes originality of spirit the assumed feature of authorship and the touchstone for property rights, one can see the author as creating something entirely new—not recombining the resources of the commons. Thus we reassure ourselves both that the grant to the author is justifiable *and* that it will not have the effect of diminishing the commons for *future* creators. After all, if a work of authorship is original—by definition—we believe that it only adds to our cultural supply. With originality first defended and then routinely assumed, intellectual property no longer looks like a zero sum game. There is always "enough and as good" left over—by definition. The distinguished intellectual property scholar Paul Goldstein captures both the power and the inevitable limitations of this view very well. "Copyright, in a word, is about authorship. Copyright is about sustaining the conditions of creativity that enable an individual to craft *out of thin air* an *Appalachian Spring,* a *Sun Also Rises,* a *Citizen Kane.*"[22] But of course, even these—remarkable and "original"—works are *not* crafted out of thin air. As Northrop Frye put it in 1957, when Michel Foucault's on authorship was only a gleam in the eye of the episteme, "Poetry can only be made out of other poems; novels out of other novels. All of this was much clearer before the assimilation of literature to private enterprise."[23]

Third, the idea/expression division circumscribes the ambit of a labor theory of property. At times, it seems that the argument is almost like Locke's labor theory; one gains property by mixing one's labor with an object. But where Locke's theory, if applied to a modern economy, might have a disturbingly socialist ring to it, Fichte's theory bases the property right on the originality of every spirit as expressed through words. Every author gets the right—the writer of the *roman a clef* as well as Goethe—but because of the concentration on originality of expression, the residual property right is only for the workers of the word and the image, not the workers of the world. Even after that right is extended by analogy to sculpture and painting, software and music, it will still have an attractively circumscribed domain.

Fourth, the idea/expression division resolves (or at least conceals) the *tension between the public and private.* In the double life which Marx described, information is both the lifeblood of the noble disinterested citizens of the public world and a commodity in the private sphere to which we must attach property rights if we wish our self-interested producers to continue to produce. By disaggregating the book into "idea" and "expression," we can give the idea (and the facts on which it is based) to the public world and the expression to the writer, thus apparently mediating the contradiction between public good and private need (or greed).

Thus the combination of the romantic vision of authorship and the distinction between idea and expression appeared to provide a conceptual basis and a moral justification for intellectual property, to do so in a way which did not threaten to spread dangerous notions of entitlement to other kinds of workers, and to mediate the tension between the schizophrenic halves of the liberal world view. Small wonder that it was a success. Small wonder that, as I hope to show in this book, the language of romantic, original authorship tends to reappear in discussion of subjects far removed from the ones Fichte had in mind. Like insider trading. Or spleens.

. . . Attachment to the idea of the individual transformative authorship is not a silly "mistake." First, it has a clear element of existential truth—our experience of authors, inventors, and artists who *do* transform their fields and our world, together with the belief (one I hold deeply myself) that the ability to remake the conditions of individual life and collective existence is to be cherished and rewarded. Second, as a basis for an intellectual property system, it seems to *work,* precisely because it makes a series

of wrenching and difficult conflicts disappear—largely by defining them out of existence rather than solving them, however. It is possible to portray the fixation on originality and the neglect of sources and audience as a technical error made by the rational guardians of the legal system or as a deep plot by the multinationals. Instead, my argument has been that we need to see the romantic vision of authorship as the solution to a series of ideological problems. For those who do not like the word "ideology," at least as applied to any group of which *they* might be a part, we could call these problems deep-seated conceptual conflicts in our ideas of property and polity. The romantic idea of authorship is no more a "mistake" than classical economics was a mistake. It is both something more and something less than that. If one is critical of a system built on its presuppositions, one must begin by understanding both its authentic appeal and the deep conceptual itches it manages to scratch. Only then can one begin the critique.

Case Study: No Electronic Theft Act

Read the following selections from the No Electronic Theft Act, which strengthened protection of copyright within the music industry. Does it embody the concept of romantic authorship? Who counts as an author within this bill? What counts as financial gain? If you trade a tape of a concert for another tape of another concert do you violate this law? If so, who could bring a complaint against you?

> Union Calendar No. 198 105th CONGRESS 1st Session
> . . .Section 101 of title 17, United States Code, is amended by inserting after the undesignated paragraph relating to the term 'display,' the following new paragraph: The term 'financial gain' includes receipt, or expectation of receipt, of anything of value, including the receipt of other copyrighted works. . . . Persons permitted to submit victim impact statements shall include: producers and sellers of legitimate works affected by conduct involved in the offense, holders of intellectual property rights in such works; and the legal representatives of such producers, sellers, and holders.

CASE STUDY: ONLINE TAPE TRADING AND THE RIAA

The following is a report on recent activities of the Recording Industry Association of America (RIAA). The RIAA maintains a Web site (www.riaa.org) where you can find more cases and reports on the impact of piracy and bootlegging on the music industry. Do you think the tape trader was engaged in unethical behavior? Do you think tape trading harms bands? Who should be able to bring a complaint—the artist, the recording company, the heirs of the artists?

> . . . Why did the RIAA single out this site—not much different from thousands of others on the Net, where traders post their "lists" in hopes of expanding their collections—threatening the site's owner with a five-year jail sentence and a $250,000 fine for copyright infringement?
>
> Unlike several Pearl Jam fan sites shut down by RIAA threats in recent months, the site—which was run by a university staffer who asked not to be identified—never featured advance, unauthorized copies of studio releases. The site was devoted strictly to the trading of high-quality concert recordings, some of which were recorded by the staffer himself, a Bruce Springsteen aficionado well-respected by other online traders.
>
> His troubles began a few weeks ago, when e-mail arrived from someone in Washington, D.C., who said they wanted to conduct a trade. The particular kind of exchange requested was what is known in trading circles as a "newbie trade," newbie being the term for someone who is just getting started in the world of trading, and who thus usually cannot offer a swap of one show for another.
>
> Newbie trades often involve the trading of one live recording for one or two blank tapes. . . . The university staffer says he spent up to 25 hours a week "spinning" tapes, many of them for newbies. The sheer volume of mail moving through his house—blank cassettes, self-addressed bubble-wrap envelopes, postage—became overwhelming.
>
> . . . Finally, he decided to streamline the operation by asking newbies to send him $6 for one tape, instead of two blanks and return postage. He didn't make any profit, he says, and his wife was happier with the reduced volume of mail. "I thought I was helping everyone," he says.
>
> To the RIAA, however, a Web site proffering unauthorized recordings for cash, even with no profit margin, smells like a professional bootlegging operation. In the eyes of the group's Anti-Piracy Unit, the site was a "commercial operation." The staffer maintains that his site was run purely "to spread the music."
>
> . . . When a trader posts his or her list to the Web, [RIAA Director Steve D'Onofrio] says, they approach the "very thin line" between commercial sites and non-commercial sites. In D'Onofrio's view, when a trader puts his list online, "then it's not just one person trading a tape. The entire world can get on the Internet. It's a much larger problem." The RIAA has also decided to target .edu sites, which it believes are hotbeds of copyright infringement and marketing of unauthorized recordings—"particularly universities that allow students to develop their own Web sites," D'Onofrio says.
>
> Thickening the plot, the RIAA regards newbie trades of one show for two blanks as a kind of profiteering. . . .[24]

CASE STUDY: MOORE V. REGENTS

James Boyle describes a case in which doctors at the University of California Medical Center discovered that a patient, John Moore, under treatment for leukemia, possessed blood products and components of potentially great commercial value. The doctors performed tests and took samples of a wide variety of Mr. Moore's bodily fluids without informing him of their commercial interest. Eventually the doctors removed Moore's spleen. Boyle remarks that the medical reasons for the operation were "arguable." The doctors also had prearranged for the spleen to be taken to a research facility. Five years later a cell line "established from Moore's T-lymphocytes was patented by the University of California, with Moore's doctors listed as the inventors."[25]

How does the listing of the doctors as inventors illustrate the idea/expression distinction? The Court ruled that ". . . Moore could not be given a property right in his genetic material because to do so would hinder research." Do you agree that recognizing Moore as having a property right in such a case would hinder medical research? How does this ruling illustrate the view that property rights are social constructs, not natural entitlements? How does the case illustrate Holmes's perspective on property rights cited by Boyle?

9.3 INTELLECTUAL PROPERTY AND POPULAR CULTURE The next article is written by one of this volume's authors. Anthony Graybosch believes in greater public access to artistic productions. His aesthetic argument could be taken as indicating that he believes that objects with intrinsic aesthetic value ought not to be privately owned. Or, alternatively, he could believe that aesthetic objects are the sort of objects Locke wished to withhold from private ownership—objects that when privately owned place other human beings at a distinct moral disadvantage. Graybosch is not a professional musician, but the other author of your text is. For that reason, Graybosch hastens to note that his view of the financial rights of musicians does not necessarily reflect the views of Joel Rudinow.

On his twelfth birthday Graybosch's cousin Helene took him to the Brooklyn Fox Theater to see the Murray the K Rock and Roll Show. The headliners were Ben E. King, the Drifters, the Barbarians, the Nashville Teens, and the Shangri-Las who came out on stage on motorcycles to sing "Leader of the Pack." (If anyone has a tape of this show, Graybosch would like to hear from you.)

QUESTIONS FOR STUDY AND DISCUSSION

1. Explain the difference between pirating and bootlegging.
2. Does Graybosch think Napster competes with official releases?
3. What is the aesthetic argument against strong protection of musical performances? To what degree does the argument appeal to rights? To utilities?
4. Does Graybosch leave any room for an artist to exercise discretion over what work is made public? What, if anything, could a musician put on tape

(perhaps personal communications?) that would not justifiably be made public in Graybosch's view?

5. Are you an aspiring musician? Do you know someone who is? What arguments can you give against circulation of recorded music?

NAPSTER: SPREADING THE MUSIC[26]

ANTHONY GRAYBOSCH

Fuck you, Lars [Ulrich, Metallica drummer]. It's our music too.[27]

Market economies sanction profit making that depends upon the creative efforts of others in diverse ways. Buying a stock is purchasing the right to a profit, or a loss, determined largely on the basis of the work of others. Some who purchased Microsoft early and became millionaires did so because of intellectual acumen and solid market research. Others were just lucky. Both reap rewards. It should not be surprising to find individuals in the art world who profit from the creative work of others. It used to be common practice for music producers to receive coauthor credit for popular music and participate in songwriter royalties. Perhaps if the producer provided support for the artists during the recording process and financed the subsequent marketing of the product then the compensation would be just despite the fact that the producer is not an author in the usual sense.

But some examples are clearly morally objectionable. A major rhythm and blues song from the 1950s was originally recorded by a minority band. Later the vocals were stripped and rerecorded with a Caucasian vocalist using the original recording as his backing track. This is perhaps the most outrageous example of white entertainers covering race records. And the practice was not always motivated by race. Some artists even argue that covering black rhythm and blues contributed to the eventual success of black artists. And sometimes black artists covered the recordings of other black artists. But certainly simply replacing the vocal track suggests a desire to profit by responding to racist preferences in the marketplace and is immoral.

Both types of cases—cover versions and coauthorship practices—should provoke a desire to know more about the transaction. Did the artists who added a producer as a coauthor do so voluntarily and receive fair compensation? Or was this simply the only way to have a record issued in a coercive music industry? Does Little Richard now agree that it was a good thing that Pat Boone covered his songs? It is not in any obvious sense always immoral to profit from the work of others. And wherever the justice of such gains lies it is not settled by knowing who authored the work in the usual sense. Investigating the morality of Napster will be more fruitful if the reader keeps in mind the complexity of the relationship of profit to creative effort.

Royalties

Recording artists receive royalties. Music royalties are split into three types: payments for unit sales (e.g., CDs), performances (radio play), and mechanical reproductions (inclusion on CD anthologies or music books). Performers receive royalties only from unit sales. Those performers who are also composers make out better because they also receive royalties from the other two categories. Since the music industry also requires that recording artists surrender the copyright on a CD and deduct various charges from royalties to recoup investments, only the most successful artists realize any additional profit from unit sales. Charles Mann remarks that session musicians who are paid flat fees for their work often do better financially than performers who are paid royalties.[28]

Lightnin' Hopkins always demanded payment for a recording session instead of a contract with royalties. Hopkins also routinely would go from company to company disregarding any contractual obligations. He acted the part of a free agent and as a result a great deal of his recorded material is available. Unlike some blues artists, he did receive some financial compensation for his creative work while he was still alive. In addition, his career was not hampered like that of other artists whose recordings were held off the market in order to manage consumption by directing the public to the works of the record company's anointed.[29] In practice, copyright is used to protect the profit of record companies, not artists. Those who criticize Napster are really complaining about a threat to the profit of the major labels and a few extremely successful artists.

Corporate profits are perhaps justified by the financial investment in record production and marketing. But the fact that such an enormous investment is required and so few artists make a profit

from sales encourages record companies to manage consumer tastes and narrow access to recorded material by keeping music in the vaults.

Metaphors are extremely important guides to moral decision making; they are even more crucial when trying to determine how to classify and approach a new moral problem. It is tempting to see Napster as analogous to radio. Americans are not accustomed to paying for radio usage except via contributions to National Public Radio. Radio broadcasters do pay performance royalties but cover the cost by selling commercial time. Radio broadcasts may be recorded for personal use. There is no law against recording a concert broadcast on the radio and playing it later at home or in your automobile. And I imagine that many people transfer such radio broadcasts to CDRs (recordable CDs) for greater security. Space and time shifting of music are no more morally problematic than recording a television program on a video for later and repeated viewing. And most people would see nothing morally problematic in copying such a recording to share with a friend. The moral line is drawn perhaps at selling the tape, although it might be moral to trade the tape with a stranger for another or a blank and postage. Using Napster, then, should be no more problematic than sharing television or radio broadcasts. But this argument breaks down in at least two places. Napster, unlike a radio station, makes music available without authorization, and Napster, unlike the radio, is not perceived as a marketing tool but as a detriment to commercial sales. I hasten to add in connection with the first point that technically it is Napster users, not Napster the company or the program that makes music available without authorization and compensation.

Napster on Trial

Not all the issues in the record industry suit against Napster are relevant to our question of the ethics of using Napster. And, after all, it could be the case that Napster itself is not violating copyright yet its application by users amounts to theft. The legal case does dramatize the seriousness of what is at issue and points toward remedies with moral implications that may be overlooked on a purely legalistic approach. But Napster is a serious problem; its usage is widespread among young consumers. I paid no attention to Napster until reading a story in *Rolling Stone* about campus police confiscating a student's computer. I asked a show of hands in two sections of Introduction to Philosophy to see how widespread Napster usage was. Almost all eighty students raised a hand.

Napster lawyer David Boies framed the case against his client with four issues: Are Napster users violating copyright when they share music? Is Napster legally responsible if some of its users violate copyright? Is Napster as an ISP (Internet Service Provider) protected from legal liability for what its users do by the Digital Millennium Copyright Act, which requires only that an ISP act to interrupt activity when notified of suspected illegal activity by a third party? And are the major record companies abusing copyright in an effort to drive Napster out of business to take over its technology for profit?[30]

Napster users share files; Napster is a file-sharing program. Common sense tells us that in order to justifiably share something the sharer must own it first. Many Napster music files are unissued live performances or studio material that is supposed to remain in the vaults. The reproduction of officially released material is generally referred to as piracy, whereas the release of unofficial material is bootlegging. Even tracks from a legitimate CD release acquired in a legitimate manner are morally problematic if placed on Napster for financial gain or to the detriment of the financial interests of legitimate owners. The purchase of a CD carries with it the moral right to perhaps play it in one's home or office for the enjoyment of family and friends, but it does not carry the right to duplicate the material for others to the financial detriment of its creator. And if the No Electronic Theft Act classifies receipt of a blank audiotape in exchange for a tape of unreleased material as profit then certainly the receipt of an MP3 file from another user should be classified as profit also. And Napster's use of "share" suggests that a Napster user sharing a file is similar to sending a tape or CDR of a new purchase to a friend. But given the number of Napster users, most sharing goes on between strangers who in the act are at best potentially friends. Individual ownership is not compatible with our current understanding of the essential social institutions of family and friend. There, intimacy is a condition of genuine sharing of the creative work one purchases in the marketplace that extends to copying. Of course, it makes no sense to say that if a CDR of an album is made from MP3s found on Napster and costs only the price of the blank on which it is burned, that the "owner" has not profited. Value is received for a fraction of its market price.

I have nothing to say in this paper about Napster's liability for the acts of its users. But it is useful to note that Napster features a search engine to locate music files and a central directory that allows tracking of file exchanges between users. An ISP can easily monitor and block use of Napster, and Napster can determine which users have downloaded a music file whose author is listed as Mungo Jerry. And Mungo Jerry or their record company could theoretically bill a user or Napster for the music file. Universities can, and have, blocked access to the Napster directories when such access degrades transmission of courses and other educational related activities due to bandwidth limitations. If Napster's legal troubles lead to its replacement by alternatives without these two features, morally relevant negative consequences will affect both recording companies and distance learners.

Napster: Old and New

In October 2000 Napster reached an agreement with Bertelsmann Music Group to develop a net-based system of music file sharing that would include a subscription fee to generate payment for artists and record companies. In January 2001 Bertelsmann chairman Thomas Middelhoff said that Napster would begin charging with a subscription service in June or July 2001. Five major music corporations sued Napster for copyright infringement, and the agreement with BMG is perceived as a step toward satisfying the major labels' concern that Napster is eroding sales. In November 2000, Napster's welcome page stated that the agreement is a step toward providing compensation for artists. Napster lawyer David Boies maintains that Napster always believed in compensating artists. Napster also maintains on its welcome page that it will continue to provide free music, presumably from emerging artists and others who consent to the sharing of music without compensation. This is the new Napster—seeking to develop a business model and align itself with major music corporations. The original idea of Napster—a community that shares music—is much more interesting aesthetically and ethically—especially because it will go on under new names.

As this book goes to press, Napster is still negotiating with the major recording companies. Napster may transform into a two-tier system. Basic Napster will allow consumers and users to share music files from independent companies but exclude files from the major companies. Premium Napster will, for an extra fee, provide music from the catalogs of the major companies. The major companies might believe that access to Napster's list of users is a worthy financial investment, but Napster users have moved on to other file sharing programs. Those who remain delight in defeating the blocking software by misspelling song titles and group names ever so slightly. Perhaps this skeptical writer will be wrong and a viable means of selling music files online will emerge. But the major music corporations hedge that bet by continuing the lawsuit against Napster.

No matter how Napster develops to satisfy BMG and other corporations, free music will continue to be shared on the Net. Gnutella, for instance, was designed to allow file sharing between computers without a central directory in order to make it harder to document its use and shut it down. The RIAA (Recording

Industry Association of America) will certainly attempt to block Gnutella, perhaps urging legislation to require ISPs to monitor for its use. But each development of software for file sharing requires more intrusive monitoring of user activities and will ultimately overreach the tolerance of users. And currently servers, which do not claim to moderate content, are not legally responsible for the content they convey. Change in this law would make things very difficult for any server that carries Usenet discussion groups. And exclusion of such discussion groups strikes at free speech.

It is also questionable whether the revolution in music delivery can be halted. A great deal of music already exists on CD and is easily translated into MP3 files. New releases could be encrypted to prevent play on CDR drives in computers, but that would strike at the profitability of both the hardware manufacturers and music companies by reducing ease of space shifting. Any attempt to encrypt music will certainly be quickly overcome as it was recently with DVDs and Windows Media Audio files.[31] Napster's March 2001 claim that it can block sharing of selected songs is specious. Those wishing to circumvent Napster's filtering of file names need only use slightly altered titles and communicate the file names via email or in chat rooms and bulletin boards. More sophisticated blocking techniques that incorporate encryption and electronic fingerprinting only issue a challenge that hackers will happily embrace. And any encrypted file offered for sale must exist in unencrypted form somewhere on whatever device plays it. And the music business cannot reasonably expect to sell a product to consumers that the consumer cannot shift from machine to machine. They would have better luck embracing an honor system.

The monthly fee being mentioned for the Napster-BMG subscription service is five dollars. This is not an extravagant expense, but why would anyone pay it for material available free elsewhere? Music download services are not new. Custom CDs made from menus of songs have been available for several years, but the selections are generally uninspiring. The subscription fee may give Napster users access to BMG's catalog, but past practice and the low fee suggest that there will be many exceptions—for hot new releases and perennial market favorites. If the choices are not restricted, the monthly fee is sure to increase to the point that it encourages the use of free alternatives. And if the corporations resist the pressure to increase subscription prices, it will be at the expense of reduced or eliminated compensation for artists, which is how they cover those record club giveaways.[32] Many users who remain content with free MP3s will resist paying for music they deem inferior to or equal to music whose commercial packaging on LPs, cassettes, and CDs features artwork and interviews. The record companies would not mind that eventuality if it resulted in increased purchases of legitimate products. But many consumers might opt for CD burners and simply exchange and copy music.

Napster is an excellent tool for finding obscure, unreleased, or out of print material. Recently I came across a reference to Esquerita in a book on the history of rhythm and blues. The author claimed that Esquerita was a major influence on Little Richard. Try to find Esquerita at your local record store.

Napster provides access in two minutes. It also facilitates preview of new and old artists unavailable on radio or at the listening station. If you are patient and persistent, you can download an item of moderate interest that you would never buy. Napster downloads are time consuming unless you have expensive DSL or cable connections, and the quality of the music files is not always the best. Perhaps newer file formats will emerge to improve quality. A subscription service would standardize file quality, but the download time can only be addressed by better connections, and that means expensive connection fees, better hardware at both the broadcast and reception sites, and more environmentally unfriendly power usage on ISPs.

I am puzzled about how Napster could be seen as a competitor for CD sales either now or in the future. Artwork is not available via Napster, and artwork is important to most fans and collectors. It could be posted and printed from the Net, but now the subscription fee has a hidden increase for a color printer, photo paper, and color ink cartridges. So, I suspect that Napster is less a threat to current sales than a potential additional source of revenue for music corporations.

Spreading the Music

One application of file-sharing programs that everyone agrees is unproblematic is making music freely available with the consent of the artists and other financial stakeholders. The problematic uses are the sharing of unreleased material, whether live performances or studio work, and commercially released material. I am going to talk about live shows first with an example that is useful in clarifying the case for spreading the music.

Pearl Jam recently released twenty separate live CDs. Each CD was made of live performances at a different venue on their recent tour. Fans of Pearl Jam, and I am not one, can purchase a CD containing the concert they attended. If I were a Pearl Jam fan, I would happily buy at least several of these at the reasonable price of $17.99, expecting mastering, artwork, and photographs superior to what I would find on a bootlegged version of the same show. An artist and the record company are always in a better position to provide such material. In 1998, the Rolling Stones, and I am a fan, released a single live CD with songs drawn from various venues on their Bridges to Babylon tour entitled *No Security*. In between selections from St. Louis and Buenos Aires are thirty seconds of crowd noise and Mick Jagger telling the crowd in Polish "I am happy to be in Poland." I was at that concert in Poland from which the Stones issued only crowd noise and a greeting. I was happy to be in Poland, too. I don't want *No Security*.[33] And I don't want Pearl Jam. I want CDs of the concert in Poland where I was almost trampled to death.

Pearl Jam's tactic of releasing recordings from multiple sites demonstrates the impact of bootlegs on legitimate releases. Pearl Jam's reaction is a sensible one—increase releases to meet a market demand. Illegal releases provoked a reaction that resulted in better quality releases and greater responsiveness to consumer interests. If other bands ignore this market niche, they have consciously abandoned the opportunity to profit from it. Napster, legal or illegal, could have similar beneficial effects upon the music industry if it is not co-opted to preserve the corporate management of consumer options. And that is just the commercial benefit. There is also the increase of aesthetic appreciation facilitated by being able to listen to the sources of popular music, which are rarely available on the radio or at listening stations. Napster encourages more releases with superior documentation, and it facilitates music appreciation through easy auditioning and location of obscure influences.

Objects with aesthetic value are commonly treated as community resources. Property rights to aesthetic objects are even more problematic than rights to control the height of the grass on your front lawn or the manner in which you can dispose of your garbage. An artist has no absolute right to withhold an object of aesthetic value from the public. Imagine that you owned a work by a major expressionist painter and an exhibit at the local museum requested a loan of your work. My intuition is that you would have a duty to make the work available under proper conditions. But perhaps you disagree? Would you go so far as to say that the owner of the work of art has the right to withhold it or dispose of it permanently over the protests of other persons who find the work aesthetically valuable? If an artist chooses not to bring a work to the market and it can be produced via other means conducive to furthering aesthetic experiences, is it not immoral to withhold or destroy the work?

The Pearl Jam CDs are available at commercial locations such as Tower Records, through pirates, and via Napster. A fan is going to select either Tower or pirated copies from a trader in most cases, because of sound quality and

artwork. And the better the artwork and more reasonable the price, the more likely Tower will be the choice of an informed consumer. Computers with CD burners, optical scanners, and color printers are the real competition for commercial sales, not Napster. Germany recently recognized this fact by placing a special tax on Hewlett Packard computers that are sold with CD burners.

Napster has not been shown to have an impact on CD sales. Its attraction to music corporations is as an additional source of revenue and not as a serious competitor. And certainly nothing is immoral in increased profits provided that the cost is not too high aesthetically and the right people profit. Napster seems like the listening stations at Tower and not a pirate's tool. Tower does not charge for this service. Tower cannot let you listen to everything, but if you purchase a CD that does not suit your tastes you can bring it right back and exchange it. Napster, like the listening station, with music samples on Web pages and a liberal exchange policy, would allow the public to make informed music choices. But Napster does not suffer from the time and space constraints that Tower does. Napster lets you listen to anything and everything. And it is commonplace in most countries other than the United States to be able to listen to any item in a music store before purchasing it. Why can the public rent a DVD at the video store to view it before deciding to buy it and not rent CDs to audition? Napster increases the amount of music available, allows more informed music selections, and has resulted in no demonstrated harm to artists by decreasing sales.

The Pearl Jam example shows how an illegal practice can provoke useful reactions in the marketplace. Now Napster should face a hard case—copying a legitimately available commercial release. Would it be morally permissible without the permission of the artists and the record company to burn copies of this CD along with color artwork made from scans of the original and trade the copies for other commercially available music? Or, alternatively, would it be permissible to place MP3 files of this CD on Napster? I say no to burning copies and yes to Napster.

Many people are happy enough with an exact digital copy of digital coded music and color copies of artwork. But Napster does not allow the production in volume of a quality item in a reasonable period of time. Placing MP3s on Napster is analogous to loaning an item to a museum for public display. The stranger uploading a file from a hard disk is a person capable of appreciating music. Unlike items that can be put on display only in museums or symphony halls, recorded music can be mechanically reproduced for maximum access in digital form without denigrating either the condition of the original or the quality of the aesthetic experience.

Napster facilitates the sharing of objects that have aesthetic value. In itself, that action is *prima facie* morally praiseworthy. Theoretically, the purpose of copyright protection for creative artists is to reward artists for the production of items of aesthetic value and to encourage additional production of such items. Napster as a facilitator of musical selection and a spur to better quality in commercial products works compatibly with copyright protection. CD burners do not.

Artistic Control

An artist might claim artistic control as a reason for withholding material from Napster. But artistic control is often abandoned in pursuit of financial success. And artists are notorious for being poor judges of the worth, financial and aesthetic, of a creation. An artist can certainly exercise the decision not to create an object. As much as it would please me to have Britney Spears record "I Can't Get No Satisfaction" I have no right to demand she does. But once created, an aesthetic object, like a child, has a right to a life of its own.

American culture overvalues the contribution, and hence the rights, of artists. Rarely does a popular artist offer anything new; rather it is old knowledge or emotion expressed in a new form. And sometimes the form is not even new in popular culture, just the performer. Ideas cannot be copyrighted, only expressions. That is the creative element an artist sometimes brings to an already existing commons of musical history and human experience. Artists have a right to be compensated, but this compensation should not be out of proportion to the contribution a new interpretation makes to the aesthetic experience of an audience. And when music corporations and artists oppose instruments such as Napster that enhance aesthetic experience they overstep their property rights and do not warrant our moral respect. They thwart both social justifications of copyright by interfering with aesthetic appreciation and discouraging the production of a wider range of aesthetic objects in the name of an inflated account of creativity.

This more modest view of popular music artists would see them as strangely like Napster. This allows for creativity and innovation on the part of artists who realize the extent to which they draw upon a cultural commons. It also makes sense of what the Metallica fan points out to Lars Ulrich—"It's our music too." Not only does the fan inherit the musical commons, the fan also, like the artists, keeps the music alive. Finally, the attack on Napster is symptomatic of a larger transformation of the Internet, which used to offer a lot more free information. Business has not only moved onto the Net, it has also fought hard in the courts to drive out free information. Napster's woes are just one part of a gradual transformation of a virtual library and museum into the mall.[34]

CASE STUDY: JOHN LENNON COLLECTIBLES

Imagine that you are an official of an economically underdeveloped nation. You notice, perhaps through a visit to eBay, that citizens of developed nations are willing to spend a great deal of money on products that bear the likenesses of popular cultural figures. You issue a series of commemorative postage stamps to honor international figures such as Robert Johnson, John Lennon, Madonna, Mick Jagger, Snoop Doggy Dogg, and Tiffany. The plan is to sell sets of these stamps to interested collectors and use the money for the basic medical needs of your population. The legal representative of one of these persons claims trademark infringement. Should you honor their right to "protect" a trademark?[35]

CASE STUDY: NAPSTER AND SOLO

The Napster case raises an issue that was also involved in the Santa Rosa Junior College SOLO case (see Chapter 2): how to apportion responsibility between user and service provider in cases where harm occurs or is alleged to have occurred. Explain specifically what this issue is in each case.

SUGGESTED READINGS:

Boyle, James. *Shamans, Software, and Spleens.* Cambridge, Mass.: Harvard University Press, 1996.

Heylin, Clinton. *Bootleg: The Secret History of the Recording Industry.* New York: St. Martin's Press, 1996.

Johnson, Deborah G. *Computer Ethics.* Englewood Cliffs, N.J.: Prentice Hall, 1994.

Litman, Jessica. "Electronic Commerce and Free Speech." *Ethics and Information Technology* 1 (1999): 213–25.

Moore v. *The Regents of the University of California,* 793 P.2d 479 (Cal 1990), *cert denied,* 111 S. Ct. 1388 (1991).

Notes

Information Access III: Intellectual Property

1. John Locke, *Of Civil Government: Second Treatise* (1689), ch. 5, sec. 27.
2. Ibid., ch. 5, sec. 33.
3. Deborah G. Johnson, *Computer Ethics* (Englewood Cliffs, N.J.: Prentice Hall, 1994), 61.

Intellectual Property Rights and Computer Software

4. Ibid., 70–9. *Computer Ethics* 2/E, by Johnson, Deborah (c) 1994. Reprinted by permission of Prentice-Hall Inc., Upper Saddle River, N.J.
5. Robert Nozick, *Anarchy, State, and Utopia* (New York: Basic Books, 1974), 174–5.
6. Richard Stallman, "Why Software Should Be Free" (1990) Free Software Foundation, Inc.
7. Helen Nissenbaum, "Should I Copy My Neighbor's Software?" *Computers and Philosophy* 2.
8. Ron Harris "Software Creates Pirating Bonanza," Associated Press Wire Service, 12 April 2000.
9. Copyright 1985, 1993, Free Software Foundation, Inc.

Authors Are Special

10. James Boyle, *Shamans, Software, and Spleens* (Cambridge, Mass.: Harvard University Press, 1996), x–xiv, 51–60. Reprinted by permission of the publishers from *Shamans, Software, and Spleens* by James Boyle, x–xiv, 51–60, Cambridge, Mass.: Harvard University Press. Copyright © 1996 by the President and Fellows of Harvard College.
11. Simon L. Garfinkel, Richard M. Stallman, and Mitchell Kapor, "Why Patents Are Bad for Software," *Issues in Science and Technology* 50 (1991).
12. See Boyle, *Shamans, Software, and Spleens*, 192–200, for the full document.
13. Boyle, *Shamans, Software, and Spleens*, discusses *LeRoy Fibre* v. *Chicago, Milwaukee, and St. Paul Ry* on pages 48–9. He presents it as a turning point in the understanding of property rights in United States jurisprudence. Oliver Wendell Holmes is cited for remarking that the company's flax piling entitlement should be removed from that portion of the property so near to the railroad tracks as to be in danger from a prudently managed engine. In other words, property owners do not have absolute freedom to conduct business on their own property if it presents a danger to others. Boyle remarks that property now becomes a bundle of entitlements that can shift at any time in response to social utilities. And so the case illustrates his claim that property rights mixes utilitarian interests with rights claims.
14. Martha Woodmansee, "The Genius and the Copyright: Economic and Legal Conditions of the Emergence of the 'Author,' " *Eighteenth Century Studies* 425 (1984): 443–4.
15. Ernst P. Goldschmidt, *Medieval Texts and Their First Appearance in Print*. 1943
16. Woodmansee, 425.
17. Ibid., 427.
18. Johann G. Fichte, "Proof of the Illegality of Reprinting: A Rationale and a Parable," quoted in Woodmansee, 445.
19. 188 U.S. 239 (1908).

20. Ibid.
21. Jessica Litman, "The Public Domain," *Emory Law Journal* 965 (1990).
22. Paul Goldstein, "Copyright," *Journal of the Copyright Society of the U.S.A.* 109 (1991).
23. Northrop Frye, *Anatomy of Criticism* (Princeton: Princeton University Press, 1957), 96–7.
24. Steve Silberman, "Trade a Tape, Go to Jail?" Reuters News Service, 7 January 1998.
25. James Boyle, *Shamans, Software, and Spleens,* 22–24. See also 103–7.

NAPSTER: SPREADING THE MUSIC

26. Anthony Graybosch is professor of philosophy at California State University, Chico. He thanks Marcel Daguerre, Paul Friedlander, and participants in the Center for Applied and Professional Ethics Napster Forum at Chico as well as the participants in the Oregon State University Conference: Computers and Philosophy, January 2001, for comments on earlier versions of this paper. Copyright © 2001 Anthony J. Graybosch.
27. Quoted from Charles C. Mann, "The Heavenly Jukebox," *Atlantic Monthly,* September 2000, 41. Ulrich spearheaded Metallica's attack on Napster to regain control over the band's music and provoked some angry reaction in fans.
28. Ibid., 50.
29. Johnny Shines is a good example of a blues artist whose career suffered from contractual obligations.
30. John Heilemann, "David Boies: The Wired Interview," *Wired* 8, no. 10, October 2000.
31. Mann, "The Heavenly Jukebox," 48.
32. This point is courtesy of Paul Friedlander.
33. The slice of Poland occurs between "Saint of Me," and "Waiting on a Friend." *No Security's* artwork does not provide venues for the songs.
34. See Jessica Litman, "Electronic Commerce and Free Speech," *Ethics and Information Technology* 1 (1999): 213–25; for a thorough discussion of the commercialization of the Internet. "To make the Internet into a viable shopping mall, merchants need to evict the riff-raff who are hanging around and giving out free stuff. It's reminiscent of the behavior that goes on over rent-controlled apartments. We can't actually throw the occupants out, but we can make their lives unpleasant." Litman, 225.
35. This case is inspired by Yoko Ono's recent suit against a Japanese subway pass offered with the likeness of John Lennon.

10

INFORMATION ACCESS IV: SECURITY

*It is clear, consequently, that war is not a mere act of
policy, but a true political instrument, a continuation of
political activity by other means.*
Karl von Clausewitz, quoted in *On War*, translated by
Michael Howard and Peter Paret (1976).

INTRODUCTION

One could argue convincingly that most information age ethics issues are in some
way issues of *access* to information. Many of the arguments you have already encountered in this book have called for liberal access to information. On the other
hand, in Chapter 8, we saw how the concepts of privacy, secrecy, and confidentiality
are each concerned with security of information—with guarding information against
unwelcome or unauthorized access. Intellectual property law also concerns itself
with the security of information in much the same sense. In this chapter we will be
exploring this concept "security," and a good place to start would be in those contexts
where the concern over security of information is at its zenith—where information is
likely to be the most zealously guarded.

"War" usually means violent conflict between agents of duly constituted governments. A government need not be a democracy to be considered duly constituted
in international law. A government entity enjoys the support of its citizens witnessed
by an ability to maintain control over its borders. If Chiapas, for example, is effectively controlled by a force labeled guerrillas by Mexico, the guerillas are still likely
to be recognized as a government by at least some international organizations on the
basis of land control.

International intervention in the affairs of another nation is increasingly justified
on humanitarian grounds. Such intervention, however, is still embraced reluctantly,
also witnessing a commitment to the view that citizens are presumed able to control

their "government" in the absence of extraordinary state tactics such as state terrorism and ethnic cleansing. When a quasi-governmental authority begins to control
a geographic area, it has taken the first, crucial step to international recognition as a
legitimate authority.

This extended idea of legitimate authority also leads to the recognition, in
practice if not in international law, of governmental entities not internally recognized
as legitimate. Sri Lanka and its supporters may label the Tamil, a group that
maintains control over an internal geographic area, rebels or even terrorists, but
externally they are treated as an independent state. Many countries, including
the United States, for instance, did not recognize Yugoslavia until the demise of
Milosevic. Its seat in the United Nations was the subject of debate. Yet Milosevic and
the Kosovo Liberation Army representatives were treated as *de facto* heads of state
by the United States at times.

So, it is impossible to provide a tight definition of what constitutes a legitimate war-making entity because of the looseness of what constitutes having the
support of citizens, the need to accommodate leaders of revolutions, and the political
advantage of bestowing or withholding formal recognition as a legitimate authority.
But it is fair to say that international law and the traditional ethics of war attempt
to restrict war fighting to entities that control geographic areas with the support
of citizens.

Just war theory divides into *jus ad bellum* and *jus in bello*—Latin expressions for
just cause and just means. Ethical questions can be raised about the justice of going
to war or engaging in actions that provoke or preempt a war, but the distinction of
these two types of moral questions recognizes that decisions about going to war are
generally made by governmental leaders whose citizens may support the war effort
but be effectively removed from the decision to go to war through a nation's political system or a lack of accurate information. Sometimes decisions about how to carry
on war are made by political leaders, such as when Winston Churchill ordered the
bombing of German cities in retaliation for the bombing of London. But the people
who make the majority of decisions about how to carry on warfare are lower in the
hierarchy of authority. Soldiers have little control over deciding whether to go to war,
but soldiers do generally have discretion over captured military opponents and civilians in war zones. The point is that the two kinds of questions in warfare distinguish
two groups of people—those who put war into motion and those who carry it out—
and hold them generally to different ethical standards.[1]

A third category of persons involved in warfare is noncombatants. Traditionally
a combatant is someone in the military involved in carrying out the war. A soldier is
justified in killing a member of the opponent's military who, for all the soldier
knows, may have opposed the war. But a soldier is not justified in killing a citizen of
the opponent nation who might be a strong political supporter of the war effort. Modern warfare has effectively extended the scope of combatant through the introduction
of technology that targets industries central to an opponent's war effort, such as munitions factories. Just war theorists disagree as to how to treat such instances of war

fighting—are the targets just the factories or also the workers in the factories? The latter perspective suggests that "combatant" includes those involved in activities crucial to a war effort that would not normally be occurring in peacetime. The idea is that farmers support the war effort by growing bananas, but the farmers would be doing that in peacetime. Munitions workers would not normally be making arms. Of course, it is easy to note that this distinction does not hold true in nations, such as the United States, France, Russia, Israel, and Yugoslavia, which manufacture weapons as a major peacetime export. Again, regardless of the slipperiness in the concepts of noncombatant and peacetime industry, there are always clear examples of noncombatants. And a basic principle of warfare is the principle of noncombatant immunity. *Jus in bello* forbids war fighting that does not, or effectively cannot, discriminate between combatants and noncombatants. Most of us have heard "I shot an arrow into the air; it fell to earth I know not where." The saying embodies the idea that arrows are not justified instruments of war.

Just war theory also incorporates the principle of double effect. The principle of double effect allows tactics that do not themselves embrace immoral ends or means but which still might have regrettable unintended side effects. Any military target, however it is discriminated, whether it is a munitions factory, a television station, or a telephone system will have noncombatant employees performing various tasks such as cleaning. Strategic bombing of such targets is considered to have satisfied the principle of the double effect if killing the noncombatants is neither the goal (end) of the operation or the means to another goal. The principle is held to apply even when the offense knows that civilians are present. Generally it is considered important to minimize civilian casualties, collateral damage. The principle has been an important tool in distinguishing terrorism from just war fighting; and it is an important tool in extending technological war fighting capabilities. The incorporation of technology into war fighting, however, puts the definition of a combatant under strain. It becomes difficult to determine who is a combatant and who is not when the major tools of war are computers.

Information warfare can be carried out by nations and by groups that would not normally be classified as government agencies. Above it was noted that "war" is primarily applied to acts of violence between nations. It is true that war is also used to describe conflicts between corporations and even individuals. Thomas Hobbes described the state of nature, the state of human life without duly constituted government, as the war of all against all. But information warfare differs slightly from these other more individualist notions of war. Technology effectively allows individuals and groups to declare war upon nations, corporations, and ways of life. Computer technology allows more entities to wage traditional war.

The incorporation of new information technology into war fighting also extends the erosion of the concept of noncombatant. Military targets now include information centers such as telephone systems, electric power plants, and software that ordinarily supports the normal activities of noncombatants. Those computer programmers that assist in the development of such war fighting tools are the new combatants.

Governments desire to classify some acts of war as terrorist acts. Sometimes hackers are described as persons who are just curious about how something works. They are just browsing the NASA control site to see if it can be done. Other hackers are more like graffiti artists. They like to deface or adjust Web pages in a comical manner, perhaps linking a page devoted to premarital sexual abstinence to *Penthouse Magazine*. But most acts of information warfare are carried out for a political purpose, and the classification of these acts as terrorist must rely upon either the notion of duly constituted authority or noncombatant immunity to be plausible. It may be that neither of these two concepts can be given more than a contextual, political interpretation. In other words, calling someone a terrorist who has similar objectives to a state and uses similar means against similar populations is merely another form of information warfare—name-calling. The readings in this chapter will help you evaluate this. First we will look at how information warfare is regarded by the United States military and by members of the security community. We also include a discussion of information warfare in the context of just war theory that also proposes a narrower definition of information warfare, distinguishing it as only a part of a larger group of activities labeled information operations, than that used by the military, the security community, and the press. And, finally, because hacking and associated activities such as the spread of computer viruses have begun to play such a large part in both warfare and public life, we will look at whether this attack on security is properly regarded as warfare or as a form of civil disobedience.

The Bill of Rights attached to the United States Constitution regards access to information as crucial to the effective functioning of democracy. The presumption in favor of open access to information has been overridden by considerations of privacy, confidentiality, intellectual property, and national security in wartime. Information warfare treats security in a Janus-like fashion. Advocates of privacy do not generally try to both protect their own privacy and justifiably compromise the privacy of others, but information warriors do play both offense and defense. It is crucial to national security to restrict access to information systems, but it is also crucial to national security to gain access to similar information resources of an opponent. It is tempting in such a situation to claim legitimate authority for oneself in playing both offense and defense and to delegitimize an opponent in order to label functionally similar activities illegal terrorism.

Given the difficulties of determining legitimate government authority and discriminating noncombatants, we can expect some difficulty in determining what constitutes cyberterrorism. Let us see what government agencies say about information warfare and cyberterrorism to determine how the concepts are evolving before we turn to a discussion of its ethical dimensions.

10.1 INFORMATION WARFARE   Here is a selection from the United States Navy addressing the importance of information technology. Note the remarks about carrying on warfare without firing a shot and the ongoing nature of information warfare. The Navy presents information technology as crucial to both offensive and defensive war. Information technology is similar to the cruise missile, enabling precision strikes against an opponent without risk to the human beings in your military. And the integration of military activities via technology makes them technology dependent, creating a new vulnerability that must be exploited in the adversary while defending your own systems from counterattack. And clearly the Navy sees information warfare as a peacetime activity. Karl von Clausewitz once remarked that war was the continuation of politics by other means.[2] Information warfare establishes an even closer continuity between diplomacy and war.

QUESTIONS FOR STUDY AND DISCUSSION

1. What is the difference between offensive and defensive information warfare?
2. Why is information warfare a priority for the Navy?
3. Why are some information operations "necessarily covert?"

INFORMATION WARFARE— CAPABILITIES FOR THE NEW MILLENNIUM[3]

Today's—and tomorrow's—challenge will involve the collection, analysis, and exploitation of information. Information Warfare (IW) will be as important to future naval operations as modern propulsion, naval aviation, and computerized data links are to today's. IW will have a profound effect on the Navy and will become central to the success of our "Forward From the Sea" strategy. For this reason, we are transitioning to Network-Centric warfare, a war fighting posture which will enable us to respond faster and more effectively to tomorrow's threats. We will do this by leveraging our information dominance to ensure we get the right information, to the right shooter, at the right time—while denying our adversaries the ability to do the same.

This Information Warfare Strategic Plan helps chart the way toward full integration of IW into our Navy's arsenal. As such, it is a critical step in realizing the full potential of this revolutionary capability; one which will rival the introduction of steam propulsion, naval aviation, nuclear power, and computers in importance to—and impact on—our profession. . . .

Military activities performed in the information age and operations conducted in the domain of cyberspace will require that we develop the ability to conduct Information Operations or Information Warfare across the spectrum from peace to conflict and return. The target of this discipline will be the adversary's decision-making ability. The target set will be comprised of information-dependent systems; and the objective, to impede the adversary's information flow, decision cycle, and battle timelines, while protecting our own.

For U.S. Naval forces, technology has expanded our target set, improved our aim point, and provided alternative means for achieving national security objectives. Information technologies offer us the potential to manipulate or degrade information systems, attack sensor systems and networks, disrupt satellite functions, interdict power grids, or negate sensor-to-shooter links, all without firing a shot. This improvement in our ability to bring force to bear in so precise a manner supports the very essence of war fighting. . . . Information Operations exploit the opportunities and vulnerabilities inherent in the dependence on information to support military activities.

Offensive IW will employ traditional methods such as precision attacks to destroy adversary key command and control nodes, and nontraditional methods such as electronic intrusion into information networks to deny, deceive, or degrade the adversary decision process. Effective Defensive IW will be our only guarantee that we can maintain information superiority in the face of similar attacks on our own information systems. . . . The unique nature of IW, the necessarily covert nature of certain offensive IW operations, and the wide range of possibilities for using IW to support military operations or as an alternative means of achieving national security goals, presents the very significant challenge of establishing IW applications for future integration in national policy.

CASE STUDY: CYBERTERRORISM: NATO AND SERBIA

The following reading is Noam Chomsky's analysis of the NATO bombing campaign against Serbia. Chomsky is concerned with the propaganda role of the democratic media. Notice the comment columnist Pfaff makes about elections and punishment of Serbian noncombatants. Does he suggest a violation of *jus in bello?* What about the bombing of the auto plant? Does that violate noncombatant immunity? Is it an act of United States terrorism? Can the principle of double effect help here?

> From the outset, Washington understood that "the demonization of Milosevic is necessary to maintain the air attacks." In conformity with this stand, strikes against civilian targets were interpreted as "Raids on Serb Elite's Property." For example, the attack that destroyed the Zastava automobile plant, whose director was a Milosevic associate—the Minister of Privatization, who, we learn in the foreign business press, was an "entrepreneur with no party affiliation [who] was courted by western governments as a leading reformist within the Serbian government and a favorite guest on the diplomatic dinner circuit." "The idea," a senior American military officer said, "is to instill fear in those whose economic standing depends on Mr. Milosevic." The plants destroyed also happened to provide the livelihood for thousands of working people, in the case of the Zastava plant, workers who had carried out a major strike with anti-regime undertones. But that was incidental, as long as the struggle was depicted as NATO vs. the demon Milosevic.
>
> As NATO bombing shifted more explicitly to attacking the civilian society directly, it became necessary to modify the propaganda framework, demonizing the people of Serbia, not merely their leader. Recognizing that "depriving Serbia of electricity, and disrupting its water supplies, communication, and civilian transport, are

part of the program," liberal columnist William Pfaff concluded that it is a mistake to describe NATO's war as "being in conflict only with Serbia's leaders," Milosevic and his cronies. "Serbia's leaders have been elected by the Serbian people," Pfaff now pointed out, and however imperfect the elections, "few suggest that the overall result failed to express the will of the Serbian electorate." We should therefore not misdescribe Milosevic as a dictator; he is a true representative of the Serbian people, who must therefore "not be spared a taste of the suffering he has inflicted on their neighbors" (presumably referring to Kosovo, Washington's deal with the criminal at Dayton having called for no such action). They too must now be demonized, not just their elected leader, if the attack on the civilian society is to be portrayed as an exercise of the New Humanism.[4]

CASE STUDY: RADIO FREE BOSNIA

Here is Chomsky's description of the NATO treatment of Serbian media in Bosnia and Serbia:

> NATO forces in Bosnia subjected Serbian Television (SRT) in Republika Srpska—the "ethnic Serb mini-state" within Bosnia—to closure and other coercion. The specific charges were that SRT had omitted thirty seconds of a statement by Madeleine Albright "discussing her warm feelings for the Serbs," "was failing to explain that NATO troops were bombing Yugoslavia to end ethnic cleansing in Kosovo, and was giving the impression that the world opposed the strikes." In short, SRT was refusing to broadcast NATO propaganda that is manifestly false, and was giving impressions that are largely true, though they received scant notice here. Another charge was that SRT was focusing on the priorities of its audience, Serbs in Bosnia, not those of NATO. In 1997 the European Union's high representative in Bosnia, Carlos Westendorp, had "seized SRT's transmitters" and "turned the station over to politicians who favored better relations with the West," including the director now under attack for insubordination. On April 7, 1999, Westendorp went further, asking NATO to "cut off the offending material at its source" by bombing Belgrade's state television, as it did the next day.[5]

Do you consider television stations legitimate military targets? If so, what conditions must such stations fulfill to be legitimately bombed? Is the fact that a media outlet lends support to a hostile government leader through the slant of its stories sufficient to justify bombing? What would the writers of the Navy document cited above say about these two cases? Would the Navy classify the incidents reported as legitimate information warfare? If so, are these examples of offensive or defensive information warfare?

EXERCISES

1. In testimony before a special panel of the United States House of Representatives Dorothy Denning defined cyberterrorism as

. . . unlawful attacks and threats of attack against computers, networks, and information stored therein when done to intimidate or coerce a government or its people in furtherance of political or social objectives. Further, to qualify as cyberterrorism, an attack should result in violence against persons or property, or at least cause enough harm to generate fear.[6]

During Gulf War I, five hackers sympathetic to the Iraqi cause breached computer security systems at thirty-four American military sites. Using the Internet they browsed through data and mail files searching with keywords of clear military significance, such as "Operation Desert Storm," and also obtained information about the capabilities and deployment of United States forces in the Gulf area. Denning reports that a United States Air Force program manager of computer crime investigations and information warfare remarked, "They didn't, but they could have; instead of sending bullets to the Gulf, they could have sent toothbrushes."[7]

Would sending toothbrushes have been an instance of cyberterrorism according to Denning's definition? How would the United States Navy have regarded this attack? Is it an instance of offensive or defensive information warfare on the part of the Iraqi supporters?

2. In 1998 Spanish protesters "bombarded the Institute for Global Communications with thousands of bogus e-mail messages."[8] The protesters engaged in other electronic activities designed to clog traffic at the IGC such as "spamming" accounts and placing bogus credit card orders on the IGC Web page. The protestors' goal was political. Their complaint was that the IGC hosted a Web site for *Euskal Herria Journal* that in turn supported Basque independence. Because the journal's Web site included information on "the terrorist group" ETA, which has claimed responsibility for assassination of Spanish political officials, the protestors argued that IGC supported terrorism. IGC pulled the Web site.

Should the IGC have pulled the Web site? If the ETA has assassinated Spanish political officials, does it follow that ETA is a terrorist group? Or do you need to know more about a group that engages in violent opposition to a government to decide if it is a legitimate revolutionary organization rather than a terrorist group? Have the protestors engaged in cyberwar or cyberterror, according to the Navy? Does the fact that the protestors did not engage in violence against persons make their actions morally superior to other alternatives such as really bombing the IGC?

10.2 JUST WAR THEORY AND INFORMATION   During Gulf War I, the United States–led coalition engaged in a wide variety of intelligence efforts in support of conventional military activities. Coalition forces destroyed Iraqi information systems with both electronic and traditional weapons, disabled air defenses with antiradiation weapons, shut down power sources with carbon fibers dropped from missiles, and decapitated the Iraqi high command by bombing the central telephone system in Baghdad. This was an all-out attack on what is called C3I—command, control, communication, and information centers. Other information operations included attacks on Iraqi radar, faked landings in Saudi Arabia carried by CNN to mislead the Iraqis and tie up some of their forces, and dispensing of approximately twenty-nine million propaganda leaflets. Iraqi prisoners of war provided advice on the composition of these leaflets. Denning, whose definition of cyberterrorism was given on pages 400 to 401, reports that they urged the elimination of the color red as well as inclusion of soldiers with beards (signifying brotherhood) and bananas in the fruit bowls. In addition to leaflets urging the soldiers to surrender, there were leaflets and loudspeaker broadcasts threatening prosecution of commanders who used chemical weapons.

The Iraqis also fed propaganda to CNN, including a fake retreat from Kuwait and radio broadcasts directed at coalition forces. Someone, perhaps Kuwait, was responsible for reports of Iraqi atrocities against Kuwaiti infants given by the fifteen-year-old daughter of Kuwait's ambassador to the United States.[9]

Some might wish to label all these actions as information warfare because "they all target or exploit information resources to the advantage of the perpetrator and disadvantage of the other."[10] Information warfare, then, is nothing really new. It is the technology that extends the scope of information-orientated tactics. But war has always involved spying, disinformation, and propaganda. Computers might facilitate the acquisition of information while leaving the opponent with the impression that security has not been breached, but spies have always tried to gain information and cover breaches of security. And when we reflect on how Gulf Wars I and II continue with the monitoring of telephone calls, debates over inspections, bombing of radar installations, and charges and counter charges over who is responsible for the deaths of Iraqi children due to economic sanctions it is clear that information plays a vital role in all these instances. It can be tempting to see the eventual solution as one that could be facilitated by information. Certainly Walter Lippman would urge that experts survey the historical record to determine if Kuwait was ever a province of Iraq, who separated them, and if Kuwait drilled sideways into Iraqi territory.

But there is good reason to treat the tactics facilitated by information technology as discontinuous with other information operations. Although information warfare is, on the surface, nonviolent, it can be so devastating to an opponent without similar capabilities that the opponent is provoked to a massive violent response or a preemptive strike. John Arquilla has a narrower definition of information warfare in part because he realizes the threat information-rich countries such as the United States can pose to rivals with significant conventional and nuclear forces. Arquilla is concerned to interpret information warfare within the framework provided by just war theory. His theoretical concerns embrace both the evaluation of information warfare and an analysis of where just war theory may be transformed by the impact of information technology. Arquilla is fully aware of the challenge information technology presents to traditional categories of just war theory such as duly constituted authority.

The reading provides an excellent introduction to the key concepts of just war theory. Just war theory is embodied in international law and is also a set of conventions that benefit the world by embodying political expectations. It is consistent with the development of just war theory to establish distinctions between weapons and tactics on the basis of convention. Even though no tenet of just war theory has not been violated in war, the principles of just war theory convey the expectations with which nations approach military and political decision making in difficult times. A critical interpretation of information warfare in light of just war theory will at the least indicate which areas of information technology an information-rich country like the United States possesses and develops will be seen as provocative, and perhaps aggressive, by potential adversaries.

Arquilla is aware that information warfare makes warfare more thinkable for a variety of reasons. Certainly the document quoted above from the United States Navy sees information warfare as an ongoing peacetime activity. The position of restraint that Arquilla advocates is one of no first use of information technology against largely civilian populations and resources.

QUESTIONS FOR STUDY AND DISCUSSION

1. What does Arquilla mean by information warfare and how does his use of the term differ from the United States Navy's?
2. What are the meanings of jus ad bellum and jus in bello?
3. What is the principle of noncombatant immunity? If the military has to choose between imposing risks upon itself or an opponent's noncombatants may the military morally place the risk on noncombatants?
4. Discuss the various meanings of proportionality.
5. What does Arquilla mean by no first use against largely civilian targets in the context of information warfare? Why does he advocate this policy?

CAN INFORMATION WARFARE EVER BE JUST?[11]

JOHN ARQUILLA

War has often driven civilization forward, but just as often has imperiled it. An ambivalence toward war has therefore developed, with acceptance of it as a sometimes necessary evil being tempered by sustained efforts to control its frequency and intensity. Thus, from the dawn of the recorded history of conflict, attempts have been made to craft ethical approaches to war. They break down into two categories: a set of guidelines regarding going to war at all; and then strictures by which combatants might fight in a just manner. These aspects of the ethical approach to war have received searching scrutiny; and, in this early period of the information age, the time has come to revisit these ethical concepts. For new forms of conflict are emerging to test our existing understanding of "just wars"—much as advanced information technologies are already requiring a rethinking of a wide range of commercial and criminal laws.

Another reason to devote some attention to ethical issues and their potential influence on future forms of conflict is that, in the large literature on information warfare (IW), there has thus far been little effort devoted to understanding the ethical dimensions of IW—though the situation is beginning to change. Part of the problem is that IW is itself a multi-faceted concept—in Martin Libicki's phrase, "a mosaic of forms."[12] IW is a concept that ranges from notions of using cyberspace as a base from which to attack communications nodes and infrastructures, to the idea of employing information media in the service of psychological influence techniques. Because it constitutes such a variety of conflict modes, IW poses problems for those who would strive to understand how to fight ethically.

This subject is important to Americans—from civilian and military leaders to the mass public. For information warfare, as it is evolving, is demonstrating a growing disruptive capacity, both against classic military command and control structures, and against many elements of the national information infrastructure. And, simply put, the United States, whose society has grown dependent upon advanced information technologies, has by far the most to lose from a wide-ranging information war—and therefore has an interest in preventing its outbreak. A well-informed ethical approach to the burgeoning problem of information warfare may even demonstrate that it is possible, in this case, to do good and to do well. Indeed, an ethical approach to conflict in the information realm may swiftly prove as practically useful and valuable—even when the opponent is a non-state criminal or terrorist organization—as it is morally desirable.

This essay uses classic just war theory as its analytic frame of reference, applying it to the phenomenon of information warfare. First, the key concepts of just war theory are explained; and then a functional definition of IW is developed. Next, the various ethical formulations are appraised in light of information age effects on the conduct of warfare. Last, insights are drawn from this analysis, and the possibility of developing guidelines for "just" information warfare is assessed.

Concepts and Definitions

. . . The key concepts of just war theory fall into the categories of criteria for going to war (*jus ad bellum*) and of fighting justly during war (*jus in bello*). They are:

I. Tenets of just war (*Jus ad Bellum*)

   A. *Right purpose.* Justifiable reasons for going to war revolve around the concept of self-defense, which Article 51 of the United Nations Charter deems an "inherent right." Notions of right purpose generally also include ideas like preemption (i.e., striking in anticipation of an oncoming attack), but are less open to the idea of preventive war (i.e., striking at a propitious time) being just. Also, this category excludes wars of conquest or annexation.

   B. *Duly constituted authority.* It is clear from all of the literature on ethics and war that a necessary condition for having a just war is that the decision to fight must come from a government, or some league of states—not from an individual. Wars waged by individuals have always fallen outside the law, the best example being provided by 19th century prohibitions on waging private wars, or "filibusters," as they were then known. In recent years, the United Nations has even used the authority concept to argue the justice of intervening in the internal affairs of sovereign states.[13]

C. *Last resort.* Simply put, war cannot be considered just unless it follows exhaustive pursuit of negotiations and other means of conflict resolution. A good example of this is given in Thucydides' depiction of the extended crisis bargaining between Athens and Sparta as both sides sought in vain to head off the oncoming Peloponnesian War. The long run-up to the Gulf War in 1991 sounded many echoes of these ancient events.

II. Concepts of just war fighting (*Jus in Bello*)

D. *Noncombatant immunity.* Wherever and whenever possible, according to just war theory, those waging the war must strive to avoid harming civilians or enemy troops that have surrendered. Fleeing troops that have no ability to fight (e.g., the Iraqi troops retreating along the "highway of death") fall into a gray area ethically, attacks upon them being allowed—but not encouraged.[14] Conventional aerial bombing, and later, nuclear war, have posed problems for the notion of noncombatant immunity that remain unresolved. One attempt to cope with this was by considering air and nuclear attacks on strategic targets as permissible, with civilian losses treated as "collateral." Needless to say, the *Universal Declaration of Human Rights* takes a strong position in support of noncombatant immunity.

E. *Proportionality.* There are several aspects to this notion. First, and best known, is the issue of using force in a manner avoiding excessive application. A second facet, though, might be that this concept requires ensuring that a sufficient proportion of one's forces, relative to the adversary, are employed, so as to enhance the probability of winning. Thus there is a built-in tension between the need for "enough," but not "too much" force. Finally, the term is often used to mean response in-kind, or in a tit-for-tat fashion.

F. *More good than harm.* This is a concept from the Thomist paradigm. This notion implies, of war fighting, that ethical conduct requires calculation of the net good to be achieved by a particular use of force. An example of such a calculation, though clouded by violation of notions of noncombatant immunity, is Truman's decision to drop the atomic bomb on Hiroshima so as to avoid a more costly conventional invasion of Japan.

As one considers these ethical constructs, it appears that ideas about the second broad category, just war fighting, might also form part of the calculations for going to war in the first place. Thus, they should all be seen as interrelated aspects of just war theory. Yet, from an ethical perspective, it seems quite clear that responding to the *ad bellum* factors should be considered a primary duty of those who would make decisions about war and peace. The *in bello* factors, while related to decisions regarding conflict initiation, should be seen, in ethical terms, as lying in the realm of decision makers' secondary duties.

. . . The need now, though, is to consider how this multi-dimensional definition of just war theory fits with current notions of information warfare.

Defining Information Warfare

In order to consider the ethical dimensions of information warfare, it is first crucial that the phenomenon be classifiable as a true form of war, as opposed to being just a manifestation of criminal or terrorist activity—or an extension of psychological operations or intelligence-oriented activities. With this in mind, it is useful to note that, in the several years since the introduction of IW, the concept has evolved and broadened to include activities that, while information-driven, are not considered warfare and therefore do not invoke the ethical constructs of just war theory.

To separate these two classes of activities, a broad view has emerged, in which the term "information operations" (IO) refers to the entire range of information intensive interactions across a spectrum that includes: psychological operations, perception management, information security and, of course, IW. Use of "information operations" thus allows us to reserve the term IW for a specific subset of war-like activities, all of which invoke just war theory. Of what, then, does IW consist? For the purposes of this paper, I shall take the popular view that, principally, this form of war means striking at communications nodes and infrastructures, with the weapons used in such attacks generally limited to those employable via cyberspace (e.g., logic bombs, computer viruses). However, this definition should also include the use of a variety of other offensive tools, from conventional explosives to high-power microwave (HPM) weapons that can also be used to strike at information-rich targets. Attacks on information-rich targets using conventional weapons, while undoubtedly an integral part of IW, present few new ethical dilemmas, as these weapons have long been used in war. Therefore, this essay focuses on the ethical implications of the new modes of attack implicit in IW, in particular those weapons deployable via cyberspace.

The range of operations that might make use of IW extends broadly, from the battlefield to the enemy home front. Thus, IW may serve as a form of close support for military forces during active operations. It may also be employed in strategic campaigns designed to strike directly at the will and logistical support of an opponent. This last notion of IW, in which it may be pursued without a prior need to defeat an adversary's armed forces, is an area of particular interest. In many respects, it resembles notions of the strategic uses of airpower that emerged in the 1920s and 1930s, and merits close scrutiny from an ethical perspective—much as air warfare was the focus of serious, prolonged ethical debate prior to and during World War II.

Though it may bear a strategic resemblance to airpower, IW has a quite different set of effects and properties. Where airpower can generally perform much destruction on fixed points (e.g., in World War II, on U-boat pens and ball-bearing plants), information attacks, even using conventional weapons, are likely to inflict far less destruction. Rather, their effects are disruptive in nature, and may occur over wide areas (e.g., knocking out a geographic power grid), even in the face of defensive redundancies emplaced in anticipation of IW attacks. Another difference is that, where strategic aerial bombardment inevitably causes civilian losses, even with today's guided weapons, information attacks will lead to far lower levels of loss of life—despite their widespread disruptive effects. This lower lethality and destructiveness may make the damage done by IW attacks somewhat harder to assess accurately—and may complicate calculations designed to craft a proportional response.

Thus, strategic information weapons have area effects that, in some respects, extend quite a bit further than even weapons of mass destruction—but with "mass disruption" being their hallmark. And it is just this prospect of having wide effects without causing very large losses of life or dire environmental consequences that makes IW such a potentially attractive form of conflict. Although the existence of these capabilities is the subject of some debate, for the purposes of this study, it is assumed that they either already exist, or soon will.

Finally, it is important to note the inherent blurriness with regard to defining "combatants" and "acts of war." In strategic aerial bombardment, it is quite clear who is making the attacks. It is also clear that the enemy combatants are military forces, too. This latter notion is relaxed a bit in guerrilla warfare, where civilians very often engage in the fighting. But in IW, almost anyone can fight. Thus, it is important, from an ethical perspective, to make a distinction between those with access to advanced information technology and those using it for purposes of waging IW. Further, the very nature of cyberspace-based attacks is such that there may often be a sort of observational equivalence between criminal, terrorist, and military acts. The ethical imperative that attaches to these concerns is, therefore, the need to determine the identity of the perpetrators of IW attacks, and to make a distinction between sporadic depredations and those actions that form part of a recognizable campaign in pursuit of discernible aims.

Just War Theory and IW

Armed with the six tenets of just war theory and their own definition of IW described above, one may now relate them to each other to help determine the extent to which information warfare can be said to be just, or may be waged justly. This form of analysis allows for a survey of the ethical issues—and elicits some surprising results.

Jus ad Bellum   In the realm of going to war ethically, the concept of "right purpose" does not appear to be put under much stress. Self-defense and preemption, both allowed under classical just war theory, may have new dimensions because of IW, as they may be applied more promptly with disruptive information weapons. The one area that may change is that of the use of force in preventive ways. Under existing just war theory, prevention (i.e., striking to prevent the rise of a threat, like the Israelis at Osirak in 1981) lies on tenuous ground. But IW might prove especially useful in derailing the rise of a threatening power—particularly those forms of information attack that might be useful in slowing a potential adversary's process of proliferation of weapons of mass destruction.

With regard to the second concept, duly constituted authority, the very nature of information weaponry may introduce new stresses for this long-established ethical concept. For the types of capabilities needed to wage an IW campaign—particularly one waged primarily in cyberspace—there is little need for the levels of forces required in other forms of war. Therefore, the state monopoly on war reflected in the concept of duly constituted authority will likely be shaken, as non-state actors rise in their ability to wage IW.

This may be part of an emerging overall phenomenon in which the information revolution is diffusing power away from states and toward non-state actors—both peaceful, civil society elements and new "uncivil society" of information-age terrorists and transnational criminal organizations (TCOs).[15] Finally, this rise of new non-state actors capable of waging IW may also encourage states to employ them. Indeed, non-state actors will likely prove useful cutouts that help to maintain deniability, or ambiguity as to the ultimate identity of an adversary. This suggests the possibility that quite weak states may be able to strike at the strong, given the lessened likelihood that they will be discovered and subjected to retaliation. However, this problem might be mitigated by improvements in cyberspace-based detection, surveillance, and tracking technologies.

This "ease of entry" into the realm of IW not only erodes the strictures against acting without "duly constituted authority." It also suggests that the convention regarding going to war only as a "last resort" will come under strain. For IW, though it may disrupt much, at great cost to the target, does little actual destruction—and will likely prove a form of warfare that results in only incidental

loss of life. In this respect, IW can be viewed as somewhat akin to economic sanctions as a tool of coercion (though probably much less blunt an instrument than an embargo). This similarity should also contribute to the erosion of the "last resort" principle. Yet, as with economic sanctions, certain non-lethal parts of IW may not be considered acts of war, and thus may be exempt from just war considerations—a status that would increase the likelihood of their use, but preserve the integrity of the "last resort" principle for those undertakings that may be unquestionably deemed acts of war.

Finally, in the case that all IW actions are considered acts of war, if IW's low destructiveness is coupled with a situation that features self-defensive "right purpose"—say, in a crisis where skillful preemption might head off a general war—then the normative inhibition against early uses of force will be eroded even further.

Jus in Bello   With regard to the issue of waging IW justly, there are also many ways in which the classical concepts will come under pressure. First, there is one approach to IW that concentrates on striking an adversary's transportation, power, communications, and financial infrastructures. This must be seen as a kind of war that targets noncombatants in a deliberate manner. They will suffer, inevitably and seriously, from such attacks. The purpose of this type of IW is to undermine the enemy's will to resist, or to persist, in a particular fight; and, in this respect, strategic IW is very similar to early notions of strategic aerial bombardment that targeted non-combatants.

In the realm of IW, it should be noted that, even as planners may be driven to wage a form of war whose effects will be most felt by noncombatants, there is another aspect to strategic attack—one strictly aimed at disrupting the movements and operations of military forces. IW may prove to be a sufficiently discriminate tool that making this distinction is possible—and just war theory implies the need to eschew the targeting of noncombatants, focusing instead upon purely military targets and effects. Thus, an apparently attractive coercive tool of force (SIW) runs hard up against the enduring ethical constraints against attacking noncombatants. This dimension of just war theory may, therefore, pose a most nettlesome policy dilemma—and require the most creative solution.[16]

Another thorny issue is posed by the just war fighting concept of proportionality, whose major concern is with avoiding using excessive force during a conflict. In one respect, the discriminate use of IW should make it possible to wage war quite proportionately. That is, it should be possible to respond to IW strikes by some adversary in a very precise, tit-for-tat fashion, neatly calculated and calibrated. However, two problems might emerge that would put notions of proportionality under some stress. First, IW attackers might strike at an opponent's critical infrastructures, but have few of their own that could be retaliated against by means of IW. This prompts the question of when more traditional military measures—including some amount or degree of lethal force—might be used in response to IW attacks without violating notions of proportionality.

Another problem might arise if the defender, or target, were struck by IW attack, and had little or no means of responding with information weaponry. Russian strategic thinkers have considered this last issue, with some of their analysts ending up recommending forceful responses—even to the extent of threatening a renewed form of "massive retaliation" with weapons of mass destruction against IW attackers. In this respect, Schelling's suggestion that varied responses can solve one dilemma of proportionality may engender yet another dilemma: the asymmetrical retaliatory response may tend toward escalation. A prime example of the sort of problem that can arise is Russian declaratory policy toward IW attacks. As one Russian defense analyst put it recently:

> From a military point of view, the use of information warfare means against Russia or its armed forces will categorically not be considered a non-military phase of conflict, whether there were casualties or not . . . considering the possible catastrophic consequences of the use of strategic information warfare means by an enemy, whether on economic or state command and control systems, or on the combat potential of the armed forces. Russia retains the right to use nuclear weapons first against the means and forces of information warfare, and then against the aggressor state itself.[17]

Thus, Thomas Schelling should be seen as providing some guidance in these issue areas; but his solution poses difficulties and risks. He has noted that proportionality is a reasonable principle, one that need not be considered as requiring the use of identical weaponry when one is engaging in retaliation. He also implicitly argues that the risk posed by escalatory threats is not necessarily credible. See, for example, his assessment of the 1950s U.S. policy of massive retaliation as a concept that "was in decline almost from its enunciation." Yet the massive retaliatory threat may be the only credible deterrent that a potential victim of IW may be able to pose. Aside from deliberately disproportionate responses, there is also the problem that gauging the comparability of damage done by radically differing weapons systems (e.g., exploding smart bombs versus computer logic bombs) is to prove quite difficult. Finally, the problem of perpetrator ambiguity further weakens proportionate response, as one may simply not have enough data to determine just who is responsible for a particular attack.

These perplexing possibilities have led the Russians to propose a broad international moratorium—a watered-down version of which was passed by the UN General Assembly—on the development and/or use of information-based weaponry. . . .[18]

The last of the just war fighting issues that must considered is even more nebulous than notions of proportionality. It consists of the admonition to engage in combat operations that do more good than harm. However, even if difficult to measure or define, this requirement for ethical calculation of costs versus benefits may be eased by the idea that IW requires effects, but little destruction, and will likely lead to scant losses of life. Unlike the terrible dilemma that faced President Truman—a choice between massive immediate casualties inflicted upon the enemy in the near-term, versus perhaps greater long-term losses for Japanese and Americans—IW may afford the prospect of use of force that causes little destruction, but that might, used properly, help to head off a potentially bloody war.

Some Guidelines for Policy

Based on the foregoing description and analysis of the ways in which notions of information warfare interact with just war concepts, it is now possible to think about establishing a general set of guidelines that will help decision makers and information warriors behave as ethically as circumstances allow—or at least to recognize and strive to resolve the apparent tension that arises here between utility—and duty-based ethical guidelines. Rectitude aside, it must also be recognized that war is about winning. Therefore, guidance for policy or doctrine must cope with the dilemmas that may emerge as a result of striving to act properly and taking those pragmatic actions that are likely to lead to victory. . . .

Policy toward Going to War   The first issue engaged, regarding "right purpose," basically boils down to the question of whether the improved capacity for preventive strikes granted by IW can overcome the ethical problems posed by offensive war initiation. The ethical problem deepens when it is recognized that preventive war—striking forcefully before an adversary has serious, threatening capabilities—will generally mean going to war before diplomatic options have been exhausted, or not as a "last resort." On the other hand, the basically disruptive rather than destructive nature of IW suggests the possibility of a "just war fighting" approach to prevention that eases the ethical dilemma.

Simply put, prevention by means of IW might be allowable if (1) strikes were aimed strictly at military targets (e.g., command and control nodes), to avoid or generally limit damage to noncombatants; (2) the amount of forceful suasion employed was enough to deter or substantially slow an attacker, without being so excessive as to have dire economic or social effects; and (3) the good done by preventing an adversary from being able to start a particular conflict, or type of conflict, could be said to outweigh the wrong of using force beyond the realm of clearly definable self-defense.[19] Thus, *jus in bello* considerations may be seen as mitigating a serious *jus ad bellum* constraint on IW.

The second policy concern, that of remaining with the bounds of notions of "duly constituted authority," poses little difficulty from the U.S. perspective, or for any state, for that matter, so long as the state actor refrains from employing a non-state "cut out" to wage IW on its behalf. The problem goes deeper, though, as the very nature of IW implies that the ability to engage in this form of conflict rests now in the hands of small groups and individuals—it is no longer a monopoly held by state actors. This offers up the prospect of potentially quite large numbers of IW-capable combatants emerging, often pursuing their own, as opposed to some state's, policies.

Finally, the just war admonition to engage in conflict only as a last resort must also be examined. Here, the previous discussion of prevention is useful, in that early uses of IW may, overall, have some beneficial effects, and may not do serious damage to noncombatants. Weighed against this, though, are longstanding normative inhibitions against "going first" in war. For policymakers, the answer is most likely that, as in the nettlesome case of "duly constituted authority," so with "last resort," there is no easily accepted answer. And, as the rise of non-state actors implies a serious, perhaps fatal, weakening of this just war constraint; so, too, the ease with which use of IW may be contemplated suggests that a sea change will occur with regard to notions of "justice" requiring that war always be undertaken as a last resort. Finally, it may prove possible to relax the ethical strictures about "last resort" if I-warmakers engaging in early use put emphasis on disruption while avoiding acts that engender much destruction.

In summary, it appears that policy perspectives on the just initiation of an information war have left a good part of "just war theory" in tatters. For IW may now make preventive war far more thinkable (and practical), straining the limits of the concept of "right purpose." And the manner in which the information revolution empowers small groups and individuals to wage IW suggests that the notion of "duly constituted authority" may also have lost meaning. Finally, the ease in undertaking IW operations, and the fact that they are disruptive, but not very destructive, weakens notions of justice as requiring that war be started only as a "last resort."

On Just War Fighting Given the ease with which entry may be made into the ranks of IW-capable states and non-state actors, and the attractiveness of targets that primarily serve civilian commercial, transportation, financial, resource, and power infrastructures, the greatest *jus in bello* concern for IW may be the problem of maintaining "noncombatant immunity." The number of actors will be (perhaps already is) large, and hardly subject to centralized control. The civilian-oriented target set is huge, and likely to be more vulnerable than the related set of military infrastructures—except to the extent that the infrastructures simultaneously serve both the military and civilian sectors. Thus, the urge to strike at targets that will damage civilians (mostly in the economic and environmental senses—but including some incidental losses of life) may prove irresistible. In many ways, IW affords the opportunity to achieve the coercive goals. . . associated with strategic air bombardment—minus much bloodshed. Indeed, strategic IW may prove ultimately to be a useful complement to airpower and economic sanctions as a tool of suasion—as it may be more effective than sanctions, and far less destructive than bombing—characteristics that may make it a very attractive policy option.

But the ease of engaging in and attractiveness of IW must be weighed, for policy analytic purposes, against both the ethical and practical concerns. The ethical problem is a clear one: a significant aspect of IW aims at civilian and civilian-oriented targets; and also, despite its negligible lethality, it nonetheless violates the principle of noncombatant immunity, given that civilian economic or other assets are deliberately targeted. In addition to the ethical dilemma posed by IW, there is the practical problem that whoever might begin the business of striking at civilian-oriented targets invites retaliation in kind—both from nation-states and from individuals or small groups that are armed with advanced information technological capabilities.

The problem is akin to the issue of the aerial bombing of cities, as conceived of in the 1920s and 1930s. The air powers of the day were in general agreement—

once it grew clear that many would have this capability—that they would avoid striking at each others' cities. Indeed, with only a few exceptions, the warring states at the outset of World War II strove to refrain from deliberately bombing civilian targets. Indeed the circumstances that sparked a shift, leading to the London Blitz and the RAF's [Royal Air Force's] retaliatory fire bombings of German cities, were accidental.[20] However, once the shift was made, all combatants went about the business of civilian targeting with a will, culminating in the nuclear attacks on Hiroshima and Nagasaki. The trend of targeting civilians was, if anything, deepened in the Korean War, at the end of which there stood only one undamaged building in all Pyongyang. But today's technologies are refining the accuracy of air bombardment, making it possible to craft campaigns that do far less damage to civilians or civilian-oriented targets.

No such technological solution appears imminent in the realm of IW. There is rather the problem of a diffusion of attack capabilities to many actors who may have the capability for mounting very precise attacks, but perhaps little incentive to limit their aggression. This implies a practical need to find ways to discourage attacks on civilian-oriented targets. From a policy perspective, there is an initiative that a leading information power, such as the United States, might take. This would consist of adopting a declaratory doctrine of "no first use" of information warfare against largely civilian targets. It is a simple, straightforward step, but one that nevertheless still allows for IW strikes against military-oriented targets (e.g., operations centers, logistics, and command and control nodes).[21] Further, it allows for retaliation in the event that one's own civilian targets have been hit (presuming that the attacker's identity may be ascertained).

The problem of ambiguity regarding IW perpetrators is indeed difficult; but is not insurmountable. For, in the context of war, there is always some purpose to such attacks, and one may add logical inference to the pool of other detection resources in parsing out just who is behind the attacks in question. This may mitigate the problem of ambiguity, which has existed in earlier eras—and has been coped with effectively. A good example of dealing with ambiguity, sixty years ago, was the case of the "phantom" submarine attacks on merchant ships bringing aid to the Loyalists during the Spanish Civil War (1936–39). Britain quickly inferred that the Italians, supporters of the Fascists, were likely suspects. Soon, a retaliatory threat was made, despite Italian denials of culpability. The British remained firm, asserting that the Italians would be struck unless the attacks were halted. "Phantom pirate" attacks stopped immediately, and never resumed.

The other potential problem with a "no first use" pledge is that it takes away an attractive coercive tool—the use of IW strikes against a potential aggressor's many infrastructures as a means of signaling, or to deter an attack during some politico-military crisis. Against this benefit, however, one must weigh the cost of initiating a behavioral regime in which such attacks are tolerated—and which would likely do enormous disruptive harm to the richest set of information targets in the world, which are to be found in the United States. Even with a pledge

of no first use against civilian-oriented targets, the option of using IW against enemy militaries still remains—which, if judiciously employed, might prove to be a good deterrent.

Compared to the problems with crafting policy approaches that will cope with the new dilemmas for noncombatant immunity, which are difficult but not duly so, the policy alternatives in the realms of "proportionality" and acting so as to do "more good than harm" seem much less daunting. With regard to proportionality, a number of very straightforward options seem available.

First, a good declaratory position on proportionality might extend to a policy by which IW attacks would engender identical retaliatory response—subject, of course, to proper identification of the perpetrator. However, in those cases where the attacker does not have a set of information targets as large as needed for there to be a proportionate response, or has no information-oriented targets, the retaliation might have take the form of a use of more traditional military force against strategic targets of the perpetrator. In this last case, proportionality may prove highly complex in practical operation.

With regard to doing more good than harm, this aspect of just war theory seems still both useful and feasible. The discriminate nature of IW should allow a very careful calibration of effects. The only difficulty that might emerge could ensue in situations where IW attacks do not have the coercive results envisioned. Indeed, it may prove very difficult to predict the psychological effects of such attacks on either elite decision makers or mass publics. In this case, if IW were used preventively or preemptively, and failed in purpose, it might even be said that an escalation to general war was the fault of taking the IW action in the first place. Therefore, the risks of escalation versus the likelihood that IW will head off a conflict must be very carefully assessed prior to relaxing any notions "right purpose," "last resort," or "non-combatant immunity."

Closing Thoughts

The key points to be drawn from this essay begin with the insight that the ethics of going to war (*jus ad bellum*) may be seriously attenuated by IW. Secondarily, though, just war fighting (*jus in bello*) issues seem to retain their currency and value.

Policy toward and doctrinal development of IW thus need to focus on this latter area, with special care given to avoid encouraging strikes against civilian-oriented targets, but with lesser consideration given—relatively—to proportionality and doing more good than harm. These latter issues are simply less nettlesome than the burgeoning problem of civilian vulnerability to strategic information warfare.

IW makes war more thinkable. This seems inescapably true—and is quite troubling. Yet it does not require that waging IW must be destructive or unjust. To the contrary, notions of just war fighting will continue to provide a useful guide to behavior, well on into the information age. This poses the possibility of giving an affirmative answer to James Turner Johnson's question about whether modern war, replete with all its new technologies, can ever be just.

CASE STUDY: HACKING INTO THE SPACE PROGRAM

Hackers regularly gain access to highly sensitive Internet sites. For instance, a hacker overloaded the National Aeronautics and Space Administration (NASA) communications system in 1997 as the United States space shuttle was docking with the Russian space station, Mir. The hacker, intentionally or unintentionally, interfered with medical monitoring and communication with the astronaut on the shuttle. NASA was forced to rely upon an alternative communications route.[22]

Because hackers have proved able at gaining access to sensitive sites guarded by the latest security systems, do you think it reasonable to protect military information systems by threat of criminal prosecution? Or should sensitive information remain off the Internet and decisions about the use of weapons systems always require a human decision maker?

CASE STUDY: THE I LOVE YOU VIRUS

The I Love You virus was ". . . estimated to have hit tens of millions of users and cost billions of dollars in damage." Cyber attacks against commercial sites such as Yahoo and e-Bay not only cause direct financial losses but shake the confidence of both corporations and consumers in electronic commerce.[23] Assume that these attacks were motivated by curiosity or spite and not by a political concern. Would Arquilla consider such attacks instances of information warfare? Would just war theory consider the attacks terrorism? Are these terrorist attacks?

CASE STUDY: ECONOMIC CYBERWAR

DCSS is a program that decrypts DVDs. It allows the DVD to be copied to a hard drive and played on a computer monitor. The files can also be copied subsequently to a blank DVD, a VCD (CD used as for video), and to an external VCR. The software was available on the Internet briefly before becoming the target of legal challenges. Many people have this now illegal software on their hard drives. The alternatives to Napster, such as BearShare and Gnutella, use disk-to-disk file-sharing software. Because those who use Napster, BearShare, and Gnutella are thought to be illegally sharing music files, it is reasonable to assume that such people are likely to have DCSS on their hard drives. It is possible to create a program that would piggyback on Gnutella and BearShare and delete DCSS wherever it finds it. What would you think of the morality of using programming to delete illegal software such as DCSS via the Internet?

10.3 CYBER CIVIL DISOBEDIENCE   Just war theory suggests that some causes are indeed worth fighting for, that not all causes are morally equal. But by separating *jus ad bellum* from *jus in bello* it not only recognizes the morality of those who fight for an unjust cause but also limits what can be justifiably done for a just cause and against the forces of an aggressor. Most of us are inclined to accept "unjust" tactics directed at nations or groups promoting an unjust cause. This inclination increases not only with the scope of the injustice but also with the powerlessness of its opponents. In other words, we do not always see terrorism primarily in terms of *jus in bello*. This accommodation is especially tempting in connection with information warfare where no direct violence will occur. Although the hint of possible violence always lurks in the background, at least part of the inclination to not label such instances "terrorism" rests on the perception that the cause is just.

Here is an example of information operations directed primarily at civilians. Certainly your perception of whether those targeting the SHO Web site were engaging in terrorism will be influenced by whether or not you think the cause is just.

> A report prepared for the Seattle Host Organization (SHO), which sponsored the [World Trade Organization (WTO)] meetings Nov. 30–Dec. 3, said there were "hundreds of illegal attempts, particularly during November 1999, to knock us off the Internet." The site contained information for visitors, including local tourist attractions and ways to get around the region, as well as information on WTO events and protests.
>
> . . . [H]ackers probed the (SHO) Web site nearly 700 times looking for weaknesses during the week of the meetings and tried to hack in 54 times "in a continuing attempt to bring down the site," the report said.
>
> On Dec. 3, the computer system repelled an e-mail assault designed "to flood the site provider and disable it," the report added.[24]

Governments and corporations have an interest in maintaining the status quo and so can be expected to classify such actions as cyberterrorism simply on the grounds that the actions are not carried out by a legitimate authority. Another perspective, however, can inform discussions of information operations carried out by non-governmental forces: civil disobedience. In the discussion so far, nongovernmental acts of information warfare have been viewed from the perspective of government policy makers and theorists sympathetic to that perspective. In this section we change the perspective slightly to one more sympathetic to computer-assisted political action. We will always have people with legalistic stances who see every act of disagreement or protest as a military revolution and threat to the government. Those with a strong attachment to government will be less likely to accept the switch of perspective Anthony Graybosch urges. In any case, trying on this different perspective should be helpful, because it is the one within which many hackers and protestors, especially those not employed by governments in information warfare, place themselves.

QUESTIONS FOR STUDY AND DISCUSSION

1. What is hacking? What is a virus? What is a worm?
2. What are the major differences between Thoreau's and King's views on civil disobedience?
3. Are the viruses directed toward kiddie porn sites reasonable forms of civil disobedience? How about viruses directed at abortion rights sites or the Hemlock Society?
4. Military planners often direct efforts toward worst-case scenarios. Does the behavior of some hackers suggest extreme caution should be used in linking the information and weapons systems?

COMPUTER-ASSISTED CIVIL DISOBEDIENCE[25]

ANTHONY GRAYBOSCH

Most people understand the weapons used by hackers and cyber protestors as tools of civil disobedience. That will be the perspective I urge here, as preferable to that of just war theory, for talking about computer assisted civil disobedience (CACD). But sometimes hackers break into computers simply to flex intellectual muscles or demonstrate that a security system can be penetrated. For instance, one hacker claims to have written a virus to demonstrate how the Pretty Good Privacy utility is vulnerable due to Microsoft's platform and lax security. Yet his testimony suggests a great deal of pride in the accomplishment.[26] Other hackers seem more like graffiti artists—invading a program or a Web site and tinkering with its operation or leaving a signature simply to place a tag on the site.

But some viruses are clearly vindictive and akin to terrorism. I was a victim of the Happy99 virus released around New Year of 1999 that ate e-mail files. I clicked on the exe file and was treated to a very colorful virtual fireworks display. Happy99 also automatically e-mailed itself as an enclosure to everyone else I subsequently e-mailed. But, as viruses go, Happy99 was a friendly one. It left behind a file in which it listed all the addresses it had mailed itself to from my address book. And so I was able to e-mail those correspondents and urge them to purge the file. It was also a friendly virus in that it delivered the fireworks display. The more recent Anna Kournikova virus reportedly did not actually contain a picture of the tennis star although the Naked Dancing Wife virus reportedly did live up to its name.

Hackers might point out that my experience with Happy99 was useful since it prevented me from opening these other two viruses. But that defense is like shooting someone to teach them not to play with guns. An effective learning experience need not be morally defensible. Hackers might also point out the humor in such viruses. The I Love You virus was quite funny as long as you did not open it yourself. Those who did lost e-mail files and a copy of the virus was mailed to all other individuals in the victim's address book. As a recipient I found the I Love You messages from some co-workers quite funny and liked knowing who had been curious enough to open an e-mail with that subject line from a co-worker. But humor was not the intent of the virus.

The intent was the destruction; the affection was the Trojan horse, and the humor was just a by-product. The conclusion is unavoidable; some hackers are just cyber terrorists.

Many viruses just automatically mail themselves to all entries in an infected e-mail address book. Some viruses activate disabling computer procedures, for instance, sending massive e-mails from a site's computers. And other viruses are fakes—warnings that if you have downloaded a particular file something terrible is going to happen and listing time consuming and expensive tasks to prevent the consequences. Finally there are virus-like programs called worms that operate independently of the cooperation of computer users. Worms do basically the same sorts of things as viruses—corrupt files, send massive e-mails—but move through computer networks independently of user actions.

There are a variety of psychological types found in the hacker community. Information warriors have to be aware of the existence of the variety of moral personalities behind the virtual visitors to highly sensitive sites and plan accordingly.

Civil Disobedience

Not all hackers are antigovernment. Some are just looking around out of curiosity and playfulness.

> . . . Synergy decided one day that it would be interesting to look at the credit history of President Ronald Reagan. He easily found the information he was looking for and noticed that 63 other people had requested the same information that day. In his explorations, he

also noticed that a group of about 700 Americans all appeared to hold one credit card, even though they had no personal credit history. Synergy soon realized that he had stumbled upon the names and addresses of people in the federal Witness Protection Program. Being a good citizen, he informed the FBI of his discoveries and the breach of security in the Witness Protection Program.[27]

We have already noted the use of massive e-mail to cripple a business. Such actions are the virtual equivalents of nonviolent sit-ins directed at shutting down an institution or drawing attention to oppression. There are Web sit-ins in which protestors point browsers toward the same address to effectively disable it and graffiti defacements of Web pages with unfriendly slogans and links. Speaking to the suggestion of an electronic national identification card, Winn Schwartau remarks, "So what is a disgruntled citizenry to do? Cyber-civil disobedience is timely, poignant, and potentially highly effective."[28] And some Seattle protestors of the WTO obviously agreed that a computer assisted disruption would be an effective yet peaceful disruption of an event so highly dependent for its success on computer technology.

It is not difficult to find examples of causes that seem to be justified instances of CACD. The same hacker who demonstrated the security problems with Pretty Good Privacy wrote a virus that "launched a 'ping flood' attack—a barrage of data packets that overloads servers and disrupts Internet connections—on four different Web sites. Two of the sites were devoted to kiddie porn; the other two were racist hangouts."[29]

Civil disobedience balances two moral imperatives—the need to respect the contribution to human well-being made by governments with the need to respect moral authority that transcends government. Martin Luther King argued that a law was unjust when it violated the law of God, violated human dignity, was formulated or applied strictly for a minority of citizens, or was formulated without participation of the affected parties.

> A just law is a man-made code that squares with the moral law or the law of God. An unjust law is a code that is out of harmony with the moral law. . . . Any law that uplifts human personality is just. Any law that degrades human personality is unjust. . . .
>
> . . . A law is unjust, for example, if the majority group compels a minority group to obey the statute but does not make it binding on itself. . . . Also, a law is unjust if it is inflicted on a minority that, as a result of being denied the right to vote, had no part in enacting or devising the law.[30]

CACD is motivated primarily by the notion that a law, culture, or corporate policy is degrading to human personality, although in some cases CACD is religiously motivated. And there is greater awareness of the environmental impact of government and corporate policy now than when King is writing. So King's view that a law was unjust when applied to a minority denied the right to vote would be extended to the environment, which cannot vote, by those who think of the environment as having intrinsic value.

King also argued that evading the law, breaking the law and avoiding punishment, would lead to anarchy. "One who breaks the law must do so *openly, lovingly*, and with a willingness to accept the punishment."[31] King goes on to say that breaking the law and accepting punishment shows the highest respect for the law. This statement testifies to one frequent difference between information operations between nations and those directed by individuals and groups against nations and corporations. Often CACD's goal is not the rejection of a nation, culture, or corporation but a reformation that is compatible with leaving the governing body more or less intact. I am not saying this is always the case. And the cases do fit on a continuum from reformation to secession to the toppling of a government. Hackers probably will not agree with King that their activities should be carried out openly and that they should accept punishment; but some forms of CACD are compatible with eventual reconciliation.

King also argued that civil disobedience was only justified after an exhaustive investigation of the facts and an attempt to negotiate an agreement. And King emphasized that protests must be nonviolent in order to hold open the possibility of eventual reconciliation.[32] I will return to these aspects of civil disobedience below.

The other prominent American advocate of civil disobedience, Henry David Thoreau, seemed to think that individual conscience was always above the law. His problem was not really when he should break the law as much as when he had an obligation to do so. Thoreau knew that breaking the law was likely to disrupt his detachment from society. Thoreau's answer was that in instances where he was made an instrument of another human being's oppression and the oppressed could not effectively gain freedom on their own, then he had an obligation to break the law.[33]

> Can there not be a government in which majorities do not virtually decide right and wrong, but conscience?—in which majorities decide only those questions to which the rule of expediency is applicable? Must the citizen ever for a moment, or in the least degree, resign his conscience to the legislator? Why has every man a conscience, then? I think we should be men first, and subjects afterward.

I mention King and Thoreau not only because they are the two most influential figures in how Americans think about civil disobedience but also because of a difference in how each would organize civil disobedience. Thoreau looked for the means by which he could act effectively as an individual against the government. He believed in the effectiveness of individual action against government if the individual could find the right tactics and was the right individual. And he was no friend of gradual change.

> Even voting for the right is doing nothing for it. It is only expressing to men feebly your desire that it should prevail. . . . When the majority shall at length vote for the abolition of slavery, it will be because they are indifferent to slavery, or because there is but little slavery left to be abolished by their vote.
>
> . . . [I]f it is of such a nature as to require you to be an agent of injustice to another, then, I say, break the law. Let your life be a counter-friction to stop the machine. What I have to do is see, at any rate, that I do not lend myself to the wrong which I condemn.

As for adopting the ways which the State has provided for remedying the evil, I know not of such ways. They take too much time, and a man's life will be gone. I have other affairs to attend to. I came into this world, not chiefly to make this a good place to live in, but to live in it, be it good or bad.[34]

This extended quote is useful because it captures the attitude toward established authority that motivates CACD. It is not enough to express your opposition to significant political evils by voting or sending e-mails to congresspersons who send back canned replies. When faced with significant evils more immediate and effective action is morally obligatory.

King was also concerned with effective action but borrowed from Gandhi the notion that a collective, military-like resistance was more effective than individual martyrdom. Thoreau lived in the nineteenth century when tax collectors still came to people's homes. So he sought face-to-face confrontation with the government in the person of the tax collector. The increased bureaucratization of government makes it increasingly difficult to find a way to confront the government, or corporate leaders, effectively without resorting to violence. So King embraced nonviolent coercion directed at essential government functions to foster social change.

Certainly there are groups of hackers who work together in cyber civil disobedience. But information technology makes the scenario Thoreau envisaged of an individual confronting the government directly a real possibility again. Certainly one appealing aspect of information technology is that it allows

protest without direct violence.[35] And, of course, it is a very effective tool for gaining governmental or corporate attention.

From the civil disobedience tradition CACD advocates draw the conclusion that an act of information warfare (CACD) will be just when nonviolent and effective, directed at entities that have violated a moral law (understood as violating human dignity and rights) as opposed to the laws of the state, and after serious investigation of the facts and attempts at negotiation. And the civil disobedience perspective is at odds with the legalistic paradigm popular with government-orientated intellectuals over the relative priority of moral and governmental law.

This perspective seems largely correct to me. First, what kinds of CACD does it classify as immoral? CACD for personal gratification or vindictive and spiteful CACD is ruled out. CACD that purports to demonstrate an imperfection in security software, even software that is adopted by military agencies, is justified only after less drastic measures have failed. By less drastic measures I mean to appeal to the equivalent of Dr. King's injunction that civil disobedience be preceded by fact finding and attempts to negotiate. A hacker should document the security problem and contact the software company, the government agency, and the media before launching a first strike. Even playful CACD might be ruled out. By playful CACD I mean viruses that make computers play silly songs when they are booted. Such viruses can make computer users paranoid.

But in some instances governments and corporations engage in projects that violate the moral perceptions of citizens and stakeholders. Projects that have a lasting environmental or economic impact also call for immediate action. They can create the sense of urgency and personal involvement that Thoreau voiced over slavery. If the CACD protestor has engaged in fact gathering, exhausted alternative means in the available time, and embraces where possible a means that targets the offending government, corporation, university, or individual in a nonviolent manner, then society should do its best to tolerate such moral opposition.

This conclusion ultimately depends on two contingent premises. One is that the American media do not effectively provide for free and open discussion. Since the media is itself part of corporate culture, this premise seems warranted. The other premise is that CACD is justifiably tolerated because it is essentially nonviolent. CACD may impose economic costs but economic costs are a reasonable price to pay to allow society to be provoked by statements of conscience.

Conclusion

CACD is here to stay, thanks to the new information technology. CACD facilitates individual action against governments and corporations. Since some CACD reflects serious moral convictions, it is more rightfully regarded as a form of civil disobedience than classified as terrorism under just war theory because individuals and groups of hackers are not legitimate government authorities. The civil disobedience approach to information operations does not necessarily conflict with the just war approach to information operations between governments and quasi-governmental agencies. And the civil disobedience approach preserves the equivalent of some concepts from just war theory. For instance, CACD for personal gain violates the notion of just cause. Its practitioners are the equivalents of terrorists. Yet not all who resort to CACD are automatically classified as terrorists.

CASE STUDY: CRASHING THE WHITE HOUSE SERVER

In 1996 a cyber protest was aimed at the White House information site to protest proposed government Internet policies deemed hostile to freedom of speech. Protestors attempted to disable the site by e-mailing copies of the Bill of Rights. Suppose the protest were aimed at a more important military communications site. Based on its greater effectiveness, would that have been a more or less moral action in the eyes of advocates of CACD?

EXERCISE

Return to the earlier exercises and case studies in this chapter and discuss them from the point of view of CACD. Use King's notion of unjust law as a means of evaluating the cause of hackers and his four steps of nonviolence to evaluate the morality of their *jus in bello*.

Suggested Readings:

Denning, Dorothy E. "Cyberterrorism: Testimony Before the Special Oversight Panel on Terrorism, Committee on Armed Services, United States House of Representatives." 23 May 2000; www.cs.georgetown.edu/~denning.

Denning, Dorothy E. *Information Warfare and Security.* New York: ACM Press, 1999.

Graybosch, Anthony J. "The Ethics of Space-Based Ballistic Missile Defense," *Monist* 70 (1987): 45–58.

Himanen, Pikka. *The Hacker Ethic and the Spirit of the Information Age.* New York: Random House, 2001.

Johnson, James Turner. *Can Modern War Be Just?* New Haven, Conn.: Yale University Press, 1984.

Petersen, John. "Information Warfare: The Future." In *Cyberwar: Security, Strategy and Conflict in the Information Age.* Edited by Alan D. Campen, Douglas H. Dearth, and R. Thomas Goodden. Fairfax, Va.: AFCEA International Press, 1996, 219–26.

Schwartau, Winn. *Information Warfare.* 2d ed. New York: Thunder's Mouth Press, 1996.

Walzer, Michael. *Just and Unjust Wars.* New York: Basic Books, 1977.

Notes

Information Access IV: Security

1. Sometimes leaders are held responsible for the tactics of soldiers in the field even in the absence of direct orders from the leaders. The idea is that military and political leaders sometimes are irresponsible in not investigating tactics in the field.

2. Peter Paret, *Clausewitz and the State* (New York: Oxford University Press, 1976), 379–80. "War is not an independent phenomenon but a continuation of politics by different means. Consequently the main lines of every major strategic plan are *largely political in nature*, and their political character increases the more the plan applies to the entire campaign and to the whole state. A war plan results directly from the political conditions of the two warring states, as well as from their relations to third powers. A plan of campaign results from the war plan and frequently—if there is only one theater of operations—may even be identical with it. But the political element even enters the separate components of a campaign; rarely will it be without influence on such major episodes as a battle, etc. . . . According to this point of view, there can be no question of a *purely military* evaluation of a great strategic issue, or of a purely military scheme to solve it." Thanks to Edward Romar for this reference.

Information Warfare—Capabilities for the New Millennium

3. DOCD 201:2 IN 3/2. Government publication.

4. Noam Chomsky, *The New Military Humanism: Lessons from Kosovo*, (Monroe, Maine: Common Courage Press, 1999), 93. Chomsky's sources include *New York Times* stories from 30 March, 14 April, and 19 May 1999.

5. Ibid., 130. Chomsky's source is Daniel Pearl, "Propaganda War: A Bosnian TV Station Staffed by Serbs Runs Afoul of U.S., NATO," *Wall Street Journal,* 13 May 1999.

6. Denning, Dorothy E., "Cyberterrorism: Testimony Before the Special Oversight Panel on Terrorism, Committee on Armed Services, United States House of Representatives," 23 May 2000.

7. Denning, *Information Warfare and Security,* (New York: ACM Press, 1999), 3.

8. Denning, "Cyberterrorism," 2.

9. Denning, *Information Warfare and Security*, 3–5.

10. Ibid., 6.

CAN WARFARE EVER BE JUST?

11. John Arquilla, "Can Information Warfare Ever Be Just?" *Ethics and Information Technology* 1 (1999): 203–12. Most footnotes have been omitted. Reprinted with kind permission of Kluwer Academic Publishers and the author.

12. Martin Libicki, *What Is Information Warfare?* (Washington, D.C.: National Defense University Press, 1996), 6.

13. Boutros Boutros Ghali, *An Agenda for Peace: Preventive Diplomacy, Peacemaking and Peacekeeping, A Report of the Secretary-General on the Work of the Organization,* UN Document A/47/277/S/2411 (1992).

14. Michael Walzer, *Just and Unjust Wars,* (New York: Basic Books, 1977), 129 notes, on this point, that the rule of thumb is to limit "excessive harm." Yet, he observes that many have argued that this restriction can be relaxed if such action contributes clearly and materially to victory.

15. On these issues, see Bruce Hoffman, "Responding to Terrorism Across the Technological Spectrum," in *In Athena's Camp: Preparing for Conflict in the Information Age,* ed. John Arquilla and David Ronfeldt, (Santa Monica: RAND, 1997), 339–67; and Phil Williams, "Transnational Criminal Organisations and International Security," *Survival* 36 (1994): 96–113.

16. It is important to distinguish here between just war theory's tolerance for collateral damage—in the event that strikes on military targets unintendedly cause noncombatant deaths and damage—and the deliberate targeting of civil systems and civilians to achieve some military purpose. The latter is, from the perspective afforded by just war theory, unethical.

17. V. I. Tsymbal, "Concepts of Information Warfare," a speech presented at the conference on Evolving Post-Cold War National Security Issues, held in Moscow, 12–14 September 1995.

18. See General Assembly Resolution 53/70, adopted 4 January 1999.

19. In this regard, the oft-stated rationales of war initiators, that they were simply starting the war to "defend" their countries against threats that would soon appear, must be viewed with some skepticism. For these are the sorts of arguments advanced by Napoleon, who felt he had to conquer all of Europe in order to defend France, and by German leaders in the first half of this century.

20. Having to do with a German pilot inadvertently jettisoning his bombs over London when he thought he was elsewhere. Though this "accident" spurred the Germans to begin bombing British cities, senior Luftwaffe leaders had been arguing for this expansion of the campaign as a means of forcing the British RAF to come out and grapple with German fighters. On this, see John Keegan, *The Second World War* (New York: Viking, 1989), 96.

21. It is the same, in many respects, as the notion of no first use in the nuclear context. However, in the nuclear setting, this type of restraint was thought to increase the risk of the outbreak of conventional war. As U.S. power today is preponderant, it is hard to conceive of an IW no first use pledge as having the effect of undermining deterrence of conventional war. The nuclear no first use debate is neatly exposited in two short essays. For the view in favor of NFU, see McGeorge Bundy, George F. Kennan, Robert S. McNamara, and Gerard Smith, "Nuclear Weapons and the Atlantic Alliance," *Foreign Affairs* (Spring 1982): 753–68. The rebuttal soon followed, from Karl Kaiser, Georg Leber, Alois Mertes, and Franz-Josef Schulze, "Nuclear Weapons and the Preservation of Peace," *Europa-Archiv* 7 (Summer 1982): 157–71.
22. "BBC: Hacker Endangered Astronauts," London: Associated Press Wire, 2 July 2000.
23. Denning, "Cyberterrorism," 2.
24. "Hackers at WTO in Seattle," Associated Press Wire, 19 January 2000.

Computer-Assisted Civil Disobedience

25. Anthony J. Graybosch, "Computer Assisted Civil Disobedience" © Copyright Anthony J. Graybosch 2001.
26. See Kim Neely, "Virus Underground," *Rolling Stone*, September 1999.
27. Michael G. Devost, "Hackers as a National Resource," in *Information Warfare*, 2d ed., Winn Schwartau (New York: Thunder's Mouth Press, 1996), 367.
28. Winn Schwartau, *Information Warfare*, 2d ed. (New York: Thunder's Mouth Press, 1996), 405.
29. Kneely.
30. Martin Luther King Jr., "Letter From Birmingham Jail," *Christian Century*, 12 June 1963, 769. King was writing about segregation.
31. Ibid., 770. Emphasis is in the original.
32. Ibid.
33. Henry David Thoreau, *Resistance to Civil Government*, originally published in 1849. This essay is sometimes anthologized with the title *On Civil Disobedience*.
34. Ibid.
35. Here we mean to point out that information warfare can result in no direct violence but still be implicated in deaths. No noncombatants may be in a power plant when it is bombed to disrupt military communications, yet the bombing may disrupt many medical services to noncombatants.

11

INFORMATION TECHNOLOGY, EVERYDAY
LIFE, AND THE FUTURE OF HUMAN
CIVILIZATION

"Read not the Times.
Read the Eternities."
HENRY DAVID THOREAU, *LIFE WITHOUT PRINCIPLE*

INTRODUCTION

The *International Herald Tribune* and *CNN* are obvious means by which travelers abroad can keep in touch with events in the United States. But even these information sources acquire a foreign flavor and in deference to their international audience omit the extensive coverage to local events and sports that make an information consumer feel right at home. Web-based publications such as InfoBeat deliver a personalized news menu that arrives at your computer with your morning cup of coffee. You can choose various editions: A Californian can choose to receive the afternoon West Coast final edition anywhere in the world. Such communications, and e-mail, might make a traveler wonder where she is waking up—in Germany or California? Sometimes technology works to preserve everyday local life and attachment to a community.

This chapter examines ways in which information technology has affected everyday life through individual electronic communication such as multi-user domains (MUDs). Cyberspace both disembodies and re-embodies; it destroys community and reconstitutes it.[1] For instance, MUD dwellers can adopt a different gender as part of constructing an identity in cyberspace. The screen allows a user to escape in virtual reality (VR) physical characteristics that play a major role in constructing an identity in real life (RL) such as gender, race, weight, and disability. Out-of-body experience facilitated by technology may lead to psychological growth in RL, but some researchers believe that RL gender characteristics may also carry over into VR. Interaction between the sexes on bulletin boards and in MUDs extends the conflicts found in everyday life. As ethicists, we are primarily interested in what light our consideration of moral issues in VR can throw on morality in RL. Yet concerns expressed about actions in VR, combined with the amount of time many people spend out of body, testify to an increased awareness that the boundaries between RL and VR—for the psychological self at least—are tenuous at best.

Many areas of everyday life are transformed by information technology and worthy of study in a course in information ethics. Perhaps all prisons will eventually be eliminated in favor of electronic home arrest. We will have little need for drivers' licenses in a world where cars drive themselves to programmed destinations. Perhaps the area of information technology most likely to have the greatest short-term effect on society is genetic engineering. But the ability to alter the self exists now through the distance created by information technology in interactions at a distance—e-mail, bulletin boards, and MUDs that allow each user extended control over access to personal characteristics.

11.1 REDESIGNING OURSELVES Sherry Turkle is a professor of sociology of science at Massachusetts Institute of Technology and a licensed clinical psychologist. The following selection is from *Life on the Screen,* which is about "how computers are causing us to reevaluate our identities in the age of the Internet" as life on the screen alters our views of politics, sex, relationships, and the self. Turkle finds that life on the Internet facilitates the development of a flexible self. The Internet facilitates psychological growth through role-playing, release from unsatisfying everyday problems, community building over large physical distances, and virtual sex. Turkle also highlights how the disembodiment allows users to alternate between incompatible selves—leading to a self that is more accurately described as plural than flexible.

This selection includes the now infamous virtual rape committed by Mr. Bungle on LambdaMOO. Certainly a virtual rape is not as significant as a real rape. Yet all of us can imagine what it would be like to come upon a story in which a character with our name and other important characteristics engaged in actions that we considered degrading. Such depictions of us, even if obviously fictional, can cause significant psychological suffering and, when directed toward someone already suffering from depression or some other psychological disorder, lead to significant physical and emotional harm. Mr. Bungle's rape of Legba in cyberspace has effects in RL. It also calls for a weighing of the significance of virtual actions. Larry Flynt, publisher of *Hustler,* once depicted Reverend Jerry Falwell as someone who had engaged in incest with his mother. Certainly the suffering Falwell felt was heightened by the fact that the illicit sex was supposed to have occurred with his mother and that his mother would hear about Flynt's characterization. Context makes a difference. MUDs are equivalent to home for many MUDders. Virtual rape in a MUD is like being insulted in front of your family, and not just a random insult from a stranger.

MUDs are places for living out fantasies. Fantasy can be a productive step toward developing relationships and talents in RL. It can also become a substitute for success in RL. The virtual world has both the potential to facilitate RL activities or provide solace in an alternative experience. VR carries no guarantees about enhancing human lives. Does VR actually foster community and participatory democracy? Does it enable more honest and meaningful communication?

QUESTIONS FOR STUDY AND DISCUSSION

1. What connection does Turkle draw between Foucault's analysis of power and the Internet?
2. What is a MUD wizard? What is a MUD voodoo doll?
3. Turkle refers to Fredric Jameson's view that postmodern life is characterized by the flattening of affect? What does that mean, and how could it be connected to MUD life?
4. Turkle refers to Radaway's view that reading romance novels may become a form of resistance. How can reading romances be a revolutionary act, and how can Internet use be seen as a step toward action for social change?

LIFE ON THE SCREEN[2]

SHERRY TURKLE

Josh is a twenty-three-year-old college graduate who lives in a small studio apartment in Chicago. After six months of looking for a job in marketing, the field in which he recently received his college degree, Josh has had to settle for a job working on the computer system that maintains inventory records at a large discount store. He considers this a dead end. When a friend told him about MUDs, he thought the games sounded diverting enough to give them a try. Josh talked the friend into letting him borrow his computer account for one evening, and then for another. Within a week, MUDs had become more than a diversion. Josh had stepped into a new life.

Now, Josh spends as much time on MUDs as he can. He belongs to a class of players who sometimes call themselves Internet hobos. They solicit time on computer accounts the way panhandlers go after spare change. In contrast to his life in RL, which he sees as boring and without prospects, Josh's life inside MUDs seems rich and filled with promise. It has friends, safety, and *space*. "I live in a terrible part of town. I see a rat hole of an apartment, I see a dead-end job, I see AIDS. Down here [in the MUD] I see friends, I have something to offer, I see safe sex." His job taking inventory has him using computers in ways he finds boring. His programming on MUDs is intellectually challenging. Josh has worked on three MUDs, building large, elaborate living quarters in each. In addition, he has become a specialist at building virtual cafes in which bots serve as waiters and bartenders. Within MUDs, Josh serves as a programming consultant to many less-experienced players and has even become something of an entrepreneur. He "rents" ready-built rooms to people who are not as skilled in programming as he is. He has been granted wizard privileges on various MUDs in exchange for building food-service software. He dreams that such virtual commerce will someday lead to more—that someday, as MUDs become commercial enterprises, he will build them for a living. MUDs offer Josh a sense of participation in the American dream.

MUDs play a similar role for Thomas, twenty-four, whom I met after giving a public lecture in Washington, D.C. As I collected my notes Thomas came up to the lectern, introduced himself as a dedicated MUD player and asked if we could talk. After graduating from college, Thomas entered a training program at a large department store. When he discovered that he didn't like retailing, he quit the program, thinking that he would look for something in a different area of business. But things did not go well for him:

> My grades had not been fantastic. Quitting the training program looked bad to people. . . . I would apply for a job and two hundred other people would be there. You better bet that in two hundred people there was someone who had made better grades and hadn't quit his first job.

Finally, Thomas took a job as a bellhop in the hotel where I had just given my lecture. "I thought that working evening hours would let me continue looking for something that would get me back into the middle class," Thomas says. "I haven't found that job yet. But MUDs got me back into the middle class."

Thomas sees himself as someone who should be headed for a desk job, a nice car, and life in the suburbs. "My family is like that," he says, "and they spent a lot of money sending me to college. It wasn't to see me bellhop, I can promise you that." During the day Thomas carries luggage, but at night on MUDs he feels that he is with and recognized by his own kind. Thomas has a group of MUD friends who write well, program, and read science fiction. "I'm interested in MUD politics. Can there be democracy in cyberspace? Should MUDs be ruled by wizards or should they be democracies? I majored in political science in college. These are important questions for the future. I talk about these things with my friends. On MUDs."

Thomas moves on to what has become an obvious conclusion. He says, "MUDs make me more what I really am. Off the MUD, I am not as much me." Tanya, also twenty-four, a college graduate working as a nanny in rural Connecticut, expresses a similar aspiration for upward mobility. She says of the MUD on which she has built Japanese-style rooms and a bot to offer her guests a kimono, slippers, and tea, "I feel like I have more stuff on the MUD than I have off it."

Josh, Thomas, and Tanya belong to a generation whose college years were marked by economic recession and a deadly sexually transmitted disease. They scramble for work; finances force them to live in neighborhoods they don't consider safe; they may end up back home living with parents. These young people are looking for a way back into the middle class. MUDs provide them with the sense of a middle-class peer group. So it is really not that surprising that it is in virtual social life they feel most like themselves.

If a patient on the antidepressant medication Prozac tells his therapist he feels more like himself with the drug than without it, what does this do to our standard notions of a real self? Where does a medication end and a person begin? Where does real life end and a game begin? Is the real self always the naturally occurring one? Is the real self always the one in the physical world? As more and more real business gets done in cyberspace, could the real self be the one who functions best in that realm? Is the real Tanya the frustrated nanny or the energetic programmer on the MUD? The stories of these MUDders point to a whole set of issues about the political and social dimension of virtual community. These young people feel they have no political voice, and they look to cyberspace to help them find one.

Escape or Resistance

In *Reading the Romance,* the literary scholar Janice Radaway argues that when women read romance novels they are not escaping but building realities less limited than their own.[3] Romance reading becomes a form of resistance, a challenge to the stultifying categories of everyday life. This perspective, sensitive to the ways people find to resist constraints of race, class, and gender, is widely shared in contemporary cultural studies. In a similar spirit, the media researcher Henry Jenkins has analyzed the cultures built by television fans as a form of resistance and as enriching for people whose possibilities for fulfillment in real life are seriously limited.

Jenkins quotes a song written by a science fiction fan, which describes how her "Weekend-Only World" at science fiction conventions has more reality for her than her impoverished "real-time life."

In an hour of make-believe
In these warm convention halls
My mind is free to think
And feel so deeply
An intimacy never found
Inside their silent walls
In a year or more
Of what they call reality.[4]

Jenkins writes that this song "expresses the fans' recognition that fandom offers not so much an escape from reality as an alternative reality whose values may be more humane and democratic than those held by mundane society." The author of the song, in Jenkins's view, "gains power and identity from the time she spends within fan culture; fandom allows her to maintain her sanity in the face of the indignity and alienation of everyday life."[5] A similar perspective can be heard in the many online discussions of addictions to virtuality.

On an Internet mailing list discussing MUDding, one player reported on a role-playing conference in Finland that debated (among other things) whether "the time spent in [the] computer (yeah, IN it, not in front of it)" was

> a bad thing or what; the conclusion was, that it is at least better than watching "The Bald [sic] and The Beautiful" for 24H a day—and here we talked about MUDs or such mostly where people communicate with real people through the machine. . . . Well, hasty judging

people might say that the escapists are weak and can't stand the reality—the truly wise see also the other side of the coin: there must be something wrong with Reality, if so many people want to escape from it. If we cannot change the reality, what can we do?[6]

One of the things that people I've interviewed have decided to do is change the reality of virtual reality. An example of this can be found in the history of the MUD LambdaMOO. LambdaMOO has recently undergone a major change in its form of governance. Instead of the MUD wizards (or system administrators) making policy decisions, there is a complex system of grassroots petitions and collective voting. Thomas, the Washington, D.C., bellhop who sees himself as a yuppie manqué, says he is very involved in this experiment. He goes on at length about the political factions with which he must contend to "do politics" on LambdaMOO. Our conversation is taking place in the fall of 1994. His home state has an upcoming senatorial race, hotly contested, ideologically charged, but he hasn't registered to vote and doesn't plan to. I bring up the Senate race. He shrugs it off: "I'm not voting. Doesn't make a difference. Politicians are liars."

One might say that MUDs compensate individuals like Thomas for their sense of political impotence. Or, if we take the perspective sketched by Radaway and Jenkins, we can look at MUDs as places of resistance to many forms of alienation and to the silences they impose. Chat lines, e-mail, bulletin boards, and MUDs are like a weekend-only world in which people can participate every day. Are these activities best understood in terms of compensation or

resistance? The logic of compensation suggests that the goal of virtual experience is to feel better; the logic of resistance suggests that it is political empowerment.

The question of how to situate users of seductive technology on a continuum between psychological escape and political empowerment is reminiscent of a similar question posed by the enthusiasm of personal computer hobbyists of the late 1970s. MUDders like Josh, Thomas, and Tanya—out of college and not yet in satisfying work—have much in common with these early computer hobbyists. Both groups express unfulfilled intellectual and political aspirations within computer microworlds. In the case of the home hobbyists, programmers who no longer had a sense of working with a whole problem on the job demanded a sense of the whole in their recreational computing. In the case of the MUDders, people who feel a loss of middle-class status find reassurance in virtual space. Although the MUDs' extravagant settings—spaceships and medieval towns—may not seem likely places to reconstruct a sense of middle-class community, that is exactly the function they serve for some people who live in them. Many have commented that one appeal of LambdaMOO may be due to its being built as a home, modeled after the large, rambling house where its designer actually lives.

There is a special irony in bringing together the stories of pioneer personal computer owners and pioneer MUDders. The politics of the hobbyists had a grassroots flavor. To their way of thinking, personal computers were a path to a new populism. NetWorks would allow citizens to band together to run decentralized schools and local governments. They thought that personal computers would create a more participatory political system because "people will get used to understanding things, to being in control of things, and they will demand more." Hobbyists took what was most characteristic of their relationships with the computer—building safe microworlds of transparent understanding—and turned it into a political metaphor. When nearly twenty years later, another group of people has turned to computation as a resource for community building, the communities they are thinking of exist on and through the computer. When Thomas talks to me about his passion for politics, about his undergraduate political science major, and how being politically involved makes him feel more like himself, he is talking about the MUD, not about life in Washington, D.C.[7]

Yet the Internet has become a potent symbol and organizational tool for current grassroots movements—of both right and left. The hobbyist dreamed that the early personal computers would carry a political message about the importance of understanding how a system worked. The Internet carries a political message about the importance of direct, immediate action and interest-group mobilization. It is the symbol and tool of a postmodern politics.

The hobbyists I interviewed nearly two decades ago were excited, enthusiastic, and satisfied with what they were doing with their machines. As an ethnographer I thought it appropriate to report this enthusiasm and try to capture a sense of the pleasures and satisfactions that these individuals were deriving from their "non-alienated" relationships with

their computers. In the same sense, it seems appropriate to report the enthusiasm of most MUD users. They take pleasure in building their virtual friendships and virtual spaces and taking on responsibility for virtual jobs. However, fifteen years ago, when reflecting on hobbyists' deeply felt populism, I also worried about a darker side:

> Will the individual satisfactions of personal computation (which seem to derive some of their power from the fact that they are at least in part responsive to political dissatisfactions) take the individual away from collective politics? People will not change unresponsive political systems or intellectually deadening work environments by building machines that are responsive, fun, and intellectually challenging. They will not change the world of human relations by retreating into a world of things. It would certainly be inappropriate to rejoice at the holistic and humanistic relationships that personal computers offer if it turns out that, when widespread, they replace religion as an opiate of the masses.[8]

These words can easily be transposed into the current context, substituting MUDs for personal computers. My misgivings are similar: Instead of solving real problems—both personal and social—are we choosing to live in unreal places? Women and men tell me that the rooms and mazes on MUDs are safer than city streets, virtual sex is safer than sex anywhere, MUD friendships are more intense than real ones, and when things don't work out you can always leave.[9]

It is not hard to agree that MUDs provide an outlet for people to work through personal issues in a productive way; they offer a moratorium that can be turned to constructive purpose, and not only for adolescents. One can also respect the sense in which political activities in a MUD demonstrate resistance to what is unsatisfying about political life more generally. And yet, it is sobering that the personal computer revolution, once conceptualized as a tool to rebuild community, now tends to concentrate on building community inside a machine.

If the politics of virtuality means democracy online and apathy offline, there is reason for concern. There is also reason for concern when access to the new technology breaks down along traditional class lines.[10] Although some inner-city communities have used computer-mediated communication as a tool for real-life community building,[11] the overall trend seems to be the creation of an information elite at the same time that the walls around our society's traditional underclass are maintained. Perhaps people are being even more surely excluded from participation, privilege, and responsibility in the information society than they have been from the dominant groups of the past.

Today many are looking to computers and virtual reality to counter social fragmentation and atomization; to extend democracy; to break down divisions of gender, race, and class; and to lead to a renaissance of learning. Others are convinced that these technologies will have negative effects. Dramatic stories supporting both points of view are always enticing, but most people who have tried to use computer-mediated communication to change their conditions of life and work have found things more complex.

They have found themselves both tantalized and frustrated.

Vanessa, thirty-four, is one of the founding wizards of a large and successful MUD. She is a skilled computer programmer whose talents and energy have always enabled her to earn good money. But she has never been happy in the computer industry because she found little support for her creative style, which she characterizes as "thinking along with people." She is the kind of person whose creativity emerges in conversation. Things went from bad to worse for her when she was forced to telework from home for a period of time. "I was going crazy. Now there was no one. I was so lonely I couldn't get myself to work." But then, a MUD-like chat window gave Vanessa some of what she wanted:

> There was one woman I was working with . . . on a project and we would always have a chat on a talk window on our machines. There we could talk about the project and the testing we were doing and say, "OK, type this," "OK, see if it works," "OK, you know I've changed this file now." . . . That talk window was an important piece of support to me.

That project and the chat sessions are over. When I meet her, Vanessa has no such intellectual companionship in her job. But she has it when she collaborates with others in MUDs. She comments, "So I think that's why I spend so much time on the MUD. . . . I am looking for environments with that sort of support." Vanessa has not yet been able to take the work style she has carved out in a virtual world and use it to enlarge her real world job. She does not find room for "that sort of support" in the company where she works. There, she describes the highly productive people as driven individualists while her preferred work style is seen as time wasting.

Vanessa's story would not read as an escape into MUDs if she had found a way to use her experiences there to model a more fulfilling style of RL work. Her story points toward new possibilities for using MUDs to foster collaboration in work settings. These are early days for such experiments, but they are beginning. For example, Pavel Curtis, the designer of LambdaMOO, is creating a new virtual space—enhanced with audio and video—for Xerox PARC in Palo Alto, California, a research facility funded by the Xerox Corporation. The MUD is called Jupiter, and Xerox PARC employees will step in and out of it depending on whom they want to talk to and what tools they want to use. Jupiter is meant to pick up where the physical workplace leaves off. Smooth transitions back and forth are a key design principle.

Xerox PARC is not the only workplace where MUDs are either in operation or being planned. The MIT Media Lab has MediaMOO, a MUD built and maintained by Amy Bruckman and dedicated to collaboration and community building among media researchers all over the world. Some veteran MUDders are building similar environments for members of international corporations, to make it easier for them to participate in meetings with their colleagues. What these situations have in common is the permeable border between the real and the virtual.

On a more widespread level, chat windows in which collaborators "talk" while editing shared documents, take notes on shared "white boards," and manipulate shared data are becoming increasingly common. Three doctors at three different physical locations, all looking at the same CAT scan images on their screens, consult together about a young child with a tumor, but the subsequent conversation about the recommended treatment will take place at the child's bedside with the family members present. Similarly permeable are virtual communities such as the WELL. In *The Virtual Community*, Howard Rheingold describes how WELL members have been able to support one another in real life. They have elicited information and contacts that saved lives (for example, of an American Buddhist nun in Katmandu who developed an amoebic liver infection). They have brought electronic consolation and personal visits in times of grief (for example, to a WELL member dying of cancer). Rheingold himself believes that this permeability is essential for the word "community" to be applied to our virtual social worlds. To make a community work "at least some of the people [must] reach out through that screen and affect each other's lives."[12]

Panopticon

Much of the conversation about electronic mail, bulletin boards, and the information superhighway in general is steeped in a language of liberation and utopian possibility. It is easy to see why. I write these words in 1995. To date, a user's experience of the Internet is of a dizzyingly free zone. On it information is easily accessible. One can say anything to anyone. Bulletin boards and information utilities are run by interested and motivated people—a graduate student in comparative literature here, an unemployed philosopher there, as well as insurance salesmen, housewives, and bellhops. These people obviously have something in common, access to the Internet and enough money or connections to buy or borrow a computer and modem, but they are a diverse enough group to foster fantasies about a new kind of social power. People who usually think of the world in materialist terms play with the idea that the somehow immaterial world of computer networks has created a new space for power without traditional forms of ownership. People who think of the world in bureaucratic terms play with the ways in which electronic communities undermine traditional forms of organization and status. Such musings are no longer restricted to professional social theorists. The August 1995 issue of *Net-Guide,* a monthly magazine written for beginning Internet users, carries the cover story "Take Charge: Create Your Own Online Service."[13]

I am talking with Ray, an MIT freshman who is discussing his first Internet experiences (an Internet account comes as part of MIT's registration package). Ray quickly turns the conversation to the issue of power and access. He is thrilled with how much there is to explore and about being able to connect with people who would otherwise be inaccessible. He says he would never dare to make an appointment to see one of his professors without something very specific to say, but would send off an e-mail to inquire about a difficult assignment. Ray is on an electronic mailing list with one of his intellectual heroes. "They say Marvin Minsky is actually on this list they let me join. He hasn't posted anything yet. But as soon as he does, I feel like I could

comment on something he said." Ray comments that the idea that he and Marvin Minsky are receiving the same e-mail makes him feel like "the two of us are sharing a *New York Times* over coffee and bagels on Sunday." Ray has also discovered LambdaMOO and is impressed with its efforts at self-governance. He says, "This is what American democracy should be."

Despite many people's good intentions, there is much in recent social thought that casts a sobering light on such enthusiasms. Michel Foucault's work, for example, elaborates a perspective on information, communication, and power that undermines any easy links between electronic communication and freedom.[14] He argues that power in modern society is imposed not by the personal presence and brute force of an elite caste; but by the way each individual learns the art of self-surveillance. Modern society must control the bodies and behaviors of large numbers of people. Force could never be sufficiently distributed. Discourse substitutes and does a more effective job.

The social philosopher Jeremy Bentham, best known for his espousal of utilitarianism, proposed a device called the Panopticon, which enabled a prison guard to see all prisoners without being seen. At any given moment, any one prisoner was perhaps being observed, perhaps not. Prisoners would have to assume they were being observed and would therefore behave according to the norms that the guard would impose, if watching. Individuals learn to look at themselves through the eyes of the prison guard. Foucault has pointed out that this same kind of self-surveillance has extended from the technologies of imprisonment to those of education and psychotherapy. We learn to see ourselves from a teacher's or a therapist's point of view, even in their absence.

In our day, increasingly centralized databases provide a material basis for a vastly extended Panopticon that could include the Internet. Even now there is talk of network censorship, in part through (artificially) intelligent agents capable of surveillance. From Foucault's perspective, the most important factor would not be how frequently the agents are used or censorship is enforced. Like the threat of a tax audit, what matters most is that people know that the possibility is always present.

Ray's attitude about being online is totally positive. But Andy and Daniella, two other MIT freshmen, express reservations about computer-mediated communication. Neither knows about Foucault's work, but their ideas resonate with his on the way social control operates through learned self-surveillance. Andy hangs out on a MUD on which wizards have the power to enter any room without being seen. This means that they can "overhear" private conversations. He is organizing a petition to put a stop to this practice. Although he has been successful in marshaling support, he does not think his efforts will succeed. "We need the wizards. They are the ones willing to do the work. Without them, there would be no MUD." His comment provokes the following remark from Daniella: "Do you know that if you type the finger command, you can see the last time someone got online? So you are responsible for your e-mail if you log on to your computer, because everybody can know that you got your messages. But you don't know who asked about

[that is, who has fingered] you." Andy nods his assent and replies, "I don't think that's the worst." He continues:

> I subscribed to a list about cyberpunk and I wrote every day. It was such a release. My ideas were pretty wild. Then I found out that the list is archived in three places. E-mail makes you feel as though you are just talking. Like it will evaporate. And then what you say is archived. It won't evaporate. It's like somebody's always putting it on your permanent record. You learn to watch yourself.

Such considerations about power, discourse, and domination have been the province of social theorists. The experience of the Internet, that most ephemeral of objects, has made these considerations more concrete. Of course, people have known for decades that each time they place an order from a mail-order catalogue or contribute to a political cause, they are adding information to a database. New catalogues and new requests for political contributions arrive that are more and more finely tuned to the profile of the electronic personae they have created through their transactions. But people are isolated in their reflections about their electronic personae. On the Internet, such matters are more likely to find a collective voice.

In discussing the parallels between hobbyists and MUDders, I have balanced a language of psychological compensation (people without power and resources in the real find a compensatory experience in the virtual) with a language of political criticism (the satisfactions that people experience in virtual communities underscore the failures of our real ones). Both approaches give precedence to events in the real world. Do MUDs oblige us to find a new language that does not judge virtual experiences purely in terms of how far they facilitate or encumber "real" ones? Perhaps the virtual experiences are "real enough."

When people pursue relationships through letter writing, we are not concerned that they are abandoning their real lives. Relationships via correspondence seem romantic to people for whom MUDding seems vaguely unsavory. Some envisage letter writing as a step toward physical presence rather than as an alternative to it. Some imagine the letter writers speaking in their own voice rather than role playing. But neither of these ideas is necessarily true of letter writing or untrue of MUDding. In MUDs it is hard not to play an aspect of oneself, and virtual encounters often lead to physical ones. What makes an eighty-hour work week in investment banking something a parent can be proud of while Robert's eighty hours a week building and administering his MUD raises fears of addiction? Would Robert seem less addicted to his MUD activities if he were being paid for them? Would they have a different feel if his relationship with Kasha—the fellow-MUDder he traveled cross-country to meet—had blossomed, as some MUD friendships do, into marriage and family? In an electronic discussion group on virtual community, Barry Kort, one of the founders of a MUD for children, argued in a similar vein: "I don't think anyone would have said that Socrates, Plato, and Aristotle were addicted to the Agora. The computer nets are the modern Agora, serving a role similar to talk radio and tabloid journalism, but with more

participation, less sensationalism, and more thinking between remarks."[15]

What are the social implications of spinning off virtual personae that can run around with names and genders of our choosing, unhindered by the weight and physicality of embodiment? From their earliest days, MUDs have been evocative objects for thinking about virtuality and accountability.

Habitat was an early MUD, initially built to run on Commodore 64 personal computers in the early 1980s. It had a short run in the United States before it was bought and transferred to Japan.[16] Its designers, Chip Morningstar and F. Randall Farmer, have written about how its players struggled to establish the rights and responsibilities of virtual selves. On Habitat, players were originally allowed to have guns and other weapons. Morningstar and Farmer say that they "included these because we felt that players should be able to materially affect each other in ways that went beyond simply talking, ways that required real moral choices to be made by the participants." However, death in Habitat had little in common with the RL variety. "When an Avatar is killed, he or she is teleported back home, head in hands (literally), pockets empty, and any object in hand at the time dropped on the ground at the scene of the crime."[17] This eventuality was more like a setback in a game of Chutes and Ladders than real mortality, and for some players thievery and murder became the highlights of the game. For others, these activities were a violent intrusion on their peaceful world. An intense debate ensued.

Some players argued that guns should be eliminated, for in a virtual world a few lines of code can translate into an absolute gun ban. Others argued that what was dangerous in virtual reality was not violence but its trivialization. These individuals maintained that guns should be allowed, but their consequences should be made more serious; when you are killed, your character should cease to exist and not simply be sent home. Still others believed that since Habitat was just a game and playing assassin was part of the fun, there could be no harm in a little virtual violence.

As the debate continued, a player who was a Greek Orthodox priest in real life founded the first Habitat church, the "Order of the Holy Walnut," whose members pledged not to carry guns, steal, or engage in virtual violence of any kind. In the end, the game designers divided the world into two parts. In town, violence was prohibited. In the wilds outside of town, it was allowed. Eventually a democratic voting process was installed and a sheriff elected. Participants then took up discussion on the nature of Habitat laws and the proper balance between law and order and individual freedom. It was a remarkable situation. Participants in Habitat were seeing themselves as citizens; and they were spending their leisure time debating pacifism, the nature of good government, and the relationship between representations and reality. In the nineteenth century, utopians built communities in which political thought could be lived out as practice. On the cusp of the twenty-first century, we are building MUDs, possible worlds that can provoke a new critical discourse about the real.

MUD Rape: Only Words

Consider the first moments of a consensual sexual encounter between the characters Backslash and Targa. The player behind Backslash, Ronald, a mathematics graduate student in Memphis, types "emote fondles Targa's breast" and "say You are beautiful Targa." Elizabeth, Targa's player, sees on her screen:

> Backslash fondles Targa's breast.
>   You are beautiful Targa.

Elizabeth responds with "say Touch me again, and harder. Please. Now. That's how I like it." Ronald's screen shows:

> Targa says, "Touch me again, and harder. Please. Now. That's how I like it."

But consensual relationships are only one facet of virtual sex. Virtual rape can occur within a MUD if one player finds a way to control the actions of another player's character and can thus "force" that character to have sex. The coercion depends on being able to direct the actions and reactions of characters independent of the desire of their players. So if Ronald were such a culprit, he would be the only one typing, having gained control of Targa's character. In this case Elizabeth, who plays Targa, would sit at her computer, shocked to find herself, or rather her "self," begging Backslash for more urgent caresses and ultimately violent intercourse.

In March 1992 a character calling himself Mr. Bungle, "an oleaginous, Bisquick-faced clown dressed in cum-stained harlequin garb and girdled with a mistletoe-and-hemlock belt whose buckle bore the inscription 'KISS ME UNDER THIS, BITCH!'" appeared in the LambdaMOO living room. Creating a phantom that masquerades as another player's character is a MUD programming trick often referred to as creating a voodoo doll. The "doll" is said to possess the character, so that the character must do whatever the doll does. Bungle used such a voodoo doll to force one and then another of the room's occupants to perform sexual acts on him. Bungle's first victim in cyberspace was legba, a character described as "a Haitian trickster spirit of indeterminate gender, brown-skinned and wearing an expensive pearl gray suit, top hat; and dark glasses." Even when ejected from the room, Bungle was able to continue his sexual assaults. He forced various players to have sex with each other and then forced legba to swallow his (or her?) own pubic hair and made a character called Starsinger attack herself sexually with a knife. Finally, Bungle was immobilized by a MOO wizard who "toaded" the perpetrator (erased the character from the system).

The next day, legba took the matter up on a widely read mailing list within LambdaMOO about social issues. Legba called both for "civility" and for "virtual castration." When chronicling this event, the journalist Jullian Dibbell contrasted the cyberspace description of the event with what was going on in real life. The woman who played the character of legba told Dibbell that she cried as she wrote those words, but he points out their "precise tenor," mingling "murderous rage and eyeball-rolling annoyance was a curious amalgam that neither the RL nor the VR facts alone can quite account for."

> Where virtual reality and its conventions would have us believe that legba and Starsinger were brutally raped in their own living room, here was the victim legba scolding Mr. Bungle for a breach

of "civility." Where real life, on the other hand, insists the incident was only an episode in a free-form version of Dungeons and Dragons, confined to the realm of the symbolic and at no point threatening any player's life, limb, or material well-being, here now was the player legba issuing aggrieved and heartfelt calls for Mr. Bungle's dismemberment. Ludicrously excessive by RL's lights, woefully understated by VR's, the tone of legba's response made sense only in the buzzing, dissonant gap between them.[18]

Dibbell points out that although the RL and the VR description of the event may seem to "march in straight, tandem lines separated neatly into the virtual and the real, its meaning lies always in that gap." He describes the way MUD players tend to learn this lesson during their early sexual encounters in MUDs.

> Amid flurries of even the most cursorily described caresses, sighs, and penetrations, the glands do engage, and often as throbbingly as they would in a real-life assignation—sometimes even more so, given the combined power of anonymity and textual suggestiveness to unshackle deep-seated fantasies. And if the virtual setting and the interplayer vibes are right, who knows? The heart may engage as well, stirring up passions as strong as many that bind lovers who observe the formality of trysting in the flesh.

The issue of MUD rape and violence has become a focal point of conversation on discussion lists, bulletin boards, and newsgroups to which MUD players regularly post. In these forums one has the opportunity to hear from those who believe that MUDs should be considered as games and that therefore virtual rape should be allowed. One posting defending MUD rape was from someone who admitted to being a MUD rapist.

MUDs are Fantasy. MUDs are somewhere you can have fun and let your "hidden" self out. Just to let you all in on what happened, here is the story:

On a MUD (who's [sic] name I will not release, like I said, you know who you are) a friend of mine and myself were reprimanded for actions we took.

We have a little thing we do, he uses emote . . . to emote "<his name> holds <victim's name> down for <my name> to rape." Then I use emote and type "<my name> rapes the held down <victim's name>."

Now this may be an odd thing to do, but it is done in a free non-meaningful manner. We don't do it to make people feel victimized, (like this GOD said we were doing) we do it for fun. OK, it is plain out sick, but that isn't the point. On this MUD the victim isn't the one who complained. It was several other PCs who complained about what we did. Let the victim complain about it. It happened to the victim, not the bystanders. The victim didn't actually mind, she thought it was somewhat humorous. Well, along comes Mr. GOD saying "raping the Player's character, is the same as raping the player."

BULL SHIT

This is a GAME, nothing more. This particular GOD needs to chill out and stop being so serious. MUDs are supposed to be fun, not

uptight. I will never return to this MUD of my own choice. There are other MUDs where we have done the same thing and even though the victim didn't like it, the GODs told the victim "too bad. it's not like they Pkilled you." [This refers to "player killing," in which one player kills another player. It is often considered different in nature from being "toaded."]

There was a postscript after the signature [Wonko the Sane] on this communication. The author asks his readers to "Please excuse my grammer [sic] as I am a Computer Science Major, not an English Major. Also excuse the no indenting as our netnews poster eats posts that have indents in them. Argh." Rape was not all that was on this MUDder's mind. Grammar and the limitations of his text formatting system also loomed large.

Discussion of the MUD rape occupied LambdaMOO for some time. In one of a series of online meetings that followed it, one character asked, "Where does the body end and the mind begin? Is not the mind a part of the body?" Another answered, "In MOO, the body is the mind." MUD rape occurred without physical contact. Is rape, then, a crime against the mind? If we say that it is, we begin to approach the position taken by the feminist legal theorist Catharine MacKinnon, who has argued that some words describing acts of violence toward women are social actions. Thus some pornography should be banned because it is not "only words." Dibbell says that he began his research on MUDs with little sympathy for this point of view but admits that "the more seriously I took the notion of virtual rape, the less seriously I was able to take the notion of freedom of speech, with its tidy division of the world into the symbolic and the real."[19] While legal scholars might disagree that any such "tidy division" is to be found in American law, no one can doubt that examples of MUD rape—of which the incident on LambdaMOO was only one—raise the question of accountability for the actions of virtual personae who have only words at their command.

Similar issues of accountability arise in the case of virtual murder. If your MUD character erases the computer database on which I have over many months built up a richly described character and goes on to announce to the community that my character is deceased, what exactly have *you,* the you that exists in real life, done? What if my virtual apartment is destroyed along with all its furniture, VCR, kitchen equipment, and stereo system? What if you kidnap my virtual dog (the bot Rover, which I have trained to perform tricks on demand)? What if you destroy him and leave his dismembered body in the MUD?

In the physically embodied world, we have no choice but to assume responsibility for our body's actions. The rare exceptions simply prove the rule as when someone with multiple personality disorder claims that a crime was committed by an "alter" personality over which he or she has no control or we rule someone mentally incompetent to stand trial. The possibilities inherent in virtuality, on the other hand, may provide some people with an excuse for irresponsibility, just as they may enable creative expressions that would otherwise have been repressed. When society supported people in unitary experiences of self, it often maintained a narrowness of outlook that

could be suffocating. There were perhaps great good places, but there was also a tendency to exclude difference as deviance. Turning back provides no solutions. The challenge is to integrate some meaningful personal responsibility in virtual environments. Virtual environments are valuable as places where we can acknowledge our inner diversity. But we still want an authentic experience of self.

One's fear is, of course, that in the culture of simulation, a word like authenticity can no longer apply. So even as we try to make the most of virtual environments, a haunting question remains. For me, that question is raised every time I use the MUD command for taking an action. The command is "emote." If while at Dred's bar on LambdaMOO, I type "emote waves," the screens of all players in the MUD room will flash "ST waves." If I type "emote feels a complicated mixture of desire and expectation," all screens will flash "ST feels a complicated mixture of desire and expectation." But what exactly do *I feel*? Or, what exactly do *I* feel? When we get our MUD persona to "emote" something and observe the effect, do we gain a better understanding of our real emotions, which can't be switched on and off so easily, and which we may not even be able to describe? Or is the emote command and all that it stands for a reflection of what Fredric Jameson called the flattening of affect in postmodern life?

. . . In a journal published on the Internet, Leslie Harris speculates on how virtual experiences become part of the perceptual and emotional background "that changes the way we see things." Harris describes an episode of *Star Trek: The Next Generation* in which Captain

Picard plays Caiman, an inhabitant of the virtual world Catanh. On Catanh, Picard lives experiences he had to forgo in order to make a career in Starfleet. He has a virtual experience of love, marriage, and fatherhood. He develops relationships with his community that are not possible for him as a Starfleet commander. "On" Catanh, the character Caiman "learns" to play the Ressiccan flute. Harris says, "He can eventually fall in love with a fellow crew member in his 'real life' because he experienced the feelings of love, commitment, and intimacy 'on' Catanh."[20] When in his real life Picard plays the flute with a fellow Starfleet officer he realizes that he is in love with her. Picard is aware that he has projected his desire for music and sensuality onto his virtual world. It is this awareness that lets him use music to link the "real" Captain Picard to the emotional growth he was to experience as the virtual Caiman.

Here, virtuality is powerful but transitional. Ultimately, it is put in the service of Picard's embodied self. Picard's virtual Catanh, like the space created within psychoanalysis, operates in a time out of normal time and according to its own rules. In a successful psychoanalysis, the meetings between analyst and analysand come to an end, although the analytic process goes on forever. It is internalized within the person, just as Picard brought Catanh inside himself. Buddhists speak of their practice as a raft to get to the other shore, liberation. But the raft, like an analytic treatment, is thought of as a tool that must be set aside, even though the process of crossing the river is conceived of as never-ending. Wittgenstein takes up a similar idea in *The Tractatus*, when he compares

his work to a ladder that is to be discarded after the reader has used it to reach a new level of understanding.

In April 1995, a town meeting was held at MIT on the subject "Doing Gender on the Net." As the discussion turned to using virtual personae to try out new experiences, a thirty-year-old graduate student, Ava, told her story. She had used a MUD to try out being comfortable with a disability. Several years earlier, Ava had been in an automobile accident that left her without a right leg. During her recuperation, she began to MUD. "Without giving it a lot of advance thought," Ava found herself creating a one-legged character on a MUD. Her character had a removable prosthetic limb. The character's disability featured plainly in her description, and the friends she made on the MUD found a way to deal with her handicap. When Ava's character became romantically involved, she and her virtual lover acknowledged the "physical" as well as the emotional aspects of the virtual amputation and prosthesis. They became comfortable with making virtual love, and Ava found a way to love her own virtual body. Ava told the group at the town meeting that this experience enabled her to take a further step toward accepting her real body. "After the accident, I made love in the MUD before I made love again in real life," she said. "I think that the first made the second possible. I began to think of myself as whole again." For her, the Internet had been a place of healing.

Virtual reality gave Ava choices. She could have tried being one of this MUD's many FabulousHotBabes. If so, she might have never felt safe leaving the anonymity of the virtual world. But instead she was able to reimagine herself not as whole but as whole-in-her-incompleteness. Each of us in our own way is incomplete. Virtual spaces may provide the safety for us to expose what we are missing so that we can begin to accept ourselves as we are.

Virtuality need not be a prison. It can be the raft, the ladder, the transitional space, the moratorium, that is discarded after reaching greater freedom. We don't have to reject life on the screen, but we don't have to treat it as an alternative life either. We can use it as a space for growth. Having literally written our on-line personae into existence, we are in a position to be more aware of what we project into everyday life. Like the anthropologist returning home from a foreign culture, the voyager in virtuality can return to a real world better equipped to understand its artifices.

CASE STUDY: VIRTUAL RAPE

One problem with ethical evaluation of the virtual rape case might be an inclination to classify the action either as equivalent to RL rape or as trivial, a game. (Criminal law no longer refers to rape. Instead it refers to degrees of sexual assault.) Mr. Bungle's actions may be more accurately evaluated if you avoid the strict dichotomy suggested by rape versus game and discuss whether it is a variety of sexual harassment or assault. Just how serious a wrong was the incident?

Also, notice that in RL, relationships often have aspects that only some "players" are aware of. One participant turns out to be married or possess some other characteristic that has been withheld. The uninformed party now perceives the past relationship as unreal. The other person was playing a game, when they were dead serious. It is also the case that playing a game usually involves public, shared rules. Surprises result in real grievances. To what extent does Wonko the Sane misuse the notion of a game in his *apologia?*

CASE STUDY: CARNIVORE

Carnivore is an electronic wiretap developed by the United States Federal Bureau of Investigation. Here is some of what Alan Davidson of the Center for Democracy and Technology had to say about Carnivore in testimony before the House Judiciary Committee on July 24, 2000.

> Recent press reports, along with testimony before this subcommittee in April, have revealed the existence of the new FBI wiretapping device known as "Carnivore." Not much is known about this device, which appears to have been developed with little or no public oversight. What is known raises serious questions about the application of electronic surveillance laws and the Fourth Amendment on the Internet.
>
> Carnivore reportedly serves at least two functions. Installed on the network of an ISP, it monitors communications on the network and records messages sent or

received by a targeted user. This is presumably designed to respond to an electronic "wiretap" order served on an ISP. Because of the intrusive nature of wiretaps, a high legal standard must be met for their issuance, requiring a showing of probable cause and strict judicial oversight.

Carnivore can reportedly also provide the origin and destination of all communications to and from a particular ISP customer. . . .[21]

How would the FBI-initiated Carnivore be analyzed by someone who agreed with the Bentham/Foucault Panopticon analysis of power?

Mr. Davidson states that one problem with Carnivore is that citizens are unsure about the extent of surveillance the program allows. His solution is that the government should allow nongovernmental experts to review the program source code and report findings to the public. Do you consider that a democratic solution?

11.2 ETHICS AND THE NEW MILLENNIUM If genetic engineering allows for "designer children" will parents be unable to take pride in the struggles of children to overcome obstacles? Perhaps parenthood will offer a merely aesthetic enjoyment of the beauty of design witnessed in optimized offspring. Certainly the parent-child relationship will face other changes occasioned by increasingly programmed offspring. Children, unless freed by genetic design from the *resentiment* gene, will be less inclined to feel gratitude to parents once they realize that parenthood has become more like picking living room furniture. Parents, faced with an environment in which genetic design is expected, will perhaps be incapable of choosing altruistically to let children just be and become. (A speculative dystopian contemporary film about the future of "natural children" is *Attica*.) The effects of technology are not merely practical but reverberate across the inner landscape of values whose felt execution determine to a large extent what it means to be human.

Turkle speculates that life on the screen may lead to a human world characterized by increased flattening of affect. Perhaps increased participation in microworlds where characters are "killed" or "raped" as part of the game and our deepest friendships are with people we meet on the Web but never in the flesh will lead to a lack of emotional reaction and attachment. It is a commonplace of utopian democratic theory that face-to-face contact is crucial to participatory democracy. Think for instance of the difference you feel when personally donating money or time to help others, perhaps working for Habitat for Humanity, and how you feel when you notice how much of your paycheck has been automatically allocated to social causes through taxation. Personal giving generally feels better than impersonal, nonvoluntary contributions. It also tends to build community.

Turkle thinks that VR is most useful when it connects by smooth transitions to RL. But imagine if the participants in LambdaMoo were no longer equipped with physical bodies—that is what RL is like when more and more of our "personal" contacts are on the screen.

Kirkpatrick Sale calls our attention to "seven lessons that one might, with the focused lens of history, take from the Luddite past." Here are two of them:

1. Technologies are never neutral, and some are hurtful.
2. Only a people serving an apprenticeship to nature can be trusted with machines.[22]

The Dalai Lama expresses concern that the increased reliance upon technology has led to isolation from community interaction, especially in developed nations. The prevalence of depression and drugs designed to alter our inner life suggests that technology is not equipped to provide humans with a meaningful existence. Pay particular attention to the personal responsibility that the Dalai Lama underlines as well as to the importance of affect, of motivation, in living a good life.

Bstan-'dzin-rgya-mtsho, His Holiness the Dalai Lama, is the spiritual leader of the Tibetan people. Among the many honors that his work for human rights and world peace have brought him is the Nobel Peace Prize in 1989.

QUESTIONS FOR STUDY AND DISCUSSION

1. Why does His Holiness think that an ethical approach to media is vital?
2. It has become increasingly popular in American politics to separate issues of personal character from public responsibility. What does the Dalai Lama think of such separation?
3. What would the Dalai Lama think of rap music? Why?

ETHICS FOR A NEW MILLENNIUM[23]

HIS HOLINESS THE DALAI LAMA

Now although it is certainly the case that if all my suggestions concerning compassion, inner discipline, wise discernment, and the cultivation of virtue were to be implemented widely, the world would automatically become a kinder, more peaceful place, I believe that reality compels us to tackle our problems at the level of society at the same time as that of the individual. The world will change when each individual makes the attempt to counter their negative thoughts and emotions and when we practice compassion for its inhabitants irrespective of whether or not we have direct relationships with them.

In view of this, there are, I believe, a number of areas to which we need to give special consideration in the light of universal responsibility. These include education, the media, our natural environment, politics and economics, peace and disarmament, and inter-religious harmony. Each has a vital role to play in shaping the world we live in and I propose to examine them briefly in turn.

Before doing so, I must stress that the views I express are personal. They are also the views of someone who claims no expertise with respect to the technicalities of these matters. But if what I say seems objectionable, my hope is that it will at least give the reader pause for thought. For although it would not be surprising to see a divergence of opinion concerning how they are to be translated into actual policies, the need for compassion, for basic spiritual values, for inner discipline and the importance of ethical conduct generally are in my view incontrovertible.

The human mind *(lo)* is both the source and, properly directed, the solution to all our problems. Those who attain great learning but lack a good heart are in danger of falling prey to the anxieties and restlessness which result from desires incapable of fulfillment. Conversely, a genuine understanding of spiritual values has the opposite effect. When we bring up our children to have knowledge without compassion, their attitude toward others is likely to be a mixture of envy of those in positions above them, aggressive competitiveness toward their peers, and scorn for those less fortunate. This leads to a propensity toward greed, presumption, excess, and, very quickly, to loss of happiness. Knowledge is important. But much more so is the use toward which it is put. This depends on the heart and mind of the one who uses it.

Education is much more than a matter of imparting the knowledge and skills by which narrow goals are achieved. It is also about opening the child's eyes to the needs and rights of others. We must show children that their actions have a universal dimension. And we must somehow find a way to build on their natural feelings of empathy so that they come to have a sense of responsibility toward others. For it is this which stirs us into action. Indeed, if we had to choose between learning and virtue, the latter is definitely more valuable. The good heart which is the fruit of virtue is by itself a great benefit to humanity. Mere knowledge is not.

How, though, are we to teach morality to our children? I have a sense that, in general, modern educational systems neglect discussion of ethical matters. This is probably not intentional so much as a by-product of historical reality. Secular educational systems were developed at a time when religious institutions were still highly influential throughout society. Because ethical and human values were and still are generally held to fall within the scope of religion, it was assumed that this aspect of a child's education would be looked after through his or her religious upbringing. This worked well enough until the influence of religion began to decline. Although the need is still there, it is not being met. Therefore, we must find some other way of showing children that basic human values are important. And we must also help them to develop these values.

Ultimately, of course, the importance of concern for others is learned not from words but from actions: the example we set. This is why the family environment itself is such a vital component in a child's upbringing. When a caring and compassionate atmosphere is absent from the home, when children are neglected by their parents, it is easy to recognize their damaging effects. The children tend to feel helpless and insecure, and their minds are often agitated. Conversely, when children receive constant affection and protection, they tend to be much happier and more confident in their abilities. Their physical health tends to be better too. And we find that they are concerned not just for themselves but for others as well. The home environment is also important because children learn negative behavior from their parents. If, for example, the father is always getting into fights with his associates, or if the father and mother are always arguing destructively, although at first the child may find this objectionable, eventually they will come to understand it as quite normal. This learning is then taken out of the home and into the world.

It also goes without saying that what children learn about ethical conduct at school has to be practiced first. In this, teachers have a special responsibility. By their own behavior, they can make children remember them for their whole lives. If this behavior is principled, disciplined, and compassionate, their values will be readily impressed on the child's mind. This is because the lessons taught by a teacher with a positive motivation *(kun long)* penetrate deepest into their students' minds. I know this from my own experience. As a boy, I was very lazy. But when I was aware of the affection and concern of my tutors, their lessons would generally sink in much more successfully than if one of them was harsh or unfeeling that day.

So far as the specifics of education are concerned, that is for the experts. I will, therefore, confine myself to a few suggestions. The first is that in order to awaken young people's consciousness to the importance of basic human values, it is better not to present society's problems purely as an ethical matter or as a religious matter. It is important to emphasize that what is at stake is our continued survival. This way, they will come to see that the future lies in their hands. Secondly, I do believe that dialogue can and should be taught in class. Presenting students with a controversial issue and having them debate it is a wonderful way to introduce them to the concept of resolving conflict nonviolently. Indeed, one would hope that if schools

were to make this a priority, it could have a beneficial effect on family life itself. On seeing his or her parents wrangling, a child that had understood the value of dialogue would instinctively say, "Oh, no. That's not the way. You have to talk, to discuss things properly."

Finally, it is essential that we eliminate from our schools' curricula any tendency toward presenting others in a negative light. There are undoubtedly some parts of the world where the teaching of history, for example, fosters bigotry and racism toward other communities. Of course this is wrong. It contributes nothing to the happiness of humanity. Now more than ever we need to show our children that distinctions between "my country" and "your country," "my religion" and "your religion" are secondary considerations. Rather, we must insist on the observation that my right to happiness carries no more weight than others' right. This is not to say that I believe we should educate children to abandon or ignore the culture and historical tradition they were born into. On the contrary, it is very important they be grounded in these. It is good for children to learn to love their country, their religion, their culture, and so on. But the danger comes when this develops into narrow-minded nationalism, ethnocentricity, and religious bigotry. The example of Mahatma Gandhi is pertinent here. Even though he had a very high level of Western education, he never forgot or became estranged from the rich heritage of his Indian culture.

If education constitutes one of our most powerful weapons in our quest to bring about a better, more peaceful world, the mass media is another. As every political figure knows, they are no longer the only ones with authority in society. In addition to that of newspapers and books, radio, film, and television together have an influence over individuals unimagined a hundred years ago. This power confers great responsibility on all who work in the media. But it also confers great responsibility on each of us who, as individuals, listen and read and watch. We, too, have a role to play. We are not powerless before the media. The control switch is in our own hand, after all.

This does not mean that I advocate bland reporting or entertainment without excitement. On the contrary, so far as investigative journalism is concerned, I respect and appreciate the media's interference. Not all public servants are honest in discharging their duties. It is appropriate, therefore, to have journalists, their noses as long as an elephant's trunk, snooping around and exposing wrongdoing where they find it. We need to know when this or that renowned individual hides a very different aspect behind a pleasant exterior. There should be no discrepancy between external appearances and the individual's inner life. It is the same person, after all. Such discrepancies suggest them to be untrustworthy. At the same time, it is vital that the investigator does not act out of improper motives. Without impartiality and without due respect for the other's rights, the investigation itself becomes tainted.

With regard to the question of the media's emphasis on sex and violence, there are many factors to consider. In the first instance, it is clear that much of the viewing public enjoys the sensations provoked by this sort of material. Secondly, I very much doubt that those producing material containing a lot of explicit sex and violence intend harm by it. Their motives are surely just commercial. As to whether this is positive or negative in itself is to my mind less important than the question of whether it can have an ethically wholesome effect. If the result of seeing a film in which there is a lot of violence is that the viewer's compassion is aroused, then perhaps that depiction of violence would be justified. But if the accumulation of violent images leads to indifference, then I think it is not. Indeed, such a hardening of heart is potentially dangerous. It leads all too easily to lack of empathy.

When the media focuses too closely on the negative aspects of human nature, there is a danger that we become persuaded that violence and aggression are its principal characteristics. This is a mistake, I believe. The fact that violence is newsworthy suggests the very opposite. Good news is not remarked on precisely because there is so much of it. Consider that at any given moment there must be hundreds of millions of acts of kindness taking place around the world. Although there will undoubtedly be many acts of violence in progress at the same time, their number is surely very much less. If therefore, the media is to be ethically responsible, it needs to reflect this simple fact.

Clearly it is necessary to regulate the media. The fact that we prevent our children from watching certain things indicates that we already discriminate between what is and is not appropriate according to different circumstances. But whether legislation is the right way to go about this is hard to judge. As in all matters of ethics, discipline is only really effective when it comes from within. Perhaps the best way to ensure that the output various media provides is healthy lies in the way we educate our children. If we bring them up to be aware of their responsibilities, they will be more disciplined when they become involved in the media.

Although it is perhaps too much to hope that the media will actually promote the ideals and principles of compassion, at least we should be able to expect that those involved will take care when there is the potential for negative impact. At least there should be no room for the incitement of negative acts such as racist violence. But beyond this, I don't know. Perhaps we might be able to find a way to connect more directly those who create stories for news and entertainment with the viewer, the reader, and the listener?

EXERCISES

1. The Dalai Lama suggests that the media themselves present no problem. Rather, he thinks that if children are raised to be compassionate, media products that celebrate violence and contribute to the production of social estrangement will find no market. Incidents like that on LambdaMoo probably will not disappear, but they will be rare and surprising. Philosopher William James urged the development of moral equivalents of war to give human beings alternative grand causes to make life feel meaningful. Does the world the Dalai Lama describes contain causes significant and attractive enough to provide substitutes for war, violence, and scientific research?

2. Would the Dalai Lama allow any video games in his home? For instance, would SimCity be more acceptable than Quake?

3. Why do the Dalai Lama's ethics for the new millennium place so much emphasis on the education children receive at home and school? Why does he rely so little upon government regulation?

11.3 OUR WIRED FUTURE Bill Joy is the cofounder and chief scientist of Sun Microsystems. Joy was co-chair of the presidential commission on the future of information technology research. He is also coauthor of *The Java Language Specification.* The following selection is from *Wired Magazine,* a useful resource for the latest thinking about technology and society by those actively involved in the industry. It serves as an extended case study in which a leading information scientist speculates on the relevance of ethics to the pursuit of technology. Notice that Joy cites the Dalai Lama as a source for ethical guidance along with Henry David Thoreau, the American philosopher whose thought figured prominently in the beginning of this book.

QUESTIONS FOR STUDY AND DISCUSSION

1. What is a dystopia; what is a utopia?
2. What is nanotechnology?
3. Why does Joy fear the combination of self-replication and nanotechnology?

4. What is the gray goo problem?
5. What lessons does Joy think society must learn from the use of the atomic bomb?
6. What is the crucial difference between twentieth- and twenty-first-century technology?

WHY THE FUTURE DOESN'T NEED US[24]

BILL JOY

From the moment I became involved in the creation of new technologies, their ethical dimensions have concerned me, but it was only in the autumn of 1998 that I became anxiously aware of how great are the dangers facing us in the 21st century. I can date the onset of my unease to the day I met Ray Kurzweil, the deservedly famous inventor of the first reading machine for the blind and many other amazing things.

Ray and I were both speakers at George Gilder's Telecosm conference, and I encountered him by chance in the bar of the hotel after both our sessions were over. I was sitting with John Searle, a Berkeley philosopher who studies consciousness. While we were talking, Ray approached and a conversation began, the subject of which haunts me to this day.

I had missed Ray's talk and the subsequent panel that Ray and John had been on, and they now picked right up where they'd left off, with Ray saying that the rate of improvement of technology was going to accelerate and that we were going to become robots or fuse with robots or something like that, and John countering that this couldn't happen, because the robots couldn't be conscious.

While I had heard such talk before, I had always felt sentient robots were in the realm of science fiction. But now,

from someone I respected, I was hearing a strong argument that they were a near-term possibility. I was taken aback, especially given Ray's proven ability to imagine and create the future. I already knew that new technologies like genetic engineering and nanotechnology were giving us the power to remake the world, but a realistic and imminent scenario for intelligent robots surprised me.

It's easy to get jaded about such breakthroughs. We hear in the news almost every day of some kind of technological or scientific advance. Yet this was no ordinary prediction. In the hotel bar, Ray gave me a partial preprint of his then-forthcoming book *The Age of Spiritual Machines,* which outlined a utopia he foresaw—one in which humans gained near immortality by becoming one with robotic technology. On reading it, my sense of unease only intensified; I felt sure he had to be understating the dangers, understating the probability of a bad outcome along this path.

I found myself most troubled by a passage detailing a *dys*topian scenario:

THE NEW LUDDITE CHALLENGE

First let us postulate that the computer scientists succeed in developing intelligent machines that can do all things better than human beings can do them. In that case presumably all work will be done by vast, highly organized systems of machines and no human effort will be necessary. Either of two cases might occur. The machines might be permitted to make all of their own decisions without human oversight, or else human control over the machines might be retained.

If the machines are permitted to make all their own decisions, we can't make any conjectures as to the results, because it is impossible to guess how such machines might behave. We only point out that the fate of the human race would be at the mercy of the machines. It might be argued that the human race would never be foolish enough to hand over all the power to the machines. But we are suggesting neither that the human race would voluntarily turn power over to the machines nor that the machines would willfully seize power. What we do suggest is that the human race might easily permit itself to drift into a position of such dependence on the machines that it would have no practical choice but to accept all of the machines' decisions. As society and the problems that face it become more and more complex and machines become more and more intelligent, people will let machines make more of their decisions for them, simply because machine-made decisions will bring better results than man-made ones. Eventually a stage may be reached at which the decisions necessary to keep the system running will be so complex that human beings will be incapable of making them intelligently. At that stage the machines will be in effective control. People won't be able to just turn the machines off, because they will be so dependent on them that turning them off would amount to suicide.

On the other hand it is possible that human control over the machines may be retained. In that case the average man may have control over certain private machines of his own, such as his car or his personal computer, but control over large systems of machines will be in the hands of a tiny elite—just as it is today, but with two differences. Due to improved techniques the elite will have greater control over the masses; and because human work will no longer be necessary the masses will be superfluous, a useless burden on the system. If the elite is ruthless they may simply decide to exterminate the mass of humanity. If they are humane they may use propaganda or other psychological or biological techniques to reduce the birth rate until the mass of humanity becomes extinct, leaving the world to the elite. Or, if the elite consists of soft-hearted liberals, they may decide to play the role of good shepherds to the rest of the human race. They will see to it that everyone's physical needs are satisfied, that all children are raised under psychologically hygienic conditions, that everyone has a wholesome hobby to keep him busy, and that anyone who may become dissatisfied undergoes "treatment" to cure his "problem." Of course, life will be so purposeless that people will have to be biologically or psychologically engineered either to remove their need for the power process or make them "sublimate" their drive for power into some harmless hobby. These engineered human beings may be happy in such a society, but they will most certainly not be free. They will have been reduced to the status of domestic animals.[25]

In the book, you don't discover until you turn the page that the author of this passage is Theodore Kaczynski—the Unabomber. I am no apologist for Kaczynski. His bombs killed three people during a 17-year terror campaign and wounded many others. One of his bombs gravely injured my friend David Gelernter, one of the most brilliant and visionary computer scientists of our time. Like many of my colleagues, I felt that I could easily have been the Unabomber's next target.

Kaczynski's actions were murderous and, in my view, criminally insane. He is clearly a Luddite, but simply saying this does not dismiss his argument; as difficult as it is for me to acknowledge, I saw some merit in the reasoning in this single passage. I felt compelled to confront it.

Kaczynski's dystopian vision describes unintended consequences, a well-known problem with the design and use of technology, and one that is clearly related to Murphy's law—"Anything that can go wrong, will." (Actually, this is Finagle's law, which in itself shows that Finagle was right.) Our overuse of antibiotics has led to what may be the biggest such problem so far: the emergence of antibiotic-resistant and much more dangerous bacteria. Similar things happened when attempts to eliminate malarial mosquitoes using DDT caused them to acquire DDT resistance; malarial parasites likewise acquired multi-drug-resistant genes.[26]

The cause of many such surprises seems clear: The systems involved are complex, involving interaction among and feedback between many parts. Any changes to such a system will cascade in ways that are difficult to predict; this is especially true when human actions are involved.

I started showing friends the Kaczynski quote from *The Age of Spiritual Machines;* I would hand them Kurzweil's book, let them read the quote, and then watch their reaction as they discovered who had written it. At around the same time, I found Hans Moravec's book *Robot: Mere Machine to Transcendent Mind.* Moravec is one of the leaders in robotics research, and was a founder of the world's largest robotics research program, at Carnegie Mellon University. *Robot* gave me more material to try out on my friends—material surprisingly supportive of Kaczynski's argument. For example:

THE SHORT RUN (EARLY 2000s)

Biological species almost never survive encounters with superior competitors. Ten million years ago, South and North America were separated by a sunken Panama isthmus. South America, like Australia today, was populated by marsupial mammals, including pouched equivalents of rats, deers, and tigers. When the isthmus connecting North and South America rose, it took only a few thousand years for the northern placental species, with slightly more effective metabolisms and reproductive and nervous systems, to displace and eliminate almost all the southern marsupials.

In a completely free marketplace, superior robots would surely affect humans as North American placentals affected South American marsupials (and as humans have affected countless species). Robotic industries would compete vigorously among themselves for matter, energy, and space, incidentally driving their price beyond human reach. Unable to afford the necessities of life, biological humans would be squeezed out of existence.

There is probably some breathing room, because we do not live in a completely free marketplace. Government coerces nonmarket behavior, especially by collecting taxes. Judiciously applied, governmental coercion could support human populations in high style on the fruits of robot labor, perhaps for a long while. [27]

A textbook dystopia—and Moravec is just getting wound up. He goes on to discuss how our main job in the 21st century will be "ensuring continued cooperation from the robot industries" by passing laws decreeing that they be "nice,"[28] and to describe how seriously dangerous a human can be "once transformed into an unbounded superintelligent robot." Moravec's view is that the robots will eventually succeed us—that humans clearly face extinction.

I decided it was time to talk to my friend Danny Hillis. Danny became famous as the cofounder of Thinking Machines Corporation, which built a very powerful parallel supercomputer. Despite my current job title of Chief Scientist at Sun Microsystems, I am more a computer architect than a scientist, and I respect Danny's knowledge of the information and physical sciences more than that of any other single person I know. Danny is also a highly regarded

futurist who thinks long-term—four years ago he started the Long Now Foundation, which is building a clock designed to last 10,000 years, in an attempt to draw attention to the pitifully short attention span of our society.[29] So I flew to Los Angeles for the express purpose of having dinner with Danny and his wife, Pati. I went through my now-familiar routine, trotting out the ideas and passages that I found so disturbing. Danny's answer—directed specifically at Kurzweil's scenario of humans merging with robots—came swiftly, and quite surprised me. He said, simply, that the changes would come gradually, and that we would get used to them.

But I guess I wasn't totally surprised. I had seen a quote from Danny in Kurzweil's book in which he said, "I'm as fond of my body as anyone, but if I can be 200 with a body of silicon, I'll take it." It seemed that he was at peace with this process and its attendant risks, while I was not.

While talking and thinking about Kurzweil, Kaczynski, and Moravec, I suddenly remembered a novel I had read almost 20 years ago—*The White Plague*, by Frank Herbert—in which a molecular biologist is driven insane by the senseless murder of his family. To seek revenge he constructs and disseminates a new and highly contagious plague that kills widely but selectively. (We're lucky Kaczynski was a mathematician, not a molecular biologist.) I was also reminded of the Borg of *Star Trek*, a hive of partly biological, partly robotic creatures with a strong destructive streak. Borg-like disasters are a staple of science fiction, so why hadn't I been more concerned about such robotic dystopias earlier? Why weren't other people more concerned about these nightmarish scenarios?

Part of the answer certainly lies in our attitude toward the new—in our bias toward instant familiarity and unquestioning acceptance. Accustomed to living with almost routine scientific breakthroughs, we have yet to come to terms with the fact that the most compelling 21st-century technologies—robotics, genetic engineering, and nanotechnology—pose a different threat than the technologies that have come before. Specifically, robots, engineered organisms, and nanobots share a dangerous amplifying factor: They can self-replicate. A bomb is blown up only once—but one bot can become many, and quickly get out of control.

Much of my work over the past 25 years has been on computer networking, where the sending and receiving of messages creates the opportunity for out-of-control replication. But while replication in a computer or a computer network can be a nuisance, at worst it disables a machine or takes down a network or network service. Uncontrolled self-replication in these newer technologies runs a much greater risk: a risk of substantial damage in the physical world.

Each of these technologies also offers untold promise: The vision of near immortality that Kurzweil sees in his robot dreams drives us forward; genetic engineering may soon provide treatments, if not outright cures, for most diseases; and nanotechnology and nanomedicine can address yet more ills. Together they could significantly extend our average life span and improve the quality of our lives. Yet, with each of these technologies, a sequence of small, individually sensible advances leads to an accumula-

tion of great power and, concomitantly, great danger.

What was different in the 20th century? Certainly, the technologies underlying the weapons of mass destruction (WMD)—nuclear, biological, and chemical (NBC)—were powerful, and the weapons an enormous threat. But building nuclear weapons required, at least for a time, access to both rare—indeed, effectively unavailable—raw materials and highly protected information; biological and chemical weapons programs also tended to require large-scale activities.

The 21st-century technologies—genetics, nanotechnology, and robotics (GNR)—are so powerful that they can spawn whole new classes of accidents and abuses. Most dangerously, for the first time, these accidents and abuses are widely within the reach of individuals or small groups. They will not require large facilities or rare raw materials. Knowledge alone will enable the use of them.

Thus we have the possibility not just of weapons of mass destruction but of knowledge-enabled mass destruction (KMD), this destructiveness hugely amplified by the power of self-replication.

I think it is no exaggeration to say we are on the cusp of the further perfection of extreme evil, an evil whose possibility spreads well beyond that which weapons of mass destruction bequeathed to the nation-states, on to a surprising and terrible empowerment of extreme individuals.

Nothing about the way I got involved with computers suggested to me that I was going to be facing these kinds of issues.

My life has been driven by a deep need to ask questions and find answers. When I was 3, I was already reading, so my father took me to the elementary school, where I sat on the principal's lap and read him a story. I started school early, later skipped a grade, and escaped into books—I was incredibly motivated to learn. I asked lots of questions, often driving adults to distraction.

As a teenager I was very interested in science and technology. I wanted to be a ham radio operator but didn't have the money to buy the equipment. Ham radio was the Internet of its time: very addictive, and quite solitary. Money issues aside, my mother put her foot down—I was not to be a ham; I was antisocial enough already.

I may not have had many close friends, but I was awash in ideas. By high school, I had discovered the great science fiction writers. I remember especially Heinlein's *Have Spacesuit Will Travel* and Asimov's *I, Robot,* with its Three Laws of Robotics. I was enchanted by the descriptions of space travel, and wanted to have a telescope to look at the stars; since I had no money to buy or make one, I checked books on telescope-making out of the library and read about making them instead. I soared in my imagination.

Thursday nights my parents went bowling, and we kids stayed home alone. It was the night of Gene Roddenberry's original *Star Trek,* and the program made a big impression on me. I came to accept its notion that humans had a future in space, Western-style, with big heroes and adventures. Roddenberry's vision of the centuries to come was one with strong moral values, embodied in codes like the Prime Directive: to not interfere in the development of less technologically advanced civilizations. This had an incredible appeal to me; ethical humans, not robots, dominated this future, and I took Roddenberry's dream as part of my own.

I excelled in mathematics in high school, and when I went to the University of Michigan as an undergraduate engineering student I took the advanced curriculum of the mathematics majors. Solving math problems was an exciting challenge, but when I discovered computers I found something much more interesting: a machine into which you could put a program that attempted to solve a problem, after which the machine quickly checked the solution. The computer had a clear notion of correct and incorrect, true and false. Were my ideas correct? The machine could tell me. This was very seductive.

I was lucky enough to get a job programming early supercomputers and discovered the amazing power of large machines to numerically simulate advanced designs. When I went to graduate school at UC Berkeley in the mid-1970s, I started staying up late, often all night, inventing new worlds inside the machines. Solving problems. Writing the code that argued so strongly to be written.

In *The Agony and the Ecstasy,* Irving Stone's biographical novel of Michelangelo, Stone described vividly how Michelangelo released the statues from the stone, "breaking the marble spell," carving from the images in his mind.[30] In my most ecstatic moments, the software in the computer emerged in the same way. Once I had imagined it in my mind I felt that it was already there in the machine, waiting to be released. Staying up all night seemed a small price to pay to free it—to give the ideas concrete form.

After a few years at Berkeley I started to send out some of the software I had written—an instructional Pascal system, Unix utilities, and a text editor called vi (which is still, to my surprise, widely used more than 20 years later)—to others who had similar small PDP-11 and VAX minicomputers. These adventures in software eventually turned into the Berkeley version of the Unix operating system, which became a personal "success disaster"—so many people wanted it that I never finished my Ph.D. Instead I got a job working for Darpa putting Berkeley Unix on the Internet and fixing it to be reliable and to run large research applications well. This was all great fun and very rewarding. And, frankly, I saw no robots here, or anywhere near.

Still, by the early 1980s, I was drowning. The Unix releases were very successful, and my little project of one soon had money and some staff, but the problem at Berkeley was always office space rather than money—there wasn't room for the help the project needed, so when the other founders of Sun Microsystems showed up I jumped at the chance to join them. At Sun, the long hours continued into the early days of workstations and personal computers, and I have enjoyed participating in the creation of advanced microprocessor technologies and Internet technologies such as Java and Jini.

From all this, I trust it is clear that I am not a Luddite. I have always, rather, had a strong belief in the value of the scientific search for truth and in the ability of great engineering to bring material progress. The Industrial Revolution has immeasurably improved everyone's life over the last couple hundred years, and I always expected my career to involve the building of worthwhile solutions to real problems, one problem at a time.

I have not been disappointed. My work has had more impact than I had ever hoped for and has been more widely used than I could have reasonably expected. I have spent the last 20 years still trying to figure out how to make computers as reliable as I want them to be (they are not nearly there yet) and how to make them simple to use (a goal that has met with even less relative success). Despite some progress, the problems that remain seem even more daunting.

But while I was aware of the moral dilemmas surrounding technology's consequences in fields like weapons research, I did not expect that I would confront such issues in my own field, or at least not so soon.

Perhaps it is always hard to see the bigger impact while you are in the vortex of a change. Failing to understand the consequences of our inventions while we are in the rapture of discovery and innovation seems to be a common fault of scientists and technologists; we have long been driven by the overarching desire to know that is the nature of science's quest, not stopping to notice that the progress to newer and more powerful technologies can take on a life of its own.

I have long realized that the big advances in information technology come not from the work of computer scientists, computer architects, or electrical engineers, but from that of physical scientists. The physicists Stephen Wolfram and Brosl Hasslacher introduced me, in the early 1980s, to chaos theory and nonlinear systems. In the 1990s, I learned about complex systems from conversations with Danny Hillis, the biologist Stuart Kauffman, the Nobel-laureate physicist Murray Gell-Mann, and others.

Most recently, Hasslacher and the electrical engineer and device physicist Mark Reed have been giving me insight into the incredible possibilities of molecular electronics.

In my own work, as codesigner of three microprocessor architectures—SPARC, picoJava, and MAJC—and as the designer of several implementations thereof, I've been afforded a deep and firsthand acquaintance with Moore's law. For decades, Moore's law has correctly predicted the exponential rate of improvement of semiconductor technology. Until last year I believed that the rate of advances predicted by Moore's law might continue only until roughly 2010, when some physical limits would begin to be reached. It was not obvious to me that a new technology would arrive in time to keep performance advancing smoothly.

But because of the recent rapid and radical progress in molecular electronics—where individual atoms and molecules replace lithographically drawn transistors—and related nanoscale technologies, we should be able to meet or exceed the Moore's law rate of progress for another 30 years. By 2030, we are likely to be able to build machines, in quantity, a million times as powerful as the personal computers of today—sufficient to implement the dreams of Kurzweil and Moravec.

As this enormous computing power is combined with the manipulative advances of the physical sciences and the new, deep understandings in genetics, enormous transformative power is being unleashed. These combinations open up the opportunity to completely redesign the world, for better or worse: The replicating and evolving processes that have been confined to the natural world are about to become realms of human endeavor.

In designing software and microprocessors, I have never had the feeling that I was designing an intelligent machine. The software and hardware is so fragile and the capabilities of the machine to "think" so clearly absent that, even as a possibility, this has always seemed very far in the future.

But now, with the prospect of human-level computing power in about 30 years, a new idea suggests itself: that I may be working to create tools which will enable the construction of the technology that may replace our species. How do I feel about this? Very uncomfortable. Having struggled my entire career to build reliable software systems, it seems to me more than likely that this future will not work out as well as some people may imagine. My personal experience suggests we tend to overestimate our design abilities.

Given the incredible power of these new technologies, shouldn't we be asking how we can best coexist with them? And if our own extinction is a likely, or even possible, outcome of our technological development, shouldn't we proceed with great caution?

The dream of robotics is, first, that intelligent machines can do our work for us, allowing us lives of leisure, restoring us to Eden. Yet in his history of such ideas, *Darwin Among the Machines,* George Dyson warns: "In the game of life and evolution there are three players at the table: human beings, nature, and machines. I am firmly on the side of nature. But nature, I suspect, is on the side of the machines." As we have seen, Moravec agrees, believing we may well not survive the encounter with the superior robot species.

How soon could such an intelligent robot be built? The coming advances in computing power seem to make it possible by 2030. And once an intelligent robot exists, it is only a small step to a robot species—to an intelligent robot that can make evolved copies of itself.

A second dream of robotics is that we will gradually replace ourselves with our robotic technology, achieving near immortality by downloading our consciousnesses; it is this process that Danny Hillis thinks we will gradually get used to and that Ray Kurzweil elegantly details in *The Age of Spiritual Machines.* (We are beginning to see intimations of this in the implantation of computer devices into the human body, as illustrated on the cover of *Wired* 8.02.)

But if we are downloaded into our technology, what are the chances that we will thereafter be ourselves or even human? It seems to me far more likely that a robotic existence would not be like a human one in any sense that we understand, that the robots would in no sense be our children, that on this path our humanity may well be lost.

Genetic engineering promises to revolutionize agriculture by increasing crop yields while reducing the use of pesticides; to create tens of thousands of novel species of bacteria, plants, viruses, and animals; to replace reproduction, or supplement it, with cloning; to create cures for many diseases, increasing our life span and our quality of life; and much, much more. We now know with certainty that these profound changes in the bio-

logical sciences are imminent and will challenge all our notions of what life is.

Technologies such as human cloning have in particular raised our awareness of the profound ethical and moral issues we face. If, for example, we were to reengineer ourselves into several separate and unequal species using the power of genetic engineering, then we would threaten the notion of equality that is the very cornerstone of our democracy.

Given the incredible power of genetic engineering, it's no surprise that there are significant safety issues in its use. My friend Amory Lovins recently cowrote, along with Hunter Lovins, an editorial that provides an ecological view of some of these dangers. Among their concerns: that "the new botany aligns the development of plants with their economic, not evolutionary, success."* Amory's long career has been focused on energy and resource efficiency by taking a whole-system view of human-made systems; such a whole-system view often finds simple, smart solutions to otherwise seemingly difficult problems, and is usefully applied here as well.

After reading the Lovins' editorial, I saw an op-ed by Gregg Easterbrook in the *New York Times* (November 19, 1999) about genetically engineered crops, under the headline: "Food for the Future: Someday, rice will have built-in vitamin A. Unless the Luddites win."

Are Amory and Hunter Lovins Luddites? Certainly not. I believe we all would agree that golden rice, with its built-in vitamin A, is probably a good thing, if developed with proper care and respect for the likely dangers in moving genes across species boundaries.

Awareness of the dangers inherent in genetic engineering is beginning to grow, as reflected in the Lovins' editorial. The general public is aware of, and uneasy about, genetically modified foods, and seems to be rejecting the notion that such foods should be permitted to be unlabeled.

But genetic engineering technology is already very far along. As the Lovins note, the USDA has already approved about 50 genetically engineered crops for unlimited release; more than half of the world's soybeans and a third of its corn now contain genes spliced in from other forms of life.

While there are many important issues here, my own major concern with genetic engineering is narrower: that it gives the power—whether militarily, accidentally, or in a deliberate terrorist act—to create a White Plague.

The many wonders of nanotechnology were first imagined by the Nobel-laureate physicist Richard Feynman in a speech he gave in 1959, subsequently published under the title "There's Plenty of Room at the Bottom." The book that made a big impression on me, in the mid-'80s, was Eric Drexler's *Engines of Creation,* in which he described beautifully how manipulation of matter at the atomic level could create a utopian future of abundance, where just about everything could be made cheaply, and almost any imaginable disease or physical problem could be solved using nanotechnology and artificial intelligences.

A subsequent book, *Unbounding the Future: The Nanotechnology Revolution,* which Drexler cowrote, imagines some of the changes that might take place in a world where we had molecular-level "assemblers." Assemblers could make possible incredibly low-cost solar power, cures for cancer and the common cold by augmentation of the human immune system, essentially complete cleanup of the environment, incredibly inexpensive pocket supercomputers—in fact, any product would be manufacturable by assemblers at a cost no greater than that of wood—space flight more accessible than transoceanic travel today, and restoration of extinct species.

I remember feeling good about nanotechnology after reading *Engines of Creation.* As a technologist, it gave me a sense of calm—that is, nanotechnology showed us that incredible progress was possible, and indeed perhaps inevitable. If nanotechnology was our future, then I didn't feel pressed to solve so many problems in the present. I would get to Drexler's utopian future in due time; I might as well enjoy life more in the here and now. It didn't make sense, given his vision, to stay up all night, all the time.

Drexler's vision also led to a lot of good fun. I would occasionally get to describe the wonders of nanotechnology to others who had not heard of it. After teasing them with all the things Drexler described I would give a homework assignment of my own: "Use nanotechnology to create a vampire; for extra credit create an antidote."

With these wonders came clear dangers, of which I was acutely aware. As I said at a nanotechnology conference in 1989, "We can't simply do our science and not worry about these ethical issues."[31] But my subsequent conversations with physicists convinced me that nanotechnology might not even work— or, at least, it wouldn't work anytime soon. Shortly thereafter I moved to

Colorado, to a skunk works I had set up, and the focus of my work shifted to software for the Internet, specifically on ideas that became Java and Jini.

Then, last summer, Brosl Hasslacher told me that nanoscale molecular electronics was now practical. This was *new* news, at least to me, and I think to many people—and it radically changed my opinion about nanotechnology. It sent me back to *Engines of Creation*. Rereading Drexler's work after more than 10 years, I was dismayed to realize how little I had remembered of its lengthy section called "Dangers and Hopes," including a discussion of how nanotechnologies can become "engines of destruction." Indeed, in my rereading of this cautionary material today, I am struck by how naive some of Drexler's safeguard proposals seem, and how much greater I judge the dangers to be now than even he seemed to then. (Having anticipated and described many technical and political problems with nanotechnology, Drexler started the Foresight Institute in the late 1980s "to help prepare society for anticipated advanced technologies"—most important, nanotechnology.)

The enabling breakthrough to assemblers seems quite likely within the next 20 years. Molecular electronics—the new subfield of nanotechnology where individual molecules are circuit elements—should mature quickly and become enormously lucrative within this decade, causing a large incremental investment in all nanotechnologies.

Unfortunately, as with nuclear technology, it is far easier to create destructive uses for nanotechnology than constructive ones. Nanotechnology has clear military and terrorist uses, and you need

not be suicidal to release a massively destructive nanotechnological device—such devices can be built to be selectively destructive, affecting, for example, only a certain geographical area or a group of people who are genetically distinct.

An immediate consequence of the Faustian bargain in obtaining the great power of nanotechnology is that we run a grave risk—the risk that we might destroy the biosphere on which all life depends.

As Drexler explained: "Plants" with "leaves" no more efficient than today's solar cells could out-compete real plants, crowding the biosphere with an inedible foliage. Tough omnivorous "bacteria" could out-compete real bacteria: They could spread like blowing pollen, replicate swiftly, and reduce the biosphere to dust in a matter of days. Dangerous replicators could easily be too tough, small, and rapidly spreading to stop—at least if we make no preparation. We have trouble enough controlling viruses and fruit flies.

Among the cognoscenti of nanotechnology, this threat has become known as the "gray goo problem." Though masses of uncontrolled replicators need not be gray or gooey, the term "gray goo" emphasizes that replicators able to obliterate life might be less inspiring than a single species of crabgrass. They might be superior in an evolutionary sense, but this need not make them valuable.

The gray goo threat makes one thing perfectly clear: We cannot afford certain kinds of accidents with replicating assemblers.

Gray goo would surely be a depressing ending to our human adventure on Earth, far worse than mere fire or ice, and one that could stem from a simple laboratory accident.[32] Oops.

It is most of all the power of destructive self-replication in genetics, nanotechnology, and robotics (GNR) that should give us pause. Self-replication is the modus operandi of genetic engineering, which uses the machinery of the cell to replicate its designs, and the prime danger underlying gray goo in nanotechnology. Stories of run-amok robots like the Borg, replicating or mutating to escape from the ethical constraints imposed on them by their creators, are well established in our science fiction books and movies. It is even possible that self-replication may be more fundamental than we thought, and hence harder—or even impossible—to control. A recent article by Stuart Kauffman in *Nature* titled "Self-Replication: Even Peptides Do It" discusses the discovery that a 32-amino-acid peptide can "autocatalyse its own synthesis." We don't know how widespread this ability is, but Kauffman notes that it may hint at "a route to self-reproducing molecular systems on a basis far wider than Watson-Crick base-pairing."[33]

In truth, we have had in hand for years clear warnings of the dangers inherent in widespread knowledge of GNR technologies—of the possibility of knowledge alone enabling mass destruction. But these warnings haven't been widely publicized; the public discussions have been clearly inadequate. There is no profit in publicizing the dangers.

The nuclear, biological, and chemical (NBC) technologies used in 20th-century weapons of mass destruction were and are largely military, developed in government laboratories. In sharp contrast, the 21st-century GNR technologies have clear commercial uses and are being developed almost exclusively by corporate enterprises. In this age of triumphant commercialism, technology—with science as its handmaiden—is delivering a series of almost magical inventions that are the most phenomenally lucrative ever seen. We are aggressively pursuing the promises of these new technologies within the now-unchallenged system of global capitalism and its manifold financial incentives and competitive pressures.

This is the first moment in the history of our planet when any species, by its own voluntary actions, has become a danger to itself—as well as to vast numbers of others.

It might be a familiar progression, transpiring on many worlds—a planet, newly formed, placidly revolves around its star; life slowly forms; a kaleidoscopic procession of creatures evolves; intelligence emerges which, at least up to a point, confers enormous survival value; and then technology is invented. It dawns on them that there are such things as laws of Nature, that these laws can be revealed by experiment, and that knowledge of these laws can be made both to save and to take lives, both on unprecedented scales. Science, they recognize, grants immense powers. In a flash, they create world-altering contrivances. Some planetary civilizations see their way through, place limits on what may and what must not be done, and safely pass through the time of perils. Others, not so lucky or so prudent, perish.

That is Carl Sagan, writing in 1994, in *Pale Blue Dot,* a book describing his vision of the human future in space. I am only now realizing how deep his insight was, and how sorely I miss, and will miss, his voice. For all its eloquence, Sagan's contribution was not least that of simple common sense—an attribute that, along with humility, many of the leading advocates of the 21st-century technologies seem to lack.

I remember from my childhood that my grandmother was strongly against the overuse of antibiotics. She had worked since before the first World War as a nurse and had a commonsense attitude that taking antibiotics, unless they were absolutely necessary, was bad for you.

It is not that she was an enemy of progress. She saw much progress in an almost 70-year nursing career; my grandfather, a diabetic, benefited greatly from the improved treatments that became available in his lifetime. But she, like many levelheaded people, would probably think it greatly arrogant for us, now, to be designing a robotic "replacement species," when we obviously have so much trouble making relatively simple things work, and so much trouble managing—or even understanding—ourselves.

I realize now that she had an awareness of the nature of the order of life, and of the necessity of living with and respecting that order. With this respect comes a necessary humility that we, with our early-21st-century chutzpah, lack at our peril. The commonsense view, grounded in this respect, is often right, in advance of the scientific evidence. The clear fragility and inefficiencies of the human-made systems we have built should give us all pause; the fragility of the systems I have worked on certainly humbles me.

We should have learned a lesson from the making of the first atomic bomb and the resulting arms race. We didn't do well then, and the parallels to our current situation are troubling.

The effort to build the first atomic bomb was led by the brilliant physicist J. Robert Oppenheimer. Oppenheimer was not naturally interested in politics but became painfully aware of what he perceived as the grave threat to Western civilization from the Third Reich, a threat surely grave because of the possibility that Hitler might obtain nuclear weapons. Energized by this concern, he brought his strong intellect, passion for physics, and charismatic leadership skills to Los Alamos and led a rapid and successful effort by an incredible collection of great minds to quickly invent the bomb.

What is striking is how this effort continued so naturally after the initial impetus was removed. In a meeting shortly after V-E Day with some physicists who felt that perhaps the effort should stop, Oppenheimer argued to continue. His stated reason seems a bit strange: not because of the fear of large casualties from an invasion of Japan, but because the United Nations, which was soon to be formed, should have foreknowledge of atomic weapons. A more likely reason the project continued is the momentum that had built up—the first atomic test, Trinity, was nearly at hand.

We know that in preparing this first atomic test the physicists proceeded despite a large number of possible dangers. They were initially worried, based on a calculation by Edward Teller, that an atomic explosion might set fire to the atmosphere. A revised calculation reduced the danger of destroying the world to a three-in-a-million chance. (Teller says he was later able to dismiss the prospect of atmospheric ignition entirely.) Oppenheimer, though, was sufficiently concerned about the result of Trinity that he arranged for a possible evacuation of the southwest part of the state of New Mexico. And, of course, there was the clear danger of starting a nuclear arms race.

Within a month of that first, successful test, two atomic bombs destroyed Hiroshima and Nagasaki. Some scientists had suggested that the bomb simply be demonstrated, rather than dropped on Japanese cities—saying that this would greatly improve the chances for arms control after the war—but to no avail. With the tragedy of Pearl Harbor still fresh in Americans' minds, it would have been very difficult for President Truman to order a demonstration of the weapons rather than use them as he did—the desire to quickly end the war and save the lives that would have been lost in any invasion of Japan was very strong. Yet the overriding truth was probably very simple: As the physicist Freeman Dyson later said, "The reason that it was dropped was just that nobody had the courage or the foresight to say no."

It's important to realize how shocked the physicists were in the aftermath of the bombing of Hiroshima, on August 6, 1945. They describe a series of waves of emotion: first, a sense of fulfillment that the bomb worked, then horror at all the people that had been killed, and then a convincing feeling that on no account should another bomb be dropped. Yet of course another bomb was dropped, on Nagasaki, only three days after the bombing of Hiroshima.

In November 1945, three months after the atomic bombings, Oppenheimer stood firmly behind the scientific attitude, saying, "It is not possible to be a scientist unless you believe that the knowledge of the world, and the power which this gives, is a thing which is of intrinsic value to humanity, and that you are using it to help in the spread of knowledge and are willing to take the consequences."

Oppenheimer went on to work, with others, on the Acheson-Lilienthal report, which, as Richard Rhodes says in his recent book *Visions of Technology,* "found a way to prevent a clandestine nuclear arms race without resorting to armed world government"; their suggestion was a form of relinquishment of nuclear weapons work by nation-states to an international agency.

This proposal led to the Baruch Plan, which was submitted to the United Nations in June 1946 but never adopted (perhaps because, as Rhodes suggests, Bernard Baruch had "insisted on burdening the plan with conventional sanctions," thereby inevitably dooming it, even though it would "almost certainly have been rejected by Stalinist Russia anyway"). Other efforts to promote sensible steps toward internationalizing nuclear power to prevent an arms race ran afoul either of U.S. politics and internal distrust, or distrust by the Soviets. The opportunity to avoid the arms race was lost, and very quickly.

Two years later, in 1948, Oppenheimer seemed to have reached another stage in his thinking, saying, "In some sort of crude sense which no vulgarity, no humor, no overstatement can quite extinguish, the physicists have known sin; and this is a knowledge they cannot lose."

In 1949, the Soviets exploded an atom bomb. By 1955, both the U.S. and the Soviet Union had tested hydrogen bombs suitable for delivery by aircraft. And so the nuclear arms race began.

Nearly 20 years ago, in the documentary *The Day After Trinity,* Freeman

Dyson summarized the scientific attitudes that brought us to the nuclear precipice:

"I have felt it myself. The glitter of nuclear weapons. It is irresistible if you come to them as a scientist. To feel it's there in your hands, to release this energy that fuels the stars, to let it do your bidding. To perform these miracles, to lift a million tons of rock into the sky. It is something that gives people an illusion of illimitable power, and it is, in some ways, responsible for all our troubles—this, what you might call technical arrogance, that overcomes people when they see what they can do with their minds."[34]

Now, as then, we are creators of new technologies and stars of the imagined future, driven—this time by great financial rewards and global competition—despite the clear dangers, hardly evaluating what it may be like to try to live in a world that is the realistic outcome of what we are creating and imagining.

In 1947, the *Bulletin of the Atomic Scientists* began putting a Doomsday Clock on its cover. For more than 50 years, it has shown an estimate of the relative nuclear danger we have faced, reflecting the changing international conditions. The hands on the clock have moved 15 times and today, standing at nine minutes to midnight, reflect continuing and real danger from nuclear weapons. The recent addition of India and Pakistan to the list of nuclear powers has increased the threat of failure of the nonproliferation goal, and this danger was reflected by moving the hands closer to midnight in 1998.

In our time, how much danger do we face, not just from nuclear weapons, but from all of these technologies? How high are the extinction risks?

The philosopher John Leslie has studied this question and concluded that the risk of human extinction is at least 30 percent,[35] while Ray Kurzweil believes we have "a better than even chance of making it through," with the caveat that he has "always been accused of being an optimist." Not only are these estimates not encouraging, but they do not include the probability of many horrid outcomes that lie short of extinction.

Faced with such assessments, some serious people are already suggesting that we simply move beyond Earth as quickly as possible. We would colonize the galaxy using von Neumann probes, which hop from star system to star system, replicating as they go. This step will almost certainly be necessary 5 billion years from now (or sooner if our solar system is disastrously impacted by the impending collision of our galaxy with the Andromeda galaxy within the next 3 billion years), but if we take Kurzweil and Moravec at their word it might be necessary by the middle of this century.

What are the moral implications here? If we must move beyond Earth this quickly in order for the species to survive, who accepts the responsibility for the fate of those (most of us, after all) who are left behind? And even if we scatter to the stars, isn't it likely that we may take our problems with us or find, later, that they have followed us? The fate of our species on Earth and our fate in the galaxy seem inextricably linked.

Another idea is to erect a series of shields to defend against each of the dangerous technologies. The Strategic Defense Initiative, proposed by the Reagan administration, was an attempt to design

such a shield against the threat of a nuclear attack from the Soviet Union. But
as Arthur C. Clarke, who was privy to
discussions about the project, observed:
"Though it might be possible, at vast expense, to construct local defense systems
that would 'only' let through a few percent of ballistic missiles, the much
touted idea of a national umbrella was
nonsense. Luis Alvarez, perhaps the
greatest experimental physicist of this
century, remarked to me that the advocates of such schemes were 'very bright
guys with no common sense.'"

Clarke continued: "Looking into my
often cloudy crystal ball, I suspect that a
total defense might indeed be possible in
a century or so. But the technology involved would produce, as a by-product,
weapons so terrible that no one would
bother with anything as primitive as ballistic missiles."[36]

In *Engines of Creation,* Eric Drexler
proposed that we build an active nanotechnological shield—a form of immune system for the biosphere—to
defend against dangerous replicators of
all kinds that might escape from laboratories or otherwise be maliciously created. But the shield he proposed would
itself be extremely dangerous—nothing
could prevent it from developing au-
toimmune problems and attacking the
biosphere itself.[37]

Similar difficulties apply to the construction of shields against robotics and
genetic engineering. These technologies
are too powerful to be shielded against in
the time frame of interest; even if it were
possible to implement defensive shields,
the side effects of their development
would be at least as dangerous as the
technologies we are trying to protect
against.

These possibilities are all thus either
undesirable or unachievable or both. The
only realistic alternative I see is relinquishment: to limit development of the
technologies that are too dangerous, by
limiting our pursuit of certain kinds of
knowledge.

Yes, I know, knowledge is good, as is
the search for new truths. We have been
seeking knowledge since ancient times.
Aristotle opened his *Metaphysics* with
the simple statement: "All men by nature
desire to know." We have, as a bedrock
value in our society, long agreed on
the value of open access to information,
and recognize the problems that arise
with attempts to restrict access to and
development of knowledge. In recent
times, we have come to revere scientific
knowledge.

But despite the strong historical
precedents, if open access to and unlimited development of knowledge henceforth puts us all in clear danger of
extinction, then common sense demands
that we reexamine even these basic,
long-held beliefs.

It was Nietzsche who warned us, at
the end of the 19th century, not only that
God is dead but that "faith in science,
which after all exists undeniably, cannot
owe its origin to a calculus of utility; it
must have originated *in spite of* the fact
that the disutility and dangerousness of
the 'will to truth,' of 'truth at any price'
is proved to it constantly." It is this
further danger that we now fully face—
the consequences of our truth-seeking.
The truth that science seeks can certainly be considered a dangerous substitute for God if it is likely to lead to
our extinction.

If we could agree, as a species, what
we wanted, where we were headed, and

why, then we would make our future much less dangerous—then we might understand what we can and should relinquish. Otherwise, we can easily imagine an arms race developing over GNR technologies, as it did with the NBC technologies in the 20th century. This is perhaps the greatest risk, for once such a race begins, it's very hard to end it. This time—unlike during the Manhattan Project—we aren't in a war, facing an implacable enemy that is threatening our civilization; we are driven, instead, by our habits, our desires, our economic system, and our competitive need to know.

I believe that we all wish our course could be determined by our collective values, ethics, and morals. If we had gained more collective wisdom over the past few thousand years, then a dialogue to this end would be more practical, and the incredible powers we are about to unleash would not be nearly so troubling.

One would think we might be driven to such a dialogue by our instinct for self-preservation. Individuals clearly have this desire, yet as a species our behavior seems to be not in our favor. In dealing with the nuclear threat, we often spoke dishonestly to ourselves and to each other, thereby greatly increasing the risks. Whether this was politically motivated, or because we chose not to think ahead, or because when faced with such grave threats we acted irrationally out of fear, I do not know, but it does not bode well.

The new Pandora's boxes of genetics, nanotechnology, and robotics are almost open, yet we seem hardly to have noticed. Ideas can't be put back in a box; unlike uranium or plutonium, they don't need to be mined and refined, and they can be freely copied. Once they are out, they are out. Churchill remarked, in a famous lefthanded compliment, that the American people and their leaders "invariably do the right thing, after they have examined every other alternative." In this case, however, we must act more presciently, as to do the right thing only at last may be to lose the chance to do it at all.

As Thoreau said, "We do not ride on the railroad; it rides upon us"; and this is what we must fight, in our time. The question is, indeed, Which is to be master? Will we survive our technologies?

We are being propelled into this new century with no plan, no control, no brakes. Have we already gone too far down the path to alter course? I don't believe so, but we aren't trying yet, and the last chance to assert control—the failsafe point—is rapidly approaching. We have our first pet robots, as well as commercially available genetic engineering techniques, and our nanoscale techniques are advancing rapidly. While the development of these technologies proceeds through a number of steps, it isn't necessarily the case—as happened in the Manhattan Project and the Trinity test—that the last step in proving a technology is large and hard. The breakthrough to wild self-replication in robotics, genetic engineering, or nanotechnology could come suddenly, reprising the surprise we felt when we learned of the cloning of a mammal.

And yet I believe we do have a strong and solid basis for hope. Our attempts to deal with weapons of mass destruction in the last century provide a shining example of relinquishment for us to consider: the unilateral U.S. abandonment, without preconditions, of the development of biological weapons. This relinquishment stemmed from the realization that while it would take an enormous effort to create these terrible weapons, they could from then on easily be duplicated and fall into the hands of rogue nations or terrorist groups.

The clear conclusion was that we would create additional threats to ourselves by pursuing these weapons, and that we would be more secure if we did not pursue them. We have embodied our relinquishment of biological and chemical weapons in the 1972 Biological Weapons Convention (BWC) and the 1993 Chemical Weapons Convention (CWC).[38]

As for the continuing sizable threat from nuclear weapons, which we have lived with now for more than 50 years, the U.S. Senate's recent rejection of the Comprehensive Test Ban Treaty makes it clear relinquishing nuclear weapons will not be politically easy. But we have a unique opportunity, with the end of the Cold War, to avert a multipolar arms race. Building on the BWC and CWC relinquishments, successful abolition of nuclear weapons could help us build toward a habit of relinquishing dangerous technologies. (Actually, by getting rid of all but 100 nuclear weapons worldwide—roughly the total destructive power of World War II and a considerably easier task—we could eliminate this extinction threat.[39])

Verifying relinquishment will be a difficult problem, but not an unsolvable one. We are fortunate to have already done a lot of relevant work in the context of the BWC and other treaties. Our major task will be to apply this to technologies that are naturally much more commercial than military. The substantial need here is for transparency, as difficulty of verification is directly proportional to the difficulty of distinguishing relinquished from legitimate activities.

I frankly believe that the situation in 1945 was simpler than the one we now face: The nuclear technologies were reasonably separable into commercial and military uses, and monitoring was aided by the nature of atomic tests and the ease with which radioactivity could be measured. Research on military applications could be performed at national laboratories such as Los Alamos, with the results kept secret as long as possible.

The GNR technologies do not divide clearly into commercial and military uses; given their potential in the market, it's hard to imagine pursuing them only in national laboratories. With their widespread commercial pursuit, enforcing relinquishment will require a verification regime similar to that for biological weapons, but on an unprecedented scale. This, inevitably, will raise tensions between our individual privacy and desire for proprietary information, and the need for verification to protect us all. We will undoubtedly encounter strong resistance to this loss of privacy and freedom of action.

Verifying the relinquishment of certain GNR technologies will have to occur in cyberspace as well as at physical facilities. The critical issue will be to make the necessary transparency acceptable in a world of proprietary information, presumably by providing new forms of protection for intellectual property.

Verifying compliance will also require that scientists and engineers adopt a strong code of ethical conduct, resembling the Hippocratic oath, and that they have the courage to whistleblow as necessary, even at high personal cost. This would answer the call—50 years after Hiroshima—by the Nobel laureate Hans Bethe, one of the most senior of the surviving members of the Manhattan Project, that all scientists "cease and desist from work creating, developing, improving, and manufacturing nuclear weapons and other weapons of potential mass destruction."[40] In the 21st century, this requires vigilance and personal responsibility by those who would work on both NBC and GNR technologies to avoid implementing weapons of mass destruction and knowledge-enabled mass destruction.

Thoreau also said that we will be "rich in proportion to the number of things which we can afford to let alone." We each seek to be happy, but it would seem worthwhile to question whether we need to take such a high risk of total destruction to gain yet more knowledge and yet more things; common sense says that there is a limit to our material needs—and that certain knowledge is too dangerous and is best forgone.

Neither should we pursue near immortality without considering the costs, without considering the commensurate increase in the risk of extinction. Immortality, while perhaps the original, is certainly not the only possible utopian dream.

I recently had the good fortune to meet the distinguished author and scholar Jacques Attali, whose book *Lignes d'horizons* (*Millennium,* in the English translation) helped inspire the Java and Jini approach to the coming age of pervasive computing, as previously described in this magazine. In his new book *Fraternités,* Attali describes how our dreams of utopia have changed over time:

At the dawn of societies, men saw their passage on Earth as nothing more than a labyrinth of pain, at the end of which stood a door leading, via their death, to the company of gods and to *Eternity.* With the Hebrews and then the Greeks, some men dared free themselves from theological demands and dream of an ideal City where *Liberty* would flourish. Others, noting the evolution of the market society, understood that the liberty of some would entail the alienation of others, and they sought *Equality.*[41]

Jacques helped me understand how these three different utopian goals exist in tension in our society today. He goes on to describe a fourth utopia, *Fraternity,* whose foundation is altruism. Fraternity alone associates individual happiness with the happiness of others, affording the promise of self-sustainment.

This crystallized for me my problem with Kurzweil's dream. A technological approach to Eternity—near immortality through robotics—may not be the most desirable utopia, and its pursuit brings clear dangers. Maybe we should rethink our utopian choices.

Where can we look for a new ethical basis to set our course? I have found the ideas in the book *Ethics for the New Millennium,* by the Dalai Lama, to be very helpful. As is perhaps well known but little heeded, the Dalai Lama argues that the most important thing is for us to conduct our lives with love and compassion for others, and that our societies need to develop a stronger notion of universal responsibility and of our interdependency; he proposes a standard of positive ethical conduct for individuals and societies that seems consonant with Attali's Fraternity utopia.

The Dalai Lama further argues that we must understand what it is that makes people happy, and acknowledge the strong evidence that neither material progress nor the pursuit of the power of knowledge is the key—that there are limits to what science and the scientific pursuit alone can do.

Our Western notion of happiness seems to come from the Greeks, who defined it as "the exercise of vital powers along lines of excellence in a life affording them scope."[42]

Clearly, we need to find meaningful challenges and sufficient scope in our lives if we are to be happy in whatever is to come. But I believe we must find alternative outlets for our creative forces, beyond the culture of perpetual economic growth; this growth has largely been a blessing for several hundred years, but it has not brought us unalloyed happiness, and we must now choose between the pursuit of unrestricted and undirected growth through science and technology and the clear accompanying dangers.

It is now more than a year since my first encounter with Ray Kurzweil and John Searle. I see around me cause for hope in the voices for caution and relinquishment and in those people I have discovered who are as concerned as I am about our current predicament. I feel, too, a deepened sense of personal responsibility—not for the work I have already done, but for the work that I might yet do, at the confluence of the sciences.

But many other people who know about the dangers still seem strangely silent. When pressed, they trot out the "this is nothing new" riposte—as if awareness of what could happen is response enough. They tell me, *There are universities filled with bioethicists who study this stuff all day long.* They say, *All this has been written about before, and by experts.* They complain, *Your worries and your arguments are already old hat.*

I don't know where these people hide their fear. As an architect of complex systems I enter this arena as a generalist. But should this diminish my concerns? I am aware of how much has been written about, talked about, and lectured about so authoritatively. But does this mean it has reached people? Does this mean we can discount the dangers before us?

Knowing is not a rationale for not acting. Can we doubt that knowledge has become a weapon we wield against ourselves?

The experiences of the atomic scientists clearly show the need to take personal responsibility, the danger that things will move too fast, and the way in which a process can take on a life of its own. We can, as they did, create insurmountable problems in almost no time flat. We must do more thinking up front if we are not to be similarly surprised and shocked by the consequences of our inventions.

My continuing professional work is on improving the reliability of software. Software is a tool, and as a toolbuilder I must struggle with the uses to which the tools I make are put. I have always believed that making software more reliable, given its many uses, will make the world a safer and better place; if I were to come to believe the opposite, then I would be morally obligated to stop this work. I can now imagine such a day may come.

This all leaves me not angry but at least a bit melancholic. Henceforth, for me, progress will be somewhat bittersweet.

Do you remember the beautiful penultimate scene in *Manhattan* where Woody Allen is lying on his couch and talking into a tape recorder? He is writing a short story about people who are creating unnecessary, neurotic problems for themselves, because it keeps them from dealing with more unsolvable, terrifying problems about the universe.

He leads himself to the question, "Why is life worth living?" and to consider what makes it worthwhile for him: Groucho Marx, Willie Mays, the second movement of the *Jupiter Symphony,* Louis Armstrong's recording of "Potato Head Blues," Swedish movies, Flaubert's *Sentimental Education,* Marlon Brando, Frank Sinatra, the apples and pears by Cézanne, the crabs at Sam Wo's, and, finally, the showstopper: his love of Tracy's face.

Each of us has our precious things, and as we care for them we locate the essence of our humanity. In the end, it is because of our great capacity for caring that I remain optimistic we will confront the dangerous issues now before us.

My immediate hope is to participate in a much larger discussion of the issues raised here, with people from many different backgrounds, in settings not predisposed to fear or favor technology for its own sake.

As a start, I have twice raised many of these issues at events sponsored by the Aspen Institute and have separately proposed that the American Academy of Arts and Sciences take them up as an extension of its work with the Pugwash Conferences. (These have been held since 1957 to discuss arms control, especially of nuclear weapons, and to formulate workable policies.)

It's unfortunate that the Pugwash meetings started only well after the nuclear genie was out of the bottle— roughly 15 years too late. We are also getting a belated start on seriously addressing the issues around 21st-century technologies—the prevention of knowledge-enabled mass destruction— and further delay seems unacceptable.

So I'm still searching; there are many more things to learn. Whether we are to succeed or fail, to survive or fall victim to these technologies, is not yet decided. I'm up late again—it's almost 6 a.m. I'm trying to imagine some better answers, to break the spell and free them from the stone.

EXERCISES

1. Here are two quotes from Thoreau that Joy included in the selection you just read. What does Joy think the quotes mean?

"We do not ride on the railroad; it rides upon us."

"[We will be] rich in proportion to the number of things which we can afford to let alone."

2. How does Joy incorporate the ethics of the Dalai Lama in his approach to the relationship of the search for knowledge and moral responsibility?

3. Is the limiting of knowledge compatible with a free enterprise society? Does either the Dalai Lama or Bill Joy have a way of ensuring that if some people limit the quest for knowledge and technology that others will also?

11.4 THE LONG NOW   One coauthor of this book lived in Oklahoma City during the 1980s. Each day on the way to the office he would pass a billboard that read, "Oklahoma City, Your Future is Now." This was in an urban area that still allowed for open fields, and the billboard stood in a field with lots of cows. It was easy to misread the sign's slogan sometimes and replace "now" with "cow." The other impression brought about by repeated sightings of the sign was that of no future—every day in Oklahoma seemed the same. The now became elongated, making all days seem equally valuable.

Stewart Brand was trained as a biologist. He won the American National Book Award for *The Whole Earth Catalog*. Brand is a founding member of the Long Now Foundation (www.longnow.org), which is dedicated to changing the way people think about their responsibilities to future generations. The foundation has built a ten-thousand-year clock to help increase people's psychological sense of the future. Another awareness-raising device is to write dates as August 12, 02000, instead of August 12, 2000. Brand's perspective on the future supports the values found in the previous two selections from Joy and the Dalai Lama both in the scope of time our responsibilities range over and in the preservation of human attachments.

QUESTIONS FOR STUDY AND DISCUSSION

1. What does Brand mean by the long now?
2. Does Brand show how long-term thinking can resist radical changes in society brought about by rapid technological change? Explain.
3. What are Dyson's six different time scales and the corresponding units and imperatives?
4. What is a Prisoner's Dilemma? What is an iterated Prisoner's Dilemma?

THE LONG NOW[43]

STEWART BRAND

In a 1994 discussion of how to think about and name Danny Hillis's millennial Clock, Eno [Brian Eno, popular musician] suggested, "How about calling it `The Clock of the Long Now,' since the idea is to extend our concept of the present in both directions, making the present longer? Civilizations with long nows look after things better. In those places you feel a very strong but flexible structure which is built to absorb shocks and in fact incorporate them."[44]

How long *is* now, usually? In the Clock discussion Esther Dyson suggested, "On the stock exchange it's today, on the Net it's a month, in fashion it's a season, in demographics a decade, in most companies it's the next quarter." . . .

For most of us most of the time I think Eno is right: "now" consists of this week, slightly haunted by the ghost of last week. This is the realm of immediate responsibility, one in which we feel we have volition, where the consequences of our actions are obvious and surprises limited. The weekend is a convenient boundary.

The sociologist Elise Boulding diagnosed the problem of our times as "temporal exhaustion": "If one is mentally out of breath all the time from dealing with the present, there is no energy left for imaging the future." In a 1978 paper Boulding proposed a simple solution: expand our idea of the present to two hundred years—a hundred years forward, a hundred years back. A personally experienceable, generations-based period of time, it reaches from grandparents to grandchildren—people to whom we feel responsible. Boulding, a mother of five, wrote that a two-hundred-year present "will not make us prophets or seers, but it will give us an at-homeness with our changing times comparable to that which parents can have with an ever changing family of children as they move from age to age."[45]

Two hundred years is good; there is emotional comfort and behavioral discipline in it. If what we want is to change mind-set, however, two hundred years is too readily imaginable, too incremental. Frames of mind change by jumps, not by degrees. . . .

. . . Other long-term frames of reference may be used as well. Geologically, the last ten thousand years is the Holocene—the thin slice in the Quaternary period of the Cenozoic era at the top of the stratigraphic epoch charts. In astronomical terms civilization is microscopic. It is best measured in comets, such as Halley's, whose seventy-five-to seventy-nine-year returns have been documented for twenty-two centuries. The name "Halley's" is only constant since 1759 C.E. The comet named "Hale-Bopp" in 1997 C.E., when it put on a dazzling show, was previously seen in 2214 B.C.E.; we do not know what it was called then. When it returns in 4377 C.E., will anyone mention the name "Hale-Bopp"? Returning comets will let us know whether civilization is developing more continuity of knowledge or less.

Might humanity pay consistent attention through one complete precession of the equinoxes, as the Earth's axis pirouettes around a point in the sky near the Pole Star? This 25,784-year cycle is known as the Great Year. How about keeping track through one rotation of our galaxy—220 million years? The Earth has existed for nearly twenty-five of those galactic rotations, life on Earth for nineteen rotations. Humans may well eventually affect the periodicity of ice ages—we have been frozen by one every one hundred thousand years for a million years and are now enjoying an "interglacial" period—but it seems unlikely that we will have much influence on the rotation of our galaxy or anyone else's, nor will we tally their spin. The human time frame is narrower than that of life, of the planet, and of galaxies.

Eno's Long Now places us where we belong, neither at the end of history nor at the beginning, but in the thick of it. We are not the culmination of history, and we are not start-over revolutionaries; we are in the middle of civilization's story.

The trick is learning how to treat the last ten thousand years as if it were last week, and the next ten thousand as if it were next week. Such tricks confer advantage. . . .

The mathematician and physicist Freeman Dyson makes a related observation about human society:

> The destiny of our species is shaped by the imperatives of survival on six distinct time scales. To survive means to compete successfully on all six time scales. But the unit of survival is different at each of the six time scales. On a time scale of years, the unit is the individual. On a time scale of decades, the unit is the family. On a time scale of centuries, the unit is the tribe or nation. On a time scale of millennia, the unit is the culture. On a time scale of tens of millennia, the unit is the species. On a time scale of eons, the unit is the whole web of life on our planet. Every human being is the product of adaptation to the demands of all six time scales. That is why conflicting loyalties are deep in our nature. In order to survive, we have needed to be loyal to ourselves, to our families, to our tribes, to our cultures, to our species, to our planet. If our psychological impulses are complicated, it is because they were shaped by complicated and conflicting demands.

In terms of quantity, there are a great many pine needles and a great many humans, many forests and nations, only a few biomes and cultures, and but one planet. The hierarchy also underlies much of causation and explanation. On any subject, ask a four-year-old's annoying sequence of *Why?* five times and you get to deep structure. "Why are you married, Mommy?" "That's how you make a family." "Why make a family?" "It's the only way people have found to civilize children." "Why civilize children?" "If we didn't, the world would be nothing but nasty gangs." "Why?" "Because gangs can't make farms and cities and universities." "Why?" "Because they don't care about anything larger than themselves."

Considered operationally rather than in terms of loyalty, I propose six significant levels of pace and size in the working structure of a robust and adaptable civilization. From fast to slow the levels are

> Fashion/Art
>
> Commerce
>
> Infrastructure
>
> Governance
>
> Culture
>
> Nature

In a healthy society each level is allowed to operate at its own pace, safely sustained by the slower levels below and kept invigorated by the livelier levels above. "Every form of civilization is a wise equilibrium between firm substructure and soaring liberty," wrote the historian Eugen Rosenstock-Huessy. Each layer must respect the different pace of the others. If commerce, for example, is allowed by governance and culture to push nature at a commercial pace, all-supporting natural forests, fisheries, and aquifers will be lost. If governance is changed suddenly instead of gradually, you get the catastrophic French and Russian revolutions. . . .

The social sector acts on culture-level concerns in the domain of governance. One example is the sudden mid-twentieth-century dominance of historic preservation of buildings, pushed by such organizations as the National Trust for Historic Preservation in America and English Heritage and the National Trust in Britain. Through them culture declared that it was okay to change clothing at fashion pace but not buildings; okay to change tenants at commercial pace but not buildings; okay to change transportation at infrastructure pace but not neighborhoods. "If some parts of our society are going to speed up," these organizations seemed to say, "then other parts are going to have to slow way down, just to keep balance." Even New York City, the most demolition-driven metropolis in America, began to preserve its downtown.

Culture is where the Long Now operates. Culture's vast slow-motion dance keeps century and millennium time. Slower than political and economic history, it moves at the pace of language and religion. Culture is the work of whole peoples. In Asia you surrender to culture when you leave the city and hike back into the mountains, traveling back in time into remote village culture, where change is century-paced. In Europe you can see it in terminology, where the names of months (governance) have varied radically since 1500 but the names of signs of the Zodiac (culture) remain unchanged for millennia. Europe's most intractable wars are religious wars. . . .

The division of powers among the layers of civilization allows us to relax about a few of our worries. We should not deplore rapidly changing technology and business while government controls, cultural mores, and so-called wisdom change slowly; that's their job. Also, we should not fear destabilizing positive-feedback loops (such as the Singularity) crashing the whole system. Such disruption usually can be isolated and absorbed. The total effect of the pace layers is that they provide many-leveled corrective, stabilizing negative feedback throughout the system. It is precisely in the apparent contradictions of pace that civilization finds its surest health.

A futurist at SRI International, a California think tank, once sculpted a "future tree." It had a fat trunk (the present), several branches indicating various major directions in which the future might go, and thirty-six *twigs* at the top, showing that many distinct futures in a few years. No wonder we discount the future: This little twig might be the future? It's nothing.

The tree's dimensions should have been inverted. The present should be a thin trunk, then fatter branches, and enormous twigs. Future considerations should dwarf the present—the same way unborn humans vastly outnumber the living, the same way the accumulative never-born of an endangered species should loom over the debate about its protection.

Virtual realist Jaron Lanier refers to this line of thinking as *karma vertigo*. "The computer code we are offhandedly writing today could become the deeply embedded standards for centuries to come. Any programmer or system designer who takes that realization on and feels the full karmic burden gets vertigo."

The karmic view of the future can be as distorting as the discounted view. Instead of the reduced responsibility of discounting, karma can impose crushing responsibility, paralyzing to contemplate.

Is there a resolution to the paradox between karma and discounting? There is at least relief from it in the pace layering of civilization (where the pace of change slows from rapid Fashion down through Commerce, Infrastructure, Governance, and Culture, to glacially slow Nature). In the fashion and commercial domains a discounted approach to the future is necessary to maintain the customary swift turnover. An increasingly karmic and careful approach, however, is appropriate to managing the slower layers of infrastructure, governance, culture, and nature. It would be nice to have one body of economics that embraces all the levels, but we don't yet.

Also, a 10,000-Year Clock offers token relief. In its perspective each future year is neither lesser in import than the present year nor greater, but exactly the same. Karma and discounting both are voided by the Clock, or perhaps balanced in its presence.

Another version of the discounting debate emerges around long-term planning. Many have noticed, these decades, that there seem to be fewer long-duration projects, even though there is growing wealth to invest in such work. Kevin Kelly once raised the question in a dinner with complexity scientists. In friendly but acerbic terms they mocked the ambitions of The Long Now Foundation. Kelly paraphrased their argument:

> Since complexity theory shows that even the fairly near future is inherently unpredictable, any polygenerational plan will guess wrong about what a future generation wants or needs. Suppose a previous generation had expended great effort planning for dirigible ports around the world in the year 2000! Inevitable technology obsolescence and economic discounting renders any long-term return of value impractical. Conservation makes sense for the long term, and so does science (because it is incremental and open-ended), but specific long-term plans

will always be based on wrong long-term predictions, and it is best to avoid them.

Danny Hillis responded to Kelly's report:

> The difference between the two examples—dirigible ports versus ecological conservation—is a great demonstration of the difference between long-term planning and long-term responsibility. I agree that the former is futile, but that's no excuse to give up on the latter. The difference is between trying to control the future and trying to give it the tools to help itself. Believing in the future is not the same as believing you can predict it or determine it. The Long Now Foundation is not about determining the destiny of our descendants; it is about leaving them with a chance to determine a destiny of their own.

Such debates indicate that the way the future is viewed and used is in transition. Some say that a sense of any future at all was extinguished for three generations in the twentieth century by the dread of nuclear Armageddon, from which we have not yet recovered. At the same time, increasing reports of incremental loss—of atmospheric ozone, of species diversity, of rural village stability—tell us that long-term maintenance issues are accumulating to crisis proportions that short-term thinking is powerless to address. "For most of civilization's history," observes Kelly, "tomorrow was going to be no different than today, so the future was owed nothing. Suddenly, in the technological age, our power of disruption became so great, there was no guarantee we'd have any future whatsoever. We now know we are stuck with having a future, and thus are obliged to it, but we have no idea what that means."

Some of what the future means can be revived from traditional ethics, such as Samuel Johnson's admonition, "The future is purchased by the present. It is not possible to secure distant or permanent happiness but by the forbearance of some immediate gratification." Some we can learn from the emerging field of future studies. "The first thing you learn in forecasting," says Paul Saffo, "is the longer view you take, the more is in your self-interest. Seemingly altruistic acts are not altruistic if you take a long enough view." In the long run saving yourself requires saving the whole world.

Governance itself is being rethought. "The proper role of government in capitalistic societies in an era of man-made brain power industries," writes the economist Lester Thurow, "is to represent the interest of the future to the present." Commerce has too short a time horizon to take the larger future seriously, therefore governance must do it. Governance can forcefully represent future Californians who might want a thriving redwood forest instead of Maxxam having once maximized its profits by clear-cutting the forest.

A major point of reference for thinkers about the future is Robert Axelrod's 01984 book, *The Evolution of Cooperation*. It reported his seminal research on the playing of a simple game called Prisoner's Dilemma, in which neither of the two players can know what move the other will make next. The game is diabolically structured so that if both act in mutual trust, they are moderately rewarded; if both defect from trust, they are mildly punished; and if one defects and the other doesn't, the defector

is richly rewarded, and the trusting one strongly punished. The apparently safest way to play the game is to always defect, but if both players do that, neither of them does as well as they would if they both cooperated. Hence the dilemma.

Axelrod proved that if the game continues over time—what is called *iterated* Prisoner's Dilemma—a strategy called *tit for tat* emerges spontaneously, allowing both players to cooperate and thus get higher scores. The game automatically generates cooperation if what Axelrod calls "the shadow of the future" is allowed to lengthen. By continuing to play each other, each player develops a reputation that the other player learns to count on and work with. Even in a game that rewards distrust, time teaches the players the value of cooperation, however guarded they may be.

To produce the benefits of more cooperation in the world, Axelrod proves, all you need to do is lengthen the shadow of the future—that is, ensure more durable, relationships. Thus marriage is common to every society, because trusting partners have an advantage over lone wolves. . . .

The great use of a continuous future, then, is its inclusiveness. Given uncertainty, we are right to use many scenarios (hence discounting any one of them), but we are also right to assume we share one world (hence karmic responsibility). Anything may happen in the future; reliable pattern only emerges in how people handle events over time. Steadily engaging the future teaches wariness about events and trust in each other. We don't know what's coming. We do know we're in it together. . . .

Except for open-ended endeavors like science, the tremendously powerful lever of time has seldom been employed. The pyramids of Egypt and Central America took only fifty years to build. Some of the great cathedrals of Europe indeed were built over centuries, but that was due to funding problems rather than patience. Humanity's heroic goals generally have been sought through quick, spectacular action ("We will land a man on the Moon in this decade") instead of a sustained accumulation of smaller, distributed efforts that might have overwhelming effect over time. The kinds of goals that can be reached quickly are rather limited, and work on them displaces attention and effort that might be spent on worthier, longer-term goals.

Danny Hillis points out, "There are problems that are impossible if you think about them in two-year terms—which everyone does—but they're easy if you think in fifty-year terms." This category of problems includes nearly all the great ones of our time: The growing disparities between haves and have nots, widespread hunger, dwindling freshwater resources, ethnic conflict, global organized crime, loss of biodiversity, and so on. Such problems were slow to arrive, and they can only be solved at their own pace. It is the job of slow-but-steady governance and culture to settle goals of solving these problems and to maintain the constancy and patience required to see them through (that is not our current model of governance).

Restorative goals such as these are the most important, but they do have a negative cast. Could their accomplishment be aided by also engaging some positive goals that operate at the same pace? Colonizing Mars has this quality. Building a 10,000-Year Clock/Library might. Assembling a universal virtual reality world on the Net feels like an achievable great work. Success in mapping the human genome should encourage the related ambition of inventorying all the species on Earth and mapping their genomes. Filling in all the gaps and blanks in the total human family tree would be a vivid experience of the Long Us.

These are first-thought blurts. We have not yet seriously asked ourselves what we might do with fifty years or five hundred years of sustained endeavor. What comes to your mind, thinking in that scale?

. . . Environmental projects, owing to the extended lag times involved and perhaps the aesthetic rewards along the way, excel at inspiring long-term ambition. I know of two North American environmental projects with thousand-year time frames. . . .

Two hours was the difference between impossible and easy. For what tasks would two hundred years make that kind of difference?

EXERCISES

1. What would the Long Now Foundation think of the winners (and losers) of the television shows *Survivor* and *Big Brother?*

2. What long-term causes do you think worthy of sustained human effort? Explain.

Suggested Readings:

Brand, Stewart. *The Clock of the Long Now.* New York: Basic Books, 1999.

Branuyn, Gareth. "Compu-Sex: Erotica for Cybernauts." *South Atlantic Quarterly* 92 (1993): 779–91.

Dery, Mark. *Escape Velocity.* New York: Grove Press, 1996.

Dery, Mark. "Flame Wars." *South Atlantic Quarterly* 92 (1993): 559–67.

Dery, Mark. *The Pyrotechnic Insanitarium.* New York: Grove Press, 1999.

Dibbell, Julian. *My Tiny Life.* New York: Holt, 1998.

Kuflik, Arthur. "Computers in Control: Rational Transfer of Authority or Irresponsible Abdication of Authority?" *Ethics and Information Technology* 1 (1999): 173–84.

Kurzweil, Ray. *The Age of Spiritual Machines.* New York: Viking, 1999.

Lanier, Jaron. "A Tale of Two Terrors." *CIO Magazine,* 1 July 2000.

McGee, Glenn. *The Perfect Baby.* Lanham, Md.: Rowman and Littlefield, 1996.

Moor, James H. "Are There Decisions Computers Should Never Make?" *Nature and System* 1 (1979): 217–29.

Moravec, Hans. *Robot: Mere Machine to Transcendent Mind.* New York: Oxford University Press, 1999.

Sale, Kirkpatrick. "Setting Limits on Technology." *Nation,* 5 June 1995.

Notes

Information Technology, Everyday Life, and the Future of Human Civilization

1. Anne Balsamo, "Feminism for the Incurably Informed," *South Atlantic Quarterly* 92 (1993): 694.

Life on the Screen

2. Sherry Turkle, *Life on the Screen* (New York: Simon and Schuster, 1995), 239–54, 262–63. Reprinted with the permission of Simon & Schuster from *Life on the Screen* by Sherry Turkle. Copyright © 1995 by Sherry Turkle.
3. Janice Radaway, *Reading the Romance* (Chapel Hill: University of North Carolina Press, 1991).
4. T. J. Burnside Clap, quoted in Henry Jenkins, *Textual Poachers: Television Fans and Participatory Culture* (New York: Routledge, 1992), 227.
5. Ibid., 280–1.
6. *Cybermind* [Electronic Mailing List] 29 March 1993.
7. Sherry Turkle, "The Subjective Computer: A Study in the Psychology of Personal Computation," *Social Studies of Science* 12 (1982): 201.
8. Turkle, "The Subjective Computer," 201.
9. The sense that virtual is better and safer and more interesting has extended even to those usually most concerned about how we *look.* The editor of *Mademoiselle* magazine, a publication chiefly concerned with fashion and beauty advice, introduces a special section on

electronic communication by declaring that if she "could live anywhere, it would be in Cyberia," i.e., cyberspace. (Gabe Doppelt, *Mademoiselle,* October 1993, 141.)

10. A spring 1995 special issue of *Time* magazine devoted to cyberspace reported:
    The fact is that access to the new technology generally breaks down along traditional class lines. Wealthy and upper-middle-class families form the bulk of the 30% of American households that own computers. Similarly, wealthier school districts naturally tend to have equipment that is unavailable to poorer ones, and schools in the more affluent suburbs have twice as many computers per student as their less-well-funded urban counterparts. [p. 25]

11. See, for example, the work of Alan Shaw of MIT's Media Laboratory. Alan Clinton Shaw, "Social Construction in the Inner City: Design Environments for Social Development and Urban Renewal" (Ph.D. diss., Massachusetts Institute of Technology, Media laboratory, Epistemology and Learning Group, 1995.)

12. Howard Rheingold, *The Virtual Community: Homesteading on the Electronic Frontier* (Reading, Mass.: Addison-Wesley, 1993), 17–37. SeniorNet, founded in 1986 by Mary Furlong, is designed to be permeable to the real. SeniorNet offers its members practical tips on home repair and advice on problems such as how to handle bouts of depression associated with aging. Members say that it has given them a sense that their "world is expanding." The organization sponsors regional face-to-face meetings, and its members regularly visit each other in person. See John F. Dickerson, "Never Too Old," *Time,* Spring 1995 (special issue), 41.

13. Daniel Ast and James Weissman, "At Your Service," *NetGuide,* August 1995, 35–38.

14. Michel Foucault, *Discipline and Punish: The Birth of the Prison,* trans. Alan Sheridan (New York: Pantheon, 1977). See also Mark Poster, *The Mode of Information: Poststructuralism and Social Context* (Chicago: University of Chicago Press, 1990), 69–98.

15. kort (Barry Kort) The WELL, conference on virtual communities (vc.52.28), 18 April 1993.

16. After a brief test period in the United States, Habitat was bought by the Fujitsu Corporation and became a successful commercial venture in Japan, with more than 1.5 million paid subscribers.

17. Chip Morningstar and F. Randall Farmer, "The Lessons of Lucasfilm's Habitat," *Cyberspace: First Steps,* ed. Michael Benedikt (Cambridge, Mass.,: MIT Press, 1991), 289.

18. Julian Dibbell, "Rape in Cyberspace," *Village Voice,* 21 December 1993, 38. [Dibbell's book, *My Tiny Life* includes an extended reflection on this event and others in cyberspace. See suggested readings at the end of this chapter.]

19. Ibid., 42.

20. Leslie Harris, "The Psychodynamic Effects of Virtual Reality," *Arachnet Journal on Virtual Culture,* February 1994.

21. www.cdt.org is the home page for the Center for Democracy and Technology.

ETHICS AND THE NEW MILLENNIUM

22. Kirkpatrick Sale, "Setting Limits on Technology," *Nation,* 5 June 1995, 785–88.

ETHICS FOR A NEW MILLENNIUM

23. From *Ethics for the New Millennium* by the Dalai Lama and Alexander Norman, copyright ©1999 by His Holiness The Dalai Lama. Used by permission of Riverhead Books, a division of Penguin Putnam, Inc.

Why the Future Doesn't Need Us

24. "Why the Future Doesn't Need Us" © April 2000 by Bill Joy. This article originally appeared in *Wired Magazine*. Reprinted by permission of the author.

25. The passage Kurzweil quotes is from Kaczynski's *Unabomber Manifesto,* which was published jointly, under duress, by the *New York Times* and the *Washington Post* to attempt to bring his campaign of terror to an end. I agree with David Gelernter, who said about their decision:

    It was a tough call for the newspapers. To say yes would be giving in to terrorism, and for all they knew he was lying anyway. On the other hand, to say yes might stop the killing. There was also a chance that someone would read the tract and get a hunch about the author; and that is exactly what happened. The suspect's brother read it, and it rang a bell.

    I would have told them not to publish. I'm glad they didn't ask me. I guess.

    From *Drawing Life: Surviving the Unabomber* (Free Press, 1997), 120.

26. Laurie Garrett, *The Coming Plague: Newly Emerging Diseases in a World Out of Balance* (New York: Penguin, 1994), 47–52, 414, 419, 452.

27. Hans Moravec, *Robot: Mere Machine to Transcendent Mind* (New York: Oxford University Press, 1999) 66-8.

28. Isaac Asimov described what became the most famous view of ethical rules for robot behavior in his book *I, Robot* in 1950, in his Three Laws of Robotics: 1. A robot may not injure a human being, or, through inaction, allow a human being to come to harm. 2. A robot must obey the orders given it by human beings, except where such orders would conflict with the First Law. 3. A robot must protect its own existence, as long as such protection does not conflict with the First or Second Law.

29. "Test of Time," *Wired* 8.03, 78.

30. Michelangelo wrote a sonnet that begins:
    Non ha l' ottimo artista alcun concetto
    Ch' un marmo solo in sè non circonscriva
    Col suo soverchio; e solo a quello arriva
    La man che ubbidisce all' intelleto.
    Stone translates this as
    The best of artists hath no thought to show
    which the rough stone in its superfluous shell
    doth not include; to break the marble spell
    is all the hand that serves the brain can do.

    Stone describes the process: "He was not working from his drawings or clay models; they had all been put away. He was carving from the images in his mind. His eyes and hands knew where every line, curve, mass must emerge, and at what depth in the heart of the stone to create the low relief." *The Agony and the Ecstasy* (Garden City, N.Y.: Doubleday, 1961), 6, 144.

31. First Foresight Conference on Nanotechnology in October 1989, a talk titled "The Future of Computation." Published in *Nanotechnology: Research and Perspectives,* ed. B. C. Crandall and James Lewis (Cambridge, Mass.: MIT Press, 1992), 269. See also www.foresight.org/Conferences/MNT01/Nano1.html.

32. In his 1963 novel *Cat's Cradle,* Kurt Vonnegut imagined a gray-goo-like accident where a form of ice called ice-nine, which becomes solid at a much higher temperature, freezes the oceans.

33. Stuart Kauffman, "Self-replication: Even Peptides Do It." *Nature* 382 (8 August 1996): 496. See www.santafe.edu/sfi/People/kauffman/sak-peptides.html.

34. Jon Else, *The Day After Trinity: J. Robert Oppenheimer and the Atomic Bomb* (available at www.pyramiddirect.com).

35. This estimate is in Leslie's book *The End of the World: The Science and Ethics of Human Extinction,* where he notes that the probability of extinction is substantially higher if we accept Brandon Carter's Doomsday Argument, which is, briefly, that "we ought to have some reluctance to believe that we are very exceptionally early, for instance in the earliest 0.001 percent, among all humans who will ever have lived. This would be some reason for thinking that humankind will not survive for many more centuries, let alone colonize the galaxy. Carter's doomsday argument doesn't generate any risk estimates just by itself. It is an argument for *revising* the estimates which we generate when we consider various possible dangers." (Routledge, 1996; 1, 3, 145.)

36. Arthur C. Clarke, "Presidents, Experts, and Asteroids," *Science,* 5 June 1998. Reprinted as "Science and Society" in *Greetings, Carbon-Based Bipeds! Collected Essays, 1934–1998* (New York: St. Martin's Press, 1999), 526.

37. And, as David Forrest suggests in his paper "Regulating Nanotechnology Development," available at www.foresight.org/NanoRev/Forrest1989.html, "If we used strict liability as an alternative to regulation it would be impossible for any developer to internalize the cost of the risk (destruction of the biosphere), so theoretically the activity of developing nanotechnology should never be undertaken." Forrest's analysis leaves us with only government regulation to protect us—not a comforting thought.

38. Matthew Meselson, "The Problem of Biological Weapons." Presentation to the 1,818th Stated Meeting of the American Academy of Arts and Sciences, 13 January 1999 http://www.potaminstitute.org/projects/Meselson.html

39. Paul Doty, "The Forgotten Menace: Nuclear Weapons Stockpiles Still Represent the Biggest Threat to Civilization," *Nature* 402, 9 December 1999, 583.

40. See also Hans Bethe's 1997 letter to President Clinton, at www.fas.org/bethecr.htm.

41. Jacques Attali, *Fraternites: une nouvelle utopie* (Paris: Fayard, 1999).

42. Edith Hamilton, *The Greek Way* (New York: Norton, 1942), 35.

The Long Now

43. Stewart Brand, *The Clock of the Long Now* (New York: Basic Books, 1999), 29, 31, 35, 38, 120–5, 157–8.

44. More than most books, this one came from conversation. The main source (unless otherwise noted) was discussion among members of the board of The Long Now Foundation, most of it via thousands of messages online.

45. Elise Boulding, "The Dynamics of Imaging Futures," *World Future Society Bulletin* (Sept. 1978): 7.

*Amory B. Lovins and L. Hunter Lovins, "A Tale of Two Botanies," *Wired* volume 8, number 4 April (2000), p. 247. This article is also available at http://www.wired.com/wired/archive/8.04/botanies.html. See also http://www.global-vision.org/misc/twobotanies.html.

CREDITS